CONTACTS

Teri Kwal Gamble
College of New Rochelle

Michael W. Gamble
New York Institute of Technology

CONTACTS

INTERPERSONAL COMMUNICATION IN THEORY, PRACTICE, AND CONTEXT

Houghton Mifflin

Boston New York

DEDICATION

For Matthew Jon and Lindsay Michele, our children, and our most important contacts. Through their spoken and unspoken messages, they repeatedly demonstrate the value of interpersonal relationships.

Senior Sponsoring Editor: Mary Finch
Developmental Editor: Julia Casson
Senior Project Editor: Fred Burns
Editorial Assistant: Lisa Goodman
Senior Manufacturing Coordinator: Marie Barnes
Senior Composition Buyer: Sarah Ambrose
Senior Art and Design Coordinator: Jill Haber

Photo Credits may be found on page 504.

Printed in the U.S.A.

Library of Congress Control Number: 2003110134

ISBN: 0-618-37963-0

123456789—DOW—08 07 06 05 04

Contents

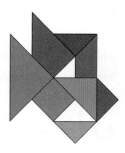

5 | *Language* **138**

6 | *Nonverbal Communication* **170**

PART 3
Discovering Interpersonal
Dynamics   231

13 | *Intimacy and Distance*   *392*

Preface

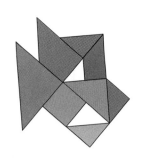

Contacts: Interpersonal Communication in Theory, Practice, and Context introduces, explores, and celebrates the central role that interpersonal communication plays in our lives. Whether it is with friends, family, or co-workers, in personal or professional contexts, enacted "up-close and personal" or with technological assistance, interpersonal communication affects the nature and development of all relationships. Our hope is that by learning about interpersonal communication, practicing key interpersonal skills, and considering how to do it better, this book's readers will discover stops to enrich their personal and professional lives.

This book rests on the following three premises:

Premise 1

A text on interpersonal communication should consider how technology and the media influence person-to-person interactions. Technological innovations and mass communication permeate our daily interactions. Whether subtly or overtly, technology and the mass media help shape our relationships, influencing our view of ourselves, what we expect from other others, and ultimately determining how we evaluate the effectiveness of our person-to-person contacts.

Premise 2

A text on interpersonal communication should consider how culture and gender influence person-to-person interactions. We can no longer expect to communicate solely with people who are mirror images of or just like us. Our world is both too complex and too small and the people with whom we interact too diverse for us even to imagine that we could limit our contacts. Consequently, an ability to interact with others in meaningful ways requires that we have a greater understanding of how culture influences relationships and communication preferences. No longer are the development of cultural understanding or sensitivity to diversity merely assets; they are now prerequisites for effective and insightful interpersonal communication.

Premise 3

A text on interpersonal communication should consider the effects of the varied contexts of our lives—that is, although it is important to consider content traditionally covered in interpersonal communication courses, it is also important to widen the scope of our consideration to include contacts occurring in the family, on the job, and in health care arenas. Our abilities to interact effectively across our life spans with friends, family members, employers, peers, and health professionals is essential for both our personal and our professional well-being.

About the Authors

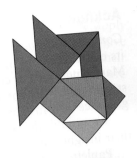

Teri Kwal Gamble and Michael W. Gamble are a husband and wife team who earned their doctoral degrees at New York University. Teri is a full professor in communication at the College of New Rochelle and Michael is a full professor in communication at New York Institute of Technology. Together, Teri and Michael have written a variety of widely used text and trade books, conducted workshops for educators and business professionals across the country, and spent their careers honing their skills as teachers, writers, and speakers. The Gambles live in New Jersey. They have two children—Matthew and Lindsay.

PART 1
BUILDING FOUNDATIONS

1

Understanding Interpersonal Communication

I truly believe that life is a contact sport. You never know just who you'll meet and what role they might play in your career or your life.

—*Ken Kragen,*
Communication Consultant

After completing this chapter, you should be able to:

▌ Define interpersonal communication.

▌ Evaluate your ability to interact interpersonally.

▌ Identify the essential elements of the communication process.

▌ Explain why we communicate interpersonally.

▌ Describe four characteristics of interpersonal communication.

▌ List and explain three principles of interpersonal communication.

▌ Identify and provide examples of Watzlawick's five axioms of communication.

▌ Describe how gender and culture affect interpersonal communication.

▌ Provide examples of the ways in which technology shapes interpersonal contacts.

▌ Describe steps you can take to become a better communicator.

3

daily contacts

The Saga of Susan and Juan

"He just walked away after our last date and said, 'Goodbye' . . . ," Susan recalled recently about the incident that so upset her.

Susan had been dating Juan for several months. They had met at a charitable function at the beginning of the year and had been seeing each other exclusively ever since. They attended parties and special events together, and she had even invited him to travel with her to her parents' home during the Thanksgiving holiday.

Then it happened. After another evening together, Juan simply said goodbye, turned, and walked away.

"What did I say or do to cause this?" Susan cried to her friend. "Has he found someone else? Has he ever been serious about me?"

She was despondent. Questions raced through her mind. Had she misjudged Juan's feelings or intentions? What could she have done differently?

Juan was sitting in his apartment, staring blankly into space, unable to do anything. He had just said goodbye to Susan for the last time. Now his phone was ringing—

he let the answering machine pick it up. It was Susan, but he still didn't budge.

"How can I tell her the truth?" he wondered aloud. Sure, they had had a wonderful relationship—that is, until Thanksgiving dinner.

He had readily accepted Susan's Thanksgiving invitation. From the moment he entered her parents' house, however, he felt uncomfortable. Susan's folks were nice enough, but he sensed a certain amount of restraint on their part.

By the time dinner was over, Juan was convinced that, as a Hispanic, he was not really welcome in Susan's parents' home. Nothing had been said directly; he just had a feeling.

Later, although Susan had told him that he was being silly, he just couldn't put it out of his mind or get over it. What should he have done? Should he have brought the issue up? Ignored it? Let time work it out? Juan didn't know.

Divide into pairs or small groups, and answer the following questions:

1. What do you think about the manner in which Susan and Juan each handled their problem?
2. What would you advise each to have done?
3. Given the current situation, what would you advise each to do next?

We do it every day. We do it with people we have known for years and with people whom we have just met. We do it with our family and with our friends. We do it with persons who are older or younger than us, and we do it with our peers. We do it with men, and we do it with women. We do it when we interview for a job, and we do it when we are being interviewed by a medical practitioner. We do it when we argue, and we do it when we make up. We do it when we give instructions and when we get them. We do it at the beginning, during, and at the end of a relationship. We do it on-line and off-line. And as we do it, we are shaped by it. In fact, there is a direct link between how good we are at doing it, and how satisfying or fulfilling we believe our life is.[1] What is it that we do? We engage in **interpersonal communication,** that is, we make personal contacts, build a connection, and establish a relationship with another individual to satisfy our social needs and to realize our personal goals.

Interpersonal communication has both quantitative and qualitative dimensions. Interpersonal communication can be quantified typically as a two-person relationship, or a **dyad,** the earliest and most frequent form of communication we experience. It is indivisible. The parties see themselves as a duo: a couple, a team, or a pair. Without a dyad, a relationship cannot exist.[2] Thus, when one person withdraws from a dyadic relationship, the relationship terminates—at least for the time being or until the person reestablishes a connection. The quality too of interpersonal communication can be measured along a continuum, with intimate communication at one end and impersonal communication at the opposite end. The more personally we interact with another individual, the more "interpersonal" is our relationship. When we engage in interpersonal communication we treat each other as genuine persons, not as objects. We respond to each other as unique individuals, not as role-players. We will explore the nature of interpersonal communication in greater depth a little later in this chapter.

Our effectiveness as spouse, partner, friend, or coworker depends on how effectively we are able to communicate interpersonally. The person you are right now is a result of all the person-to-person contacts you have had throughout your life. Each of our contacts is an experience, and as such, helps to shape us. None of our

professional contacts

Gloria Steinem on Finding Your True Self

Gloria Steinem is the founder of both *Ms.* magazine and the National Women's Political Caucus. One of her books, *The Revolution from Within: A Book of Self-Esteem,* was translated into eleven languages. In this brief excerpt from it Steinem discusses how a series of person-to-person contacts and experiences helped her gain greater insight into herself and her world.

> When I was living in India on a fellowship after college, a kind Indian friend took me aside and suggested I might consider saying "South Asia," "Southeast Asia," and the like, instead of the "Near" and "Far East." It was the first time I'd ever realized that "Near" and "Far" assumed Europe as the center of the world.
>
> . . . No matter who we are, the journey toward recovering the self-esteem that should have been our birthright follows similar steps: a first experience of seeing through our own eyes instead of through the eyes of others (for instance, the moment when an Algerian first looks in defiance at a French soldier, or when a woman stops being defined by the male gaze); telling what seemed to be shameful secrets, and discovering they are neither shameful nor secret (from the woman who has survived

childhood sexual abuse to the man whose bottomless need for power hides weakness); giving names to problems that have been treated as normal and thus have no names (think of new terms like *homophobia, battered women,* or *Eurocentrism*); bonding with others who share similar experiences (from groups of variously abled people to conferences of indigenous nations); achieving empowerment and self-government (from the woman who has a room and income of her own to the nation that declares its independence); bonding with others in shared power (think of democratic families, rainbow coalitions, or the principles of the United Nations); and finally, achieving a balance of independence and interdependence, and taking one's place in a circle of true selves.[*]

1. Steinem identifies some of the steps she took that resulted in her discovering new ways of thinking about herself and the problems that characterized her world. Identify insights and experiences you have had that changed the way you view yourself, your relationship to others, and the world.
2. For each change you cited, discuss how your change in thinking played itself out in your behavior and the behavior of others.

[*]Gloria Steinem, *Revolution from Within: A Book of Self-Esteem.* New York: Little, Brown, 1992.

contacts is fixed in time. Rather, just like each of us, they ebb and flow and change through the years.

Interpersonal communication plays a key part in building our sense of personal identity. When it is effective, it helps us work through problems and ultimately enhances our sense of self-worth. When it is ineffective, however, rather than enlarge us, it limits our growth and frustrates the realization of our unique potential. Because the United States is a society in which the very civility of individuals is brought into question, especially now, we need to commit to paying greater attention to interpersonal communication and its effects. Consequently, we would be well served to investigate how adept we are at forming and maintaining relationships. For example, we need to ask and answer the following questions:

> How effective are we at communicating with people from diverse cultures? Are we able to interact equally well with males and females or with individuals whose sexual preferences differ from our own?

Using this Gordon Allport quote, discuss the relationship between unfamiliarity and prejudice.

> See that man over there?
> Yes.
> Well, I hate him.
> But you don't know him.
> That's why I hate him.

literary contacts

Are You in a Disguise?

In the following poem, Samuel Menashe suggests that too often when interacting with another person we pretend to be someone we are not. Have you ever asked a question like the one he asks when interacting with someone? Do you suppose that anyone has ever asked it about you?

Anonymous

Truth to tell,
Seldom told
Under oath,
We live lies
And grow old
Self-disguised—
Who are you
I talk to?

Next, read "We Wear the Mask," by poet Paul Laurence Dunbar.

We wear the mask that grins and lies.
It hides our cheek and shades our eyes,—
This debt we pay to human guile;
With torn and bleeding hearts we smile,
And mouth with myriad subtleties.

Why should the world be over-wise,
In counting all our tears and sighs?
Nay, let them only see us, while
*   We wear the mask.*

We smile, but, O great Christ, our cries
To thee from tortured souls arise.
We sing, but oh the clay is vile
Beneath our feet, and long the mile;
But let the world dream otherwise,
*   We wear the mask.*

1. What aspect of the relationship they share might lead a person to assume a disguise or wear a mask when interacting with another person?
2. What steps can we take to amend a person's desire to assume such a relational disguise or mask?
3. How would you handle the pain, frustration, and anger caused by having to suppress your cultural identity or hide your real feelings?

SOURCES: Samuel Menashe, "Anonymous." By permission of the author from *The Niche Narrows: New and Selected Poems*, Talisman House, 2000; first appeared in *The New Yorker*; Paul Lawrence Dunbar, "We Wear the Mask" from *Lyrics of the Lowly Life*. New York: Dodd, Mead, 1896.

How easy is it for us to relate to people our own age and those of different ages?

To what extent are we able to maintain control of ourselves when we interact with others? Under what conditions do we lose control?

How is technology changing our interpersonal interactions?

Societal problems related to factors such as ethnocentrism, sexism, violence, and health can be alleviated, at least to some degree, if we improve our ability to adapt to a changing world and connect interpersonally with others in more effective ways. To this end, it is necessary to examine interpersonal communication. We need to explore the field's theories, consider relevant research, and apply what we learn to our own practice of interpersonal communication skills. The more we learn, the more extensive our repertoire of acceptable behavioral choices will become, and the more flexible we will be, thereby improving our chances to sustain rather than sever needed relationships.

What happens in our own world of interpersonal contacts depends on the communication choices we make. Through communication we present ourselves to others and we work out or compound relationship problems. Relationships of all kinds are important to both your personal and your professional well-being. Thus, a key goal of this book is to help you build and maintain effective interpersonal connections with a broad array of individuals.

Meet the Interpersonal Communicator

We are social beings. During our lifetimes each of us will experience a large number of relationships. Many of these will develop into lasting friendships, whereas others will never progress beyond mere acquaintances. Some of our relationships will become intimate, while others will remain much less personal. Some will change or end. Whatever their nature, however, implicit in every one of our person-to-person contacts is the dyad, the two individuals interacting to create it.

The dyad is always central to our consideration of interpersonal communication.[3] From an interpersonal perspective, even groups of three or more individuals are viewed as a series of dyads. In effect, dyads serve as the foundation for possible interpersonal coalitions. Whenever we are part of a dyad we experience some kind of a relationship. For example, Lamar, Mark, Nobuko, and Sara share a three-bedroom apartment and thus comprise a

Developing effective interpersonal skills and relationships is a process that begins at birth and continues throughout the lifespan.

Theory

Rating Relationships

Think about some of the relationships you have had over your lifetime.

1. Identify an extremely satisfying interpersonal relationship you have experienced. Identify an extremely frustrating relationship. For each, indicate who the other person was and how long you have known him or her.

2. Now think about the various aspects of the relationship that have worked to make it satisfying or frustrating.

3. What characteristics and qualities appear to differentiate the most satisfying from the most frustrating relationship? Be specific.

foursome. Within a group of four people, six possible dyads exist:

Mark/Lamar
Mark/Nobuko
Mark/Sarah
Lamar/Nobuko
Lamar/Sarah
Nobuko/Sarah

Thus, how each individual in the foursome feels about and gets along with each of the other three will determine which individuals will spend more time with each other, what topics they will discuss, and what activities they will engage in. Even when all four persons are present at the same time, preferred or stronger friendships may influence the kind of interaction that occurs.

Every time we consciously or unconsciously send a verbal or nonverbal message to a relative, friend, lover, stranger, employer, or coworker, interpersonal communication occurs. Every aspect of our lives, including every one of our transitions, from birth to death, depends on and is influenced by interpersonal communication. We depend on our relationships to help us meet our needs, overcome adversity, attain personal happiness, and adjust to change. In fact, the relationships we typically find most satisfying are usually those that help us fulfill our sense of self and reflect similar levels of commitment. Thus, each of us can benefit from discovering more effective ways of relating to others. This is where interpersonal communication comes into play.

Because of its pervasiveness and significance, interpersonal communication is a lifelong project that requires a lifelong commitment. While we may be born communicators, we are not born with effective interpersonal skills—those we need to learn. Effective interpersonal skills are not static; the same techniques may not work with all people or in all situations. The culture of the interactors, their gender, their environment, and their goals will determine how they approach and process interpersonal communication.

Have you ever suffered from the malady Saul Bellow describes below? If so, how did you remedy the problem?

What's Humanitis? It's when the human condition is suddenly too much for you.

Simply communicating a lot does not necessarily mean communicating well. Having many interpersonal contacts daily doesn't guarantee that we acted appropriately, adjusted to the special needs of each, overcame obstacles that impeded the development of more meaningful relationships, or achieved our objectives. What happens between us when we relate interpersonally cannot be fully measured or described by any one member of the dyad. Rather, it is only understood when the interaction created by both parties is shared and processed. Because we are all unique, we need to examine how our differences influence our interactions.

Among the things that distinguish us from one another are our physical, psychological, educational, gender, and cultural characteristics. Each new relationship we experience can teach us a little bit more about the nature of people and interpersonal communication. Each new contact we open ourselves to can increase our comfort at interacting not only with those who share our characteristics, but also with those who have internalized different values, attitudes, and perspectives; had different life experiences; and thus developed different personal communication styles. Personal theories of what works during interpersonal contacts must be constantly revised and updated or our assumptions will compel us to repeat interpersonal scenarios or scripts that are doomed to failure.

Interpersonal communication helps us develop a sense of self. As we revise the way the way we think about ourselves, we also revise our behavior and how we relate to others. The self–other relationship is both intriguing and involved. In Chapter Two we will explore how self-concept affects interpersonal communication. For now, keep in mind that the effective interpersonal communicator does not take others for granted. Rather than following stereotypes, the effective interpersonal communicator is guided by knowledge and skill. How knowledgeable and how skillful are you as an interpersonal communicator?

Essentials of Interpersonal Communication

Why do we need to study interpersonal communication when we have been communicating interpersonally since we were born? Even as infants, when we took our first breaths and cried, interpersonal communication has played a critical role in our lives. For much of our lives, we are unaware of why we act or react as we do. We tell ourselves communication comes naturally. We know what to do and we know how to do it. Most of us would agree, however, that while this is partially true, certainly we can always do it better!

We use interpersonal communication to accomplish what is important to us and to achieve our personal goals. If we are adept at interacting with others and are sensitive to their needs and goals, then we are likely to realize more of our needs and goals as well.[4] Sometimes to accomplish our goals we form dyadic coalitions—that is, we form two-person relationships by uniting with another member of a larger group. We may, for example, develop a coalition with a particular coworker in an effort to improve our chances to receive a coveted assignment, or we might form a coalition with a fellow student in an effort to conduct extensive research for a class project. On reality-type television programs such as *Survivor*, forming temporary dyadic coalitions helped the winners achieve their goals. Television shows that compel players to prevail over one or more opponents suggest that we are in the midst of an era of hyper-competitiveness where the only way of winning is to prevent other persons from attaining their goals. Such an arrangement is not conducive to lasting interpersonal relationships. Whether a coalition is productive or unproductive depends on how satisfying the relationship is and how much attention we pay to its health. Good interpersonal skills can mean the difference between success and failure in multiple arenas—home, job, school, heath-care settings, and society—and across cultures and generations.

Enhancing our awareness and understanding of the numerous factors at work when two individuals communicate with each other can increase our chances of developing our **interpersonal competence**—the ability to communicate effectively.[5] We can learn to be more competent communicators by observing ourselves and others, assessing what we observe, practicing specific behaviors, and then predicting and evaluating the outcomes of our own interactions with the goal of improving our interpersonal skills.

The kinds of relationships we create depends on how good we are at interacting with others. Whether we are able to exchange messages and negotiate or share meaning during our person-to-person encounters is a result of the interrelationships of an array of essential elements in the process. For example, when we pat someone on the back it may be perceived as friendly or supportive or as a form of sexual harassment. Among the elements that will influence the act's interpretation are the *people involved,* the *messages* they send, the *channels* they use, the amount of *noise* present, the communication *context,* the *feedback* sent in response, and the act's *effect* (see Table 1.1). The better we understand these essential elements, the more likely we are to increase our communication competence and improve our communication performance. In other words, the more we understand how interpersonal communication works, the greater the chances that we will make it work the way we want it to.

People

The communication we will address in this course involves people. Whereas *intrapersonal communication* involves a single person, *group communication* requires three or more people, and *public* and *mass communication* require many more people, *interpersonal communication* requires only two people. These communication transactions occupy a space on an imaginary communication continuum that ranges from an **impersonal relationship** at one end to an **intimate relationship** at the other.

When you respond *impersonally* to another individual, you communicate with him or her based on your knowledge of the categories in which you place the person—that is, the social groups or the culture to which you believe the individual belongs, rather than on your personal knowledge and experience with the specific individual. In contrast, when you respond to a specific person as an individual, you include your knowledge of various elements unique to that individual's personality that guide your interactions with the person. In other words, your

---

TABLE 1.1
The Essential Elements of Interpersonal Communication

People	*the senders and receivers of communication messages*
Messages	*the content of our communication*
Channels	*the media through which a message travels*
Noise	*interference with our ability to send or receive messages*
Feedback	*information received in exchange for messages*
Context	*the environmental, situational, or cultural setting in which the communication takes place*
Effect	*the result of the communication episode*

past experience with this particular individual allows you to differentiate him or her from the groups to which he or she belongs. You now take this *unique* person and his or her needs into account when you communicate.

As your relationships with individuals develop and you get to know them better, not only can you *describe* their behavior (actually you can offer a description of anyone's behavior), but you can also more accurately *predict* their behavior when faced with a particular situation or set of circumstances. When you know people well, you can also sometimes *explain* their behavior, offering *reasons* for their actions. For instance, when you share an impersonal relationship with someone at work, you can probably describe that person's behavior, for example, his procrastination in completing an assignment. When you see him given a project to work on, you may be able to predict that he will not complete it on time. Were you to share a more personal relationship with your coworker, however, you might also be able to explain the reasons behind his procrastination—why he is unable to meet a deadline—such as concerns about his child, or feelings of inadequacy, for instance.[6]

Both persons in an interpersonal relationship perform message-sending and message-receiving functions. Each simultaneously functions as sender and receiver, both giving out and taking in messages at the same time. For instance, in the following interchange both parties give and receive messages:

JANA: I'm so tired, I wish we didn't have to go to the Joneses' party.

KARL: You always feel tired whenever we have plans to go to a party for someone I work with.

JANA: Why do you have to attack me when I say how I feel?

KARL: What's the matter with you? I'm not attacking you. I'm only commenting on what I observe and experience directly.

JANA: Is that all? Give me a break. Don't I have a right to be tired?

KARL: Sure you do. Just tell me one thing. Why do you never feel tired when we're going someplace that you want to go?

This role duality is an important concept. During interpersonal communication, the roles of sender and receiver don't belong to any one member of a dyad. Instead, these roles are constantly performed by each. How the individuals perform the roles, or how good they are at sending and receiving, depends on what they bring to the relationship, including their feelings about themselves; their knowledge about communication; and their attitudes, values, and goals. All these elements influence how well they encode (put their thoughts, feelings, emotions, and attitudes into a form another can relate to), and decode (interpret and attach meaning to the thoughts, feelings, emotions, and attitudes of others) messages. Because the interpersonal communication process is *transactional* in nature, it is a process in which source and

I . . . have never been the same person alone that I am with people.

—*Philip Roth*

How do you change in the company of different people? What brings about the change in you?

During a face-to-face encounter, as we code our thoughts and feelings into verbal and nonverbal messages, we simultaneously receive and decode the verbal and nonverbal messages of the other person.

receiver influence each other; during this process, transmission and reception occur simultaneously. What we think of each other and what we believe each other to know influence the interpersonal messages we send.[7]

Messages

The meaning derived from interpersonal communication is negotiated by sending and receiving verbal and nonverbal **messages.** Whom we choose to speak to, what we choose to speak about, what we do as we interact, the words we use, the sound of our voices, our posture, our facial expressions, our touch, and even our smell constitute the message or the *content* of our communication. Thus, everything we do as a sender or a receiver has potential message value for a person who is interacting with us or observing us interacting.

Messages can be auditory (heard), visual (seen), gustatory (tasted), olfactory (smelled), tactile (felt), or situational-manipulational (communicated by the environment). Some of the messages we send are more personal than others (a caress, a kiss, or the words "I love you"); others are less personal and might be sent to any number of persons. Some of our messages are sent purposefully ("I want to be very clear about this . . .") while others, such as nervous tics, are sent accidentally or unconsciously ("I didn't know you knew how I felt about . . ."). Consequently, everything we do when interacting with another person has potential message value as long as the other person is observant and interprets or gives meaning to the behavior we exhibit. Whether we grimace, emphasize a point, shout for joy, move closer, turn away, chat briefly, or go on and on, we are communicating, and the messages being sent and received are having some effect.

Channels

A **channel** is simply the medium through which a message travels. Every channel connects a sender and receiver, much as a bridge connects two locations. As noted, we send and receive messages with and through all of our senses. In effect, we can simultaneously use a multitude of channels to communicate a single message. In fact, under most circumstances, interpersonal communication is a multichanneled interaction using visual, auditory, tactile, and olfactory channels to convey both verbal and nonverbal messages.

Channels connect individuals, each one functioning as a link between sender/receiver and receiver/sender. In cementing this link, a hug and a sincere smile may communicate as much as saying, "It's great to see you again." Effective interpersonal communicators are adept at switching channels. They know how to use sound, sight, touch, taste, smell, and the environment, as well as traditional words and nonverbals to get their message across. Get stuck using one channel and you could tune yourself into the wrong part of a message, missing the most important part. While we may prefer to send or receive messages through a particular channel, we should pay attention to all of them.

Today, we have such a richness of communication channels available to us. In addition to face-to-face contact, we have chat rooms, instant messaging via computers, and text messaging via cell phones at our disposal. If one channel is closed, we can open another. If one channel is damaged, we can use others to compensate. For example, rather than assuming that a blind or sight-impaired person will be able to recognize us by our voice, we should also name ourselves. Since the blind person is unable to see the visual cues we may be using to color in or shade the meaning of our verbal message, we will also need to take special care to ensure that the meanings we want conveyed are contained in the words we choose and the expressiveness of our voice.

Noise

Noise is anything that interferes with or impedes our ability to send or receive a message. Noise distracts communicators

We deliver our messages via pathways known as channels. What channels do you see these graduates using as they celebrate with one another?

and focuses their attention on something extraneous to the communication act. Effective communicators find ways to make sure their messages get through accurately despite the interfering noise.

Among the creators of noise are the *environment, physical discomfort, psychological states,* and *intellectual ability.* If there is a lot of noise, it becomes less likely that interactants will be able to successfully negotiate or share meaning. Noise can emanate from both internal and external sources.

Among the external sources of noise are the sight, sound, smell, and feel of the environment. A drab room, an overly warm space, a loud siren, an offensive odor, as well as two or more conversations occurring at the same time, are all examples of environmental noise.

Among the internal factors of noise are our personal thoughts and feelings. Racism, sexism, feelings of inadequacy, hunger, excessive shyness, excessive extroversion, deficient knowledge, or excessive knowledge can also interfere with our ability to send and receive messages effectively. Most people find that it is easier to cope with external noise than with internal noise factors because closing a window, for example, is usually a lot easier than changing a personality (see Table 1.2).

Feedback

Feedback is information we receive in exchange for messages we have sent. It can be both verbal and nonverbal. Feedback lets us know how we are doing, or how another individual is responding to us. It tells us "how we are coming across," whether we were heard through the noise and interference, and how the receiver has interpreted our communicative efforts. It reveals whether the meaning of our message has been interpreted as we hoped it would be and, if it was not, lets us know what portions of our message we need to reencode.

Feedback can be positive or negative, internal or external. *Positive feedback* enhances behavior in progress. It serves a reinforcing function, causing us to continue behaving or speaking as we have been. In contrast, *negative feedback* stops

TABLE 1.2
Types of Noise

Semantic noise	noise due to the failure to understand the intended meaning of one or more words or the context in which the words are being used (persons speaking different languages, using jargon and "technicalese")
Physiological noise	noise due to personal illness, discomfort, or a physical problem including speech, visual, auditory, or memory impairment (difficulty articulating, hearing or sight loss, fatigue, disease)
Psychological noise	noise due to anxiety, confusion, bias, past experience, or emotional arousal that interferes with communication (sender or receiver prejudice, close-mindedness, rage)
Intellectual noise	noise due to information overload or underload (over- or under-preparedness)
Environmental noise	noise due to the sound, smell, sight, and feel of the environment or physical communication space that distracts attention from what is being said or done (cars honking, garbage rotting, people talking at once, cellular or computer interference)

behavior in progress. It serves a corrective function, prompting us to discontinue one or more behaviors because of their apparent ineffectiveness. Thus negative feedback helps us eliminate behaviors others find inappropriate or unwarranted.

Because we constantly communicate with ourselves (even when we communicate interpersonally), feedback emanates from both internal and external sources. *Internal feedback* is the feedback you give yourself as you assess your own communication during an interpersonal transaction. *External feedback* is feedback you receive from the other party. To become a more competent communicator you need to be sensitive to both types of feedback; both serve important functions.

When we provide feedback, the response we provide can focus on the person or on the message. We can talk about a person's appearance or we can talk about the effectiveness of the message. In addition, we can be totally honest about the feedback we offer (*low-monitored* feedback) or we can carefully craft a response designed to serve a particular purpose (*high-monitored* feedback). Whether we are spontaneous or guarded in offering feedback depends on how much we trust the other person and how much power they have over our future. With whom would you be spontaneous in the delivery of feedback? With whom would you be more guarded?

We can also offer immediate or delayed feedback. Immediate feedback instantly reveals its effect upon us. For example, after someone tells us a joke, we may convulse in laughter. Other times, however, a gap occurs between the receipt of a message and the delivery of feedback. For example, we can offer a speaker immediate feedback by applauding every time the speaker makes a remark with which we agree. This often happens when Congress listens to the president's State of the Union address. Or, as is more often the case, we can withhold applause until after a speaker has finished delivering a speech. When we interview for a job, we are rarely told immediately after the interview whether we will be given the position. Instead, sometimes days, weeks, or even months pass before we know whether or not our interview was successful. The same is true of many mediated situations and events. An advertiser rarely knows the success of a particular campaign until it is well underway. Similarly, while the Nielsen overnights give immediate feedback as to how the airing of a show has done, the overall viability of a series may not be known until nearly the end of a season.

Feedforward is a variant of feedback. Instead of being sent after a message is delivered, it is sent prior to a message's delivery as a means of revealing something about the message that is to follow. Feedforward introduces messages by opening the communication channel and previewing the message. Phatic communication (see Chapter 12), or messages that open communication channels, as in the preface and the cover of this text and the introduction of a chapter, are examples of feedforward.

Context

The environmental, situational, or cultural **context,** or setting, in which the communication takes place can also affect the outcome of the interpersonal transaction. The environmental context refers to the physical location in which an interaction occurs. The situational or cultural context refers to the life space or cultural backgrounds of the communicators. In many ways, culture and physical, social, psychological, and temporal settings are integral parts of communication.

The *physical setting* includes the specific location for the interaction, that is, the setting's appearance and condition. A candlelit communicative exchange may have a different feel and outcome from one held in a busy, brightly lit office. The *social setting* is derived from the status relationships and roles assumed by the interactants. Some relationships seem more friendly and are less formal than others. The *psychological setting* includes the emotional dimension of the interactants. It influences how persons feel about each other and respond to each other. The *temporal setting* includes not only the time of day the interaction takes place, but also the history, if any, that the interactants share. Any previous communication experiences communicators have had with each other will influence the way they treat each other in the present. The *cultural context* is composed of the beliefs, values, and rules of communication that affect the behaviors of the communicators. If interactants are from different cultures, the rules that each follows may confuse the other or lead to missed chances for effective and meaningful exchange. Sometimes the context is so obvious or intrusive that it exerts considerable control over the way we interact by restricting or dominating the way we relate to each other; other times it seems so natural that we virtually ignore it.

Effect

As we interact with each other, we each feel an **effect**—we are influenced in some way by the interaction. One interactant may feel the effects more than the other. One person may react more quickly than the other. The effects may be immediately observable or initially not observable at all.

The effect can be emotional, physical, cognitive, or any combination of the three. As a result of interacting with another you can experience feelings of elation or depression *(emotional);* you can fight and argue or walk away in an effort to avoid a fight or argument *(physical);* or you can develop new ways of thinking about events, increase your knowledge base, or become confused *(cognitive).*

There is a lot more to interpersonal communication and the ultimate effects of your interpersonal connections than you may immediately discern. In large measure, the outcomes of interpersonal communication are related to the level of your interpersonal interaction. In fact, your current relationships may best be considered examples of "unfinished business."[8]

A Model of Interpersonal Communication

One way to visualize how these elements interact with and relate dynamically to each other is to examine the model of interpersonal communication (see Figure 1.1). The model shows that the sender and the receiver of the message are both active participants; that each party to the interaction performs both sending and receiving roles, typically simultaneously; and that the sending and receiving processes are continuously reversed, making neither role the exclusive property of any one participant. The sender and receiver are shown as irregular shapes to indicate that both individuals are in a process of constant change and development. Every experience we have is unique (not necessarily bad or good) and changes us in some way.

Noise or interference can enter at any point in the transaction; it may be present in the people, the message, the channel(s) used to carry a message, or the environment. We see that communicators are affected by fields of experience or psychological frames of reference (including culture) that they carry with them wherever they go. A person's psychological frame of reference (which can also be a form of noise) influences the meanings given to messages. By depicting communication as a circular rather than a linear relationship, and by showing the presence of feedback, the model also reveals that communication is continuous, that it evolves or progresses over time, that it accumulates, and that it has neither

FIGURE 1.1
Model of Interpersonal Communication

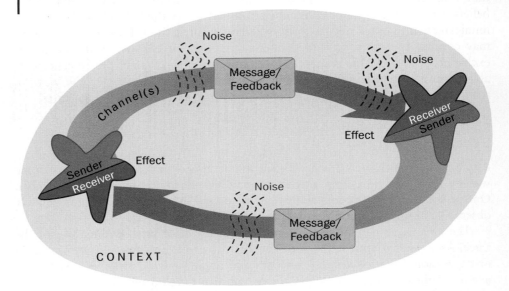

Practice

Making Model Sense

Use the model of interpersonal communication in Figure 1.1 to analyze the following interpersonal scenario. Identify how each of the factors included in the model—people, messages, channels, noise, feedback, context, and effect—makes its presence felt during the interaction.

SARAH *(approaching a restaurant table):* Hi, Kevin. I thought I recognized the back of your head. How ya doing? Long time no see.

KEVIN *(turning, somewhat startled):* It sure has been a long time, hasn't it? When was the last time we got together? Could it already be a year?

SARAH *(smiling):* Longer than that. I haven't seen you since your divorce from Jeanie.

KEVIN: I recognize your perfume—it used to drive me crazy when Jeanie wore it. Haven't seen me since the divorce. Hmmm . . . that makes it almost two years and twenty-four days, then.

SARAH: Time sure goes fast when you're having fun, doesn't it? Well, you look great. Life's been good to you, huh?

KEVIN: Yeah. I just got back from six months' troubleshooting in Singapore. I got a promotion,

too. I'm finally making the kind of money I deserve.

SARAH: Good for you! Dante and I still see Jeanie, you know.

KEVIN: Do you? How's she doing? I haven't spoken to her in two years, either.

SARAH: You haven't even spoken to your ex since the divorce? Actually, I'm meeting her for lunch today.

KEVIN: Didn't seem to be anything left to say to her. *(Does a double-take.)* Did you say you're meeting Jeanie here? Listen, I'd really love to talk, but I've got to get back for an important client conference. It sure was a surprise running into you.

SARAH: Bet it was. I'll tell Jeanie you say hello.

KEVIN: No. Don't even tell her that you saw me. It would just open up her old wounds.

SARAH: Why would it do that? I'm sure she'd be glad to know you're doing so well. Anyway, she's got a great job and is seeing one of Dante's friends.

KEVIN: So she picked up the pieces, did she? I didn't think it would happen that fast. She was so broken up, so devastated by my leaving.

SARAH: Life goes on.

KEVIN: Guess it does. Well, gotta go. Be good.

SARAH *(Under her breath, as he walks away):* What a conceited jerk.

a clearly observable beginning nor a clearly observable end. The situational/cultural context depicted in the model is irregular in shape to indicate that it, too, is constantly changing and evolving, and to be effective at interacting interpersonally we must be ready to adapt to it.

Thus it is clear from the model that all the parts of the communicative act continuously interact with and affect each other. The effect of an interaction becomes part of the total **field of experience** that an individual brings to every communication.

Why We Communicate Interpersonally: Motivation

Interpersonal communication can help us discover who we are, meet our needs for personal contact, and cause us to change our own attitudes and behaviors or the attitudes and behaviors of others. In these ways interpersonal communication serves *psychological, social, information,* and *influence functions.*

Psychological Functions

A primary function served by interpersonal communication is self–other understanding. When we get to know another person, we also get to know ourselves. When we get to know ourselves, we learn how others affect us. In fact, we depend on interpersonal communication to develop our self-awareness and maintain our sense of self. To quote communication theorist Thomas Hora: "To understand oneself, one needs to be understood by another. To be understood by another, one needs to understand the other."[9]

As previously mentioned, interpersonal communication affords us numerous chances both to get feedback from others and to give feedback to them. As such, it presents us with myriad opportunities for self–other discovery. Interpersonal communication helps us know who likes or dislikes us and why, when and why we trust or distrust others, which behaviors elicit strong feelings on our part, under what conditions we have the power to influence others, and whether we have the ability to resolve conflicts that confront us.

Social Functions

Just as we need water, food, and shelter, we need people. When we are isolated or cut off from human contact, our health suffers. In fact, being in at least one good relationship appears to be necessary for both physical and mental well-being.[10]

Through interpersonal communication we begin and work to maintain meaningful relationships with others. To various degrees, our key social needs are met through our interpersonal contacts. Although we vary greatly in the extent to which we experience these needs, according to psychologist William Schutz our relationships reflect three needs in particular: our need for *affection*—to express or receive fondness; our need for *inclusion*—to be included or include others as full partners in dyads of various kinds; and our need for *control*—to be directed or to exert influence over ourselves and others so that we feel responsible and can prove to ourselves that we are able to deal with and manage our environment.[11] When we interact with someone whose needs complement or balance our own, each of us is able to have our needs met. When our needs are not complementary, however, we are more apt to experience relationship struggles or conflicts.

Interpersonal communication also gives us the chance to share our reality with another person, as well as to enter into and experience that person's reality. More than ever before, there is the likelihood that we will share interpersonal relationships with people from cultures other than our own. Our interpersonal styles may differ from theirs. We will need to adapt to the sound, form, and content of messages delivered to us

Interpersonal communication is a dynamic, mutually reinforcing, interactional activity that affects each of the parties to it.

during interpersonal contacts with members of different cultures. While we may more easily identify with and understand those who are like us, not sharing a common culture does not preclude our learning to share similar meanings.[12] To do so, we must learn how the members of different cultures feel about displaying affection, exerting control, defining roles, and meeting goals.

Interpersonal communication can also fulfill our needs to befriend others and to feel needed. Thus, in many ways effective relationships can alleviate our feelings of isolation; fulfill our desire to be with people; give us the chance to feel loved, wanted, and capable; and, in general, give us personal satisfaction by helping us feel more positive about ourselves.

 Theory

Tell Me Why

By looking at our relationships we can learn how they help us fulfill various communication functions.

1. Compile a list of key relationships you enjoy.

2. For each, identify the prime function(s) served by the relationship.

3. Provide one or more examples that illustrate the function(s) provided. For instance, your relationship with your sister might serve psychological, social, and information functions if she acts as a sounding board for you when you have a problem, meets you for lunch, or lets you know how your mother is doing.

Information Functions

During interpersonal contacts we have the opportunity to share information and reduce the amount of uncertainty in our lives. As we take in information, our need to acquire knowledge is met. When we relate interpersonally, we both give and receive information.

Information is not communication. While interpersonal communication can help us satisfy our desire for knowledge, can we be given too much information? The answer is yes. More information is not necessarily better information. More communication is not necessarily better communication. Sometimes no information and no communication may be the best course. We can, after all, talk a problem or issue to death. And in the process we can talk ourselves deeper and deeper into trouble. Thus, just as there is a time to talk, there is a time to stop talking and listen.

Influence Functions

During interpersonal contacts, we have the opportunity to influence each other subtly or overtly. As we exert influence, our need to gain compliance is met. When we relate interpersonally, we are sometimes the users of and sometimes the target of persuasion.

As we noted earlier in this chapter, interpersonal communication is goal-directed. Because of this, even though we may neither admit it nor be conscious of it, we often use strategic communication to achieve our goals. We methodically plan how to achieve the ends we desire. We seek contact with and advice from persons who we believe can assist us. This is not to say that we are manipulative or deceptive. Neither of those practices support the interdependent and transactional nature of interpersonal communication.[13] Communication isn't something we do to others. It is a mutually reinforcing activity we engage in together. How we interact with each other is a two-way affair. We mutually influence each other.

Mutual influence means that not just one party is affected by what we do and say; we are both affected.

Thus, interpersonal communication has evolved from a linear process in which one receiver influences another, to an interactional process in which communication by each person precipitates a reaction in the other person, to a mutually interactive transaction deriving meaning from the simultaneous sharing of ideas and feelings. From a transactional perspective, no single cause explains how you interpret or make sense of experience. Communication is more complex than that.

Making Interpersonal Contact: Characteristics, Principles, and Axioms of Communication

As noted, every interpersonal communication contact shares certain essential elements and serves one or more functions in our personal lives. Every interpersonal communication contact also shares:

1. *Key characteristics*, that is, descriptions of the communication that tend not to vary from situation to situation or from context to context;

2. Core *communication principles*, that is, every communication episode illustrates identifiable behavioral patterns and motivations; and

3. The ability for the communication to be analyzed or explained using one or more of five basic communication *axioms*.

Characteristics of Interpersonal Communication: Taking a Closer Look

Let's explore a number of noteworthy characteristics of interpersonal communication (see Table 1.3).

TABLE 1.3

Communication Is . . .	In Other Words . . .
A dynamic process	It is ongoing, continuous, and in a constant state of flux.
Unrepeatable and irreversible	It is unique.
Learned	We find out over time what works for us and what does not work if we remain conscious of the communication.
Characterized by wholeness and nonsummativity	It operates as a complete entity, much like a team functions.

Interpersonal Communication Is a Dynamic Process

When we say that interpersonal communication is a **dynamic process** we mean that it is ongoing or continuous, and in a constant state of flux. All the components continually interact with and affect each other. They are interdependent or interconnected. They depend on and influence one another. What one person says or does during an interpersonal contact affects what the other person says or does. Everything is cumulative. In many ways, every interpersonal encounter is a point of departure for a future encounter.

Interpersonal Communication Is Unrepeatable and Irreversible

Every interpersonal contact is unique. It has never happened in just that way before, and it will never happen in just that way again. Why? Because every contact changes us in some way and, as a result, can never be exactly repeated or replicated. Thus, try as we might, we can never recapture exactly the same feelings, thoughts, or relationship that existed at a specific point in time. We and the person with whom we shared that relationship are no longer exactly the same persons we were before we made contact.

In addition to being unrepeatable, interpersonal communication is also irreversible. Once we have said or done something to another, we cannot erase its impact. After we exhibit behavior, we cannot merely say, "Forget that!" and substitute a better or more appropriate behavior in its place (though we sometimes might like to try). Human beings, unlike cars or tape recorders, cannot be put in reverse or rewound. We cannot unhear words we have heard, unsee sights we have seen, or undo acts we have displayed. Such stimuli are irretrievable. Presenting a new stimulus does not change the previous stimulus. It merely becomes part of a behavioral sequence.

"Un-communicating" is impossible on-line as well as off-line. For one thing, a message that is in writing provides evidence of the message sent. E-mails are difficult if not impossible to erase. They remain on servers and workstations. You may try to soften their effects, but you cannot reverse their existence any more than you can try to squeeze the toothpaste back into a tube.

Describe a time when the irreversibility of communication posed problems for you. What feelings or emotions caused you to want to take back what you said or reverse what you did? What feelings or emotions occurred when you realized that was impossible?

Interpersonal Communication Is Learned

Over time we learn what works for us in an interpersonal relationship and what does not. Our communication with another person can be hindered if we remain unconscious of the ways in which we affect him or her, and vice versa. Part of the art of interpersonal communication involves recognizing how our words and actions affect others, how their words and actions affect us, and then, based on our observations, making the necessary adjustments.

Interpersonal Communication Is Characterized by Wholeness and Nonsummativity

When we say that the interpersonal relationship is characterized by wholeness we are saying that it operates as a complete entity. It is similar in operation to a team, in that when a team competes, in theory, individuals do not win or lose; the team wins or loses. Likewise, when we examine interpersonal communication, we consider more than the individuals involved; we look at the unique ways in which the individuals affect each other. When we say that interpersonal communication is characterized by *nonsummativity* we are saying that the whole is more than the sum of its parts; in other words, interpersonal communication is about more than just its participants per se. We cannot understand a couple by looking at only one-half of the partnership. We cannot understand a family by looking at only one child. The nature of the relationship itself must be examined. The "us" must be explored. The relationship takes on a quality that cannot be explained merely by possessing information about its parts. The whole of a system is simply different from the sum of its components.[14]

Principles of Interpersonal Communication

Interpersonal communication involves understanding patterns of behavior, predicting the behaviors of others, and providing reasons for their behaviors, as well as our own.[15] **Behavioral patterns,** not individual behavioral acts, provide the basis for understanding interpersonal communication. In interpersonal communication, a behavior is viewed as part of a series of behavioral events. In other words, interactions are viewed as behavioral sequences. No single behavior is interpretable in and of itself; its meaning becomes clear only if it is interpreted as part of a series of behaviors that occurs within a given context.

As noted in the discussion of the essential elements of communication, interpersonal communication involves not only interpreting, but also predicting and accounting for the behavior of another person. If we are able to distinguish individuals from the groups they are members of, then we will recognize their uniqueness and we will be able to base our understanding of them on psychological cues. For example, were we to interact with a number of different professors over time, yet treat all of the professors alike, or were we to date a number of different men or women, yet not distinguish one date from another, we would not be very effective interpersonal communicators. To the extent that we can predict the behavior of a particular professor or a specific woman or man, and account for that behavior, what we term **reasoned sense making,** we understand that individual more than we might understand other professors, other dates.

We also reason retrospectively. **Retrospective sense making** involves making sense of our own behavior once it has occurred. We interpret our own actions in light of the goals we have or have not attained. We look back on interactions and continually redefine the relationships we experience, which is our way of making sense of them. As the interactions progress, the events of a relationship increase in number, and as a result, the relationship continues to change. Thus, interpersonal communication can also be defined as a relationship: it is human interaction; it is the process of behaving with one another.

Five Communication Axioms

Exploring communication characteristics and principles has shown what an interpersonal contact is like and how it can help us predict and understand our own and others' behavior patterns. Now let's turn our attention to the five **axioms of communication** or universally accepted principles, identified in a classic study by Paul Watzlawick, Janet Beavin, and Don Jackson.[16] Each axiom helps us more fully understand the interpersonal interactions that we experience (see Table 1.4).

> **TABLE 1.4**
> Axioms of Communication
>
> 1. *You cannot not communicate.*
> 2. *Interactions have content and relationship dimensions.*
> 3. *Interactions are defined by how they are punctuated.*
> 4. *Messages are verbal symbols and nonverbal cues.*
> 5. *Exchanges are symmetrical or complementary.*

Axiom 1: You Cannot Not Communicate

Behavior has no opposite. Whenever we are involved in a person-to-person inter-action, of necessity we respond in some way. We cannot voluntarily choose to stop behaving. Even if we consciously decide not to respond, even if we do our utmost not to move a muscle or utter a sound, our lack of a response is itself a response. As such, it has message value, influences others, and therefore communicates.

Watzlawick, Beavin, and Jackson identified four basic strategies we typically use when trying *not* to communicate—that is, when we seek to avoid rather than commit ourselves to interpersonal contact. The first strategy is to *reject the communication efforts of the other person.* We make it clear that we do not want to converse. By doing this, however, we do not actually avoid communicating, and we may increase our own discomfort as well as embarrass ourselves and the other person as a result of our directness. With the second strategy, even though our desire is to not communicate, to avoid feeling uncomfortable, we take the easy way out and *accept* the communication efforts of the other person. We make conversation, hoping that it will be short-lived and that the other person will relent and go away. The third strategy requires us to *disqualify* communication. In other words, we communicate in a way that invalidates message sending and receiving. We contradict ourselves, switch subjects, utter incomplete sentences, and spurt out non sequiturs with the expectation that the other person will be so stymied by our responses that he or she will give up. When we use the fourth strategy, we use the *symptom* as a means of communication. We pretend that we would love to interact, but unfortunately, because we are too tired, upset, or otherwise dis-tracted, we simply cannot communicate at present. Despite our ability to use each of these strategies, no matter how hard we resist, we cannot *not* communicate. All behavior has potential message value; behavior communicates whenever it is given meaning.

Axiom 2: Every Interaction Has a Content Dimension and a Relationship Dimension

The content dimension of a message refers to the behavioral response expected, and the relationship dimension indicates how the message is to be interpreted and reveals what one party to the interaction thinks of the other. For example, a hus-band says to his wife, "Come here right now." This message has both a content level that refers to the expected response (the wife will approach her husband immediately), and a relationship level, which reveals something about the relationship between the husband and the wife and indicates how the communication is to be handled. The message can be delivered in a number of ways: as an order, a plea, a flirtation, or an expression of sexual desire, for example. Each way suggests a different kind of relationship. It is through such variations that we offer clues to others regarding how we see ourselves in relationship to them.

Paul Watzlawick, Janet Beavin, and Don Jackson identified three types of responses that we use to reveal how we feel about each other. First, we can practice *confirmation*—we can confirm another's self-definition or self-concept and treat that individual as he or she believes he or she ought to be treated. If, for example, your friend Elana considers herself capable and intelligent and if those around her reward her by asking for her advice or seeking her help, her image of herself is confirmed. Alternatively, we can practice *rejection*—we can reject another individual's definition of self by simply refusing to acknowledge its validity. If your friend Carlos perceives himself to be a leader but no one around him treats him with respect, he may, in time, be compelled to revise his image of himself. Finally, we can practice *disconfirmation*—we can disconfirm the way another defines him- or herself. If confirmation says, "I accept your definition of self; I see you as you see you," and rejection says, "I disagree with your definition of self; I fail to see you as you see you," disconfirmation says, "You do not exist; you are unimportant and inconsequential." When we disconfirm others we indicate to them that we do not care enough about them to reveal how we feel about them one way or another. We treat those persons as nonentities, never changing our reaction to them no matter what they do. We fail to supply these individuals with any clues whatsoever to indicate whether we believe they are performing well or not. For us they do not exist; therefore, we ignore them.

Axiom 3: Every Interaction Is Defined by How It Is Punctuated

Communication is a continuing process. Though we often feel as if we can label the start and the finish, or point to a traceable cause for a specific reaction, in actuality, communication has no definitive beginning or end. Consequently, it is hard to determine exactly what is stimulus and what is response. Consider this example:

> A woman is usually late getting home from work. When she does arrive home, her spouse is frequently asleep. Both are angry with each other. The woman might observe that she works so much because all her husband does is sleep. The husband might say that he sleeps so much because she's never home.

Notice that both husband and wife interpret their own behaviors as responses to the behaviors of the other. To the wife, her husband's behavior is the stimulus and hers is the response; he causes her behavior. For the husband, it's just the opposite. Whereas the husband sees the sequence as going from working to sleeping, the wife sees it as going from sleeping to working. Which is it, really?

We all segment experience somewhat differently because we each see it differently. This division of communication into segments is called *punctuation*. As we saw in the above example, the way a communication is punctuated usually benefits the person doing the punctuating. It also reveals how the individual interprets the

---

No more fiendish punishment could be devised . . . than that we should be turned loose in a society and remain absolutely unnoticed.

— William James

Have you ever been given the silent treatment? How did you respond? How do you respond when others ignore you or pretend you do not exist?

Communication is a continuous stream in which everything is simultaneously a reaction and an instigation, an instigation and a reaction.

— Deborah Tannen

situation, and offers insight into the nature of an interpersonal conflict in particular and the interpersonal relationship in general. However, keep in mind that whenever we suggest that a certain communication began because of a particular stimulus, we are forgetting that communication is continuous and that is has no clearly distinguishable starting or end points.

Axiom 4: Messages Consist of Verbal Symbols and Nonverbal Cues

When we interact with another person we emit two kinds of messages: discrete, digital verbal symbols or words; and continuous, analogic, nonverbal cues. Language is a digital code composed of discrete words, and nonverbal communication is analogic, composed of continuous behavior. Watzlawick, Beavin, and Jackson tell us that the content of a message is more apt to be carried via the digital system, whereas the relationship level of the message is typically carried via the analogic system. Although we can usually control our use of verbal symbols and utter only those words we intend, many of the nonverbal cues we send are not under such tight control. Thus, while we may not speak the angry words we are thinking, our face will reveal our rage. Consequently, it is easy to lie with words, but hard to produce the behavior that supports the lie. Nonverbal cues often give you away.

Axiom 5: Interactions Are Either Symmetrical or Complementary

Relationships can be categorized as either symmetrical or complementary. These terms are not descriptive of "good" and "bad" relationships; they simply represent the two basic types of relationships into which all communication interactions can be divided. Each serves important functions, and both are used in healthy relationships.

In a *symmetrical relationship,* the parties mirror each other's behavior. If one person is amorous, the other is amorous. If one person whines, the other responds similarly. If one expresses envy or anger, so does the other.

In contrast, in a *complementary relationship,* the two interactants engage in opposite behaviors, with the behavior of one precipitating the behavior of the other. If one person is docile, the other is assertive. If one person is a leader, the other is a follower. Complementary relationships maximize the differences between the parties. The communicators occupy different positions: one partner is loud, the other meek; one dominant, the other submissive; one strong, the other weak.

Neither symmetrical nor complementary relationships are trouble-free. Parties to a symmetrical relationship run the risk of experiencing *symmetrical escalation.* Believing they are "equal," each person might assert, for example, the right to exert control. Once this starts, each may feel compelled to engage in a battle to demonstrate his or her equalness. In time, a status struggle ensues. Thus, the main danger faced by interactants in a symmetrical relationship is a runaway sense of competitiveness.

In contrast, the problem that is familiar to those who share complementary relationships is extreme rigidity, or *rigid complementarity.* This problem surfaces when one party to an interaction begins to feel that control is automatically his or hers, that neither alternation nor negotiation is necessary. For example, an overly protective mother who cannot accept that her son or daughter is no longer a child,

When did I become the mother and the mother become the child?

— *Erma Bombeck*

a teacher who cannot learn from his or her students, or an employer who is unable to share leadership of an organization all illustrate the rigidness that befalls interactants who have become locked into self-perpetuating, unchanging, unhealthy patterns of behavior. Switches in power are natural; we need to be prepared for them.

Taken together with the characteristics and principles of communication we have spoken about, the five axioms of communication provide additional knowledge as we seek to enhance our understanding of others and increase the effectiveness of our interpersonal contacts. Now let's widen our focus.

Diversity and Culture Contacts

Diversity and Communication Style

Because U.S. society is becoming increasingly multicultural in makeup, and cultural values help shape our acceptance of and preference for a specific communication style, it is important that we understand the role cultural prescriptions play in shaping our interpersonal contacts. For example, even though the United States is now the most demographically diverse country in the world, how regularly do you take cultural differences into account when you communicate interpersonally?

What steps have you taken to facilitate interaction with people from different cultures? What do you do to promote the discussion of different points of view and to see events from the perspective of the other person?

Developing **cultural awareness,** the ability to understand the role that cultural prescriptions play in shaping communication, is necessary because it is intercultural ignorance, not cross-cultural understanding, that frequently slows our ability to develop meaningful interpersonal relationships with persons who are culturally different from us. We need to become more comfortable and adept at sharing ideas and feelings with individuals from diverse cultures.

Whenever cultural variability influences the nature and outcomes of interpersonal communication, culture is having an effect. To facilitate person-to-person interaction we need to learn not only about our own culture but about other cultures as well. When we learn about a culture we learn about its typical system of knowledge, beliefs, values, customs, behaviors, and artifacts.[17] Every culture can be subdivided into subcultures or cocultures; these consist of members of the same general culture who differ in some ethnic or sociological way from the dominant culture. In the United States, African Americans, Hispanic Americans, Japanese Americans, Korean Americans, the disabled, homosexuals, adolescents, and the elderly are examples of cocultures. To engage in effective interpersonal communication with members of these and other groups it is important to enhance your knowledge of the norms and rules that characterize person-to-person interactions. The lessons taught to you by your culture are not necessarily the lessons others have been taught by theirs.

Among the lessons taught by a culture are how to say hello and goodbye, when to speak and when to remain silent, how to behave when angry, how much eye contact to make when interacting, and how much gesturing and touching is appropriate. If cultural anthropologist Edward T. Hall is right in saying that culture is communication and communication is culture, then culture guides behavior, and we must make the effort to understand someone's culture if we are to stand any chance of being able to understand the individual.[18]

Ask yourself these questions when you communicate interpersonally with an individual whose cultural background differs from your own:

1. How do this person's feelings about socialization differ from mine?

2. How does his or her concept of self differ from mine?

3. To what extent do our attitudes, values, and thinking processes differ?

4. To what degree is he or she more or less competitive than I am?

5. In what ways did his or her use of nonverbal cues differ from mine?

Orientation and Cultural Context

Two variables are used to distinguish cultures: (1) individual and collective orientation, and (2) high-context and low-context communication.[19] Cultures that are more individualistic in nature, such as the United States, Canada, Great Britain, and Germany, stress individual goals. In contrast, cultures that are more collectivistic in nature, such as those represented by many Arabic, African, Asian, and Latin American

in Theory

How Prepared Am I to Interact with Persons from Other Cultures?

To assess your personal preparedness to communicate with individuals from different cultures, respond to each of the following statements as either True or False.

1. I prefer to interact as often as I can with people who are like me.

2. After interacting with a person from another culture I frequently feel confused.

3. I fear developing a close relationship with a person from a different culture.

4. I believe that my culture is superior to all other cultures.

5. I am more comfortable with the way my own culture defines gender roles than with the ways other cultures define them.

By thinking about your responses to statements such as these, you begin developing greater cultural awareness.

countries, stress group goals. Whereas *individualist cultures* nurture individual initiative and achievement, *collectivist cultures* nurture loyalty to a group. While in an individualist culture you are responsible for yourself and maybe your immediate family (the "I" is dominant); in a **collectivist culture** you are responsible for the entire group (the "we" is dominant). Likewise, whereas competition is promoted in individualist cultures, cooperation is stressed in collectivist ones.

Cultures also distinguish themselves from each other by using high- or low-context communication. *High-context cultures* are tradition bound; cultural traditions guide members' interactions, causing them to appear to outsiders as overly polite and indirect in relationships. In contrast, members of *low-context cultures* usually exhibit a more direct communication style; they are verbally explicit. While members of Western cultures tend to exhibit the use of low-context communication, members of Asian and other Eastern cultures typically use high-context communication and interact indirectly, leaving much unstated. Because they also place a premium on face-saving behavior, members of high-context cultures are much less confrontational than members of low-context cultures. They are more apt to avoid arguing because they prefer to preserve harmony, for fear that the other person might lose face. For similar reasons, members of high-context cultures are also reluctant to say "no" directly to another person. Thus, members of low-context cultures may have a difficult time deciding when and if the "yes" of a member of a high-context culture really means yes.

Gender Contacts

Gender and Communication Style

Culture also shapes gender, and gender shapes communication.[20] Socially accepted variations in the definitions and views of masculinity and femininity, **gender differences,** are taught to us as we grow up. As historian Elizabeth Fox-Genovese writes, "To be an 'I' at all means to be gendered."[21] As a result, men and women are pressured subtly or overtly to conform to societal norms, encouraged to learn accepted interaction scripts, and usually develop a preference for using different communication styles. Thus, gender is a social creation, and reflects a sense of social order. In our society, for example, women are generally expected to be more nurturing, sensitive to the needs of others, and emotional than men, whereas men are expected to be more independent, assertive, and emotionally restrained than women.[22] Many families divide responsibilities along gendered lines, assigning physically demanding outdoor chores to males, while females are expected to clean the interior of the house, cook, and care for younger siblings or aging parents. From the delivery room of the hospital, which often wraps baby girls in pink blankets and baby boys in blue blankets; to the playground, where girls and boys are provided with different kinds of toys—perhaps dolls for girls (remember, girls are supposed to be caring, sensitive, and responsive) and action figures for boys (boys are supposed to be active, competitive, and tough); to the school, which encourages males and females to pursue different curricula; to romantic relationships; to career paths; we see gender helping to shape lifestyle. Yet communication can alter the way men and women define themselves and behave. As we become more conscious of arbitrarily created gendered meanings, we can work to reconstruct and broaden our understanding of the meaning of appropriate behavior. You can use your understanding of the cultural and gender differences discussed in this text to help you adjust to differences and reduce the number of misunderstandings you have when interacting interpersonally.

We all express our gender through behavior that we believe is normal for a member of our sex. What defines "normal," however, shifts and changes. By identifying how arbitrarily created gendered constructions, or conventions, affect interpersonal communication and relationships, we take a step toward understanding what we hope for when it comes to our interpersonal lives. What do we see as our options? What tasks do we feel free to perform? What limits, if any, do we think should be set on the role gender plays in our social, professional, and family relationships? All societies promote gender ideologies that specify

in Context

Gender's Impact

When growing up, boys and girls tend to play with different toys. They also often assume different roles when engaging in creative play.

1. What kinds of toys did you play with while growing up?

2. What kinds of roles did you assume when playing creatively with others? For example, were you a teacher? a mother or a father? a nurse? a doctor? a lawyer? an action hero? a space warrior?

3. To what extent, if any, were the games you played and the roles you assumed shaped by culturally gendered expectations?

4. To what extent, if any, are culturally gendered expectations influencing your career choice? Explain.

appropriate behaviors for males and females. How can we tell when a gendered construction is privileging, disadvantaging, empowering, or paralyzing us? What are appropriate ways for men and women to communicate and interact with each other? As you proceed through this text, you will have numerous opportunities to answer questions like these. Gender, after all, is a relational construct that we clarify through person-to-person interaction.

Media and Technology Contacts

Interpersonal Interaction and the Technological Embrace

"The medium is the message." "The medium is the massage." Both of these sayings are owed to the musings of media critic and communication theorist Marshall McLuhan. According to McLuhan, the channels of communication affect both the sending and receiving of messages. The same words sent using face-to-face interaction, print, radio, or television convey different messages. The medium changes things, altering the message, massaging its contents. Ending a relationship in person is different from terminating it via e-mail or telephone.

More than three decades ago McLuhan predicted that the introduction of new technologies would transform our world into a mobile global village.[23] His prophecy has certainly come true. Technological advances have made it increasingly possible for us to watch and listen to, introduce ourselves to, and have continuing contact with individuals across the country and around the world without ever leaving our own homes. Technology and the media are altering our sense of self, the social norms we adhere to, our view of reality, our images of success and failure, and the interpersonal communication options available to us.

Today, many of us are spending increasing amounts of time with computers, music, television, video, and film. As a result, our real-life experiences are influenced by our exposure to **mediated reality**, the reality depicted for us in all the media we see, hear, and read. Mediated reality is frequently sexier, funnier, and significantly more violent than our real-life experiences. Despite this, we often attempt to apply what we learn from the media to our own lives. Often, we end up disappointed. Our love affairs are rarely as poignant or as passionate as those depicted in the media. Our friends are rarely as attractive, giving, or fun to be with as those we "meet" on television. Physicians and lawyers are rarely as successful treating or working with us as are their fictional counterparts. Somehow, real life falls short of the worlds brought to us by television and film.

… *Theory*

Meet the New Stranger

When you were a young child your parents probably cautioned you not to speak to strangers. However, today's on-line services make talking to strangers acceptable, even ordinary. Consider the following questions.

1. Are you more willing to talk to a stranger in cyberspace than at the mall?

2. Does the anonymity or privacy of on-line relationships increase or decrease your level of personal comfort?

3. Should parents restrict on-line chat time much as many restrict television viewing hours?

4. In your opinion, which is more likely to result in a lasting interpersonal relationship—an on-line friendship or the old-fashioned penpal relationships, which depended on the mail for message delivery? Explain.

Computer-mediated communication and the Internet are also altering the nature of our interactions. By participating in online chat rooms (the equivalent of cyberspace pen pals)[24] and bulletin boards, we are also revolutionizing the ways in which we move through social space and interact with others. We now go places without having physically traveled.[25] We can send and receive e-mail; reveal our private fears, desires, and visions; hold forums; and discuss a wide array of subjects of interest with people in diverse locations. We then use the conversations and interactive relationships we share on the global communication highway as input to shape our own lives.

The extent to which the Internet is personalizing or depersonalizing our person-to-person interactions—fostering or impeding the development of an interpersonal community—is debatable. While the Internet, instant messaging, and text messaging may be increasing some kinds of interaction, they may be decreasing others. At least one survey reveals that approximately one-quarter of persons who use the Internet regularly spend less time talking face-to-face or on the telephone with important persons in their lives and more time working as a result of the time spent online.[26] On the other hand, other researchers contend that CMC (computer mediated communication) is not having the adverse effect on interpersonal communication that was feared. At least one survey demonstrates that rather than harming them, the Internet can help relationships thrive. Seventy-two percent of Internet users report having communicated with a relative or a friend within the past twenty-four hours, compared with 61 percent for non-Internet users. Internet users were also more likely to have spoken on the telephone to a friend or relative. In addition, 55 percent of users reported that e-mail had improved their communication with family members, and 66 percent noted that it had promoted their contacts with friends.[27] With which group do you side?

Early proponents of the Internet also claimed that it would dissolve race, class, and gender distinctions, but more recent research suggests that has not been the case. Our concept of community has changed: we now speak of virtual communities, and we have surrogate neighborhoods. The reality is that only a minority of the world's population currently uses the Web. In addition, African Americans, the elderly, and the poor remain underrepresented online. What is more, when we do interact online, we tend to gravitate to cliques of persons who share similar proclivities; we find a Web "tribe" that shares our interests.[28] There is also a digital backlash. Within the last five years, for example, some 30 million Americans have chosen to stop using the Internet, preferring to lead a more simple life by withdrawing from using technology that they feared was complicating their lives.[29] Internet skeptic Steve Woolgar believes that in the end the Internet will probably be like the telephone— "this huge new revolution that didn't make much difference to existing social structures."[30] Do you agree? Is the Internet making a difference in your interpersonal relationships? Do you think Steve Jobs of Apple Computer was right when over a decade ago he noted that computers are really personal and should be renamed "inter-personal computers"?[31]

What we do know, however, is that new technologies are causing some of us to redefine ourselves as "plugged-in technobodies;"[32] Some people feel less worthy in person than they do online, where they are unconstrained by personal contact. Yet at the same time, these new technologies are increasing the options that human beings have to relate to each other and form diverse communities of interest.[33] Whether these options prove to be real or "virtual," beneficial or harmful, is still open to question. What is certain is that they are being incorporated into contemporary social life and thereby altering our communication experiences. Observing this trend, media critic Neil Postman noted that a new technology does not merely add or subtract something from our culture; it changes it. According to Postman, we are the members of a **technopoly**—a culture whose thought-world is monopolized by technology.[34] What is the impact of this? Postman maintains that the continued acceleration of communication is causing us to value immediate gratification and emotional involvement over sequential understanding and logic. He fears that because we are overwhelmed with information but "underwhelmed" by a lack of credibility, we are in danger of becoming tools of our tools. How depersonalizing and impersonal is that?

Gaining Communication Competence

Improving Your Effectiveness as an Interpersonal Communicator

Even though interpersonal communication is virtually inevitable, few—if any—of us are as effective or as successful at it as we could be. Consequently, we hope you treat this class in interpersonal communication as your laboratory. Use the information you gain and the skills you practice as guides when you interact with others. Certainly there is no such thing as becoming too good at interpersonal communication. To help yourself become a better communicator, whatever your capabilities are right now, promise yourself you will do the following.

Add to Your Storehouse of Knowledge about Interpersonal Communication

The chances that you will be able to influence what happens during interpersonal encounters is based, at least to some extent, on your knowledge of how interpersonal relationships work. While interpersonal relationships vary significantly, with some being plagued by problems and others proceeding smoothly, one of our objectives in this book is to share with you a number of techniques you can use to enhance the quality of your relationships and the satisfaction you and the people with whom you communicate derive from them.

Recognize How Your Relationships Affect You

Each of your interpersonal contacts affects you in some way. Some may influence your sense of self; others may change the quality of your life. Some enhance your feelings of confidence; others diminish your belief in your abilities. While healthy interpersonal relationships can enrich your life, unhealthy ones may rob you of your energy and leave you demoralized and apathetic. Another goal of this book is to help you understand the complex ways in which interpersonal communication changes you and the complex forces at work during person-to-person contacts. If you can identify the challenges you face when interacting interpersonally, identify alternative modes of responding, and learn how to think about interpersonal relationships both in general and in particular, then you will be better able to deal effectively with a wide variety of interpersonal experiences.

Recognize the Behavioral Options Open to You

The choices you make during interpersonal contact have an impact not only on you but also on your cocommunicator and the relationship you share. Rather than responding automatically, take time to think about the options available to you. What happens in a relationship is usually not beyond your control; in most situations you do have the freedom to respond in any number of ways. Every contact you engage in offers opportunities to improve it if you remain flexible and open. Another goal of this book is to help you learn to take advantage of such opportunities.

Interact Ethically, Respect Diversity, and Think Critically about Your Person-to-Person Contacts

Effective interpersonal communicators act ethically in their relationships, demonstrate their respect for diversity, and think critically about the interaction itself. Interpersonal communicators who are ethical demonstrate the ability to adhere to standards of right and wrong. They follow appropriate interaction rules, treat others as they themselves would like to be treated, and do not knowingly contribute to the harm of someone else in an effort to achieve personal goals.

Interpersonal communicators who respect diversity understand the role culture plays in person-to-person interactions, tolerate difference and dissent, interact willingly with persons from a variety of cultures, demonstrate a decreased use of stereotypes to guide behavior, process experience from another's viewpoint, avoid imposing their cultural values on others, and refrain from racist or sexist attitudes or behaviors. Individuals who think critically about the interpersonal relationships they share know that they do not know it all. They are open-minded; reflect on the ideas of others rather than respond impulsively; open themselves to new ideas and new ways of perception; challenge themselves to reexamine their beliefs, values, and behaviors; and concern themselves with unstated assumptions in addition to outright discourse.

Practice Skills That Improve Interpersonal Performance

In this book we will share with you skills that you can practice in an effort to enhance your effectiveness as an interpersonal communicator. Commit to practicing them. How you present yourself, how you perceive others, how you use words and nonverbal cues, how you listen, how you progress in a relationship and overcome relationational obstacles, how you demonstrate trust and trustworthiness, and how you handle your emotions—all affect your abilities to interact with family members, coworkers and health providers. The extent to which you practice and apply the skills we discuss will determine in large measure whether you are able to increase your behavioral repertoire and develop your versatility and resourcefulness as an interpersonal communicator.

daily
contacts

Wrap-Up

Meet again in pairs or with your discussion group to re-examine the case study featured at the beginning of this chapter. Reconsider the questions that follow it. How have your answers changed or become more focused? Based on what you have learned in this chapter, what advice would you give Susan and Juan now?

Critical Thinking Contacts

Examine the following cartoon. Then, based on your understanding of this chapter, discuss the advice you would offer to Calvin and Hobbes regarding the role interpersonal communication plays in life.

That's Life

Summary

Our effectiveness as spouse, partner, friend, and coworker depends on how effective we are at communicating interpersonally. In addition, societal problems related to ethnocentrism, sexism, violence, and health can be alleviated to some degree if we improve our ability to relate to others.

During our lifetimes, we each experience a multitude of dyadic relationships. Some will be short-lived and impersonal, while others will develop into lasting friendships or intimate entanglements. The dyad is of central importance in interpersonal communication.

In order to become more adept interpersonal communicators, we need to understand: (1) the relationship among the essential elements of communication (people, messages, channels, noise, feedback, context, and effect); (2) the psychological, social, and informational/influential functions of communication; and (3) the key characteristics, principles, and axioms of communication. Our knowledge of interpersonal communication would be incomplete without an examination of how gender, diversity, and technology influence our relationships.

To improve our effectiveness as interpersonal communicators and demonstrate communication competence, we need to add to our storehouse of knowledge, recognize how relationships affect us, realize the behavioral options open to us, interact ethically, respect diversity, think critically about our person-to-person contacts, and practice basic interpersonal communication skills.

Terms to Talk About

interpersonal communication *(p. 4)*
dyad *(p. 5)*
interpersonal competence *(p. 9)*
impersonal relationship *(p. 10)*
intimate relationship *(p. 10)*
messages *(p. 12)*
channel *(p. 12)*
noise *(p. 13)*
feedback *(p. 13)*
feedforward *(p. 15)*
context *(p. 15)*
effect *(p. 15)*
field of experience *(p. 17)*

dynamic process *(p. 21)*
behavioral patterns *(p. 22)*
reasoned sense making *(p. 22)*
retrospective sense making *(p. 22)*
axioms of communication *(p. 22)*
cultural awareness *(p. 26)*
collectivist culture *(p. 27)*
gender differences *(p. 28)*
mediated reality *(p. 29)*
computer-mediated communication
    (p. 30)
technopoly *(p. 31)*

Suggestions for Further Reading

Michael Benedikt, *Introduction to Cyberspace: First Steps,* Cambridge, MA: MIT Press, 1991. Acquaints us with this rapidly growing communication arena.

Stephen R. Covey, *The Seven Habits of Highly Effective People,* New York: Simon & Schuster, 1989. A very readable personal effectiveness guide.

William B. Gudykunst, *Bridging Differences,* 4th ed., Thousand Oaks, CA: Sage Publications, 2004. Valuable reading for anyone who interacts within multicultural environments and wants to improve her or his ability to communicate effectively with persons from different groups.

Philip N. Howard and Steve Jones, eds., *Society Online: The Internet in Context,* Thousand Oaks, CA: Sage, 2004. Explores how new media are making their presence felt in the different spheres of our lives.

Paul H. Watzlawick, Janet Beavin, and Don D. Jackson, *Pragmatics of Human Communication: A Study of Interactional Patterns, Pathologies and Paradoxes,* New York: Norton, 1967. A classic work that provides a comprehensive analysis of the nature of communication and the pathologies that impede the development of healthy relationships.

The Impact of Self-Concept

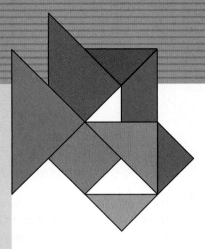

Know thyself.

—Socrates

After completing this chapter, you should be able to:

▮ Define self-concept, reflected appraisal theory, and self-fulfilling prophecy.

▮ Compare and contrast the self and the self-concept.

▮ Discuss the ways others shape a person's self-concept.

▮ Explain social comparison theory.

▮ Distinguish among confirmation, rejection, and disconfirmation.

▮ Describe how cultural diversity and gender influence self-concept.

▮ Distinguish between positive and negative Pygmalions.

▮ Discuss how collectivist and individualist cultures differ in their views toward the self.

▮ Describe the ways in which the media and technology help shape self-concept.

▮ Identify how to change and strengthen self-concept.

daily
contacts

Aisha's Term Paper Problem

"I'll never be able to pass this course," Aisha moaned to herself as she sat in front of the computer with her text opened beside her. "I've been trying to write this paper all weekend and I'm still on the first page." She sighed, and then rose to get a cup of tea.

As Aisha sipped her tea, she began to thumb through the Sunday paper. She stopped to read an article about the Efficacy Institute, a school that provides students with instruction on self-concept. The studies on "efficacy" suggest that any person can succeed if he or she is motivated and works hard. The efficacy program, now being tried experimentally in several schools across the United States, repeatedly delivers this message to students: "Work hard! Think you can! Believe in yourself!" One teacher calls their approach a "recipe to get smart."*

Aisha began to think about her own situation. She had dropped out of college years earlier and had only recently returned to school. Now she found herself stuck in the same old trap—she didn't think she could do the work. Aisha wondered—would the recipe work for her? She recalled how she had felt when she dropped out of college, and how she was now experiencing those same feelings of failure about the course for which she had to write a term paper. Could the "success" techniques advocated by efficacy experts work for her?

Aisha sat down at her computer and typed the following:

RECIPE FOR SUCCESS IN COLLEGE
1. Believe in Your Abilities to Succeed
2. Work Hard on All Assignments
3. You Can Do It!

She placed her sign above the computer and again began to work on her term paper.

Suddenly she was writing. Her head was filled with so many new ideas that her fingers could barely keep up. Could all of these ideas have come from the "recipe" she had just posted above her computer?

Aisha didn't care. She was working too hard and too fast to ponder that possibility.

Divide into pairs or discussion groups and answer the following questions:

1. Do you believe that improving a college student's self-esteem will enable him or her to earn better grades? Why or why not?
2. Are there recipes students should follow to succeed in college? In the world of work? In life? If so, describe them and compare and contrast them.
3. In your opinion, does what you tell yourself influence your chances of succeeding? Explain.

*Lynda Richardson, "Dr. Crew's Prescription: 'Efficacy' Looms as New York's Next Educational Philosophy," *New York Times,* November 26, 1995, p. 39.

Do you know who you really are?

Who are you? What do you think of yourself? What kind of relationship do you have with yourself? When you evaluate yourself do you characteristically give yourself a thumbs up or a thumbs down? This chapter offers you the opportunity to find out more about yourself. It allows you to explore the nature of the self; to analyze how culture, gender, the mass media, and technology influence its development; and to examine how the intrapersonal level of communication (the individual level, communication with oneself) and your intrapersonal view of yourself (the view of communication that comes from your perspective) affect the choices you make, the actions you take, and the interpersonal relationships you have.

As poet–philosopher Alan Watts notes, "Trying to define yourself is like trying to bite your own teeth." Exactly how confident are you that you really know yourself? And how willing are you to try to get to know yourself better?

literary contacts

"The Clown"

Think for a moment. Do you, like the subject in the following poem by Teri Gamble, ever wonder who you really are?

The rubber man in the spotlight
Propels himself
Beyond the reach
Of reality.
Midway between today and tomorrow
He pauses
Suspended in his reverie by the crowd.

The rubber man in the spotlight
Warmed by laughter

Finds a face
To play to.
Dancing upon an ever-turning spindle
He plays to another
And another and another.

The rubber man in the spotlight
Sweeps up the dreams
That remind him
Of yesterday.
Then tumbling out of the ring
His face frozen in a rainbow smile
He wonders who he is.

— Teri Gamble

Who you think you are and how you think about yourself in relationship to others influences every one of your interpersonal contacts. In many ways, what you think of yourself is your *baseline,* or starting point for communication.

The Self-Concept: Your Answer to Who You Are

Where does self-concept come from? While we are not born with a self-concept, over time we certainly do develop one.[1] The day a child first says "me," the day she recognizes herself as separate from her surroundings, life begins to change as she strives to fit into the world as she sees it. In short order, our concept of self—that relatively stable set of perceptions each of us attributes to ourselves— becomes our most important possession.

Beginning in childhood, our **self-concept** is composed of everything we think and feel about ourselves. It is a composite of the roles we claim and the attitudes and beliefs we use to describe who and what we are to others. It is important to use available opportunities to think carefully about the nature of our self-concept.

Are you happy with yourself? With your self-concept?

The ways in which you complete the sentence "I am . . . " in the "In Theory" box and the categories into which your answers can be grouped offer clues to your self-concept. For example, you might conceive of yourself in reference to your *gender* (male or female), *religion* (Buddhist, Muslim, Jewish, Christian), *race* (African American, Hispanic, Asian), *nationality* (United States citizen, Canadian, Russian), *physical attributes* (tall, stout), *roles* (spouse, daughter, sibling, employee), *attitudes and emotions* (optimistic, dejected, personable), *mental*

in Theory

Who Are You?

You can begin the exploration of your self-concept by answering the following question: "Who am I?" How many answers can you give? Complete the sentences below with the many different ways you view yourself.

I am _____
I am _____
I am _____
I am _____
I am _____
I am _____
I am _____
I am _____
I am _____
I am _____

There were many ways to complete the sentence. For example, did you give information about personal traits, such as, "I am spiritual," "I am attractive," or "I am friendly"? Did you describe your social identity, such as, "I am a Christian," or "I am Chinese"? Taken together, your answers describe the elements or specific beliefs that comprise your self-concept. What do your responses reveal to you regarding the way you define yourself? What roles did you see yourself playing? How did you define yourself socially? How did social comparisons influence your answers? To what extent, if any, did past successes and failures as well as other people's judgments play a part in determining your responses?

FIGURE 2.1
The Self and the Self-Concept

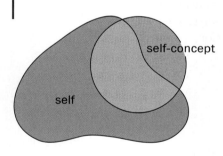

What kind of self-concept have you built? Would you like to reconstruct it?

abilities (brilliant, academically challenged), or *talents* (musically or artistically gifted). The kinds of descriptors you use to express your self-perceptions reveal to you and to others what you think you are like. In many ways, your answers represent a theory or *construct* that you have built to help you make sense to yourself. Keep in mind, however, that the self-concept is not necessarily the same as the self.

According to industrial psychologist William Haney, the self and the self-concept differ from each other in a number of important ways. First, the self is very fluid and in a state of constant change, whereas the self-concept is more highly structured and difficult to change (see Figure 2.1). Second, a portion of our self-concept may not actually be included in the self; this area represents the part of the self that we invent. Third, there is much more to the self than is included within the self-concept; this area represents our untapped potential. For example, you may think of yourself as friendly and outgoing, while others see you as snobbish and reserved. You may have the potential to become a leader, but because of your inability to persuade others that you really want to work with them, you might not have had the opportunity to demonstrate this talent.

To put it another way, the self-concept is a "map" that we create to chart the "territory" that is the self.[2] Our map or mental picture is, at least in part, a result of our interpretations of the messages others send us. As such, it may be accurate or inaccurate, positive or negative. The self-concept is depicted as a rigid, geometric design to indicate that we like to make sense to ourselves. Experiencing uncertainty about the self is not a comfortable state for us to exist in, and so we work hard to develop consistency in the way we perceive ourselves.

What are some of the factors that come into play as we develop feelings about self-worth?

Despite the fact that change is a constant in life, this thirst for constancy causes us to cling to outdated self-notions even in the face of evidence that renders these notions obsolete. Instead of revising our self-concepts to conform to new information, we do our best to acquire information that confirms what we already believe to be true. Such cognitive conservatism on our part allows outmoded notions about the self to persist. It is understandable that we might resist changing an inaccurate self-concept when the new information available to us is negative (for example, we're no longer considered to be as bright or hardworking as we once were) because our self-concept could become more negative. Nevertheless, it is hard to comprehend why we similarly resist changing when the information is positive (for example, we're no longer perceived to be gawky or "a nerd") and would enhance our self-concept. By rejecting such information, we deny ourselves a chance for growth and self-renewal. Defending an unrealistic negative or positive self-concept keeps us from making efforts to redefine ourselves. Whether that redefinition would result in a more positive or negative picture of who we are does not matter; our cognitive conservatism keeps us from seeing the real need for change and allows us to continue deluding ourselves. Refuting new information that could lead us to change only limits us and obscures our view of how others see us. Conducting a reality check is necessary to validate or invalidate who we think we are. Have you conducted one recently? What did you discover?

As we go through life, each of us builds feelings of self-worth. The questions we must answer are: What is our feeling of self-worth? Why? What, if anything, do we want to do about the way we feel about ourselves?

Self-Esteem: Feelings of Self-Worth Affect You

Feelings of self-worth are important. When we feel good about our achievements and what we have earned, we also tend to value and feel good about ourselves. **Self-esteem,** our positive or negative evaluation of our self-concept or sense of personal worth, is important because it both nurtures and feeds success. According to social historian Barbara Dafoe Whitehead, "Self-esteem is rooted in achievement and acquiring new competencies."[3] In other words, we build real and durable self-esteem as a result of overcoming obstacles, acquiring specific tangible skills and achievements, being given and fulfilling progressively increasing responsibilities, and seeking and finding opportunities to give to others.[4] As a result of feeling good about ourselves and what we are capable of doing, we tend to perform well.

Since self-esteem is a measure of the value we place on ourselves, we carry it with us from one interpersonal transaction to another. What is more, we relay it to others by the way we interact with them. High self-esteem and low self-esteem persons differ from each other in communication style. They tend to maintain different eye contact, posture, and expression. Think about both your friendly and romantic relationships. How does your opinion of your self-worth affect them?

Persons who have high self-esteem are likely to think better of others, expect others to like them, evaluate their own performances favorably, perform well in front of others, work harder for those who demand it, feel comfortable interacting with superiors, and defend themselves against others' negative appraisals.[5] In contrast, persons with low self-esteem are more apt to disapprove of others, expect others not to like them, evaluate themselves unfavorably, perform poorly in the presence of others, feel threatened by their superiors, and find it hard to defend themselves against those who view them critically, equating criticism with rejection.[6]

When we perceive ourselves as failures, we are more apt to exhibit behaviors that will indeed cause us to fail. When we perceive ourselves as successes, we are more likely to act successful, and thereby act in ways that will bring about our success. Every success we have helps to build our self-esteem.

However, if self-esteem is not connected to performance, it can be self-defeating. Feeling good about yourself when you have no reason to—that is, when you have added to neither your achievements nor your competencies—can lead you to develop a favorable self-appraisal that will not be matched by the views others have of you. Thus when we talk about the importance of developing self-esteem, we are not talking about merely praising yourself or becoming a cheerleader for yourself; rather, we are talking about opening yourself to opportunities that will help you to develop your skills and abilities to their fullest potential.

We also need to sound another cautionary note: recent research reveals that persons having

 *Theory*

Feelings about the Self

As we overcome obstacles and develop new skills, we tend to enhance our sense of self-esteem. In contrast, when we perceive ourselves to be incapable of achieving either our goals or new competencies, our self-esteem suffers.

1. Provide an example of how believing in your ability to overcome an obstacle or acquire a new skill enhanced both your performance and your sense of self-worth.

2. Provide an example of how failing to believe in your ability to overcome an obstacle or acquire a new skill impeded both your performance and your sense of self-worth.

high self-esteem may pose more of a threat to those around them than persons with low self-esteem.[7] It is feared that overemphasizing the importance of reinforcing self-esteem in those whose self-esteem is already high precipitates a culture of bullying characterized by persistent teasing, name-calling, or social exclusion. Researchers contend that such bullying behaviors derive from an unrealistically inflated self-appraisal.[8] Responding to this, some now call for a balance in the amount of praise we give to prevent inflated perceptions of self-importance in already self-centered persons. These researchers note that it is resilience rather than self-esteem that we should be fostering in others, because it is resilience that helps persons recover from personal defeats and disappointments.[9]

How Others Shape Our Self-Concept

While your experiences help to shape your self-concept, your self-concept, in turn, helps to shape your future experiences. In every instance, how you see yourself in relation to others both guides and modifies your behavior. Thus, you probably do not act the same way with all people. You may act outgoing when in the presence of one friend, but be intimidated by another. You may feel like a star in art class, but inferior in biology, or vice versa. At any given moment, the nature of your self is affected by the nature of the situation in which you are interacting. And your view of your self is shaped during these interactions. Consequently, your language, your attitudes, and your appearance are apt to change as you move from one set of conditions to another. In a way, you become different selves as you adapt to perceived changes.

> In order to get at any truth about myself, I must have contact with another person.
>
> —Jean-Paul Sartre

We Reflect the Appraisals of Others

Psychologist William James put it this way: "A man has as many social selves as there are individuals who recognize him and carry an image of him in their mind."[10] In similar fashion, in his **reflected appraisal theory** psychologist Charles Cooley described the mirrorlike image we derive from our contacts with others and then project into our future experiences. According to Cooley's theory, we build a self-concept that reflects the way we believe others see us.[11] Thus, as our assessments of situations and people change, we show different sides of ourselves. In fact, we use the views of others to develop a view of ourselves. According to the reflected appraisal theory, the self we present is in large part based on the way others categorize us, the roles they expect us to play, and the behaviors or traits they expect us to exhibit. Cooley believes that by reflecting back to us who we are and how we come across, other people function as mirrors for us. He coined the term *looking-glass self* to represent the self that comes to us from others. For example, if others communicate that they see you as a leader, capable or outgoing, you may reflect their appraisals by viewing yourself in those ways. Of course, the roles we play and how we play them affect both the way we communicate and with whom. They also influence the content, object, and frequency of our communication contacts.

literary
c o n t a c t s

The Roles Others Play in Your Self-Concept

What do the following lines from *There Was a Child Went Forth* by Walt Whitman and *Cat's in the Cradle* by Harry and Sandy Chapin tell us about the roles others play in influencing our self-concept and behavior? To what extent do your own experiences confirm or contradict these perceptions?

There Was a Child Went Forth
Walt Whitman

There was a child went forth every day,
And the first object he look'd upon, that object
    he became,
And that object became part of him for the day
    or a certain part of the day,
Or for many years or stretching cycles
    of years. . . .

His own parents, he that had father'd him
    and she that had conceiv'd him in her womb
    and birth'd him,
They gave this child more of themselves
    than that.
They gave him afterward every day, they
    became part of him.

The mother at home quietly placing the dishes
    on the supper table.
The mother with mild words, clean her cap and
    gown, a wholesome odor falling off her
    person and clothes as she walks by,
The father, strong, self-sufficient, manly, mean,
    anger'd, unjust,
The blow, the quick loud word, the right
    bargain, the crafty lure,
The family usages, the language, the company,
    the furniture, the yearning and swelling heart,
Affection that will not be gainsay'd, the sense
    of what is real, the thought if after all it
    should prove unreal,

The doubts of day-time and the doubts of
    night-time, the curious whether and how,
Whether that which appears so is so, or is it
    all flashes and specks?
Men and women crowding fast in the streets, if
    they are not flashes and specks what are they?

The streets themselves and the facades of
    houses, and goods in the windows,
Vehicles, teams, the heavy-plank'd wharves,
    the huge crossing at the fences,
The village on the highland seen from afar at
    sunset, the river between,
Shadows, aureola and mist, the light falling on
    roofs and gables of white or brown two miles
    off,
The schooner near by sleepily dropping down
    the tide, the little boat slackrow'd astern,
The hurrying tumbling waves, quick-broken
    crests, slapping,
The strate of color'd clouds, the long bar or
    maroon-tint away solitary by itself, the spread
    of purity it lies motionless in,
The horizon's edge, the flying sea-crow, the
    fragrance of salt marsh and shore mud,
These became part of that child who went forth
    every day, and who now goes, and will always
    go forth every day.

Cat's in the Cradle
Harry and Sandy Chapin

My child arrived just the other day.
He came to the world in the usual way.
But there were planes to catch, and bills to pay;
He learned to walk while I was away.
And he was talkin' 'fore I knew it, and as he
    grew, he'd say,
I'm gonna be like you, Dad. You know I'm gonna
    be like you.

And the cat's in the cradle and the silver spoon.
Little boy blue and the man in the moon.

When you comin' home, Dad? I don't know when,
But we'll get together then, son;
You know we'll have a good time then.

My son turned ten just the other day.
He said, "Thanks for the ball, Dad.
Come on, let's play.
Can you teach me to throw?"
I said, "Not today. I got a lot to do." He said,
* "That's OK," and he walked away,*
But his smile never dimmed and said,

"I'm gonna be like him, yeah,
You know I'm gonna be like him."

Well, he came from college just the
* other day,*
So much like a man, I just had to say,
"Son, I'm proud of you. Can you sit for a while?"
He shook his head, and he said with a smile,

"What I'd really like Dad is to borrow the car keys.
See you later. Can I have them, please?"

I've long since retired. My son's moved away.
I called him up just the other day.
I said, "I'd like to see you if you don't mind."
He said, "I'd love to Dad, if I can find the time.
You see my new job's a hassle, and the kids
* have the flu,*
But it's sure nice talking to you, Dad.
It's sure nice talking to you."
And as I hung up the phone, it occurred to me,
He'd grown up just like me.
My son was just like me.

SOURCES: Walt Whitman, "There Was a Child Went Forth" from *Leaves of Grass*. Philadelphia: David McKay, 1990; "Cat's in the Cradle," words and music by Harry Chapin and Sandy Chapin. © 1974 (Renewed) Story Songs Ltd. All Rights administered by WB Music Corp. All Rights Reserved. Used by Permission. WARNER BROS. PUBLICATIONS U.S. INC., Miami, FL 33014.

To be sure, not all messages sent to us by others about our nature carry the same weight. Those sent to us by a *significant other*—someone whose opinion we respect and trust—normally exert more influence than do the opinions of strangers or acquaintances. Consider the following questions: Who are the significant others in your life? How have they influenced who you think you are?

We Compare Ourselves to Others

According to **social comparison theory**,[12] we compare ourselves to others to develop a feel for how our talents, abilities, and qualities measure up to theirs; in other words, in an effort to learn more about ourselves, we use others as measuring sticks, and then we evaluate ourselves in terms of how we perceive we measure up to them. As a result, we form judgments of our own skills, personal characteristics, and so on. We can, for example, decide that we are better or worse, stronger or weaker, superior or inferior to, more or less creative, or the same or different than those with whom we compare ourselves. Often, as we assess our similarities and differences, we also make decisions regarding what groups we think we fit in. In general, research shows that we are most comfortable interacting with others who are like us.[13]

If we continually feel that we fall short when we gauge ourselves in relation to others, our self-esteem will suffer. It may well be, however, that we have chosen to compare ourselves to an inappropriate reference group. For example, if we compare our looks with those of a supermodel, our musical ability with those of a Grammy winner, or our athletic prowess with that of an Olympic champion, we probably are making an unfair comparison and, as a result, will develop an unrealistic assessment of our own appearance, talent, or ability. If, on the other hand,

> Part of knowing who we are is knowing we are not someone else.
>
> —*Arthur Miller*

we were to compare ourselves to a more appropriate reference group, we might then be able to inflate rather than deflate our sense of self.

How accurate we are at assessing our self-concept and self-esteem depends on how successful we are at processing experience and feedback. If we pay more attention to our successes than our failures and more attention to positive reactions than negative ones, our sense of self could overinflate. On the other hand, if we pay more attention to our failures and also give more credence to negative reactions, then our sense of self could deflate. In neither instance would our sense of self conform to reality. Rather than achieving congruence, our sense of self would be inconsistent with both real life experiences and feedback.[14]

We possess a perceived self, ideal or possible self, and an expected self. Often, these views of the self may conflict with each other. The perceived self is a reflection of your self-concept. It is the person you believe yourself to be when you are being honest with yourself. Usually there are a number of aspects of the perceived self that you wish to keep secret from others. For example, you might be hesitant to let others know that you do not think you're good looking or intelligent, that you are fixated on becoming wealthy, or that you're more concerned for your own welfare than for theirs. Your ideal self is the self you would like to be. For example, you may want to be likeable, and so you try to be a likeable person. To accomplish this you engage in **impression management;** you exercise control over selected behaviors in an effort to make the desired impression.[15] The possible self is the self we might become—the one we dream of becoming. We may, for instance, want to be a thin self, a passionately loved self, or a rich self. The expected self is the one others expect us to exhibit. It is based on behaviors they have seen us exhibit in the past.

The Self in Relation to Others: Confirming, Rejecting, and Disconfirming Responses

As we interact with others, the way we feel about ourselves changes. Some people with whom we interact **confirm** (support or agree with) our opinion of ourselves by communicating with us in ways consistent with our own appraisal of ourselves. How they treat us during our interpersonal contacts with them reflects the way we think we are. For example, if you believe yourself to be intelligent, confirmers might reflect this by asking you for help. Others with whom we interact **reject** (negate or disagree with) our self-appraisals by treating us in ways inconsistent with our sense of self—whether that treatment is good or bad. For example, if you believed yourself to be hard working, but rejecters treated you as if you were lazy, in time their treatment of you might cause you to revise the picture you hold of yourself. Still others **disconfirm** (show lack of regard for) our self-appraisals by sending us messages that tell us that as far as they are concerned, we are not even important enough for them to think about; in their eyes, we do not exist—we are irrelevant. Disconfirmers ignore you, fail to pay attention to your needs, and go about their business as if you were not present. By treating human beings like nonentities, consistent disconfirmers eventually rob individuals of their sense of self, without which it becomes virtually impossible for them to relate to the world effectively.[16] Thus, those around us help shape our self-concepts in both positive and negative ways. Indeed, virtually every interpersonal contact we share sends us

Practice

Ups and Downs

Because self-concept is a product of person-to-person interactions, it is important to understand what people do to help shape it. In order to understand how others affect us, we need to be able to analyze the extent to which the messages they convey confirm, reject, or disconfirm our sense of self.

1. Identify individuals who have confirmed, rejected, or disconfirmed your self-concept, whether intentionally or inadvertently. Describe the nature of your interactions with these individuals and your impressions of both the short- and long-term effects their actions had on you.

2. Describe an instance in which you deliberately or accidentally confirmed, rejected, or disconfirmed the self-concept of someone else.

Describe what you did or said and the effects your words and actions had. How did you feel once you became aware of the impact of your behavior?

3. What behaviors do you need to practice to be able to demonstrate your recognition of another person's humanity? What skills do you need to exhibit to be able to determine if the messages you send to another person have positive or negative effects on the other person's sense of self? What words can you express and what behaviors can you display to indicate your positive regard for that person? What impact do indifference (exhibiting silence, mindless responses, or interrupting the person when speaking), imperviousness (inattentiveness), or disqualification (a general lack of awareness of the other) have on that person's sense of self?

How do the actions and words of others function to confirm, reject, or disconfirm our self-concept?

TABLE 2.1	
The Self in Relationships	
Confirming response	supports self-appraisal
Rejecting response	negates self-appraisal
Disconfirming response	robs the individual of a sense of self

a message regarding our importance, our capabilities, and how others view both our potentials and our inadequacies.[17] (See Table 2.1.)

The Self-Fulfilling Prophecy: The Influence of Positive and Negative Pygmalions

Are you a pessimist or an optimist? Optimists believe they will succeed and persevere; pessimists tend to give up when confronted with challenges. Consequently, pessimists fail more frequently than do optimists, whose expectations of success often precipitate success. What is unfortunate is that the pessimist's outlook may lead to failure even as success is within reach. In many ways, both pessimists and optimists live out self-fulfilling prophecies.

A **self-fulfilling prophecy** occurs when we verbalize a prediction or internalize an expectation that comes true simply because we act as if it were already true. Thus, our behavior increases the likelihood of particular outcomes. For example, have you ever been invited to a function that you did not want to attend because you expected to be bored? Were you? If you were, to what extent is it possible that your prediction of boredom increased the likelihood of its occurrence?

There are five basic steps in the self-fulfilling prophecy cycle[18] (see Figure 2.2). First, we form expectations of ourselves, other people, or events. (For example, Monica won't like me.) Second, we communicate these expectations by exhibiting various cues. (I'll keep my distance from Monica.) Third, people respond to the cues we send by adjusting their behavior to match our messages. (Monica tells herself: "Ed is stuck up. I want nothing to do with him.") Fourth, the result is that our initial expectation comes true. Because we act as if our belief is true prior to its being confirmed, eventually it *is* confirmed. (It seems that, in fact, Monica does not like me.) Fifth, we attain closure as we complete the self-fulfilling prophecy cycle. The way we interpret the actions of others only serves to strengthen our original belief. (Every time I see Monica, I am reminded that she does not like me.)

A self-fulfilling prophecy can occur because of either a self-imposed or an other-imposed prophecy. When your own expectations influence your behavior, the prophecy is self-imposed. When the expectations of others help direct your actions, the prophecy is other-imposed. Either way, the tendency is for us to become what we ourselves or others expect us to become.

Among the most widely reported examples of the self-fulfilling prophecy is that reported by psychologists Robert Rosenthal and Lenore Jacobson in their classic study *Pygmalion in the Classroom,* named for George Bernard Shaw's

FIGURE 2.2
The Self-Fulfilling Prophecy Story

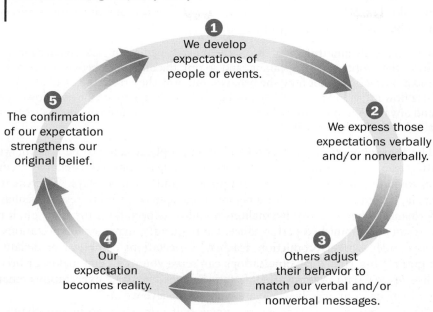

1 We develop expectations of people or events.

2 We express those expectations verbally and/or nonverbally.

3 Others adjust their behavior to match our verbal and/or nonverbal messages.

4 Our expectation becomes reality.

5 The confirmation of our expectation strengthens our original belief.

play *Pygmalion*.[19] Researchers told a number of teachers that certain of their students were expected to "bloom"—that is, perform exceptionally well—during the academic year. What the teachers were unaware of was that since student names had actually been selected randomly, there was no real basis for the prediction of who would succeed. Despite this, the students who were singled out to bloom did so, improving their IQs and performing at higher levels than would otherwise have been expected. Apparently teachers functioned as **positive Pygmalions.** Just as playwright Shaw's character Henry Higgins transformed Cockney flower girl Liza Doolittle into a duchess by believing that he could help her learn to speak and act like one, the teachers had caused the students to live up to the labels given them. The teachers' positive expectations had positively influenced their treatment of the students. The teachers gave the "about to bloom" students extra positive verbal and nonverbal reinforcement, waited patiently for the students to respond if they hesitated, and did not give them negative feedback when they offered incorrect answers. Thus, the way the teachers

in Context

The Pygmalion Effect

Consider the people who have been influential in your personal, educational, or professional life, as well as the people whom you may have influenced.

1. Identify individuals who have intentionally or unintentionally functioned as positive or negative Pygmalions. Describe the behaviors exhibited by the individuals and their effects on you. Be as specific as possible.

2. Identify instances when you believe you functioned as a positive or a negative Pygmalion for yourself.

3. Identify instances when you functioned as a positive or a negative Pygmalion for another. How were you able to determine the impact of your actions?

4. Does your personal experience conform to the research presented in this section? If not, what do you think accounts for the differences?

behaved positively influenced the students' perceptions of their own abilities. The "about to blooms" responded to the teachers' prophecies by fulfilling them. Like Liza Doolittle, the students acted like the persons others perceived them to be. As Liza so aptly put it:

Who are the positive and negative Pygmalions in your life?

> You see, really and truly, apart from the things anyone can pick up (elegant dress, the proper way of speaking, and so on), the difference between a lady and a flower girl is not how she behaves, but how she's treated. I shall always be a flower girl to Professor Higgins because he always treats me as a flower girl, and always will: but I know I can be a lady to you, because you always treat me as a lady, and always will.[20]

The *Pygmalion effect*, as this self-fulfilling prophecy came to be known, works to affect subject performance in a variety of settings, from work-related to educational to social, and it does so in both positive and negative ways. Whereas when others hold high expectations for a person, their opinions tend to result in enhanced performance; when **negative Pygmalions** hold low expectations for a person, it typically results in diminished performance. Consequently, managers' expectations can help or hinder worker production, teachers' expectations can boost or deflate student grades, and your own expectations can serve you as an ego maker or breaker. We live up to—and down to—expectations, whether these expectations emanate from others or from ourselves. We are what we believe we are.

What is important is that we recognize that our self-concept can change. At any point, we can work to strengthen our sense of self-worth.

Changing Your Self-Concept: Revising Impressions and Conceptions

The way others treat us and the way we treat ourselves influence who we think we are. Thus, if we wish to change our self-concept, we need to do our part to break with old ways of thinking. We need to update the way we think about ourselves and assess the accuracy of our self-concept. Figuratively speaking, we need to turn on a light inside ourselves so we can become more self-aware, can recognize the kinds of messages others send us, and can be cognizant of messages sent to us that we typically ignore, discount, or purposefully misinterpret.

While we all share the tendency to hold onto our existing self-concept—even when it is proven false—this doesn't mean that we can't change it. It's just that we have to work hard to overcome our natural resistance to change. In fact, some of us will need professional therapy to help make meaningful changes. What is curious is that the urge we exhibit to accept a faulty impression of ourselves from another, or to cling to an erroneous self-concept, is present whether the change in the way we think of ourselves would be positive or negative. To combat this tendency, we need to exhibit the drive and develop the skills to reevaluate or reinvent ourselves. If we possess such courage, then we, like snakes, will be able to shed and regrow our skins over and over during our lifetimes; unlike snakes, however, we must accomplish this one impression at a time, rather than all at once.

To start this process, we need to understand how we manage to maintain a self-image that others may regard as unrealistic. For example, we might suppose we're great thinkers while others believe our thoughts lack depth. Perhaps because we are overly concerned with how we are coming across to others, we put all our energy into presenting ourselves in as favorable a light as possible. When our entire focus is on ourselves, however, we concentrate less on others' actual reactions to us. Thus, we may fail to pay attention to feedback from them that reveals how they really see us. In addition, sometimes we are able to persist in holding onto an unrealistic self-image because others are reticent to reveal what they really think about us for fear that if they told us the truth our feelings would be hurt. So they tell us instead what they think we want to hear. Other times, we base our assessment of ourselves on obsolete information—we opt to cling to memories rather than face present realities.

professional
contacts

Changes

As you read these words from best-selling author, philosopher, and former salesperson Robert Fulghum's book *Uh-Oh,* ask and answer his questions. What do your answers tell you about your view of yourself today and yesterday? How do you account for any changes you observe?

Over the last couple of years I have been a frequent guest in schools; most often invited by kindergartens and colleges. The environments differ only in scale. In the beginners' classroom and on university campuses the same opportunities and facilities exist. Tools for reading and writing are there—words and numbers; areas devoted to scientific experiment—labs and work boxes; and those things necessary for the arts—paint, music, costumes, room to dance—likewise present and available. In kindergarten, however, the resources are in one room, with access for all. In college, the resources are in separate buildings, with limited availability. But the most apparent difference is in the self-image of the students.

Ask a kindergarten class, "How many of you can draw?" and all hands shoot up. Yes, of course we can draw—all of us. What can you draw? Anything! How about a dog eating a fire truck in a jungle? Sure! How big you want it?

How many of you can sing? All hands. Of course we sing! What can you sing? Anything! What if you don't know the words? No problem, we make them up. Let's sing! Now? Why not!

How many of you dance? Unanimous again. What kind of music do you like to dance to? Any kind! Let's dance! Now? Sure, why not?

Do you like to act in plays? Yes! Do you play musical instruments? Yes! Do you write poetry! Yes! Can you read and write and count? Yes! We're learning that stuff now.

Their answer is Yes! over and over again, Yes! The children are confident in spirit, infinite in resources, and eager to learn. Everything is still possible.

Try those same questions on a college audience. A small percentage of the students will raise their hands when asked if they draw or dance or sing or paint or act or play an instrument. Not infrequently, those who do raise their hands will want to qualify their response with their limitations: "I only play piano, I only draw horses, I only dance to rock and roll, I only sing in the shower."

When asked why the limitations, college students answer that they do not have talent, are not majoring in the subject, or have not done any of these things since about third grade, or worse, that they are embarrassed for others to see them sing or dance or act. You can imagine the response to the same questions asked of an older audience. The answer: No, none of the above.

What went wrong between kindergarten and college? What happened to YES! of course I can?

SOURCE: From *Uh-Oh* by Robert Fulghum, copyright © 1991 by Robert Fulghum. Used by permission of Villard Books, a division of Random House, Inc.

Just as we can view ourselves more favorably than others do, we can also function as our own worst critics and view ourselves more harshly than is warranted. For example, we might be convinced that we are fat despite the insistence of others that we are a perfect weight. Why would we do this? We might act on the basis of outmoded data, information that was true at one time but is no longer true today. Or we might be the recipient of distorted feedback; perhaps an overly critical friend or relative gave us information that warped our view of ourselves. Or we might criticize ourselves simply because we believe that society expects such behavior from us. We might feel that society prefers us to 'fess up to our inadequacies but downplay our strengths.

Do you view yourself more positively or more negatively than you believe is valid? Being too harsh on ourselves can keep us from fulfilling our potential. Instead, we need to assess our strengths and shortcomings honestly, freeing ourselves to reshape our image of self and grow.

Diversity and Culture Contacts

How Important Is the "I"?

In what ways has your culture influenced your sense of self?

People in most, if not all, cultures have a notion about the self, although specific notions of self vary across cultures.[21] These variations or cultural differences influence person-to-person interactions in sometimes subtle and sometimes dramatic ways, affecting how we conceive of "self," the expectations we have for ourselves and others, and our behavior.

In North American and western European cultures, for example, the word *self* usually reigns supreme. People from these cultures reflect the importance placed on individuals as they work toward the realization of personal goals. Persons in individualist cultures value uniqueness and personal identity; they tend to believe in themselves, seek to do their own thing, and shun conformity. In contrast, peoples in Asia, Africa, and Central and South America, places where **collectivist cultures** (cultures in which group goals are given a higher priority than individual goals) are dominant, are more apt to "downplay their own goals," emphasizing in their place goals set or valued by the group as a whole.[22] Japanese parents, for example, do not "lavish praise on their children because they are concerned that if they do they will end up being self-centered and not focus enough on the needs of the group."[23] For members of collectivist cultures, the self is not the center of the universe. In their eyes, the group—not the individual—is the primary social unit. Whereas **individualist cultures** (cultures in which individual identity is paramount) link success with personal achievement, collectivist cultures link success to group cohesion and loyalty. This basic difference is underscored by the fact that the "I" in the Chinese written language looks very much like the word for selfish.[24] For this reason, members of collectivist cultures gain a sense of identity through their group memberships, not by stressing their self-importance or promoting themselves, as members of Western cultures are apt to do.[25] Thus, while some of us have been raised to call attention to ourselves and to sing our own praises, others of us have been reared to avoid such behaviors. For these persons, the self is

In collectivist cultures, group goals are a priority. To what extent, if any, does your cultural orientation support this tendency?

not developed at the expense of the group; loyalties are directed at others instead of at the self. Persons in these cultures are more self-critical, nurturing the interdependent self instead.[26]

Researchers define those of us who are primarily individualist in our way of thinking and behaving as having an **idiocentric orientation.** Those who are primarily collectivist in their way of thinking and behaving are defined as having an **allocentric orientation.**[27] To which group do you belong?

Do the "'I' versus the 'We'" assessment in the "In Practice" box. Clearly, our self-concept—how we define ourselves—is influenced by our unique personal experiences as well as by shared membership in groups. Together with culture these factors play integral parts in helping us formulate a sense of self. However, we do need to be cautious about rigidly categorizing people from a culture within an individualistic or collectivist orientation. It is important to recognize that variations occur within countries. For example, in the United States, persons from the South exhibit higher levels of collectivism than do those who live in the West.[28] In addition, cultural orientations moderate as persons from the West and East interact with each other. For example, after Japanese exchange students live in Western countries, their self-concepts tend to become somewhat more individualized.

In addition to possessing individualistic or collectivistic orientations, persons from different cultures also vary in the communication style they prefer to use. Persons from high-context cultures tend to be extremely polite and indirect in their communication when interacting with others. In contrast, persons from

.๛ *Practice*

The "I" versus the "We"

Describe the extent to which you display a tendency to exhibit an individualist (idiocentric) or collectivist (allocentric) orientation by evaluating how much the following statements reflect the way you think and act in regard to yourself and others. If the statement is very important to you, rate it a 5; somewhat important, a 4; neither important nor unimportant, a 3; somewhat unimportant, a 2; and not at all important, a 1.

A

_____ 1. I want to prove my personal worth.
_____ 2. I need to be myself.
_____ 3. I want others to view me as important.
_____ 4. I want to achieve my personal goals.
_____ TOTAL

B

_____ 1. If I hurt you, I hurt myself.
_____ 2. I want all my relationships to be harmonious.
_____ 3. I am concerned for the welfare of others, even if it hurts me.
_____ 4. I act according to tradition.
_____ TOTAL

To determine your score, total the numbers you entered under A and B. The higher your A score, the greater are your idiocentric tendencies. The higher your B score, the greater are your allocentric tendencies.

low-context cultures tend to exhibit a more direct communication style.[29] When meeting someone for the first time, a person from a low-context culture is likely to ask direct questions in an effort to gather background information and get to know the person. The discovery and expression of individual uniqueness becomes a priority. As a result, persons from individualistic cultures also feel they have to explain everything and feel compelled to speak out. They value assertion. In comparison, persons from high-context cultures hesitate to ask others direct questions, preferring instead to rely on nonverbal, contextual information. They value silence and reticence, believing that persons of few words are thoughtful, trustworthy, and respectable. Thus, persons from collectivistic cultures are likely to find unsolicited self-disclosures inappropriate. They also are less likely to criticize each other publicly, as they would view such behavior as a sign of disrespect or disloyalty. When their words hurt another person, they believe they hurt themselves.

Attitudes toward the self also differ along the dimension of **power distance,** or the extent to which individuals are willing to accept power differentials. Persons from high-power-distance cultures, such as Saudi Arabia and India, perceive power as a fact of life. In these cultures, persons in low-power positions are very likely to defer automatically to persons in authority. In contrast, persons from low-power-distance cultures, such as the United States and Sweden, are more likely to emphasize and value their independence even when in the presence of superiors.[30] A general feeling of equality prevails (see Table 2.2).

Even though they may differ in orientation, young people throughout the world still share many attitudes regarding the self. Most hope to develop and sustain social relationships, especially with their peers, and most are optimistic regarding their abilities to assume responsibilities for themselves in the future. Although the majority of teens exhibit such confidence, on average between 25

TABLE 2.2
Culture and Influences on the Self

Persons with Individualistic Orientations	Conceive of the individual as the basic social unit Make individual goals a priority Link success and individual achievement
Persons with Collectivist Orientations	Conceive of the family/group as the basic social unit Make interdependence/group goals a priority Link success and group achievement
Persons from High-Context Cultures	Exhibit an indirect communication style Make face-saving a consideration
Persons from Low-Context Cultures	Exhibit a direct communication style Seldom think of face-saving
Persons from High-Power-Distance Cultures	Defer to superiors
Persons from Low-Power-Distance Cultures	Value independence

and 30 percent of them also describe themselves as lonely, overwhelmed by life's problems, and frequently sad.[31] Interestingly, Japanese teens are even more likely to attribute these traits to themselves, with 55 percent of them reporting that they are frequently sad and 39 percent describing themselves as lonely. Similarly, Japanese young people are almost twice as likely to fear that they will disappoint their parents or that their parents will be ashamed of them than are young people from other cultures.

According to clinical psychologists Darlene Powell Hopson and Derek Hopson, such discontent with the self is shared by African Americans. The Hopsons report that as early as the age of three, black children begin to express a desire to be white.[32] The experiences of writer Yvonne Lamb echo these findings. One day four-year-old William Lamb surprised his mother by stating: "I want to be white. Whites are good. Being black . . . being an African American isn't good. That's the reason why."[33] Where does such a self-perception come from? From infancy on children are fed a steady diet of negative messages about being African American and positive messages about being white from a variety of sources, including the media, peers, and relatives. Psychologist Alvin F. Poussaint notes that even traditional fairy tales instill in some children the belief that kings, queens, princes, and princesses are white and that white people control and run the world. Thus it is not surprising that when given a choice of whether to play with white or black dolls, children of both races overwhelmingly choose to play with the white dolls, with a significant number of African American children noting that the black dolls "looked bad."

In his book *Losing the Race,* John McWhorter explains that African Americans have developed a "cult of victimology."[34] According to researchers, African Americans, by perceiving themselves as victims of discrimination, are prone to experiencing "debilitating psychiatric and physical health symptoms," including low self-esteem.[35] Researchers advise that, to combat this, the members of marginalized groups focus on positive thoughts of self.

⁞ *Practice*

Young and Old

1. With a partner, interview two senior citizens, a male and a female. Ask them these questions:
   (a) Who are you? What roles do you see yourself performing? What adjectives describe you?
   (b) How has the way you see yourself today changed from the way you saw yourself as a child, as a young adult, and as middle-aged?
   (c) How have the ways your family and friends see you changed through the years?
   (d) Is there any era of your life you would not want to repeat? Why?
   (e) Is there any era of your life you would want to repeat? Why?

2. The following quotations reveal the perceptions that two, aged persons have of themselves. These quotations are not meant to characterize the elderly or to quantify the perceptions elderly persons have; rather they are meant to illustrate, from their point of view, how aging affects self-perception.

   (a) "The young want everything to move fast. They let their impatience show in their eyes. . . . When you are hard of hearing it is worse. People get impatient when you try to join in. They yell in your face. Finally, they just give up on you and act like you are not there because it is too much trouble to try and keep you in the flow of things."*
   (b) "You ask me if I enjoy remembering things from the past. Well I do. I was born in 1898 and it is as if there are reels of movies in my head, all starting at different times in different eras. I can go back and start one up any time. Different people, dressed differently, living in rooms and houses without electricity. And all starring a different me, of course . . . the past— what I did and accomplished and endured and loved—are all part of who I am."†

3. Compare and contrast your discoveries with the preceding perceptions.

   *Joel Wells, *Who Do You Think You Are?* Chicago: Thomas More Press, 1989, pp. 92–93.
   †Ibid., p. 93.

Like some African Americans who internalize the racism inherent in our society, many elderly persons are likely to accept society's **ageism.** Just as there are a variety of ways of coping with racism, there are myriad ways to cope with ageism. In light of the fact that old age is viewed negatively by our society, maintaining a positive view of self as we age is not without its challenges. Too often, the elderly report that they feel lonely, bored, and isolated.[36] Negative self-images among the elderly, at least to some extent, can be attributed to their being talked down to, treated as incompetent, or perceived as getting frail. In order to preserve their self-esteem, many elderly view themselves as exceptions, deny that such behavior occurs, confront the perceiver directly, and/or work to preserve their youthful appearance.

Like African Americans and the elderly, some physically and mentally challenged persons are also prone to assimilate society's devalued appraisals of them and reflect this with lowered self-esteem.[37] While the elderly try to come to terms with their identity in a youth-dominated society, so the disabled "struggle for identity in an able-bodied world."[38] People with disabilities typically do not want to be viewed as helpless or sick—they want to be treated like other people. As a case in point, when nine-year-old Amy Hagadorn was asked what she wanted more than anything else, the child, who had cerebral palsy, asked for one day without teasing. "I have a problem at school," wrote Amy. "Kids laugh at me because of the way I walk and run and talk. I have cerebral palsy. I just want one day where no one laughs at me or makes fun of me."[39]

 ## *Gender Contacts*

Gender and Self-Concept

If you awoke one day to discover that you had changed into the opposite sex, how would that affect you? How, for example, would it affect your plans for the day? The week? The month? The year? The rest of your life?

Sex is a variable that influences how others treat us and how we treat others. For instance, we typically dress male and female babies differently, and we provide them with different toys. Young girls are often given Barbie dolls that say things like, "Let's go shopping," while young boys are given G.I. Joe dolls that order, "Attack." Recently, one group, calling itself the "Barbie Liberation Organization," attempted to call attention to such sexual stereotyping and make a statement about the way toys can influence behavior by switching G.I. Joe voice boxes with Barbie voice boxes, thereby surgically altering the dolls to say the unexpected. The result? "A mutant colony of Barbies-on-Steroids who roar things like 'Attack!' 'Vengeance is mine!' and 'Eat Lead, Cobra!' The emasculated G.I. Joes, meanwhile, twitter, 'Will we ever have enough clothes?'"[40] It is certain that the experiences we have during our formative years influence our views of masculinity and femininity and affect our identities in later years. This is because our gender becomes integrated into our self-concept, providing us with a gender identity, that is, our inner sense of being male or female. As we internalize the attributes of maleness and femaleness, what we have come to believe about our gender affects the way we conceive of our self. Men and women both see and describe themselves differently. Males characterize themselves as possessing initiative, control, and ambition. In contrast, females see themselves as sensitive, concerned for others, and considerate. While appearance plays a major role in the self-image of women, until recently, it was not considered integral to the self-image of a man. Greater emphasis is placed on how a woman looks. Women, more frequently than men, are often teased about both their looks and weight. The macho male, muscular and fit, is making a comeback, placing pressure on men "to bulk up" or be thought of as unmanly.

Unfortunately, in our society, women frequently develop a less positive self-concept than men do.[41] Societal expectations help create this. Our society expects those who are feminine to be nurturing, unassertive, deferential, and emotional. As a result of such expectations, society rewards young women for having a pleasing appearance, revealing their feelings, being forgiving, and being nice or helpful to others. In contrast, our society expects men to be strong, ambitious, in control of their emotions, and successful; men, unlike women, are reinforced for displaying these qualities and for achieving results.[42] It is significant that our society values the male characteristics more than it values the female characteristics. Thus, men typically feel better about themselves than do women. The upshot is that many women try harder and harder to attain success by attempting to be it all and do it all.[43] As comedian Carol Leifer so aptly puts it: "I just had a baby an hour ago and I'm back at work already. While I was delivering I took a course in tax-shelter options."

Why do women tend to develop less positive self-concepts than men do?

Beauty Meets the Beast

What role do the cosmetic and diet industries play in feeding a woman's desire to attain a self that mirrors the ideal presented in media offerings? Together, the cosmetic and diet industries gross more than a billion dollars a year, primarily because American women are driven to pursue an industry "ideal" when it comes to appearance.* Unrelenting in their pursuit of the ideal, women deprive and even starve themselves — all in an effort to conform. The following excerpt is from "The Girl Who Could Never Be Thin Enough: One Family's Tragedy," by Gene Wojciechowski, a special to the *Los Angeles Times.*

There it was again . . . that noise. Tom Asbury squinted through the darkness and found the bedside alarm clock. It was 3 A.M. — and someone or something was downstairs.

Careful not to awaken his wife, he slipped out of bed and moved slowly, quietly down the steps. As he neared the family room, he saw her. She was soaked in sweat and strands of her long blond hair were matted against her workout clothes and pressed along her frail neck and shoulders.

Who knows how many jumping jacks or sit-ups she had done this time — 100 . . . 1,000? However many, it never would be enough. There always was another pound to lose, another ounce to be starved away.

Asbury stared helplessly at his oldest daughter. "Stacey?" he said.

When their eyes met, it was as if someone had pierced Tom Asbury's heart. Anorexia nervosa can do that. It can render a father and mother useless. It can make a daughter sneak downstairs in the middle of the night and do jumping jacks until she can no longer raise her hands above her waist. It can glorify hunger.

That's what eventually happened to Stacey Asbury. In the wee hours of Sept. 12 — doctors estimated it was a little after midnight or so — she made her way down those same stairs, reached the bottom step, sat down and died. Her heart, no longer able to support even a starved 70-pound body, simply gave up.

Paramedics were called to revive her, but it was too late. Stacey was 22.

"Her body just couldn't take it anymore," her mother, Carlie, said.

The night before, mother and daughter talked about the anorexia, that insidious and mysterious eating disorder that had preyed on the Asbury's oldest daughter for nearly six years.

Once a healthy 5-foot-8, 130 pounds, Stacey weighed almost half that during those final days. Beginning in 1990, she never allowed herself to weigh more than 90 pounds.

By September, Stacey's condition had worsened to the point that another hospitalization seemed imminent. In the end, though, Stacey's illness consumed her, overpowered her both mentally and physically. She would look at herself in the mirror, see nothing more than a stick figure and still think she was too fat. To compensate, she would eat even less, exercise in secrecy even more.

"You could have put her in a cheese box and she would have found a way to exercise," said Dr. Joel Yager, who specializes in anorexia nervosa research at University of California Los Angeles' Neuropsychiatric Institute, where Stacey was a frequent patient.

So now she is gone, now part of the 3 to 5 percent who are afflicted with anorexia nervosa and ultimately die of it within 10 years.

Don't ask how it happened, because nobody knows. Not the parents. Not the doctors. It is, as Churchill once said of Russia, a riddle wrapped in a mystery inside an enigma.

Dr. Michael Strober, who oversees the eating disorder program at UCLA, says, "I still feel humbled in its presence."

Not long after she turned 16, Stacey decided she needed to lose weight. Not much, she said at the time, just a few pounds. Tom and Carlie thought nothing of it.

A year passed and as it did, Stacey began eliminating sugar, red meat, and most dairy products from her diet. She would eat chicken or fish, salads, and fruits — that was it. A candy bar? Never.

The illness had begun to take hold. Carlie didn't realize it until she was called out of town to attend the funerals of her grandmother and grandfather. Carlie was gone a week and when she returned and saw Stacey, "it was like somebody hit me in the stomach."

Stacey had lost too much weight, enough so that the Asbury's family physician referred her to a local psychologist. The therapy seemed to work.

"She looked great," Carlie said. "We thought, 'Oh, we're fine. Isn't this wonderful!'"

Four months later, Stacey began restricting her diet even more. Rice cakes and yogurt replaced poultry and fish. There were long stretches when she would eat nothing at all. Exercising became a treasured ritual, eating a necessary evil to be monitored precisely.

The textbook symptoms of anorexia nervosa had revealed themselves. Stacey fit the profile to the letter: adolescent . . . pathological willingness to diet to the point of malnutrition . . . exaggerated and inexplicable sensitivity to weight and body shape.

According to the best estimates and that's all they are—one-half to 1 percent of college-age women suffer from some form of anorexia. In all, about 100,000 people are afflicted with the eating disorder, although the illness is most often linked to women.[†]

In your opinion, is it for any industry to send women the message that beauty and thinness are requisites for suc-

cess? When women are bombarded with ideals of how they should think, look, and act, is it any wonder that they feel inferior or inadequate by comparison?

Are the messages being sent to women any different from the messages being sent to men regarding athleticism and the ideal muscular build? Today men are expected to spend time working out in the gym in order to develop that well-toned look. Many are unsatisfied with the results they attain. Are the dimensions men are expected to attain when it comes to shoulder:waist proportionality any more realistic than the measurements women seek to mirror? What, if anything, should we do to counter the effects of such media messages and campaigns?

[*]Naomi Wolf, *The Beauty Myth.* New York: Morrow, 1991.
[†]From Gene Wojciechowski, "The Girl Who Could Never Be Thin Enough: One Family's Tragedy," special to *Los Angeles Times,* December 27, 1993. Copyright, 1993, Los Angeles Times. Reprinted with permission.

Media and Technology Contacts

Seeing the Self through the Media and the Technological Looking Glass

The products of our media culture provide the programs, films, and music that help us forge our identities, our sense of self, and who we want to be. Along with this, what we view or listen to also endows us with our sense of ethnicity and race, gender, and class. From the media we learn how "to dress, look, and consume."[44] We learn who has power and who does not, what force and violence accomplish, and how the oppressed are kept in their places.

The Impact of the Media

Media portrayals help us assess what the general public's preferred patterns of behavior and appearance are. They help shape our opinions about how our bodies should look, how males and females should interact, and the meaning of success. The way we interpret what we observe reinforces or negates our own sense of self by influencing our sense of who we are and who we should aspire to be.

Often we don't consciously realize the extent to which the media work us over, how much they are "**make-believe media; they make us believe.**"[45] Our concept of what we should be like or, for that matter, what our relationships should be like, or even more specifically what African and Mexican Americans, or males and females are supposed to be like, is conveyed to us via the media, so much so that some critics complain that the media preempt real life, offering us a fabricated view of our world in its place.

If video games are any indication, males and females are being fed very different messages regarding the nature of the self. When it comes to being a hero, girls do not get their fair share of the action. According to Marsha Kinder, a professor of critical studies at the University of Southern California in Los Angeles, "That's very disturbing because video games provide an entry into the world of computers." Instead, observes Kinder, a young girl is the weaker princess who waits to be rescued. "If you want to be in an empowered position," she notes, "you have to adopt a male position. Being feminine and being empowered seems to be an oxymoron in video games."[46]

Among the other messages the media carry are that appearance counts for women; that violence against women is commonplace; that men are hard, tough, and independent; that minorities are even less visible than women; and that African American males are frequently athletes, entertainers, lazy, or unlawful. These messages often cause us to distort the way we see ourselves and influence our perception of what is normal and desirable behavior.

Even toys get into the self-image act. In 1992, Mattel introduced a new Barbie doll, one equipped to utter, "Math class is tough." Though protests resulted in the doll's recall, the message was all too clear: women were being fed another message of inadequacy, and a cultural assumption about how females should think was being presented through one of society's popular culture icons. In an effort to combat

literary contacts

Trading Places

Think about these words, spoken by a character in Paddy Chayefsky's award-winning movie *Network*:

Television is not the truth. . . . We lie like hell. . . . We deal in illusions, man. None of it is true. But you people sit there day after day, night after night. . . . We're all you know. You're beginning to believe the illusions we're spinning here. You're beginning to think that the tube is reality and that your own lives are unreal. You do what the tube tells you to do. You dress like the tube, you eat like the tube, you raise your children like the tube. In God's name, you people are the real thing; we're the illusion!

1. What does this quotation tell us about our relationship to the media?
2. Divide your life into three approximately equal parts. (For example, if you are 21 years old, your life would be divided into these segments: ages 1–7, 8–14, and 15–21.) From each life segment, select a television program, film, video, or book that you believe exerted a significant influence on the way you conceived of yourself and interacted with others. Give specific examples.
3. Finally, compare and contrast the image you have of each of the following with the image portrayed in the media. Which image do you prefer and why?

a nurse
a corporate executive
a teenager
the elderly
the police
the homeless
the wealthy
conservatives
African Americans
Arabs

If you could trade places with any media personality or character, past or present, who would it be and why?

some of the negative or unrealistic images presented to young girls by Barbie, a company called High Self-Esteem Toys Corporation introduced a fashion doll named "Happy to Be Me," whose scale measurements of 36–27–38 represent a more realistic figure for a female than Barbie's scale 18-inch waist and 33-inch hips.[47]

The media provide us with models—often holding up standards of appearance or living that few of us can expect to achieve. Our evaluations of ourselves as attractive, successful, or smart can be adversely affected by what we see and hear in the media. And all too often, the thirst we acquire from the media for "beautiful thinghood" turns abruptly into an affliction and results in painful and enduring feelings of inadequacy.[48]

The Impact of Technology

We are in the midst of participating in the creation of new worlds and new ways of finding out about ourselves. When we interact in cyberspace, we can choose to be ourselves or someone else. Because others cannot readily identify us, the identity we have in a cybersociety can be different from our real-world identity. In cyberspace we can exist as a persona.

For some of us, the lives we live are more virtual than real. According to media critic Neal Gabler, "This idea that you can live essentially a virtual life is a very powerful idea, and we are the first generation that has the capability to do that in a whole host of ways."[49] The Internet makes it feasible for users to inhabit virtual worlds, participate in simulations, and assume different personas. According to a Pew Internet and American Life Project, it is not uncommon for teenagers to have a number of e-mail addresses and screen names. They employ multiple personas to conceal their real identities from both friends and strangers. The use of multiple personas makes it possible for us to pretend to be someone we are not. We can use the Internet to experiment with multiple identities.[50] Some persons fake personal data in their e-mails or instant messages or construct imaginary selves that inhabit various chat-rooms in an effort to experiment with various kinds of online social relationships. They might, for example, pose as a member of the opposite sex, conceal their ethnicity, hide physical characteristics, or otherwise pretend to be someone who they are not. According to psychologist Sherry Turkle, "The obese can be slender, the beautiful plain, the

Technology enables us to interact in a virtual world. Has going online contributed to your being more or less social? More or less knowledgeable about yourself?

'nerdy' sophisticated."[51] Since they can remain anonymous, it becomes easy to construct and reconstruct identities that are not part of their authentic selves.[52]

Who are you when you communicate in an online virtual world? Do you try on or invent different versions of yourself so that you may more readily engage in interactions you otherwise would not have an opportunity to experience? To what extent are you able to remain genderless, raceless, rankless, and appearanceless? Have you considered how this opportunity for egalitarianism changes the way you communicate with others and how others communicate with you? Do you become more or less social? More or less inhibited? More or less anonymous? More or less yourself? In discussing the nature of identity online, a 14-year-old user who identified himself as "the Professor" observed, "You can make the character behind the alias exactly like you, nothing like you, a combination of both, or even make it vary depending on the situation."[53] Thus, when participating in an online world, and interacting with numerous online others, we can either assume multiple identities, negotiate our identities, or relate as ourselves. By playing with the self, perhaps we will able to discover more about it.

Gaining Communication Competence

Ways to Strengthen Your Self-Concept

We all carry a figurative snapshot of who we think we are wherever we go. Depicted in our snapshot is an impressionist collage of merged images: what we think we were like in the past, what we wish we had been like, what we think we are like right now, and what we expect to be like in the future. In many ways our photo is also a composite of how we see ourselves, how we wish we saw ourselves, and how we imagine others see us.

Although changing the mental image you attribute to yourself is not easy, it is possible. What you need to do is remind yourself that a snapshot captures but a moment in time and is linked to a particular environment and communication context. Each picture you take, however, reveals a somewhat different you. Unlike photographs, we need not be frozen in time. We change from moment to moment, person to person, year in and year out. Thus, while our memories are important and help us construct our sense of who we are, we need to keep the mental pictures that we carry with us current and up to date. Only by doing this will we be able to discount images that no longer accurately describe us, and thereby avoid focusing on what psychologists refer to as regrets—"the lost lives, lost selves a person could have lived or been if he had done a few things differently."[54] The following suggestions will help you turn regret into creative thought. They will help you enhance your life by improving your mental picture-taking ability and thus enable you to develop a clearer sense of self.

Never Stop Taking Self-Snapshots

While you can't erase past memories and self-conceptions, or even pretend they did not exist, you can continue to develop your self-awareness and a clear sense of who you are now by watching yourself in action. Periodically reassess the roles you perform, the statements you use to describe yourself, and the extent to which you approve of your own values and behaviors. Examine the composite photo that emerges. Are you satisfied with it? If you expect too much of yourself, you might experience feelings of dissatisfaction and inadequacy. If this happens, check to see if your goals are realistic. If, on the other hand, the mental picture that emerges reflects your actual capabilities, then that which you aim for is worth striving for. It takes courage to develop more accurate pictures of the self. It takes even more strength to be open-minded while examining them.

Explore the Pictures Others Take of You

Others frequently see in us strengths or weaknesses we tend to either overlook or underplay. While we need not become what others think we are, if we are willing to explore their perceptions of us, we at least open ourselves to the possibility of change. If we are receptive to how others see us, we may be able to make adjustments to become more effective in other person-to-person contacts.

Picture the Possibility

The self is flexible and changeable. In a constant state of transition, it has the capacity to adapt to changing circumstances and conditions. Your self-concept need not remain as it is. By continually asking yourself "Who am I now?" instead of "Who am I always?" you will be able to take picture after picture of a changing you, someone who has opened him- or herself to the possibilities offered by today and tomorrow. As Claudette Mackay-Lassonde, vice president for corporate affairs of Xerox, so aptly noted in a speech entitled "Butterflies, Not Pigeonholes":

> In a knowledge-driven economy, self-confidence means a willingness to champion new ideas . . . and the resilience to roll with the punches when ideas turn out to be better in the abstract than in reality. Plus, self-confidence provides the persistence to try again from another angle. Self-confidence enables an individual to withstand the criticism of colleagues, to live with the fact that not everyone will like everyone else.
>
> And it gives one the ability to listen to others, to work as part of a team, to be willing to let others share the load . . . and the spotlight, confident that one's contribution to the success of the whole will be recognized.
>
> In short, self-confidence enables people to feel comfortable outside the pigeonholes, to contribute in an ever-changing environment. Without it, the most gifted individual can toil in the shadows, the gifts of provenance never fully realized.[55]

Isn't it better to picture yourself as a butterfly, free, than stuck in a pigeonhole?

Wrap-Up

Meet again in pairs or with your discussion group. Turn back to the case study at the beginning of the chapter and reconsider the questions that followed it. How have your answers changed or become more focused? Based on what you have learned in this chapter, what advice would you give Aisha now?

Critical Thinking Contacts

Examine the following cartoon. Then, based on your understanding of chapter concepts and principles, discuss what Ziggy can do to enhance his self-concept.

Thinking Positively

Summary

Self-concept, the baseline for communication, is that relatively stable set of perceptions we attribute to ourselves. Composed of everything we think and feel about the self, it guides our communicative behavior.

The relationship between the self and the self-concept is much like that between a territory and its map. It may be accurate or inaccurate, positive or negative. Whatever its nature, however, it drives behavior and shapes relationships.

Self-concept is affected by the nature of the interactional situation. The term *reflected appraisal* describes the mirrorlike image we derive from our contacts and project into future relationships. The self-concept we build reflects the way we think others see us. In addition, according to social comparison theory, we regularly compare ourselves to others and then evaluate ourselves to determine how we measure up.

Cultural diversity, gender, the media, and technology also influence the nature of self-concept. Whether we are from an individualist or a collectivist culture, display an idiocentric or an allocentric orientation, are young or old, are white or African American, are able bodied or physically or mentally challenged, are male or female, we are affected by the lessons our society teaches us.

The self-fulfilling prophecies we and others make also affect self-concept. Once communicated, expectations increase the likelihood that anticipated outcomes will actually occur. As the Pygmalion effect illustrates, we tend to live up and down to labels.

To strengthen our sense of self-worth, we need to periodically reassess the nature of our self-concept, visit and revisit others' perceptions of us, and keep ourselves open to the possibility of change.

Terms to Talk About

self-concept *(p. 39)*
self-esteem *(p. 42)*
reflected appraisal theory *(p. 43)*
social comparison theory *(p. 45)*
impression management *(p. 46)*
confirm *(p. 46)*
reject *(p. 46)*
disconfirm *(p. 46)*
self-fulfilling prophecy *(p. 48)*

positive Pygmalions *(p. 49)*
negative Pygmalions *(p. 50)*
collectivist cultures *(p. 52)*
individualist cultures *(p. 52)*
idiocentric orientation *(p. 53)*
allocentric orientation *(p. 53)*
power distance *(p. 54)*
ageism *(p. 56)*
make-believe media *(p. 59)*

Suggestions for Further Reading

Nathaniel Branden, *The Six Pillars of Self-Esteem,* New York: Bantam, 1994. An exploration of both our need for self-esteem and the foundations on which self-esteem is built.

Steve Craig, ed., *Men, Masculinity, and the Media,* Newbury Park, CA: Sage, 1992. Discusses the ways the media construct ideas of masculinity and explores how men respond to such images.

Daniel Goleman, *Emotional Intelligence,* New York: Bantam Books, 1995. Considers why emotional intelligence is more important than IQ; explores the impacts of self-awareness, self-motivation, empathy, and social deftness.

Ronald L. Jackson, II, ed., *African American Communication and Identities,* Thousand Oaks, CA: Sage, 2004. Explores aspects of African American communication behaviors as they relate to how African Americans define themselves culturally.

Derek Layden, *Social and Personal Identity,* Thousand Oaks, CA: Sage, 2004. Explorations and discussions of the self in context.

Robert Rosenthal and Lenore Jacobson, *Pygmalion in the Classroom,* New York: Holt, Rinehart and Winston, 1968. A now-classic work that offers an insightful discussion of how self-fulfilling prophecies function in life.

Myra Sadker and David Sadker, *Failing at Fairness: How America's Schools Cheat Girls,* New York: Scribners, 1994. Describes the different educations boys and girls receive in the same classrooms.

daily contacts

Dax on Trial

Dax couldn't believe what was happening. Would it never end?

Dax had not been happy when he received the notice that he was to appear at the courthouse for jury duty. He was even less happy when he found out that he did not have a valid excuse to be recused from the obligation.

The first day things went just fine. He was called as a member of a panel for a case, but the case was quickly resolved and the jury was dismissed. The second day he was not called during the morning, so he was able to finish a novel. Then it all began.

Dax was called to meet in the voir dire—jury selection—phase of a murder trial. Before Dax knew it, he was on the jury and the trial had started.

Two days into the trial, Dax began to wonder about the entire process. Could each of the witnesses called by the attorneys really have seen the same thing? Twelve different witnesses had been called to testify about what had happened on the street corner where the murder

had occurred. All twelve witnesses had reported different versions of the event.

Was it possible? Could so many people not agree on what had taken place? Dax wished he could have a chance to question the witnesses himself. Was each of them certain of his or her perception? To what degree did the relationship each did or did not share with the defendant influence what was reported?

Dax was really getting into the trial when the defendant changed his plea to guilty and the jury was dismissed. Though he was released from duty, Dax continued to mull over his confusion about witnesses' perceptions.

Divide into pairs or discussion groups and answer these questions:

1. Do you think several people observing one event will perceive it the same way? Why or why not?
2. What is there about the process of perception that enables us to observe different realities?
3. Were the twelve witnesses who testified in the preceding case lying?

*T*he Matrix movies provide a case study in perception, causing us to ask if "the real world" could merely be a simulation that is programmed into our brains. What, after all, is reality? What is illusion? According to Cornel West, a professor of religion at Princeton University, through *The Matrix* films we explore "modes of being that allow us to get outside of the mask-wearing and the role-playing that are so pervasive in our society. . . . It's this quest to be a real individual, a real person in the face of these systemic attempts to render us superficial and inauthentic."[1]

Where is the line between the real and the virtual to be drawn? Is reality TV real? Are news anchors really our friends? Are congressional bills whose names mean the opposite of what they propose to accomplish acceptable? When should we believe our eyes? Our ears? The intersection between real life and illusion is becoming more difficult to detect. It is so easy to reproduce images from real life visually today that we are becoming skeptics regarding whether we can even perceive what reality is.[2]

Much of what we see today is not really there. For example, the yellow line scribbled down the TV screen's football field with a digital pen is not really there. The computer-generated ads behind home plate are not really there. Dead celebrities

BABY BLUES   *BY RICK KIRKMAN & JERRY SCOTT*

Reprinted with special permission of King Features Syndicate.

in contemporary commercials are not really there. Keeping this in mind, look at the *Baby Blues* cartoon pictured here. What do you see? The cartoon illustrates a key aspect of perception: that different people do not always view the same situation in the same way. The perceptions we have are a consequence of who we are, where we are, and what we choose to see. Our culture, race, age, gender, geographical location, life experiences, and ideological preferences combine to create perceptual gulfs between ourselves and those whose culture, race, age, gender, geographical location, life experiences, and ideological preferences differ from our own. Confronted with issues such as race relationships, gender equity, the murder of gay student Matthew Shepherd in Wyoming, the first and second Gulf wars, and the war on terrorism,

 in Theory

Can You Walk in My Shoes?

Recently, Circuit Judge Lynn Tepper sentenced a 12-year-old, Raymond Thomas, to get a feel for the life he created for his gunshot victim, a 16-year-old named Reggie Haines. For shooting Haines point blank in the forehead, Judge Tepper ordered to Thomas a series of punishments: first, he must serve time in a wheelchair for a set period; second, he would have to walk with a walker; and third, he would have to use a cane. In an effort to explain his rationale for the unusual sentence, the judge told Thomas: "You're going to be moving around in Reggie's world, which you created. You will go to the bathroom in a wheelchair. . . . You will get in and

out of bed, eat, try to drink from the water fountain in a wheelchair." The judge continued, "Perhaps you will appreciate what Reggie had to go through to get where he is today, which is a miracle."*

1. In your opinion, will such "punishments" really allow Raymond Thomas to understand what Reggie Haines is going through?

2. Do you believe the sentence will enable Thomas to empathize with Haines—that is, feel what he feels?

3. Do you think the sentence is appropriate? Why or why not?

*"Boy Who Shot Teen Ordered to Spend Time in Wheelchair," January 9, 1994, *The Sunday Record* (Hackensack, NJ), A16.

many of us see different realities. Why do our perceptions of events and people differ? Why do we sometimes see what is not really there? How can we account for discrepancies in the observations of what exists and what occurs?

Differences in the way we see, hear, taste, smell, or feel specific stimuli—that is, *differences in the way we perceive*—occur all the time. Whether the object of our consideration is a country, an event, another person, the impact of technology, or ourselves, we may disagree with others regarding what exists. Is it because we cannot perceive what is really there? Is it because we perceive what we *want* to perceive? Is it because we don't ever experience the exact same reality as anyone else?

This chapter will explore questions like these as we describe how we perceive our world and the people in it. By learning more about the process of perception you will prepare yourselves to better handle the continuing interpersonal communication problems posed by perceptual variations. By exploring why we see stimuli differently, you will better understand why we think and act differently as well. Only by getting behind the eye of the "I" do we understand why "where we stand depends on where we sit."[3]

Our perception is affected by our social circumstances, the experiences and interactions we have every day. The way we perceive situations, people, and ourselves is shaped by the experiences we have had as members of particular groups. This perception is explained by what is known as the standpoint theory: the point where we stand influences our perception. For example, it is easier for the powerless to feel inequities than it is for those who are empowered. Why is this? Because **standpoint theory** tells us that persons in positions of power have an overriding interest in preserving their place in the social hierarchy; therefore, they develop more distorted views of social life than do persons who can gain little, if anything, from the position they occupy in the social hierarchy. In contrast, persons in less powerful, subordinate, or marginalized positions develop better insights into how society works if only because they need to develop these understandings to survive.[4] To develop better-balanced perception, it is important for us to become more aware of diverse perspectives and interact with people whose standpoints are significantly different from our own.[5]

> Our morning eyes describe a different world than do our afternoon eyes.
>
> —*John Steinbeck*

Perception in Action: The Process at Work

Perception is the process we use to make sense of our experiences. Through perception, we make an effort to give meaning to our world and make it our own. We actively *select* or choose to focus on relatively few stimuli, *organize* or give order to the stimuli, and *interpret* sensory data or explain what has been selected and organized. While waiting to order in a bustling restaurant, for example, we may observe two people meeting for lunch, size them up as businesspeople, and decide that they are meeting to close an important deal.

Interpersonal perception is the process we use to decide what people are like and to give meaning to their behavior. We form impressions of others based on the sensory data we take in. When we engage in interpersonal perception, we also ask questions about the relationship others have to us, draw conclusions about their personalities, and make judgments about their intentions. According to **uncertainty**

reduction theory it is through monitoring our social environment that we learn more about each other. We seek to learn about each other because if we lack such knowledge, we could fail in our efforts to predict behavior and its consequences. Thus, upon meeting someone, we will choose certain cues to attend to: we might note, for example, that the person is female, older than we are, speaks with a foreign accent, is well groomed, and seems approachable. Our next step would be to organize the information we took in so that we are able to store it and/or use it. This will be followed by an effort to evaluate and interpret the meaning of our perceptions to be placed in our memory for retrieval whenever we need or choose to respond.

According to information theorists, although our senses can process approximately 5 million bits of data every second, our brains can handle only about 500 bits per second. Because of our inability to perceive everything, we are compelled to select the stimuli we become aware of. As a result, we focus on certain cues and ignore others. Figure 3.1 illustrates the process of perception in action.

If to people, crickets appear to hear with their legs, is it possible that to crickets, people appear to walk on their ears?

Selection

As you read this chapter, stop and look around you. What do you notice? What captures your attention? Is it the sound of the refrigerator; the feel of the chair, sofa, bed, or floor on which you are seated; the color of the walls; or voices coming from another location? Consciously turn your attention to something different. What did you fail to notice initially that now makes an impression on you? Since we can attend to only a limited number from an array of randomly competing stimuli at one time, we must choose which persons, situations, or events to perceive. We use all our senses to gather information. Multiple factors influence what we will pay attention to and what we will ignore, what enters our level of awareness and what exits unobserved and unnoticed.

When we interact with others, we select the cues we will focus on. Some of us focus on appearance, others on the strength of a handshake, and still others on the sound of the voice or the look in the person's eyes. Whatever we select to focus on, we direct our attention to certain qualities and not others.

In the environment, usually we focus on a stimulus that is more intense than others or that reflects our motives or interest more than others. For example, we pay attention to a loud noise that disrupts our concentration. Likewise we overhear two people conversing behind us in a restaurant if they are speaking about a topic that concerns us. Our interests also influence what we perceive.

Our motives or needs also influence the impressions we select to notice. When we are concerned with our finances, we notice more information about how to save money. When we are considering buying a car, we notice the kinds of cars our relatives, friends, and acquaintances drive. When we are hungry we

FIGURE 3.1
The Perception Process

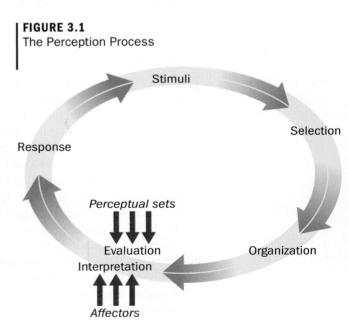

become more aware of food establishments or we notice the smell of what someone else is eating. When we're late for an appointment we might run right by a close friend without even seeing her.

Once our attention is captured, we can organize the sensory data to better interpret and evaluate them. As we attempt to make sense out of the flood of stimuli that compete for our awareness, the personal nature of our selective processes takes over. We do not all experience the same stimuli in the same way. We all have different thresholds of arousal that need to be crossed before a stimulus captures our attention. The cues we select to attend to depend more on the kind of perceiver we are and less on what is actually occurring. In addition to our sensory acuity, our loves, hatreds, and desires also come into play during the selection process.

When we direct our attention to some stimuli while choosing to ignore other stimuli, we demonstrate our selectivity. What are the specific cues you tend to focus on when you first meet someone? What do you look for? What do you listen for? Four different selective processes concern us: **selective exposure**—our preference for exposing ourselves to people and messages that confirm our existing beliefs, values, or attitudes; **selective attention**—the means by which we focus on certain cues but ignore others; **selective perception**—the tendency to see, hear, and believe what we want to (such as downplaying negative qualities in a person we like); and **selective retention**—the practice by which we recall things that reinforce our thinking and forget things we find objectionable (such as recalling positive qualities of persons we like and negative qualities of persons we dislike). In using any of these processes, we may bias the perceptual process of selection and end up with distorted views of people or events. For example, think about a relationship you shared that has ended. Once you made the decision to terminate the relationship, did you begin to notice more about the person that you disliked? We call this the **horn effect.** Compare the horn response to what happens when you decide to take a personal relationship to a more serious level. Once we make this kind of decision, instead of perceiving what is negative about the person, we are more likely to perceive additional things that we like about her or him. We call the reverse of the horn effect the **halo effect.**

Organization

Just as we use a number of different strategies to select what impressions we will notice, so we use a number of different strategies to facilitate our meaningful organization of these impressions. One strategy is to categorize a stimulus according to the principle of **figure–ground.** What we choose to focus on becomes the figure and the rest of what we experience is the ground. Figure 3.2 illustrates the figure–ground concept. What do you see when you look at each example? In A you see either an old woman or a young woman. In B you see a duck or a rabbit. While you can't see both stimuli in each illustration simultaneously, if you are able to switch your attention and focus, you will be able to see both stimuli alternately. In other words, you are able to alternate the figure or ground of what you perceive. In a classroom, for example, if you were to focus on what a fellow student was doing while the professor was lecturing, the student would be the figure, while the professor would recede into the background.

A second organizing strategy we rely on is **closure.** Every time we fill in a missing perceptual piece we exhibit closure. Look at the stimuli pictured in Figure 3.3. What

FIGURE 3.2
Figure–Ground Principle

SOURCE: Mitsuko, Saito-Fakunage: "General Semantics and Intercultural Communication," *ETC,*
vol. 46, no. 4, Winter, 1989, p. 297.

do you see? Most see a dog and a circle. Because we seek to close gaps, we simply mentally fill in incomplete figures. We want to perceive a completed world, as it were, so we supply what is not really part of the stimuli or messages we process. For example, the assumptions we make about others' motivations help us make sense of our own relationships. We might conclude that a friend invited us to a party only because she needed our help in passing a course. Whether the sense we make is right or wrong, justified or unjustified, we did fill in certain gaps. Just as what you choose to notice is up to you, so is how you choose to organize what you perceive.

FIGURE 3.3
Closure Principle

A third organizational strategy we use is **perceptual constancy**—the tendency we have to maintain the same perception of stimuli over time. The constancy principle helps explain why we find it difficult to alter a perception once we form it. As a consequence, we often see people not as they are but as we have been conditioned to see them. A large number of our perceptions are learned and then reinforced over time.

This third strategy is facilitated by our use of **schemata** (the mental templates or knowledge structures we carry with us) and **scripts** (the general ideas we have about people and situations and how things should play out). We develop schemata and scripts based on both our real and vicarious experiences. It is by reverting to schemata that we are able to classify people into manageable categories, such as appearance, psychological traits, group memberships, and so on. Sometimes schemata, as we will soon see, also contribute to stereotyping, which can lead us to see what is not there while too often causing us to ignore what is there.

in Theory

How Real Is Real?

In the U.S. polls are conducted and released virtually hourly on almost every subject from the state of the nation to media coverage of the Iraqi war. Never mind that persons responding to the polls sometimes offer opinions on matters they know little or nothing about. In fact, in one now infamous poll students cheerfully revealed their opinions on three completely fictional nationalities (the Pireneans, the Danireans, and the Wallonians). The net effect of all this spinning and sculpting oftentimes is an air of unreality; interpretation replaces fact.* Snapshots in time supplant understanding of the big picture.

Understanding the big picture is complicated in other ways as well. For example, the media were given unprecedented opportunities to cover the 2003 Iraqi war. Reporters were imbedded with the troops. Some critics contended that the media served as cheerleaders for the U.S. war effort. Others contended that they were too negative about the war.

Some journalists perceived the troops they were with as their protectors. Others filed raw and unflattering accounts. The reality is that the embedded correspondents "were only able to see little slices of the pie." And our view of the battlefields of the war was through their individual eyes, making it difficult to contextualize it. "The war effort was stalled," we were told. "The war effort wasn't stalled," said someone from a different vantage point. In an effort to replicate what had occurred in Iraq so that we would understand it, a commentator for National Public Radio arranged to play a giant chess game on the streets of New York City. Players were selected, assigned individual roles as chess pieces, and assigned to specific positions throughout metropolitan New York. They wore transmitters and ear-pieces and moved according to the orders they received from the game's directors, who were sequestered far from where the action would occur. Thus, when ordered to do so, a castle would move from one assigned location to where a pawn might be waiting, and without any warning the pawn

Reporters embedded with U.S. troops during the war against Iraq only saw "little slices of the pie." Despite this, our view of the war effort was through their eyes.

would be captured and removed from where it had stood. The surprise that registered on the pawn's face when it realized that, for it, the game had ended was a reward of the battle. And so it was in Iraq. Central command, situated somewhere in Qatar, moved pieces of an armed forces in and around Iraq at will. A wrong move and the members of an entire regiment were put in harm's way. But the various units only saw their piece of the battlefield. The big picture often remained blurry—for them and for us.

Al-Jazeera, or "the island" in Arabic, is an Arab network that also covered the Iraqi war. In contrast to American networks, they covered images of injured Iraqi citizens and heated antiwar protests. Instead of calling the war a fight for liberation, this network's journalists referred to it as an invasion.

Al-Jazeera called its coverage "War on Iraq," whereas CNN titled its coverage "War in Iraq."[†] The world and America watched different wars.

1. What do the preceding examples reveal about the nature of perception?

2. What dangers do we face when we allow opinion to replace truth?

3. What steps do we need to take to widen our perception and ensure that we do not view critical situations through an opening the size of a straw?

*Michiko Kakutani, "Opinion vs. Reality in an Age of Pundits," *New York Times*, January 28, 1994, pp. C1, C27.

†Eman Varoqua, "A Different Point of View from Al-Jazeera," The *Record*, March 31, 2003, A-10, and Rami G. Khouri, "The War Americans Don't See," *The New York Times*, April 4, 2003, A21.

Evaluation and Interpretation

As we evaluate and interpret experience, the meaning we assign to experience is influenced by a number of individual **affectors**—factors that color our responses. These may include our culture, roles, biases, present emotional state, past experiences, and physical limitations or capabilities. If you are looking for a fight, you may perceive an insult. If you are hungry, you may smell food. If you are looking for a date, you are more likely to interpret a statement as an overture to ask someone out. We are likely to view people with whom we seek a relationship more positively than those we have no feelings about one way or the other.[6] If, on the other hand, we are in an unhappy relationship, we will most likely interpret the behavior of our partner more critically than if we were impartial.[7]

Among other variables that influence the interpretation–evaluation process are the degree of involvement we have or expect to have with a person, the knowledge we have relative to the person's intentions, our feelings about ourselves in relation to the other person, and the assumptions we make about human behavior in general and this person's behavior in particular.

Memory

How we interpret and evaluate a stimulus determines whether or not what we experience enters our memory. That which we remember we can retrieve for later use. The question is: how reliable is what we remember? Can we count on our perceptual abilities to supply us with accurate memories of what we have experienced? Consider this: when Americans were asked to recall their memories of what they observed on September 11, 2001, they spoke of watching television broadcasts of the two planes that struck the twin towers of the World Trade Center. This recollection, held by 76 percent of the New Yorkers surveyed and 73 percent of

literary contacts

Young and Old

In "Childhood" by Frances Cornford, a child's initial perception of old age matures.

> *I used to think that grown-up people chose*
> *To have stiff backs and wrinkles round their nose,*
> *And veins like small fat snakes on either hand,*
> *On purpose to be grand.*
> *Till through the banisters I watched one day*
> *My great-aunt Etty's friend who was*
> *going away,*
> *And how her onyx beads had come unstrung.*
> *I saw her grope to find them as they rolled;*
> *And then I knew that she was helplessly old,*
> *As I was helplessly young.*

First, working alone or in dyads, account for the changes in the child's perception. Why is it possible to perceive a person, situation, or event one way at a particular point in time and differently at another point in time? What did it take for the child to discover that what she or he saw did not tell the entire story?

Then, give examples from your own life to demonstrate the deceptive nature of appearances — that what you see may not be the whole story. Identify the challenges that stand in the way of your accurately evaluating people, situations, or events. What steps can you take to ensure that what you see in a person, situation, or event is not just what you are looking for?

SOURCE: "Childhood" from *Frances Cornford: Selected Poems*, ed. Jane Dowson. London: Enitharmon Press, 1996. Reproduced by permission of Enitharmon Press.

persons surveyed nationwide, was a false memory. In fact, on that day there was no video of the first plane hitting the tower.

What is memory? It is a human construct, a composite of what we read, piece together, experience, and/or want to be true. While we may have confidence in what we remember, that confidence may be misplaced, if only because at least some of what we think is true turns out to be false.[8]

When we try to remember something we have stored in our memory, we don't simply reproduce it. Rather, instead of objectively recalling what we experienced, we attempt to reconstruct a memory at the time of withdrawal. As we engage in retrospection or backward reasoning, however, inaccuracies may creep in. As we seek to remember, we infer past occurrences based on who we now are, what we now believe, and what we now know. We tend to remember information consistent with our schema and discount or forget information that is not. On the other hand, if information dramatically contradicts a schema, compelling us to think about it, it may lead us to revise the schema we use.

Response

Perception is a mixture of external stimulation and an internal state, and we actively participate in it as we exercise control over what we do with or how we respond to the stimuli that affect us. In many ways we are both the cause and the controlling force of what we perceive. The processes we employ affect the ways we make sense of our world and relate to others.

Attribution theory facilitates our understanding of why we respond as we do to persons and events. Underlying the theory is the fact that we like to be able to explain why things happen. Why, for example, did Eric Harris and Dylan Klebold slaughter thirteen of their classmates at Columbine High School in Colorado? Was it because they were mentally ill? Were their parents at fault because they neglected to pay attention to them? Were violent video games to blame? Did the cause lie in the boys' bullying by the school's athletes? In an effort to make sense out of what occurred, we make educated guesses about what motivated the boys to behave as they did. We do the same with people we know. We assign meaning to the behavior of others by prescribing motives and causes to their behaviors. For instance, suppose a couple seated near you in a restaurant get up in the middle of their meal and leave. Why did they leave? Did they have an argument? Did they feel ill? Was the food bad? We can attribute their behavior to something in their disposition (an internal cause) or to something about the situation or environment (an external cause).

We use a number of principles to guide us in making sense of the behavior we observe: consensus, consistency, distinctiveness, and controllability. When we use the first principle, *consensus,* we ask a question such as: "Do the friends of people I know behave the same way as my friend?" If the answer is no, we are more apt to decide that the exhibited behavior had an internal cause. When we focus on *consistency* to make an attribution, we ask if the behavior occurs frequently. If the answer is no, then there is low behavioral consistency, and we are more apt to attribute the behavior's cause to external causes. When we focus on *distinctiveness* we ask if the person displays similar behavior in different situations. If the answer is yes, we're likely to conclude the behavior had an internal cause. Finally, when we focus on *controllability,* we are seeking to determine if the person was in control of the behavior.

A common mistake in making attributions occurs when we assume that the primary motivation for behavior is in the person, not in the person's situation, a tendency known as the **fundamental attribution error.** When, for example, a friend disappoints us by failing to arrive for a surprise party, we are more apt to conclude that the friend is inconsiderate or doesn't care than to believe that external factors interfered with her or his ability to attend. We overemphasize internal or personal factors and we deemphasize or discount the role played by the situation or factors external to the person.[9] Things change dramatically, however, when we provide reasons for our own behavior. In offering reasons for why we behave as we do, we overemphasize external factors and downplay internal factors. We label this tendency the **self-serving bias.** The self-serving bias functions as a barrier to accurate perception while, at the same time, it helps to raise our own self-esteem during the self-attribution process. We take credit for the positive while denying culpability for the negative. Instead we attribute the negative to factors beyond

 Theory

Attribution Errors in Action

1. Explain how we can use the fundamental attribution error to explain the following excerpts from a speech by the Reverend Jesse Jackson.

   Most poor people are not lazy. . . . They catch the early bus . . . They raise other people's children. . . . They clean the streets. No, no, they're not lazy.

2. Explain this statement: *We find causes where we look for them.* Provide examples from your own experience.

our control. A second perceptual barrier is **overattribution**—the attributing of everything an individual does to a single or a few specific characteristics, such as when we attribute an individual's lack of interest in close relationships to the fact that she or he was sexually abused when young.

The Role of Schemata, Sets, Selectivities, and Stereotypes

How have the life lessons you have learned conditioned you to perceive?

As we noted, the mental templates and life experiences we bring to any situation strongly affect how we process experience and relate to others.

Schemata

Four perceptual schemata, or cognitive frameworks, help us decide what others are like and whether we want to get to know them better. Schemata are general ideas about people. Physical constructs enable us to classify people according to their characteristics, including age, weight, and height. Interaction constructs point us toward social behavior cues, for example, whether they are friendly, arrogant, or aloof. Role constructs focus on their social position. Are they professors, students, administrators? And psychological constructs lead us to classify people according to such things as their generosity, insecurity, shyness, or sense of humor. Which of these schemata are you conscious of using when you first meet someone?

Perceptual Sets

Each of us learns to make sense of the world by organizing the stimuli we perceive uniquely. These organization frameworks are known as our **perceptual sets** and are established gradually over time. The perceptual sets we internalize not only help us decide which stimuli we should attend to, they also help us construct our social reality. In other words, the lessons taught us by society and our family and friends condition us to perceive stimuli in set ways. For example, if we are raised in a family that values learning, we are apt to perceive learning-related activities more positively than we would if we had been raised in a family that dismissed learning as unimportant. Likewise, if we grow up in a home where a particular religious or ethnic group is consistently demeaned, we would be more likely to believe in that group's inferiority.[10] Because past lessons and experiences are part of us at every new encounter, our past also influences how we interpret and evaluate the present.

Selectivities

Another factor that determines the way we make sense of our environment is the selection of stimuli that are significant to us. Education, culture, and motivation are selectivities that play a part in influencing our perception. For

in Practice

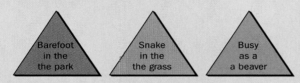
example, although Americans support the open expression of opinion, the Japanese believe that talk is not necessarily good but rather a sign of shallowness.[11] If our culture values competition, we might find it problematic to relate to members of a culture who stress the benefits of cooperation. Culture helps to condition us to communicate in different ways. As you will see later in this chapter, it also influences our communication preferences and style.

Similarly, our motivation or internal state also causes us to exhibit perceptual selectivities. For instance, just as thirsty people lost in the desert tend to see water mirages, so hungry people are more apt to see food before their eyes when shown ambiguous pictures than are satiated individuals. Similarly, our financial position can influence our positive or negative perceptions of matters such as the U.S. welfare system or clothing fads. Stimuli look different to us as our experiences with them change.

The lessons life teaches each one of us will never be exactly like the lessons life teaches others. As a result, no two people will perceive the same stimulus in exactly the same way. Our position in life, in a relationship, or in a job influences our evaluation and reaction to events and people. By altering our view of reality, perception also influences our behavior.

When we have narrow perceptions, we exhibit a rigid repertoire of behaviors, and our communication effectiveness will be reduced by what are called ethnocentric tendencies. **Ethnocentrism** is the tendency to perceive what is right or wrong, good or bad according to the categories and values of our own culture. If we exhibit ethnocentric tendencies, we mentally formulate categorizations that make up the perceptions that are familiar and comfortable to us (in-group) and other categorizations that are unfamiliar and awkward (out-group). While such a process can help us make sense of our world, it also can lead us to take perceptual short-cuts and to stereotype.

What are some of the stereotypes you hold? Can you easily and quickly complete the following generalizations?

Math teachers are . . .
Immigrants are . . .
Latinos are . . .
Arabs are . . .
Asians are . . .
Women are . . .
Men are . . .

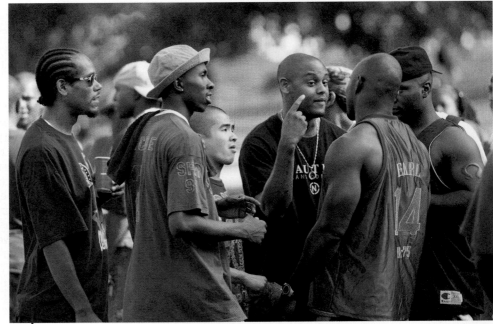

Racial profiling, a form of stereotyping, can bias perception. Problems can arise if we revert to stereotypes when thinking about each other.

Stereotypes

Stereotypes are "rigid perceptions which are applied to all members of a group or to an individual over a period of time, regardless of individual variations."[12] The stereotypes we hold affect how we process stimuli around us. Generalizations can help us make sense of our world by allowing us to apply what we already know to different situations. As long as the generalizations are accurate, they are extremely useful. However, when they turn into rigid stereotypes, they become responsible for our losing touch with the real world.

The stereotypes that cause us to lose touch with reality share two key characteristics: (1) they lead us to categorize others on the basis of easily recognized, but not necessarily significant, qualities (for example, noticing a person's ethnicity before anything else), or (2) they lead us to ascribe an array of qualities to most or all members of a group (for example, assuming that all persons of Asian descent are soft-spoken and shy). When the generalizations we make harden, they cause us to disregard any differences individuals have that set them apart from the stereotyped group.

Stereotypes like those just described plague both interracial and intercultural communication. For example, The front cover of one major city's daily newspaper depicted fifteen photos of fugitives wanted for murder by that city's police department. Although there were a number of Caucasian fugitives on the list, the only suspects prominently featured on the cover were African American, Hispanic, or Asian American fugitives.[13] Racial profiling, a form of stereotyping, biases perception. Surveys of African American students reveal that many of them perceive Caucasian students as manipulative and demanding. In comparison, many Caucasian students perceive African American students as loud and showy.[14] Too frequently, both Americans and residents of predominantly Islamic countries revert to stereotypes when picturing each other. Although most Americans perceive themselves and their country as trustworthy, friendly, caring about poorer nations, and respectful of Islamic values, most people living in Muslim countries perceive just the opposite.[15] Thus, the skewed pictures we carry around in our heads can lead us to think more negatively of each other. The very fact that we remember more favorable information about in-groups and more negative information about out-groups demonstrates this.

When we stereotype, instead of responding to the communication or cues of individuals, we create expectations, assume they are valid, and behave as if they have already occurred. We judge people on the basis of what we believe regarding the group in which we have placed them. We emphasize similarities and overlook discrepancies. Stereotyping leads us to oversimplify, generalize, and grossly exaggerate what we observe.

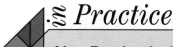

You Be the Judge

Imagine the following situation: You have a campus job working nights from 6:00 P.M. to midnight in the campus computer lab. It is late and you are alone. You feel particularly uncomfortable because there has been an increase in campus crime and students have been warned to travel in pairs. You are relieved when 12:00 comes and you can leave for home. As you close and begin to lock the door to the computer lab, you hear someone yell, "Wait! Don't lock the door!" A person runs down the hall towards you and pleads with you to let him into the computer room so that he can complete a class project that is due the next day. In his haste to get to the lab, he tells you that he forgot his ID. You do not recognize the student. Do you trust what he is telling you? Do you let him in?

How would the decision you make change if the student was female? Had a baby face? Was elderly? Was an African American? A Latino? An Asian? An Arab? Was poorly dressed? Well dressed? Was wearing a lab coat? Had tattoos? Had body piercings?

We often find ourselves in situations that require us to make decisions based on little information other than appearance. Unfortunately, too frequently we make feature–trait associations, relying on physical appearance to make judgments regarding both the categories people belong to and the traits they possess. While we may believe we are responding to a particular person, what we are really responding to is a stereotype. For example, for many years a person with dark skin, coarse hair, full lips, and a wide nose signaled to some people that the person was African American. This was a stereotype that produced a stereotypic judgment. And the more "Afrocentric" their features, the more these persons were ascribed traits stereotypic of African Americans.[16] Colorism researchers similarly report that more prejudice and discrimination are directed against dark-skinned African Americans than light-skinned African Americans. Light-skinned African Americans are more likely to have better jobs and attain higher levels of education than are group members with darker skin.[17] Researchers caution that although we may see more African American lawyers and doctors in prime-time dramas, those characters are lighter skinned than the African Americans who are still shown on the evening news as less exemplary characters.[18]

Lazy perceivers rely on stereotyping as their key perceptual process. Because it discourages careful observation and encourages pigeonholing, stereotyping discourages the noting of differences and encourages categorization, leading some to observe that stereotyping brings on a malady called "hardening of the categories."

professional
contacts

Understanding the Pain

Reporter Jerry Bembry tells of the following incident:

At a basketball media day at the Naval Academy, a ranking Navy official was greeting the news media. Each journalist received a gracious hello, but when the Navy man got to me, I was asked a question.

"So," the official said, extending his hand. "Where did you play ball at to get this job?"

His assumption: Because I'm an athletic-looking African-American male, my education must have come

in combination with an athletic scholarship. It's a question I'm often asked, although I've never played collegiate sports.

No matter how many times such instances happen to me, it's unsettling.*

1. In your opinion, why does such behavior exist?
2. How can we stop ourselves and others from acting this way?

*Jerry Bembry, "The Pain that Whites Don't See," *The Record* (Hackensack, NJ), January 23, 1994, p. E3.

When we suffer from such a malady, we insist on having everyone fit into a particular niche, and we fail to recognize that every person is unique in some way and in fact comprises his or her own category.

Exploring Other Barriers to Accurate Perception

A number of barriers can interfere with the development of accurate perception by causing us to behave unreflectively—that is, act only on the basis of our personal interests, make erroneous assumptions, and so forth. Perhaps the best way to succeed in razing such barriers is to learn to recognize them in our own behaviors as well as in the behaviors of others. Among the factors that interfere with our developing our perceptual abilities are:

What are some of the stereotypes you hold? What are some that people you know hold?

1. Our failure to recognize the influence of age,
2. Our failure to distinguish between facts and inferences,
3. Our tendency to think we know it all,
4. Our penchant for indiscrimination,
5. Our fondness for freezing our evaluations,
6. Our tendency to respond to events or persons with an undelayed reaction,
7. Our ability to wear blinders,
8. Our tendency to judge others more harshly than we judge ourselves, and
9. Our penchant for clinging to first impressions.

Let us consider each in turn.

Age and Person Perception

The only constant when it comes to age and perception is change. This is because we continually change age-group memberships throughout our life span. The age we are, at any point in time, influences our perception of other persons.[19]

According to category-based processing, if we are younger and identify an individual as belonging to the category of older adults, then our attitudes toward the person may be affected by the attitudes we have toward older persons in general. On the other hand, if we are older and view the target individual as similar to ourselves, then rather than rely on stereotypic category-based processing, we may rely on person-based processing instead. This action reduces the influence of group attitudes on our perceptual judgments of the target and may help explain why older people have more complex representations of people their age compared with other age groups. Older persons are more familiar with persons in their age group and are motivated to use person-based processing when forming an impression of a member of their group.[20]

In contrast, younger people tend to place older adults into a number of different stereotypes. As a group, young people perceive older people more negatively than they do young and middle-aged adults. Along these same lines, as a group, young adults are more apt to rate a negative elderly target as more typical of the group than they would rate a positive elderly target.[21]

Older people, in contrast, rate characteristics associated with older people more positively than their younger counterparts. They have more positive attitudes about their own aging process than do younger persons. Older people perceive other older adults as exhibiting more instrumentality and autonomy than do either adolescent or middle-aged persons. This may be because people display biases that favor the members of their own group, demonstrating an in-group favoritism effect. This may also explain why younger people rate characteristics associated with young people more favorably than do older adults. The attitudes they have are reflective of the fact that young people have the highest level of anxiety about aging.[22]

Attitudes toward aging influence whether or not a person engages in stereotyping. These attitudes are also affected by gender. Young women who attribute any negative attitudes toward older people to their own fear of aging stereotype older people less than do other women. On the other hand, young men who consider their own fears about aging stereotype older adults more than do other men. The fact that men and women have different mental representations for aging may account for this disparity.[23] Thus, attitudes toward aging play a key role in perception of elderly people.

Fact–Inference Confusion: Can You Assess What Happened?

A fact is something you know to be true on the basis of observation. Your hair is brown; Joe's Place serves only Chinese food. An inference is simply a conclusion you draw. Your neighbor is having an affair because an unfamiliar car comes every few days for an hour or so; the bulb must have blown because the light's not working. When we mistake what we infer for what we observe, we experience *fact–inference confusion*. Inferences have varying degrees of probability of

in Practice

Facts and Inferences

To test your understanding of facts and inferences, read the following brief story and the statements accompanying it. If you think a statement is true, circle T; if it's false, circle F. For an inference that might be either true or false, circle the question mark.

You arrive at school one day and see that a number of police cars and an ambulance are parked at the front gate of the campus. Also parked there is a car with "Dr. Smythe" on the license plate.

1. Police cars are parked at the front gate of the campus.   **T F ?**

2. Someone at the college has been shot.   **T F ?**

3. The ambulance was summoned by the police.   **T F ?**

4. The car with "Dr. Smythe" on its license plate was not parked at the front gate.   **T F ?**

5. Dr. Smythe is the car's owner.   **T F ?**

Answers appear on page 486.

Which are more interesting—facts or inferences?

being correct; their validity depends on the facts that underlie them. For example, saying "The sun will rise tomorrow" is technically not a fact; it is an inference with a very high probability of being correct. In contrast, if you saw a friend talking and laughing with a member of the opposite sex, and you concluded that they were dating, that would be an inference. It cannot be verified by your observations to this point.

Acting as if an assumption is a fact can have serious consequences. It can cause us to jump to erroneous conclusions, create embarrassing moments, and result in our responding inappropriately and perhaps even violently to people or circumstances.

It is important to take the time we need to evaluate whether we are relying on facts or on inferences when we perceive and interpret. The question is not whether we make inferences, but whether we are *aware* of the inferences we make. It is when we don't recognize inferences and thus fail to consider that we could be wrong, instead acting as if we were dealing with "sure things," that we are more likely to encounter problems. If we are aware that we are inferring rather than observing and we assess the degree of probability that our inferences are correct, we will take a giant step forward in improving the accuracy of our perceptions.

Allness: Can You Know It All?

Allness, or thinking that we can know all there is to know about a given topic, is an attitude that some people carry with them as they attempt to make sense of their world. Because they mistakenly think they can know everything, they exhibit very little tolerance for ambiguity. Thus, they display a lack of willingness to withhold judgment, preferring instead never to doubt themselves but to react on the basis of what they know. That's just what the six blind men in John G. Saxe's poem "The Blind Men and the Elephant" did (see the "Literary Contacts" box).

By thinking we know it all, we limit our ability to perceive accurately. In addition, when we insist that our viewpoint alone is correct, we are saying that any differing perception is incorrect. In effect, we build an

in Theory

The Plot Thickens

Fiction and drama frequently revolve around stories based on fact–inference confusion.

1. Think of a TV show or film or novel plot that revolved around a fact–inference confusion.

2. Analyze specifically what occurred, why it occurred, and what the involved characters could have done or said to avoid it.

"all-wall."[24] Instead, we would be wiser to open ourselves to alternative ways of perceiving; by so doing we would also open ourselves to new experiences. Once we raze the "all-wall" it becomes feasible for us to keep on learning. While we may know a great deal, we also need to acknowledge we do not know it all and that an implied "et cetera" follows every one of our perceptions—a recognition that there's more than what we see.[25]

> The belief that one's own view of reality is correct is the most dangerous of all delusions.
>
> —*Paul Watzlawick*

literary contacts

Is That All There Is?

Explain how this poem by John Godfrey Saxe helps illustrate the perceptual fallacy of allness.

It was six men of Indostan
    To learning much inclined
Who went to see the Elephant
    (Though all of them were blind),
That each by observation
    Might satisfy his mind.

The First approached the Elephant,
    And happening to fall
Against his broad and sturdy side,
    At once began to bawl:
"God bless me! but the Elephant
    Is very like a wall."

The Second, feeling of the tusk
    Cried, "Ho! what have we here
So very round and smooth and sharp?
    To me 'tis very clear
This wonder of an Elephant
    Is very like a spear."

The Third approached the animal
    And, happening to take
The squirming trunk within his hands
    Thus boldly up he spake:
"I see," quoth he, "the Elephant
    Is very like a snake!"

The Fourth reached out an eager hand,
    And felt about the knee:
"What most this wondrous beast is like
    Is very plain," quoth he;
"Tis clear enough the Elephant
    Is very like a tree!"

The Fifth, who chanced to touch the ear,
    Said: "E'en the blindest man
Can tell what this resembles most;
    Deny the fact who can
This marvel of an Elephant
    Is very like a fan!"

The Sixth no sooner had begun
    About the beast to grope
Than seizing on the swinging tail
    That fell within his scope:
"I see," quoth he, "the Elephant
    Is very like a rope!"

And so these men of Indostan
    Disputed loud and long,
Each in his own opinion
    Exceeding stiff and strong.
Though each was partly in the right,
    They all were in the wrong!

1. What does this poem suggest about the dangers of allness?
2. Can allness ever prove accurate?
3. To what extent does allness affect future evaluations? Provide specific examples.

in Practice

Dots

Without lifting your pen or pencil from the paper or backtracking over a line, draw four straight lines that connect all the dots.

· · ·
· · ·
· · ·

If you are having trouble solving the puzzle, ask yourself this question: "What do I see before my eyes?" If you are like most people, instead of seeing only nine dots, you also see a square. By seeing a square you unconsciously add a restriction—one that doesn't really exist. Seeing a square blinds you in your attempt to find a solution; it prevents you from realizing that the boundaries you have created are imaginary and exist only in your mind. Turn to page 486 for the solution.

Indiscrimination: Can You Perceive Difference?

Semanticist Irving J. Lee said, "The more we discriminate among, the less we will discriminate against."[26] In other words, the more we are discriminating and look for differences in all individuals, the less likely it is that we will be prejudiced against the members of any one group or treat them unfairly. Do you think that following Lee's suggestion will improve your ability to perceive others more accurately?

Accurate perception depends on the identification of differences, not just the recognition of similarities. Too frequently, however, we are prone to neglect differences and overemphasize similarities.[27] When this happens, the categories into which we place things become rigid, increasing our tendency to stereotype. To improve our ability to perceive clearly, we need to remind ourselves that no two people are absolutely the same; each is unique. Noting differences can completely alter our perceptions.

As Lee notes, being discriminating is the opposite of practicing discrimination. It is when we fail to discriminate *among* persons that we may end up discriminating *against* them. When we ignore individual differences and act instead on the basis of a preconceived judgment or generalized perception, we then display our prejudice. Using stereotypes as the basis for social exchanges can lead to miscommunication. Our prejudicial behavior can cause us to act in ways that harm the person with whom we are interacting. Too frequently, the way stereotypes play out in behavior leads us to decide that we do not like or approve of someone before we have even gotten to know her or him. Our expectations influence the judgments we make.

Frozen Evaluations and Undelayed Reactions: Can You Perceive Change? Can You Wait?

We are apt to assume that things, situations, and people stay the way they are . . . always. We therefore make **frozen evaluations,** judging people and events, and we are prone to stick with them. "Once a poor student," we think, "always a poor student." "Once a thief," we reason, "always a thief." Statements like these, however, fail to acknowledge that people can change. If our perception does not permit us to be flexible but instead freezes our judgment, then we fail to perceive the constant change that characterizes all of us.

Just as we are apt to make frozen evaluations, we often exhibit **undelayed reactions,** or snap decisions. In our rush to give meaning to what we perceive, instead of delaying our responses, we jump to conclusions and exhibit an

When you experience difficulty interacting with another person, are you more likely to blame yourself, the other person, or share the blame?

instantaneous and reflexlike—often dangerous—response to events. For example, if we see our friend talking with a police officer, we may rush to judgment and conclude that the officer was giving him a ticket. Accurate perception, however, usually takes time. Better perceivers do not rush to respond; rather, they try to synthesize as much data as possible, explore alternative evaluations of each situation, and thus increase their chances of understanding what really has happened.

Putting on Blinders: Do You Add Unnecessary Perceptual Restrictions?

What we tell ourselves about what we perceive can also limit our ability to perceive accurately. In effect, we put **blinders** on when we force ourselves to see situations only in certain ways. To understand the concept of putting on blinders, try the experiment in the "In Practice" box.

Accurate perception depends on your ability to see what is there without being limited by imaginary boundaries. When, for example, scientists stopped searching for the cause of malaria in the air (*malaria* comes from the Italian for "bad air"), and looked for other causes, they soon traced its origin to the anaphales mosquito and were then able to find a cure.

We Judge Others More Harshly Than We Judge Ourselves

Point your finger at a person sitting near you. The gesture feels natural, doesn't it? Now point that same finger at yourself. That doesn't feel quite so natural, does it?

When perceptual disagreements or discrepancies arise, we tend to assume that the problem is due to a deficiency in the other person, rather than to a deficiency in ourselves. We are quite comfortable evaluating ourselves and our perceptual capabilities more charitably than we judge others.

When people are asked to compare their ability to communicate with that of their peers, parents, professors, or siblings, most report that they communicate at least as well if not better than others. Thus, whenever communication goes awry, that finger points outward—directly at another individual—rather than inward to the self. We thereby shift responsibility for communication problems and perceptual distortions away from ourselves and place it with those with whom we interact.

Clinging to First Impressions

Once we form an opinion of someone or perceive something in a particular light, we tend to adhere to it, and do our best to manipulate or distort any information that appears to contradict or conflict with our evaluation so that it conforms with our view. Sometimes, for example, we forget that time means change. When this happens, because we evaluated a person as having certain attributes or saw that individual a specific way at one time does not mean that we should see that individual the same way or attribute the same qualities to him or her always. We need to put dates on our perceptions to remind ourselves that adopted perspectives need not be permanent. How we see something or someone now is not necessarily the way we need to see that something or someone always. Everything changes—people, situations, events—even our perceptions.

While maintaining an open mind is a goal, actually realizing that goal can become a challenge. Yet it is important to reach if we are to develop more valid perceptions. For example, consider the following initial description and then the reevaluation of one person's perception:

For years I had seen octopuses as terrible, evil creatures that were intent on grabbing swimmers with their tentacles and dragging them under water to be crushed and drowned.

Now I perceive them as being gentle, inoffensive, intelligent creatures who enjoy playful contacts with swimmers.

Probably I have changed my perception of octopuses because of changes in the filters of past experience and mind-set. My early experiences were reading horror stories and seeing horror movies. My mind-set was to believe, as truth, what I read and saw in those media. Also I wanted to believe the horrible stories were true

 in Theory

Reexamination of Experience

Think of an experience in your life that you once had a strong opinion about, which was changed when something happened. For example, you might have believed that a disheveled person seen frequently was homeless until you discovered that a building at the college was named for him.

1. How difficult was it to reevaluate your perception?

2. What caused you to do so?

because that enhanced my enjoyment. Later experiences were seeing undersea documentaries by Cousteau and reading books by him. My mind-set now is that I respect what scientists tell me and I expect that they will give me accurate accounts of their research. I saw a movie of one of Cousteau's divers doing a little ballet dance with an octopus he had made friends with. Then I saw the octopus and the diver embrace affectionately as they parted. I also read about a young woman biologist who has made friends with giant octopuses near Seattle. She tickles them and they love it.[28]

Diversity and Culture Contacts: Interpreting through Different I's

Most of us persist in maintaining the way we see the world—not necessarily as it is but as we have been conditioned to perceive it. Our culture and our past experiences create in us a quest for perceptual constancy—it is easier for us to keep seeing things as we have in the past than it is to revise our perceptions. We are more comfortable managing stimuli the way we have done so before. Once we learn to make sense of our world, we resist changing how we make that sense.

The more our life experiences are like those of others, the more similarly we tend to perceive the world. The more dissimilar our life experiences are compared to others', the wider the gap between us becomes with respect to the way we see things and make sense of them.[29] The fact is, not everyone makes sense out of experience in the same way. Cultural habits or selectivities see to that.

Every culture develops in its members particular cultural perspectives or ways of looking at the world. As we have seen, most Americans perceive it important to express their uniqueness and independence, whereas in Asian cultures the family and not the individual are paramount. These contrasting orientations have implications for interpersonal communication. Persons who are taught to be interdependent tend to be more sensitive and attentive to others. American children are taught to separate from their parents and develop self-reliance, but in cultures that value interdependence over dependence, cooperation, helpfulness, and loyalty are nurtured instead. Thus, persons from these cultures tend to have more closely knit relationships and expect more from others.

We see such differences play themselves out in how people process information. The Japanese, for example, develop a wider-angle view of experience than do Americans. They do not place themselves at the center of the universe. When students at the University of Michigan and Kyoto University were shown an animation of an underwater scene with a "focal fish" and other fish swimming among an array of undersea objects, the Japanese students made more references to the background elements while the Americans focused on the "focal fish." Americans believe that each person has a separate identity that needs to be identified and reinforced. They value the ethic of competition, the need to be number one. This orientation often causes difficulties for Americans when they interact with persons from other cultures who do not share this value, perceiving it to threaten them.

In the U.S. we have a culture that values youth and rejects the notion of growing old. Persons in Arab, Asian, Latin American, Native American, and African cultures do not share this perception.

Practice

Culture teaches us a world view. For example, when looking at the moon, a North American might report seeing a man on the moon while an American Indian is apt to say there's a rabbit, a Chinese person is likely to see a lady fleeing her spouse, and a Samoan will find a woman weaving.[30] Whether we are judging beauty, describing snow, or evaluating the meaning of success, our culture influences our assessment of reality. Individuals from different cultures are simply trained to observe the same cues differently; they interpret what they perceive through a **cultural lens.** Some years ago, researchers employed an apparatus resembling binoculars to compare the perceptual preferences of Native Americans and Mexicans. Each subject was shown ten pairs of photographs—one photo in each pair was of an element of Native American culture and one was of Mexican culture. After viewing the paired images through the device, the subjects reported their observations. Results revealed that both Native Americans and Mexicans were more likely to report having seen a scene from their own culture.[31]

Similarly, culture teaches us to behave in a particular manner when faced with a given set of conditions and to expect others to do the same. Misunderstandings can result, however, when one person operates according to a different set of assumptions and rules than another. Consider, for example, an American who expects that when conversing, acquaintances will maintain approximately an arm's length distance from each other. What if that American is interacting with Arabs? In contrast to Americans, Arabs prefer to stand close enough in conversation to smell each other's breath. In fact, some Arabs feel insulted when they are restrained from approaching this closely; not to permit such closeness is akin to an insult. If we simply follow the rules and expectations of our own culture, without making an effort to understand whether those rules and expectations support or conflict with those of another culture, more than likely we will misinterpret or misconstrue the other person's intent. Sometimes such misunderstandings can lead us to distrust others. For example, imagine a white teacher questioning an African American student. As she answers her instructor, the African American student does not make eye contact with him. Because of the lack of eye contact, the teacher is apt to evaluate his student's behavior as disrespectful and may even conclude that the student is keeping something from him. On the other hand, the student keeps her eyes downcast because she has been taught that by exhibiting that behavior she is being not rude but respectful.

Because we have not all experienced the same life lessons, even within a culture, we do not attribute the same meanings to the same behavioral cues. Our cultural nearsightedness, however, keeps us from recognizing this. Such deficient perceptual vision contributes to our misreading cues and missing opportunities to use the differences among people as a means to help ourselves perceive each other more accurately.

Provide examples of cultural nearsightedness.

Our perception of reality, then, is not necessarily reality at all. Our interpretation of what we see may not be what is there. The more we make ourselves aware of the extent to which culture conditions us, the more we become willing to acknowledge our perceptual selectivities and open ourselves to alternative ways of perceiving. Once we do this, we will be able to better understand each other.[32]

Media Contacts

The Media and Perception

The media also influence how we perceive social experience. In fact, because they tend to depict us in ways that reinforce cultural views of gender, the more media we use, the more accepting we tend to become of social stereotypes, and the more likely we are to help perpetuate the unrealistic and limiting perceptions presented to us. In what ways do the stereotypes or overly simplified portrayals that the media present us influence our expectations for ourselves, others, and our relationships?

First, they help us identify and generalize about what we consider to be appropriate behavior. They offer us categories into which people fit, and they provide us with an array of models in action so that when similar situations arise we think we know how to deal with them. Second, they provide us with **perceptual shortcuts;** they cause us to forget that we communicate with individuals, not stereotypes, and they contribute to our becoming *lazy perceivers*—too accepting of the inaccurate or false images presented to us.

What are some of the specific lessons we learn from the media that help shape our perceptions of gender? One important lesson is that due to the significant underrepresentation of both women and older people in the media, we come to believe that males matter more and that women and older people are either unimportant or invisible. During prime-time television programming, for example, we

Theory

How Risky Is It?

Some researchers assert that by distorting our perception of risk, the media induce us to experience fear that is out of proportion with actual danger. In other words, they are virtually scaring us to death.

The more attention the media pay to a particular risk factor, the worse we assume the risk to be. For example, Dr. Baruch Fischoff, a psychologist at Carnegie-Mellon University and an expert in the study of risk perception, reports, "If scientists are studying it and the news reports it, people assume it must be worth their attention."* Another risk researcher, Dr. Paul Slovic, reports that adding to this effect is the finding "that people put more stock in reports of bad news than in reports that might increase their trust."†

1. In what ways and regarding what topics have the media contributed to your being fearful?

2. To what extent, if any, was the risk you perceived greater than the reality?

*See Daniel Goleman, "Hidden Rules often Distort Ideas of Risk," *New York Times,* February 1, 1994, pp. C1, C10.

†Ibid.

see three times as many white men as women.[33] When we watch broadcast news, stories about men outnumber stories about women approximately 10 to 1.[34]

A second media lesson involves our internalization of the stereotypic portrayals of gender the media offer us. Whereas media offerings present men as active, independent, powerful, and sexually virile, they portray women as passive, dependent, incompetent, and the objects of the males' sexual desires. The media show men taking care of business, but more typically, they show women concerned with their looks, other people, and family members. From the point of view of the media, males dominate and females are subservient.[35] Males are providers; females are caregivers.

A third media lesson concerns the extent to which the media lead us to perceive minorities inappropriately. Minorities occupy an even smaller presence in media offerings than women do. For the most part, minorities play supporting rather than leading roles, and often, instead of being depicted in complimentary ways, they are portrayed as lazy, unlawful, or dumb. Writer David Evans, for example, criticized television for stereotyping African American males as athletes and entertainers. Doing this, wrote Evans, causes the young African American viewing public to conclude that success "is only a dribble or dance step away," thereby preventing them from developing more realistic expectations.[36]

The media, particularly television, affect us in other ways as well. According to researchers, television also influences perception by molding our conceptions of the real world and people in a way that is inconsistent with actual facts. While we may think the media exert less influence on us than our peers, research tells a different story.[37] According to cultivation theory heavy television viewers (those who watch four hours of television a day or more) are more likely to be fearful and to exaggerate the amount of violence in the world than are light viewers (those who view two hours or less of television). Heavy viewers perceive the world to be meaner and a more dangerous place.[38] They believe, for example, that their chances of being a crime victim are 1 in 10 when the actual risk is much, much less. Perceptions such as this one affect real-life judgments of where it is safe to go, how late it is safe to stay out, whom we should fear, and whom it is safe to be with. What steps can you take to counteract the false sense of reality brought to you by the media?

Our online interaction is also influenced by judgments we make about a person's culture or gender. According to the Social Identity Model of Deindividuation Effects (SIDE), we have different identities that make themselves visible in different situations. When we chat online, the lack of nonverbal cues, especially those that would have revealed information about our appearance and sound, causes us to hold on more tightly to visible cues about each other, such as our group affiliations.[39] This may compel us to become more judgmental, make overattributions (single out one or two characteristics of the person), or exaggerate the importance of the minimal information we have. We practice closure, often filling in the gaps by using stereotypes. If we assume people share social categories with us, making them like us, we will tend to find them more likeable than if we believe they are different.

Thus media lessons, which appear innocuously to weave their way into our consciousness, also function to limit the way we perceive ourselves in relation to each other and, what's worse, they often cause us to misperceive reality. As they perpetuate what is unreal and untrue, they encourage us not to reach for what is possible. Because we use the media as reference points for what's normal, we are more likely to perceive ourselves, our relationships, and our lives as inferior by comparison. The media present the human body in perfect forms and convince us that no one could love us the way we actually are, thus causing us to develop negative images of ourselves. Because they tend to focus on images of violence, the media make us think the world is a very scary place. The media's unreal images perpetuate in us unrealistic perceptions of what our life should be like and cause us to internalize and anticipate unreasonable outcomes from relationships.

Practice

Online Chatting

Enter a chat room and begin to interact with someone you do not know. After a few moments of chatting, answer these questions:

1. What do you think your chatting partner is like?

2. How is what you think influencing your online behavior?

3. What online cues are you using to form your perception of the other person?

4. What stereotypes, if any, are you using?

When you have finished answering these questions, continue chatting. To what extent, if any, do you think that consciously considering the preceding questions improved your ability to see the person more accurately and communicate more effectively?

Gender Contacts

Gender and Perception

Gender, like ethnicity, influences the way we make sense of our experiences. Men and women are conditioned to perceive different realities, are encouraged to perform in different ways, and prefer to use different communication styles. In addition to influencing how men and women *perceive* each other, beliefs about gender-appropriate behavior influence how men and women *relate* to each other. From early childhood, both boys and girls are rewarded for using behaviors that conform to their gender; for example, boys are commended for displaying strength and independence, whereas girls are commended for expressing their feelings and being kind to others. Women are categorized as emotional; men are classified as rational.[40]

As a result of our interaction with parents, teachers, peers, and others, we internalize the lessons of appropriate gendered behavior. These lessons frame our perceptions and instruct us in how society would like us to behave. Such constructs, however, can limit the way each of us is perceived and may lead to the judging of men and women based on gender expectations rather than on observed cues.[41]

Interweaving and working in combination, the expectations of others, the behavioral cues exhibited by role models, the promotion of stereotyped notions of sex roles by traditional educational institutions, and the repeated confirmation of male and female stereotypes by the media provide us with repeated confirmation of "acceptable" images of male and female behavior.[42] If we want to change the perception of the kinds of behavior appropriate for men and women, we need to change the messages fed us by society.

To what extent have you internalized gendered behavior lessons?

As we perceive experience, we also monitor ourselves. We sort stimuli, selecting some and rejecting others. The information we store in our internal database helps us build our view of reality and gives our lives a sense of stability. For example, if we develop the perspective that men are persistently more dominant than women, then we use that belief to categorize both genders and predict their actions. However, when our expectations cause us to misperceive others and their intentions, undesirable consequences can result. All too frequently, rigid categorizing creates communication problems and precipitates interpersonal fiascoes.

As thinking men and women, we don't have to accept all the **gender prescriptions** a culture provides—we may reject those that limit our development. By doing so, we can elicit changes in the behavior of others toward us. When we refuse to support a gender-based definition, we in effect participate in its redefinition. For example, when one woman encourages another to be more autonomous, she may help that woman to expand her definition of behaviors appropriate for women. As women change their behavior and roles, men may perceive both women and themselves differently and may change as well. As we enlarge our perceptions of others by experiencing a greater variety of situations and people, we alter our expectations, and we may also revise our views of what males and females can do. In the process, we recast what masculinity and femininity mean.

Technology Contacts

Technology and Virtual Reality

Technology is altering the way we perceive others, our world, and ourselves. How do we perceive the new social connections we have forged with computer-mediated communication? Do we view them as pulling us together into new kinds of communities, or pulling us apart by their ability to separate us from more local, personal interactions, thrusting us into the realigned world of distance relating? Is it possible for us to reproduce real social interactions in the virtual medium of cyberspace?

How do others perceive us when they interact with us online? How do we perceive the different form of social contact online relationships provide? Some say we are simply seeking community by whatever means are available to us—the lack of a sense of meaningful community in our lives has fueled our desire to create **virtual communities** in cyberspace.[43] **Cyberspace** and computer-mediated communication make the distances between us vanish, causing us to perceive each other as closer than we actually are. Because it gives us the illusion of closeness, the computer may also be changing our concepts of time and space. We can now move through social space and from relationship to relationship without actually leaving the physical space we are in. Whereas in years past our lives were made up of face-to-face relations with friends, in the future our lives may be characterized by "distant, impersonal contact among strangers."[44] Will we perceive them to be strangers, though, or friends? As we eliminate the social constraints created by location, will life online be happier for us? Once we are able to link ourselves specifically with those who share the same interests and goals, will we become bored with the sameness and lack of serendipity or lulled into a false sense of companionship by the comfort provided us by interacting with those who confirm our way of thinking? Will our impersonal associations really substitute for traditional interpersonal ones? Will we possess the same sense of personal commitment to those we meet in cyberspace? Will we be able to tell when someone we interact with online is being sincere or telling the truth? Will we perceive those we interact with differently when we are no longer concerned with what they look like, but are more focused on how they think? Again, who we are, and what online site we choose to visit, will determine what we see.

How does life online influence offline perceptions?

Technology is changing us in other ways as well. Researchers have shown that playing violent video games increases aggressive behavior by causing people to perceive annoying provocations as hostile in nature. The games also have been criticized for expanding the repertoire of aggressive behaviors used by players and for emotionally desensitizing players to aggression and violence.[45] More recent reports, however, reveal that the playing of action video games such as *Grand Theft Auto, Counter Strike,* and *Spider Man* enhance the ability to pay attention to objects and changes in the environment. Experienced video game players are 30 percent to 50 percent better than nonplayers at perceiving everything happening around them. While earlier studies demonstrated that playing video games precipitated better spatial skills, we now learn that it also improves attention skills and facilitates the development of an accurate understanding of a visual landscape.[46]

Gaining Communication Competence

Enhancing Your Perceptual Abilities

Your ability to communicate is affected by your ability to perceive accurately. How can you improve those abilities?

Recognize the Part You Play

Because we are all unique, we each experience a somewhat different reality. Until we recognize the part we play in perceiving and making sense of reality, we are apt to experience numerous relational and communication problems. Just because others may not see the world the way we do doesn't mean their view is wrong. They are merely expressing an alternative outlook. Variations in physiological, psychological, and cultural factors lead us to adopt different perspectives and attribute different meanings to experience. Perception is not something that happens to us. It is something we do.

You may like a person who seems similar to you and dislike someone who seems different. Your friend's jokes may strike you as funny when you're in a good mood and tasteless when you're preoccupied with a personal problem. By taking stock of yourself, including your emotional state and your biases, you accept responsibility for what you bring to the perception process.

Be a Patient Perceiver

Because people tend to live at an accelerated pace in U.S. society, they expect things to happen quickly. The emphasis placed on speed may diminish our ability to be patient and may contribute to our proclivity for jumping to conclusions. Patient perceivers, however, do not jump to conclusions, cling to first impressions, or believe they know it all and, as a result, have a corner on the truth. They open their minds to possibilities, look beyond the obvious, and genuinely attempt to check the accuracy of their interpretations.

To do this, question your perceptual acuity. Ask yourself if there is any chance you could be wrong. By acknowledging that you could have made an error in judgment or misevaluated the behavior you observed, you motivate yourself to seek further validation. If you take the time as well as make the effort either to verify your judgment or prove yourself wrong, you increase your chances of forming more accurate impressions of both others and the situations in which you find yourself.

Become a Perception Checker

In order to avoid treating interpretations as if they were facts, develop the skill of perception checking. When you exhibit perception-checking behavior you observe the behavior of the person with whom you are interacting, describe and interpret what her or his behavior means to you, and put your interpretation into words in an effort to determine if your perception is correct. Interpretation does not involve assessment or evaluation; it does call on you to relay a nonevaluative, descriptive statement of what you have observed.

For example, imagine you are a participant-observer of the following scene:

> Leila walks into the classroom and flings her books down on the desk. As she takes her seat, you notice that her eyes are narrowed and her face is in a scowl. You are seated directly to her right. You quietly say to her, "Leila, I get the feeling that you're angry about something. Am I right? Can I do anything to help?

Making these statements is better than asking: "Why are you angry with me?" (Who said she was?) Your goal as a perception checker is to explore Leila's thoughts and feelings, not to prove that your interpretation of what you observed is right. For example, in response to your comments, Leila might state, "I'm not angry. I'm upset with myself for not getting the paper done on time." By seeking verification of the impression you received from Leila's nonverbal behavior and giving her the opportunity to share her thoughts and feelings, you reduce your uncertainty about what she's feeling as well as take some of the guess-work out of perception.

Keep in mind that perception checking works best with persons who belong to low-context cultures. Typically, it involves straight talk and direct statements of observation. Persons from high-context cultures might experience embarrassment when asked so directly about their feelings and the meaning of their actions.

Widen Your Perception

Keep the big picture in mind as perceptual clues surface. Don't jump to a conclusion based on a single piece of evidence. You are not in "the spin zone." By this we mean you want to ensure that you cautiously assess what is occurring so that you refrain from overattributing meaning to an exhibited behavior or circumstance based on a lack of additional data. While what you may see or hear first (primacy effect) or hear last (recency effect) may make a great impression on you, you need to search for more evidence so that you do not draw an inaccurate conclusion based on the partial picture to which you have access.

See through the Eyes of Another

Try to see things from behind the eyes of the other person. That means you need to take the focus off yourself (socially decenter) and place it on the other (consciously think about her or his thoughts and feelings). Doing this allows you insight into the other person's state of mind and lets you see things from her or his perspective, enabling you to empathize with her or him (re-create or vicariously experience what she or he is feeling). When you empathize you develop a personal sense of what the person is going through. You are able to imagine what it would be like to be in that person's position. Can you imagine, for example, how your significant other feels when you forget his birthday? Can you sense how the boss feels when every few weeks you take a day off? While it is easier to feel empathy for those with whom we identify, it is equally important to be able to put yourself into the shoes of a person with whom you may have little in common.

Build Perceptual Bridges, Not Walls

Although perceptual disagreements can drive us apart, if we exhibit a willingness to experience the world from another person's perspective, we can enhance communication. Rather than argue over whose point of view is right or whose behavior is wrong, it is more productive for us to understand the factors that create differences in our interpretations of experience and then work to adapt to and bridge those differences.

Consider How Technology Is Changing the Way We Perceive

While it is hard to imagine how new online relationships will alter the way we perceive our more traditional relationships, it is important that we try to understand how our linking via computers is influencing and changing our desire for actual versus virtual contact. We need to become aware of the benefits and consequences of the social transformations that are now occurring.

daily
contacts   **Wrap-Up**

Meet again in pairs or with your discussion group. Turn back to the case study at the
beginning of the chapter and reconsider the questions asked. How have your answers
changed or become more focused? Based on what you know about perception, what
advice would you give Dax now?

Critical Thinking Contacts

Examine the following cartoon. Why do the perceptions of the two anchors differ?
Use the perpectual principles discussed in this chapter to support your answer.

**Can You
See It My
Way?**

"Now here's my co-anchor, Nancy, with a conflicting account of that very same story."

Summary

Perception is a personally based process. Because the perceptions we have depend both figuratively and literally on where we sit, differences in the way we perceive occur all the time. Perception is the process we use to make sense of experience. When we perceive, we select, organize, and interpret sensory data in an effort to give meaning to our world. The principles of figure–ground and closure are among the strategies we use to facilitate this process. Affectors, unique to each of us, also influence what we perceive.

Our perceptions tend to persist. Our culture, gender, and past experiences create in us a desire for perceptual constancy. Culture teaches us acceptable ways of looking at our world, as well as acceptable ways of behaving. So does gender, which conditions men and women to perceive different realities, exhibit different behaviors, and use different communication styles. The media also influence how we perceive ourselves, each other, and the social experiences we share. Because the media tend to reinforce cultural views of gender, they contribute to our becoming more accepting of social stereotypes.

Our perceptual sets develop over time. Each set helps us decide what stimulus to focus on and how to construct our social reality. Various barriers, including the tendency to confuse facts and inferences, think we know it all, exhibit indiscrimination, freeze evaluations, display undelayed reactions, and put blinders on ourselves, make it difficult for us to perceive people and events accurately.

Technology is another factor influencing the way we perceive. By altering the way we perceive ourselves, each other, and the nature of our social connections, technological innovations are also changing our view of what is real.

To improve our chances of developing more accurate perceptions, we need to recognize the part we play in perception, develop patience as a perceiver, work to bridge perceptual differences, and carefully consider how technological changes are changing the way we perceive our world.

Terms to Talk About

standpoint theory *(p. 70)*
perception *(p. 70)*
uncertainty reduction theory *(p. 70)*
selective exposure *(p. 72)*
selective attention *(p. 72)*
selective perception *(p. 72)*
selective retention *(p. 72)*
horn effect *(p. 72)*
halo effect *(p. 72)*
figure–ground *(p. 72)*
closure *(p. 73)*
perceptual constancy *(p. 73)*
schemata *(p. 73)*

scripts *(p. 73)*
affectors *(p. 75)*
attribution theory *(p. 77)*
fundamental attribution error *(p. 77)*
self-serving bias *(p. 77)*
overattribution *(p. 78)*
perceptual sets *(p. 78)*
ethnocentrism *(p. 79)*
stereotypes *(p. 80)*
fact–inference confusion *(p. 83)*
allness *(p. 84)*
frozen evaluations *(p. 86)*
undelayed reactions *(p. 86)*

blinders *(p. 87)*   gender prescriptions *(p. 94)*
cultural lens *(p. 90)*   virtual communities *(p. 94)*
perceptual shortcuts *(p. 91)*   cyberspace *(p. 94)*

Suggestions for Further Reading

Edmund Blair Bolles, *A Second Way of Knowing: The Riddle of Human Perception*, Englewood Cliffs, NJ: Prentice-Hall, 1991. An exploration of the perception process with special attention on how the way we construct our perceptual realities affects our lives.

Patricia G. Devine, David L. Hamilton, and Thomas M. Ostrom, *Social Cognition*, Orlando, FL: Academic Press, 1994. Provides thorough coverage of impression formation, person perception, and stereotyping.

William V. Haney, *Communication and Organizational Behavior:* Homewood, IL: Irwin, 1973. A now-classic work that explores the "misevaluations" we tend to make in processing experience and how to avoid them.

Addie Johnson, *Attention*, Thousand Oaks, CA: Sage, 2004. Explores the nature and complexities of attention.

Hernant Shah and Michael Thornton, *Competing Visions of America*, Thousand Oaks, CA: Sage, 2004. An overview of the perceptions people from different countries have of the United States.

Daya Kishan Thussu, *War and the Media*, Thousand Oaks, CA: Sage, 2004. Discusses the media's role in communicating the nature of war.

PART 2
SHARING MESSAGES

Listening

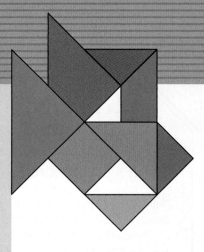

Most people never listen.
Nor do they observe.

— Ernest Hemingway

After completing this chapter, you should be able to:

▮ Describe the amount of time you spend listening.

▮ Define and distinguish between hearing and listening.

▮ Identify and explain the six stages and four types of listening.

▮ Compare and contrast effective and ineffective listeners.

▮ Evaluate your own ability to listen.

▮ Describe and provide examples of nonlistening behaviors.

▮ Use a system to help you overcome listening problems.

▮ Define feedback.

▮ Describe the benefits of effective listening.

▮ Provide examples of gender's and diversity's influence on listening.

▮ Discuss how media and technological advances influence listening.

daily contacts

Flora's Nonlistening

"I didn't mean to do it," Flora told Fred, her boss, at the factory outlet. "I just misunderstood you."

Tuesday had begun as a fairly typical day in Flora's busy life. She had attended her morning classes, eaten a late lunch with several friends, and then left campus for a nearby factory outlet store where she was working as an assistant manager on the evening shift to help pay her way through school.

As she arrived, Flora's boss said, "Be sure and mark the blouses down to $17.99." It seemed a little low, but who was she to question his call? She told Joe, one of the stock workers, to adjust the price.

About an hour later, Adel, a sales clerk, told her that the blouses were moving very quickly. Flora instructed Joe to bring out another case. Indeed, before her shift's end, five more cases of blouses had been purchased by eager shoppers.

As she prepared to close, Flora looked over to the now-depleted blouse display and saw the problem: the blouses were erroneously marked $7.99.

Just then Fred, the store manager, called to see how things were going. "I told Joe, the stockboy, to mark the blouses down to $17.99 like you said, but he mistakenly marked them down to $7.99. He just didn't listen. Should I fire him?" Flora asked.

"Fire him?" came the reply. I told you to mark them up to $77.99. We've now lost $70 for every blouse sold tonight! You and Joe are two of the worst nonlisteners I have met!"

Flora and her boss reached an agreement. The listening mistake would not be paid for out of Flora's check all at once; it would be deducted over several weeks.

Flora felt terrible. How could such a costly mistake be her fault?

Divide into pairs or discussion groups and consider these questions:

1. Was Flora really a "nonlistener"?
2. What specific listening problems are exhibited in this case study?
3. What steps can you take to ensure that you don't experience such a problem?

How much of your day do you spend listening?

What is listening? Listening is "the process of receiving, attending to, and assigning meaning to aural and visual stimuli."[1] During the act of assigning meaning to a spoken message, other components involved in the multi-faceted behavior of listening come into play; among the other elements that we need to consider as we investigate the process of listening are remembering, evaluating, and responding. Are you a proficient listener? We hope so, if only because most of us spend more of our communication time listening than doing anything else. You're probably thinking, "That's not possible! I spend most of my time speaking!" But that's not what communication research reveals. According to the experts, the average college student spends over 50 percent of the possible communicative time in an average day listening, and the average employee spends over 60 percent of an average workday listening.[2] Listening clearly consumes more time than any other communication-related behavior.

That we spend a great deal of each day listening is undeniable. Whether we do it well, however, is another issue. Unfortunately, research shows that while the average person hears a great deal, he or she actively processes only approximately half of what is said, understands about a quarter of it, and retains even less than that. Too frequently, we take listening for granted, and that's not good news for our relationships.

Listening is just as important as other communicative behaviors when it comes to making relationships work. But can we afford not to improve our listening ability when we are faced with facts such as the following?

1. We are exposed to millions of words every year.

2. We spend a much larger percentage of our waking day listening than we do speaking, writing, or reading.

3. On average, we listen at only 25 percent efficiency; that is, instead of retaining most of what we listen to, we lose approximately 75 percent of it over a very short period.[3]

4. Errors in listening are common. While listening is our most pervasive activity, it is also our least developed communicative skill.

professional contacts

The Listener's Intention

In this excerpt from *The Seven Habits of Highly Effective People,* Stephen R. Covey describes a behavior that interferes with effective listening. Identify the problem behavior and cite examples that illustrate how you or someone you know has been guilty of acting in the way described.

"Seek first to understand" involves a very deep shift in paradigm. We typically seek first to be understood. Most people do not listen with the intent to understand; they listen with the intent to reply. They're either speaking or preparing to speak. They're filtering everything through their own paradigms, reading their autobiography into other people's lives.

"Oh, I know exactly how you feel!"

"I went through the very same thing. Let me tell you about my experience."

They're constantly projecting their own home movie onto other people's behavior. They prescribe their own glasses for everyone with whom they interact.

If they have a problem with someone—a son, a daughter, a spouse, an employee—their attitude is, "That person just doesn't understand."

A father once told me, "I can't understand my kid. He just won't listen to me at all."

"Let me restate what you just said," I replied. "You don't understand your son because he won't listen to you?"

"That's right," he replied.

"Let me try again," I said. "You don't understand your son because *he* won't listen to *you?*"

"That's what I said," he impatiently replied.

"I thought that to understand another person, *you* needed to listen to *him,*" I suggested.

"Oh!" he said. There was a long pause. "Oh!" he said again, as the light began to dawn. "Oh, yeah! But I do understand him. I know what he's going through. I went through the same thing myself. I guess what I don't understand is why he won't listen to me."

This man didn't have the vaguest idea of what was really going on inside his boy's head. He looked into his own head and thought he saw the world, including his boy.*

*Steven R. Covey, *The Seven Habits of Highly Effective People,* New York: Simon & Schuster, 1989, pp. 239–240.

5. Whether we want to gain information or critically evaluate a message or the messenger, listening requires our active participation. Passive receivers are not really listening.

6. If we don't give people with whom we interact honest feedback, we forfeit our right to complain about them.

7. It pays to listen. Listening mistakes carry both a personal and a monetary cost. In fact, if each of us in the United States made just one ten-dollar listening mistake a year (much smaller than the mistake in the case study at the beginning of the chapter), the total national cost would accrue to over one billion dollars annually.

8. Our very existence, as well as the effectiveness of all our person-to-person contacts, depends on our ability to listen and respond appropriately. Listening is the primary process through which we make sense of what we hear. It is through listening that we gain the insights we need to: (1) develop relationships, (2) make personal and professional decisions, (3) formulate attitudes and opinions, (4) mentally store data for later use, and (5) provide feedback to others.

9. You will spend more time listening in this course than you will speaking.

10. One purpose of this course is to develop your listening skills.

It is because of the many ways that listening affects us and our relationships that we will take the time to explore not only what we can do to enhance our own listening abilities, but also how we can help those with whom we interact to listen more effectively. It is essential that we develop our abilities to understand and critically evaluate what we listen to, but it is equally important for us to develop our abilities to empathize with and provide feedback to those with whom we share relationships. In addition, our relationships will benefit from our learning to recognize those factors that cause us to turn off and stop listening, when that is the last thing we should be doing.

Differences between Listening and Hearing

Effective listeners don't use just their ears to listen—they also rely on their minds. If you listen well, you also think well. Yet listening and hearing are very different processes. Although **listening** is a *voluntary, psychological process,* **hearing** is an *involuntary, physiological process.* In other words, just as we don't need to think to breathe, neither do we need to think to hear. As long as our eardrums are functional, when sound waves hit them, the subsequent vibrations cause the hammer, anvil, and stirrup, located in the middle ear, to vibrate and produce sound. Once these vibrations reach our auditory nerves, they are transformed into electrical impulses and automatically processed by our brains, and we hear. However, it is what we do with these impulses once we have received them that takes us into the complex arena of listening. If we do not function well as listeners, we likely will not understand what we hear, and we may pass misinformation on to others.

We can learn a lot about listening by considering the extent to which we listen to those with whom we make contact. Far too often, instead of listening

. . . to understand another person, you need to listen to him.

— *Stephen Covey*

actively to others, we only *hear* them. Our minds are asleep rather than alert, and thus we passively receive, rather than actively process, another's message. When we listen, however, we not only hear the message—we also make sense of it, or try to.

The Stages of Listening

The HURIER model of listening developed by Judi Brownell is a behavioral approach that suggests that listening is a system of interrelated components composed of both mental processes and observable behaviors. There are six skill areas on which the model focuses: hearing, understanding, remembering, interpreting, evaluating, and responding (see Figure 4.1).

Stage One—Hearing

We exist in a world filled with the stimuli of sounds. Sounds surround us and compete to be noticed. Some sounds we choose to ignore because we see nothing in them for us. We select other sounds to focus on because they interest us. Eugene Raudsepp of Princeton Creative Research explains the hearing/sensing process by telling the story of a zoologist who was walking with a friend, down a busy street filled with the sounds of honking horns and screeching tires. Turning to his friend, the zoologist says, "Listen to that cricket!" The friend, with astonishment, replies, "You hear a cricket in the middle of all this noise?" The zoologist takes out a coin and flips it in the air. As the coin falls to the sidewalk, a dozen heads turn in response to its "clink." The zoologist responds, "We hear what we listen for."[4]

Attending involves our willingness to organize and focus on particular stimuli. Once we select a sound, we have the opportunity to attend to it and concentrate on it. Here again, of course, we have a choice. Although sound may capture our attention, our focus may be momentary, and unless our attention is held, we will soon choose to refocus our attention on something else. It will simply drift away. Consequently, it is not enough to capture the attention of another; attention needs to be maintained. This requires that we develop sensitivity to the interest of those with whom we make contact.

Stage Two—Understanding

During the understanding stage our focus is on learning what the speaker means. During this stage we relate what the speaker tells us to what we already know, and we refrain from judging the message until we are certain we comprehend it. In an effort to ensure understanding we might ask the speaker questions that when answered help clarify the speaker's message. Rephrasing or paraphrasing what we believe the speaker said also helps us comprehend the message.

FIGURE 4.1
Listening Stages

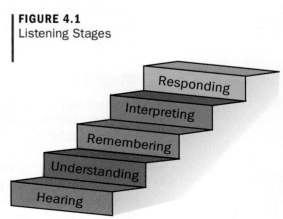

Stage Three—Remembering

During the remembering stage, our brain assigns meaning to that which we have paid attention. We now try to remember what we have gained from the message for further use. Here again, we make choices as we decide what has value and is worth storing in memory and what we can discard. Of course, if we have intense feelings for the person with whom we are interacting or if the message is reinforced, our chances of remembering it are increased. Our memory allows us to retain information and recall it when we need to. On the other hand, some forgetting is necessary to our mental health.

While we usually remember only what we have directly experienced, memories attributed to vicarious experiences or the instilling of false memories are possible. Most frequently, however, memory requires the raw material produced by attention, our listening ally.

Two key kinds of memory concern us: short-term memory and long-term memory. Most of what we hear is stored, if only briefly, in our brain's short-term memory depository, which has limited space. Unless we continually use and apply what we have stored in short-term memory, we will forget it before we can transfer it into our long-term memory bank for use at a much later date. This helps explain why we remember only 50 percent of a message immediately after listening to it and approximately 25 percent after a brief period of time has elapsed. On the other hand, long-term memory, as a more permanent memory-storage facility, plays an important role in listening by connecting new experiences to previous images and information. We tend to remember personal and public events of significance. For example, you probably remember the birthdays of persons close to you, as well as where you were when you learned of the terrorist attacks of 9/11 or the destruction of the space shuttle.

Some of us remember more of what we hear first (a primacy effect), while others of us are better at recalling what we heard last (a recency effect). There is no middle effect because that's the part of a message we tend to recall least.

Stage Four—Interpreting

During the interpreting stage, we attempt to make sense of the listening event. In order to interpret a message effectively we need to engage in dual perspective taking (a critical ingredient in interpersonal communication), which involves considering the message received from the sender's perspective. When we accomplish this, we refrain from imposing our meanings onto another person's message, making the effort to learn how the other person views the situation instead.

Stage Five—Evaluating

During stage five, evaluating, we weigh the worth of and critically analyze what has been communicated; we appraise what we have heard and understood. We decide whether the message has relevance for us or is valid based on what we know or feel. As with all the stages, we face tough choices. Separating facts from inferences, weighing evidence, and identifying prejudices and faulty arguments are part of the evaluation process. If we fail to evaluate a message effectively, we risk agreeing with ideas or supporting actions that violate our values or have been slanted to garner our support.

Stage Six—Responding

Stage six, responding, finds us reacting and providing feedback. We communicate our thoughts and feelings about the message we have received. We let the other person know whether we thought the message was successfully communicated or flawed and whether it was "on target" or "missed its mark." During this stage we act as the other person's radar.[5] We will cover responding in greater depth when we cover feedback.

Types of Listening

Listening theorists identify four different types of listening.

Type One: Appreciative Listening

How recently have you listened to music, seen a movie, or spent an evening at the local comedy club? What was your main reason for doing so? Probably because you wanted to have a good time; you wanted to be entertained. Often we listen simply because doing so enables us to unwind or escape. When we listen to music, a comedy routine, or a television show, we take part in **appreciative listening** to enjoy ourselves. We are listening because it gives us pleasure.

Appreciative, informational, deliberative, and empathic are four types of listening. Which of these listening types do you believe the listeners pictured here are engaged in?

Type Two: Comprehensive or Informational Listening

When you listen to gain knowledge you engage in **comprehensive listening.** Thus, when you listen to directions; a friend's description of his or her job; someone's position on religion, abortion, or another topic; or simply in class, you are listening to derive information, and your purpose is primarily a comprehensive or informational one. This requires that you listen with an open mind, that you suspend judgment and delay evaluating what you hear. If you succeed in doing this, you will better understand the messages sent to you.

Type Three: Critical or Deliberative Listening

How much of each day do you devote to each type of listening?

Have you ever doubted the truth of a message, the message's usefulness, or the reliability of the individual who provided it to you? Frequently, in addition to working to understand the content of a message, we must also analyze it; assess its worth, validity, soundness; and, ultimately, decide whether to accept or reject it. We perform these functions when we engage in **critical listening.**

Type Four: Empathic/Therapeutic Listening

In the chapter on perception, we introduced the topic of empathy. Because empathy is a skill needed for effective listening, we'll explore it in greater depth in this chapter.

When another person depends on us to understand her or his feelings and point of view, we need to engage in empathic listening. For example, when was the last time you called a friend because you needed a sounding board, someone to whom you could tell your troubles? When was the last time you helped someone else work a problem through by offering an ear? Empathic listening serves a therapeutic function. It facilitates problem solving, fosters the development of a clearer perspective of the situation, and aids individuals in restoring emotional balance. When you listen empathically, you understand the dilemma another is facing from his or her viewpoint rather than your own. You do your best to interpret the dilemma as if you were the other person.

According to psychologist Daniel Goleman, persons who score high in emotional intelligence are generally better at listening, being empathic, and de-centering, in order to place the focus on others so that one can understand them as they desire to be understood. Empathic listening functions as a relationship enhancer.[6]

While for some people empathizing comes naturally, others need to work at it. In general, women are more likely to describe themselves as being empathic (able to feel what another feels) than are men. Women are more likely to cry with another person or report feeling distressed when another person shares their distress with them. This may explain why when someone wants empathy, another person to whom they can tell what's bothering them or exciting them, that person, whether male or female, is likely to turn to a woman.[7]

The word empathy *has both Greek and German roots. It comes from the Greek word for "passion" and is also related to the German word* Einfuhling, *meaning "to feel with."*

Good listening is an other-oriented behavior. Sometimes in order to listen well all we need to do is to show that we respect and have compassion for a person. When you listen empathically, your goal is to seek to understand the speaker's thoughts and feelings, so you need to put aside your own thoughts and feelings and listen from the speaker's point of view. Three different skills are necessary to be able to empathize: empathic responsiveness, perspective taking, and sympathetic responsiveness.[8]

When we exhibit **empathic responsiveness** we experience an emotional response that corresponds to the emotions the speaker is experiencing. For example, when Samira tells Latifah that she has to leave school because her family needs her at home, if Latifah feels the emotion that Samira is feeling, she will have done so by using her powers of empathic responsiveness.

When we employ **perspective taking,** we place ourselves in the speaker's shoes. If Latifah had been able to imagine herself in Samira's position and experienced some of the same emotions, she would have fulfilled the expectations of perspective taking.

Finally, if Latifah had felt concern and compassion for Samira because of the situation Samira faced, then Latifah would also have succeeded in demonstrating sympathy, or **sympathetic responsiveness.** Sympathetic responsiveness is different from and falls short of empathy because, while the receiver *feels for* the speaker, without perspective taking and empathic responsiveness she does not *feel with* the speaker.

What can we do to increase our empathic abilities? For those of us who are individualistically or "I"-oriented, empathizing doesn't typically come easy. We may be so used to being the center of attention that we may find it challenging to look at the world from anyone's point of view but our own. Yet, if we want to improve our effectiveness at developing meaningful interpersonal relationships, empathizing is a skill we need to practice. There are six steps we can take to improve our empathy quotient.

Step One

We need to make a concerted effort to become other-oriented and pay careful attention to what others are saying and feeling. If, for example, your significant other comes home depressed after being demoted at work, try to imagine how you would feel if you were in your partner's situation, or how you did feel when face to face with a similar situation, or how your partner felt when previously faced with a situation like this.

Step Two

We need to take in the whole scene. We need to focus not just on words but on the nonverbal cues that are part of another person's message. We need to tune in to how the person walks, sits, looks, and sounds.

Step Three

We need to work to understand the other person's emotions by questioning the other person and then paraphrasing how we think the other person feels. We ask one or more questions in an effort to obtain more details, clarify the nature of their situation, or get at the root cause of what they are feeling. When we paraphrase, we might say something like, "You are probably feeling . . . ," "I guess you are feeling . . . ," or "So now you're likely feeling . . . ." Questioning and paraphrasing let us check our perceptions and ensure that we accurately comprehend how the person is feeling.

Step Four

While processing the other person's information, we need to repeatedly ask ourselves why we believe that is what the other person is experiencing and make a continual effort to identify what it is that makes us think and feel that is so. Is it what the person says, the person's facial expressions, or something else? By focusing on the person's emotions and the cues we use to draw conclusions, we also increase our attentiveness and become better at sensing another person's emotional state.

Step Five

Again, we need to use the skill of perception checking, which we discussed above and in the preceding chapter, to facilitate the answering of this last question.

Step Six

Once we fully understand the other persons' feelings, we may still need to provide them with emotional comfort and support (we help them feel better and/or show that we care about what happens to them). When we comfort and support others we provide affirmation, acknowledging their right to feel as they do. We also offer them reassurance, consolation, and assistance and, if appropriate, try to cheer them up or divert their attention. This may be done with verbal as well as nonverbal cues.

When we fail at empathizing with others, usually we do so for one of the following reasons: (1) We deny others the right to their feelings, suggesting that what they are feeling is either wrong or inappropriate. "It's nothing," we say. "Don't worry about it." Or we might say something like, "You shouldn't be so upset," or "You're foolish to let that get you down." By uttering such statements we unwittingly indicate that the person should feel differently, in effect, "delegitimizing" the person's emotions. (2) We minimize the importance of the situation to the other person by saying, "It's no big deal," or "Why are you making a mountain out of a molehill?" Statements like these reveal we really don't understand what the other person is experiencing. (3) We pass judgment on another person by saying something foolish such as, "Well, you asked for it," or "It's your own fault." Statements like these do little other than make the other person defensive. (4) We feel the urge to defend ourselves and say something self-centered like "I didn't do it," or "Don't blame me." Defending ourselves does nothing to help or support the other person. (5) We place the focus on tomorrow rather than on today. Scarlett O'Hara did it to herself in *Gone With the Wind*, when she said, "Tomorrow is another day." Empathizing occurs in the present, not in the future. While the person who needs your empathy may not remember how bad they will feel a decade or a day from now, that's not what they want to hear you tell them now.

The closer we feel to another person, and the more familiar we are with the particular situation she or he faces, the easier it should be for us to demonstrate empathic responsiveness. In order to exhibit genuine empathic responsiveness toward those persons we know only briefly, we will probably need to work harder.

Each of these types of listening is of value when we communicate interpersonally. Listening for pleasure can relax us as well as entertain us and help us experience new insights into a range of relationships. Listening to empathize helps us understand what we need to do to help someone see things through our eyes and what we need to do to enable another person to appreciate our

in Context

How's Your LQ (Listening Quotient)?

The following quiz can help you determine your effectiveness as a listener. First answer questions 1–4 yourself; then ask two people with whom you interact regularly to help you fill in questions 5–8. You can then answer question 9.

1. On a scale of 0 to 100, I give myself a rating of _____ as a listener.

   0   25   50   75   100

2. I would use the following three words to describe myself as a listener:

   _____   _____   _____

3. Others would give me a rating of _____ as a listener.

   0   25   50   75   100

4. Others would use the following three words to describe me as a listener:

   _____   _____   _____

5. One person I asked gave me a rating of _____ as a listener.

   0   25   50   75   100

6. He or she used the following three words to describe me as a listener:

   _____   _____   _____

7. Another person I asked gave me a rating of _____ as a listener.

   0   25   50   75   100

8. He or she used the following three words to describe me as a listener:

   _____   _____   _____

9. How did your rating of yourself compare to the ratings others gave to you?

   _____

perspective. By listening to derive information, we can sensitize ourselves to the ways we should provide information to another if we want to simplify the comprehension process for him or her. And by listening to evaluate information, we realize that just as we evaluate the behavior of another, so will that person evaluate our behavior.

Active and Inactive Listening

Active listening has a lot in common with perception checking since it involves feeding back to the speaker your understanding of what the speaker communicated, both in content and in feeling. Active listening holds the key to engaging one another in mutually understood messages, both on a cognitive and emotional level. By providing the speaker with feedback, we help the speaker clarify his thoughts and emotions.[9] To listen actively, we pay attention to both the speaker's verbal and nonverbal cues. When we listen actively, we respond both verbally and nonverbally to the speaker. We identify what the speaker said and what we think the speaker meant. Doing this gives us the chance to ensure our understanding and the speaker the chance to clarify any misunderstandings or misperceptions of the message we may have. But active listening also goes further. When we listen actively we also let the speaker know that we understand her or his feelings and ask questions that provide her or him an opportunity to talk further.

Consider the following responses that three friends give to Kahlil in response to his stating: "I'm done for! Dr. Rodriguez wants me to redo this entire paper. I put a lot of time into researching it, but somehow it's not up to his standards. He's giving me two days to improve it or I'll get a C. Where am I going to find the time to do this now? Does he have any idea how strapped I am for time?" Which of the responses do you think demonstrates active listening?

DAVILLA: Lucky you. At least you got two days. I just got the C.

DAWN: Two days isn't so horrible. You can do it. All you need to do is focus.

DORETTE: You need to improve the paper you worked so hard on? So you feel really stressed. Is that it?

Davilla focuses on herself. Dawn attempts to lessen the problem facing Kahlil. Only Dorette attempts to promote a meaningful exchange with Kahlil. Darette also reflects Kahlil's feelings, recognizing the legitimacy of what Kahlil feels, while the other two listeners did not.

What exactly did Dorette accomplish with her simple response? First she paraphrased Kahlil's original message. She identified what she thought he meant. Second, she showed interest in how he was feeling by expressing her understanding of what he must be experiencing. Her response does something else, however. Because she made the attempt to cross-check her interpretation, her response also affords Kahlil the chance to let her know if she has gotten it right.

The Differences between Effective and Ineffective Listeners

Think of the worst listeners you know. What behaviors do they exhibit that suggest to you that they are not listening? Picture each of them interacting with you. What words would you use to describe their behaviors? Typically, words like *inattentive, close-minded, daydreamer, bored, impatient, nonresponsive,* and *rude* come to mind. Now think of the best listeners you know, and select adjectives to describe their behavior. Probably among the words you've chosen to describe the best listeners are *concerned, open-minded, intelligent, attentive, interested,* and *respectful.* Then compare and contrast the words you have selected to describe the best and the worst listeners. Which words would others use to describe your listening behavior?

How have effective and ineffective listening behaviors affected your relationships?

You need to reflect on whether you are the best listener you could be. We know that we stand to lose by listening ineffectively and to gain by listening effectively. But what exactly is it that we stand to lose or gain? To find out, first ask and answer the following questions on your own, and then ask them of two other people.

The Losses:

1. What consequences have you suffered when you showed a lack of respect for someone with whom you were conversing?

2. What problems have you encountered when you lost your temper when interacting with another?

3. What challenges have you faced when you failed to understand what another person was telling you?

4. How has jumping to an incorrect conclusion caused problems for you?

5. What occurred on an occasion in which you missed a key conversational segment because you were distracted?

6. How did the person you were interacting with respond when he or she became aware that you weren't really listening?

The Gains:

1. What benefits have you derived from showing real interest in what another person shared with you?

2. What benefits have you derived from maintaining control of your emotions when someone was telling you something you really did not want to hear?

3. What benefits have you derived from correctly understanding instructions?

4. What benefits have you derived from concentrating fully on what someone was sharing with you instead of giving in to distractions?

5. How has patience aided you when interacting with another?

6. How has listening effectively to another helped facilitate the development of your relationship with that person?

Listening increases relationship satisfaction. When individuals fail to listen to each other, relationships usually experience problems. On the other hand, effective listening can help cement a relationship by:

Decreasing stress. The stress levels of individuals are reduced as ideas and feelings are communicated clearly and understood as intended.

Enhancing knowledge. People learn more about each other. Each learns more about what the other responds to and how the other reacts to his or her ideas.

Building trust. We all need someone to listen to us. We appreciate those who listen much more than those who fail to give us their complete attention. In fact, we don't like to be around those who don't listen to us for very long. In turn, we tend to listen more to those who listen to us.

Improving decision making. Listening effectively to another person provides you with the kind of input you need to determine whether this is someone with whom you want to continue a relationship. Listening to another person can also provide you with information and insights you can use to develop better judgment.

Improving the person with whom you are interacting and raising his or her level of self-esteem. When another individual perceives that he or she has your rapt attention and that you are open, alert, and actively involved, he or she will be more comfortable interacting with you and more able to share his or her thoughts and feelings effectively.

The greatest compliment that was ever paid me was when one asked me what I thought, and attended to my answer.

— Henry David Thoreau

literary contacts

"The Dangling Conversation"

Putting ourselves into the shoes of characters in poems, songs, stories, plays, or films can enable us to experience vicariously situations that we may or may not have experienced in our own lives. Can you imagine what the characters in this Paul Simon classic song are feeling? How would you describe each character's emotional state? What kind of relationship do they share? Based on your understanding of the song, what behaviors does each character need to exhibit to improve their relationship? Why do you think it takes more than two good ears to listen empathically?

It's a still life watercolor,
Of a now late afternoon,
As the sun shines through the curtained lace
And shadows wash the room,
And we sit and drink our coffee
Couched in our indifference,
Like shells upon the shore
You can hear the ocean roar
In The Dangling Conversation
And the superficial sighs,
The borders of our lives.

And you read your Emily Dickinson
And I my Robert Frost,
And we note our places with bookmarkers

That measure what we've lost.
Like a poem poorly written
We are verses out of rhythm,
Couplets out of rhyme,
In syncopated time
And The Dangling Conversation
And the superficial sighs,
Are the borders of our lives.

Yes, we speak of things that matter,
With words that must be said,
"Can analysis be worthwhile?
Is the theatre really dead?"
And now the room is softly faded
I only kiss your shadow
I cannot feel your hand,
You're a stranger now unto me
Lost in The Dangling Conversation
And the superficial sighs
In the borders of our lives.

1. How often and for what reasons have you been left dangling or have you left someone else dangling during a conversation?
2. What do such conversations tell you about the relationship you share?

SOURCE: "The Dangling Conversation." Copyright © 1966 Paul Simon. Used by permission of the Publisher: Paul Simon Music.

Improving yourself. When you listen effectively you increase your confidence and understanding. Because you are better able to comprehend the ideas and feelings of another, you gain confidence in your ability to respond appropriately to him or her.

Protecting yourself. When you listen critically to the messages sent to you by another, you don't just accept what is presented to you at face value. Rather, you can spot faulty reasoning and identify invalid arguments or gross appeals to prejudice. As a result, you protect yourself against those who interact irresponsibly. It is the uncritical listener who often has to face the consequences created by the unscrupulous talker. If you are ill-prepared to analyze and evaluate the motives and messages of someone with whom you interact, you are much more likely to accept the unacceptable.

The Ethics of Listening: A Look at Nonlistening Behaviors

If we are to become more effective listeners, we need to recognize those internal and external factors that contribute to deficient listening behavior (**nonlistening**) and do our part to eliminate them. How exactly do we behave when acting like nonlisteners? What causes us not always to listen as effectively as we could (see Table 4.1)?

"Are you telling me something?"
"Are you listening?"
"Of course not."

— *Edward Albee*

Nonlisteners Tune Out

Nonlisteners have the ability to tune out what another is sharing with them simply by not paying attention to the other person. When someone is trying to start a conversation, share ideas, or influence them, nonlisteners act as though their ears and minds are "out to lunch" or "on vacation." Nothing the other person says or does penetrates. Nonlisteners are preoccupied—they are too busy thinking about their own problems or something else. Consequently, they fail to focus fully or actively on the messages sent by another.

This kind of behavior is quite common. At one time or another, we have all committed a nonlistening act by preferring to pursue our private thoughts, reminisce, worry about something personal, or silently plan for an event rather than concentrate on the other person. In fact, as far as nonlisteners are concerned, their own thoughts are more worthy of their attention than are the thoughts of

TABLE 4.1
Behaviors of Poor Listeners

Tuning Out	Listener's loss of focus and preoccupations make understanding less likely
Faking Attention	Listener's pseudo-listening looks and behavior deceive the speaker
Losing Contact Opportunities	Listener's misjudging potential for both message relevance and relationship
Losing Control	Listener's emotions and lack of patience lead to ambushes, message distortions, and defensiveness
Laziness	Listener's lack of effort and refusal to work at listening make comprehension unlikely
Selfishness	Listener's focus is on the self rather than on the other person
Being Distracted by External Factors	Listener's oversensitivity to setting or context interferes with listening
Wasting Time	Listener's failing to use the thought–speech differential to advantage
Apprehensiveness	Listener's fear of the new leads to defensiveness
Burnout	Listener's inability to cope with information overload closes down the mind

the person with whom they are interacting. They let their own thoughts compete with the thoughts of another for their attention. Unfortunately, their own thoughts generally win.

Nonlisteners Fake Attention

Nonlisteners have mastered the art of pseudo-listening: they know how to fake attention. They pretend they are listening to the individual with whom they are interacting, when nothing could be further from the truth. How do they feign attention? They look at the person, smile or frown appropriately, nod their heads, and even utter remarks such as "hmmm," or "uh huh." All their external cues tell the speaker that they are listening. But nonlisteners are only pretending to listen. In fact, they let no meaning through.

What causes you to stop listening?

Think of the last time you pretended to listen when communicating interpersonally. Perhaps you were bored with the conversation or otherwise preoccupied. What did you miss? How do you know—you weren't listening!

Nonlisteners Lose Opportunities for Meaningful Contact

Before even giving their cocommunicator a chance, nonlisteners decide that the other person looks uninteresting or sounds dull, or that there is no future for a relationship with him or her. By prejudging, the nonlistener usually misses opportunities for relationship development. Prejudgment, whether positive or negative, seriously impedes interpersonal communication. It causes us to uncritically accept or unfairly reject others and their ideas.

Nonlisteners Are Overly Emotional

Sometimes nonlisteners let disagreements with the person with whom they are conversing get in the way of effective listening. Nonlisteners go out of their way to avoid listening to anyone with whom they do not agree, ideas that they believe have little relevance to them, or information they feel will be too complex to comprehend. Instead of listening to what another person expresses as he or she actually expresses it, nonlisteners hear it as they *want* the speaker to express it. When was the last time you distorted another's comments because you didn't like the other person or what he or she was saying? Nonlisteners manufacture rather than process information. Personally threatened by another's ideas, they don't really listen to what is said, preferring to work instead on defending themselves.

We listen selectively. Whenever possible, we expose ourselves to opinions that agree with our own. We interpret these opinions however we want, often making them fit our preconceptions. We better remember the ideas that support our personal point of view, forgetting those that do not. Figuratively speaking, we wear earmuffs to shield ourselves from comments we would rather not hear at all.

Nonlisteners also allow particular words uttered by another to interfere with their ability to listen. These words, referred to by listening researcher pioneer

When we feel threatened by another person, we often concentrate on defending ourselves instead of listening to the other person.

Ralph Nichols as **red-flag words,** trigger an emotional deafness among nonlisteners, causing listening efficiency to drop to zero as they go off on an emotional side trip. Among the words and phrases contributing to the emotional deafness of nonlisteners are *AIDS, welfare, Nazi, you should, you're so slow,* and *what's wrong with you?* Are you aware of any specific words or phrases that cause you to erupt emotionally, thereby disrupting your ability to continue meaningful interaction with another?

What words or other stimuli cause you to become a nonlistener?

Nonlisteners Seek the Easy Way Out

Listening is voluntary and, unfortunately, nonlisteners don't usually volunteer to listen to people whose ideas or manner of expression challenge them. Believing they won't understand the other person anyway, they fail to even give themselves a chance to exercise their minds.

When was the last time you dismissed another person or his or her ideas as uninteresting or unimportant because you told yourself, "I won't understand them anyway"? Do you turn off possible relationships because you assume that you would have to work too hard to make them succeed? To what extent are you willing to stretch your mind to accommodate the challenge of new ideas instead of merely focusing on those people or ideas that validate your preconceived notions?

Nonlisteners Are Egocentric

When was the last time you tuned out and turned off someone you were conversing with because you felt his or her ideas were irrelevant to your life? Nonlisteners do this regularly. They are egocentric, viewing themselves as the center of the universe. Seeking only self-satisfaction, nonlisteners are so wrapped up in themselves that they fail either to realize or value their interconnectedness with others. Of course they expect everyone to listen to them. Because they are intrigued with their own thoughts and ideas, nonlisteners want you to "give them your ears and mind," while not providing you with theirs. Thus, they deny your desire to be listened to but attempt to monopolize your attention by focusing it on them. They remain self-focused rather than other-directed or other-oriented.

in Theory

Tuning Out

Look at the Peanuts cartoon.

1. Have you ever been so "tuned into yourself" that you failed to pay attention to the personal appeals made to you by another?

2. Is it appropriate to be so self-absorbed? To what extent, if any, is such nonlistening behavior justifiable? Explain.

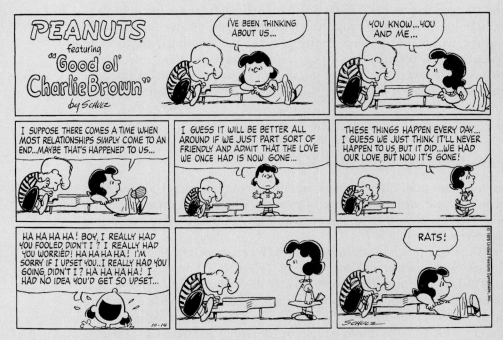

Peanuts reprinted by permission of United Feature Syndicate, Inc.

Nonlisteners Are Overly Sensitive to Setting or Context

Think of the story of Goldilocks and the three bears. Momma and Pappa Bear's things were either too cold, too hot, too big, too small, too high, or too low for Goldilocks. Nonlisteners let themselves be distracted by physical factors such as the temperature, the room, or the general setting of their interaction. Instead of working to overcome any such difficulties, they give in to them and use them as nonlistening excuses. Once they succumb to external distractions, nonlisteners are unlikely to listen.

Nonlisteners Are Time Wasters

We think a lot more quickly than we speak. When we converse, we typically speak at a rate of 150 to 200 words per minute. However, we can comprehend upward of 400 to 600 words per minute. The difference between the two is referred to as the **speech–thought differential.** Nonlisteners waste this extra time by daydreaming instead of focusing on, summarizing, and asking themselves questions about the substance and meaning of the remarks made by the person with whom they are interacting. They would rather drift off than use the energy it takes to closely attend to what someone else is saying.

Nonlisteners Are Overly Apprehensive

Apprehensive listeners are fearful of processing or psychologically adjusting themselves to the messages sent to them by others.[10] They are so fearful of new situations, new people, or new information that they become overly anxious when faced with such stimuli; their anxiety causes them to become overly defensive, which, in turn, inhibits their ability to listen effectively.

Nonlisteners Exhibit Symptoms of Listening Burnout

At times, listeners turn into nonlisteners because they are burned out. When exposed to too much new information at one time, our minds, unable to cope with the information overload, simply close. For instance, individuals who must listen daily to clients' disclosures, as therapists or psychiatrists, may also experience listening burnout and seek to spend their free time not listening so attentively.

Certainly we cannot listen at full capacity all the time. What we need to do, however, is to become aware of how often and why we fail to listen and determine what we can do to become better listeners.

A System for Hurdling Listening Roadblocks

Listening is hard work. When you listen actively, your body temperature rises, your palms become moist, and your adrenaline flow increases. Your body actually *prepares* itself to listen. You are the catalyst in this operation—you set the listening process in motion. Making a conscious effort to listen has its benefits;

refusing to listen has its costs. By remembering the following principles, you will find it easier to avoid exhibiting poor listening habits and make your listening more effective.

Principle One. Listening is a conscious process. It requires your full attention. You can't half-listen—the half you miss could be critical.

Why is listening hard work?

Principle Two. Evaluation should follow, not precede, reception. Effective listening takes time and patience. Effective listeners withhold their evaluation until they are certain they have understood the entire message. Anger and hostility, like rapture and hero workship, can impede understanding. A heightened emotional response—whether positive or negative—can decrease your ability to comprehend what another person is saying to you. Never allow what a person says or how he or she says it to close your mind.

ℹ️ *Practice*

Listening Roadblocks and Payoffs

Identify five listening roadblocks—problems that you have encountered that contributed to ineffective listening on your part.

1. _____
2. _____
3. _____
4. _____
5. _____

Identify five listening payoffs—benefits that you have personally realized as a result of effective listening.

1. _____
2. _____
3. _____
4. _____
5. _____

Now, analyze your listening behavior by responding to the following questions:

	Yes	No
1. Do you ever find yourself labeling either the person you are interacting with or his or her subject uninteresting?	☐	☐
2. Do you ever find yourself getting overstimulated by what someone says to you?	☐	☐
3. Do you ever jump ahead of the person speaking to you?	☐	☐
4. Do you ever fake paying attention?	☐	☐
5. Do you ever try to avoid listening to complicated information?	☐	☐
6. Do you ever daydream when you should be listening to someone?	☐	☐
7. Do you ever try to process every word another person says?	☐	☐
8. Do you ever let someone's manner of delivery or mannerisms interfere with your reception of his or her remarks?	☐	☐
9. Do you ever let the environment or personal factors distract you from paying attention?	☐	☐
10. Are there some people or subjects you refuse to listen to?	☐	☐

Every "yes" is a listening behavior that can serve as a listening roadblock; each merits additional work on your part.

Principle Three. Neither the appearance nor the delivery of another person provides you with a legitimate reason not to listen. Focus instead on the person as a potential source of information. Every contact presents you with an opportunity to learn something new. Use—don't abuse—that opportunity. At times, you might need to overlook a person's monotone or lack of eye contact. Instead of being distracted by someone's rough or unpolished demeanor, try to concentrate on the message. Realize that ineffective delivery is not the only detractor you need to be aware of. A smooth, polished manner of speaking can be equally harmful if you let it blind you to an absence of substance. Again, focus on the message, not just the messenger.

Principle Four. Negative and positive prejudices close ears. Negative or positive prejudices toward either a person or a topic can cause you unconsciously or consciously to judge them too quickly. You will be either too busy arguing against them or too quickly impressed by what they say to listen accurately to the message being sent.

Principle Five. The way we listen affects how others feel about interacting with us. The better we become at reflecting the feelings of those with whom we interact, and the more adept we are at exhibiting empathic and supportive behaviors, the more they will want to interact with us.

Principle Six. Good listeners hear major points. Effective listeners focus their listening efforts; rather than working to absorb every isolated fact, they concentrate on identifying key ideas and the reasons given to justify or support them.

Principle Seven. If you seek opportunities to practice skillful listening, you will become a more skillful listener. The listener is like an athlete: daily practice improves performance.

The Feedback Factor

Feedback and listening are related processes. Developing your abilities to send and receive feedback can also improve your listening skills.

The Speaker as Listening Facilitator or Roadblock

Speakers need to think of listening as a collaborative process that requires the participation of both speaker and listener if it is to be effective. Speakers have the power to facilitate or complicate the listener's role. Remember, it is a mistake to conceive of people as functioning solely as speakers or receivers. In most of our interpersonal encounters, we do both. Thus, speakers need to speak so that listeners can listen, and listeners need to keep in mind that they are not just waiting to speak but need to be actively involved in listening to speakers. In effect, listening is a dialogic process in which speakers do not deliver monologues, but should be intimately involved in helping their listeners participate in and coordinate what is a joint activity.[11] Both listening and speaking include verbal and nonverbal cues.

Speakers who work to facilitate the tasks of listeners are insightful—they try to tap into the interests, needs, and concerns of listeners. They take the time to analyze with whom they are interacting by standing in the shoes of listeners. Similarly, listeners are expected to stand in the shoes of speakers, contemplating the perceptions that speakers have of them. Effective speakers are culturally sensitive to the many ways that situations and culture can influence both the encoding and decoding process. They also are true to their values and tolerant of disagreements.

Feedback Defined

When we listen actively or responsively to other people, we provide them with feedback. The term **feedback** implies that we are returning or feeding back to others our reactions to the verbal and nonverbal messages we received from them. Whenever you consciously or unconsciously emit a verbal or nonverbal message that another perceives to be a response to something he or she said or did, that message serves as feedback. As an interpersonal communicator, you continually provide others with feedback—and you're probably not totally honest when you provide it, either. At times, when you are unhappy in a relationship or bored by

 in Theory

The Relationship between Communication Style and Feedback

Members of different cultures view feedback differently. In the United States and western Europe, for example, we expect the feedback given to us to be honest and to reflect the feelings of the person with whom we are interacting. In Asian cultures, however, communicators expect the feedback given to be more positive than honest. They value politeness and the maintenance of a positive image. Thus, when compared with people from Asian cultures who prefer and practice an indirect style of communication, people from the U.S. and western Europe tend to give feedback that is significantly more direct and truthful. Why is this? In part, because persons from Asian cultures believe that bluntness could damage or injure the self-esteem of the person to whom the feedback is directed. In order to help the person with whom they are communicating save face and not feel threatened by what they are about to hear, persons from Asian cultures are likely to provide

feedback that is vague and indirect. For example, when an employee delivers a report to an Asian manager, the manager's immediate feedback will probably be somewhat positive and complementary, even if the manager knows that there are problems with the report. In an effort to promote face saving, persons of Asian heritage will sometimes tell another person one thing when they really mean something else. If you understand this, you have a better chance of understanding what the other person is actually telling you.

In addition, in Asian cultures, silence rather than talk may inspire feedback. Asian culture instills in its members a respect for silence. Thus, rather than breaking the silence with talk, persons from other cultures need to learn to use the quiet in a way that is conducive to feedback once the silence ends.

1. How would you adapt the offering of feedback when interacting with persons from cultures other than your own?

2. To what extent, if any, has the way you typically offer feedback posed problems for you? Explain.

a conversation, you may nevertheless don an "I care for you" face or an "I'm interested" expression and nod adoringly or approvingly. Unfortunately, individuals who are given dishonest feedback may well be misled by it. Consequently, our goal when we provide feedback should be to reveal to others how their behavior affects us. The nature of the feedback you give to another affects his or her interpretation of your relationship.

Offering and Receiving Feedback: Exploring the Options

Feedback is a continuous process. We constantly send feedback, whether or not we intend to. Everything we do or fail to do, every word we speak or fail to speak, can be interpreted as feedback by another. Sometimes we send feedback purposefully, hoping to evoke a specific response. For instance, if you laugh heartily at a joke shared with a partner, you may do so because you want him or her to know you genuinely enjoyed it and would like him or her to feel comfortable telling you more. On the other hand, some feedback is sent unintentionally and elicits unexpected reactions. Without our consciously realizing it, our words or behaviors may provoke responses in others that we never intended. When faced with such an occurrence, we spout phrases like, "That's not what I meant!" or "Don't take it that way!" Other times, an individual we're interacting with may simply refuse to acknowledge the feedback we send, choosing to ignore it. How many times have you sent someone a message you hoped would turn him or her off when the opposite happened? Thus, before consciously giving feedback, we need to ask ourselves of the person to whom we are providing feedback: What are their expectations regarding feedback? Why are they interacting with us? Are they ready, willing, and able to process our honest reactions?

As with all kinds of messages, the feedback we intend to send may not be the feedback perceived or received by another. Despite this, it is important for us to be able to distinguish among the feedback options available to us. To provide others with effective feedback, we need to be willing to follow certain guidelines. For example, the type of feedback we offer and the content of the feedback messages we give often depend on the kind of relationship we share with the feedback's recipient. Our friend, for example, probably expects us to provide feedback on his or her appearance; our boss probably does not. Our significant others are apt to give us feedback regarding our relationship strengths; our teachers probably won't. Well-given feedback has positive consequences for our relationships; poorly given feedback does not. Whether the feedback you provide elicits positive or negative reactions from those you give it to depends on three key factors. First, are you offering feedback at the right time? Second, are you clear and specific about the feedback you give? And third, is the feedback appropriate, tactful, and conducive to sustaining the relationship?

Have you ever misinterpreted feedback? What happened?

Feedback Can Be Immediate or Delayed

When we communicate interpersonally, much of the feedback we send is immediate; our reactions occur virtually simultaneously with our reception of a message. Immediate feedback is generally the most effective because praise or punishment loses its impact if we wait too long to give it. Sometimes, however, we may consciously withhold responding. For example, it is wiser to cool down before offering a response to a message that angers you. Feedback sent in anger can damage a relationship.

Other kinds of communication, such as public speaking or mass communication, often involve delayed feedback. We rarely interrupt speakers during their presentation by shouting out our approval or disapproval for what they have shared or by interrupting them with a question. We typically wait until a presentation has ended before we applaud, withhold applause, or ask questions. Some feedback comes during media programs in the form of audience Internet or phone surveys, Nielsen ratings, and an analysis of viewer watching and purchasing patterns.

Feedback Can Be Person or Message Focused

We can give feedback centered on either the person or the message. Feedback such as, "You're just about the most compassionate person I know," focuses on the person, while a statement such as, "While I understand your position, I believe the reasons you offer are flawed," focuses on the message.

Feedback Can Be Low- or High-Monitoring

Feedback that is sincere and spontaneous is low-monitored feedback. It occurs constantly throughout the interpersonal communication process. As we exchange messages, we allow our responses to be revealed without consciously monitoring or censoring them. Much of the low-monitored feedback we send may be sent unintentionally and without our carefully planning it. In contrast, feedback that we deliver to serve a specific purpose is high-monitored feedback. We are more guarded and think about whether our feedback will serve a desired purpose of ours before we send it. When we send a response, we consciously intend to do so. For example, if your instructor asked you what you think of the course, you will probably monitor the feedback you offer before offering a response.

Feedback Can Be Evaluative

When we provide **evaluative feedback** to someone, we announce our opinions or feelings about the matter being discussed. For example, if someone asks whether you like his haircut, your response will most likely be perceived by him as evaluative. A slight pause before you say, "It looks great" might be interpreted as meaning you don't really like it. When we give evaluative feedback, we provide positive or negative assessments to another; we let him or her know what we think of his or her ideas, abilities, looks, and so on. By its very nature, evaluative feedback is judgmental; it either rewards or punishes another.

Positive Evaluative Feedback. Positive evaluative feedback keeps people and their communicative behaviors moving in the direction in which they are already proceeding. For example, if you are flirting with someone who is receptive to your advances, you will tend to continue behaving in that manner. Positive evaluative feedback serves a reinforcing function; it causes us to continue acting as we already are by enhancing our desire to do so.

Negative Evaluative Feedback. Negative evaluative feedback serves a corrective function—it helps reduce undesirable communicative behaviors. When we perceive feedback as negative, we are apt to change or modify our behavior accordingly. For example, if you told an off-color joke that someone else found offensive, you probably would not tell another. Negative evaluative feedback alerts us to discontinue behavior in progress.

Feedback Can Be Nonevaluative

Unlike evaluative feedback, which tends to be judgmental, **nonevaluative feedback** does not function to direct the actions of another. Instead, we use it when we want to find out more about another person's feelings or when we seek to help another person work through his or her feelings. When we provide nonevaluative feedback, we refrain from revealing our own personal opinions or judgments. We simply question, describe what we observe, or demonstrate our interest in listening to that person.

Nondirective in style, nonevaluative feedback often is perceived as positive in tone. That is because others' behaviors are apt to be reinforced when we probe or support them as they work through a problem. In reality, however, nonevaluative feedback goes beyond positive feedback, because it does more than simply reinforce behavior; it also enables others, without direction from us, to explore their own thoughts and feelings and arrive at their own solutions. Let's look at four kinds of nonevaluative feedback: probing, understanding, supporting, and the use of "I" messages.

Probing. Probing is a nonevaluative technique in which we solicit additional information from another person in an effort to draw him or her out as well as to demonstrate our willingness to listen. For example, suppose a friend who is concerned about a job-related conflict tells you, "I'm really over the edge. My boss keeps pushing me and pushing me. I'm going to snap." If you are probing, you might inquire, "What, specifically, is your boss doing?" or "What is it about your boss's behavior that particularly concerns you?" or "Why do you believe this is happening?" By responding in this way you give the other person the opportunity to think through the problem while also offering him or her the chance for emotional release. On the other hand, responses like "Oh, they're all like that"

Effective listening requires your full attention. How often do you achieve that objective?

or "Who cares what the boss does?" or "You're stupid for getting upset" could cause your friend to become defensive and prevent him or her from thinking through and discussing the troublesome situation with you.

Understanding. An alternative kind of nonevaluative reaction is **understanding.** When we offer understanding to another, we try to comprehend what the other person is telling us, and we check our interpretation by paraphrasing (restating in our own words) what we heard. By paraphrasing we show that we care enough about the other person and the problem he or she is facing to be sure we understand what the message means.

The following are examples of paraphrases:

PERSON 1: I don't think I'm good enough to get the job.

PERSON 2: You mean you think you lack the skills to get the promotion?

PERSON 1: I am so hurt that John trusts Sheila more than he trusts me.

PERSON 2: You mean you're jealous of the attention John is paying Sheila?

If we use understanding early in our relationship with another person, we communicate to him or her our willingness to listen and his or her importance to us. Understanding responses could encourage a relationship's development in part by demonstrating our sensitivity to and concern for another person, but also by allowing the other person more time to describe and detail his or her feelings and perceptions to us.

Supportive Feedback. A third nonevaluative feedback response is **supportive feedback.** When we respond supportively we indicate that we share another person's perception of a problem as important. For instance, suppose your friend comes to you with a problem she believes is extremely serious. Perhaps your friend's concern for the situation has caused her to become agitated, and she says that you couldn't possibly understand the predicament she is in. If you wanted to offer supportive feedback you would do your best to calm down your friend by assuring her that you understand the problem, that her world is not ending, and that you are there to help her work through it.

When we offer supportive feedback we accomplish a number of things: First, we do what we can to reduce the intensity of another person's feelings; second, we let him or her know we consider the problem real. Instead of uttering comments like, "Why are you worrying about that?" or "It's ridiculous to care about that," we say things like, "I can tell you're upset. Let's sit down and discuss it. I'm sure you can find a way to work it out." A friend who is distraught because he or she has just been fired or has just broken up with a lover doesn't need to be told, "Next time you'll handle things differently," "There's no reason to be so upset," or "I warned you about this." It's much more productive to say instead, "I can tell you're upset. I don't blame you for feeling the way you do." When we provide supportive feedback, we acknowledge the importance of another person's problem, but we don't attempt to solve it; we simply listen, show that person we care, and in so doing, help him or her to discover a solution.

"I" Messages. Finally, a fourth nonevaluative feedback response is **"I" messages.** By delivering "I" messages, we refrain from passing judgment on the

in *Context*

It's in the "I"s

When phrased appropriately, "I" messages contain three parts: (1) a description of the other person's behavior, (2) a description of how you feel about the behavior, and (3) an explanation of how the behavior of the other affects you—its consequences. "You" messages begin with the word *you* and often express blame.

1. Divide into groups of four to five people. Group members take turns responding to the following situation, first using a you message and then using an "I" message. Be sure to include all three parts of the "I" message in your response.

    You and a colleague have been assigned the joint task of completing a complex project. You find your partner difficult to work with because he or she will not spend the time you think necessary to complete the task.

2. What different effects do you think the two types of messages would have on your working relationship?

other person's actions; however, we do reveal our own feelings about the nature of the situation.

Every time we interact with someone, we have a choice of providing them with evaluative or nonevaluative feedback. Neither type is always right or wrong. Sometimes, however, the choice we make adversely affects the tenor of a relationship. Do any of these remarks sound familiar? "You're a pain in the neck!" "You infuriate me." "You're a filthy pig." "You're no damn good." "You're such a waste." What do statements like these have in common? They all contain the word *you*. When we utter such statements, we place blame for something on someone else. When we experience relationship problems, at times we resort to name-calling and blame-placing as a means of coping with the situation. Feedback like that, however, tends to build bigger barriers between us, which then become increasingly difficult to raze.

To avoid building such barriers, try replacing "you" messages with "I" messages. For example, if a friend says, "You're really getting on my nerves," a "you" message, your interpretation may well be, "I'm not liked," which will then precipitate some defensiveness toward your friend ("I'm not doing anything to get on your nerves"). On the other hand, if your friend had used an "I" message, such as "Your asking about our plans for tonight as soon as I walk in the door makes me feel stressed. I need to have time to unwind before talking about that," your reaction is more apt to be, "She's had a really tough day." The alternative response is much less likely to evoke a defensive or self-serving reaction in you.

Each of the types of feedback we discussed has its place in our person-to-person contacts. Whether you opt to respond evaluatively or nonevaluatively depends on the person with whom you are interacting, the nature of the situation, and the kind of relationship you share.

Diversity and Culture Contacts

Diversity's Influence on Listening

How do you feel about silence?

Listening plays a vital role in the development of social relationships. **Dialogic listening** focuses on what happens between people as they respond to each other, work toward shared understanding, and create a relationship.[12] The pressures of life in the United States today seem to push people away from adopting an open-ended, tentative, and playful attitude toward conversation; instead, all too often, people find themselves pushed in the opposite direction as they opt for certainty, closure, and control. Individuals from Western cultures tend to prefer "hard" focused and concrete thinking, whereas those from Eastern cultures prefer "soft" speculative, metaphoric thinking. Thus, members of the Western world tend to be less open and tentative in their listening behaviors than do members of the Eastern world.

Attitudes toward silence also play a role. Cross-cultural differences regarding when to talk and when to remain silent are common. People from Eastern cultures think silence signals respectability and trust, that words can corrupt an experience, and that it is through heart-to-heart communication that people can intuitively grasp meaning. Thus, Westerners need to listen to Easterners with more than their ears. They need to remember that from the Eastern perspective, people should listen more than talk.[13] When interacting with Easterners, Westerners need to listen between the lines.

If we are to listen effectively, it is important for us to understand what the members of another culture think about the nature of talk. Whereas some cultures value succinctness and directness, others value elaboration and exaggeration. For example, members of Arabic cultures commonly use verbal exaggerations and forceful assertions when interacting with others. Rather than being verbally restrained, they release their emotions through language. For example, the Arabic proverb "A man's tongue is his sword," suggests that Arabs use language as a means of offense, to chastise or punish others, and to boast about one's abilities. Arabs typically spend hours expounding on the faults and failures of others. They pepper their speech with overassertions and repeat themselves numerous times, contributing to impressions among non-Arabs that they are aggressive or threatening. If we are unaware of this, we may well misinterpret their intentions.[14]

Thus, as we interact with and listen to members of different cultures, we need to remind ourselves that the meanings they are giving to the words they use vary based on their experiences and backgrounds. Because culture influences our use of language, it also influences the way we listen to and interpret language.

Gender Contacts

Gender's Influence on Listening

To what extent, if any, do the listening behaviors of men and women differ? According to sociolinguist Deborah Tannen, women and men exhibit different listening styles and listen for different reasons. According to Tannen, women listen to confirm the relationship as well as the person with whom they are in contact.[15] While she processes information, a woman's real goal is to zoom in on an emotional level. Thus, women excel at empathizing and at identifying the mood of communication; they are ready, willing, and able to allow other individuals to open themselves and reveal what is important to them.

Why are women considered better at listening to open communication? First, they are perceived as more responsive and supportive. This encourages others to seek women out as listeners. Women also value receiving emotional revelations. It is important to them to be good listeners, to be considered receptive and open.[16]

In contrast, research reveals that men are more at home with comprehensive listening, hearing a message's facts or informational dimension, and less at home with its emotional content.[17] Men prefer to maintain power and control; they try to dominate. Thus, they listen for solutions so they can give advice rather than empathize. They also tend to turn off their listening when they come across a problem they can't solve right away. They prefer talk and explanation over empathic listening. Unlike women, men listen to solve problems, not to relay support.

Do men and women listen differently?

However, empathic listening is essential for a meaningful relationship. Empathy has three relevant aspects: **perspective taking** (the ability to adopt the viewpoint of the other person), **emotional contagion** (the ability to respond in kind or to exhibit a parallel response), and **empathic concern** (the ability to convey an altruistic concern for the other person).[18]

As we noted earlier in this chapter, perspective taking finds you picturing yourself in the shoes of another person. For example, when your friend reveals to you how upset he is after being laid off, you would put yourself in your friend's position and personalize what has happened to your friend by imagining what you would feel like were you to lose your job. Emotional contagion finds you mirroring the verbal and nonverbal cues of your friend so that you are better able to feel, with your body, not just your mind, what your friend is feeling and going through. And finally, when you display empathic concern, you might not feel what your friend is feeling after being fired but sympathize with or communicate your compassion or emotional concern for your friend's plight instead. Most people again perceive women as more empathic than men, in part because of the way they listen and respond on an emotional level.

One way to help men develop empathic listening skills might be to tell them to use more vocal cues when listening, to interject "uh-huh"s and "hmmm"s. Doing so would help the person they are in contact with feel listened to.[19]

As we can see, a number of asymmetries exist in the ways women and men listen. Men tend to spend more time in the speaking role and women in the listening role. If women want to disengage themselves from the role of listener or responder, they probably need to take action rather than wait for men to end their monologues. If women exercise their right to enter the conversation, they may also relieve men from feeling that they have to give a solo conversational performance. Each can expand their behavioral repertoire when it comes to listening.

Not only do men and women listen differently, we also listen to them differently. For example, when men and women speakers use an equal number of tag questions or qualifiers, we still perceive the women to use these speech forms more frequently.[20] Listeners perceive the speech of men as stronger, more active, and more aggressive than the speech of women, which they perceive as more polite, pleasing, and sweet.[21] Even when women talk like men, they are evaluated more negatively and perceived to be aggressive rather than strong. Perhaps if listening were not perceived as a source of power differences between men and women but as a means of relationship building, our ability to process the speech of men and women equitably would improve.

Media and Technology Contacts

Media and Technological Influences on Listening

The mass media and technological innovations are part of our communication landscape. We regularly watch television and film, we use our computers, and we listen to the radio and CDs. With the increasing popularity of cell phones, we are able to exercise our ears and mouths more than in years passed. How we consume what we hear is affected by our interactions with family and friends. Our daily contacts influence the way we experience mediated messages, as well as how receptive we are to new modes of communication.

Except for films shown in theaters, mediated or computer-generated messages are typically processed by individuals alone or in small groups. For example, we usually watch a video or TV show or listen to music alone or with a few friends or family members. Although it is doubtful that watching television or listening to CDs would ever replace listening to real person-to-person interaction or live concerts, the content of what we listen to may influence how we communicate interpersonally.[22] Global media such as CNN, MTV, and the Internet cross national boundaries and are thus changing the way we respond to people from different countries. Popular music, for example, serves as an international language transcending national borders and uniting its audiences. Cultural, informational, and personal barriers may continue to fall as our ears open wider.

How are the media and technology changing the way we listen to each other? Because we spend more time listening to or being entertained by the media, do we spend less time listening to each other? Have you ever responded passively to another person because you were preoccupied with the sounds or messages emanating from a mass medium? On the other hand, to what extent have newer media made it possible for you to respond to or seek a response from others? For

in Practice

Illusionary Listening

If it is possible for the television to be on, and for people to sit facing it but not really viewing it, and for the radio to be on and for people to hear it but not really react to it, is it equally possible for people to speak to each other but not really listen?

1. Think about how often you have been oblivious to the fact that someone to whom you were speaking, while still there before your eyes, had stopped paying attention to you?

2. Do you prefer to have illusionary listeners (persons around you who do not listen to you) the way broadcast stations prefer to have illusionary viewers or receivers (persons whose TVs or radios are on but who do not watch or listen) as long as they are counted in their program ratings?

3. Working in pairs, generate strategies to ensure that your listeners are truly listening.

4. Can you think of situations in which you may lose your listeners no matter what you do?

example, the availability of cellular telephones and recent advances in telephone technology mean that whenever we want to, no matter where we are, we can always reach someone to listen to us.

On the other hand, some believe that our connections to computers and e-mail, together with our obsessions with the Internet and cell phones, are impeding our ability to listen. For example, the contention is that by focusing our attention on the visual rather than the aural, computers lead us to emphasize the eye over the ear. Do you agree or disagree with this premise?

Advances in technology also make it more likely that we will be multitasking when listening. For example, how often do you find yourself checking your e-mail while talking with friends over the phone? Unfortunately, as a result of multitasking we find ourselves not focusing exclusively on any sole communication channel. As a result, we fail to give a person with whom we are interacting our full attention. In your opinion, should we develop rules specifying when multitasking is and is not socially acceptable? If so, what kinds of rules should we develop? If not, why do you believe such rules are unnecessary?

Gaining Communication Competence

Following are seven steps to ensure that you become a more effective listener.

How to Become "All Ears"

Step One: Catch Yourself Exhibiting a Bad Habit

Recognition of a fault precedes correction of it. If you monitor your listening behavior, you can catch yourself before you display an undesirable trait. That's the first step toward positive change.

Step Two: Substitute a Good Habit for a Bad Habit

Think about the new listening habits you would like to have. For example, if you are a daydreamer and mentally wander off while others speak to you, encourage yourself to exhibit greater attentiveness and concentration. Visualize yourself listening effectively when conversing. Imagine the positive impact your new behavior will have on your relationships.

Step Three: Use Your Whole Body to Listen

Take steps to ensure that your physical mannerisms do not distract or confuse the person with whom you are interacting. Instead of leaning back with your arms crossed, fidgeting, playing with your hair or jewelry, gazing repeatedly at your watch, or otherwise signaling that you are not interested in what he or she is saying, make a commitment to convey a more positive listening demeanor. Display an attentive posture, make good eye contact, and exhibit appropriate facial expressions. In other words, get physically ready to listen. If you look more like an effective listener, you will be more apt to behave like one.

Step Four: Consistently Use Your Ears, Not Just Your Mouth

When you converse with another, you need to be able to shift naturally and frequently from a speaking mode to a listening mode. Rather than monopolizing the speaking role or spending your time planning what you will say once you get the floor, make a sincere effort when you're not speaking to focus on what the other person is saying to you. Rather than completing his or her statements because you "know for sure" what he or she is going to say, let the person complete his or her own thoughts. Conversing with another compels us to develop not just a speaking presence, but also a listening attitude.

Step Five: Be Willing to See the Other Side

Because one of the greatest detriments to listening is an unwillingness to look at a situation from another's point of view, if you begin a conversation by telling yourself you are willing to see and feel from the other individual's perspective, you increase your chances for more meaningful interaction. You may not end up agreeing with what you have heard, but you will be more likely to understand where the thoughts and feelings came from.

Step Six: Avoid the Tendencies to Distort Messages or Listen Assumptively

Every message delivered by one person to another exists in at least four different forms:

FORM 1: The message as it exists in the mind of the person speaking to you (his or her thoughts)

FORM 2: The message as it is spoken (encoded by that person)

FORM 3: The message as it is interpreted by the listener (decoded by you)

FORM 4: The message as it is ultimately remembered by the listener (influenced by your personal selectivity or rejection biases)

When passed from person to person, messages become distorted. This happens because, first, we usually try to simplify the messages we hear as we process them. Second, because of our apprehensiveness, we may not want to admit that we didn't understand what someone said to us; instead, we may try to make sense of what we were told on our own by making certain assumptions. Typically we do this by adding to, subtracting from, or otherwise altering what was said.

Step Seven: Participate Actively

Ask questions. Paraphrase. Listening is an active and responsive process, not a passive behavior. It requires that you paraphrase—restate in your own words—what you have heard another say to you. Doing this lets you know whether you have correctly processed the words and feelings—the actual meaning—of another's message.

Keep in mind that developing yourself as an effective listener is a basic step in developing yourself as an effective communicator.

Wrap-Up

Meet again in pairs or with your discussion group. Turn back to the case study at the beginning of the chapter and reconsider the questions that followed it. How have your answers changed or become more focused? Based on what you know about listening, what advice would you give Flora now?

Critical Thinking Contacts

Examine the following cartoon. Based on your understanding of the listening process, advise Peppermint Patty and Charlie Brown what each needs to do to encourage or exhibit effective listening behaviors.

Who's Listening?

Peanuts reprinted by permission of United Feature Syndicate, Inc.

Summary

Although listening consumes more time than any other communicative activity, research reveals we do not do it very well. Although our very existence depends on our ability to listen, on average, we listen at only 25 percent efficiency.

Listening and hearing are different processes. Listening is a voluntary psychological process and hearing is an involuntary physiological process. The listening process involves six stages: sensing, attending, understanding/interpreting, evaluating, responding, and remembering.

Listening positively influences our relationships by helping us decrease stress, enhance knowledge, build trust, improve decision making, improve the person with whom we are interacting, improve ourselves, and protect ourselves.

Unfortunately, due to our propensity to nonlisten or exhibit deficient listening behaviors, we do not always listen as effectively as we could. As nonlisteners, we may tune out, fake attention, miss opportunities for meaningful contact, become overly emotional, seek the easy way out, exhibit egocentric behavior, become overly sensitive to setting, waste time, become overly apprehensive, or exhibit symptoms of listening burnout.

Feedback and listening are related processes. Whether or not we intend to send feedback, we constantly provide it to those with whom we interact. Feedback can be evaluative or nonevaluative, positive or negative. Among the nonevaluative forms of feedback are probing, understanding, supportive feedback, and "I" messages.

Listening theorists have identified four types of listening: appreciative listening, empathic listening, comprehensive listening, and critical listening. Each is of value when we communicate interpersonally.

As we have seen, gender, culture, the media, and technology each play a role in influencing our listening behavior.

By eliminating listening roadblocks and practicing good listening habits, we take steps to ensure we listen more effectively.

Terms to Talk About

listening *(p. 106)*
hearing *(p. 106)*
attending *(p. 107)*
appreciative listening *(p. 109)*
comprehensive listening *(p. 110)*
critical listening *(p. 110)*
empathic responsiveness *(p. 111)*
perspective taking *(p. 111)*
sympathetic responsiveness *(p. 111)*
nonlistening *(p. 117)*
red-flag words *(p. 119)*
speech–thought differential *(p. 121)*

feedback *(p. 124)*
evaluative feedback *(p. 126)*
nonevaluative feedback *(p. 127)*
probing *(p. 127)*
understanding *(p. 128)*
supportive feedback *(p. 128)*
"I" messages *(p. 128)*
dialogic listening *(p. 130)*
perspective taking *(p. 131)*
emotional contagion *(p. 131)*
empathic concern *(p. 131)*

Suggestions for Further Reading

Diane Bone, *The Business of Listening*, Los Altos, CA: Crisp, 1990. Offers guidelines and activities designed to improve listening. Also available with a video program.

Deborah Borisoff and Michael Purdy, *Listening in Everyday Life: A Personal and Professional Approach*, Lanham, MD: University Press of America, 1991. Explores the role of listening in both personal and professional lives.

Carol A. Roach and Nancy J. Wyatt, *Successful Listening*, New York: HarperCollins, 1988. Identifies behaviors that contribute to effective listening.

Lyman K. Steil, Larry L. Barker, and Kittie W. Watson, *Effective Listening: Key to Your Success,* Reading, MA: Addison-Wesley, 1983. A readable guide to improving listening skills.

Deborah Tannen, *The Argument Culture: Moving from Debate to Dialogue,* New York: Random House, 1998.

Andred D. Wolvin, and Carolyn Gwynn Coakley, *Listening,* 4th ed., Dubuque, IA: Wm. C. Brown, 1992. A highly readable survey of the listening process.

5

Language

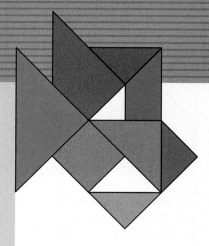

Almost everything we do that concerns other people involves us in conversation.

—Robert E. Nofsinger

After completing this chapter, you should be able to:

▌ Define language and explain its uses, and the role it plays in the formation of social identity.

▌ Draw and explain the triangle of meaning.

▌ Provide examples of how words can wear masks and give an example of a word wall.

▌ Compare and contrast denotative and connotative meaning.

▌ Describe how the semantic differential can be used to measure meaning, and how time and place influence meaning.

▌ Distinguish between offensive and inoffensive language and give an example of a euphemism.

▌ Identify and provide examples of two types of bypassing.

▌ Describe the ways in which language helps express and reinforce gender.

▌ Discuss how culture influences expression.

daily contacts

Words That Wound

Like many college students, Aiden gave little thought to how his words affected others. He was shocked to discover that his uttering of only a few words could actually precipitate demonstrations on and off campus. What had Aiden said?

One day when disturbed by a group of students who were socializing, in his opinion, much too loudly, beneath his window, Aiden yelled "Shut up, you water buffalo." Though it was later learned that Aiden had previously attended a yeshiva where the Hebrew term for "water buffalo" was slang for "foolish person," Aiden was threatened with prosecution for racial harassment. Eventually, the case died down when the women so addressed by Aiden claimed that they were being persecuted by the press and dropped their charge against him.

When speaking at a meeting that was organized to discuss campus sexual harrassment policies, one participant, we'll call him or her Lindsay, used a number of hypothetical scenarios to make a point. Featured in the scenarios were two fictional persons referred to as Dave Stud and Diane Sex Object. While a number of persons at the meeting laughed when they heard the names, others were offended and objected vocally, noting that Lindsay's choice of words were sexist.

Divide into pairs or small groups and answer the following questions:

1. How do you feel about political correctness?
2. Are some words so offensive or sexist that no one should use them? Explain.
3. In what ways can words be used to change our views of people? Give examples.
4. If you were Aiden's or Lindsay's friend, what advice would you offer each?

In this chapter, we're going to talk about talk. Talk comprises words, and words are what we use to symbolize reality. The words we use affect the feelings, thoughts, and actions of others. Words can comfort and inspire just as easily as they can annoy and alienate. Words can help us gain interpersonal closeness or ensure that others keep their distance. We use words to speak of things we have not seen or experienced, to share what we have seen and experienced, to learn about history, and to share perceptions of the present. We use words to clarify as well as confuse, to make meaning apparent or to conceal meaning from others. When we exchange words, we may exchange meaning or we may misunderstand each other and, literally, miss meaning. Either way, our interpersonal effectiveness is related to our mastery of words and their use. How we use words and how others use words when interacting with us affect both our sense of self and the development and nature of our relationships. Let's explore how and why.

Language makes it easier for us to converse with others. We rely on it to facilitate message encoding and the sharing of meaning. It is through language that we express our ideas, our hopes, our fears; attempt to inspire others to action; or win others' approval. The words we use have the ability to make us laugh and cry; they can cause us to be joyful or experience despair. It is through words that we make social contact, share our perceptions, and negotiate reality. Our words can clarify or conceal, mask or reveal meaning. Thus, the nature of language helps account for matched meanings and missed meanings, shows us why our attempts to communicate succeed or fail, and humbles us by causing us to feel, at times, that none of us speaks the same language.

Despite these challenges, our ability to use language allows us to form, maintain, and end relationships, and for these reasons, language is central to our humanness. In addition, language makes it feasible for us to cooperate with others, make plans, and talk about ideas and events. Were it not for language, we would be far less effective communicators, more isolated from each other, less apt to converse, and therefore significantly less social than we in fact are.

Getting into and behind the Words We Use: The Meaning of Meaning

The verbal messages we encode are composed of words. But how did the words we use develop their meanings? To explain how words come to have meaning, we need to set the scene by introducing a trio of language codes: the semantic code, the syntactic code, and the pragmatic code (see Table 5.1).

The semantic code, which we will explore in greater depth as we proceed through this chapter, indicates that words have both denotative and connotative levels of meaning, vary through time and place, and only represent or symbolize reality. Under the semantic code, we agree to use the same symbols. Were we unable to agree on semantic rules, it would be impossible for us to understand each other. Were we to use symbols in unpredictable ways, perhaps arguing over whether an apple was something to eat or wear on your foot, we would be unable to communicate in a meaningful way with each other.

The syntactic code establishes that there are conventions, or syntactic rules, which guide our use of words, even if we are unable to state those rules explicitly. When proper syntax is lacking, that is, when we disregard grammatical rules, our words can be misconstrued or rendered nonsensical. When someone fails to follow widely accepted linguistic rules or violates the syntactic rules that we typically follow, our impressions of that person may be negatively

TABLE 5.1
The Language Code Trio

Semantic Code	Syntactic Code	Pragmatic Code
Denotative and connotative meaning	Conventions and rules (grammar)	Appropriateness based on context
Variability through time and place		

affected. For example, Black English has been described by the "Eurocentric" community as a deviant form of Standard American English. Ebonics, African American Vernacular English, and African Mainstream American English are more acceptable synonyms for Black English. To avoid being stigmatized or labeled in negative ways, African Americans may engage in code or style switching (using either Ebonics or Mainstream American English), depending on the situation in which they find themselves.[1]

Until popularized by the music industry, the rappin' syntax of the hip-hop community was neither widely accepted nor understood by most European Americans, who initially maligned it and blamed it for promoting violence. For example, the hip-hop expression "I'm keeping it ghetto," was not understood as meant: "I'm keeping it real." We all must try to understand another person's mode of expression regardless of whether we share the same grammatical conventions.

Communication works when the persons involved understand and adhere to the same rules. To be pragmatic, participants coordinate their efforts and cooperate with each other in order to agree on an appropriate code. When, for example, is it appropriate to tell a joke, and what kind of joke may be told? Are there jokes that you might consider tasteless or denigrating to others? How do you know how a conversational partner will interpret your attempt at humor? The pragmatic code requires that to decipher meaning, we rely on the context of the interaction, the interdependent nature of our relationship, and the goal of the exchange. If, however, we begin by holding dissimilar perspectives, then our interpretations of meaning will also likely diverge. For example, have you ever observed how the same words can take on different meanings depending on the perspective a person holds? Consider this: You work for a computer company that is about to fire fifty workers. Your boss walks by and says: "You look like you've been through the wringer. Why don't you take the rest of the week off?" If you feel secure in your position, you would probably understand that your boss was appreciative of how hard you had been working and was rewarding you with a well-deserved rest. If, on the other hand, you feared being one of the fifty to be laid off, you might view the boss's suggestion as the beginning of the end of your employment. How do you think the boss's words were meant? What pragmatic rules would you use to guide your interpretation if you were the worker? Do you think you would jump to the wrong conclusion?

Since our focus in this chapter is on how words are able to influence the thought, behavior, and actions of communicating persons, the pragmatic code will also come into play. Let's continue by exploring the nature of language in greater depth.

Language: A Definition

Language is a code or system of arbitrary symbols shared by a group to communicate. Were it not for our facility at using words to create verbal messages, communicating would be far more difficult and certainly more frustrating than it is.

For example, how would we discuss our career goals, sports, politics, or the media with a partner if we were unable to use words to communicate? If you think it would be a cinch, try it!

Sharing ideas and meaning with each other using language can be a challenge; however, expressing ourselves clearly without using language is virtually impossible. Yet, like so many other things, we take words and our ability to use them for granted. It is only when we are prevented or restrained from communicating that we come to value its utility and importance.

We use language to negotiate meaning, and negotiating meaning is at the heart of communication. Words are **symbols**. In and of themselves, they don't have any meaning. Actually, the words we use are letter combinations or spoken sounds that were arbitrarily selected at some point to stand for the things or referents about which we speak. If enough people agreed, we could create new symbols—new words—to use in their place. The word *water* is not drinkable. The word *dog* does not bark. The word *love* is not loveable. The word *snow* is not colder than the word *coffee* any more than the word *coffee* is hotter than the word *pepper*.

Meanings for words do not reside in their symbols—their letters or their sounds—but rather in the minds of those who use them. Thus, words are not reality; they merely *represent* reality. In order to understand each other, people must understand the realities represented by the words they use. Meaning exists in *people,* not in *words*. You have your meaning, and other people have their meanings. To the extent that you can negotiate your meanings so that they overlap, you will be able to decode each other's messages and understand each other. We can use the model developed by C. K. Ogden and I. A. Richards to help us comprehend this process.

The Triangle of Meaning: Gaining Perspective

In *The Meaning of Meaning,* C. K. Ogden and I. A. Richards use the **triangle of meaning** to illustrate the relationship among words, things, and thoughts (see Figure 5.1).[2] Ogden and Richards use a broken line to connect the word and the thing to which it refers. This broken line underscores that there is an arbitrary relationship between a symbol and its referent; it lets us know that the word is not the thing and that there is no direct connection between these two points on the triangle. In contrast, by showing that a direct connection exists between words and thoughts and things and thoughts, Ogden and Richards show that people attach personal meanings to words and things. Thus, meanings exist in the thoughts or references that people have, not in the symbols or their referents. When you say the word *wealth,* for example, it does not necessarily mean the same thing to you that it does to the individual with whom you are conversing. Each of you has different associations that you attach to the word, based on your stored mental images and personal experiences. Thus it is quite possible for two of us to use the same word or look at the same referent

FIGURE 5.1
The Triangle of Meaning

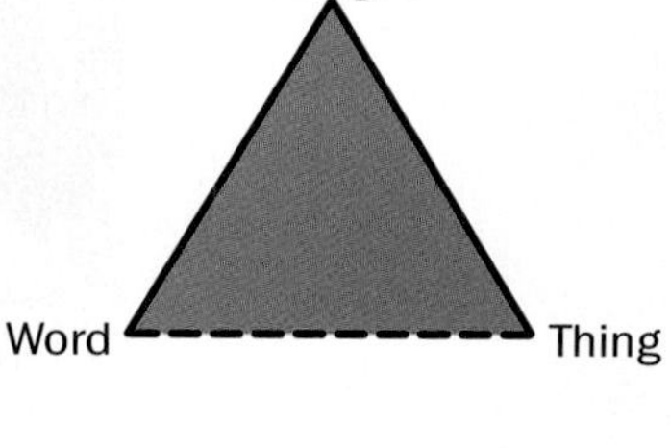

.⋚ *Theory*

Would You Let Your Words Wear a Mask?

During political campaigns, politicians sometimes try to evade scrutiny of a controversial position by handling a probing question with a vague, "Oh, don't worry about my stance on that issue; I'm okay on that." The hope is that listeners will interpret their words to mean "I agree with you," rather than "We're on opposite sides of the fence on this issue."

1. Is it ethical to use words that you know will contribute to another's misunderstanding of your position, if doing so makes it possible for you to continue interacting without apparent overt disagreement?

2. You have probably seen or heard of the psychological tests devised by Rorschach, in which a person says what is visually suggested to him or her by a series of ink blots. Is providing verbal Rorschach tests, in which persons are encouraged to project what they *wish* you had said into your response, fair? For example, is it ethical when you are asked how you feel about gay marriages for you to avoid a clear enunciation of your feelings and offer instead the noncommittal "I'm okay on that"?

> Whatever we call a thing, whatever we say it is, it is not. For whatever we say is words, and words are words and not things.
>
> — *Harry Weinberg*

and give it the same or different meanings. No one will react to a stimulus— whether a word or a thing—exactly as you do, because no one has had your exact experiences.

The significance of the triangle is quite clear: *Meaning exists in thoughts, not in words or things.* For you and those with whom you interact to understand each other, the sense you attribute to the words used must overlap. That is, you must both attribute the same meaning and sense to the words you use to communicate.

In your opinion, is it ethical for a politician to deliberately use language that might mask the true meaning of his or her words in order to win a campaign?

When your language is ambiguous or contains what is known as **word masks,** misunderstandings may result.

When words wear "masks," listeners are apt to misunderstand them. Although relationship disagreements may be avoided in the short run, in the long run, when the mask is finally taken off the words, the viability and honesty of the relationship may be called into question.

Semantic Barriers: Unlocking Person-to-Person Understanding

When we use language in a way that impedes understanding, we construct a **word wall.** In Lewis Carroll's *Through the Looking Glass,* Humpty Dumpty explains to Alice how easy it is to build a word wall:

> "I don't know what you mean by 'glory,'" Alice said.
> Humpty Dumpty smiled contemptuously. "Of course you don't—till I tell you. I meant, 'There's a nice knock-down argument for you!'"
> "But 'glory' doesn't mean 'A nice knock-down argument,'" Alice objected.
> "When I use a word," Humpty Dumpty said in a rather scornful tone, "it means just what I choose it to mean—neither more nor less."

When we think we can make words mean whatever we want them to, we usually fail to share our meaning with others. If we consider only our meaning for a word without stopping to think about how others may interpret it, we are apt to experience communication problems. Although there are a number of semantic barriers that complicate the sharing of meaning, we can overcome them for the most part if we identify the kinds of problems we face when using language, recognize them when they are present, and take steps to facilitate rather than mask the transference of meaning.

The Meaning of Word Meaning: Connotation versus Denotation

Words have both denotative and connotative meanings. **Denotative meaning** refers to a word's standard dictionary definition. It is the general or objective meaning that the members of a particular language community attribute to a word. Although the number of denotations applicable to a word is limited by the number of dictionary definitions, the more denotations a word has, the greater the possibility for confusion in the word's use. A run in baseball is different from a run in a stocking, which is different from a 10K run. When our listeners do not understand the denotative meaning of words we use, we have set up a potential semantic barrier.

Connotative meaning, in contrast, is much more subjective, personal, and temporary in nature. Unlike denotative meaning, it is influenced by an individual's personal experiences with a word and its referent. Thus the connotative meaning you have for a word may not be shared by others with whom you interact, and it is even more likely that a semantic barrier may exist. In fact, a word can have as many connotations as there are people who use it. Thus, its meanings are limitless. To understand just how limitless, take some time to explore the meanings of commonly used words such as *college, sex, tests,* and

In Practice

Measuring Meaning

Below is a seven-point *semantic differential scale* composed of bipolar terms used to measure how you feel about particular words. Developed by Charles Osgood, George Suci, and Percy Tannenbaum, this scale measures the meaning the words *college, sex, tests,* and *athletes* have for you.

1. Score each of the four words, *college, sex, test,* and *athletes,* according to the semantic differential scale below. Using the word *college* and the good–bad scale as an example, the seven positions should be interpreted as follows: If your personal meaning for the word *college* gives you an extremely good feeling, place your X as follows:

good   X __ __ __ __ __ __ bad

1 extremely
2 quite
3 slightly
4 neutral
5 slightly
6 quite
7 extremely

If your meaning of the word *college* gives you an extremely *bad* feeling place your X as follows:

good   __ __ __ __ __ __ X bad

Proceed in this manner for each word and each polar scale, scoring the four words with four different colored markings on the scale below.

SEMANTIC DIFFERENTIAL SCALE

good   __ __ __ __ __ __ __ bad

1 extremely
2 quite
3 slightly
4 neutral
5 slightly
6 quite
7 extremely

happy   __ __ __ __ __ __ __ sad
strong __ __ __ __ __ __ __ weak
honest __ __ __ __ __ __ __ dishonest
hot   __ __ __ __ __ __ __ cold
active __ __ __ __ __ __ __ passive
valuable __ __ __ __ __ __ __ worthless
sweet   __ __ __ __ __ __ __ bitter
fast   __ __ __ __ __ __ __ slow

2. Fill in the numerical score you assigned for each word and each bipolar set of terms in the table below.

Scale	college	sex	tests	athletes
good/bad				
happy/sad				
strong/weak				
honest/dishonest				
hot/cold				
active/passive				
valuable/worthless				
sweet/bitter				
fast/slow				

3. Compare your scores with others in your class. How do your feelings for each word compare with the feelings expressed by other students? To what extent, if any, does the sex or age of the respondent appear to affect ratings?

athletes have for you and your classmates (see the "In Practice" box). Because you and others in your class probably have not shared the exact same experiences with college, sex, tests, or athletes, it is quite likely that you will not share the same connotative meanings for these terms. It is important to keep in mind how personal experience influences the connotative meaning carried from encounter to encounter.

Meanings Change: Time and Place

The meanings words trigger in people's minds can change through time. Just because we used a word one way at a particular time doesn't mean that people from another generation or era would use it in the same way or even be able to understand our message. Our language system is open to expansion and alteration. Many words lose their old meaning and evolve new ones, sometimes as often as every year.

Consequently, especially if you are interacting with someone older or younger than yourself, it is important to find out whether the meaning each of you gives to a word matches or misses the other's meaning. The word *gay* for example, is now an acceptable term for "homosexual," and is well on its way to shedding its past meaning of "happy," "bright," or "merry." Consider, for instance, how three audiences, one of young adults, one of middle-aged adults, and one of elementary school children, might interpret these words and phrases: radical, kick the ballistics, rap, gross, red, the Net, straight, chill, bite moose, parallel parking, far out, surfing, awesome. The point is that definitions do not necessarily stay with words indefinitely, and because time can affect a word's meaning, it is important for us to be aware of a word's current meaning.

The meanings of words change not only through time. They also change by geographic region. Thus, a driver whose curiosity causes him or her to slow traffic is called a "rubbernecker" in Texas, a "lookie-Lou" in Los Angeles, and a "gonker" in Detroit.[3] Similarly, a soft drink is referred to as a "soda" in some parts of the country, a "phosphate" in others, "tonic" elsewhere, and "pop" in other regions. Because of these differences, to determine meaning, you have to consider where you are. Unless you are sensitive to how regional differences affect word meaning, you could find yourself facing a communication gap.

Offensive versus Inoffensive Language: Feelings and Effect

Word choice matters. The words we choose can be candid and explicit or vague and misleading. Similarly, they can announce or conceal our true feelings. We may revert to using euphemisms, emotive language, or politically correct language to help accomplish our message objectives.

Euphemisms

Sometimes we elect to substitute less direct or inoffensive language for language that is too blunt or that may be potentially offensive to people. Such substitutions, called **euphemisms**, mask a communicator's meaning by "softening the blow" of an offensive message, but they also frequently obscure or fog the actual meaning and thereby affect the receiver's response. Consider, for example, being asked how you feel about someone by that person, whom you happen to dislike. Would you blurt that out, or would you attempt to be somewhat more tactful and say something like, "I could grow to like you" instead? By being less blunt (though also perhaps less honest), you take the punch out of the first message's impact. As a case in point, few people are "fired" today; instead, we speak of them being selectively separated or redundantly eliminated.

While people in most cultures value politeness, there are cultural variations in how important politeness is when contrasted with honesty. Asian cultures, for example, value politeness in interpersonal relations more than do people in the United States.[4] Eager to spare the feelings of those with whom they interact, they are prone to using euphemisms to soften the impact of words.

Politicians also use euphemisms to soften the impact of policy changes. A tax increase becomes "increased revenue," a missile becomes a "peacemaker," a "war" becomes a "freedom operation," an environmentalist becomes a "conservationist," and global warming becomes a "climate change."

While euphemisms can spare feelings, they can also obscure or mislead receivers by camouflaging the truth. According to William Lutz, euphemisms wage "linguistic fraud and deception."[5] Sometimes, however, using euphemisms can defuse a crisis, as it did after the United States found itself in a diplomatic crisis with China when a U.S. spy plane collided with a Chinese EP-3E fighter that had been tailing it. The Chinese wanted the U.S. to issue a formal apology, something the Bush administration did not want to do. The solution was found in linguistic ambiguity—via the writing of a nuanced note in which the U.S. expressed one "sincere regret" over the incident and two "very sorry's," one "sorry" for the loss of the Chinese pilot, and another for making an unauthorized landing—expressions satisfactory to both the U.S. and China.

Emotive Language

While we use euphemisms to mask our real feelings, we use emotive language to editorialize on our feelings. Emotive language announces your attitude toward a particular subject. If, for example, you approve of a friend's cutting back on expenses, you might call her thrifty; if you disapprove, you might call her cheap. While the behavior you are describing is the same, the terms you use to describe that behavior expresses your opinion by eliciting favorable or unfavorable connotations. Notice, for example, how your reactions are changed by the words in the following trios, each meaning the same thing.

Third World	*underdeveloped*	*backward*
corpse	*dead body*	*loved one*
war	*defensive response*	*massacre*
coffin	*casket*	*slumber chamber*
heavy	*overweight*	*obese*
handkerchief	*cloth tissue*	*nose rag*
laying off	*firing*	*downsizing*
cheat	*evade*	*use loopholes*

In many ways, the word you select to describe a person or an action can be more a matter of personal opinion than one of objective fact. Now, using the following statements descriptive of a person, demonstrate how you can editorialize on the given description by helping others view the subject either more favorably or more unfavorably merely by altering the italicized word:

She's *messy.*
He's *principled.*
I'm *reserved.*
She's *stocky.*
He's *tactful.*

The Power of Polarization: The Case of the Missing Middle

Although the vast majority of cases exist between extremes, our language leads us to think in extremes. When you view the world and describe it in terms of extremes, you exhibit a tendency to polarize; that is, you describe experience in either–or terms. How many of these expressions sound familiar to you? "Either you're for us or against us." "You're our ally or our enemy." "For richer or poorer." "He's a genius or an idiot." "She's either a patriot or she's a traitor." Either–or thinking conditions us to categorize experience and people according to polar positions.

Our language makes it too easy for us to think and talk in opposites. Just see how easy it is to fill in the opposites for each of the following words:

Fat   _____
Happy   _____
Bold   _____
Brave   _____
Tall   _____

Then try filling in two or more words between each pair of opposites. It's more diffi-cult, isn't it? It's harder to find words that express all possibilities, not just the extremes. The world is not black and white, good and bad, beautiful or ugly. It comes in a plethora of shades. Because polarizing leaves out the middle ground, it does not reflect reality but creates monumental, artificial divisions instead. Overstating the divide between positions causes people to perceive gulfs where none really exist.

Politically Correct Language

The words *political correctness,* like many words, mean different things to different people—the words may have different connotations for each of us. For some of us, being *politically correct* means we use words that convey our respect for and sensi-tivity to the needs and interests of different groups. Thus, when we find ourselves discussing sensitive issues with people who are culturally different from us, we may also find ourselves adapting our language so that it demonstrates our sensitivity to the perspectives and interests of those with whom we are conversing. For others, however, political correctness means feeling compelled by societal pressure not to use some words for fear that doing so would cause others to perceive us as either racist or sexist. Thus, we might opt to clothe our words in political correctness in an effort to avoid offending. Still others view political correctness as a very real danger to free speech. Which of these three views comes closest to your own?

We need to recognize that many people judge the users of politically incorrect language to be sexist (displaying a value for one sex over another), heterosexist (displaying a value for one sexual orientation over another), ageist (displaying a value for one age group over another), or racist (displaying a value for one race over another)—not just noninclusive or insensitive. In addition to disparaging a person's sex, sexual orientation, age, ethnicity, or race, politically incorrect lan-guage also may demean a person's social class or physical or mental abilities. When, for example, you call someone "white trash," "a retard," or "a spastic," you are announcing your attitude towards the person and excluding her or him from your group, as well as establishing your sense of superiority. These words tend to impede a relationship. Politically incorrect language indeed tends to be divisive; some even believe it is unethical.

Using sexist language such as *congressman* ignores the reality that a woman may also serve in Congress. Similarly, labeling someone a "fag" or a "dyke" is offensive, announces an antipathy toward sexual orientation, and is hurtful. In like fashion, using ageist language such as "old geezer" indicates that you have little regard for or respect for a person who is older than you are. Using language that is ethnically or racially biased indicates your disdain for the person and also reveals the stereotypical image you hold of the members of a particular ethnic or racial group different from your own. Because they demean and disparage others, words like these promote distance rather than interpersonal approachability. For example, corporate advertisers and educational institutions have used Indian names such as "redskins," "braves," and "Seminoles," and logos that featured images of severed heads, tomahawk cops, or Indian princesses to sell products. Native Americans object to such symbol uses as racist.

Language can have repercussions depending on the words and symbols used and who is using them. For example, while one African American may, without blinking an eye, casually refer to another African American as a "nigger" and not have that reference taken pejoratively, it would be highly unlikely for a white person's use of the word to be construed in the same way. In your opinion, is it the prerogative of the African American to use the word? What is interesting is that members of a group may reclaim and redefine words that were once used to stigmatize or degrade them. Illustrating this, it is increasingly common for gays and lesbians to use the term *queer* as a means of making positive references to themselves, and it is more common for women to refer to themselves as girls.

Members of various groups were asked what words they prefer that others use to describe them. The term *"older persons"* is preferred to *elderly* or *senior citizen,* *"gay"* and *"lesbian"* are preferred for a man and a woman who have affectional preferences for members of their own sex, *"African American"* is preferred to *black* (*African American* places the emphasis on cultural heritage, while *black* focuses on a color), *"Hispanic"* is preferred to *Latina(o),* *"Inuit"* is preferred to *Eskimo,* *"Muslim"* is preferred to *Moslem,* *"Asian"* is preferred to *Oriental,* and *"Native American"* is preferred to *Indian.*[6]

The language we choose to use also conveys our feelings and attitudes toward the object of discussion. Thus, the words we select, to a large extent, depend on our point of view. As a result, we use words to express and alter perceptions of events, objects, people, and society. Language is one means of expressing and shaping attitudes. We should be aware of the words we use so we can accurately communicate our meanings. Language helps us create the world we want to share with those with whom we interact.

Bypassing: Equivocal Language Can Confuse

Bypassing occurs when individuals think they understand each other but actually miss each other's meaning because one or both are using **equivocal language,** words that can have more than one interpretation. In other words, instead of meeting, their meanings simply pass by one another, leaving both parties confused.

When has bypassing caused problems for you? for someone you know?

Two types of bypassing concern us.[7] The first occurs when people are unaware that they are talking about the same thing or fail to see that they agree with each other because they are using different words or phrasing. For example, a husband and wife argued vehemently over proposed changes in the health care system.

in Context

The Power of Politically Incorrect Speech

In December 2002, incoming Senate Majority Leader Trent Lott was forced to resign his position soon after attending a 100th birthday and retirement celebration for Strom Thurmond, during which Lott bemoaned all the problems the United States might have avoided if it had followed Thurmond's lead in 1948, elected him president, and taken the segregation route. Said Lott:

I want to say this about my state: When Strom Thurmond ran for president we voted for him. We're proud of it. And if the rest of the country had followed our lead we wouldn't have had all these problems over all these years, either.

Lott initially defended himself by contending that his remarks about Thurmond were based on Thurmond's promotion of a strong national defense, supporting law enforcement, and opposing budget deficits. Subsequently, he apologized for his remarks, noting, "A poor choice of words conveyed the impression that I embraced the discarded policies of the past. Nothing could be further from the truth, and I apologize to anyone who was offended by my comment." Earlier, he had also said: "My comments were not an endorsement of his positions of over fifty years ago, but of the man and his life."

In your opinion, were Lott's *politically incorrect* remarks made at the event honoring Thurmond racist? Do you agree that Lott needed to be removed as majority leader for uttering words judged to have both negative moral and social consequences? To what extent, if any, do you believe that the political correctness movement interferes with the First Amendment that was expressly designed to protect unpopular speech? How, in your opinion, should we balance our right to say what we want—no matter how provocative or controversial—with those who believe we need to watch what we say so that we do not offend others or speak insensitively without regard for how our remarks might play in another context? How do you differentiate and where do you draw the line among politically incorrect speech, unpopular speech, and freedom of speech?

One insisted that the health care system should be "revamped," while the other said that that was foolish, since all that was called for were "small changes." They didn't realize that what one meant by "revamped" was what the other meant by "small changes." Far too often, we argue with others because we are unaware that, although we appear to disagree, in fact we basically agree. We are simply using different words.

The second and more prevalent type of bypassing occurs when the words people use suggest that they are in agreement with each other when in fact they substantially disagree. While this form of bypassing is often harmless, it can and sometimes does have more serious consequences. Consider the man who was driving on a parkway when his engine stalled. He succeeded in stopping another driver, who, after listening to his tale of woe, agreed to push the stalled vehicle in an effort to start it. "My car has an automatic transmission," the stuck driver explained, "so you'll have to get up to 30 or 35 miles an hour to get me moving." The driver who had agreed to help nodded in understanding, and the driver of the stalled vehicle climbed back into his own car and waited for the other car to line up behind him. After waiting what seemed an interminable amount of time, he turned around, only to see the other driver coming at him at 30 to 35 miles per hour! While the drivers thought their meanings matched, they really had a very basic misunderstanding—the meanings just were not immediately apparent. This was also the problem for the young

British man who was astonished that he was slapped when on a visit to the States he told his American acquaintance that he would "knock her up" before he returned home to Britain. It was only after he explained to her that in Britain "knock her up" meant "come and see her" that the young woman apologized.

But not all bypassing is so humorous. During World War II, it was thought that the Japanese had decided to ignore the Potsdam Declaration, which called on them to surrender, when the Japanese announced that they were adhering to a policy of "mokusatsu." It was only after the atomic bomb was dropped on Hiroshima that interpreters realized that "mokusatsu" could also have been translated as "make no comment at the moment" rather than "reject" or "ignore," its initial translation. The cost of this seeming interpretational error is incalculable.

A first step in limiting the damage that bypassing can do to our relationships is to develop an awareness that it can and does occur. If it is possible for someone with whom we are interacting to misunderstand us, they probably will. With this in mind, it is important for both conversants to be "person minded," to take the time needed to ensure that the meanings each gives to words overlap. Don't get caught being "word minded" by protesting, "I never thought you'd think I meant . . ." or "I was sure you understood me." Recognize the responses your words can precipitate. If you anticipate these responses, then you'll do your part to prevent mismatched meanings from interfering with effective communication.

Labels Can Obscure Meaning: Confusing Words and Things

How label conscious are you? To what extent do you respond to labels themselves, rather than to what they represent?

Are you extensionally or intensionally oriented? How do you know?

Linguistic researcher Benjamin Lee Whorf notes that the way we define a label or situation dramatically affects our behavior. According to Whorf, words help shape our perceptions of reality and at times even determine the reality we are able to perceive.[8] Thus, because the Inuit are able to perceive many more different types of snow than most of us, they use different words to label different types of snow. For instance, they have one name for falling snow, *gana*, and another for fluffy fallen snow, *akilukah*. Similarly, avid skiers can label and distinguish a wide variety of snow types, in contrast to the nonskier, to whom snow is simply snow.

At times, the words we use as labels do not clarify reality but obscure it. When we respond to a label rather than to what the label actually represents, we display what is known as an **intensional orientation**. Individuals who are intensionally oriented are easily fooled by words and labels and as a result fail to inspect whatever is represented by the label. In contrast, when we inspect the item referred to by the label instead of being blinded by the label's words, we exhibit what is known as an **extensional orientation**. Extensionally oriented individuals are "show me," reality-based people who refuse to be conned by language. For example, perfume and cologne manufacturers take advantage of our tendencies to display intensional orientations when they give their products names like "Intimate," "Brut," and "Obsession." They count on us to buy the product based on our desire to become intimate with another, to be perceived as a brute, or to have another obsessed with us.

Have you ever been hurt by a word?

Other manufacturers follow suit with a whole range of consumer products and marketing messages. Likewise, some teachers react to student labels, responding to

literary
contacts

Do Hurtful Words Have Power?

Bill Maher, the former host of *Politically Incorrect,* found his show cancelled not long after uttering the following words during a post 9/11 on-air discussion of whether the terrorists who flew the planes that crashed into the World Trade Center and the Pentagon were cowards. Contrasting the horrific acts of these members of Al Qaeda with the U.S. practice of long-range aerial attacks, Maher said: "We have been the cowards, lobbying cruise missiles from 2,000 miles away. That's cowardly. Staying in the airplane when it hits the building—say what you want about it, it's not cowardly."

How powerful were Maher's words? Upon learning of Maher's remarks, FedEx and Sears immediately pulled their ads from Maher's show, and at least seventeen TV stations suspended *Politically Incorrect,* with some noting that they were expressing their First Amendment rights.

Subsequently, Maher apologized for his comments, noting: "In no way was I intending to say, nor have I ever thought, that the men and women who defend our nation in uniform are anything but courageous and valiant, and I offer my apologies to anyone who took it wrong."

According to the old nursery rhyme: "Sticks and stones will break my bones but words will never harm me." Do you agree? In your opinion do the words we use or misuse affect thinking and behavior? Have you ever been hurt by the words of others? Now, rethink the Maher incident. Do you believe that the words Maher uttered were harmful, merely insensitive, or neither? Defend your position with reasons.

When talking to receivers, it is important to use words they'll understand. It does not matter if you understand what you're saying if others do not.

their associations with student names or descriptions, rather than to their knowledge of the actual individual. When we confuse labels with reality, or words with things, we can make major misinterpretations.

Mastering Meaning

When we are sensitive to communication context, the words we use reflect the needs of those with whom we are communicating. If you are to master meaning, you need to use words that your receivers will judge to be clear, appropriate, and concrete.

Are Your Words Clear?

Far too often we use words we understand but others do not. If we choose words with our listeners in mind, our listeners will be more apt to respond as we had hoped. Ask yourself the following questions when considering the clarity of your words:

> Are the words I am using reflective of the educational level of the individual with whom I am interacting?
> Will the individual with whom I am interacting be familiar with any technical language (jargon) or sublanguages (special language used by members of a particular subculture)?

Are Your Words Appropriate?

Our word choice should change as the situation we are in changes and as the people with whom we are interacting change. For example, we might use slang when speaking with friends, but we probably would not use it when conversing with our employer or a professor. Whereas obscenities might spew from our mouths when we are letting off steam around a close pal, we probably would censor our remarks when in the presence of a parent, grandparent, or school or corporate officer. Ask yourself the following questions when assessing the appropriateness of your word choice:

It is through words that we are made human, and it is through words that we are dehumanized.

—Ashley Montagu

> Would my receiver find my words offensive?
> Have I used the right words in the right place at the right time?

Are Your Words Concrete?

The words we use are concrete when they enable us to describe a feeling, an event, or a circumstance unambiguously—that is, they let us communicate precisely what we mean. When we eliminate vague and confusing words from our conversations and substitute more exact ones, we are able to more effectively shape the meaning we transmit to others. Ask yourself the following questions when evaluating the concreteness of your expression:

> Do my words enable my receiver to formulate a clear picture of my thoughts?
> Do my words communicate my intended feelings?

professional
contacts

The Nature of Language

In his essay "Sweeping Changes," commentator Charles Osgood explores the nature of language. How can you use his observations to improve person-to-person understanding?

Lawyers talk funny. They write funny, too. Legalese is like another language in which you and I become two other people: to wit, the Party of the First Part, and the Party of the Second Part. There has been an effort in recent years to get lawyers to use plain English, so that anybody could understand what a given contract, law, regulation, etc., was trying to say, radical a notion as that may be. Some government agencies have rewritten their regulations to make them clearer and easier to understand.

Poets and lawyers have exactly opposite intentions. Poets want to write so that their language is subtle and nuanced, rich with possible interpretations. Lawyers are supposed to write so that later (when somebody sues) there will be no question as to what was meant by a certain phrase. The ideal is that there should be only one possible meaning.

One way to unsnarl the convoluted gobbledygook of government is to make more use of simple, declarative sentences, omitting needless words. (See *The Elements of Style*, by Strunk and White.) However, as Albert Einstein once pointed out, you should make things as simple as possible, but not simpler. There is such a thing as omitting one word too many.

The U.S. International Trade Commission omitted three words too many. In trying to streamline its regulations, the ITC took an editor's pencil to the section that deals with the importing of brooms made of corn bristles. To protect the American corn-broom industry, there were restrictions and heavy tariffs on brooms made "wholly or partly from broom corn." The words "wholly or partly" seemed unnecessary, and so in the revised edition, out they went. In trying to sweep away the extra words, however, the ITC may have swept away the business.

Recently, the Customs Service was asked whether, under the new language, a broom with 28 percent to 43 percent corn bristles would be subject to the tariffs and import limitations. The answer was no.

In other words, broom makers in Mexico, let us say, can now stuff their brooms with cheap materials, use a lot of vegetable fibers or grass, and still market their products here in the U.S. as corn brooms, competing with the fifty or so American broom companies, and selling their brooms for about half what a quality U.S. maker would have to charge for the real McCoy. "It's absolutely unbelievable," says one broom-maker. "It's thrown our industry in turmoil!" says another. There are some fifty American companies making roughly twenty million corn brooms a year. Floor brooms, whisk brooms. All sorts of brooms.

Although Congress went along with the word changes, there's now an effort being made on Capitol Hill to correct what was obviously an error. The folks who re-wrote the regulations never intended to say what the words ended up saying. David B. Beck, a Commission official, has written a letter to the Customs people, saying: "The consequences this would have on the tariff treatment of these products were never brought to our attention when we could have done something about it. . . ."

The moral is: It's a good idea to make language simple. But don't make it *too* simple.

SOURCE: "Sweeping Changes" from *The Osgood Files* by Charles Osgood, copyright © 1986, 1987, 1988, 1989, 1990, 1991 by Charles Osgood. Used by permission of G. P. Putnam's Sons, a division of Penguin Group (USA) Inc.

Language and Relationships: Communication Style, Words, and Feelings

Language plays an integral part in the formation of social identity.[9] As such, speaking style often reflects people's values and helps emphasize similarities and differences. For example, Japanese and Americans display contrasting communication styles. The qualities valued by the Japanese—reserve, formality, and silence—are discouraged by Americans, who prefer self-assertion, informality, and talkativeness.[10] To Americans, the prevention of silence is a key function of speech.

Unlike Americans, who typically use a direct conversational style, the Japanese favor conversational indirectness. The Japanese also assert that communication failures are due to deficiencies in the receivers, and not in the message, even when it contains imprecise and ambiguous words. Because of these cultural differences, when Japanese and American people communicate, there is a potential for tension and bad feeling.

For Americans, social conversation aids in the establishment of friendships. It is talk that brings us together. The words we use have emotional content. That is, although language serves an information function (it lets us get things done), it also helps us express our feelings. Thus the words we use to describe a subject display our attitude toward it. We can refer to someone as a *substance abuser,* an *addict,* or a *junkie.* We can call a person *homeless, displaced,* or a *bum.* Through our word choice, we announce our attitude. The words *mangy animal, adorable puppy, goofy pup,* and *vicious beast* may all refer to the same dog. The descriptions demonstrate our tendency "to snarl" (register disapproval) or "purr" (register approval). In actuality, when we use **snarl** and **purr words,** we are not describing anything but our own preferences.

In addition to facilitating the expression of feelings, language can be used specifically to exclude or include others in conversation. Groups of people who share a profession or a language different from our own, for example, often make use of "in-group" discussions during which anyone else privy to their conversation may feel quite left out. In contrast, persons who use language that is more inclusive enable everyone present to feel more of a connection to the conversation because they explain terms that may be confusing, translate foreign terms, or use analogies that make it possible for all involved to understand the content more readily.

Language also can be used to positively or negatively influence perceptions of power. For example, compare the following two statements:

> Um, could I talk to you for a second? I probably shouldn't mentions this, and I'm not really sure it's your fault, but I'm kinda upset about the fact that you didn't meet with me at the restaurant like you were supposed to. Can you meet me tomorrow—maybe, that is, if you're free?

> I'd like to talk to you. I waited for you at the restaurant and I'm upset that you didn't call when you realized you would be unable to meet me as planned. While I am willing to set another date, I hope that you will demonstrate greater consideration for my time, should you again discover that you are unable to keep our appointment.

The speaker in the second example sounds stronger, more in control, and more self-confident than does the speaker in the first example, who comes across as weak, powerless, and certainly nonauthoritative.

Don't confuse powerful speech with rude speech. They are quite different. Imagine if the second speaker had instead stated:

> *What's wrong with you? You kept me waiting at the restaurant without so much as a phone call. If you know what's good for you, you'll never do that again!*

Effective speakers can state their feelings clearly without being rude or offensive.

Diversity and Culture Contacts

Culture Speak

Understanding language can help us share our experiences with others. However, the more diverse our experiences, the more difficult it becomes for us to achieve mutual understanding.

One of the key theories concerning how language reflects our culture is the **Sapir–Whorf hypothesis,** which states that language reveals social reality. According to Edward Sapir:

> The real world is to a large extent unconsciously built up on the language habits of the group. No two languages are ever sufficiently similar to be considered as representing the same reality. The worlds in which different societies live are distinct worlds, not merely the same world with different labels attached.[11]

The Sapir–Whorf hypothesis can be viewed as an expression of linguistic determinism or as an expression of linguistic relativity, depending on how strongly you adhere to it. According to Sapir and Whorf, words are not neutral vehicles conveying meaning but rather tools that structure our perception of reality and participate in the construction of our social world. Not everyone speaks or thinks in the same way. Language is not just the content of talk; it is also the content of thought (see Table 5.2).

According to linguistic relativists, language influences both human thought and meaning. It mediates between symbols and the ideas they represent.[12] In fact, Whorf, in the same vein as his student, Sapir, states: "We cut up and organize the spread and flow of events as we do largely because through our mother tongue, we are parties to an agreement to do so, not because nature itself is segmented in exactly that way for all to see."[13] From this perspective, language defines, rather than reports, experience. It influences how we think and perceive the world around us.

Those who are extreme advocates of the Sapir–Whorf hypothesis believe that we are "at the mercy of the particular language which has become the medium of expression" for our society.[14] Believing that language determines reality, they contend that our language conditions us to process experience in a certain way. For example, the Hopi language has no concept of time as an objective entity. This, according to adherents of extreme Whorfianism, affects their conceptualization of the world. They claim that the way the Hopi rely on preparation, announcing events well in advance, shows a concept of continuous time instead of segmented

TABLE 5.2 Sapir–Whorf Hypothesis

Are you a Relativist, Determinist, or Nonbeliever?

Relativist:	Language influences thought and feeling
Determinist:	Language conditions us to process experience
Nonbeliever:	Language does not influence thought

time in Western societies. Similarly, famed speech therapist Wendell Johnson observed that very few Indians in one tribe stuttered. Soon after discovering that their language contained no word for stuttering, he concluded that the reason they did not stutter was because the possibility of stuttering never occurred to them.[15]

Those who disagree with the premise of the Sapir–Whorf hypothesis do so by expressing the belief that language does not influence thought. In support of this, they cite a number of reasons, including the following two: (1) translatability, that is, although languages may differ in grammar and syntax, it is still feasible to translate meaning from one language to another; and (2) universals, that is, they support Noam Chomsky's claim that there are deep grammatical structures that are common to all languages.[16]

Despite having its critics, the Sapir–Whorf hypothesis has influenced the way we conceive of language. For even its weak and moderate supporters, while language may not mandate or determine thought or reality, it does influence us by functioning as a barometer of cultural behavior and offering ways of perceiving and interpreting reality. We may study a culture by examining the words that the members of a culture use. In effect, the language used by groups of people mirrors their experiences. For example, if your talk abounds with words like "instant message," "download," or "text message," receivers are able to learn something about what is important to you and what your culture is like. However, if the culture of receivers was one that was not as technologically advanced as yours, they might have trouble understanding what the terms mean.

We might say that language affects thought, and thought affects language. Language viewed from this perspective does not imprison its users but rather is something that has the ability to influence the perspective the users of a language adopt, which affects how they interpret experience and reflects their world view. In Brazil, for example, a country whose economy depends on coffee, there are many words used for coffee, reflecting how important the product is to the Brazilian culture. Similarly, Arabs, who are dependent on camels for transportation, have many words for what most of us would simply refer to as a camel, and the Inuit, as noted previously, who must be able to differentiate different types of weather conditions for survival reasons, have approximately twenty-five words for snow. According to the Sapir–Whorf hypothesis, the language we use reflects our world view, our interests and concerns, and what we believe to be important.

Language also reflects reasoning patterns and expression preferences. For example, people in Western cultures rely on inductive and deductive reasoning to make and understand points; the Arab world relies on emotions. Thus, Westerners frequently have difficulty locating the main idea in an Arab's message, and vice versa.[17] Arab speech is peppered with exaggerations and repetitions. Its stress patterns often confuse Western listeners, causing them to interpret messages as either aggressive or disinterested when that is not their intent. Likewise, whereas members of Asian cultures are apt to use language sparingly and carefully, preferring to keep their feelings to themselves in an effort to preserve social harmony, members of Spanish cultures eagerly engage in conversation, and are typically open and willing to share their feelings with others. Thus, our cultures influence the way we use language.

Clearly, language and the way we use it can become a barrier to understanding the ways members of a culture communicate.[18] Similarly, language can function as an obstacle to effective communication among diverse individuals. Statements such as

By your mouth you shall perish.

—Japanese proverb

.Σ *Theory*

The Link between Language and Culture

The advertisements in a country provide clues regarding the nature and effectiveness of interpersonal relationships there. In *Intercultural Communication Training: An Introduction,* Richard Brislin and Tomoko Yoshida offer the example of a Japanese ad for frozen breaded pork, which they observe can be translated literally as "A 'bento' [box lunch] that can be made with an oven toaster: Strong in the morning delicious at noon." While this statement may make little or no sense to the uninitiated perceiver, Brislin and Yoshida note that once you understand the culture, the ad's meaning becomes clearer:

To fully understand this advertisement it is necessary for people to know that the Japanese take fairly elaborate lunches to work, school, picnics, and other outings, and that it is important for the lunches to look as though plenty of time had been spent on them. Traditionally, women are expected to make bentos *for their children, their husbands or, perhaps, for someone they love. If a woman is seen with an elaborate* bento, *many men interpret it as signifying that she will probably make a good wife.*

Although things are rapidly changing in Japan, and many working women do not have the time to make bentos, *there is still some romantic significance attached to them. Two other factors that need to be understood is that most Japanese households do not have full-size ovens and that it is extremely time consuming and messy to make breaded pork from scratch. It is, therefore, a strong selling point to emphasize the fact that it can be made in an oven toaster in a matter of minutes. In addition, the phrase "strong in the morning" needs to be understood. The functional equivalent of the phrase in English would be "a morning person," suggesting that even women who are not "morning people" can appear as though they are with the help of this product.**

1. Working with a partner, locate an example of an advertisement from another country (try foreign newspapers and magazines in your library).

2. In what ways does your ad demonstrate, as Brislin and Yoshida have, how an understanding of the culture can help us interpret the ad's meaning more accurately?

*Brislin and Yoshida, *Intercultural Communication Training,* pp. 48–49.

"Eric is a Jew" or "Sima is an Arab" lead some people to confuse the descriptive words with the actual individuals. Remember, some people are blinded by labels and are led to confuse the pictures they carry around in their heads with the actual people. The words they use lead them to become so busy noticing the stereotype the word brings up, they never come to understand the people who are actually present.[19] It is important that we develop sensitivity to differences and refrain from using words like *Arab* or *Jew* as if they accurately represented commonly held stereotypes.

It can also be helpful for us to understand how language functions within cocultures. **Cocultures** are groups of people who live within a society but outside its **dominant culture** (the mainstream culture, the one in power). Thus, the language they use will differ in a number of ways from the language used by members of the dominant culture because it will reflect their reality, including their lifestyle, values, and behavior. The language that evolves, an **argot**, enables them to develop both an identity and a sense of community.

Argots are composed of special or unique vocabularies used by particular groups. In American society, African Americans, gays, drug users, and prisoners are just some of the cocultures that use argot to communicate with members of their own groups. The use of argot can help them use language to conceal behavior as a means of self-defense, to release hostility toward members of the perceived dominant culture, and to assist the development of cohesiveness within the group.

In time, some words pass from the coculture and are used by the dominant culture. When this happens, members of the coculture often will stop using them. Thus argots undergo constant change. Language is a part of identity.

Gender Contacts

Gender Speak

How does our use of language affect social relationships and gender? Language is a prime means of communicating cultural views of gender to males and females, who may then internalize the transmitted social prescriptions and exemplify them via their interaction with others. Thus, our use of language may both express and reinforce gender stereotypes. Again, language is not neutral but exerts a powerful influence on the ways we perceive one another.

The way we use language may symbolize a devalued perception of women by presenting the experiences of men as the norm, showing women as departures from the perceived standard. Thus, language helps shape what we see as "normal," "appropriate," or an exception to the rule.[20] Consequently, although male generic language, in theory, is inclusive of both women and men, research reveals that many of us interpret male generics as including men but excluding women.[21] For example, the use of male generics like *mankind, businessmen,* and *he* to refer to men *and* women, or accolades such as *Man of the Year* causes us to perceive men as more prominent and more numerous than women. Although there are more women than men, the way we use language can trick us into thinking that men are the dominant population group.[22] To combat this perception, many dictionaries, book companies, and individuals now adhere to a policy of not using male generics or other sexist language.[23]

In addition, while men are rarely referred to as boys, women are commonly referred to as girls. Girls, however, are defined as children, not adults. Similarly, the highlighting of a person's sex, referred to as **spotlighting**, also reinforces the perception that men set the standard. Although we rarely hear the following combinations: male physician, male lawyer, male physicist, terms like these *are* widely used: woman doctor, female mathematician.[24] Women are thus defined as exceptions to a norm established by males. If we refrained from spotlighting, perceptions would be easier to revise.

Language also distinguishes between men and women when it is used to define them differently. Men tend to be defined by their independence and by their activities, status, or accomplishments. Women tend to be defined by their appearance or their relationships to others. Defining a person by physical quality or appearance diminishes that person's achievements. Definitional biases only reinforce the idea of women as decorative accessories whose claim to fame is how they look and of men as capable and qualified individuals whose claim to fame is how they perform.

It is not just how language is used to describe women and men that is of consequence. The communication practices of females and males also demonstrate key constrasts in the ways each gender uses language. Some research has determined that, in general, men and women use language to accomplish different goals.[25] Typically, males use language to achieve something or assert themselves, whereas women use it to create and sustain relationships. Men use language to attract and keep an audience, whereas women use it to indicate that they are paying attention to others. Men use language as a means to compete; women use it to collaborate. For women, talk is at the very core of a relationship. It is not, as it is with men, a means to achieve conversational dominance.[26]

Since women tend to exhibit an affiliative orientation, they find it harder to use language as a means of asserting their status. Unlike most men, who express their ideas firmly and then wait to see if someone challenges them, many women prefer to use language that fosters connections, garners support, and exhibits understanding. Women, in contrast to men, are also more likely to interpret challenges to their ideas as personal attacks. Because women are socialized to weigh the opinions of others, they also are likely to ask others for their ideas before offering a decision. Whereas men interpret questions as requests for information, women characteristically use questions to keep conversations going. When a man provides the requested information, the woman then asks another question, which frequently succeeds in frustrating the man. Why is this? When neither party understands the other's behavior, frustration is the likely result.[27]

The sensitivity women display to the reactions of others probably explains their unobtrusive and smoothing style. It also helps explain why women's speech often is labeled as deferential, as well as why women are prone to offering ritual apologies—saying an "I'm sorry" on numerous occasions during the course of a day.

Differences in male and female orientation precipitates differences in the very structure of their utterances. Tentative phrases such as "I guess," "I think," and "I wonder if" characterize the speech patterns of women but not of men. Unlike men, women frequently tend to turn statements into questions. Thus, a woman might ask: "Don't you believe it would be more effective to put this paragraph in the introduction rather than in the conclusion?" A man, in contrast, would issue a more definitive statement: "It would be more effective to put this paragraph in the introduction rather than in the conclusion."

According to linguist Robin Lakoff, unlike men, women don't try to lay claim to their utterances. In addition, their tendency to ask "tag questions" contributes to their being perceived as more tentative than men. While a woman may say, "Mel is right, isn't she?" or "It's a great day, isn't it?" men usually make such statements minus the "isn't she" or "isn't it" question tags. Women also frequently reinforce their reputation for tentativeness by prefacing utterances with phrases like, "This probably won't matter, but . . ." or "This probably isn't important, yet . . . ." While some researchers contend that such habits further weaken the impact of the messages women send, others suggest that the tentativeness noted in women's speech is not a sign of powerlessness but rather reveals their desire to keep conversation open and inclusive.

Linguist Deborah Tannen affirms that men and women speak different **genderlects.** According to Tannen, women hear and speak a language of connection and intimacy, seeking to preserve relationships. Men, in contrast, speak and hear a language of status and independence.[28]

> To a great extent, power is just a matter of how you express yourself.
>
> —*Jeffrey Eisen*

Age and Language

Just as gender and culture help account for language use variations, so does age. Persons who grew up in different generations may experience more difficulty understanding each other than people who grew up in the same generation. Significant differences in age may make individuals more prone to misunderstanding one another or to misperceiving what is being said to them.[29]

Research also reveals that younger people tend to adjust the language they use when conversing with older people. Sometimes, younger persons will feel they have to overaccommodate when interacting with someone who is significantly older than they are. Reacting on the basis of their stereotype of older persons, younger persons may consciously alter their choice of words by making them simpler and more concrete, believing erroneously that the older persons with whom they are relating have a diminished capacity for conversation. Younger persons also are likely to think that they have to speak slower and use a more nurturing tone when interfacing with elderly persons, making the older persons feel child-like and less capable. Because the younger persons speak as if the older persons are incompetent, the older persons soon feel incompetent, which contributes to both parties, young and old, feeling unfulfilled by their interactions.[30]

The message here is not that one should not be prepared to make individual accommodations. Accommodations are necessary when needed. However, even if an older person has a hearing loss, this does not correlate with diminished mental ability. The message is that our use of language should be related to the needs of the persons with whom we are interacting rather than being based on stereotypes that may cause us to interact in ways that older persons may find demeaning. Persons of any age group need to be treated as individuals rather than as members of a social category.

Media and Technology Contacts

Distorted Reflections

As we have seen, the way we and others use language reveals both our attitudes toward and our assessments of the subjects of our discussions and each other. For example, we are much more likely to define women by appearance or relationships and men by activities or positions than vice versa. This tendency is reflected in countless examples throughout the media.

Experiencing the Media

News coverage of female politicians and athletes often focuses on their physical appearance, whereas stories about their male counterparts typically stress their accomplishments instead of their hair, dress, weight, or physical appeal.[31] The language used in these media stories thus reflects societal judgments of what is important for each sex. In part, this is seen in the more frequent placement of stories about women newsmakers in the leisure or lifestyle pages of newspapers rather than on the front pages.[32]

Unlike men, who tend to be defined by their activities, women tend to be defined by their appearance.

Similarly, when women are mentioned in news stories, explicit references to their marital status appear far more frequently than in articles about males. Also noteworthy is the depiction of female prime-time television characters first as wives and mothers, even when they have careers as physicians or lawyers. In large measure, the media persist in portraying women in stereotypical ways, defining them by their marital and familial status.

Experiencing Technology

The increasing popularity of computer-mediated communication is facilitating the development and cultivation of new kinds of online relationships based on the expression of mutual interests and areas of expertise. Internet users connect with others to express opinions, research areas of concern, argue, or swap notes on various subjects. By combining aspects of both mass and interpersonal communication, technology is providing us with a new communication environment, one in which we can now separate ourselves from others based on our needs and affiliate ourselves with others based on our mutual concerns; in other words, we are now able to join or "get together" with a select community of others in a virtual world.[33] When we interact in an online environment, we encode our identities as words on a screen: "The way we use these words, the stories (true and false) we tell about ourselves (or about the identity we want people to believe us to be) is what determines our identities in cyberspace. The aggregation of personae, interacting with each other, determines the nature of the collective culture."[34]

.≋ *Theory*

Is It Time to Reengineer Media Images?

The stereotyping of any group by the media may lead to increased sexism and racial and ethnic prejudice.*

1. Identify a list of specific words or phrases used in media offerings that you currently find particularly degrading to you or the members of a specific group.

2. In your opinion, should we hold the media more accountable? What steps, if any, can we take to ensure that the media alleviate the gulf between the stereotypes they present us with and reality? For example, if the images they gave us and the words they used were reengineered in an effort to deliberately eradicate stereotypical portrayals, how do you imagine that would affect our day-to-day interactions? In what ways might such a reengineering contribute to the elimination of barriers among whites, people of color, and various groups like gays, the elderly, and the disabled?

3. How would less conventional mediated images and words enhance your ability to make more fair value judgments regarding society's individual members? How do we know that old stereotypes won't merely be replaced with new ones?

*See Louis A. Day, *Ethics in Media Communication,* Belmont, CA: Wadsworth Publishing Co., 1991.

The word *community* has special meaning online. Members of an online community speak a special language, the online equivalent of jargon. They also share the use of truncated speech and acronyms for phrases such as IMHO (in my humble opinion), BTW (by the way), and FAQ (frequently asked questions). Members of various online communities participate in ongoing conversations; at least initially, these online interactants are most concerned with what members of their community think, not with what they look like. Users are also encouraged to adhere to other Net conventions, including that a new posting should be linked by attribution and subject heading to the posting for which it is a response. Thus, postings are linked to others and in this manner dialogues are interlocked, relationships are forged.

As in face-to-face communications, individuals from virtual communities are cautioned about using language that is inflammatory, insulting, imprecise, or sexist. Consider, for example, the following admonition: "We would like to remind the frequent posters here that what we say is going out to a potential readership of between 25,000 and 40,000 individuals. . . . So words do have meaning and what you write in haste or in anger may have more influence than you realize."[35] Language use violations may cause members to lose interest or refrain from participating; as such, it can precipitate the destruction of the virtual community itself. Thus, "netiquette" attempts to ensure that even as we transcend our own experiences and realities, language use on the Internet in many ways mirrors language use in society.

The language of expedience is not just limited to Internet use; it has spread to cell phones. Mobile text messaging also uses shorthand expressions such as RUOK (Are you okay?), CUL8R (see you later), TAH (take a hint), and BIL (Boss is listening). Are you a text-messaging user? When and where do you text-message others? Some text-messaging aficionados text-message others when at the movies, at a sporting event, or on public transportation. People appear to long for private conversations even when they are in public places surrounded by others.

Gaining Communication Competence

It can be dangerous to take language for granted. With this in mind, what can you do to show that you are taking it seriously?

Work Your Way Carefully and Sensitively through the World of Words

Recognize that people may use words differently than you do. When this happens, do not assume that they are wrong. Rather, keep in mind that their experiences may have led them to develop different points of view or different ways of thinking about something or someone. When the meanings you and others have diverge, question the sources of their meanings in an effort to develop greater understanding between yourselves. When you are sensitive to the person and the context, you increase your chances of "talking the same language."

Keep in mind that the meaning of a word can change from one time period to another and from one culture to another. Until Steve Jobs created Apple Computer, when people heard the word *apple* they probably imagined the fruit. When someone refers to an apple today, the fruit is probably not the first thing that comes to mind. When Ford attempted to sell its car, the Pinto, in Brazil, it failed miserably. Could the failure have been due to the fact that in Brazilian slang, the word *pinto* means "tiny male genitals"? Along these same lines, the Dr. Pepper company no longer runs its well-known "I'm a Pepper" ad in the U.K. In British slang, *pepper* means "prostitute." We all use symbols, just not necessarily in the same way.

Share Your Meanings and Your Words

Words can confuse or clarify, conceal or reveal meaning. Not everyone thinks the same way or uses the same words to mean the same thing. When you take the time to share your perception of the "to me" nature of language with another, you let him or her know that you are aware that he or she may not be processing experience the same way you are. That person then also becomes more willing to share his or her "to me" perceptions with you.

You share "to me" meanings by eliminating the accusatory "you" from your vocabulary. By using the word *I* in place of *you*, you effectively describe your own feelings and thoughts instead of berating others for theirs. This simple strategy also allows you to take ownership of your words.

If the parties who are interacting share their "to me" meanings, this behavior will also actualize the communication strategy of dual perspective talking. Once you acknowledge that everyone has a "to me" meaning and that we all own our own feelings and thoughts, you take responsibility for yourself while you allow others to take responsibility for themselves. We don't need to give up our "to me" perspective to respect and understand the perspectives of others. Using "I" or "to me" language decreases the defensiveness of others, opens the door to dialogue, and empowers the self.

Respect Uniqueness

No two people, events, or things are exactly alike. Dog 1 is not dog 2. Student 1 is not student 2. Political rally 1 is not political rally 2. When we talk in generalities, our words can trip us up and lead us to stereotype. Identifying differences enables us to demonstrate our respect for uniqueness.

Whenever we make a blanket judgment about anything such as, "Lawyers are liars" or "Guidance counselors are teachers who just want out of the classroom," we are thinking in generalities and ignoring differences. Because expecting a behavior can help to precipitate the behavior, we must consciously avoid forming fixed mental pictures of anyone or any group. When we form a fixed mental picture, we fail to notice the unique characteristics that distinguish one person or group from another.

What steps can we take to ensure we look beyond the category? Indexing the generalizations we make can prevent us from using language to conceal important distinctions between people or things. When we index observations, we acknowledge individual differences within a group. Group member 1 is different from group member 2, who is different from group member 3, and so on. An action as simple as this can help us avoid the problems that stereotyping encourages.

Look for Growth

People change. Situations change. We and the world are in the process of becoming. Your authors are not the same people we were fifteen years ago; our children, Matthew and Lindsay, are not the same people they were last year. Just as people are not fixed in time, neither are ideas.

Take the opportunity to allow your words to reflect this growth. Demonstrating such flexibility will facilitate more effective interpersonal communication. Language may be an imperfect tool, but we have to be able to work with it if we are to make and sustain our person-to-person contacts.

Thus, keep in mind that when we make general and/or static evaluations of people and events, we deny the reality of change. Static evaluations limit interpersonal effectiveness because they prevent us from acknowledging the changes that occur in people and situations. For example, when predatory fish are kept for long periods in tanks with a glass partition that prevents them from eating other fish that in a natural environment would be their food source, they learn that their attempts to eat the fish bring them "pain" and frustration. Then, even when the partition is removed, the predatory fish no longer pose a danger to the other fish because their pattern of behavior has been set. They do not grow or change. They retain their original evaluation of the situation, imprisoning themselves where they have been rather than where they could be.

Check yourself periodically to see if you're holding onto any static evaluations about people or situations that are no longer valid. Dating your observations will remind you that nearly everything—even language—changes with time.

Wrap-Up

Meet again in pairs or with your discussion group. Turn back to the case study at the beginning of the chapter and reconsider the questions that followed it. How have your answers changed or become more focused? Based on what you know about language, what advice would you give the case study characters at this point?

Critical Thinking Contacts

Examine the following cartoon. Use your understanding of language to explain why the attitudes of the two characters differ and what each can do to facilitate understanding of and being understood by the other.

Can We Talk?

Summary

Language is a symbol system used by a group of people to communicate. It facilitates social contact, the sharing of perceptions, and the negotiation of reality.

Ogden and Richards's triangle of meaning illustrates the relationship that exists among words, things, and thoughts. The triangle's broken line indicates that there is no direct connection between a symbol and its reference. It underscores the fact that the word is not the thing—that meaning exists in thoughts, not in words or things.

Sometimes—inadvertently or intentionally—we build word walls between ourselves and others. Word walls impede understanding and make it difficult for a transference of shared meaning to occur. Contributing to the creation of word walls are the predilection to confuse denotative (dictionary) and connotative (personal) meaning, our use of euphemisms to mask meaning, our propensity to bypass each other's meaning, and our tendency to display intensional rather than extensional orientation.

Language also helps to express and reinforce both gender and culture; as such, it exerts a powerful influence on the way we perceive each other and helps reveal our social reality. In addition, the language used in the media and in computer-mediated communication by men and women, as well as to describe men and women, can facilitate the persistence or eradication of stereotypes.

To use language more effectively, we need to ensure that the words we use are clear, appropriate, and as concrete as possible. We also need to work our way carefully and sensitively through the world of words, be committed to sharing meaning, respect the uniqueness of every individual with whom we interact, and seek opportunities for growth through words.

Terms to Talk About

language *(p. 142)*
symbols *(p. 143)*
triangle of meaning *(p. 143)*
word masks *(p. 145)*
word wall *(p. 145)*
denotative meaning *(p. 145)*
connotative meaning *(p. 145)*
euphemisms *(p. 147)*
bypassing *(p. 150)*
equivocal language *(p. 150)*

intensional orientation *(p. 152)*
extensional orientation *(p. 152)*
snarl words *(p. 156)*
purr words *(p. 156)*
Sapir–Whorf hypothesis *(p. 157)*
coculture *(p. 159)*
dominant culture *(p. 159)*
argot *(p. 159)*
spotlighting *(p. 160)*
gender-lects *(p. 161)*

Suggestions for Further Reading

Michael Agar, *Language Shock,* New York: Morrow, 1994. Discusses language as a part of culture.

Janet Beavin Baveals, Alex Black, Nocile Charil, and Jennifer Mullet, *Equivocal Communication,* Newbury Park, CA: Sage, 1990. Focuses on equivocal communication, its nature and consequences.

Derek Bickerton, *Language and Human Behavior,* Seattle, WA: University of Washington Press, 1996. Explores how language makes abstract thought possible.

S. I. Hayakawa and Alan R. Hayakawa, *Language in Thought and Action,* 5th ed., Orlando, FL: Harcourt Brace Jovanovich, 1990. A highly readable and comprehensive study of general semantic principles.

Steven Pinker, *The Language Instinct: How the Mind Creates Language,* New York: Morrow, 1994. An insightful examination of how language works, how we learn it, and how it changes.

Deborah Tannen, *Talking from 9 to 5,* New York: Morrow, 1994. Explores the causes of miscommunication between the sexes.

Nonverbal Communication

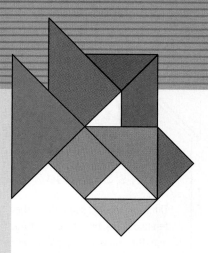

Beware of persons whose bellies do not move when they laugh.

— Chinese Proverb

After completing this chapter, you should be able to:

▌ Define nonverbal communication and explain its metacommunicative functions, and identify the characteristics nonverbal messages share.

▌ Discuss why an analysis of communication is incomplete without a consideration of nonverbal cues.

▌ Define and distinguish among the following kinds of nonverbal communication: kinesics, paralanguage, proxemics, haptics, and chronemics.

▌ Identify the key cues revealed by face, eyes, body alignment, and movement.

▌ Distinguish among emblems, illustrators, affect displays, regulators, and adaptors; describe the basic elements of paralanguage.

▌ Compare and contrast the nonverbal communication styles of men and women.

▌ Distinguish between contact and noncontact cultures.

daily contacts

Sam's Surprise

Things just didn't seem right when Sam entered the conference room, but he couldn't put his finger on the problem. The company president was sitting at the head of the mahogany conference table. The senior vice presidents were positioned on either side of the president, and several managers—including Sam's immediate supervisor—lined the table's sides.

As Sam approached the seat left for him, he couldn't help but feel uneasy. Sure, everyone was drinking coffee, smiling, and chatting as they spread their papers out before them. Yet something felt weird.

As he sat down, Sam realized that there were a number of cues contributing to his discomfort. The president had not looked up to acknowledge Sam when he had walked into the room and taken his seat. For that matter, neither did anyone else. The only person to nod a greeting to him was his immediate supervisor, and she appeared to have suddenly developed a facial tic. Maybe she hadn't acknowledged his presence after all. Sam felt like an outsider.

Then the president looked up—directly at Sam. Everyone else stopped chatting and looked his way.

The president called the meeting to order, explaining that there was but one major agenda item. That item was Sam.

Sam's heart sank. How could he have missed it? Had there been other nonverbal cues besides the lack of eye contact that he had overlooked? Was this going to be the end of his career? Here they were, he told himself, about to fire him, and he had had no clue that any problem existed before today.

With that the president reached under the table and brought out a bottle of champagne. Sam, he announced, was being promoted and would now be a senior vice president in charge of his entire division. Slowly, a smile appeared on Sam's face, and Sam rose to shake hands with all assembled, including his soon-to-be former supervisor.

Divide into pairs or discussion groups to consider the following questions:

1. Have there been times when you have felt just as uncomfortable as Sam did on entering a room but could not identify what caused you to feel that way?
2. What steps can we take to ensure that we do not misread nonverbal cues?

> What you are speaks so loudly that I cannot hear what you say.
>
> — *Ralph Waldo Emerson*

The twinkle in his eye. The edge in her voice. The knowing look of your smile. The rigidity of your posture. The confidence in his walk. Your hairstyle. Your dress. Where you sit. How closely you stand to another. Their eagerness to arrive early. Each of these cues contains clues regarding the attitudes, feelings, and personality of the person(s) exhibiting them. Despite such cues, often we are virtually unaware of the messages we send with our body, our voice, or the space around us when we interact with others. We simply act and react without considering how our actions modify, reinforce, or distort the messages we are communicating.

In this chapter we will focus on nonverbal communication, the cues people see and hear when they interact with each other. Thus, our focus is moving from *what* we say to *how* we say it, for words alone rarely, if ever, compel another to initiate, sustain, or terminate a relationship. By taking time to explore how we can use nonverbal cues to enhance interpersonal communication, you will develop a greater sensitivity to the contributions of nonverbal messages, and you take another step forward in expanding your ability to understand the meaning of person-to-person contacts.

Nonverbal Communication: A Definition

The meaning of interpersonal communication is found in more than just the words we use to express ourselves. As communicators, we are also the message. When we interact with someone else, it is not merely words that compose the messages we send and receive. Before, during, and after our interactions we use a kaleidoscope of channels that reveal our state of mind, expectations, and sense of self. The nonverbal cues we send add to or detract from the impact our words have. We might say that our entire being chatters incessantly during interpersonal contact, revealing to others what we really think about ourselves, them, and our relationships.

For example, how do you assess the honesty of those with whom you interact? How do you assess their feelings toward you? On what basis do you judge others to be sincere or insincere, trustworthy or untrustworthy? The meaning of each of these variables is carried predominantly through nonverbal messages, which often are emitted without the conscious control of the communicator.[1] For this reason, such messages are less likely than words are to be deceptive in their intent.

Nonverbal communication is that form of communication that doesn't include words. It is composed of messages that are expressed by nonlinguistic means. Indeed, *it is the actions or attributes of humans, including their use of objects or sounds, time and space, that have socially shared significance and stimulate meaning in others.* Nonverbal communication includes visual/kinesic cues such as facial expressions, gestures, and body orientation; vocal/paralinguistic cues such as volume, pitch rate, and inflection; proxemic cues such as space and distance; artifactual cues such as clothing and appearance; chronemic, or time, cues; and color. Although nonverbal cues may be sent deliberately or accidentally, they derive meaning based on another's interpretation of them. Consequently, they fulfill **metacommunicative functions,** meaning that they communicate about communication. In other words, when used with language, nonverbal cues help to clarify both the nature and the meaning of our verbal messages for receivers. In fact, researchers conclude that nonverbal cues carry approximately two-thirds of the communicative nature of a message. Even when used alone, as long as an observer is able to derive meaning from them, nonverbal messages speak volumes. Of course, the amount of information conveyed by nonverbal means varies according to how receptive and perceptive the receiver is and how clear or ambiguous the nonverbal signals provided by the source are. Thus, the setting, the use of objects and artifacts, space, touch, movements and gestures, voice, and time, in addition to one's appearance and demeanor, interact to convey meaning. As these cues are interpreted, others may decide to like or dislike us, listen to or reject our ideas, or sustain or terminate the relationship we share. Our ability to understand and respond to nonverbal messages can help us unlock the door to meaning.

Understanding Nonverbal Communication: Functions and Characteristics

To fully understand the meaning of verbal messages, we also need to understand the meaning of the nonverbal cues that accompany them. The meaning of many words can be changed by the wink of an eye, a certain facial expression, voice tone, bodily movement, use of space, or touch. As our ability to use nonverbal behaviors as contextual cues improves, so does the accuracy of our interpretation of meaning in interpersonal communication.

The Functions of Nonverbal Cues

1. The little boy who hides behind his mother as he says, "I'm not afraid of the dog."
2. The woman who says "I love you" to her husband while hugging him and smothering him with kisses.
3. The teacher who asks, "Any questions?" and fails to wait for a response before moving on to the next lesson.
4. The child whose eyes are downcast and shoulders are rounded as she says, "I'm sorry for breaking the vase."
5. The speaker who, when asked a question by an audience member, leans forward with a hand cupped behind one ear.

Each of these messages contains nonverbal clues that help reveal what an individual is feeling as words are uttered. Thus, as we see, nonverbal cues comprise an important part of the communication process. They may, as illustrated in the situations above:

1. contradict words,
2. emphasize or underscore words,
3. regulate the flow of communication,
4. complement words, or
5. substitute for or take the place of spoken words (see Table 6.1).

Whereas words are best at conveying thoughts or ideas, nonverbal cues are best at conveying information about relational matters such as liking, respect, and social control. To be sure, the meaning of neither verbal nor nonverbal messages should be interpreted without carefully considering the other. Let us review each of the preceding functions.

1. Nonverbal cues can *contradict* or *negate* verbal messages. When this happens, what is said and what is done are at odds. Imagine the man who repeatedly says, "Hold me," but backs away to avoid being held, or the salesperson who has just lost a deal, screaming, "I'm not angry!" Each of these verbal messages is negated by the nonverbal behavior of its source. Each interaction represents a **double message**—the words say one thing, the nonverbal cues another.

2. Nonverbal cues can *emphasize* or *underscore* a verbal message. For example, when you raise or lower your voice, or slow down your rate of speech so you can deliberately stress a series of words, you are using nonverbal cues to accentuate the meaning of your words.

TABLE 6.1
Functions of Nonverbal Communication

Function	Example
Contradicting	Your face is contorted into a grimace. Your eyes are narrowed and eyebrows furrowed. Yet, you are yelling, "I am not upset!" You are sending a mixed/double message.
Emphasizing	You wave your finger accusingly and raise your voice to demonstrate your anger as you say, "It is *your* fault, not *mine.*" Your behavior provides the italics.
Regulating	After explaining your stance on an issue, you raise and then lower your intonation as you say, "And that's why I feel the way I do." This together with your silence signal you are finished speaking and another person may comment. Your behavior influences the flow of verbal interaction.
Complementing	Your head is bowed and your body posture is slouched as your boss tells you how unhappy she is with your job performance. Your nonverbal cues provide clues to the relationship you and your boss share; they also help convey your attitude toward your boss.
Substituting	A friend sees you, and asks: "So, how do you like your new job?" You just roll your eyes, using nonverbal cues in place of words.

3. Nonverbal cues can *regulate* or *control* person-to-person interaction. We establish the rules of order or "turn-taking" during talk with nonverbal cues. With eye contact, gestures, and voice we control who should talk next and thus direct the flow of verbal interaction. The regulatory skills of others influence our judgments of them. For example, if we feel that talking to John is like talking to a wall or that when we talk to Joyce we can't get a word in edgewise, it may be because we do not get the turns or attention that we feel we deserve when we interact with John or Joyce.

4. Nonverbal cues can *reinforce* or *complement* a verbal message. In effect, they add redundancy to a message. When someone asks, "How are you?" and you reply "Great!" and smile and make an OK sign with your fingers, or when you wave and say "Hi," you are using nonverbal cues as reinforcing tools.

5. Nonverbal cues can *substitute for* or *replace* verbal messages. For example, when we don't know what to say to express our sorrow at the death of a relative or a friend, an embrace often suffices. Similarly, when someone asks, "What do you want to do tonight?" a shrug of the shoulders is frequently used in place of "I don't know." Often when actions substitute for words, the nonverbal cues function as symbols of the verbal messages because they are widely understood by others. The up and down nod is understood to mean "yes," just as forming a T with your hands during a sports event is understood to mean "time-out."

Characteristics of Nonverbal Communication

Nonverbal communication is an integral part of the total communication package. From a nonverbal perspective, each of us is a lighthouse of information continually sending messages from which others derive meaning.

All Nonverbal Behavior Has Message Value

While we can refrain from speaking—we can literally shut our mouths—it is impossible for us to refrain from behaving. Behavior, whether intentional or unintentional, is ongoing. Each of us continually emits a wealth of nonverbal information.

You cannot stop sending nonverbal messages. As long as someone is aware of your presence and is there to decode your nonverbal communication, it is impossible for you not to communicate. Even if you turn your back on the observer and remove yourself from his or her sight, you are communicating. With this in mind, if someone were to enter the space in which you are now reading, what messages would they derive from your nonverbal behavior? Are you seated at a desk or reclining on a bed? What does your face suggest regarding your level of interest and degree of understanding?

Nonverbal Communication Is Ambiguous

Although nonverbal cues are continuous and frequently involuntary, they may also be evaluated by others in different ways—that is, what we communicate may be ambiguous and subject to misinterpretation. One nonverbal cue can trigger a variety of meanings. For example, wearing blue jeans can be symbolic of a relaxed mode of dress typical of college students, or it can be construed as a statement of support for the gay community, as when gay organizations without warning surprise blue jeans wearers by posting signs that say, "Wear blue jeans if you advocate gay rights."

The nonverbal cues you emit may not mean to others what you think they do. There could be any number of reasons why an individual looks at his or her watch, coughs, or rubs his or her eyes. All nonverbal behavior must be interpreted within a specific context.

Nonverbal Communication Is Predominantly Relational in Nature

Frequently, it is easier for us to communicate our emotions and feelings nonverbally than with words. We convey liking, attraction, anger, and respect for authority through nonverbal messages. Nonverbal communication is our primary means of revealing those inner

in Context

It's Not What You Say . . . But What You Do When You Say It!

Behavioral slip-ups can betray those who commit them. For example, if an individual is attempting to communicate an aura of confidence, but his or her foot shakes uncontrollably, then chances are that the listeners will determine that the individual is anxious and uptight rather than confident and in control.

1. Cite an example of how a coworker's behavior contradicted what he or she was saying to you or to another person. Specifically, what behaviors exhibited by the person leaked his or her true feelings?

2. To what extent, if any, have you attempted to use nonverbal messages to conceal your actual feelings or intentions? Were you successful? Why or why not?

states that are not readily transmitted through words. Therefore, more accurate information can be derived from nonverbal than from verbal cues. For example, we typically look to the face to assess emotional state. We look to the eyes to evaluate both dominance and competence. We base our judgments of confidence and relationship closeness on our reading of gestures and posture, and we listen to the voice to help us evaluate both assertiveness and self-confidence.

Frequently we are unaware of our own nonverbal cues as senders. We inadvertently reveal information we would rather conceal from others. Without our intending it, our nonverbal messages let others know how we feel about ourselves and about them. As our awareness of our nonverbal communication increases, its informational value decreases. In effect, a conscious intention to manage the impression we convey to others means that we will do our best only to communicate messages that are in our own best interest.[2]

Nonverbal Behavior Provides Clues to Deception

When an individual says one thing but means another, we can use our **deception detection** skills to see that the behavior contradicts the words. Under most circumstances, when there is a discrepancy or inconsistency between verbal and nonverbal messages, researchers advise that

Why do you think it is sometimes easier to communicate our feelings and emotions nonverbally than with words?

you believe the nonverbal cues, which are more difficult to fake.[3] Deception clues or leakage can be detected in changes in facial or vocal expression, gestures, or slips of the tongue.[4] In fact, once strong emotions are aroused, these changes may occur automatically, and attempts to conceal feelings may well be betrayed by the words, voice, or body. Thus, by focusing on how emotion is communicated by speech, voice, body, and face, the astute communicator may be able to spot false emotional portrayals.

Researchers David Buller and Judee Burgoon have conducted an array of studies in which they ask subjects to deceive another person. For example, imagine you face the following situation:

> You and your best friend have agreed that you would see a new film together during winter break. Prior to your winter break, however, your significant other surprises you by taking you to see the movie you had agreed to see with your friend. What do you do when you return home from college and

your friend comes over and says, "We're going to be the last people to see that movie, but I didn't want to see it without you. Can we go tonight?" How do you respond?

According to Buller and Burgoon, formulators of **Interpersonal Deception Theory**,[5] if you decide not to tell the truth you could lie to your friend by telling him or her how excited you are to finally be able to go see the movie. You engage in *falsification* by creating fiction. Or you could say, "I changed my mind. Let's see something else. I heard that movie got bad reviews." You engage in *concealment* by keeping from your friend your real reason for not wanting to go to the film. Or you could engage in *equivocation* by changing the subject and dodging the issue of movie-going altogether. All three responses, however, involve deception on your part. Looking at things from your friend's point of view: do you think you could spot the deception if you were not the person lying but the person being lied to? Buller and Burgoon believe that human beings make poor lie detectors, that many liars strategically monitor and control their deceptive displays, that you have only a 60 percent chance of being able to identify when someone is lying to you, and that your ability to spot the deception depends on how suspicious you are.

In contrast to the preceding researchers, psychologist Paul Ekman believes that with training it is possible for all of us to become more skilled at detecting dissemblers. Ekman and his co-researcher, Wallace Friesen, have identified forty-three muscular movements that we are capable of making with our face. They have also identified more than 3,000 facial expressions that have meaning, compiling them into the Facial Action Coding System, or FACS, a virtual taxonomy of facial expressions. Ekman and Friesen have worked both for the C.I.A. and the F.B.I. to create experimental scenarios for studying deception that would not only facilitate the counterterrorism work of these organizations but also help their agents correctly identify untruths.[6]

Theatrical and media performances demonstrate that it is possible for skilled communicators to control the nonverbal cues they exhibit, thereby persuading audience members to suspend their disbelief and accept the facade. Yet most of us do not spend weeks, days, or hours consciously rehearsing for our daily interpersonal encounters. Nevertheless, when interacting with others we sometimes may wish to misrepresent our real feelings or intentions, perhaps by dressing differently, by lying, or by masking an actual facial expression so that we do not insult or embarrass another person. In general, persons are more successful at such deceptions if the others with whom they are interacting trust them than if the others suspect they are hiding something. The more a person plans and rehearses a deceptive message, the more confident the person is, and the less guilty the person feels about the deception itself, the less likely it is that others will suspect or uncover the person as a liar. Some people are more adept at deceiving people than others. For example, some occupations such as the law, the diplomatic corps, and sales require that professionals be able to act differently than they may actually feel.[7] This can pose problems for those of us trying to uncover deception in others.

If we are watchful, however, we can improve our ability to detect attempts at deception. Unskilled liars leak clues. It may be a change in facial expression, a shift in posture, a change in breathing, an unusually long pause, a slip of the

TABLE 6.2
Nonverbal Clues to Deception[*]

When telling a lie, you are more apt to:

Smile falsely, using fewer facial muscles than when exhibiting a genuine smile

Blink more frequently

Have dilated pupils

Rub your hands or arms together, scratch the side of your nose, or cover your mouth

Shift body posture frequently

Articulate and pronounce words more carefully

Speak more slowly and say less than you otherwise would

Exhibit speech that contains more errors and/or hesitation than is typical for you

Raise your pitch

Deliver a mixed message

Your lie is more apt to be discovered if you:[†]

Intentionally want to conceal your emotions

Feel intensely about keeping the information hidden

Feel guilty

Are unfulfilled by lying

Are unprepared and unrehearsed

[*]R. G. Riggio and H. S. Freeman, "Individual Differences and Cues to Deception," *Journal of Personality and Social Psychology,* 45, 1983, pp. 899–915.
[†]Paul Ekman and Mark G. Frank, "Lies That Fail," in Michael Lewis and Carolyn Saarni, eds., *Lying and Deception in Everyday Life,* New York: The Guilford Press, 1993, pp. 184–200.

tongue, a false smile, an ill-timed gesture, or other inappropriate nonverbal cue that gives them away.[8]

Types of Nonverbal Messages: Kinesics, Paralanguage, Proxemics, and Beyond

To improve your ability to interact effectively with others, it is necessary to explore a number of different cues, including *kinesics, paralinguistics, proxemics, haptics, clothing and artifacts, color,* and *chronemics.* Though for purposes of examination we will explore each category separately, the meanings stimulated by behavioral cues that fall within these categories do not occur in isolation; instead, they interact with each other, whether reinforcing or diminishing the impact of perceived cues (see Table 6.3).

TABLE 6.3
Types of Nonverbal Cues

Messages are sent by:	
Kinesics	*facial expressions, gestures, eye movement, posture, rate of walk*
Paralinguistics	*how words are spoken, variations in the voice*
Proxemics	*how space and distance are used*
Haptics	*different types of touching*
Clothing and artifacts	*appearance, style*
Color	*variations in clothing and environmental colors*
Chronemics	*using time to communicate*

 Theory

Are You a Deception Detector?

Can you distinguish a liar from a truth teller? A number of reality-type television programs such as *Meet My Folks* and its spin-off *Who Wants To Marry My Dad?* use polygraph or lie-detector tests to assess the honesty of prospective suitors and identify when a potential date or mate is lying to relatives or the show's subject. The popularity of programs like these demonstrates our fascination with the detection of deception. However, even experts acknowledge that polygraph machines may give false readings.

In your opinion, should the media be popularizing the use of technologically based truth-telling tactics, or should they be encouraging us to rely on other means, including the overall impression communicated by the nonverbal cues of individuals? According to researchers, the latter are the most important sources of information when individuals are called upon to make judgments about deception.

Think of the last time you interacted with someone who you thought was telling you the truth but who you now know was lying to you. How many of the following nonverbal clues to deception do you recall the person exhibiting during your interaction?

Pausing

Nonfluencies

Rapid speaking rate

Self-adaptors, such as touching the face and body

Object-adaptors, such as touching or playing with objects

Deficient eye contact

Averted gazes

Excessive blinking

Pupil dilation

Masked smiles

What was it about the person's behavior during the initial interaction that caused you to believe that he or she was being truthful?

With which theorists do you side: Buller and Burgoon or Ekman and Friesen? Why?

Kinesics: The Messages of Movement

Kinesics is the study of human body motion. It includes such variables as facial expression, gestures, eye movement, posture, and walking speed. Valuable communicator information is contained in the look on your face, whether you stare at or avert your gaze from another, whether your shoulders are straight or drooped, whether your lips are curved in a smile or a sneer, and whether your gait suggests eagerness or anxiety.

Face and Eye Talk

Picture yourself in the following situations:

> Your spouse had an operation. You are meeting with the doctor to discuss the prognosis. You search the doctor's face, looking for clues.

> You are returning home a day late from a business trip. Your spouse meets you at the door. As you approach, your eyes focus on your spouse's face.

Almost immediately, either of the above faces could cause us to cry, put us at ease, or terrorize us.

The Face. The face is the main channel we use to decipher the feelings of others. In many ways, faces talk. Chatter oozes out of their every movement. In fact, we would be wise to depend on messages derived from facial cues to facilitate person-to-person interaction.

According to nonverbal researchers, facial cues reveal:

1. whether parties to an interaction find it pleasant or unpleasant,
2. how interested an individual is in sustaining or terminating contact,
3. the degree of involvement,
4. whether responses during contact are spontaneous or controlled, and
5. the extent to which information is understood and shared.[9]

The face is also the prime communicator of emotion. Our ability to read the emotions depicted in facial expressions determines whether we will be able to respond effectively to others' feelings. How good are you at reading faces? Do your interpretations of facial expressions have a high or a low degree of accuracy? In general, the ability to read another's face increases with familiarity, an understanding of the communication context, and an awareness of behavioral norms. Research has determined that not everyone is adept at reading facial cues. Deficiency in interpreting the nonverbal messages sent by the faces of peers and teachers, for example, may be a factor contributing to unpopularity and poor grades in school. According to psychologist Stephen Norwicki, "Because they are unaware of the messages they are sending, or misinterpreting how other children are feeling, unpopular children may not even realize that they are initiating many of the negative reactions they receive from their peers."[10]

In addition, facial features are the most visible and reliable means of identifying a person.[11] Just as victims describe suspects' faces for police artists to draw and aggrieved parents describe the faces of their missing children, so do relatives, friends, and acquaintances describe your facial features to others when identifying

Are you aware of the facial cues you send? Are you able to accurately read the facial cues sent by others?

you. People use the face more frequently than any other bodily feature to distinguish one individual from another.

Besides identifying you, your facial appearance also influences judgments of your physical attractiveness.[12] In addition, it exerts an impact on whether others assess you to be dominant or submissive.[13] Thus we speak of a baby face, a face as cold as ice, a face as strong as a bull dog's, and so on. What words would you use to describe your face?

professional
contacts

More from Charles Osgood

A two-time Peabody Award winner, writer, speaker, and broadcast anchor, Charles Osgood offers us advice in this essay, "Read My Eyes, Not My Lips."

This is the age of "your lips tell me yes, yes, but there's no, no in your eyes."

Just think about it. You used to be able to tell what people were thinking by listening to what they say. Nowadays, for one reason or another, many people will tell you one thing when they are thinking exactly the opposite.

You ask the boss for a raise or a promotion, for example, giving him the full sales pitch about how long it's been and how much you've been contributing these days.

And what he tells you is that the home office has put a freeze on raises and promotions just now, but that as soon as the right opportunity presents itself, he'll do everything he can to see that you get what you've got coming.

While he is saying this, however, his face and tone of voice are saying:

"You know what I hate about this job? It's having to listen to whiners like you. Why don't you just go back and do your job and stop complaining. Go away and leave me alone!"

We are trained not to say unpleasant things to each other, so the words may come out sounding polite and civilized enough. But watch the face.

"I'd love to go out with you tonight, George," says Cybil, "but I have to wash my hair."

Meanwhile her face and tone of voice are saying: "Get out of my life, creep, I wouldn't go out with you if you were the last man on earth."

Three classic lines are:

"You're looking great!"

"It was swell running into you!"

"Let's have lunch!"

Meanwhile, the face and eyes are saying:

"God, she looks like death warmed over."

"Just my luck to run into this turkey when I'm running late."

"Let me out of here!"

It's almost as if one believed that someday a higher court would be reading a transcript of the conversation, in which all the words would be taken at face value, and the facial expressions and tone of voice completely removed.

"See, Your Honor? I did not tell the plaintiff to 'go stuff it.' All I told him to do was 'have a nice day.'"

It's not what you say, but the way that you say it.

If you are such an accomplished dissembler that you can think one thing and say another with your words and voice and facial expressions all at the same time, then I would say there is only one vocation for you—and I am not referring to the used-car or aluminium-siding business.

A person with your gifts and inclinations is ideally suited for the U.S. Congress.

Have you ever conversed with someone whose words and facial expressions contradicted each other? Which message channel did you believe?

SOURCE: "Read My Eyes, Not My Lips" from *The Osgood Files* by Charles Osgood, copyright © 1986, 1987, 1988, 1989, 1990, 1991 by Charles Osgood. Used by permission of G. P. Putnam's Sons, a division of Penguin Group (USA) Inc.

The Eyes. "Shifty eyes." "Goo-goo eyes." "The evil eye." "Eye to eye." Eye behaviors are a key part of interpersonal communication; by using our eyes we can establish, maintain, and terminate contacts.[14] As with all nonverbal cues, any eye behavior you exhibit may be interpreted in a variety of ways, but there are three central functions served by eye movements. Eyes

1. reveal the extent of interest and emotional involvement,

2. influence judgments of persuasiveness and perceptions of dominance or submissiveness, and

3. regulate person-to-person interaction.

The pupils of our eyes are a reliable indicator of emotion. When we take an interest in what someone is saying, our blinking rate decreases and our pupils dilate. On the other hand, when we are *not* interested in a subject, our pupils contract.[15] Our pupils also dilate when we experience a positive emotion and contract when we experience a negative one. They rarely — if ever — lie, because regulating the size of our pupils is a nonverbal cue beyond our conscious control.

In order for others to find us persuasive, we need to refrain from excessive blinking and maintain a steady gaze — that is, neither look down nor look away from the individuals we are trying to convince and not exhibit eye flutter. In many cultures, including Arab, Latin American, and Southern European,

To what extent does eye contact affect your interactions?

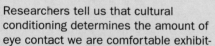

Context

Culture Cues

Researchers tell us that cultural conditioning determines the amount of eye contact we are comfortable exhibiting. This means that the frequency and duration of looking behavior varies across cultural groups.

For example, we know that Arabs, Latin Americans, and Southern Europeans typically tend to look directly into the faces of those with whom they are interacting, while Chinese, Japanese, Northern Europeans, and Pakistanis avoid focusing on the faces of those with whom they are conversing. In addition, African Americans tend to use more eye contact than whites when performing speaking roles, but less when functioning as receivers.[*]

1. Working in pairs or small groups, set up a role-play situation of a sales representative making a call on a potential customer. Assign class members to play the roles, alternating the various cultural heritages for each part. Follow the eye contact rules outlined above.

2. What conclusions can you draw about eye contact behavior for different cultures? How did you feel when you changed your usual eye contact rules? What problems would someone outside the dominant culture have adjusting to different eye contact? Keep in mind that a member of one cultural group will be less apt to establish personal credibility and/or develop an effective relationship with a member of another cultural group when nonverbal cues send messages that are likely to be misconstrued. Thus it is particularly important for members of one culture to avoid sending nonverbal messages that members of another culture will consider inappropriate.

[*]See Larry A. Samovar and Richard E. Porter, *Communication between Cultures*, 5th ed., Belmont, CA: Wadsworth, 2004, p. 195.

people judge those who look them in the eye as more honest and credible than those who do not. When individuals avoid meeting our eyes or avert their gaze from us, we often assume that they have something to hide, that they lack confidence, or that they are not knowledgeable on some matter.[16] Visual dominance correlates with increased eye contact, whereas frequently averted eyes lead to impressions of submissiveness. Humans, like apes, can "stare down" each other to establish dominance. Look away first, and you may well find that you have become the less powerful player in an interaction. However, when we are interacting with people from different cultures, we may, at times, draw the wrong conclusions by observing eye behavior.

Eye contact also indicates whether a communication channel is open or closed. It is much easier to avoid interacting with someone if we have not made eye contact with him or her. Eye contact makes interaction virtually an obligation.[17] Eye contact also increases when two people like each other.

Eye behaviors let us know when it is our turn to talk and when it is time to yield the floor. Our eyes communicate such messages more subtly than such verbal expressions as "Shut up! It's my turn to talk," or "What's your problem? Can't you let me finish a sentence without butting in?"[18]

The eyes provide another cue that we can use to enhance the establishment of behavior synchrony (behavioral mirroring) with another person in an effort to establish or advance a relationship; we establish behavioral synchrony by using nonverbal cues that are in sync with the other person's. According to Richard Bandler and John Grinder, a relationship exists between eye movements and thought or cognitive processing—including whether a person is primarily a visual, auditory, kinesthetic, or emotional processor. As a result of their research, Bandler and Grinder were able to identify eye movement patterns and their meanings for right-handed people (the reverse tends to be true for left-handed people) (see Figure 6.1.) Since these eye movements reflect a person's preferred sensory modality, you can use them to get on the same wavelength and promote interaction with that person.

A person's eye movements can also be used to determine how truthful the person is. If, for example, a person is describing an event that was experienced first hand, the person's eyes should move primarily to his or her left (if right-handed) suggesting memory access. If, however, the person looks up and to the right a lot, it may be that the person is constructing the experience, not recalling it.[19] The eyes, in addition to providing a mirror into the soul by revealing one's emotions to others, may also provide a window into how a person thinks.

Putting on a Face: Is What You See True or False?

"Put on a happy face!" instructs the well-known maxim. Have you ever done so when you didn't really feel happy inside? Could others tell? Why or why not?

When we use our facial movements to communicate our genuine inner feelings we exhibit **representational facial expressions.** Conversely, when we consciously control our face to communicate a message meant only for public consumption, we are, for all practical purposes, giving a performance; hence our facial expressions are termed **presentational.**[20] It is when we consciously control our facial expressions that we may end up participating in interpersonal deception.

FIGURE 6.1
Eye Movements and Cognitive Processing

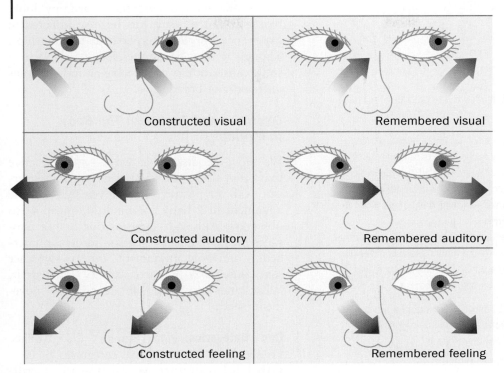

What techniques do individuals use when putting on a face? First, they may qualify their facial expression—that is, they add another expression that modifies the impact of the original expression. Second, they may modulate their facial expression. They simply change it to reflect feelings that are somewhat more or less intense than what they actually feel. Third, they may falsify directly. This requires either that they simulate an unfelt emotion, neutralize an emotion by showing none when they actually feel some emotion, or mask a felt emotion by displaying one that they don't actually feel.[21]

When we fake a face we usually leave an array of clues for astute observers to decipher. For example, our "facework" may lack spontaneity or be out of sync with our words or actions, or we may exhibit involuntary microfacial cues, in which an expression appears for only a fraction of a second. In effect, what begins as a smile ever so briefly is turned into a grimace and then is reengineered back into a smile. Researchers call these fleeting emotional changes, which last no more than one-eighth to one-fifth of a second, **microfacial or micromomentary expressions.** They assert that the expressions reveal true emotional states and typically occur when an individual is consciously or unconsciously attempting to disguise or conceal a feeling. Thus, a twitch of the mouth or eyebrow can suggest that the message being communicated is not the message actually being felt.

Sometimes the simple act of smiling actually evokes a positive mood change in the smiler. Still, the extent to which people demonstrate susceptibility to deliberately engineered facial expressions varies greatly.

Facecrime

Novelist George Orwell alluded to the practice of masking in his novel *1984:*

> It was terribly dangerous to let your thoughts wander when you were in any public place or within range of a telescreen. The smallest thing could give you away. A nervous tic, an unconscious look of anxiety, a habit of muttering to yourself—anything that carried with it the suggestion of abnormality, of having something to hide. In any case, to wear an improper expression on your face (to look incredulous when a victory was announced, for example), was itself a punishable offense. There was even a word for it in Newspeak: facecrime, it was called.*

1. When was the last time you committed a facecrime or observed someone else committing one? What factors led you or another to do it?

2. What was the outcome of the act?

*George Orwell, *Nineteen Eighty-Four,* New York: New American Library, 1983.

It is the total lack of an ability to smile, a condition called Moebius syndrome, that leaves one with a perpetually grumpy look, that makes it difficult for those so afflicted to experience normal interpersonal relationships. Though it may be unintended, the lack of a smile causes others to perceive an individual as unfriendly or bored.[22]

Gestures and Postures: The Body in Motion

We move in distinctive ways—so distinctive that often others can identify us by a characteristic walk or posture. The movements and the alignment of a body communicate meaning to observers. Although some of our body's messages facilitate effective person-to-person interaction and goal attainment, others—whether sent consciously or unconsciously—impede it. What kinds of cues do different bodily movements send?

Cue Categories. Paul Ekman and Wallace Friesen have identified five categories of nonverbal behavior that we can use to describe bodily cues: emblems, illustrators, regulators, affect displays, and adaptors.[23] Let us explore each in turn (see Table 6.4).

TABLE 6.4
Types of Bodily Cues

Cue category	Description	Examples
Emblems	Deliberate body movements that can translate into speech	Thumbs up, wave hello
Illustrators	Body cues that support or reinforce speech	Direction pointing
Regulators	Intentional cues to influence turn taking	Head nods, breaking eye contact
Affect displays	Unintentional movements of the body that reflect emotional states of being	Slumping body; relaxed, confident body
Adaptors	Unintentional movements that are frequently interpreted as signs of nervousness	Nose scratches, hair twirling

Emblems, such as a wave and a high-five sign, are consciously sent and easily understood.

Emblems. **Emblems** are movements of the body that are consciously sent and easily translated into speech, such as a wave that means "come here," a thumbs-up gesture that means "okay," and a wave that means "hello" or "good-bye." They are used most frequently when oral communication is undesirable or when noise or distance makes it less feasible. When many emblems are used regularly in the course of a day, as they are by traders on the floor of the stock exchange or in sports events by umpires and coaches, they then compose a gesture system.[24]

Illustrators. **Illustrators** are bodily cues designed to enhance receiver comprehension of speech by supporting or reinforcing it. Like emblems, illustrators are used consciously and deliberately by communicators. For example, when you give someone directions, you use illustrators to facilitate your task. When you want to stress the shortness of a member of a basketball team compared to the average height of team members, you would use your hands to emphasize the difference.

Regulators. **Regulators** are cues intentionally used by communicators to influence turn taking—who speaks, when, and for how long. For example, gazing at a speaker and head nods on your part usually encourage that person to continue speaking, while leaning forward in your seat, tensing your posture, and breaking eye contact traditionally signals that you'd like a turn. If we choose to ignore or remain unaware of someone else's use of regulators, we may find ourselves accused of rudeness or insensitivity. Thus your use or misuse of regulators reveals much about your social skills.[25]

in Context

Creating an Impression

Trial consulting is a growing industry. Many of the services trial consultants perform for lawyers involve communication. For example, consultants work with defendants and witnesses in an effort to ensure that the nonverbal behaviors they exhibit help them to create as favorable an impression on the jury as possible.

Likewise, career, college, and political consultants work with individuals like you to help you learn to present yourself in as favorable a light as possible when interviewing for a job, applying for admission to graduate school, or campaigning for public office.

1. Imagine you have been hired as a consultant to help yourself build a more successful image. What changes would you suggest regarding your own nonverbal behavior?

2. Is it ethical to employ consultants to train people to use nonverbal displays that don't come naturally just so they will be able to make a specific impression or achieve a desired goal? In other words, should we be training defendants to appear more credible, job applicants to appear more assertive, or politicians to appear more likable than they actually are? Why or why not? Whatever your feelings, it is important to recognize the importance nonverbal cues play in impression formation.

Affect displays. **Affect displays** are movements of the body that reflect emotional states of being. While the face, as noted, is the prime indicator of the kind of emotion being experienced, it is the body that reveals the emotion's intensity. Typically, we are less aware that we are exhibiting affect displays and thus often we do not intentionally mean to send many of the cues we send. People who "read" our bodies on the basis of its demeanor can judge how we genuinely feel.[26] For example, is the listener's body slumping and defeated, stiff and motionless, relaxed and confident, or proud and victorious? Those of us who characteristically show a lack of affect or feeling make it especially difficult for others to relate meaningfully to us.

Adaptors. Like affect displays, **adaptors** are often sent unintentionally and thus reveal information involuntarily about an individual's psychological state. Adaptors include movements such as nose scratches, hand over lips, chin stroking, and hair twirling. These are frequently interpreted either by those with whom we are interacting or by those observing us as signs of nervousness, tension, or lack of self-assurance. By habitually using various adaptors, we also try to meet our own physical or emotional needs.

The Body's Messages

Based on observations of our physical behavior, receivers form impressions of us and may judge us to be more or less likable, assertive, or powerful.[27] Observing nonverbal behavior can help us to answer a number of the following questions.

Do Individuals Like or Dislike Each Other?
People who like each other tend to exhibit open postures and more direct body orientation, and stand more closely together than those who do not. Their bodies are also relatively relaxed, and their gestures

are uninhibited and natural. In general, cues like these stimulate person-to-person contact. In contrast, if interactants do not like each other, their bodies emit very different cues. Instead of facing each other directly, they exhibit body orientations that are both incongruent and indirect. They avoid sustained eye contact, and exhibit a high degree of bodily tension and rigidity. It is more difficult to like someone who is closed off or all wrapped up in him- or herself.

Are Individuals Assertive or Nonassertive? The nonverbal behavior of an assertive communicator is more relaxed and expansive than that characteristically displayed by someone who is nonassertive. Typically, nonassertive communicators adopt a rigid posture, exhibit an array of nervous gestures, avoid sustained eye contact, and hunch their shoulders in a protective or closed stance. Their assertive counterparts, in contrast, exhibit comfortable eye contact and employ illustrators in place of confidence-deflating adaptors that announce their vulnerability to others.

Are Individuals Powerful or Powerless? Communicators who exhibit an erect but relaxed posture, gesture dynamically, feel free to stare at others, and interject their own thoughts even if it means interrupting others are likely to be perceived as powerful. In contrast, visible bodily tension, downward gazes, and closed postures contribute to perceptions of powerlessness.

Thus, whether or not we want to approach or avoid another communicator, assess him or her to be confident or anxious, powerful or powerless, is often determined by the bodily cues he or she communicates. Our bodies talk constantly about how we feel about ourselves and others. Even when we attempt to "stonewall" another in an effort to cut off communication between us, our body talks as we strive to realize our objective.

Paralinguistics: The Messages of the Voice

The messages that you send with your voice are known as **paralanguage.** Often it is not *what* you say but your paralanguage, or *how* you say it, that determines the outcome of an interaction. In effect, we use vocal cues to determine the *real* meaning of the words spoken to us. Such cues are especially important to our deciding whether or not another person is being sarcastic when interacting with us. The words, "Yeah, right" convey different meanings depending on whether they are spoken sincerely or sarcastically, and our interpretation of these words will influence how we respond to the person who speaks them. Your voice can help you convey your thoughts, or it can convey thoughts you mean to conceal. It can reinforce the words you speak or negate them. The sound of your voice communicates, revealing to others your emotional state, attitudes, personality, status, and interaction maintenance, or turn-taking needs. How you speak influences how those with whom you interact interpret your intentions, as well as how credible, intelligent, or attractive they judge you to be.[28] With this in mind, respond to the following questions:

> Does my voice enhance or detract from the impression I make?
> Does my voice support or contradict my intended meaning?
> If I were interacting with me, would I want to listen to the sound
>   of my voice?

Vocal Cues

Among the elements of paralanguage are pitch, volume, rate, articulation and pronunciation, hesitations, and silence. Each plays a part in the impression others form of you.

Pitch. Pitch is the highness or lowness of the voice; it is similar to pitch on a musical scale. We tend to associate higher pitches with female voices and lower pitches with male voices. We also develop vocal stereotypes. We associate low-pitched voices with strength, sexiness, and maturity, and high-pitched voices with helplessness, tension, and nervousness. Although we each have a modal or habitual pitch—one that is used the most frequently when we speak—we also vary our pitch to reflect our mood and generate interaction. For example, we often lower our pitch when sad and raise it when excited. In contrast, if we are bored, we may use a monotone to reflect our lack of interest in conversing. Whereas a lively animated pitch encourages interaction, a monotone discourages it.

It is the voice's pitch that others use to determine whether you are making a statement or answering a question or whether you are expressing concern or conviction. Your pitch expresses your emotional state; for example, it can communicate anger or annoyance, patience or tolerance.

Volume. The power of your voice, its loudness or **volume**, also affects perceptions of intended meaning. While some whisper their way through encounters, others blast through them. People who are typically loud may alienate others and often are viewed as overbearing or aggressive; in contrast, the behavior of soft-spoken individuals is often interpreted as a sign of timidity. Thus, your volume level can over- or underwhelm others, thereby causing others to turn you off in an effort to turn you down or to lose interest in your words simply because they are unable to comfortably hear them.

Effective communicators regulate volume in an effort to promote meaningful interaction. The volume you use should reflect the nature of your message, the size and acoustics of the space in which you are conversing, your proximity to your receivers, and any competing noise or conversations. Typically, we increase the volume to stress particular words and ideas and to reflect the intensity of our emotions. Similarly, sudden decreases in volume add suspense or sustain receiver attention. Volume is most effective when it is varied.

Rate. Your **rate** of speaking is the third vocal cue affecting the communication of meaning. Most of us speak at an average rate of 150 words per minute. When we speed up our speech, exceeding 275 to 300 words per minute, it is difficult for others to comprehend us, and our message thus becomes virtually unintelligible. In contrast, if we speak too slowly, others often perceive us as tentative or lacking in confidence or intelligence. An overly deliberate speaking pace contributes to receiver boredom, lack of attentiveness, and unresponsiveness. Rate also affects receiver judgments of speaker intensity and mood. As a speaker's rate increases, so do our assessments of his or her level of emotional intensity.[29] When discussing more serious subjects, communicators often slow down; on the other hand, the speaking rate usually accelerates as conversation shifts to lighter topics. In many ways, your rate

Practice

Ummmmmm . . .

Read the following excerpt from an article in the *Los Angeles Times*.

> To "er" is human. You may think you are articulate. You may see yourself as socially graceful. Even so, forget about trying to rid the "ums" from your patter.
>
> Everyone uses several hundred filled pauses—"um," "er," and "like" are prime examples—every day and sometimes as many as 900 an hour, said Nicholas Christenfeld, who at 29 is the youngest member of the psychology department at the University of California at San Diego.
>
> He studies the um phenomenon, which also includes "eh," "well," and "you know." These filled pauses signal a time-out while the speaker grapples for the next word or thought, he said.
>
> It is the verbal equivalent of "bouncing a tennis ball before you serve," Christenfeld said.
>
> Based on analysis of speech patterns around the world, the pauses are universal, said Christenfeld, who claims he is a man of few ums.
>
> But he is still trying to figure out what he calls the fundamental question: why people utter um, especially because most believe it makes them sound fuzzy-headed.
>
> "Why do people say 'um' instead of sitting quietly—given that people don't admire people who um?"
>
> Christenfeld believes such utterances signal the individual's desire to speak—though words may elude the tongue. It is also a sign the speaker is weighing his verbal options and ideas.

1. Count the number of "ums" you utter during a specific one-hour period. Try not to become too self-conscious while you're counting.

2. Begin counting "ums" and related nonfluencies uttered by others around you. How many do you estimate each person makes per minute?

3. How does "uming" affect your perceptions of the credibility and likeability of the person with whom you are interacting?

---

reflects the pulse of the words you speak. It quickens to communicate agitation, excitement, and happiness, and it falls to convey seriousness, serenity, or sadness.

Articulation and Pronunciation. The sound attributes of articulation and pronunciation affect the intelligibility of your message, as well as others' perceptions of your credibility. **Articulation** is the way you pronounce individual sounds. Ideally, even during person-to-person contact, you speak the sounds of speech sharply and distinctly. When you fail to utter a final sound (a final *t* or *d*, for example), fail to produce the sounds of words properly, or voice a sound in an unclear, imprecise way (*come wimme* versus *come with me*, *dem* versus *them*, *idear* versus *idea*), perceptions of your credibility drop.

While the focus of articulation is on the production of speech sounds, the focus of **pronunciation** is on whether the words themselves are said correctly. When you mispronounce a word, you may suffer a loss of credibility, and those with whom you are conversing may find it more difficult to make sense of your remarks.

Nonfluencies and Silence. Nonfluencies and silence are the final paralinguistic variables to be considered here. Knowing when to pause during speech is a critical skill. When nervous or tense, we exhibit a tendency to fill all pauses, often by inserting meaningless sounds or phrases such as *uh, you know,* or *okay* in the

What's the difference between "hmmm" and "ummm"? How does each influence interaction?

voids. These **nonfluencies,** or hesitation phenomena, disrupt the natural speech flow and adversely affect others' perceptions of our competence and confidence.

Besides slowing the rate of speech and emphasizing key ideas, brief periods of **silence** or pauses also give us a chance to gather our thoughts. This is not to suggest that the message of the pause is a purely positive one. Sustained pauses— significantly extended periods of silence—allow us to give another person the "silent treatment," a means by which we ignore someone's presence, saying to him or her without using words, "As far as I am concerned, you do not exist." We also become silent during moments of extreme anxiety or annoyance.[30]

Proxemics: The Messages of Space and Distance

Our use of space and distance also reveals how we feel about ourselves and others. Like kinesics and paralinguistics, space and distance communicate.

In general, we use physical proximity and distance to communicate either our desire or our disdain for contact.[31] The closer we stand to someone else, the greater the chances are that we like each other. Proximity or lack of it also signals our dominance or submissiveness in a relationship. The more dominant we feel, the more likely we are to move closer to another; in contrast, the more submissive we feel, the less apt we are to decrease the interaction distance that exists between ourselves and another. Perceptions of friendliness or unfriendliness and extroversion or introversion, as well as our privacy and social contact needs, are also revealed by how we relate to others spatially.

Our proxemic behavior has message value. As we study the ways we use space to communicate, we need to keep in mind that a gap may exist between the messages we intend to communicate through our use of space and distance and the messages actually received by others.

The father of proxemic research, Edward T. Hall, coined the term **proxemics** to indicate that "proximity" influences human interaction. The word itself refers to how we use the space around us as we communicate with each other (personal space), as well as how we structure the space around us in our homes, offices, and communities (territory).[32]

Spatial Relationships: Near or Far

Hall identified four distances that distinguish the kind of interaction we are involved in and the relationship we share during it. Hall's research was based only on white Americans.

Intimate distance	*Contact to 18 inches*
Personal distance	*18 inches to 4 feet*
Social-consultative distance	*4 to 12 feet*
Public distance	*12 feet to the limit of sight*

Intimate distance ranges from skin contact to 18 inches from the other person. At this distance physical touching is normal. While we usually share such a distance (or lack of distance) with those we trust and with whom we share an emotional bond, it is also the distance used for physical combat and sexual harassment. Have you, for example, ever had someone physically close to you whom you wished would just "back off"? At times—in crowded spaces like elevators, buses, or theater lobbies—we have to put up with intimate distance between ourselves and strangers—people we would not ordinarily stand so near.

Personal distance, which ranges from 18 inches to 4 feet, is less proximate or personal than intimate distance. At this distance, while we can still hold or shake the hand of another, we are most likely merely to converse informally. This is the distance used at receptions or when talking between classes or during coffee breaks. If we unilaterally close the gap between personal distance and intimate distance, we may make the person with whom we are interacting feel uncomfortable. On the other hand, if we widen the distance gap between us, we may make him or her feel rejected.

Social distance extends from 4 feet to 12 feet. At this distance we are less apt to talk about personal matters, more able to keep people at arm's length, and thus more likely to conduct business or discuss issues that are neither private nor of a personal nature. Many of our discussions during meals, conferences, or meetings are held within the social distance range. Often we use objects such as desks or tables to maintain an appropriate degree of distance. Usually, the more distance we keep between us, the more formal our interaction becomes.

Public distance (12 feet and beyond) is the distance we use to remove ourselves physically from interaction, to communicate with strangers, or to address large groups. Public distance is much less likely to involve interpersonal communication. Other peoples maintain the same four categories, but the distances vary from culture to culture. For example, Latin Americans use the smallest conversational space, European Americans use more space than Latin Americans do, and African Americans use even more impersonal space than European Americans do.[33]

In addition, as common sense tells us, our cultural and family background will also influence our use of space and personal body boundaries. Unlike the U.S., where land tends to be plentiful and family size averages three or four, in countries where land is scarce and families larger, people live in tighter spaces, spaces that by our standards might be small or confining.

What happens when we violate distance norms? Researchers tell us that the outcomes of such violations can be positive. For example, if the approaching person—who closes the distance—is perceived as attractive or a high-reward source, our evaluation of him or her may become more favorable, especially if the distance violation is accompanied by other behaviors, such as compliments.[34] More frequently, however, we feel uncomfortable or violated when our personal space is invaded.

An understanding of proxemics presents us with opportunities to improve our relationships. By becoming aware of the messages communicated by space, we attune ourself to the nature of acceptable and unacceptable proxemic behavior. Although a number of studies suggest that spatial "invasions" may, under some conditions, achieve positive results, let us not be too quick to discount the spatial violations that have led to lawsuits or violence.

Places and Their Spaces: The Meaning of the Environment

Nonverbal communication researchers identify three key types of environmental space: fixed feature, semi-fixed feature, and informal.[35] Each affects our communication in different ways.

Fixed feature space refers to the permanent characteristics of an environment, including walls, doors, built-in cabinets, windows, in-ground pools, roads, or paths, that functionalize it and determine how we will use it. For example, window

The design of a room can promote or inhibit interaction.

placement often determines the front of a classroom, swimming pools provide opportunities for increased interaction, and aisles in shopping malls and stores route customers in an effort to promote sales.

Semi-fixed feature space uses movable objects such as furniture, plants, temporary walls, and paintings to identify boundaries and either promote or inhibit person-to-person interaction. For instance, desks can reduce contact, while chairs facing each other can increase it. Compare the amount of interaction that occurs in a physician's waiting room, where chairs line a wall, with the amount of interaction that occurs in restaurants, where chairs are positioned to encourage conversation. Compare the room that says "use me" and succeeds in bringing people together with the one that says "look at me" and succeeds in keeping them out.

Informal or **non-fixed feature space** is the space we carry around with us. It is invisible, highly mobile, and enlarged or contracted at will as we try to keep individuals at a distance or bring them closer. The amount of personal space we claim, the size of our personal bubble, changes as we move from situation to situation, contact to contact.

Territoriality: Yours and Mine

Related to our use of informal space is another proxemic variable—**territoriality**. Each of us lays claim or identifies as our own spatial areas that we then seek to protect or defend from intrusion by others. We devise various means to accomplish this, some more formal than others: nameplates, fences, stone walls, assigned chairs, or signs that say things such as "My Room." While it may not be logical to claim certain areas of an environment, it is typical. Think of the number of times that you wouldn't let someone take a specific seat, saying, "That's my chair," or "Don't sit there—that's my dad's seat."

Problems can develop when people invade territory we have identified as ours. Sometimes we fight over spaces, or we get angry when someone uses space we think is ours without our permission. To restore our comfort and prevent others from continuing to occupy our space, we may chastise people who, without our authorization, put their things on our desk or in our room.

In professional settings, the territory claimed is a reflection of status. For example, CEOs and company presidents are accorded more favorable and larger spaces than those allotted to managers. Traditionally, the former also are able to employ more markers, such as outer offices with secretaries, to keep others out. While higher-status people can enter the spaces of lower-status people unannounced, the opposite is rarely true.

Touch: Haptics

In the discussion on proxemics, we noted that intimate space extends from the point of touch to 18 inches. Touch, or **haptics,** is usually involved in our closest contacts. While it is always involved in sexual communication, it also plays a role in helping us develop closer contacts with others and is a key ingredient in the establishment and maintenance of many of our personal relationships.[36]

Hugging is a lot like waltzing. Somebody has to take the lead.

— *Russell Baker*

It is touching that usually signals our desire for closeness. Though we may have been told on numerous occasions as children not to touch, and we are all familiar with various touching no-nos, the fact is that touch is an important tool in interpersonal communication, and the messages it communicates, as we shall see, are varied.

The amount of touching we do or find acceptable is, at least in part, culturally conditioned. As with proxemic behavior, our touching behavior is governed by a set of norms. When these norms are violated, we usually experience discomfort. Although some cultures promote only limited touching, others promote more frequent touch. Communicators belonging to a given culture generally conform to its established norms. In the United States, for example, it is more acceptable for women to touch each other than it is for men.[37] In general, women are more accessible to touch than men. Touch also correlates positively with openness, comfort with relationships, and the ability to express feelings.[38]

We use touch for different purposes: to communicate attitude or affect, to encourage affiliation, and to exert control or power.[39] When we want to demonstrate our affection or concern for others, we often touch them. In many ways, touch serves a therapeutic function that begins early in our lives. Infants wither emotionally and physically when not touched and thrive when picked up and held. Our entrance into this world and our exit from it typically involve touch. Unfortunately, although touch is the most effective means of demonstrating affect or support, as we get older we are often touched less. It is touch that helps us maintain both our physiological and psychological well-being and thus plays a part in our health.

Touch also helps us exert status or power in our relationships. Nancy Henley notes that people of higher status usually initiate touch. Thus, a boss is more apt to pat a worker on the shoulder than vice versa.[40] When you are the one to initiate touch, you are also usually the one who controls or directs the interaction. The toucher is perceived to have more power and to be more assertive than the person who is touched. Thus, the touching act itself implies power. Sometimes, however, rather than communicate liking or concern, touch communicates dislike, dominance, aggression, or abuse; shoves, pokes, and slaps fall into this category.

> You cannot shake hands with a clenched fist.
>
> — *Golda Meir*

The amount of touch individuals engage in consensually is also an indicator of how much they like each other. Touch is part of relationship development and is used as a guide to gauge the amount of intimacy desired. We touch those we like and try not to be touched by those we dislike.

Touch is also used to mark greetings and leave-takings. Even a handshake can be social and polite, or friendly and warm. Clearly, touch has message value.

Clothing and Artifacts: The Control of Personal Appearance

What kinds of clothing or jewelry do you like to wear? What do your appearance, hairstyle, and mode of dress suggest to others about who you are? Are your choices of clothing or bodily adornments appropriate? To what extent do your choices meet or disappoint the expectations of those with whom you interact?[41]

We react to people based on their clothing. In the early stages of a relationship, clothing and appearance affect first impressions and exert influences that lead to the acceptance or rejection of others. In addition, judgments regarding our success, character, power, and competence are made based on the type of clothing and jewelry we wear.[42] Typically, we respond more positively to those we perceive to be well dressed than we do to those whose attire we find questionable or unacceptable. We are also more likely to respond to requests from or follow the lead of well-dressed individuals, including people in uniform, than we are to listen to or emulate those whose dress suggests lower status or lack of authority.[43]

> It is impossible to wear clothes without transmitting social signals.
>
> — *Desmond Morris*

Color: Meanings and Associations

The colors we surround ourselves with and the colors we wear affect us both physically and emotionally. Color talks both to us and about us.

Color theorist Max Luscher observes that when subjects are exposed to pure red for extended periods of time, the nervous system is excited, and blood pressure, respiration rate, and heart rate rise. In contrast, when similarly exposed to dark blue, a calming effect occurs, and blood pressure, respiration, and heart rate fall.[44] Color can also compel us to move more quickly or slowly, help us relax, or cause us to become agitated. People who regularly wear red tend to be more active, outgoing, and impatient than people who avoid wearing it.

Fast-food chains, product marketers, department stores, and law enforcement officials use our predictable reactions to various colors as behavioral conditioners. For example, because the color green encourages oral interaction, it is common practice for investigators to question suspects in a green room or in a room lit with a green light. Similarly, color influences purchasing decisions. The colors of detergent boxes are designed to create positive perceptions about products in the minds of consumers. The chart on color personalities indicates how marketers use color to target consumers (see Table 6.5).[45] To which group do you belong?

Colors do not have the same meanings in all cultures. For example, while persons in the U.S. and European countries routinely wear white at weddings, white

TABLE 6.5
Color Matters

First, look at the following color palette.* Then, rank the colors shown according to the color you prefer most (your favorite) to the color you prefer least.

Once you have completed ranking the colors, consider the following color preference descriptions. To what extent, if any, do you think they accurately describe you?

Gray	the color of neutrality	communicates noninvolvement, concealment, or lack of commitment
Blue	the color of calmness	communicates contentment, being at peace
Green	the color of growth	communicates persistence, high self-esteem, constancy
Red	the color of energy	communicates intensity, conquest, fullness of living
Yellow	the color of happiness	communicates lack of inhibition, a desire for change
Violet	the color of enchantment	communicates a longing for wish fulfillment, a desire to charm others
Brown	the color of security	communicates a need for physical ease and contentment, for release from discomfort
Black	the color of nothingness	communicates surrender, renunciation

*Based on Max Luscher, *The Luscher Color Test,* ed. Translated and edited by Ian Scott, New York: Random House, 1969.

could be an inappropriate color for a wedding in China and Japan because in those and other Asian countries it is the color of mourning. Even in India, should a bride wear white, the color is usually relieved by at least a touch of another color. While blue in Ghana signifies joy, in Iran it has negative connotations. And while the color yellow in the U.S. suggests caution or cowardice, in China it represents wealth, as does red, a color which Korean Buddhists use when writing a person's name upon their death. What meanings do different colors have for you?

Chronemics: The Communicative Value of Time

Chronemics is the study of how we use time to communicate. Some of us are preoccupied with time, while others regularly waste it. Some of us are typically early, while others are chronically late. Some of us travel through life with a sense of urgency, while others prefer to amble through it at a much more leisurely pace. Some of us function best in the morning (the early birds), while others perform best at night (the night owls).

Misunderstandings, miscalculations, or disagreements involving time can create communication and relationship problems. What is meant by the words "on time" or the concept of punctuality is one such factor. To be "on time" for a job interview may be interpreted differently from what it means to be "on time" for a cocktail party. The latter usually allows more flexibility than the former.

We also structure time in an effort to ensure that the tasks we need to perform are accomplished. How long we are willing to wait to meet with someone or for something to occur is also a reflection of our status and the value we place on what we are waiting for. Status affords us greater power to control both our own time and the time of others. The more status a person has, the longer others with less status will wait to see him or her.[46]

The way we use and think about time depends on our culture. In some cultures people live for today, but in others they are waiting for tomorrow. Thus even the meaning of the phrase "a long time" is influenced by how the members of a culture view time.

 Diversity and Culture Contacts

Cultural Patterns in Nonverbal Behavior

Throughout the world, people use nonverbal cues to facilitate self-expression. To a great extent, however, the culture of a people modifies their use of such cues. For example, individuals who belong to **contact cultures**, which promote interaction and encourage displays of warmth, closeness, and availability, tend to stand close to each other when conversing, seek maximum sensory experience, and touch each other frequently. In contrast, members of **noncontact cultures** discourage the use of such behaviors. Saudi Arabia, France, and Italy are countries with contact cultures; their members relish the intimacy of contact when conversing. In contrast, Scandinavia, Germany, England, Japan, and the

Researchers report that persons from high-contact cultures stand closer to each other than do persons from low-contact cultures. What social distance are you most comfortable with?

He who hesitates is lost.

— *Native American proverb*

Think three times before you act.

— *Chinese proverb*

United States are low- or lower-contact cultures whose members value privacy and maintain more distance from each other when interacting.[47]

Individuals who grow up in different cultures may display emotion or express intimacy in different ways. It is normal, for example, for members of Mediterranean cultures to display highly emotional reactions that are uninhibited and greatly exaggerated; it is common for them to express grief or happiness with open facial displays, magnified gestures, and vocal cues that support the feelings. On the other hand, neither the Chinese nor the Japanese readily reveal their feelings in public, preferring to display less emotion, maintain more self-control, and keep their feelings to themselves; for these reasons, they often remain expressionless.

Even when different cultures use the same nonverbal cues, their members may not give the cues the same meaning. In the United States, for example, a nod symbolizes agreement or consent, while in Japan it means only that a message was received.

Misunderstandings can occur when people fail to understand that persons around the world and from different cocultures use nonverbal cues in different ways because they adhere to different cultural rules. For example, persons from Latino cultures avoid making direct eye contact with another individual as a sign of respect or attentiveness, a cue that persons from the main culture may misinterpret as a sign of inattentiveness or disrespect. Like persons from Latino cultures, persons from Asian cultures also lower their eyes as a means of signaling respect. While African Americans are apt to use more continuous eye contact than European Americans when speaking, they tend to use less when listening.[48] They also prefer that authority figures avert their gaze.[49] When it comes to public displays of fervent emotion, however, members of African American groups are comfortable with such behavior, while members from the main culture may regard such displays as inappropriate because they violate the expectation they have for self-control and restraint.[50]

If we hope to interact effectively with people from different cultures, it is important that we make the effort to identify and understand the many ways culture shapes nonverbal communication. We need to acknowledge that one communication style is not intrinsically better than any other; it is that awareness that can help contribute to more successful multicultural exchanges.

Gender Contacts

Masculine and Feminine Styles in Nonverbal Behavior

Just as we learn language from others, we pick up the proper use of nonverbal cues while interacting with others. In fact, our nonverbal interaction style probably contributes to our gendered identity because the preferred styles of men and women tend to reflect a number of gendered patterns. Researcher Judith Hall suggests that "'male and female' are roles, each with its set of prescribed behaviors."[51] As a result, men and women commonly use nonverbal communication in ways that reflect societal expectations. For example, men are expected to exhibit assertive behaviors that demonstrate their power and authority; women, in contrast, are expected to exhibit more reactive and responsive behaviors. Thus, it should not surprise us that men talk more and interrupt women more frequently than vice versa.[52]

Men are also usually more dominant during interactions than women. **Visual dominance** is measured by comparing the percentage of time spent looking while speaking with the percentage of time spent looking while listening. When compared with women, men display higher levels of looking while speaking than women do, and lower levels than women when they are listening. Thus, the visual dominance ratio of men is usually higher than that of women, and again reflects the use of nonverbal cues to reinforce perceptions of social power.[53]

Men and women also differ in their use of space and touch. Men use space and touch to assert their dominance over women. As a result, men are much more likely to touch women than women are to touch men. Women are thus more apt to be the recipients of touching actions than they are to be the initiators of such actions. Men also claim more personal space than women usually do, and they more frequently walk in front of women rather than behind them. Thus, in general, males are the touchers, not the touchees, and the leaders rather than the followers. In general, when it comes to same-sex touch, it is considered more appropriate for women to touch other women than for men to touch other men. Men, it appears, have more of a concern with being perceived as homosexual than women do.[54]

There are nonverbal behaviors that women display more than men do. Women tend to smile more than men. Accustomed to using a smile as an interactional tool, women even smile when under stress.[55] In contrast, men, who are customarily taught to display less emotion than women, are likely to suppress their facial expressions, thereby conveying more a sense of reserve and self-control. Gender differences in such behaviors as smiling do not necessarily cross over to cocultures. Unlike their Caucasian counterparts, African American women do not tend to smile more than African American men. Feminine socialization functions differently in the African American community. Women also commonly display their feelings more overtly than men. In general, women are more expressive than men and exhibit higher levels of involvement when engaged in person-to-person interaction than men. Women also use nonverbal signals to draw others into conversation to a greater extent than men do. While women demonstrate an interest in affiliation, men are generally more interested in establishing the strength of their own ideas and agendas than they are in sharing the floor with others.[56] Women also are better interpreters of nonverbal messages than men are.

When it comes to the use of artifacts, use of color, and clothing, men and women tend to reflect the stereotyped characteristics attributed to the sexes. For

 Practice

It's in the Mail

Our increasing reliance on e-mail has led to the creation of combinations of keyboard characters that allow communicators to punctuate their messages with nonverbal nuances. Because they are not actually hearing the sounds of each other's voices, seeing each other's faces, or observing each other's physical demeanor, e-mail users have had to add new nonverbal communication to their messages. Called *emoticons,* these symbols function as a form of nonverbal shorthand. Following is a sample:

:-1)	*smiley with a mustache*
:D	*big smile*
;-	*wink*
:*	*kiss*
:**:	*returning kiss*
:-J	*tongue in cheek or joking*

()	*hug*
:-(	*sad*
:'(	*crying**

In addition, writing in all caps connotes yelling, B) means wearing shades, LOL stands for laughing out loud, :P indicates that you are sticking out your tongue, :X means my lips are sealed, and O:) indicates an angel.

1. Working in groups, collect as many emoticon samples as possible.

2. Identify how frequently these and other nonverbal conventions are used during on-line conversations.

3. Do you think emoticons are a valuable part of the e-mail message that would not otherwise be communicated?

*See Charles Bowen. *HomePC* (January 1995): 109.

example, artifacts women use such as jewelry, cosmetics, and objects for their hair help reinforce the image of a woman as a decorative object. Similarly, the clothing of males tends to be less colorful and more functional than women's clothing. Because male clothing is likely to promote utility, activity, and ease of movement, it does not limit movement or call the same kind of attention to the male's body that feminine attire is likely to elicit regarding the female's body. As a result, women are perceived to be more sexual than men.[57] According to Standpoint theory, it was women's subordinate societal status that compelled them to become better message-decoders so that they could accurately predict the behavior of the more dominant or powerful men.[58] On the other hand, as Carol Gilligan notes, since women are more concerned with relationship maintenance, it follows that they are likely to develop an enhanced sensitivity to nonverbal cues that facilitate and sustain the development of relationships.[59]

 ## Media and Technology Contacts

Nonverbal Messages Communicated by the Media and by Computer-Mediated Means

All too often, the media and technology help legitimize stereotypical nonverbal displays. The contents of various media contain a plethora of open sexual appeals, portrayals of women obsessed with men, and male-female interactions that portray the man as physically dominant and the female as subordinate. They also include numerous repetitions of the message that "thin is in."[60]

For example, in her video "Killing Us Softly," Jean Kilbourne explores how media representations help convey gender norms for dominance and subordination. Kilbourne argues that advertising, the primary storyteller in American culture, takes agency away from women. According to Kilbourne, by exploiting the social anxieties women have and espousing the American value that transformation is possible, advertisers encourage women to be excessively thin. At the same time, Kilbourne warns that the images advertisers use undermine how women see themselves while, at the same time, participating in the normalization of violence directed at them by men. In support of her position, she offers examples of how advertisements sexualize women, turn women into body parts, contain numerous instances of silenced women, depict women competing against one another, trivialize the power women have, appear to condone violence against women, and feature few older women. At the same time, Kilbourne observes that advertising's objectification and sexualization of men is also on the rise.

After repeated exposure to such media messages, men and women come to believe and ultimately emulate what they see and hear. Thus, females are primed to devote considerable energy to improving their appearance, preserving their youthfulness, and nurturing others, while males learn to display tougher, more aggressive take-charge cues, trying all the while to control their emotions.

Nonverbal power cues echo the male dominance/female subservience message. In advertisements, for example, men are typically portrayed superior to women, who are usually shown in various stages of undress. In the media, nonverbal behaviors portray women as vulnerable and men in control.[61]

in Theory

The Assumptions Behind Ads

Create a collage of advertisements that prominently feature women and/or men. For each ad, answer the following questions:

1. What product is the advertisement selling?

2. Who is the ad targeting?

3. What feeling is the ad trying to generate?

4. What is the promise of the ad?

5. How would you describe the appearance of women and/or men in the ad?

6. In your opinion, could a man or woman have been used to convey the ad's message in an ad that more prominently displays one sex or the other? Why or why not?

7. To what extent, if any, do you believe the ad reflects cultural expectations of women and/or men?

8. Does the ad portray a woman and/or a man from a subculture or foreign culture in a way that is different from the way a person from the primary culture might be portrayed?

9. Of the ads you have collected, which ad do you find most offensive?

10. What consequences, if any, do you believe the image of a woman and/or a man in the ad has for women and men in our culture?

11. Do you believe that advertising encourages women and men to live up to impossible ideals? If so, why? If not, why not?

The repetition of such myths can make us feel dissatisfied and inadequate. If we rely on the media as a reference point for what is and is not desirable in our relationships and interactions, we may find it difficult to be ourselves.

Even mediated vocal cues suggest that it is the male and not the female who is the authority. In up to 90 percent of all advertisements male voices are used in voice-overs—even when the product being sold is aimed at women.

Further complicating the situation is the continued growth of the use of computer-generated virtual reality simulations. In addition to allowing us to feel as if we were really interacting in different, but make-believe environments and even giving us the opportunity to change our gender, such simulations are also being used to enforce violent gender scenarios resulting in women being threatened and killed. Even when erotic rather than violent, the media offerings all too often reinforce the notion that men have physical control over women.[62]

Gaining Communication Competence

Harnessing the Power of Nonverbal Communication

If we are to enhance our abilities to interact with others and develop effective interpersonal relationships, we must try to be more aware of the nonverbal cues we and others send.

Pay Attention to Nonverbal Cues

We use nonverbal cues to express ourselves. By tuning into nonverbal messages, we can learn how individuals respond to us, each other, and the world around them. Nonverbal communication is "relationship language." It expresses how people feel about one another. Even though it may be a challenge to interpret how people really feel, if only because they may not want you to know, the key to understanding people is to observe them in action and listen to the sound of their voice as they interact with you. For example, when in your company, does another person lean towards you or pull away? Face you directly or indicate their desire to avoid interpersonal involvement by facing away from you? Do their facial expressions suggest they are happy you are around, interested in pursuing a relationship, fearful to approach you, or angry with you? Is their posture relaxed, indicating they feel comfortable, or tight, indicating that they may feel threatened by you or by the situation they find themselves in? What does their voice reveal? Do they speak in a friendly manner? Are they trying to use their voice to hide what they are really feeling? Similarly, what does their use of touch, space, and distance suggest about the relationship you share? What about their use of clothing, color, and time? As you observe others, you pick up and interpret nonverbal cues that reveal both attitudes and feelings.

When You Are Uncertain about the Meaning of a Nonverbal Cue, Ask

What a particular nonverbal cue signifies in one culture may not transfer to another culture. For example, psychologist Aaron Wolfgang reports:

> *I remember when I was doing some filming in a marketplace in Palermo, a group of men motioned to my crew with their arms extended, palms down and fingers moving back and forth. We thought it meant "go away." As we prepared to leave, one of the men came forward, smiled, and taking our arms invited us for some wine. We found out later that the gesture meant "come here."*[63]

To avoid misinterpretation, it is important to pay attention to differences in cultural background.

Even if you come from the same culture, it is important to remember that nonverbal cues can have multiple meanings. Since nonverbal cues can be ambiguous, you'll want to check your perception, perhaps by paraphrasing, to determine if you are correctly interpreting the nonverbal cues you observe. Accurately interpreting the meaning of nonverbal behavior is key in building meaningful relationships. By asking for verbal clarification of your observations, you increase the chances for mutual understanding.

Recognize the Communicative Value of Inconsistent Messages

When words and facial expressions, gestures, postures, or vocal cues contradict each other, rely more on the nonverbal information you are receiving than on the words. Even though the words may be precisely what we want or expect to hear, we must also heed unintended mixed or inconsistent messages to help us decide whether the person with whom we are conversing is incompetent, nervous, or a liar.

Match the Degree of Closeness Sought with the Nonverbal Behaviors You Exhibit

Nonverbal behavior should be compatible with the kind of relationship sought. Touch, for example, typically varies according to duration, location, and strength, depending on the kind of relationship we share with another person. Similarly, intimacy and distance also correlate with relationship type. Thus, your proximity to the other person and the amount of touching you use should be compatible with the kind of relationship you seek. The more intimate your relationship with another person is, the closer you will want to be to each other. The less intimate a relationship with another person is, the greater the distance you are likely to keep between you. Should we find ourselves in close proximity with someone with whom we are not emotionally close, we use nonverbal cues to compensate for the discomfort we may feel. For example, we may decrease eye contact with the other person, helping to psychologically increase the distance between us. Similarly, if we are separated from someone with whom we feel emotionally close, we can find ways to close the distance gap between us, perhaps by using increased eye contact, waving, or smiling. Among the other nonverbal cues we can use that reveal the closeness of a relationship is chronemics or time. Our closeness to and comfort with another person is often revealed by how much time we spend with them.

Monitor Your Nonverbal Cues and Those of the Person with Whom You Are Communicating

Nonverbal behaviors affect the credibility of all of us. Successful communicators learn to use nonverbal cues to enhance personal credibility, likability, and attractiveness, and to establish dominance. The appropriate use of nonverbal cues can create a more favorable impression and aid in the development of more effective relationships.

Monitoring your own nonverbal behavior is a critical component of interpersonal goal attainment. By engaging in self-reflection, you are better able to ascertain if you are using nonverbal cues to project the message you hope to send. For example, does your use of facial expressions and body movements foster relationships you want to pursue and the termination of relationships you want to end? Does your use of the environment invite or interfere with person-to-person interaction? What does your proximity to the other person and your use of touch suggest about the nature of your relationship? When you want to change the tenor of a relationship from one that is close to one that is more restrained, or vice versa, what nonverbal cues do you use? What effect did they have on your partner?

Recognize That We Vary in the Ability to Encode and Decode Nonverbal Messages

Some of us are better at regulating, expressing, and interpreting nonverbal behavior than others. There appears to be a positive correlation between our ability to enact nonverbal messages and our ability to receive and decipher them—skills that are also linked with a positive home environment,[64] as well as the ability to empathize (discussed in the chapter on listening). Those of us who are extroverted also have an advantage when it comes to picking up nonverbal cues because we tend to be more comfortable in making contact, participating in social encounters, and observing others.

Even more important, the more we hone our nonverbal abilities, the more likely it is that we will be perceived as socially adjusted, exert social influence, and have satisfying relationships.[65]

Wrap-Up

Meet again in pairs or with your discussion group. Turn back to the case study at the beginning of the chapter and reconsider the questions that followed it. How have your answers changed or become more focused? Based on what you have learned in this chapter, what advice would you give Sam now?

Critical Thinking Contacts

Examine the cartoon. It details one kind of nonverbal cue interactants need to understand if they are to be able to relate effectively to each other. Based on your knowledge of nonverbal communication, discuss other nonverbal cues that can influence the development of our relationships.

SALLY FORTH

Beyond Words

Reprinted with special permission of King Features Syndicate.

Summary

Nonverbal communication consists of the actions or attributes of human beings, including their use of objects, sounds, time, and space that have socially shared significance and stimulate meaning in others. Because it helps clarify the nature and meaning of verbal messages, nonverbal communication also fulfills metacommunicative functions.

Nonverbal cues can add to, negate, accent, regulate, or replace verbal messages. As such, they are an integral part of the total communication package. Though they may sometimes be ambiguous, all nonverbal cues have message value, are predominantly relational in nature, and can provide cues to deception. Among the main categories of nonverbal communication are kinesics, paralinguistics, proxemics, haptics, clothing and artifacts, color, and chronemics.

Men and women display different nonverbal communication styles that typically reflect societal expectations, which are reinforced by the media and technology. In addition, throughout the world, culture modifies and helps direct the use of nonverbal communication.

Terms to Talk About

nonverbal communication *(p. 173)*
metacommunicative functions *(p. 173)*
double message *(p. 174)*
deception detection *(p. 177)*
kinesics *(p. 181)*
representational facial expressions *(p. 184)*
presentational facial expressions *(p. 184)*
microfacial or micromomentary
    expressions *(p. 185)*
emblems *(p. 187)*
illustrators *(p. 187)*
regulators *(p. 187)*
affect displays *(p. 188)*
adaptors *(p. 188)*
paralanguage *(p. 189)*
pitch *(p. 190)*
volume *(p. 190)*
rate *(p. 190)*

articulation *(p. 191)*
pronunciation *(p. 191)*
nonfluencies *(p. 192)*
silence *(p. 192)*
proxemics *(p. 192)*
intimate distance *(p. 192)*
personal distance *(p. 193)*
social distance *(p. 193)*
public distance *(p. 193)*
fixed feature space *(p. 193)*
semi-fixed feature space *(p. 194)*
territoriality *(p. 194)*
haptics *(p. 194)*
informal feature space *(p. 194)*
chronemics *(p. 197)*
contact cultures *(p. 197)*
noncontact cultures *(p. 197)*
visual dominance *(p. 199)*

Suggestions for Further Reading

Robert E. Axtell, *Gestures: The Do's and Taboos of Body Language Around the World*, New York: Wiley, 1991. A practical guide to what gestures to use and avoid when interacting with members of various cultures.

Paul Ekman, *Emotions Revealed: Recognizing Faces and Feelings to Improve Communication and Emotional Life,* New York: Times Books, 2003. Offers insight into emotions and nonverbal cues that give them away.

Paul Ekman, *Telling Lies,* New York: Norton, 1992. An interesting overview of lying and deception detection.

Paul Ekman, *Telling Lies: Clues to Deceit in the Marketplace, Politics, and Marriage,* New York: W. W. Norton & Co., 2001. Delves into nonverbal cues that may reveal when a lie is being told.

Stanley E. Jones, *The Right Touch,* Cresskill, NY: Hampton Press, 1994. Insights and observations on the language of physical contact.

Mark L. Knapp and Judith A. Hall, *Nonverbal Communication in Human Interaction,* 3rd ed., Orlando, FL: Harcourt Brace Jovanovich, 1992. A comprehensive survey of nonverbal communication.

daily **contacts**

Talk, Talk, Talk

It would be one of those company parties—the kind where you stand around, don't really know anyone, and feel awkward and totally unconnected. Alberto knew he had to go. He told himself that he would just have to talk to people with whom he really wasn't interested in conversing and who really weren't interested in conversing with him. He just wasn't the chit-chatty type.

Alberto had tried to get out of attending the party. Perhaps, Alberto had reasoned, he could use the old "car trouble" excuse. But he dismissed the idea quickly because it was trite and seemed just too obvious. He had mentioned in passing to a coworker that he didn't feel well, but he knew that not going would only create more problems for him. So after a few hours, he'd said he felt better.

Alberto was trapped. He had to go. He had even gone so far as to briefly consider quitting his job to avoid having to put himself in these uncomfortable situations time and again. But that really wasn't feasible.

From the moment he arrived, Alberto felt out of place, just as he'd expected. No one approached him, and he approached no one. He longed to find a quiet little corner, sit down, and do his best to look introspective. He thought about talking to the catering staff so that he wouldn't stand out as unapproachable.

Suddenly, seemingly out of nowhere, a person Alberto had never spoken to before stood before him. But Alberto was dumbstruck. He had no idea what to say. He opened his mouth, hoping some interesting words would come out, but his nerves got the better of him. Alberto was a wreck. As he excused himself and hurried to leave the room, an even sicker feeling consumed him. Alberto realized that the person he had just turned his back on was the company's president and chairman of the board.

Divide into pairs or small groups and answer the following questions:

1. If you were Alberto's friend, what advice would you have given him about how to survive and thrive at a company party or similar function?
2. Have you ever been in a situation similar to the one Alberto found himself in? How did you handle it?

Who is the best conversationalist you know? the worst? What qualities distinguish one from the other?

Although making **small talk** or engaging in spontaneous conversation with others may come naturally to some of us, for others it may not be so easy. Yet it is talking to others that lays the foundation for most of our interpersonal relationships. Because most people enjoy being in the company of a good communicator, one of the most important skills you can master is learning to carry on an effective conversation. A good conversationalist is adept at approaching others, starting a conversation, listening, changing a topic to one of interest or importance to him or her, and gracefully terminating a conversation.

| *The Importance of Conversational Contact*

Conversation facilitates our making contact with others. As such, it plays a critical role in our lives. For example, some years ago, in an effort to reduce the likelihood that prison inmates would succeed in educating each other about how to commit

Theory

Do You Like to Talk?

Take a few moments to assess how you feel about striking up a conversation with another person. Using a scale of 1 to 5, where 1 represents an extremely negative response and 5 represents an extremely positive response, answer each question as honestly as possible.

1. How much do you enjoy yourself in situations that compel you to mingle and strike up conversations with people you don't know well or at all?

2. How much do you enjoy engaging in small talk?

3. Do you like spending a lot of time talking to others?

4. How comfortable are you around people who don't like to talk a lot?

5. How at ease are you sharing personal information with others?

6. What do your answers suggest regarding whether or not you are conversation apprehensive?

different crimes, prison reformers reduced the amount of conversation inmates were able to have with each other. The result was very interesting: "The prisoners spent much of their time tapping out coded messages on walls and pipes, devising means of passing information to one another, and working out other clever ways of communicating."[1] Another example that illustrates the extent to which individuals go to compensate for **conversation deprivation** is described by retired Navy Captain Gerald Coffee, who was one of hundreds of American pilots shot down over North Vietnam and held as a prisoner of war in a facility known as the "Hanoi Hilton" during the Vietnam War. In *Beyond Survival* Coffee describes an ingenious method prisoners used to communicate with each other within the prison walls. A five-by-five grid had been scratched into the wall of his small cell by the prisoner who had occupied it before Coffee. The grid displayed a system for using taps to represent the letters of the alphabet; letters were indicated by tapping their location down and then across. "Hi," for example, would be tapped as follows:

$$XX\ XXX \qquad XX\ XXXX$$
$$(2-3) \qquad\qquad (2-4)$$
$$H \qquad\qquad\qquad I$$

After learning this system, prisoners were able to maintain contact with each other by covertly tapping coded messages.[2]

	1	2	3	4	5
1	A	B	C	D	E
2	F	G	H	I	J
3	K	L	M	N	O
4	P	Q	R	S	T
5	U	V	W	Y	Z

Because of the grid, the prisoners were able to compensate for a lack of aural communication and thereby maintain their sense of connection to others.

To what lengths have you personally gone to maintain your ability to converse with another?

Practice

Tap It Out

1. Try using the "Hanoi Hilton" grid to tap out some simple words to a partner.

2. How important would this system be to you if this were the only means you had to carry on conversations?

What Is Conversation?

Conversation has been defined as a "relatively informal social interaction in which the roles of speaker and hearer are exchanged in a nonautomatic fashion under the collaborative management of all parties."[3] *Nonautomatic* means that during conversation there is no set time limit for each party to speak or listen; the participants determine this themselves during the course of their interaction. However, the fact that the exchange is described as nonautomatic does not mean that the conversations we hold are random or without rules. In fact, researcher Susan Shimanoff suggests that communication is indeed regulated by **conversational rules** that reveal which behaviors are preferred and prohibited in various social situations or conversational exchanges.[4] For instance, if someone says "Hello," how do you respond? Typically, with a "Hi," or a "Hello, how are you?" Rules, according to Shimanoff, guide much of person-to-person behavior. Reflect for a moment on the rules you use to guide you in answering the following questions: Do American fathers kiss their sons on the lips? When you are angry with your employer, how do you speak to him or her? We tend to rely on learned social and conversational rules to guide us as we interact with others.

in Context

The Elevator

What rules do you follow regarding conversing with others in an office building elevator?

1. Working in pairs, break the rules you usually follow and observe how your partner responds to the change.

2. Does he or she respond in kind, merely refrain from responding, or exhibit some other noteworthy behavior?

As we explore conversation we can also apply what we have learned about verbal and nonverbal messages directly to our daily interactions with others and our efforts at relationship building. After all, as relationship expert and researcher Steven Duck notes, "If you were to sit and list the things that you do with friends, one of the top items on the list would surely have to be 'talking.'"[5] By exploring the dynamics of conversational exchange, we can enhance our ability to engage in everyday talk wherever our conversations occur—whether on the playing field, at work, at home, during a date, or at a social gathering. While many of our conversations are primarily spontaneous, casual interactions with others and involve no preplanned agenda, others are more pragmatic and involve a specific goal on the part of at least one of the conversational parties. Which kinds of conversations do you engage in more?

Conversation: Games and Players

Some theorists suggest that conversation is a kind of game and that we can therefore apply the same rules we use when playing a game or a favorite sport to our conversational interactions.[6] Adopting this approach, Robert Nofsinger notes: "The idea is to apply what we know about ordinary, everyday games (chess, checkers, tic-tac-toe, card games, competitive sports, and so on) to the conduct of conversation."[7] When we use this analogy, we find people making moves, taking turns, and aiming to achieve some goal. We also find them deciding what to do (using tactics) and devising a game plan (employing strategies).

Some suggest that conversation is like a game. Do you agree? Reflect on the aspects that make them similar and/or different.

 Practice

Conversation Analysis

Watch and tape a brief segment of a film or television show focusing on interpersonal relationships in which two characters are shown conversing. For example, you might use an excerpt from a film such as *Capturing the Friedmans, Bend It Like Beckham, When Harry Met Sally,* and *The Breakfast Club,* or a cutting from a TV show such as *LA Law, Friends, The Simpsons,* or any soap opera. Be prepared to present your analysis of the conversation orally and/or in writing.

1. Describe the nature, purpose, and results of the conversation.

2. Describe how the communicators regulated their interaction with each other, including who appeared to be in control of interaction ebb and flow. Be sure to note how turn-taking was managed, who asked questions, who interrupted, and who shifted topics.

3. Discuss the extent to which the characters conversing appear to be involved in the conversation, identifying the cues you relied on to distinguish involved from uninvolved characters.

4. Evaluate the adaptability (flexibility) of participants, responsiveness (the extent to which

parties to the conversation appeared to know what to say, understood their role, and felt part of the interaction), perceptiveness (the extent to which parties to the conversation demonstrated an awareness of how others perceived them and responded to them), and attentiveness (the extent to which parties to the conversation listened carefully to the other party or was preoccupied with personal thoughts).

5. Decide if any party to the conversation displayed **conversational narcissism**—that is, exhibited cues suggesting that he or she was overly self-concerned—and how the presence or absence of this quality affected the outcome of the interaction.

6. Identify which conversational participant exhibited more empathy, that is, was able to show his or her conversational partner that emotions were shared and the situation was understood.

7. Evaluate whether the goals of the conversation were achieved and at what, if any, cost.[*]

[*]Robert E. Nofsinger, *Everyday Conversation*. Newbury Park, CA: Sage, 1991, p. 6

According to Nofsinger, it is talk that primarily produces the moves of conversations. When we talk, however, we don't simply *say* something, we also *do* something. The talk we use, for example, may direct others, invite others to approach us, signal our acceptance or rejection of another, or insult another. How we act and respond or subsequently conduct our conversations depends on our understanding or interpretation of conversational events.

While the rules of board games and sports games are codified and written down so that they may be easily enforced—and violators can be corrected or penalized when they break the rules—rules of everyday conversation do not usually appear in print. There are topics that we may consider taboo when we interact with some people but that we consider acceptable when we converse with others. We simply are able to change the rules we use to guide our conversations from day to day and minute to minute.

Conversational Structure

If we were to analyze conversations, we would find that most people adhere to a general **conversational structure** as they speak: the greeting, topic priming, the heart of the conversation, preliminary processing, and the closing (see Table 7.1).

TABLE 7.1
The Stages of a Conversation

The Greeting	*Ask a question*
	Or
	Tell something about yourself
	Or
	Deliver a compliment
	Or
	Make a cute/flippant statement
	Or
	Say something innocuous
	Or
	Issue a direct invitation
Topic Priming	*Provide feedforward by previewing the nature of and reason for the conversation*
	And
	Asking one or more open-ended questions
The Conversation's Heart	*Introduce and then discuss the conversation's focus or goal by exchanging comments*
Preliminary Processing	*Reflect back on the conversation in an effort to evaluate conversational progress*
The Closing	*Let the other person know the conversation is ending*
	Express appreciation
	Summarize topics discussed

The Greeting

Phatic communication is a message that opens up the communication channel, thereby enabling two people to begin interacting. By creating an opening for conversation, the greeting serves that function. The interpersonal greeting is our routine way of beginning or initiating conversation with someone, and we are usually able to adjust it based on our perception of a relationship with a specific person, our mood, or how we imagine the other person will respond to us. Our opening lines, however, cannot necessarily be scripted in advance. There are no lines that are guaranteed to establish a relationship. "Didn't I meet you in Istanbul?" and "Do you have an aspirin?" and "Bet I can make you laugh" have all been tried and worked some times but not others. Even our favorite line to use at a business function: "You look like someone I should know. My name is X" doesn't come complete with a guarantee.

Conversational analyst T. E. Murray identifies three different categories of conversational openers:

1. Questions ("How are you?"),
2. Advertisements ("My name is . . . "), and
3. Compliments ("I like your suit").[8]

Researcher Chris Kleinke also identifies three types of openers:

1. Cute/flippant ("Is that really your hair?"),
2. Innocuous ("What do you think of the band?"), and
3. Direct ("Since we're both eating alone, would you like to join me?").

While men and women both seem to prefer using opening lines that are either innocuous or direct, women particularly tend to dislike the use of cute and flippant openers by men.[9]

Whatever type of greeting we employ, we use it to let others know that we are accessible and would like to converse with them. Normally the person we greet will return our greeting in a similar way. When this doesn't happen—when the other person responds coolly or with caution to our greeting or conversational overture—we can usually tell that something is wrong, that he or she doesn't want to establish contact, that he or she is shy or fears establishing contact, and/or that we will have to work harder and be more creative if we hope for a more sustained conversation.

Topic Priming

We prime a conversation by keeping the communication channels between us open and by previewing for the other person what the topic or focus of our conversation will be. For example, we might say, "I need your input. What do you think of X?" or "I need to share some bad news with you," or "This isn't easy for me to say, and you may not like to hear it, but . . . ." Priming prepares the person we are conversing with for what is to follow.

Should we not have or be able to find a topic to discuss with another person, our conversation ends after the greeting. In general, we usually end up talking about one of three kinds of topics: ourselves, the other person, or a situation.[10] Often we test a particular topic not by merely making a statement, but by asking a question: "I liked what you said today at lunch. What do you think businesses should be doing to avoid having to downsize their operations?" or "I've been looking for a place to buy a new computer. Your computer skills are great. Do you have any suggestions?" or "I notice you're reading a book by John Naisbitt. What do you think of his work?" By asking **open-ended questions** (questions that allow the respondent free rein in answering) rather than **closed-ended questions** (questions that force the respondent to choose a specific response), we are better able to involve and interest another person in conversing with us.

Gregory Stock, author of *The Book of Questions*, notes that far too frequently we exchange small talk without being involved in the conversation we are having. To combat this dilemma, he suggests that we ask questions that are more "dangerous," that perhaps we've never been willing to ask before, but that might provoke more interesting reactions in others. The following are examples of such questions:

> *For a person you loved deeply, would you be willing to move to a distant country, knowing there would be little chance of seeing your friends or family again?*
>
> *Would you accept $1,000,000 to leave the country and never set foot in it again?*
>
> *What would constitute a "perfect" evening for you?*[11]

We err when we cut short or extend the priming stage beyond what is considered appropriate. If we get stuck in the priming stage, our conversational partner may begin to wonder if we really have anything to discuss, that is, if we have a purpose or focus or are totally disorganized. On the other hand, if we omit this stage and head straight for our goal, the other person may judge us as rude, insensitive, or interpersonally deficient.

The Heart of the Conversation

At the heart of our conversation, we find our conversation's focus or goal. Perhaps we want to converse with another person to share new information with him or her. Or perhaps we want to persuade him or her to act or think in a specific way. Maybe we want to offer the person our help—perhaps even just a friendly ear. Whatever our specific goal, in this part of our conversation we get to the heart of the matter— why we opened the conversation in the first place, and why we did our best to prepare him or her for what was to come next.

How good we are at getting to and explaining the heart of our conversation is directly related to **conversational maintenance** skills. (We will discuss conversational maintenance a little later in this chapter.) The substance of the conversation involves conversational partners exchanging speaker and listener roles.

Preliminary Processing

The preliminary processing step is the flip side of topic priming. Here, instead of preparing the person for what is to come, we process what has just occurred between us. We consider the effect that our conversation has had on each of us and, based on our assessment of the other person's response, we may decide to adjust or alter our message and strengthen or modify our content. During this stage we may also assess how much more we have learned about the other person in an effort to determine the extent to which our uncertainty about him or her has been reduced.

As we review the progress of our conversation, we may realize that while we may feel that we have accomplished our conversational purpose, our partner may not feel that way. Thus, we may need to take a step back instead of forward and complete our discussion.

The Closing

The closing is the reverse of the greeting. We now take our leave, say good-bye, signal that we are no longer accessible, and separate ourselves from the other person, sometimes for a short period and sometimes forever. How we take our leave often lets the other person know whether we intend to meet with him or her again. "Gee, it was good seeing you and hearing about your date with Joe, but I've got to go now, or I'll be late for my date" or "I really enjoyed hearing about your trip. When can I see you again?" or "I'm sorry to hear you haven't been feeling well. I'll call you tomorrow to see how you're doing," for example, all send very different messages than a mere good-bye.

Can you divide a conversation you've recently had into segments?

Mark Knapp and his colleagues note that a good closing to a successful conversation serves three functions:

1. It lets the other party know that the conversation is nearing an end and thus signals the impending inaccessibility of one party.

How we say goodbye offers clues about our intentions for a relationship's future.

2. It is supportive in tone and contains expressions of appreciation for the conversation and the desire to renew contact.

3. It summarizes the main topics discussed.[12]

Closings based on these three rules leave both parties feeling good about the possibilities for continued contact.

Sometimes we merge conversational stages—the processing and closing stages may be combined, for example—or we may mutually agree to skip a stage because the time we will have together is short. Thus, our five-stage model of conversation is just that—a model—a representation of how a conversation forms, builds, and concludes. Not all conversations we are party to will contain all five steps. However, if you listen and observe carefully, you should be able to identify at least some, if not all, of these stages during many of your conversations with others. You will probably realize that the conversations you find most fulfilling and least frustrating are those that develop sequentially according to the five-stage model.

Conversational Management

When a conversation flows smoothly and naturally, the roles of speaker and listener are constantly reversed. In other words, each participant engages in **conversational turn-taking**—the changing of the speaker or listener role during conversation as each takes a speaking turn, as they cooperate and engage in dialogue to fulfill the conversation's purpose.

Are you a good turn-taker? How do you know?

How does one get a turn to speak during a conversation? Is this something that can be determined ahead of time? Is it affected by perceptions of one's wealth or status? Do we stand in line to do it? How do we cooperate? What behaviors promote conversational dialogue?

Turn-Taking: Maintaining and Yielding the Floor

We regulate our conversations by using and responding to **turn-maintaining** and **turn-yielding signals**.

Turn-maintaining signals include both paralinguistic and kinesic cues. For example, we may vocalize pauses (*ummm, uhhh*) to indicate we have not yet completed a thought, inhale a breath to suggest we have more to say, exhibit a gesture

in Practice

Whose Turn Is It, Anyway?

Keep a log of all the significant conversations in which you are involved for one day. Every time you converse with someone, note the following:

1. With whom you spoke

2. How contact was initiated and terminated

3. The topic of your conversation

4. The cues you used to determine when it was your turn to talk

5. Your ratings of the extent to which the conversation satisfied both you and the other person, where 1 represents completely dissatisfied and 5 represents completely satisfied.

6. Your reasons for each rating.

Relationship Turns

Read the following excerpt from Lorraine Hansberry's *A Raisin in the Sun.*

MAMA: (*Still quietly*) Walter, what is the matter with you?

WALTER: Matter with? Ain't nothing the matter with *me!*

MAMA: Yes there is. Something eating you up like a crazy man. Something more than me not giving you this money. The past few years I been watching it happen to you. You get all nervous acting and kind of wild in the eyes — (*Walter jumps up impatiently at her words*) I said sit there now, I'm talking to you!

WALTER: Mama — I don't need no nagging at me today.

MAMA: Seem like you getting to a place where you always tied up in some kind of knot about something. But if anybody ask you 'bout it you just yell at 'em and bust out of the house and go out and drink somewheres. Walter Lee, people can't live with that. Ruth's a good, patient girl in her way — but you getting to be too much. Boy, don't make the mistake of driving that girl away from you.

WALTER: Why — what she do for me?

MAMA: She loves you.

WALTER: Mama — I'm going out. I want to go off somewhere and be by myself for a while.

MAMA: I'm sorry 'bout your liquor store, son. It wasn't the thing for us to do. That's what I want to tell you about —

WALTER: I got to go out, Mama —

MAMA: It's dangerous, son.

WALTER: What's dangerous?

MAMA: When a man goes outside his home to look for peace.

What do the turn-taking and turn-yielding behaviors of Mama and Walter tell us about the relationship between the characters?

SOURCE: From *A Raisin in the Sun* by Lorraine Hansberry, copyright © 1958 by Robert Nemiroff, as an unpublished work. Copyright © 1959, 1966, 1984 by Robert Nemiroff. Used by permission of Random House, Inc.

that suggests we are not yet finished, or avoid making direct eye contact with the listener until we are fully ready to surrender our speaking turn to him or her.

Turn-yielding signals let our fellow conversationalist know that we are prepared to exchange the role of speaker for the role of listener. For example, we may make direct eye contact with our partner, ask him or her a question that requires a response, nod in his or her direction, drop our pitch, or keep silent. When someone interrupts or overlaps what we consider to be our turn, we may become upset or agitated, fight to maintain our turn allocation, or reluctantly yield it prematurely.

Are you better at sending turn-maintaining or turn-yielding signals?

Turn-taking control does not rest with the speaker alone. Listeners can also exert regulatory controls over conversational turn-taking by emitting **turn-requesting** or **turn-denying** signals that let the speaker know whether the listener would like to switch roles. To signal his or her interest in having a turn, the listener might use a vocalized filler such as "umm" or "ah," merely open his or her mouth as if to interject a thought, lean forward and look directly at the speaker, or gesture for attention with his or her hand. Similarly, the listener could signal a reluctance to take over the speaker's role by avoiding eye contact with the speaker, shaking his or her head as if to indicate that he or she has nothing to add, engaging in some activity that is incompatible with a speaking role such as taking copious notes, closing one's eyes, coughing, or exhibiting a gesture that encourages the speaker not to yield the floor but to continue speaking instead. The use or absence of **backchannel signals** (verbalizations we use to tell another person that we are listening) also contributes to the continuing or ending of talk.

Which is harder for you to do: request a turn for yourself, or deny a turn to someone else? Why?

The Cooperation Principle

In order to have a good conversation, the parties to a conversation need to cooperate with each other. According to the cooperation principle, conversations are most satisfying when the comments made by conversational partners are consistent with the conversation's purpose. Based on this premise, researchers offer the following conversational maxims or truths: quality, quantity, relevancy, and manner.[13]

According to the quality maxim, persons engaged in conversation do not offer a comment if they know it to be false. The parties to a conversation should offer only information that they know is truthful. Information that is deceptive, deliberately misleading, or distorted has no place in conversation. Giving an opinion when you have no knowledge of the topic or are only speculating is inappropriate. Violating this maxim leads to distrust.

The quantity maxim tells us to provide as much information as is needed to communicate the meaning of our message and continue the conversation. That means neither talk too much nor too little. Avoid single word responses but say what is needed to deliver the message while allowing the other person to continue the conversation. Persons who fail to provide others with the information they need violate this maxim. Monopolizing the conversation and failing to give others their chance to engage in a normal conversational exchange undermines cooperation.

in Theory

It's My Turn

Think about the last time you missed a turn to speak either because you failed to exert your right to have one or because the other person failed to request your participation or input.

1. With whom do you find it a challenge to get a word in edgewise? What does he or she do that makes requesting a turn frustrating for you? Be specific.

2. What methods do you typically find yourself using in an effort to "get the floor" from someone else?

The relevancy maxim asks that we not go off on tangents or purposefully digress and switch subjects when the other party to the conversation still wants to actively discuss our initial topic. Interjecting irrelevant comments illustrates uncooperativeness. Effective conversationalists work instead to sustain conversational coherence[14] by relating their comments to previous remarks and by rarely interrupting to switch subjects. They prefer to ask relevant questions that others enjoy answering.

According to the manner maxim, diction should be appropriate to the receiver and the context of the interaction; that means using terms the receiver understands and providing the receiver with background information to clarify any confusion. Just because conversation is informal doesn't mean it should be disorganized. Adherence to this maxim requires organizing thoughts to facilitate the sharing of meaning.

These four maxims apply to conversations that occur between persons living in the U.S. Persons from other cultures may also adhere to other maxims such as the *maxim of face-saving,* which would require the parties to a conversation to not argue, contradict, embarrass, or correct each other. In addition, the *maxim of politeness* might also require that persons avoid self-praise or taking credit for an accomplishment, focusing the spotlight on the other person instead.[15] Although persons from Asian cultures are the primary adherents to the foregoing two maxims, all cultures value face-saving and politeness.[16] Being impolite or committing a face-threatening act (an FTA) would likely jeopardize any relationship.

While effective conversations are dialogic, some seem more like monologues.

The Dialogue Principle

When we converse with another person, we can exhibit a preference for **monologue** (we speak, the other person listens) or **dialogue** (we both speak and listen). Unlike dialogue, monologue involves little, if any, conversational ebb and flow, lacks interactivity, and expresses minimal concern for the thoughts and feelings of the other person. Instead, the monologist is self-centered, spends a lot of time talking about himself or herself, and exhibits an obsession with achieving personal conversational goals and objectives.

Effective communication, however, is dialogic and requires that communicators exhibit concern for each other and their relationship. The conversational parties display respect for each other, invite each other to participate actively in the conversation, display an accepting manner, request clarification of the other person's perspective, and empathize with one another by adopting an other-oriented perspective that makes the other person feel understood.

Repairing Conversational Damage

Every now and then we commit or are on the receiving end of a **conversational blunder**—a faux pas—during which something we or others find objectionable is said. When this occurs, a prime means of repairing the damage done by the blunder is to offer an excuse or a disclaimer that is designed to lessen the potential negative consequences of the remark.

What was the last conversational blunder that you committed? What did you do to repair the damage?

For instance, after insulting a friend or being overly critical of a peer, we might offer an excuse such as: "I'm really sorry. It's been a long day, and my exhaustion got the better of me" or "I don't know why I said that. Can you forgive me? I'm just stressed because of what's happening at work."

To avoid committing such blunders we need to continually remind ourselves that, as we converse with another, it is important that we engage in dual perspective taking. This requires that, while we not abandon our own feelings, we also make a concerted effort to take the other person's feelings into account as we interact with him or her. Our conversations help define the relationships we share.

Insensitivity is not the only cause of the conversational blunders we commit. At times, **prejudiced talk** may also damage our conversations. What is prejudiced talk? It includes the making of racist, sexist, or ageist comments in public.[17] Racist, sexist, or ageist talk is when one individual disparages an individual of another race, sex, or age group. Because it emphasizes differences rather than similarities, such talk functions to separate, distance, and enhance feelings of power for the user of the questionable language rather than unite, bring individuals from diverse groups closer together, or equalize the perceived power bases from which they operate. Because most of us try to present ourselves as unprejudiced when we interact with others, we are apt to preface our remarks with a disclaimer in which we claim not to be prejudiced. As noted earlier, however, once spoken aloud, a word cannot easily be taken back.

Diversity and Culture Contacts

Differences and Conversation

What has your culture taught you about the nature and value of conversation?

Culture and conversation are related. Our culture influences our beliefs about the nature and value of conversation. For example, conversation is more important to European Americans than it is to native-born Chinese or Chinese Americans. For that reason, European Americans are much more likely to initiate and engage in conversations with others than are the Chinese. Whereas European Americans view talk as a tool to gain social control, the Chinese view the absence of talk, or silence, as a control strategy.[18] From their collectivist perspective, talk is not a necessary ingredient for relationship development, while from the individualist perspective held by European Americans, it is.

The difference between high-context cultures such as Asia and Africa and low-context cultures such as the U.S. and most Western European countries is also reflected in the word choices of members. During their conversations, members of low-context cultures are more likely to utter words such as *absolutely, positively,* and *most definitely,* while members of high-context cultures are more likely to use fewer categorical words while employing more provisional language, such as *maybe, possibly,* or *probably.* Do your experiences confirm this observation?

The Japanese share the collectivist perception; in general, they tend to trust those who are silent more than those who talk a lot. The Japanese value social discretion; they believe that talking can be dangerous to a relationship because it may precipitate social disapproval that may unnecessarily contribute to the embarrassment of others.[19] Consequently, rather than face interpersonal consequences or express disagreement or anger with another person, the Japanese prefer to remain silent.

In contrast, people from Arab cultures tend to engage others in conversation much more directly and to use an abundance of overassertions or exaggerations when conversing with others. Often, for example, a simple "no" is construed by other Arabs to mean "yes," and thus the Arab must rely on verbal exaggeration to make or drive home a point.

Puerto Rico, a collectivist, high-context culture, shares a number of characteristics with Asian cultures. Like Asians, Puerto Ricans typically do their best to reduce the risk of any conversational confrontation, preferring to be imprecise and indirect when it comes to clarifying a message's meaning rather than explicit and direct. What is *not* said during a conversation with someone from Puerto Rico may be more significant than what is said.[20]

Feelings about turn-taking also vary among cultures. Because they value succinctness rather than verboseness, for example, people from Asian cultures tend to take short turns when interacting with others and try to distribute their turns evenly.[21] In contrast, North Americans tend to take longer turns, which they distribute unevenly, with the participant who initiated a topic characteristically attempting to monopolize the conversation. To the extent that we understand such differences, we enhance our chances of facilitating effective communication when conversing with people from diverse cultures.

Gender Contacts

Differences and Conversation

There are important differences in the way men and women view and define conversation. Many of these differences can be attributed to the value men place on instrumental behavior and their preference for engaging in organized activities or interacting in groups and the value women place on talk and their preference for engaging in one-on-one, person-to-person communication.[22] Underscoring this basic difference, linguist Deborah Tannen notes that for men, conversations "are negotiations in which people try to achieve and maintain the upper hand if they can, and protect themselves from others' attempts to put them down and push them around," whereas for women, conversations "are negotiations for closeness in which people try to seek and give confirmation and support, and to reach consensus. They [women] try to protect themselves from others' attempts to push them away."[23] As a result, women and men often misunderstand each others' intentions. Women wonder why men fail to have an interest in discussing the details of a situation, and men wonder why women want to waste their time talking about trivial matters.

Conversation is a collaborative effort. Everything that happens during conversation is the doing of the participants, including interrupting. For interruption to succeed, one speaker begins speaking before being yielded the floor, and another speaker must stop speaking as a result. Men and women also differ in the amount of interrupting they do during conversations with each other. Interrupting provides the interrupter with an opportunity to violate the turn-taking system, exercise his or her conversational power, and assume greater conversational control. At the

What has your gender taught you about the nature and value of conversation?

What percentage of your conversational time is spent being interrupted or interrupting others?

professional contacts

Interruptitis

In this excerpt from her book *Gender and Discourse,* Deborah Tannen focuses on a gender-based conversational perception.

A joke has it that a woman sues her husband for divorce. When the judge asks her why she wants a divorce, she explains that her husband has not spoken to her in two years. The judge then asks the husband, "Why haven't you spoken to your wife in two years?" He replies, "I didn't want to interrupt her."

This joke reflects the commonly held stereotype that women talk too much and interrupt men. On the other hand, one of the most widely cited findings to emerge from research on gender and language is that men interrupt women far more than women interrupt men. This finding is deeply satisfying insofar as it refutes the misogynistic stereotype and seems to account for the difficulty getting their voices heard that many women report having in interactions with men. At the same time, it reflects and bolsters common assumptions about the world: the belief that an interruption is a hostile act, with the interrupter an aggressor and the interrupted an innocent victim. Furthermore, it is founded on the premise that interruption is a means of social control, an exercise of power and dominance.*

1. To what extent do your experiences support or contradict these observations?
2. Explain your answers, using specific examples.

*Deborah Tannen, *Gender and Discourse,* New York: Oxford University Press, 1994, pp. 54–55.

same time, interruptions can also be construed not as a power play but as a sign of conversational or social comfort, where one party feels free to interrupt the other, and the interrupted party does not feel infringed on and does not resent the interruption.[24] When this occurs, there is a conversation duet or supportive or cooperative overlapping, which actually greases a conversation's wheels, encouraging and reinforcing the speaker, rather than an attempt at conversational domination, which can and often does bring conversation to a halt.[25]

Media and Technology Contacts

Media and Technology Talk

What messages do the media and technology present us with regarding the nature of talk?

Media Talk

The nature of conversation on radio and television talk shows has coarsened over the years. Now, instead of mirroring the "constructive buzz of the public square," too frequently they offer us "a noisy, messy melee."[26] On programs such as "Imus in the Morning," "O'Reilly Factor," and "Scarborough Country" hosts and guests commonly use insults, speech that degrades, and pronouncements that encourage defensiveness or even hostile reactions. On one talk show a guest referred to a

literary
contacts

Don't Finish My Thoughts

In this selection from *A Doll's House* by Henrik Ibsen, Torvald Helmer and his wife, Nora, whom he has always treated like a child, are engaged in a conversation.

NORA: (*Looking at her watch.*) It's not so late yet. Sit down, Torvald; you and I have much to say to each other. (*She sits at one side of the table.*)

HELMER: Nora—what does this mean? Your cold, set face—

NORA: Sit down. It will take some time. I have much to talk over with you. (*Helmer sits at the other side of the table.*)

HELMER: You alarm me, Nora. I don't understand you.

NORA: No, that is just it. You don't understand me; and I have never understood you—till tonight. No, don't interrupt. Only listen to what I say.—We must come to a final settlement, Torvald.

HELMER: How do you mean?

NORA: (*After a short silence.*) Does not one thing strike you as we sit here?

HELMER: What should strike me?

NORA: We have been married eight years. Does it not strike you that this is the first time we two, you

and I, man and wife, have talked together seriously?

HELMER: Seriously! What do you call seriously?

NORA: During eight whole years, and more—ever since the day we first met—we have never exchanged one serious word about serious things.

HELMER: Was I always to trouble you with the cares you could not help me to bear?

NORA: I am not talking of cares. I say that we have never yet set ourselves seriously to get to the bottom of anything.

HELMER: Why, my dearest Nora, what have you to do with serious things?

NORA: There we have it! You have never understood me—.

1. What does this excerpt reveal about Torvald and Nora's relationship?
2. Have you ever initiated a conversation similar to this one that signaled a turning point in a close relationship you shared?
3. Did the individual with whom you were conversing attempt to interrupt you? Did you attempt to interrupt him or her? How did each of you respond?

---

famous African American tennis star as an "animal," noting that it would be more appropriate for her to appear nude in *National Geographic* than in *Playboy.* The host responded by referring to the guest as a "moron."[27] Hosts and guests repeatedly verbally attack and chronically interrupt each other, exhibit little patience for alternative points of view, belittle each other, raise their voices so that they literally yell at and curse one another. Moreover, hosts cut off guests' answers with strategically placed commercial breaks. By providing too few examples of genuine, well-mannered, and well-informed conversation, the media provide us with a multitude of negative models of conversation for listeners and viewers to emulate when interacting with each other.

 Practice

Squawk Talk

Listen to or view a talk show. Count the number of times the show's host or guests attack, embarrass, or insult each other; raise their voices; interrupt each other; or otherwise display anger, frustration, or impatience with one another.

In your opinion, does poor conversational behavior make "good" radio or television? If yes, why? If no, how do you account for its popularity?

Of course, we also learn about the nature of conversation from media offerings other than talk shows.

.:: *Theory*

Viewer Values

Think about the ways your conversation or your expectations for conversation with a partner have been influenced by characters you've seen conversing in movies, sitcoms, television dramas, and talk shows.

1. Cite examples of conversation initiation, topic focusing, and termination that you have copied or used.

2. To what extent, if any, do you think we use these shows to learn how we are supposed to talk to each other and what we are supposed to talk about?

Certainly, although the media present us with myriad interaction styles and expose us to different kinds of greeting styles, dialect differences, and reactions people (if fictional) have to those differences, they also help perpetuate stereotypes about dialects. Today's media offerings reinforce in us the belief that individuals may be socially stigmatized by mainstream society because of how they sound and what they say when conversing with others. As a result, we are apt to believe that some dialects are more prestigious than others, and we may persist in forming opinions of others based on their speech. For example, in movies characters with Southern accents have been portrayed as less intelligent and were often the butt of others' jokes. Similarly, Italians were characterized as intimidating and aggressive in conversations with others.

In addition to reinforcing cultural stereotypes, the media reinforce gender stereotypes. Media and gender researcher Phyllis Japp asserts that rarely is the working woman's professionalism the focus of a show's plot line. Instead, the typical conversation subjects for working women are their relationships with men and the tension that is generated when an attempt is made to juggle work and a relationship. Consequently, instead of being shown conversing about professional issues, women characters are depicted sitting in their places of business talking about clothing, food, relationships with men, and problems with children. According to Japp, making such subjects the only focus of conversation serves to dichotomize or widen the gap between women and work.[28]

At the same time that we are introduced to negative images, however, we are also shown examples of how dialects can serve important prosocial functions within a community by promoting feelings of group solidarity, trustworthiness, and friendliness. The media also suggest how people are able to adjust the tone and tenor of their conversations based on the context in which they find themselves. We are shown portrayals of people conversing one way on the job and another way when interacting with friends.[29]

Technology Talk

On-line services and the Internet also affect who we are able to converse with, as well as the kinds of conversations we are able to have. People around the world now have virtually immediate access to anyone else who is on-line. While some people have resisted the lure of on-line interaction, others are succumbing and adding it to their communication repertoire. One recent convert put it this way: "I was made to feel out of it because I didn't have an e-mail address."[30] According to one Internet provider, "In the cyberspace age, those who have access will find themselves with more listeners and greater respect than those who try to communicate in other ways."[31] One user explained, "I don't get discrimination on the Internet."[32] Others echo the satisfaction that the ease of communication on the technological freeway affords: "It's a lot easier to communicate on-line," says a user. "We talk about life. We talk about anything and everything."[33] For some of us today, even the telephone is passé; we prefer computer chat to phone chat. According to educators, e-mail is helping shy students come out of their shells and facilitating interaction among students of different races, socio-economic levels, and capabilities.

Partly because we can remain anonymous when using it, the Internet gives us a chance to vent without fear of retribution. It also offers those who feel isolated the chance to simply log on and search for emotional support. In addition, while people engaged in face-to-face conversation may feel compelled to tell us only what they know we want to hear, people on-line are apt to be more blunt and tell it like it is.[34]

 in Theory

On-Line versus Off-Line

Think about how on-line interactions might translate into better off-line relationships.

Do you think that because the Internet is color blind and gender blind it will facilitate the development of face-to-face relationships that are also gender and color blind? Explain.

This does not mean that Internet chat rooms and e-mail always function as conversational boosters. To the contrary, some fear that as we come to rely on machines to a greater extent, we are actually putting ourselves in danger of losing our voices. Indeed, digital manipulation not only alters pictures, it also alters the human voice, even simulating it. However, in increasing numbers, people are finding it difficult to imagine person-to-person contact apart from electronic connections, especially such technology innovations as instant messaging via computer and text messaging (also known as SMS or Short Message Service) via cell phones.[35] For members of both generations X and Y, distance appears to help precipitate conversational intimacy. In addition, users report that with instant messaging and text messaging there are no "awkward voices, no quavering voices, no hint of embarrassment. . . ."[36] Both technologies are changing the way people communicate. Indeed, instant messaging adherents report that it is a great way to communicate when you want to converse with many people at once. And text messaging adherents believe this medium is of benefit when you are too busy to talk, or reluctant to make a call because doing so would be rude or impractical. More than one billion text messages are sent annually. Cyberspace is now in all our hands, not just at our desks. New technologies are expanding the way we think and interact.

Is it a benefit to be physically absent during an electronic or cellular conversation? Media critic James Katz believes that cell phones "hollow out people," and are responsible for what he calls the "ghosting of America." More and more, people walk down a street or sit in a café communicating with other people who are not physically present in the same space.[37]

Gaining Communication Competence

Developing a number of skills can facilitate your ability to participate in and manage conversations more effectively.

Improving Your Conversational Skills

Commit to Developing Metaconversational Abilities

Metacommunication is communication about communication. **Metaconversation** is conversation about conversation. Be willing to talk with your conversational partner about *how* you talk with each other. Share your insights about intentions, messages sent, perceived contradictions or inconsistencies, and impressions of each others' thoughts and feelings. It is important to be committed to developing a greater understanding of the factors that contribute to effective conversation.

Develop Awareness of Culture and Gender Differences

In practicing your skills, be aware of how culture and gender differences may influence both the conversational style and the reactions of conversants. What works in China may not work in the United States or in Arab countries. To facilitate interaction with people whose cultural background or gender differs from our own, we need to take steps to ensure that we are able to open ourselves to and respect the differences that exist, that we maintain a flexible rather than a rigid outlook, and that we are creative in finding ways to increase our understanding of each other through meaningful conversational exchanges. This means that we need to be unconditionally accepting of differences; we should not make others feel that they have to conform to our preferences for us to interact with them.

Strive to Improve Conversation Initiation, Management, and Termination Abilities

Every communicator shares responsibility for beginning, managing, and terminating conversations. This means that we are each responsible for performing speaking and listening functions, and we are each responsible for ensuring that we feel we have the opportunities needed to participate in a total communication package—that is, to share ideas and to process them.

To that end, we need to be able to monitor our own behavior in addition to monitoring the behavior of the person with whom we are conversing. We have to demonstrate our concern for others in addition to demonstrating our concern for ourselves. We need to practice active listening; be sensitive to expressions that signal turn-taking preferences; find ways to communicate our personal involvement and our interest—or our lack of personal involvement and disinterest—in appropriate ways; and terminate or attain conversational closure in a manner that is confirming, nonoffensive, and leaves the door open for possible future encounters.

daily **contacts**

Wrap-Up

Meet again in pairs or with your discussion group. Turn back to the case study at the beginning of the chapter and reconsider the questions that followed it. How have your answers changed or become more focused? Based on what you have learned about interpersonal dialogue, what new advice would you now offer to Alberto?

Critical Thinking Contacts

Read the cartoon below. Based on your understanding of conversation, discuss those factors that contribute to and take away from our ability to converse effectively with others.

Look Who's Talking

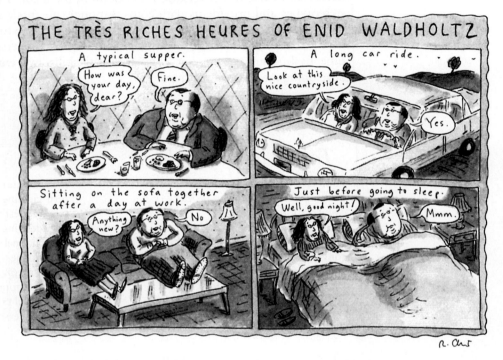

© The New Yorker Collection 1996 Roz Chast from cartoonbank.com. All Rights Reserved.

Summary

Carrying on small talk or holding spontaneous conversations lays the foundation for many of our important relationships. It is conversation that facilitates our making contact with others. When we are deprived of conversation, we go to great lengths to find some way to maintain a connection to others.

Conversation is a "relatively informal social interaction in which the roles of speaker and hearer are exchanged in a nonautomatic fashion under the collaborative management of all parties." Like a game, conversations are guided by rules and have a structure. Most conversations contain five parts: greeting, topic priming phase, heart of the conversation, preliminary processing, and closing. Each phase serves different functions and occupies an important place in the conversation's life.

Conversational turn-taking facilitates the maintenance and flow of a conversation. Affecting turn-taking are turn-maintaining and turn-yielding signals, turn-requesting and turn-denying signals, and backchanneling signals.

Every now and then a conversational blunder disrupts a conversation. When this occurs, we often use excuses to attempt to repair the damage that results from insensitivity.

Both cultural and gender differences influence the attitudes we have about the nature and value of conversation. In addition, the media reinforce conversational stereotypes and provide us with conversational role models, while new technologies are enhancing the kinds of conversations we are able to have.

By working to increase our understanding of conversations and taking the time to further develop our conversational skills, we enrich our potential for developing meaningful relationships.

Terms to Talk About

small talk *(p. 210)*

conversation deprivation *(p. 211)*

conversation *(p. 212)*

conversational rules *(p. 212)*

conversational narcissism *(p. 213)*

conversational structure *(p. 214)*

open-ended questions *(p. 216)*

closed-ended questions *(p. 216)*

conversational maintenance *(p. 216)*

conversational turn-taking *(p. 218)*

turn-maintaining signals *(p. 218)*

turn-yielding signals *(p. 218)*

turn-requesting signals *(p. 219)*

turn-denying signals *(p. 219)*

backchannel signals *(p. 219)*

monologue *(p. 221)*

dialogue *(p. 221)*

conversational blunder *(p. 221)*

prejudiced talk *(p. 222)*

metaconversation *(p. 227)*

Suggestions for Further Reading

Michael Agar, *Language Shock: Understanding the Culture of Conversation,* New York: Morrow, 1994. Explores the relationship between cultural values and conversation.

Robert E. Nofsinger, *Everyday Conversation,* Newbury Park, CA: Sage, 1991. Addresses important processes and characteristics of conversation; illustrated with segments of real-life talk.

Bret Saxon and Steve Stein, *The Art of the Schmooze,* Charlotte, NC: SPI Books, 1998. Explores the art of small talk, conversation, and relationship building.

Deborah Tannen, ed., *Gender and Conversational Interaction,* New York: Oxford University Press, 1993. Papers on gender-related patterns in conversational interaction.

Deborah Tannen, *You Just Don't Understand: Women and Men in Conversation,* New York: Ballantine Books, 1990. Explores key differences in the ways women and men approach conversation.

PART 3

DISCOVERING INTERPERSONAL DYNAMICS

8

Emotions

Emotions are contagious.

— Carl Jung

Anyone can be angry — that is easy. But to be angry with the right person, to the right degree, at the right time, for the right purpose, and in the right way — this is not easy.

— Aristotle

After completing this chapter, you should be able to:

▌ Distinguish between emotional ineptitude and emotional intelligence.

▌ Define emotion and discuss emotional contagion.

▌ Distinguish between emotion states and traits.

▌ Compare and contrast the emotions associated with relationship facilitation and relationship debilitation.

▌ Discuss how culture and gender affect the expression of emotion.

▌ Discuss how the media and technology serve as both models and channels for the emotions we exhibit.

▌ Identify steps you can take to facilitate the effective sharing of emotions.

daily **contacts**

Time Troubles

John was furious. Jean had promised she would be home for dinner for once. But, once again, she was over an hour late.

John had rushed from work just so that they would be able to spend some time together, but here he was spending it alone. Obviously, he told himself, Jean did not consider their relationship as important as he did. Clearly, he reasoned, work came before him.

John felt dejected. His emotions mixed together: annoyance fused with resentment, exasperation turned into outrage. His once adoring and caring spouse had for some reason chosen to abandon him, depriving him of her company. She was like a boarder, he told himself, not a wife. Feeling forlorn and almost desperate, he phoned her at work.

Just as he finished dialing, the front door opened. It was Jean—and she was carrying his favorite bottle of dinner wine.

"Sorry honey," she said. "I meant to be here an hour ago, but one thing led to another, and before I knew it time got away from me."

Divide into pairs or small groups to answer the following questions:

1. If you were John, what would be the next words out of your mouth? Why?
2. Does dinner wine solve the problem? Does it help alleviate it? Or does it camouflage or conceal it?

I n his best-selling book *Emotional Intelligence*, author Daniel Goleman relates the following incidents from the news:

> *At a local school, a nine-year-old goes on a rampage, pouring paint over school desks, computers, and printers, and vandalizing a car in the school parking lot. The reason: some third-grade classmates called him a "baby" and he wanted to impress them.*
>
> *Eight youngsters are wounded when an inadvertent bump in a crowd of teenagers milling outside a Manhattan rap club leads to a shoving match, which ends when one of those affronted starts shooting a .38 caliber automatic handgun into the crowd. The report notes that such shootings over seemingly minor slights, which are perceived as acts of disrespect, have become increasingly common around the country in recent years.*
>
> *For murder victims under twelve, says a report, 57 percent of the murderers are their parents or stepparents. In almost half the cases, the parents say they were "merely trying to discipline the child." The fatal beatings were prompted by "infractions" such as the child blocking the TV, crying, or soiling diapers.*
>
> *A German youth is on trial for murdering five Turkish women and girls in a fire he set while they slept. Part of a neo-Nazi group, he tells of failing to hold jobs, of drinking, of blaming his hard luck on foreigners. In a barely audible voice, he pleads, "I can't stop being sorry for what we've done, and I am infinitely ashamed."*[1]

Academic intelligence has little to do with emotional life.

—Daniel Goleman

Can you define what it means to be emotionally intelligent?

Each of these incidents represents an example of out-of-control, poorly handled emotions. **Emotional ineptitude,** or the inability to handle and control one's emotional responses, is the cause of many relationship problems. Once we have an emotional outburst, we may regret it, but the relational damage is done. What steps can we take to prevent this from happening to us? How can we learn to recognize what we are feeling? How can we learn to better understand our emotions so that when we respond to them, we don't end up hurting ourselves and others? How can we learn to shape our emotional habits so that we are better able to handle our relationships smoothly rather than destroy them overtly or insidiously? How can we develop what Goleman calls **emotional intelligence** (the ability to motivate ourselves or persist in the face of frustration, to control impulse and delay gratification, to regulate our moods and keep distress from swamping the ability to think, to empathize, and to hope)[2] in lieu of falling prey to the forces created by emotional toxicity?

What Are Emotions?

Emotions are the feelings we experience in reaction to our surroundings. They are our impetus for responding to the differences we perceive between ourselves and our environment.[3] For example, if we sense a personal gain from a relationship, we are apt to feel confident. On the other hand, if we feel threatened by the relationship, we are apt to feel anxious. Thus, it is how we feel about the interpersonal situation that influences the emotions we generate, our interpretations of the feelings we experience, and, as a result, our emotional response to the situation itself.

The emotions we feel are accompanied by physiological changes within our bodies and physical changes in our appearance. Some emotions, such as anger, increase respiration and heart rate and may cause us to become tense and flushed and to raise our voices or strike out at those around us; other emotions, including depression, slow respiration and may cause us to visibly pale, sit sullenly, or cry uncontrollably.

By becoming more aware of our emotional responses to people and events and their responses to us, we become more aware of what it is about the relationships we share that is important to us. As noted in Chapter 3, not everyone responds to the same stimulus in the same way or with the same intensity. We each experience unique physical and psychological sensations as our emotions affect us in complicated ways. By focusing on both response differences and response similarities, we can also learn how to better cope with our own feelings and those of others. As one theorist observes, "The joyful person is more apt to see the world through 'rose colored glasses,' the distressed or sad individual is more apt to construe the remarks of others as critical, and the fearful person is inclined to have **tunnel vision,** that is, to see only the frightening object."[4] Thus our emotions help color our relationships. According to Howard Gardner, at the very core of intrapersonal and interpersonal intelligence are the ability to gain "access to one's own feelings and the ability to discriminate among them and draw upon them to guide behavior," and the "capacities to discern and respond appropriately to the moods, temperaments, motivations, and desires of other people."[5]

Are you aware of your feelings as they occur?

Why Emotional Intelligence Is Important

Emotional intelligence is a form of social intelligence—the ability to understand and relate to people.[6] According to Howard Gardner, author of *Multiple Intelligences,* both intrapersonal and interpersonal intelligence are integral components of social intelligence.[7] When we are emotionally intelligent we are able to monitor our own and others' emotions, to discriminate among the emotions we experience, and to use what we discern to guide our thinking and actions.[8] Thus, in addition to demonstrating self-awareness (intrapersonal intelligence), which helps us to recognize our own emotions, we also manage our emotions by finding ways to handle such feelings as fear, anxiety, anger, and sadness. What is more, we motivate ourselves to display emotional self-control that frees us to channel our emotions in the service of a goal. Additionally, the ability to empathize enables us to recognize emotions in others as well as to harness interpersonal intelligence.

Managing our emotions is a full-time job.

The monitoring of our emotions is critical if we are to develop self-understanding. If we can get in touch with our true feelings, we can learn to control them. However, if we fail to develop an awareness of them, we are at their mercy. Learning to manage our emotions enables us to bounce back from setbacks and upsets. We become more adept at shaking off feelings that debilitate and de-energize us.

Employing the appropriate emotions to help us reach a goal is also a skill. By displaying emotional self-control, a willingness to delay gratification and refrain from acting on impulse, we facilitate goal realization.

As you learned in Chapter 4, empathy, the ability to tune into what others are feeling and to feel with them, is an important interaction skill. The "emotionally tone-deaf" usually do not have as many fulfilling relationships as do the emotionally attuned. If we are to develop interpersonal effectiveness, we need also to develop our ability to manage emotions in others.[9]

The Look and Feel of Emotions

Ninety percent or more of an emotional message is nonverbal.

Some years ago a hit song was titled "The Look of Love." Have you ever stopped to consider what love actually looks like? Our face and our body help reveal our emotions to others. (See the discussion in Chapter 6 about face and eye expressions and body gestures and postures.) In fact, while different cultures may have rules that guide the display of emotions, the physical expressions associated with particular emotions appear to be virtually universal. For that reason, even without understanding another's language, we are often able to identify the emotion the person is expressing—we can tell whether he or she is angry, feels threatened, or feels at ease and is having a good time.

According to researchers Carroll Izard and Paul Ekman, particular facial patterns support the expression of each emotion.[10] For example, *surprise* is the briefest of all emotions, flitting quickly across our faces. We express surprise by lifting our eyebrows, creating horizontal wrinkles across the forehead, slightly raising our upper eyelids, and usually opening the mouth in an oval shape. This lifting of the eyebrows also allows us to take in a larger visual area and enables more light to strike the retina. Surprise may transform itself into happiness if the stimulus that precipitated it leads to something favorable; it also may transform itself into anger or fright if the event that caused it in the first place leads to a perceived threat or outrage.

The face and eyes usually reveal more about emotions than words. What emotions are revealed in this photo?

We feel *anger* when someone interferes with our ability to pursue or attain a goal. That person can restrain us physically or psychologically, respectively, by holding us back or by causing us to feel that we are incapable or unworthy. Actions that reveal another's disregard for our feelings or disdain for us may produce anger and feelings of hostility in us. When we experience anger or hostility, we usually lower our eyebrows and draw them together to create a scowl or frown. Often we stare at the object or person that elicited these feelings and tightly compress our lips or draw them back in a

 Practice

Face the Emotion

Display each of these emotions: surprise, anger, happiness, sadness, and fear. As you create each one, note the specific feelings you experience.

1. To what extent—if any—were you able to create the sensations of any or all of the emotions merely by creating the look of the emotion?

2. To what do you attribute this ability or inability to create emotional sensations?

Do you have any doubt about the emotion this baby is feeling? What facial clues did you use to decide?

squarish shape to reveal our clenched teeth. Our face may redden, and the veins on our neck and head may become more visible to others. As anger surges through us, blood flows to our hands, making it easier for us to grasp a weapon or, should we desire to do so, strike out; our heart rate increases and adrenalin prepares us for possible action.[11]

Because contemporary society discourages overt expressions of anger, we might conclude that expressing anger is dangerous and unhealthy. If communicated properly, it is neither. In fact, while it may be unhealthy to express a lot of anger often, it is better to express some anger than no anger at all. The expression of moderate anger when compared to little, if any, expression of anger cuts the risk of heart attack and stroke in half.[12] Unexpressed anger is more likely to precipitate passive-aggressive behavior or a negative and hostile personality. What is important is learning constructive ways to express anger, that is, finding ways to express angry feelings in assertive rather than aggressive ways. Also of value is learning how to redirect angry feelings and calm down.

When we express our feelings aggressively to a person or situation that angers us, we lash out unthinkingly at other persons involved, escalating both our and the other person's anger and aggression. Our hotheadedness and low tolerance for frustration cause us frequently to respond inappropriately. Prolonged anger is unhealthy. On the other hand, when we respond to persons or situations that anger us by keeping our feelings hidden, suppressing them, and turning them inwards, we often find ourselves feeling chronically grumpy and irritable as a result. Repressed anger is also unhealthy. A more effective response to anger is to figure out what triggered our anger so that we can express our angry feelings assertively by clarifying for the

Practice

Anger Management

The film *Anger Management,* starring Adam Sandler as timid businessperson Dave Buznik and Jack Nicholson as anger management therapist Dr. Buddy Rydell, explores what happens when Dave Buznik, due to a misunderstanding that escalated out of control aboard an airplane, is ordered by the court to seek treatment from Dr. Rydell. Like Dave Buznik, we all know what anger is, and we have all felt it. It is not anger, but *out of control anger,* that can cause problems for us in any context. In fact, the ultimate test of our emotional intelligence quotient may be the way we handle anger.

In order to understand the emotional state of anger, answer the following questions:

1. Identify the last time you felt angry.
2. Explain the cause(s) of your anger. For example, were you angry with another person, at a situation, personal problems facing you, or yourself?
3. Other than angry, how else did the situation and person(s) involved make you feel?
4. What, if anything, did you do to express your anger? Be specific.
5. What did your angry feelings suggest to you regarding what you value, need, lack, or believe?

person(s) involved what our needs are and how they can be met without harming anyone else. This requires that we be able to calm down before responding so that we are able to control not just our outward behavior but also our internal responses. By relaxing, perhaps by doing some deep breathing or visualizing appropriate imagery, we can calm down angry feelings. Expressing angry feelings in assertive ways—ways that are respectful of our needs and feelings as well as of the needs and feelings of others—rather than in aggressive or suppressive ways is the healthiest means of expressing anger.

We can call on a number of techniques, including cognitive restructuring, problem solving, and humor to help us manage anger. Cognitive restructuring involves changing the way we think. If, for example, we commonly react by swearing when we become angry, primarily because we exaggerate the situation by telling ourselves that this is the worse thing that could happen, we need to change that dramatic response by toning it down and reminding ourselves that this is not the end of the world. While we may feel frustrated, getting angry isn't going to help. Instead we need to adopt a more balanced perspective, identify the problem, and focus on facing and handling it. This involves mapping out a plan and monitoring progress toward it. Humor can also diffuse anger that is in danger of escalating out of control. Relying on humor is not to suggest that you make light of the situation, become overly sarcastic, or laugh away the problem. Rather, try not to take yourself too seriously.[13]

In contrast to anger, happiness is the feeling that pulls our lips back and curves them gently upward in a smile. Our cheeks rise and the corners of our lips create wrinkles (some call them dimples) that run from the nose and eyes and out beyond our lips and cheeks. The key biological change during a happy state is increased activity in the brain center that inhibits negative feelings and increases our sense of energy. After the terrorist attacks of September 11, 2001, feeling happy became more important to many of us. We reordered our priorities, making happiness our "new bottom line."[14]

Practice

Emotion Checklist

1. Which of the emotions listed below do you recall experiencing during the past month? List them on a separate piece of paper.

accepted	angry	anticipatory
anxious	apathetic	apprehensive
ashamed	bewildered	bored
calm	concerned	confident
confused	contemptuous	curious
depressed	desperate	disappointed
disgusted	eager	ecstatic
embarrassed	envious	excited
fearful	guilty	happy
hostile	hurt	impatient
insecure	jealous	joyful
loving	optimistic	outraged
paranoid	pessimistic	proud
rejected	relieved	remorseful
sad	shy	supported
surprised	stressful	sympathetic
tense	useful	useless
vengeful	vicious	violent
worried		

If necessary, add other emotions not listed here.

2. Go back through your list and put a check mark next to those emotions you experienced most often.

3. Think about the specific people you tend to be with when you experience your most frequent emotions. Write their names next to the appropriate emotions.

4. Look back over the emotions and the names you have written. What relationship variables can you point to as being the cause or precipitating factor for each emotion?

5. Finally, complete these sentences:

I am anxious when I interact with _____

I am confident when I interact with _____

I am frustrated when I interact with _____

I am embarrassed when I interact with _____

I am happy when I interact with _____

I am stressed when I interact with _____

Answering such questions helps us identify who makes us feel which emotions. The term we use to label our feelings is based on our interpretation of the situation.

When we experience the opposite of happiness, *sadness,* we often exhibit a loss of facial muscle tone. We arch the inner corners of our eyebrows upward and draw them together. We may also raise our lower eyelids and draw down the corners of the mouth, and our lips may tremble. Accompanying sadness are a drop in energy and a slowing of the body's metabolism.

On the other hand, when we experience *fear,* we raise our eyebrows slightly as we draw them together. We open our eyes wider than usual, and our lower eyelids tense. We stretch our lips back tightly, and the center of the forehead wrinkles. Our body tells us that something is wrong.

Sometimes putting on an emotion actually precipitates the feelings that the facial expression represents. In other words, expressions are not merely the visible sign of an emotion: in some instances, they may in fact be the *cause* of the emotion.[15] As our mind can influence our body, so can our body influence our mind.

The emotions just discussed are primary emotions. According to Robert Plutchik, there are eight primary emotions, the aforementioned four plus disgust, acceptance, anticipation, and joy. Plutchik believes that the eight primary emotions combine to form mixed emotions. Included among mixed emotions are remorse (a mixture of disgust and sadness), love (a mixture of joy and acceptance), awe (a mixture of fear and surprise), submission (a mixture of acceptance and fear), disappointment (a mixture of sadness and surprise), contempt (a mixture of anger and disgust), optimism (a mixture of anticipation and joy), and aggressiveness (a mixture of anger and anticipation).[16] (See Figure 8.1.) Does your experience support or contradict Plutchik's hierarchy of primary and secondary emotions? In your opinion, are his amalgams of mixed emotions accurate?

It is also possible for us to catch a mood much as we catch a cold. We call this **emotional contagion.** People give us moods in much the same way that they pass their germs on. The better able we are to tune in to the moods of others—the more empathic we are—the better our chances of catching the mood of the person with whom we are communicating. Highly empathic people tend to develop greater emotional rapport and unconsciously mirror or imitate the moods and emotions of those with whom they interact.[17] People who are weak at both sending and receiving moods tend to have more relationship problems than do those who are more emotionally expressive and receptive.

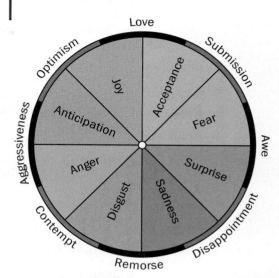

FIGURE 8.1
Wheel of Emotions

Primary emotions are inside the wheel.

Source: Based on R. Plutchik, "Emotions: A General Psychoevolutionary Theory," in K. R. Scherer and P. Ekman, eds., *Approaches to Emotion.* Hillsdale, NJ: Lawrence Erlbaum Associates, 1984, pp. 197–218.

Emotions Affect Evaluations

Although our relationships affect the emotions we feel, each relationship itself does not experience emotions—we do. When we feel good or experience what we perceive to be a positive emotion when interacting with another person, we tend to attribute that feeling to the other person and to the kind of relationship we share.[18] Were we always to feel a particular emotion, however—were we to persist, for example, in a chronic state of depression or rage—we would then be exhibiting an **emotion trait.** An emotion trait means that we have a tendency to experience a specific emotion during our person-to-person interactions.[19]

We are constantly experiencing some emotion. During any interpersonal encounter, we have various thoughts or feelings about the person with whom we are interacting and the situation itself. These thoughts elicit what we call an **emotion state,** an emotional process of limited duration that lasts from seconds to hours and varies in its

in *Context*

Coping on the Job

How we handle our emotions at work can directly affect both our ability to work with others and our promotion potential.

1. Describe an instance in which your emotions interfered with your ability to do a good job. Be specific.

2. Describe an instance in which effectively handled emotions diffused a potentially difficult work situation.

level of feeling from mild to intense.[20] This contrasts with the emotion trait, which persists for a long time. Examples of emotion states are temporary sadness or happiness that comes from hearing certain news, for instance.

Women report being in negative moods or emotion states about twice as often as men and, as conflicting as it may seem, in positive moods about twice as often as men. One reason cited for this disparity is that women's moods simply tend to be more intense than men's.[21] In addition, we generally seek to interact with those who share our mood. As a result, our moods tend to perpetuate themselves. Further, our moods influence our perceptions of the future. After seeing a comic film, for example, we tend to evaluate our relationships and our careers more positively than we do after seeing a tragic film. Thus, a good or a bad mood can create in us an optimistic or pessimistic frame of mind and, in turn, influence how positively or negatively we view others and our future.

Means of Coping with Emotions

We are most inventive when trying to escape the blues.

Coping involves the management of our emotions. We use two key coping strategies: first, we can try to remove the problem. This is often difficult—if not impossible—to accomplish when it involves another human being. For example, when we are angry with another person, it is not always practical or desirable for us simply to remove him or her from our surroundings. The second, more feasible and usually more effective means of coping involves changing the way we interpret a situation and our emotional response to it. In the following sections, we will look at ways to cope with emotions.

Relationships and Emotions

Emotions can facilitate or impede the development of healthy relationships. When we perceive our interactions to facilitate our well-being, we usually experience positive or **facilitative emotions,** and we act in ways that permit our emotions to help our relational goals. When we perceive that others impede our well-being, we usually experience negative or **debilitative emotions,** and the actions that accompany these feelings typically get in the way of our developing a healthy relationship or realizing our relational goals.[22]

Complaining and personally criticizing someone are not the same thing.

Although we all experience an array of emotions in relationships with others, those most closely associated with relationship facilitation or goal attainment are compassion, happiness, hope, love, pride, and relief. Those most closely associated with debilitation that lead to our failing to attain our relational goals are extreme anxiety, disgust, envy, terror, guilt, jealousy, paranoia, rage, sadness, and shame. Both facilitative and debilitative emotions run the gamut of different types of feelings, but they differ from each other in two important ways. The two characteristics that help distinguish emotions that are facilitative from those that are debilitative are intensity and duration. We tend to feel debilitative emotions even more intensely and for longer periods of time than facilitative emotions. Because of their intensity and duration, debilitative emotions interfere with our ability to engage in productive interactions. For example, although some anger can serve as a motivational force and even propel us to take needed action, anger that is out of control—rage—typically reduces our ability to act rationally and, therefore, usually impedes our ability to make matters better. Thus, how we experience and express our emotions can be facilitating or debilitating and can significantly affect our relationships with others.

How you interpret events often holds the key to handling your emotions. Consider the following two situations:

Imagine you are walking by a friend's house. Suddenly your friend opens the door, throws a rock at you, and starts shouting obscenities at you. How do you respond?

Imagine that instead of walking by a friend's house, you are walking by a mental institution in which your friend is a patient. When your friend hurls the same rock and shouts the same obscenities at you, will your reaction be the same?[23]

The ways you think about and react to each of these situations would probably differ. Although you might feel angry and upset as a result of the first situation, most likely you would feel saddened and distraught by the second. Your interpretation of each incident causes you to experience different feelings. What you tell yourself about the nature of your experiences determines whether you feel outrage or sympathy, compassion or disdain for another person. We interpret the actions of others based on our feelings and the reasons we use to explain their behaviors. According to attribution theory, which describes how we infer and explain the causes of social behavior, whether we believe a specific behavior is due to someone's personality or to the situation a person finds herself or himself in affects our evaluation of that person. In other words, what we determine to be the reasons for someone else's behavior—rightly or wrongly—directly influence our perception of that person.[24]

Should You Tell?

What do these lines from a poem by William Blake reveal about the power of our emotions?

I was angry with my friend:
I told my wrath, my wrath did end.
I was angry with my foe.
I told it not, my wrath did grow.

1. Do you agree with Blake? Is the expression of anger always beneficial?
2. Do you think verbally expressing your anger helps you purge yourself of it or does it cause you to feel even more angry? Explain.

in Context

Processing Reactions

How you respond to various emotional situations can provide insight into the role each emotion plays in your more and less successful relationships.

1. Think about how you tend to respond when you experience facilitating emotions: compassion, happiness, hope, love, pride, and relief.
2. Now think about your responses to experiencing goal-inhibiting emotions: anger, anxiety, disgust, envy, fright, guilt, jealousy, sadness, and shame.
3. Identify the conditions under which you typically experience each emotion and how you react once that emotion takes hold.

The Value of Explaining Feelings

To feel with another is to care.

How do you tell others what you are feeling? How do you explain your anger without becoming angry? How do you explain your disappointment without withdrawing into a shell? By making the effort to describe your feelings—rather than enact them—you increase your chances of keeping lines of communication open and improving your relationship.

When we describe our feelings, we are also describing how we would like others to treat us. As we reveal what we are feeling, we also indicate the effect their behavior is having on us. By sharing such information, we give those with whom we relate the information they need to decide whether their behavior toward us is appropriate or is having the effect they intended. For example, if you politely tell Lindsay that you get exasperated when she doesn't stop talking long enough to listen to you, maybe next time you interact she'll seek a response from you instead of merely delivering a monologue. If you tell Ken that you are delighted to go with him to his friend's party, he's more likely to ask you again than if you said you'd go but weren't really happy about it. When we share feelings, we make others more aware of how their actions affect us. But remember, **describing feelings** and **displaying feelings** are not the same thing. When we describe our feelings, we are not judging the other person. In contrast, an overt *display* of our feelings—such as shouting, "That was the most stupid thing you've ever done!"—implies an evaluation.

Emotions help us structure our view of the world. When we are angry, we see the world as offensive; when we are fearful, we see it as threatening; when we are in love, we see it as beautiful. Those who don't share our perception of an act as offensive or threatening will not get angry or experience fear. Yet they are probably still capable of understanding our perceptions.

Though we find it easier to share positive emotions than negative ones, and we are reluctant to send messages that could hurt or embarrass others, it is important that we let others know when we are angry or disappointed in them. Because emotion is one of the most consequential outcomes of interaction, it is important that we let others know what causes us to feel as we do.[25] Our feelings help reveal the current temperature of a relationship. When our relationship partners understand this, they should be in a position to make more appropriate interpersonal choices regarding how to interact with us.

Diversity and Culture Contacts

The Expression of Emotions

As we discussed, there are basic emotions that we all experience. No matter what our cultural background, at one time or another we all feel anger, disgust, fear, happiness, and sadness. What generates these feelings, however, and how expressive we are at displaying or revealing them to others are affected, in part, by the rules and norms of our culture. For instance, the Japanese generally

professional
contacts

Do You Help Others Save or Lose Face?

Consider this example of a negotiation between Japanese and U.S. businesspeople. As you read it ask yourself what the subject failed to understand and why.

> Phil Downing . . . was involved in setting up a branch of his company that was merging with an existing Japanese counterpart. He seemed to get along very well with the executive colleagues assigned to work with him, one of whom had recently been elected chairman of the board when his grandfather retired. Over several weeks of discussion, Phil and the chairman of the Japanese branch had generally laid out some working policies and agreed on strategies that would bring new directions needed for development. Several days later . . . the young chairman's grandfather happened to drop in and he began to comment on how the company had been formed and had been built up by the traditional practices, talking about some of the policies the young executives had recently discarded. Phil expected the new chairman to explain some of the innovative and developmental policies they had both agreed upon. However, the young man said nothing; instead, he just nodded and agreed with his grandfather. Phil was bewildered and frustrated . . . and he started to protest. The atmosphere in the room became immediately tense. . . . A week later the Japanese company withdrew from the negotiations.*

Phil had failed to understand that the fact that the young chairperson of the Japanese company had saved face for his grandfather by agreeing with him did not negate the agreements that he had earlier negotiated with Phil. Because he overtly protested and disagreed with the grandfather, Phil had threatened the grandfather, and the young chairperson was now unwilling to do business with him.

*R. W. Brislin, K. Cushner, C. Cherrie, and M. Yong, *Intercultural Interactions: A Practical Guide,* Beverly Hills, CA: Sage, 1986, pp. 155–156.

refrain from expressing negative emotions in public. This is because members of collectivist cultures, such as Japan and India, place great value on preserving harmony and consequently discourage the expression of any negative feelings that could create disharmony among the group's members. In contrast, members of highly individualist cultures, such as the United States and Canada, are comfortable "telling it like they see it"—revealing their feelings to others. In such cultures, always withholding feelings or keeping them secret so that others are unable to tell when you are hurt, happy, or sad is, for the most part, regarded as both inappropriate and an ineffective way to manage feelings. As a result, when people from these different cultures communicate with each other, members of collectivist cultures might easily perceive members of individualist cultures as too frank or direct. The perception that members of collectivist cultures are not completely forthcoming is partly due to the importance collectivist cultures place on helping members save face. **Face saving,** or the preservation of dignity, is so important that should persons from individualist cultures violate this norm when interacting with members of collectivist cultures, the relationship they share can suffer.

In a multicultural society and world we must understand our own cultural filters when assessing the behaviors of persons from another cultural group. To do so helps us in judging the propriety of emotions displayed by persons from other ethnic/cultural groups. Climate may affect cultural variations of emotional expressiveness. It appears that persons from warmer places tend to be more emotionally expressive than persons living in cooler climates.[26]

Gender Contacts

The Expression of Emotions

How comfortable are you expressing your emotions to others? Are you more or less comfortable sharing your feelings with males or with females?

There are numerous differences in the ways women and men handle feelings. Most men are taught to be more emotionally reserved than are women. Consequently, instead of practicing emotional disclosiveness, many men tend to be more inexpressive. As a result, some researchers say that men's friendships lack the emotional depth that characterizes women's friendships.[27] However, others counter that men neither lack feelings nor emotional depth, but rather prefer to express their feelings and develop closeness with others through *doing* rather than through talking, through activities rather than through self-disclosure.[28]

Men and women vary in both expressiveness and sensitivity to the emotions of others. Women are more likely than men to reveal a wide range of feelings, precipitating the stereotype of them as overly expressive and of men as inexpressive. Men are also less willing than women to reveal feeling frightened, sad, lonely, or embarrassed. As a result, observers are able to discern women's emotions more accurately than men's.[29] Men tend to unabashedly reveal their strengths,[30] whereas women are better at discerning the clues that others provide regarding their emotions.[31] Thus, women tend to outperform men at decoding the emotions of others.[32]

Most women tend to prefer intimate talk, whereas most men prefer instrumental demonstrations of commitment instead. By recognizing and understanding this stylistic difference, both sexes take a giant step forward in being able to relate effectively with each other. This difference may also account for the reason why, when under stress, both men and women report wanting to be with a woman friend, and why both men and women are in general more comfortable revealing feelings to women than to men.[33] We see these differences played out on the Internet as well, with women more likely to use emoticons as emotional clarifiers than men.[34]

Media and Technology Contacts

Channeling Feelings

The media and technology provide both the models and the channels we use daily to form attitudes about the most effective ways of handling and displaying our feelings.

Media Models

Many people have found that **media models,** the images that we see depicted in the media, have the potential to affect our emotions. Researchers have found that heavy television viewers (those who watch more than four hours a day) have different attitudes and hold different beliefs than do light television viewers (those who watch fewer than two hours a day). For example, heavy television viewers perceive women as having more limited abilities and interests than men, hold an exaggerated view of the prevalence of violence in society, and believe that old people are fewer in number and less healthy today than in years past. In general, heavy television viewers perceive the world to be a meaner and more sinister place than do light viewers, believing that, if given the chance, people will take advantage of you because they are looking out only for themselves. The opinions heavy viewers hold reflect the fictional world that television brings to them, not the world that they actually live in.[35] As you learned in Chapter 3, perception often becomes reality.

What we see influences what we believe, which in turn influences how we evaluate experience, which finally influences how we feel and how we express those feelings. For example, heavy television viewers are less likely to presume

Heavy TV watchers are generally more depressed after watching TV.

∷ *Practice*

Sharing Feelings

Think of a specific male and a specific female (friend, sibling, parent, etc.). Using a scale of 1 to 10, where 1 represents little if any comfort and 10 represents complete comfort, indicate how comfortable you are sharing the following feelings with each:

	Male	Female
A problem you have with him or her		
A problem you have with someone else		
Anger directed toward him or her		
Anger directed at someone else		
A recent disappointment directed at him or her		
A recent disappointment directed at someone else		
Fears about him or her		
Fears about someone else		
What he or she does that makes you feel insecure		

	Male	Female
What someone else does that makes you feel insecure		
What he or she does that causes you stress		
What someone else does that causes you stress		
What he or she does that makes you happy		
What someone else does that makes you happy		

Working in mixed-sex pairs or small groups, compare your ratings for each person, and then pool your results by gender.

1. With which person are you most comfortable sharing your emotions? Does it have anything to do with gender?

2. Which emotions are easiest for you to share with a female? with a male? Which are the hardest to share with a female? with a male? How do you account for the differences?

3. Based on the pooled results, what general conclusions can you draw about individuals sharing emotions with the same or the opposite gender?

in Theory

Persuasive Models

Identify a media offering that you believe convinced you that a certain way of behaving was legitimate or appropriate. For example, have any shows or films affected your way of dressing or manner of speaking?

1. Explain how that offering altered your perception of reality by influencing the way you felt and expressed those feelings, and as a result influenced the way you ultimately chose to respond to a real-life situation.

2. To what extent, if any, did the emotional rewards obtained by the mediated characters also accrue to you?

3. If given the opportunity, would you act the same or differently today? Explain.

innocence and tend to take more of a hard line when serving on juries than do light viewers. This helps them handle the anger they feel about the perceived prevalence of societal violence. They also develop more fear of crime than do light viewers and, due to repeated exposure to slasher-type programming, have less sympathy or empathy for victims of rape. For heavy viewers, television serves as a vital source of information for constructing their image of the world.[36]

Mass media models have the potential to influence our behavior. We are simply more likely to do what we have seen. After viewing a televised suicide, we may come to feel that suicide may be a reasonable way to deal with the problems life presents; after watching a televised fight, we may conclude that physical violence is an acceptable way to deal with disappointment.

Technological Channels

We are gaining control of the channels of mass and personalized communication. We now have the capability to call up television programs and movies on demand. Some of us can use our remote control devices to order programs, pizzas, or clothes or do our banking whenever we want. With the aid of various multimedia systems, we now can control and create our own interactive experiences.

We no longer just watch; we also participate. We can experience media versions of real worlds or we can enter a virtual world. While we have always

in Theory

Anger in Media

Outrage has become an increasingly popular entertainment form, whether on television and radio talk shows that feature partisan and opinionated hosts and guests such as Curtis Slewa, Bill O'Reilly, and Ann Coulter, on the Internet with such commentators as Matt Drudge, or in music CDs and videos with lyrics provided by anger-venting artists such as Eminem. In these media we find ourselves witnessing a plethora of very angry human beings attempting to communicate

by name-calling, spouting series after series of overgeneralizations, and generally exhibiting their incivility in settings where civility should be the norm.

What effects, if any, do you believe that listening to extremely angry hosts, guests, and artists have on the viewing and listening public? In your opinion, does it harm us or educate us to listen to media personalities who make a living demonstrating their inability to handle their emotions by becoming aggressive, lashing out, and giving into verbal impulses that trample on the rights of others?

entered other worlds by watching a television program or movie or playing a computer game, virtual reality does something these media do not; virtual reality endows us with **telepresence**—it takes our body with us into that world, giving us the sense of physically being in a different place or time—and allows us to more fully participate in sensory experiences that elicit feelings and emotions we might otherwise never have experienced. Just as NASA astronauts have used virtual reality to train for space flights, so can we use virtual reality to train for future communication encounters unlike any we have had to date. Will virtual reality enable us to escape from reality into a world of fantasy, or will it help us more fully process the human experience and, rather than emotionally bankrupting us, emotionally enrich us? Time will tell.

Gaining Communication Competence

A number of factors can facilitate the accurate communication of our feelings. Among these are our ability to use precise language, our acceptance of ownership and responsibility, our willingness to reveal the breadth of our range of feelings, and our penchant for gauging the right time and place to discuss our feelings.

Guidelines for Sharing Emotions

Recognize That Thoughts Cause Feelings

The rational-emotional approach to emotion management posits that in order to turn off debilitative feelings and replace them with feelings that are more facilitative, we first need to learn how to change unproductive thinking.[37] According to rational emotive behavior therapy founder and cognitive-behavior

in *Theory*

The Right Word

Using specific language can help us describe our emotions so that others can understand them.

1. Think about people or situations in your life that have triggered feelings of anger, happiness, disappointment, excitement, and fear. For each instance, be as specific as possible in thinking about the *kind* of emotion you experienced. Indicate what you perceive to have been the cause or trigger for your feeling.

2. Indicate the words you might use to describe each emotion. For example, perhaps a thought-ful invitation from a friend triggered your feeling of happiness. You might say, "I appreciate your invitation. I'm *ecstatic* to be going there with you." Or after your spouse criticized your efforts to make dinner, you might say, "I feel nervous when you yell at me after I've worked so hard to have dinner ready on time; I'm even more *petrified* about what you'll do if you don't like it."

Remember, you can also use descriptions of what's happening to you as well as descriptions of what you'd like to do to further individualize your responses.

psychologist Albert Ellis, the *beliefs* we hold about events and people, and not the events or actual people, cause us mental anguish and lead to mental and even physical discomfort. How we react emotionally to a person or event, that is, how we interpret the event or the behavior of a person, elicits different feelings in us and different consequences in our behavior. The key to understanding our feelings is to review our self-talk—the thoughts we have about what is occurring, the thought process that takes place before an emotion is expressed—and analyze whether the thoughts we have debilitate or facilitate our interactions and relationships.

By taking responsibility for our own emotions and actions and by monitoring our emotional reactions to specific persons or situations, we can get in touch with our feelings. Once we realize how we feel, we can look for factors that trigger a debilitative reaction in us. We need to record our self-talk, the continuous internal monologue we spoke of above; specifically, we need to identify the irrational beliefs we hold, explain why they are a product of irrational thinking, and choose as an alternative a more rational and realistic way of thinking for the next time we are faced with the same person or situation. Are we suggesting that we try to talk ourselves out of feeling bad? Yes, we are. Why should we allow our feelings to debilitate us when we can use our feelings as facilitators instead? As Albert Ellis believes, we create our own moods and emotional state with the words we use during self-talk.[38] We can reframe events by using different words to describe what occurred. A person who persistently places a pessimistic frame around events will debilitate him- or herself, whereas a person who places an optimistic frame around events helps to facilitate instead. Persons who are optimists when young are in better health in middle age than those who had been pessimists.[39]

Choose the Right Words

Many of us have a hard time letting others know exactly what we are feeling: we say we feel "good," "okay," or "bad." By relying on words that are not as specific as they could be or that do not adequately describe our emotions, we make it more difficult for others to understand us. If we can figure out what triggered a particular emotion, we can often be more specific when we talk about it. We can also try to find words to describe what we feel happening to us: for example, we might say, "I feel like a robot, robbed of my personal identity"; "I feel like a trained seal"; or "I feel like an eagle." In addition, we can describe what we would like to do in response to our feelings: "I feel like sticking my head in the sand" or "I feel like coming right over and kissing you." It is important that we work hard to describe our feelings and their intensity.

Show That You Accept Responsibility for Your Feelings

Acknowledge that you own your feelings. To do this you need to identify yourself as the feelings' source. This means that you need to start your comments with "I," not "you." Instead of saying, "You're always embarrassing me," say, "I get embarrassed when . . . ." Remember, no one can make you feel an emotion that you refuse to feel.

Share Feelings Fully

Often what we feel is an amalgam of feelings rather than one single feeling. For example, we may feel anger, confusion, embarrassment, and sadness at the same time. To simply call the feeling anger would be misleading and not candid. To refuse to discuss it at all could be even worse. Once the feelings have surfaced they will continue to exist, and they won't go away even when we try to ignore them. You must be sure to share all feelings fully in the interest of openness.

Decide When and Where to Reveal Feelings

When you are angry is not necessarily the best time to let others know just how angry you are. Often it is wiser to wait a bit, collect your thoughts, and consider the best way to express your feelings to whoever you believe triggered your anger.

Deciphering our emotions and deciding how to deal with them can be a lengthy process. Be sure that once you start a discussion of your feelings you have the time needed for a fair consideration of them.

Describe the Response You Seek

It is important that the person you are speaking to understands how you want him or her to respond to your expression of feelings. For example, you might end your statement by noting: "I need you to help me unwind after a busy day." By revealing how we feel, how we see things, and how we would like to change them, we take steps toward achieving a greater state of relational health and we set the stage for continued relational growth.

daily
contacts   Wrap-Up

Meet again in pairs or small groups. Turn back to the case study at the beginning of the chapter and reconsider the questions that followed it. How have your answers changed or become more focused? Based on your knowledge of emotions, what advice would you give John now?

Critical Thinking Contacts

Examine the following cartoon. Based on your understanding of interpersonal communication, what advice would you offer Calvin and Hobbes about the importance of emotions and properly handling them?

Triggers

Summary

By learning to understand and handle our emotions—that is, by making a commitment to become emotionally intelligent—we increase our potential for sharing meaningful, effective relationships. On the other hand, when we display emotional ineptitude, our inability to discuss or cope with our emotions contributes to continued relationship difficulties.

Emotions are reactions that influence our appraisals of interpersonal situations. The emotions we feel are accompanied by physiological changes in our bodies and physical changes in our appearances. By becoming more aware of our emotional responses and the emotional responses of others, we become more aware of what is important to each of us in our relationships as well as the extent to which our emotions help color our relationships.

We use our faces and our bodies to help reveal our emotions to others. Some people are better at communicating and reading emotions than others are. Emotions are also contagious. The more empathic we are, the better are our chances of sharing someone else's emotion.

We are always experiencing some emotion. An emotion state is an emotional process of limited duration that varies in both duration and intensity. An emotion trait is an emotion state that persists beyond what is considered appropriate.

Because emotions can either facilitate or impede both the development of healthy relationships and our sense of well-being, we must learn to better manage them. The way we think about and react to situations triggers specific feelings in us and affects how we respond to others.

As we have seen, culture and gender both influence the expression of emotions. In addition, the media and technology function as models for us to emulate and channels for us to use as we make sense out of and express our feelings. By working to facilitate the accurate communication of emotion, we also increase our chances for realizing greater relationship satisfacation and health.

Terms to Talk About

emotional ineptitude *(p. 234)*
emotional intelligence *(p. 235)*
emotions *(p. 235)*
tunnel vision *(p. 235)*
emotional contagion *(p. 241)*
emotion trait *(p. 241)*
emotion state *(p. 241)*
coping *(p. 242)*

faciltative emotions *(p. 242)*
debilitative emotions *(p. 242)*
describing feelings *(p. 244)*
displaying feelings *(p. 244)*
face saving *(p. 245)*
media models *(p. 247)*
telepresence *(p. 249)*

Suggestions for Further Reading

Paul Ekman, *Emotions Revealed: Recognizing Faces and Feelings to Improve Communication and Emotional Life,* New York: Times Books, 2003. Aids in developing greater skill in reading and processing emotions.

Daniel Goleman, *Emotional Intelligence,* New York: Bantam Books, 1995. Explores how a lack of emotional intelligence can sabotage relationships and careers.

Richard S. Lazarus, *Emotion and Adaptation,* New York: Oxford University Press, 1991. Explores how emotions are derived from an individual's appraisal of relationships and his or her connection to the environment.

Michael Lewis and Jeanette M. Haviland, eds., *Handbook of Emotions,* New York: Guilford, 1993. Provides both an overview and an in-depth look at the role emotions play in our lives.

Sandra Metts and John W. Bowers, "Emotion in Interpersonal Communication," in Mark L. Knapp and Gerald R. Miller, *Handbook of Interpersonal Communication,* 2nd ed., Newbury Park, CA: Sage, 1994. A readable overview of the theories of emotion.

Jean-Didion Vincent, *The Biology of Emotions,* Cambridge, MA: Basil Blackwell, 1990. Discusses the links between our physical and emotional selves.

daily
contacts

Trust Troubles

Fifty houses! Angela was devastated. She had shown the Williams family fifty houses during her summer vacation — and now this!

At the end of the spring term, Angela had completed a real estate sales course. A summer job selling houses had seemed like a great idea. She liked people, the hours were flexible, and the potential for earning high commissions as a sales agent with a company in her hometown was great. Of course, the down side was that there would be no pay if she failed to make a sale. Angela figured that was too remote a possibility for her to take seriously.

Selling homes was not an easy job. There were houses to inspect, owners to call, and buyers to show houses to seven days a week. After working days and evenings for six weeks with no success, Angela finally found "live" buyers — Rita and Tom Williams — who desperately wanted to buy a $600,000 home in an upscale neighborhood. All was not lost. The fee she would earn from selling them a house would pay most of her school expenses for the next year.

Angela worked tirelessly taking Rita to houses in the morning and showing Tom the same houses in the evening. She got to know their three-year-old son, Evan, better than she knew her own nieces and nephews. Evan was a nice kid; it wasn't his fault that he often got car sick and threw up in her back seat. . . .

Rita and Tom had finally narrowed it down to two houses. Angela was sure she could close the deal before September, when she would return to college.

Showing them fifty houses had been exhausting, but now that she could see the bright light at the end of the real estate tunnel, she decided it had been fun.

Then Rita called. She and Tom had also been looking at houses with another real estate agent. In fact, they had already made an offer on a house that had been accepted several days ago; they would be closing on it soon. They had continued to look at houses with Angela just to convince themselves that the one they had made the offer on was the best they could find. Now they were convinced that they had made the right choice. Unfortunately, nothing Angela showed them had compared to it. Rita thanked Angela for all her help.

Angela dropped the phone. How could they do this to her? Because of the time she'd spent with them, Angela had worked the entire summer without earning a cent.

"Who can you trust?" she cried to her sales manager.

Just then, the door opened and a couple walked in. They wanted to look at homes. The sales manager introduced them to Angela.

Divide into pairs or small groups to consider these questions:

1. Should Angela trust the new couple and show them houses?
2. What could she do to ensure that the trust she would place in these buyers would not be misplaced?

≋ *Theory*

Can We Depend on Each Other?

Take a moment to identify three people you recently trusted or depended on and three people who recently trusted or depended on you.

1. Consider the three relationships in which you trusted another person, and enter the information below.

Names	Behaviors you expected each person to exhibit	Extent to which your expectations were fulfilled
a. _____	_____	_____
b. _____	_____	_____
c. _____	_____	_____

2. For each person, indicate whether your trust in the person was justified. Explain your rationale for each.

3. Now consider the three relationships in which another person trusted you and enter the following information:

Names	Behavior expected of you	Extent to which you believe you fulfilled each expectation
a. _____	_____	_____
b. _____	_____	_____
c. _____	_____	_____

4. For each person, explain why you think they should or should not have trusted you.

Whom do you trust? How can you tell when you should or should not trust another person? What behaviors lead you to place your trust in some individuals but not others? What occurs that enables people to answer questions like these?

What Is Trust?

We all think we know what it means to trust or depend on another person and to have another individual trust or depend on us. Sometimes our trust in each other is merited and we are rewarded for it; other times, however, our trust is misplaced and causes us to feel disappointment or become disillusioned with that relationship.

We rely on others for a variety of reasons. Sometimes we rely on others because we expect them to perform basic services for us, such as make breakfast or drive us to work. Sometimes we expect others to give us direction, such as helping us pick out what to wear for an interview or helping us choose our classes. Still other times we expect others to meet our emotional needs—commiserate with us when we are sad or celebrate with us when we are happy. The degree to which our expectations are fulfilled determines whether we will depend on or trust that particular individual again. As the maxim says:

In general, do you consider yourself trusting? trustworthy?

Fool me once
Shame on you.
Fool me twice
Shame on me.

The amount of trust we place in someone is based on our perception of his or her character.

Is it easy to define what trust means to you? Why?

Although we all freely use the word "trust," it is a difficult concept to put into words. Try to express what it means to you now. As you do so, consider the following excerpt from Antoine de Saint-Exupery's *The Little Prince,* in which the fox tries to explain to the prince what trust means to him.

> *"I am looking for friends. What does that mean—'tame'?"*
> *"It is an act too often neglected," said the fox, "it means to establish ties."*
> *"'To establish ties'?"*
> *"Just that," said the fox. "To me, you are still nothing more than a little boy who is just like a hundred thousand other little boys. And I have no need of you. And you, on your part, have no need of me. To you, I am nothing more than a fox like a hundred thousand other foxes. But if you tame me (if we establish ties), then we shall need each other. To me, you will be unique in all the world. To you, I shall be unique in all the world."*

The Bases of Trust

Like the Little Prince, we all need to establish a basis for **trust.** The amount of trust we place in another person is, to a large extent, based on our perception of that individual's character. In other words, when we judge someone to be of good character, we are more likely to display trust in the integrity of the person, trust in his or her motives, trust in the consistency of his or her behavior, and trust in his or her discretion.

When we trust someone because of his or her *integrity,* we think the individual possesses a basic honesty that permeates our relationship. When we trust another's *motives,* we trust that individual's intentions—that is, we do not believe that he

To what extent are any of the relationships you share affected by a fear of betrayal?

or she would exhibit malevolent behavior toward us. When we trust someone on the basis of the *consistency of his or her behavior,* we feel that we know that person well enough to be able to predict his or her actions. Finally, when we trust another on the basis of his or her *ability to be discreet,* we conclude that he or she will neither intentionally violate our confidence nor disclose to anyone else information that could harm us.

To foster the development of a relationship based on mutual trust, we need to work to create an interpersonal climate that reduces each interactant's fear of rejection or betrayal. This is not always easy. Yet, as we are well aware, the establishment of trust is essential for the maintenance and well-being of our relationships.

The Components of Trust

Trust consists of two basic components: *trusting behavior* and *trustworthy behavior.* Only when both components are present can trust be said to exist. In fact, trusting and trustworthy behaviors are reciprocal: trusting precipitates trustworthiness, and vice versa. Trust therefore either grows or weakens over time.

Trusting Behavior

Trusting behavior involves three elements. First, we expect another person to behave in a way that can have either harmful or beneficial results, and we acknowledge that if that individual's actions lead to negative results, they will probably be more damaging to us than the positive results would be rewarding. Second, we are aware that the outcome depends on the other person's actions. Third, we think the other person's behavior will produce beneficial results; we are confident that the positive outcomes are more apt to occur than the negative outcomes. In other words, we think the behavior of the other person has "positive" predictability.

Trustworthy Behavior

Like trusting behavior, **trustworthy behavior** demands that three conditions be satisfied. First, we become aware of the motivational preferences of another person. Second, we recognize that the other person has confidence in us and is relying on us to confirm his or her expectations. Third, we respond by exhibiting the expected behaviors.

Failed Trust

If any ingredient for trusting or trustworthy behavior is lacking, trust, in the real sense of the word, does not exist. It should be evident from our discussion on the components of trust that trust is difficult to develop. However—unfortunately—trust is relatively easy to destroy. Trust requires that each party in a relationship be willing to risk something; the element of risk means that either party to the relationship could be personally harmed or diminished. When we trust others we recognize that it is possible for others to use our trusting behavior against us. When this happens, trust is usually shattered.

Unfortunately, not everyone we know can be trusted.[1] Inappropriately trusting another individual can sometimes cause us as many problems as not trusting someone who merits our trust. Thus, it is wise to avoid trusting another person if he or she repeatedly behaves in a way that brings you pain or causes you to feel rejected or betrayed. When you say, "I don't trust Ralph," for example, you probably mean that when you trusted him in the past, he disappointed you. In effect, you no longer feel you can predict what Ralph will do in a given situation. In contrast, it makes sense for you to continue trusting those whose behavior you believe you can predict with relatively consistent accuracy.

To what extent, if any, have you made growth choices?

Trust is a gamble and thus always involves some risk. According to psychologist Abraham Maslow, people who trust themselves and others tend to make "growth" choices. Maslow believes that those individuals who make "growth" choices are self-actualizers who are close to fulfilling their unique potential as human beings.[2] The trusting behavior of self-actualizers permits them to experience the world fully and vividly, for they have the ability to be open and honest with others as well as themselves. Because trust can lead us to reveal important information about ourselves, it can also help us improve our self-understanding and awareness. Thus trust, openness, and self-actualization go hand-in-hand.

Have you ever played or been the target of a "get the guest" experience?

As you have probably learned from experience, there are numerous reasons for sustaining or ending a relationship. Once we feel we can no longer trust another person, our relationship with that individual is in jeopardy. The absence of trust, an ingredient essential to the sharing of intimate information, causes reciprocation of disclosures to cease, thereby precipitating relationship failure. Trust is somewhat like interpersonal glue. When it is present, parties psychologically stick together. The relationship is perceived to have value. When it is missing, however, the potential costs of a relationship are perceived to outweigh its potential benefits.

Misplaced Trust

An example of the negative outcomes of misplaced trust is in Edward Albee's play *Who's Afraid of Virginia Woolf?* During the course of an evening spent at the home of George and Martha, Nick and Honey and their hosts engage in some rather heavy "social" drinking. When the wives are elsewhere, George discloses some personal information about his youth to Nick. Nick reciprocates by telling George that because of Honey's hysterical pregnancy, he was forced to marry her. As the evening progresses, George perceives that Nick has humiliated him; he therefore decides to "get the guest." In the presence of Honey and Martha, George reveals the story Nick had confided in him. Honey, quickly sickened, rushes from the room. The scene ends with Nick vowing revenge for George's behavior.

1. Cite an incident in which you witnessed or participated in an interaction in which someone who was trusted acted in an untrustworthy manner. What did you and others learn as a result?

2. Describe a relationship you share that is based on trust. Identify the trusting and trustworthy behaviors exhibited by both partners, and determine the factors in your relationship that permitted a climate of trust to develop.

3. Describe a second relationship you share that you mistakenly believed was based on trust. Identify the trusting and trustworthy behaviors that were missing, and describe the negative consequences that resulted from the situation. Determine the factors in your relationship that prevented or inhibited the development of a climate of trust.

Forgiveness: Rebuilding a Relationship After Trust Is Betrayed

What happens when you are hurt as the result of an interpersonal transgression committed against you by someone close to you? Are you likely to respond by holding a grudge and being resentful or by forgiving the other person? The choice of whether to forgive or not to forgive another person is ours, and no one can force us to do either. According to researchers, forgiveness can be defined as the "peace and understanding that come from blaming that which has hurt you less, taking the life experience less personally, and changing your grievance story."[3] While forgiveness does not mean condoning unkindness, it is a manifestation of the personal control we have over our lives. So is deciding whether or not we take offense in the first place.[4]

In order to repair and rebuild a relationship that has been jeopardized by the betrayal of a person whom we trusted, we need to find a way to forgive the person who has hurt us so that we are able to let go of the active and submerged "black cloud of anger."[5] According to forgiveness researcher Fred Luskin, people establish strict rules of relationship fair play such as "Don't cheat on your partner" and "Don't lie," and when individuals violate those norms or choose not to follow our rules, we are apt to label them "bad persons" and find it challenging to deal with them. Luskin believes that the act of forgiveness involves a multistage problem solving process, similar to the one associated with grief. In the forgiveness process, initially the person feels anger and hurt, but then finds a way to forgive the specific offense by "taking less personal offense, blaming the offender less, and offering more personal and situational understanding of the offender and of oneself."[6] Luskin identifies four stages in the forgiveness process:

1. Experiencing self-justified anger,

2. Recognizing that anger does not feel good to you and desiring to repair the damage to the relationship,

3. Realizing that forgiveness has beneficial effects and choosing to let go of your anger fairly quickly, and

4. Making the proactive choice to rarely if ever get angry.

He also notes that we will not all follow these four stages in the same way. There are some people for whom we have such love that we will always be at stage four. And there are other people who have hurt us so badly that we might spend years at stage one. The choice, however, should be ours.[7]

Persons who are unable to forgive a violation of trust put themselves in danger of experiencing not just emotional difficulties and interpersonal problems, but also impaired cardiological, neurological, and immune systems. Notes Luskin, "When we get hurt, we get hurt not just in our minds but also in our bodies. The more readily we experience anger or hurt, the more our bodies secrete 'stress chemicals' that, over time, take a toll."[8] Persons who are unwilling to forgive experience more depression and are likely to have less fulfilling relationships. Holding onto resentment can adversely impact health. In the words of Nelson Mandela, "Resentment is like drinking poison and waiting for it to kill your enemy." In contrast, giving up grudges improves both emotional and physical well-being. By accepting not only the flaws that others have, but our own flaws as

Theory

The Forgiveness Factor

First, identify one unresolved hurtful interpersonal experience that continues to elicit from you negative behavioral, cognitive, or emotional responses. What keeps you holding a grudge toward or being unable to forgive the person?*

Next, take a position on each of the following questions and defend each position with reasons:

1. Who is more willing to forgive a breach in trust—a man or a woman?

2. Is being unwilling to forgive the same thing as continuing to hold a grudge?

3. Is forgiveness about the future or the past?

Interestingly, when Stanford psychologists solicited volunteers to participate in a study on forgiveness, they found it easy to attract female participants but had difficulty attracting men. In an effort to determine why men were hesitant to participate, one of the researchers, Dr. Carl Thoresen, randomly asked a group of men about it. The consensus among the men was that the word *forgiveness* was too soft and acquiescing, suggesting that the person was being a doormat. They advised that the researchers substitute the harsher, more masculine sounding word *grudge* in place of the word *forgiveness*. Once researchers began distributing flyers reading "Got a grudge?" male participants surfaced.

*F. Luskin, C. Thoresen, A. Harris, S. Benisovich, S. Standard, J. Bruning, and S. Evans, "Effects of Group Forgiveness Intervention on Perceived Stress, State and Trait Anger, Symptoms of Stress, Self-Reported Health and Forgiveness," August 2001, **http://www.learningtoforgive.com/Research.htm.**

well, we increase our chances of deriving more satisfaction from our relationships. Learning to forgive the self is as important as learning to forgive others.

Cost–Benefit Theory: The Price We Are Willing to Pay for a Relationship

According to **cost–benefit** or **social exchange theory,**[9] we work to sustain relationships that give us the greatest total benefit. We can represent this concept by constructing a relational balance sheet on which we keep track of the rewards we receive from our relationships and the costs we must pay to obtain the rewards. We can represent the relational equation as follows:

Perceived relationship rewards − Perceived relationship costs = Perceived relationship benefits

The perceived relationship rewards are the positive outcomes we hope to acquire from our relationships. The perceived relationship costs represent the price, or personal energy, that we must expend if we hope to reap any of the rewards. The perceived relationship benefit is the net gain (or loss, if the costs turn out to be more than the rewards) from the relationship.

We can see how this equation works by looking at some sample relationships. For example, to acquire a benefit of intimacy in a relationship, we have to be willing to trust another person enough to self-disclose or reveal personal information to him or her. To acquire social acceptance, we have to adopt certain beliefs, attitudes, and values. To acquire friends, we need to work at being a good friend. In each case, to obtain any benefit we have to pay a price; that is, we need to expend energy to ensure that we receive a desired result.

This couple's happy relationship is their reward for the energy they've expended over the years to maintain it.

Calvin and Hobbes © 1993 Watterson. Reprinted with permission of Universal Press Syndicate. All rights reserved.

in Practice

Relationship Balance Sheet

Consider two relationships: one that recently ended and one that you currently are in.

1. Conduct a cost–benefit analysis for each relationship by identifying both the rewards you receive(d) and the costs you accrue(d). Estimate what you consider your net benefit to be.

	Relationship you ended	Relationship you currently are in
Rewards you received		

Costs you accrued		
Net benefit		

2. On the basis of your analysis, what do you think led you to end the first relationship? What is your forecast for the future of the present relationship?

In fact, our relationships thrive or falter as a consequence of the energy we are willing to expend on them; they succeed or fail based on what we are willing to do with and for one another. For example, we may expect a high level of trust, commitment, respect, and, when appropriate, love to characterize a relationship when we have worked to hold up our side of it. When expectations like these are

Sharing, interdependent efforts, and trust are characteristics of a cooperative relationship.

fulfilled, we find the relationship satisfying; however, when they go unfulfilled, we find the relationship lacking.

Cost–benefit theory tells us that we will work to continue a relationship only as long as the benefits we perceive ourselves to be receiving outweigh our emotional expenditures. Typical benefits include increased self-esteem, an enhanced sense of security, and better coping skills. In comparison, the typical costs we must pay to get these benefits include the time we need to invest to make a relationship work, psychological and physical stress, and a damaged self-image. As we compare and contrast the profits and costs of one relationship, we also establish a **comparison level for alternatives** with which to weigh the profits and costs of one relationship against those we might derive from another. If we believe we will easily find another person to give us whatever a current partner is not providing, we are likely to extricate ourselves from an unsatisfactory relationship and enter a new and potentially more rewarding one; in contrast, if we believe such a person *cannot* easily be found, we are more likely to stay in the relationship even though it carries with it great costs and the potential for significant personal loss.[10]

Theory

How Competitive Are You?

Generate a list of three people with whom you interact regularly.

1. Think about three recent encounters with each person and how each encounter made you feel.

2. Characterize your interactions with each person as predominantly competitive (X) or cooperative (O) in nature by placing the appropriate symbol next to each name.

3. Describe how your feelings about each relationship are reflected in your behavior. In other words, how do you act in situations you define as competitive? In situations you define as cooperative? Are there times when it would have been or would be more productive for you to cooperate rather than compete? What kept or keeps you from doing so?

4. To what extent, if any, does the sex or the ethnicity of the other person appear to make a difference in your perception of the relationship? Explain.

Defining the Relational Situation

Trusting and trustworthy behaviors will thrive or wither depending on the relationship situation or climate.

Cooperative and Competitive Relationships

How we define the relational situation plays an important role in determining whether we develop trust. If individuals view their relationship as primarily a **competitive relationship,** then both are more likely to attempt to protect themselves when communicating with each other, and the rule of "everyone for him- or herself" may play itself out. If, on the other hand, individuals view the relationship between them as primarily a **cooperative relationship,** the dog-eat-dog nature of the situation is eliminated, and sharing, interdependent efforts, and trust are more likely. Defining an interpersonal relationship as competitive precipitates defensive and threatening behavior on the part of the communicators, whereas defining it as cooperative precipitates supportive, nonthreatening behav-

With which friends do you tend to compete and cooperate? How does your definition of a relationship affect its nature?

iors and the exchange of messages that are more honest. In cooperative interpersonal relationships communication channels are opened rather than closed.

The goals we bring to each of our relationships affect the amount of trust we exhibit in each other. If we perceive our goals to be congruent, then it is easier for us to create an atmosphere of cooperation. But if we perceive our goals to be contradictory, then we are more likely to display competitive mind-sets.

In order for both parties in an interpersonal relationship to cooperate, certain requirements must be met. First, both parties must agree that each has an equal right to satisfy his or her needs. Second, conditions have to allow each person to get what he or she wants at least some of the time. Third, power plays that rely on techniques such as threatening, yelling, or demanding are discouraged. Finally, neither party attempts to manipulate the other by holding back information or dissembling. When engaged in cooperative interaction, one individual does not aim to "win," "beat," or "outsmart" the other. Unlike competition, cooperation does not depend on one person gaining an edge over another, and also unlike competition, cooperation does not promote defensiveness or lying.

Supportive and Defensive Relationships

One of the first problems we face when we enter into a new relationship is developing an ability and willingness to trust the other person.[11] For trust to develop we have to feel valued by each other. Valuing is communicated by messages a person sends that make us feel recognized, let us know that our ideas and feelings are important, and project interest in what we think and how we feel. When valuing is not communicated, we usually take steps to protect ourselves from being hurt. The result can be a **defensive climate** because a party to the relationship perceives or anticipates a threat. The kind of threat we are talking about is not necessarily physical, but rather a comment or behavior by one person that the other person perceives as a direct attack on the image that he or she is trying to project. When we feel psychologically unsafe, we are likely to experience a negative feeling and respond by exhibiting a defensive reaction. For example, we might respond to a threat to our image by counterattacking and becoming verbally aggressive towards the other person: "Who made you king?" we might say. "What gives you the right to say what I should and should not do!" In effect, with our response, we take the focus off ourselves, shifting the blame to the other person. We could also defend ourselves from attack by distorting what the other person says in such a way that we are able to preserve our sense of self. We rationalize the attack—we create an explanation that is untrue but self-protective. Or we try to compensate for the criticism by pointing out one or more strengths we have that we contend are more important than the weakness that was pointed out to us. Instead of deflecting an attack, we could choose simply to avoid one by avoiding people we believe pose a threat to our image. None of these attempts at image preservation are particularly healthy responses.

Analyze how nonverbal cues have contributed to the creation of defensive or supportive climates in relationships you share.

To minimize or eliminate the arousal of defensiveness in our own interpersonal relationships, we need to understand the stimuli that can cause us to become defensive in the first place and substitute supportive behaviors. In a classic article Jack R. Gibb identified six such defense-causing behaviors and isolated six contrasting behaviors that, when exhibited, help create a **supportive climate** that will reduce the level of threat individuals experience (see Table 9.1).[12]

> **TABLE 9.1**
> Categories of Behavior Characteristic of Defensive and Supportive Climates
>
> | *Defensive climate* | *Supportive climate* |
> |---|---|
> | 1. Evaluation | 1. Description |
> | *Judgmental statements impede communication* | *Neutral statements promote communication* |
> | 2. Control | 2. Problem orientation |
> | *Promotes resistance* | *Promotes cooperation* |
> | 3. Strategy | 3. Spontaneity |
> | *Presence of a hidden agenda* | *Deception-free* |
> | 4. Neutrality | 4. Empathy |
> | *Communicates indifference* | *Communicates concern* |
> | 5. Superiority | 5. Equality |
> | *Encourages jealousy or resentment* | *Encourages trust* |
> | 6. Certainty | 6. Provisionalism |
> | *Encourages perceptions of inflexibility* | *Encourages perceptions of flexibility* |

Evaluation versus Description

A relationship can run into trouble if one party makes judgmental or evaluative statements. If, as a result of our manner of speaking, tone, or words, we seem to be evaluating or judging the person with whom we are interacting, that individual is likely to be wary of our intentions. For example, once we label the actions of another with a judgmental term such as "stupid," "ridiculous," or "absurd," that action can impede the development or continuance of a positive communication climate. The following statements are judgmental in tone and phrased in a way likely to evoke defensiveness:

> "You have no idea what you're talking about!"
> "This car is filthy!"
> "Your sense of humor sucks!"

In contrast to evaluative behaviors, descriptive behaviors recount particular observable actions of an individual without labeling those behaviors good or bad, right or wrong. When we use descriptive language, we do not admonish the other person to change his or her behavior but simply report or question what we saw, heard, or felt. The following statements are descriptive, nonjudgmental, nonevaluative, and focused on the speaker's thoughts and feelings:

> "I would like to understand how you came to that conclusion."
> "I get upset when the car looks like this because I'm the one who cleans it up."
> "When you tell jokes that embarrass me I turn all red."

It is usually more productive to describe what concerns you than to go on the attack. Thus, instead of telling someone that a marketing report is poorly done, be descriptive and say: "The marketing analysis doesn't include background on the competition."

Control versus Problem Orientation

Communication perceived as an effort to exert control over another also provokes defensiveness rather than trust in the target. In other words, if our intent is to control the individual with whom we are interacting—that is, to get that person to do something or change his or her beliefs—we are apt to encounter resistance. The amount of resistance we meet depends, in part, on the openness with which we approach the individual and the degree to which our behavior causes the other person to question or doubt our motives. Once we conclude that someone is trying to control us, we tend also to conclude that the individual believes that we are ignorant and unable to make decisions. A problem orientation, on the other hand, promotes just the opposite response. Because the sender communicates that he or she has not already formulated a solution and is not going to attempt to force his or her opinions on us, we feel free to cooperate to solve the problem. For example, consider asking the other person to decide where to dine, what movie to see, how to use a job bonus, or for whom to vote rather than issuing a directive such as, "Well, I like Barbados more than Aruba, and since my bonus is paying for the vacation, I'll decide where we go."

A controlling orientation is not just communicated with words; we can also generate hostility in others via voice tone, gestures, or facial expressions. Whether using words or nonverbal cues, the person exerting control sends a clear message that he or she has more power, has secured more rights, or is more intelligent than we are— a message we are likely to find disconfirming and objectionable. A problem-solving demeanor, accompanied by problem-solving words, is much less likely to trigger a defensive reaction. Say something such as, "It appears that we both have different vacation destinations in mind. Let's see if we can identify a locale where we can enjoy ourselves together." This keeps the relationship intact rather than provoking interpersonal disharmony.

Strategy versus Spontaneity

The level of defensiveness we experience is likely to increase if we feel another individual is trying to put something past us. No one likes to be conned or made the victim of a hidden agenda. We become suspicious of strategies we discover have been concealed or are underhanded. We do not look with favor on someone who makes a decision for us and then tries to make us feel that we made the decision. Once we feel we have been manipulated, we tend to become defensive and self-protective. In contrast, honest, spontaneous behavior, free of deception, helps reduce defensiveness. Under such conditions, we will doubt less the motivations of another person, and trust is more likely to develop.

With this in mind, consider if a person says to us, "Would you help me out if I told you it was really important?" and also fails to tell us what helping out means. We might feel that something is being kept from us, and we might begin to feel that we were being set up. We might develop a similar feeling if someone began a request for help with words like these: "Remember when you needed me to help move?" Instead of trying to manipulate us with premeditated comments, others should be open and honest with us. For example, saying, "I could really use your help to prepare for this exam," is a more natural and straightforward way of asking for someone's assistance.

On the Defensive

Defensive behaviors abound in the communicative strategies employed by Blanche DuBois in Tennessee Williams's *A Streetcar Named Desire*. Blanche holds a false picture of herself and a set of values contradicted by reality. As she puts it, "I don't want realism. I want magic. I try to give that to people. I misrepresent things to them. I don't tell the truth. I tell what ought to be truth." Blanche feels the need to act defensively to maintain her false image. She can't "stand a naked light bulb" any more than she can stand the truth. Blanche's inner feelings and outward acts tend to create equally defensive postures in her brother-in-law, Stanley. Their resulting circular response pattern becomes increasingly destructive.

STANLEY: This millionaire from Dallas is not going to interfere with your privacy any?

BLANCHE: It won't be the sort of thing you have in mind. This man is a gentleman and he respects me. (*Improvising feverishly*) What he wants is my companionship. Having great wealth sometimes makes people lonely! A cultivated woman, a woman of intelligence and breeding, can enrich a man's life—immeasurably! I have those things to offer, and this doesn't take them away. Physical beauty is passing. A transitory possession. But beauty of the mind and richness of the spirit and tenderness of the heart—and I have all of those things—aren't taken away, but grow! Increase with the years! How strange that I should be called a destitute woman! When I have all of these treasures locked in my heart. (*A choked sob comes from her*) I think of myself as a very, very rich woman! But I have been foolish—casting my pearls before swine!

STANLEY: Swine, huh?

BLANCHE: Yes, swine! Swine! And I'm thinking not only of you but of your friend, Mr. Mitchell. He came to see me tonight. He dared to come here in his work clothes! And to repeat slander to me, vicious stories that he had gotten from you! I gave him his walking papers . . .

STANLEY: You did, huh?

BLANCHE: But then he came back. He returned with a box of roses to beg my forgiveness! He implored my forgiveness. But some things are not forgivable. Deliberate cruelty is not forgivable. It is the one unforgivable thing in my opinion and it is the one thing of which I have never, never been guilty. And so I told him, I said to him, "Thank you," but it was foolish of me to think that we could ever adapt ourselves to each other. Our ways of life are too different. Our attitudes and our backgrounds are incompatible. We have to be realistic about such things. So farewell, my friend! And let there be no hard feelings . . .

STANLEY: Was this before or after the telegram came from the Texas oil millionaire?

BLANCHE: What telegram? No! No, after! As a matter of fact, the wire came just as—

STANLEY: As a matter of fact there wasn't no wire at all!

BLANCHE: Oh, oh!

STANLEY: There isn't no millionaire! And Mitch didn't come back with roses 'cause I know where he is—

BLANCHE: Oh!

STANLEY: There isn't a goddamn thing but imagination!

BLANCHE: Oh!

STANLEY: And lies and conceit and tricks!

BLANCHE: Oh!

STANLEY: And look at yourself! Take a look at yourself in that worn-out Mardi Gras outfit, rented for fifty cents from some rag-picker! And with the crazy crown on! What queen do you think you are?

BLANCHE: Oh—God . . .

STANLEY: I've been on to you from the start! Not once did you pull any wool over this boy's eyes! You come in here and sprinkle the place with powder and spray perfume and cover the light-bulb with a paper lantern, and lo and behold the place has turned into Egypt and you are the Queen of the Nile! Sitting on your throne and swilling down my liquor! I say—*Ha!*—*Ha!* Do you hear me? *Ha—ha—ha!* (*He walks into the bedroom*)

1. Describe the defensive behaviors exhibited by the characters in this exchange.
2. Consider what the results of the encounter might have been if either or both parties had taken a supportive stance.

In *A Streetcar Named Desire,* playwright Tennessee Williams shows us how the defensive postures exhibited by Blanche DuBois and Stanley Kowalski become increasingly destructive.

Neutrality versus Empathy

Another behavior that can increase defensiveness is neutrality. For the most part, we like and need to feel that others see us as worthwhile, value our presence, like us, and are willing to take the time to establish a meaningful relationship with us. If instead of communicating warmth and concern the person with whom we are interacting communicates neutrality or indifference, we may interpret this as worse than rejection, concluding that the individual has no interest in us or that he or she perceives us as a nonperson. Comments such as, "In that class, I'm only a number" or "The boss doesn't even know me by my name" indicate that someone is bothered by a perceived indifference. In contrast, empathy erases feelings of indifference by implying care and regard for others. When you accept another person's feelings, you send a message of concern and respect. "I can see that you're hurting and I understand why" and "It sounds like you're feeling undervalued by your boss" are empathic statements.

Superiority versus Equality

The fifth set of behaviors fostering the development of either defensiveness or trust in interpersonal relationships is superiority and equality. Our defensiveness is aroused if the person with whom we are communicating expresses feelings of superiority about social position, power, wealth, intellectual aptitude, appearance, or other such characteristics. Upon receiving such a message, we are apt to react by competing with the sender, becoming jealous, or ignoring the message altogether. On the other hand, by communicating a message of equality, another person can forestall defensive reactions in us and encourage our trust.

Persons with whom we are communicating are likely to become defensive of any message that we send suggesting that we are in a one-up position and that they are not as good as we are. Sometimes the way we deliver a message conveys our feelings of superiority and lets others conclude that we literally are "turning our nose down at them." Consequently, saying something such as "I know more than you do on this subject" or "You should shop where I shop" convey an attitude of superiority and are likely to elicit from us a response protecting our self-esteem. If the remarks had been communicated to us in a way that did not make us feel inadequate, we would probably be less apt to get our guard up. The more secure we feel, the easier it is to treat someone as an equal.

Certainty versus Provisionalism

The last set of behaviors is certainty and provisionalism. When someone expresses absolute or total certainty about a disputed issue, we may become defensive. We suspect individuals who think they have all the answers, view themselves as our "guides" through life rather than our fellow travelers, and belittle or reject ideas we have to offer. In contrast, an attitude of provisionalism (openmindedness), by not requiring someone to win an argument, defend ideas to the bitter end, or be right all the time, is more likely to encourage the development of trust.

When we communicate an attitude of provisionalism, we make it possible for others to perceive us as flexible and open. We do not want to feel or convey "the need to be right." Saying something such as "Only an idiot would think this assignment is fun" or "You're not going to get me to change my mind, because I know my decision is right" closes the door to continued discussion because the speaker appears to be unwilling to consider other positions. Alternatively, saying something such as "The way I look at the assignment . . ."or "The way I came to my decision is . . ." encourage further discussion.

 Practice

On the Defensive

First, think of several interpersonal encounters you have shared during which you believed that the person with whom you were interacting successfully challenged the image you were trying to project. For example, how would you respond if a professor or employer criticized you for performing poorly? Or how would you feel if a friend told you that you were never there when needed but always put yourself first? If the criticism was justified, you would more than likely feel defensive. Compile a list of persons with whom you most frequently feel on the defensive. Identify the aspects of yourself that these people cause you to defend and the means you use to protect yourself from their perceived attacks.

Next, think of several interpersonal encounters during which you sent one or more messages to the persons with whom you were communicating that led them to feel a threat to their image. How did they respond to your criticisms? What consequences did your behavior have for your future relationship with those persons?

Consider the defense-producing situations from the perspective of both persons. What advice would you give to the person whose image was threatened regarding how to handle feelings of defensiveness more effectively? What would you say to the person doing the threatening regarding how to reduce the level of threat projected?

TABLE 9.2
Nonverbal Symbols That Can Contribute to the Development of a Supportive or Defensive Climate

Behavior producing defensiveness	*Behavior producing supportiveness*
1. Evaluation	1. Description
Maintaining extended eye contact *Pointing at the other person* *Placing your hands on your hips* *Shaking your head* *Shaking your index finger*	*Maintaining comfortable eye contact* *Leaning forward*
2. Control	2. Problem Orientation
Sitting in the focal (central) * position* *Placing hands on hips* *Shaking your head* *Maintaining extended eye contact* *Invading the personal space of* * the other person*	*Maintaining comfortable personal distance* *Crossing your legs in the direction of the* * other person* *Leaning forward* *Maintaining comfortable eye contact*
3. Strategy	3. Spontaneity
Maintaining extended eye contact *Shaking your head* *Using forced gestures*	*Leaning forward* *Crossing your legs in the direction of the* * other person* *Maintaining comfortable eye contact* *Using animated natural gestures*
4. Neutrality	4. Empathy
Crossing your legs away from the * other person* *Using a monotone voice* *Staring elsewhere* *Leaning back* *Maintaining a large body distance* * ($4\frac{1}{2}$–5 feet)*	*Maintaining close personal distance* * (20–36 inches)* *Maintaining comfortable eye contact* *Crossing your legs in the direction of the* * other person* *Nodding your head* *Leaning toward the other person*
5. Superiority	5. Equality
Maintaining extended eye * contact* *Placing your hands on your hips* *Situating yourself at a higher* * elevation* *Invading the other person's* * personal space*	*Maintaining comfortable eye contact* *Leaning forward* *Situating yourself at the same elevation* *Maintaining a comfortable distance*
6. Certainty	6. Provisionalism
Maintaining extended eye contact *Crossing your arms* *Placing your hands on your hips* *Using a dogmatic voice*	*Maintaining comfortable eye contact* *Nodding your head* *Tilting your head to one side*

Various nonverbal cues support the development of either a defensive or a supportive interpersonal climate; Table 9.2 summarizes them. As you review the cues, consider the extent to which a defensive or supportive climate characterizes each of your relevant social or job-related relationships.

Gender, Risk, and Trust: Today's Dilemma

One way we can better understand the importance of cooperation, reliance, dependence, and trust is by using the game–theoretical model known as the "prisoner's dilemma,"[13] which illustrates how people evaluate a decision-making situation in terms of how much to trust another person. In the game, two prisoners are being held for a crime. Each has the opportunity to better his or her own position at the expense of the other person. However, if both players implicitly trust each other, both can better their positions. But by taking the trusting approach, each runs the risk that the other player might violate that trust and take advantage of him or her. Scores are assigned to the various situations and plotted on a matrix game board. Each decision represents a change in the game board and the scores are recalculated. The possibilities are for both parties to maintain the status quo (a_1b_1), for a to change but not b (a_2b_1), for b to change but not a (a_1b_2), or for both to change (a_2b_2). The four situations are illustrated in the matrix in Figure 9.1.

The actual numbers used in Figure 9.1 and subsequent paragraphs are just for illustration. The factor to focus on is the relative value of each of the payoffs. When both parties in the relationship choose to cooperate, the perceived reward for cooperating must be greater than the perceived temptation for defecting. In any prisoner's dilemma–like situation, both parties involved can cooperate, one can defect and thereby harm the other party who cooperates, or both can defect and proceed without the support of the other. The "winning or losing" part comes with the payoffs/rewards and/or the temptations/defections (represented in the relationship matrix by the assigned numbers).

Whom to trust is a question faced not just by prisoners but by anyone making interpersonal decisions. Consider the following hypothetical situation involving a man and a woman that can be illustrated by the prisoner's dilemma. Anne (a) and Rafael (b) were recently married. Both are employed, represented on the matrix as a_1b_1, and happy (+5 +5 are the scores for both players at the start of the game). Anne has been given a chance at a new job, but to do so, she must relocate. If she takes the new job and convinces Rafael to go with her (a_2b_2), she would receive a substantial increase in salary, work fewer hours, and gain status and power. Her score would move from +5 to +20, but Rafael's would change from +5 to −2. But if Anne accepts the new position without the support of Rafael (a_2b_1), she could lose him and much of her happiness and move from a score of +5 to a score of

In general, whom do you trust more: men or women? Why?

FIGURE 9.1
Relationship Matrix

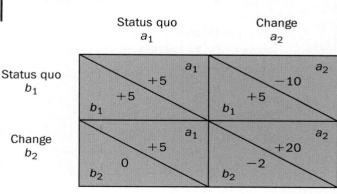

	Status quo a_1	Change a_2
Status quo b_1	$+5$ / $+5$ (a_1/b_1)	-10 / $+5$ (a_2/b_1)
Change b_2	$+5$ / 0 (a_1/b_2)	$+20$ / -2 (a_2/b_2)

−10. Thus, Anne must convince Rafael that it is to their mutual advantage to relocate. To succeed, she has to persuade him that the negative effects he sees in the move—his having to look for another job, leaving friends—are far outweighed by the fact that he will not have to work as hard as he does in his present job; nor will he have to work as many hours, since the pay increase Anne will receive will permit Rafeal to "take it easy." To be sure, Anne has to convince her husband that she will really share the rewards of her new job with him, because after he consents to change from b_1 to b_2 his score will change from +5 to −2 and he will feel vulnerable. In fact, Rafael believes that once Anne rises to the top he only stands to lose, because he thinks she may grow to feel that she no longer needs him. On the other hand, he knows that if he opposes her taking the new job and they stay where they are (a_1b_1; +5 +5), Anne will not be able to achieve her career goals.

Now, consider this, Aaron (a) and Barbara (b) were recently married. They are quite happy (+5 +5), and both planned to work to save money before going to college (a_1b_1). However, Aaron has just been given an opportunity to attend a top college (+20). If he accepts, Barbara will have to work full-time to pay the tuition and their living expenses (a_2b_2). This means she won't be able to pursue her own college education until after Aaron receives his degree. If Aaron decides to enter college without the support of his wife (a_2b_1) he could lose Barbara, her income, and much of his happiness (−10). Thus, it is important for Aaron to convince Barbara that it is to their mutual advantage that he attend school before she

in Context

Who Supports Whom?

1. Divide into male–female pairs, and discuss the situations faced by Anne and Rafael and Aaron and Barbara in the text. When your discussions are complete, secretly indicate your decisions regarding the characters of your gender, writing them on separate slips of paper. Your pair's responses for each situation should be labeled to indicate sex, clipped together, and passed to the instructor for tabulation.

2. Enter the results of each set of deliberations on the following charts:

   A. Anne and Rafael

   Analysis of individual decisions by gender

   Number of males choosing b_1 _____   Number of males choosing b_2 _____
   Number of females choosing a_1 _____   Number of females choosing a_2 _____

   Analysis of decisions

   Number of pairs choosing a_1b_1: _____   Number of pairs choosing a_2b_1: _____

   Number of pairs choosing a_1b_2: _____   Number of pairs choosing a_2b_2: _____

   B. Aaron and Barbara

   Analysis of individual decisions by gender

   Number of males choosing a_1 _____   Number of males choosing a_2 _____
   Number of females choosing b_1 _____   Number of females choosing b_2 _____

   Analysis of decisions

   Number of pairs choosing a_1b_1: _____   Number of pairs choosing a_2b_1: _____
   Number of pairs choosing a_1b_2: _____   Number of pairs choosing a_2b_2: _____

3. Was there a difference in the numbers of males and females who were willing to cooperate for the betterment of their partners? Why?

4. What do the results reveal about gender perceptions?

5. What do the results reveal about trust?

does. However, Barbara fears that once Aaron graduates, he will no longer be interested in her because she will not be his equal. In addition, she has no guarantee that he will pay for her college tuition when the time comes.

What would you suggest in each case? Explain.

For real trust to develop in a relationship, both partners need to be supportive and honest with each other and be willing to take risks and cooperate for mutual gain. This is not always as easy as it appears, however. Many of us simply don't trust each other enough to select the alternative most beneficial to both. At times, we prefer either to "play it safe" or to "go for personal gain" at the possible expense of the other person. What types of choices do you or those with whom you interact make? Do you frequently trust other people to cooperate with you? Can you envision yourself or any of your friends or relatives trying to obtain personal gain at someone else's expense?

Relationship Ethics: Deception and Relationships

An old Moroccan proverb reads: "Why are you lying to me who is your friend?" What does the word "lie" mean to you? To whom have you recently lied? Who has recently lied to you? What kinds of situations do you feel justify lying on your part? Being lied to? How do you react when you catch someone in a lie? How do you react when caught in a lie? How does lying or being lied to affect a relationship? How common is it? Complete the five sentences below.

Is misrepresenting the truth ever justifiable?

1. A lie is _____

2. I would lie to _____

3. I would lie if _____

4. In the past week I lied _____ times.

5. In the past week I was caught lying _____ times.

Why Do We Lie?

Deliberately lying by distorting (committing an *overt lie*) or concealing sensitive information (committing a *covert lie*) is a practice all too common in person-to-person interaction. Whenever we hope to convey a false impression or convince another individual to believe something about us, someone else, or something else that we ourselves do not believe, we are **lying.** Whether we want to admit it or not, our goal is to intentionally deceive the other person into accepting what we know to be untrue; our verbal and nonverbal communicative intent is to mislead the other person either by providing him or her with false information or by purposefully failing to provide him or her with the relevant information he or she needs to make a decision or come to an understanding.[14] When we lie we can manipulate someone into making choices he or she would not otherwise make. By manipulating the truth, partners manipulate each other.

Once we tell a lie, it is rare for us to tell only a single lie. We are compelled to work hard to cover our tracks. Our own experience probably reveals that to sustain a lie, we frequently have to tell another, and another, and another. . . . Thus, whenever we lie, we usually are left with a significant amount of mending. A lot of our time and energy is spent concentrating on who we told what lies to and why. Many people think that lying, whatever the reason, is morally and ethically wrong. Others hold that it is the individual's motives that really matter: was harm intended? Still others believe it is the lie's outcome that merits consideration.

At times we fail to realize that under some circumstances a truth that hurts someone can be as harmful as a lie. Sometimes we succeed in taking away false beliefs from those who need them to survive. Wittingly or unwittingly, when we do this we can do as much damage as callous liars. For example, if someone believes she is attractive to others, but you find her unappealing and a bore, would you say so? Some people need illusions. If you analyze your own life it will probably be clear that some of your relationships rely on the silent agreement made between parties that certain illusions will be sustained and certain memories will be suppressed. This, too, is a form of trust.

White Lies: Are They Little Lies?

What does the phrase "white lie" mean to you? Do you remember the last white lie you told? What motivated you to tell it? What effect did it have? Have you ever encountered a situation in which you might have told a white lie but did not? What stopped you? What were the effects of your telling the truth? To what degree do you think telling white lies can be justified? Do you mind being told white lies?

A *white lie* is a minor falsehood that is not meant to harm or injure anyone. Such lies are sometimes used to provide moral support or cheer, or to maintain the "humanness" of the social relationship itself. An example is telling your roommate you like her haircut even if you don't because you know she does, or telling your little brother you didn't go by the toy store on your way home because you know he'd be upset.

Lying to Ourselves: Defensive Strategies

Individuals do not lie only to others; they also lie to themselves, employing a number of defensive strategies to protect themselves from having to face the truth. It seems we need illusions to feel good about ourselves and to maintain a sense of continuity in our lives.[15] Three commonly employed defense mechanisms are displacement, repression, and rationalization.

To whom do you lie more: yourself or others?

Displacement

Displacement is when we release our anger or frustration by communicating our feelings to people or objects who are perceived to be more accessible and less dangerous than whoever precipitated the feelings in the first place. For example, you yell at a younger brother or sister when you really want to yell at your boss.

Repression

We use the self-protective strategy of **repression** when situations are too painful or unpleasant for us to face. We "forget" the stimulus that disturbs us by denying its very existence. For example, if someone had been verbally abused as a child, he or she might "solve" the problem by pretending that it never happened. Although the facade erected would say "nothing was wrong," in reality, feelings of anger and aggression would be building, and in time, resentment might surface and affect his or her relationships today.

SALLY FORTH   **BY GREG HOWARD**

Reprinted with special permission of King Features Syndicate.

Rationalization

Rationalization is another frequently employed self-protection strategy. When we engage in rationalization, we give ourselves a logical or reasonable explanation for the unrealistic pictures, thoughts, or feelings we have. For instance, workers who receive poor assessments from their managers might tell themselves that "everyone gets poor assessments." Or individuals who interview for a position only to be turned down might convince themselves that they didn't really want the job.

Thus, beneath deception and lying are strong feelings and the desire to protect our emotional well-being or that of another. Our lies may be self-serving or they may be motivated by our desire to demonstrate caring and support for others.[16]

Relationship Counterfeiters

What moves us to create a **counterfeit relationship**—one based on deception that invariably leads us down the road to interpersonal failure? What causes us to lie to another? While there are many reasons we lie, two appear most prevalent: We hope as the result of a lie (1) to gain a reward, or (2) to avoid a punishment. Specifically, we are motivated to lie to protect our self-esteem, continue to meet our basic needs, initiate or preserve desired affiliations, and attain personal satisfaction.[17] Achieving these goals is

in Theory

Under What Conditions Do You Lie?

1. Compile a list of lies you have committed (overtly or covertly) during the past month. Be honest.

2. For each incident, identify your motivation for lying.

3. Did the recipient of each lie discover the deception?

4. What were the lie's effects on your relationship with the person you deceived?

5. Is lying ever ethical? If you think lying is always unethical, explain why. On the other hand, if you think lying can be ethical, identify the ethical guidelines you propose for telling lies.

professional contacts

The Case for White Lies

More than two decades ago, psychologist Richard S. Lazarus reported that when he started practicing as a psychologist, the prevailing view was that accurate reality testing was the hallmark of mental health, an opinion he did not share. Do you accept his rationale? Is it still valid today?

To live successfully meant to face the truth, however painful. This ideology is around today; the latest form of this doctrine is that to have an "authentic" relationship with another person you have to be absolutely honest with that person, and with yourself about how you feel. . . . Paradoxically, poets, playwrights, and novelists have been saying just the opposite: we need our illusions. As Don Quixote puts it in *Man of LaMancha*, "Facts are the enemy of truth." . . .

My own research on how people actually deal with life crises has brought me around to the view that illusion and self-deception can have positive value in a person's psychological economy. Indeed, the fabric of our lives is woven in part from illusion and unexamined beliefs. There is, for example, the collective illusion that our society is free, moral, and just, which, of course, isn't always true. Then there are the countless idiosyncratic beliefs people hold about themselves and the world in which they live — for example, that we are better than average, or doomed to fail, or that the world is a benign conspiracy, or that it is rigged against us. Many such beliefs are passed down from parent to child and never challenged.

Despite the fixity with which people hold such beliefs, they have little or no basis in reality. One person's beliefs are another's delusions. In effect, we pilot our lives in part by illusions and by self-deceptions that give meaning and substance to life.[*]

[*]Richard S. Lazarus, "Positive Denial: The Case for Not Facing Reality," *Psychology Today* (November 1979): 47.

When was the last time you discovered you had been lied to by someone you trusted? How did you respond?

rewarding; having them taken away can be punishing. While we lie, most frequently, to protect ourselves, many lies are designed to protect the person with whom we are interacting, and an even smaller number are committed to benefit some third party (see Table 9.3). Thus, lies help us negotiate situations that have exposed us or someone else to levels of vulnerability that exceed our comfort zone.

The Effect of Lying

How does lying affect a relationship? If discovered, it can chill it by destroying the relationship's very fabric and trust. Imagine sharing a relationship, no matter how effective in other respects, in which you could never trust the authenticity of the other person's messages — never believe his or her words or gestures. Imagine feeling you had been treated unfairly, taken advantage of, or, because of your gullibility, duped. Such a relationship would be difficult to sustain simply because you would probably suspect the other person's motives, resent the way he or she treated you, feel disappointed in him or her as well as in yourself for believing what was told you, and, as a result, be much more likely to question the veracity of any and all future information passed on to you by him or her. Because you feel wronged, you will reinterpret and evaluate your past, present, and future relationships with this individual in light of the lies, and you will be wary of ever fully trusting him or her again.

TABLE 9.3
Who Lies?

Where do you fit into the following statistical analysis of lying?

10,000,000+ taxpayers "lie on their tax forms" according to the IRS.

Approximately 80% of all resumes are misleading.

It is estimated that 70% of all doctors lie on their bills to health insurance providers.

100% of dating couples surveyed reported lying to each other in about a third of their conversations.

20%–30% of middle managers surveyed admitted to writing fraudulent internal reports.

95% of participating college students surveyed were willing to tell at least one lie to a potential employer to win a job, and 41% had already done so.

We are lied to about 200 times each day.

Most people lie to others once or twice a day and deceive about 30 people per week.

The average is 7 times per hour if you count all the times people lie to themselves.

We lie in 30% to 38% of all our interactions.

College students lie in 50% of conversations with their mothers.

The numbers provided are derived from information contained in the 2000 Census Web site and the Bureau of Labor Statistics.
http://www.census.gov/population/www/index.html
http://www.bls.gov/home.htm

Although "bending the truth" to keep the peace in a relationship may be a common practice, doing so can also reveal that the relationship is in trouble and not likely to last. By sucking trust out of a relationship, lies destroy it; after discovering a partner's lies, it is much less likely that you will take the risk and display the vulnerability required for you to trust that person in the future. Once this occurs a climate of distrust can be said to characterize the relationship. In fact, an inability to trust in one's partner is the reason most commonly given for a relationship's deterioration and dissolution, and it is the partner who discovers that he or she has been lied to who typically ends things.

Thus the issue is not just whether you lie in an interpersonal relationship but the *reason* why you lie, the *nature* of the lie you tell, and the *effect* of the lie. Whether to lie or tell the truth is often a difficult decision to make.

The Effects of Gossip

How do you feel about gossip? Have you ever begun a conversation with a friend with words such as these: "Have you heard the latest?" If you have, then more than likely you have gossiped to a friend about another person. Whether you are a man or a woman, telling a friend a juicy story or sharing a rumor lets the other person know that you trust him or her enough to share your confidence. While many believe that gossip is negative, much of it is benign small talk, peppered with statements such as, "Did you know Kaleisha got a really great grade on her presentation?" or "Can you believe that Paula and Sean are engaged? I never thought they'd get back together, after she left him for Raul." This kind of gossip is basically harmless because no secrets are being revealed. What is being talked about is public information. Although many erroneously believe that women gossip more than men, the opposite is actually true. Men gossip at least as much as women, especially on mobile phones. Men, however, give gossip another label—calling it "shop talk."[18] While some consider gossip evil, it is interesting to know that until the 1800s gossip denoted friendship. Today, over two centuries later, a number of psychologists once again contend that it is a natural activity and critical to our survival. Although many of us may think gossip is "wrong," chances are we all gossip. In fact, if you review the conversations you held during the past twenty-four hours, you may discover that a large number of them consisted of gossip. Gossip can be a powerful socializing force.[19]

According to the book *Gossip—The Inside Scoop,* gossip functions like social grooming, setting the boundaries of social behavior and letting us know when we have crossed over a line. As such, it holds the key to our understanding of the social environment, helps us develop and maintain relationships, cement social ties, and bond with other members of our social group.[20] This view is supported by another book, *Grooming, Gossip, and the Evolution of Language,* in which the author contends that verbal communication evolved from a need to indulge in gossip, ultimately reducing stress and enhancing feelings of social cohesion.[21] According to author Robin Dunbar, we humans gossip because, unlike primates, we do not groom each other. Instead, we use speech to maintain contact with one another. For Dunbar gossip is a synonym for social communication. He believes that we learned to talk so that we could talk about each other.

All this is not to deny that gossip does have a darker side. Contemporary e-mail and "chat rooms," for example, are filled with rage and hate messages. Gossip can also be unethical, malicious, and vicious. It is particularly egregious when the information being shared is inaccurate and directed at those who are not present to defend themselves. Sometimes the gossiper is particularly subtle and deceptive by pretending to be sympathetic to the subject of his or her remarks while actually attempting to harm him or her. When used in this way, gossip can do untold damage to relationships. Have you ever been the target of such gossip? What do you believe motivated the gossiper to target you? How did the gossiper's message impact you? What steps did you have to take in order to repair the damage done by the rumors the gossiper spread about you? Were you successful at regaining the trust and respect of those to whom the gossiper spoke? If you were successful at dispelling the rumors, how was the gossiper affected? Gossip, in some instances, functions much like a boomerang—the characteristics the gossiper attributes to you or another person end up rebounding back to the gossiper.

Diversity and Culture Contacts

Influences on Trust

Our expectations and predictions regarding how members of various cultural groups will communicate with us can facilitate or impede the development of trust when we actually relate to a member of the group. Some of us are much less apt to trust someone whom we perceive to be different from us than we are to trust those we think are similar. For example, consider that people from Western cultures expect friends to maintain approximately an arm's length distance when conversing. When people enter our private space, we feel uncomfortable and violated and are unlikely to enter a trusting relationship. In contrast, many members of Arabic cultures expect friends to stand so close that they can smell each other's breath. In fact, some people in Arabic cultures believe that to not allow a friend to smell your breath is viewed as an insult and can lead to decreases in trust and intimacy.[22]

The presence of ethnocentrism also impedes the development of trusting relationships with people from different cultural groups. *Ethnocentrism* is the perception that one's own culture is superior to all others; it leads us to conclude that our way of doing things is the best way, that members of other groups have inferior values, and that, therefore, we should maintain a social distance from them. Thus, rather than try to understand members of other groups, which would facilitate our trust in them, we simply evaluate their behavior and manner of communicating negatively. Feelings of ethnocentrism can make it difficult for individuals to dispel preconceptions, impede the personalizing of communication, make satisfying conversations of self-disclosure difficult, limit the acceptance of "outsiders," and hinder the development of trusting relationships between individuals.[23]

The more ethnocentric you are, the more anxious you are about interacting with other cultures; when we are fearful, we are less likely to expect a positive outcome from such interactions, and less willing to trust someone from another culture. If relationships between people from diverse cultures are to thrive, then the individuals involved at least "need to act *as if* a sense of (trust) were justified, and set their doubts aside."[24] Unfortunately, unless interactants feel they can trust one another, it is unlikely that their relationship will become close.

People from different cultures also differ in the amount of emotional expression they are apt to exhibit. In the United States people operate from the premise that expressing feelings is a positive act and, as a result, are particularly emotionally expressive, but it is important to realize that other cultures are much less likely to act emotionally, preferring to mask their emotions and behave in a way that may not signify how they actually feel. It becomes difficult for us to trust such people if we think their lack of expressiveness is a form of deception that will enable them to lead us astray.

In Practice

Trust and Diversity

Use the following series of statements to gauge the degree to which you are prepared to trust people whom you perceive to be significantly different from yourself.

1. Label each statement True or False. Be honest.

_____ I usually trust most people whom I perceive to be like me more than those who are different.

_____ I am more apt to cooperate with someone whom I perceive to be like me than someone who is different.

_____ I fear interacting with people from other cultures.

_____ I believe people from other cultures create problems for me.

_____ I use my values as a standard against which I judge the values of others.

2. If your answers are mostly True, you will need to work on becoming more prepared to trust others who are different from you.

Gender Contacts

Influences on Lying and Trust

Is the Internet, as a sociologist suggested, like a "backyard fence, a place for virtual neighbors to build trust and intimacy?"[25] For example, if you need to talk to someone you trust, you can go online, see which of your "buddies" is currently online, and chat with him or her.

The kinds of lies we tell may be gender based. Whereas the lies of men tend to be self-centered, the lies of women tend to focus on the feelings of others. Women will generally put a positive spin on events, or falsely derogate themselves to make another feel more confident, whereas men may pretend to be more put off than they actually are in order to manipulate others into acting the way they want.[26]

Just as women use talk to preserve relationships, at times they will also pretend not to detect a lie so they don't have to put the relationship in jeopardy. Because of this quality, some believe that women are more self-deceptive than men. Men, in contrast, tend to be more likely to confront the deception, or at the very least to let on that they are aware that another person is trying to deceive them.[27]

Men and women both want to have close friends they can trust. Yet women focus primarily on the sharing of feelings, while men focus primarily on the sharing of activities.[28] Yet both kinds of interaction can engender trust and may be considered alternate paths to its development. Unless there is reason to doubt trust in a relationship, men assume trust and rarely discuss it, whereas women are likely to talk about a relationship's dynamics more overtly.

Having mismatched perceptions of communication, men and women can hurt each other and impair trust by failing to recognize each other's concerns and to interpret each other's behavior appropriately. However, because trust develops as people support each other, making each other emotionally reliable, mutual attentiveness tends to enhance trust. Women are more likely than men to sense when a partner is in trouble and provide an empathic response. Men, upon sensing something is wrong, tend to respond by attempting to change the subject. While from a female perspective such a response may be interpreted as a lack of caring or understanding, when viewed from a male perspective it is construed as appropriate.[29]

Media and Technology Contacts

Lessons about Trust

The media and technology influence the amount of trust we place in others.

The Media and Trust

Of the many influences on how we view different groups in society, the media are among the most powerful. Integrated into our daily lives, media messages are repeated to us incessantly. They communicate images of the sexes, senior citizens, business people, medical professionals, ethnic groups, and so forth. However, a significant percentage of the messages they encode help sustain stereotypical or unrealistic perceptions regarding who is trustworthy.[30]

For example, the media categorize women as good and bad. "Good" women are typically portrayed as deferential and focused on home and family, while "bad" women are depicted as hard, cold, aggressive, ambitious, embittered, and not to be trusted.[31] In addition, because of their portrayals of women, the media may be undermining the ability of women to trust each other.[32] For example, in advertising, film, and television, women and girls are often presented as being in competition with each other—often for men. Such depictions may cause women to become suspicious of one another, contributing to their inability to trust each other and leading others to stereotype women as "catty."

Similarly, the media have all too frequently handled minority groups by either stereotyping them or neglecting them.[33] For instance, until recently, the portrayal of Native Americans in the U.S. media has been inaccurate, depicting them as blood-thirsty, marauding savages who were not to be trusted.[34] Likewise, the media still all too frequently portray people from less-developed countries in extremes: African Americans as incapable, shiftless, or inferior; Hispanics as illegal aliens; and Italians as mobsters. Journalists are depicted as unprincipled investigators who will stop at nothing to get a story. The media also show overweight people as lazy, the elderly as childlike and helpless, and the disabled as useless. By unfairly labeling individuals, media portrayals negate the human value of honesty, perpetuate misinformation, lead to human degradation, and adversely influence person-to-person understanding.

Technology and Trust

According to a news report, "more and more people are meeting on line—flirting with their fingertips, sharing their deepest secrets in e-mail messages, and falling in love at Pentium speed."[35] Technology, as has been noted, is facilitating the ease with which we are able to contact each other. It even can help speed up romance by compelling people to communicate verbally at the same time that it deemphasizes distracting visual signals such as frowns, smirks, and rolling eyes, which can inhibit in-person contact.

For many, e-mail is rapidly replacing the traditional letter as the medium of preference. As a result, people reveal secrets and share vulnerabilities much sooner than they would in traditional relationships. Yet e-mail lacks the security or inherent privacy of the sealed letter. E-mail, in fact, may be more like the postcard: we shouldn't be surprised when the e-mail we send is read by individuals other than the person to whom it was addressed. People who thought they were disclosing personal information to one intended recipient have been devastated to find that others to whom they had no intention of revealing such information were privy to their message. Consequently, while making us more accessible to each other, e-mail may also make us more accessible to everyone. We need to consider what kinds of personal messages we are sending by e-mail and who is reading them.

When we communicate on-line we may be giving others personal information we never imagined they would possess. For example, one woman who had used the newspaper personals as a means to find a date always required respondents to provide her with an e-mail address. If one failed to provide an address, she would not communicate with him. However, when her curiosity got the better of her, she would also run the name of a potential date through Alta Vista, a searchable index of every word on every publicly accessible Web site in the world. Based on what she was able to find out about the messages a prospective date had previously posted, she made a decision regarding whether to pursue a date. Certainly, none of us is proud of everything we have posted on the Net, but probably few of us imagine that what we have posted actually has the ability to follow us around, be accessed by others, and embarrass us when we least expect it. Alta Vista provides such on-line memory—for better or worse.[36]

On the other hand, e-mail may do a lot to encourage the sharing of personal information that some of us might have found too difficult were we actually required to talk face-to-face. E-mail may help reduce inhibitions and free us to reveal information we would otherwise hesitate to tell another person.

However, there are three questions concerning e-mail that we need to ask before entrusting to it our more intimate disclosures:

1. If we would not discuss something on the richest channel available to us— face-to-face communication—should we actually be revealing this personal information?

2. How much of the real meaning of our disclosures is being lost in the electronic translation of personal information?

3. To what extent should we trust the computer to ensure our privacy at the same time it reduces our inhibitions and links us more closely to each other?

Whereas we may have been taught to assume that members of the community in which we live are trustworthy, on-line it has been a different story. Many of the people we interact with on-line we know only by their on-line aliases, making it more difficult for us to establish genuine trusting relationships. As one writer queried, "Is technology making us intimate strangers?"[37] When we otherwise interact with persons who surrender their fictional identities so that we can verify who they really are, the establishment of trust becomes easier.

Gaining Communication Competence

Nurturing a Trusting Relationship

As our examination of trust reveals, being trustworthy means working to build a real relationship, not working to get to know the other person just so you can take advantage of his or her vulnerabilities. When you use your knowledge to harm a partner in a relationship, you destroy your partner's trust in you. Fear, distrust, and other defensive feelings are common blocks to the functioning and self-actualizing abilities of an individual, as well as barriers to the development or maintenance of a good relationship. Thus the key to building trust in a relationship is to behave in a trustworthy manner.

Be Willing to Disclose Yourself to the Other Person

Trust, like self-disclosure, is a reciprocal process. Trusting behavior on your part can often lead to trusting behavior in the person with whom you are interacting. Thus, self-disclosing to another can help the other come to know you, understand you, and realize that he or she must also take a risk if a relationship based on mutual trust is to develop.

Let the Other Person Know You Accept and Support Him or Her

When you reduce threats to the ego of another individual, you increase the level of trust between you and create a supportive environment. If the other person feels accepted by you and feels that you perceive him or her as a significant human being who is worthy of your time and attention, then he or she will be less likely to experience anxiety about being placed in a vulnerable position. Such feelings of acceptance will also deter others from attempting to defend themselves by lying or concealing the truth. They simply will have no reason to do so. Thus, support and acceptance encourage trust and honesty.

Develop a Cooperative Rather Than a Competitive Orientation

Working to "win" in a relationship can destroy it. The definition of a relationship affects how easily trust may be built—indeed, whether it will be built at all. If you aim only to increase your own immediate gain, even though it means sacrificing the well-being of a partner, the degree of trust your partner is willing to put in you will rapidly diminish. You will be perceived as a manipulator. In contrast, healthy relationships depend on the problem-solving abilities of the individuals involved. Problem solving presupposes a nonmanipulative orientation. If individuals choose to compete with each other instead of cooperating with each other, trust simply will not develop.

Trust Another Individual When It Is Appropriate

Taking inappropriate risks can cause as many problems as never being willing to take a risk. In other words, always trusting people who don't merit your trust is as dysfunctional as never trusting anyone. People who consistently trust exploitative people find themselves taken advantage of and will not build relationships based on trust. Instead, you must be willing to question the other person's motivations and behaviors openly. The other person may learn to respect you for feeling strong enough or capable enough to call a halt to the duplicity. Remember, trust is sustained only if both parties to a relationship behave in trustworthy ways.

daily **contacts**　　　　　　　　　　　　　**Wrap-Up**

Meet again in pairs or small groups. Turn back to the case study at the beginning of the chapter and reconsider the questions that followed it. How have your answers changed or become more focused? Based on your knowledge of trust, what advice would you give Angela now?

Critical Thinking Contacts

Examine the following cartoon. Based on your understanding of trust and how its presence or absence affects relationships, discuss the advice you would offer the two characters.

Are You Honest or "Fairly" Honest?

"Look, Ellen, haven't I always been fairly honest with you?"

Summary

Trust consists of two basic components: trusting behavior and trustworthy behavior. Whether trust exists influences the nature of a relationship.

The amount of trust individuals are willing to place in each other is based in large measure on each person's perceptions of the other's character. Among character-based sources of trust are trust in the integrity of another, the consistency of his or her behavior, and trust in his or her discretion.

Trust is difficult to develop but relatively easy to destroy. The presence of trust strengthens relationships; its absence causes relationships to deteriorate. According to the cost–benefit theory, we work to sustain relationships that enable us to maximize the profit side of our relational balance sheets. As long as the benefits received from our relationships outweigh emotional expenditures, we will work to sustain them.

Whether a relationship is defined as cooperative or competitive plays a part in determining whether individuals develop trust. Defining an interpersonal relationship as competitive precipitates defensive and threatening behavior in interactions, and defining it as cooperative tends to precipitate more honest communication.

Deception, or the effort to manipulate truth, also influences a relationship's nature and outcomes. Whereas some people differentiate between white lies and big lies, others maintain that all lies help us negotiate situations that expose us to levels of vulnerability exceeding our comfort zones.

Culture, the media, and gender each play a role in determining whom we trust. The presence of ethnocentrism, mediated stereotyped portrayals, and gender preferences influence perceptions of who can be trusted.

The key, then, to building trust in a relationship is to behave in a trustworthy manner.

Terms to Talk About

trust *(p. 258)*
trusting behavior *(p. 259)*
trustworthy behavior *(p. 259)*
cost–benefit theory (social exchange theory) *(p. 262)*
comparison level for alternatives *(p. 265)*
competitive relationship *(p. 265)*
cooperative relationship *(p. 265)*

defensive climate *(p. 266)*
supportive climate *(p. 266)*
lying *(p. 275)*
displacement *(p. 276)*
repression *(p. 276)*
rationalization *(p. 277)*
counterfeit relationship *(p. 277)*

Suggestions for Further Reading

Sissela Bok, *Lying,* New York: Pantheon, 1978; *Secrets,* New York: Random House, 1989. Both books offer interesting insights into lying, truth telling, and the effects of both on relationships.

Stephen R. Covey, *The Seven Habits of Highly Effective People,* New York: Simon & Schuster, 1990. Presents strategies for developing trust in relationships.

Barry L. Duncan and Joseph W. Rock, *Overcoming Relational Impasses,* New York: Insight Books, 1991. Explores relational problems from a systems perspective.

Jack Gibb, *Trust,* North Hollywood, CA: Newcastle, 1991. Explores the nature of trust and offers an insightful discussion of fear and the barriers it creates between people.

James Jaska and Michael S. Pritchard, *Communication Ethics: Methods of Analysis,* Belmont, CA: Wadsworth, 1991. Discusses the ethical dilemmas posed by truth telling and whether lying is ever justified. Explores ethical theory, the perplexities of moral decision making, and the causes and complexities of deception.

Alan J. Kimmel, *Rumors and Rumor Control,* Mahwah, NJ: Lawrence Erlbaum, 2004. Sheds light on the phenomenon of rumor.

Michael Lewis and Carolyn Saarni, eds., *Lying and Deception in Everyday Life,* New York: Guilford Press, 1993. Explores factors that cause people to construct lies and illusions about their own lives.

10

Power and Influence

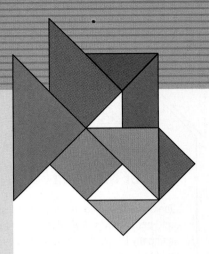

To be nobody but yourself in a world which is doing its best, night and day, to make you everybody else — means to fight the hardest battle which any human being can fight; and never stop fighting.

— e. e. cummings

After completing this chapter, you should be able to:

▌ Define power.

▌ Compare and contrast the following types of power: reward, coercive, expert, legitimate, referent, and persuasive.

▌ Define and distinguish among attitudes, beliefs, and values.

▌ Discuss the persuasive forces that help create compliance.

▌ Discuss balance theory and its role in interpersonal persuasion.

▌ Discuss the extent to which gender differences influence the exercise of power.

▌ Explain how different cultures view power.

▌ Discuss the extent to which the media and technology influence the perception and exercise of power.

daily contacts

Power Moment

Tonja was assigned the task of assessing the productivity and performance of people in various divisions of the company for which she worked. Included among those she had to report on was her live-in boyfriend, Larry, who was a division head. Tonja's boss told her to deliver to division heads copies of a preliminary report once it was complete, prior to its being disseminated to him and to a wider company audience.

After reading Tonja's preliminary report, which was somewhat critical of a number of people in his division, Larry hit the roof. If his people were being criticized, the clear implication was that he was not doing his job. When Larry told Tonja his reaction and concerns, she became defensive and insisted that the information in her report was accurate. Larry cautioned Tonja that if she didn't alter her report, he would end their relationship. It was that important to him.

Larry didn't want his anger to become evident to others at work. Thus he interacted with Tonja at work with the same level of professionalism he had always exhibited. Their private communication was another matter, however. All week, when they were alone at home, Larry pressured Tonja to revise the report, pointing out time and again the errors he believed she was making, and reminding her of the consequences she would face if she failed to comply.

Tonja was in emotional turmoil. What should she do?

Divide into pairs or small discussion groups to answer the following questions:

1. How would you respond to Larry's demand?
2. What steps can Tonja and Larry take to resolve their impasse?

Power, or the potential to influence others, permeates our interpersonal contacts and plays an important role in every one of our relationships. **Power** influences whose company we seek, whom we respect, whom we fear, and how confident or dependent we feel. It determines those individuals we are able to control, those who are able to control us, and whether we are comfortable being in or out of control. Although the amount of power we are able to exert depends on with whom we are interacting, we can all learn to increase the personal power we are perceived to have.

Interpersonal Control: Exploring the Balance of Power in Relationships

Power is present in all relationships.

Do you feel in control in your relationships? If you find yourself feeling powerless a lot of the time, chances are that you are unhappy and unsatisfied by the relationships you currently share. When we lose our ability to control what happens to ourselves, we also lose our ability to direct our future, and others end up directing it for us. When that happens, others influence our decisions, and they also can make choices for us—which may or may not be in our best interest.

Our emotions can influence how powerful or powerless we feel. For example, if we feel nervous or overly emotional in social situations, we may suffer from social anxiety, which can make it more difficult for us to project a powerful image. When we feel socially anxious, we also typically feel socially powerless, which makes it impossible for us to enjoy ourselves in public. We are likely to feel that others are evaluating us, finding fault with us, or "judging" us in some way. Because the anxiety felt by the socially anxious is so very painful, some of us who experience this problem decide to stay away from social situations and avoid other people altogether, which makes it unlikely that we will be able to influence others. The socially anxious are especially fearful of authority figures such as bosses and supervisors at work, or anyone whom they perceive to be "better" than they are. Upon meeting an

Theory

What's Your Power Orientation?

The amount of Machiavellianism you possess influences whether you are more or less likely to try and control others when interacting with them. Persons who score high on the Machiavellianism test are apt to be more strategic and manipulative in their personal persuasion efforts than are persons who score low. The latter are more likely to exhibit a problem-solving orientation when faced with an interpersonal power moment.

For each statement below, select one of the following responses and place it before the question number:

Disagree			Agree	
A lot	A little		A little	A lot
1	2	3	4	5

1. The best way to handle people is to tell them what they want to hear.

2. When you ask someone to do something for you, it is best to give the real reason for wanting it rather than giving reasons that might give more weight.

3. Anyone who completely trusts anyone else is asking for trouble.

4. It is hard to get ahead without cutting corners here and there.

5. It is safest to assume that all people have a vicious streak, and it will come out when they are given a chance.

6. One should take action only when it is morally right.

7. Most people are basically good and kind.

8. There is no excuse for lying to someone else.

9. Most people more easily forget the death of their father than the loss of property.

10. Generally speaking, people won't work hard unless they're forced to do so.

To determine your score, follow these steps.

A. Reverse the scores on items 2, 6, 7, and 8 as follows:

If you responded with	Change it to
5	1
4	2
3	3
2	4
1	5

Add together your answers for all questions, being certain to use the reverse numbers for questions 2, 6, 7, and 8. If you score between 35 and 50, you are likely a high Mach; if you score between 10 and 15, you are probably a low Mach. The majority of respondents fall between these extremes.

Do you think the results of the test accurately describe you? Do your results support or contradict research findings that men are generally more Machiavellian than women, older adults tend to have lower Mach scores than younger adults, and higher Machs tend to be in professions that require one to exert control over others? To what extent, if any, do you see your score reflected in how you interact with others and your decision whether or not to exert power over the choices others make?

SOURCE: The Power Orientation Test, at http://www. humanlinks.com/personal/power_orientation.htm. Adapted from Richard Christie, "Scale Construction," in Richard Christie and Florence L. Geis, eds., *Studies in Machiavellianism*, pp. 17–18. Copyright © 1970 by Academic Press, Inc. Reprinted with permission from Humanlinks.com and Elsevier.

authority figure, people with social anxiety describe getting a lump in their throat and having their facial muscles freeze up. Because their focus is on "not failing" and "not giving themselves away," they are unlikely to even remember what was said in the conversation.[1]

On the other hand, some of our emotions can send us on a *power-trip*—we feel so capable and so secure that we imagine we can manipulate others to do whatever we want with little effort. The term *Machiavellian* refers to people who use a variety of tactics to make choices for and control others. If you score high in Machiavellianism, you have the drive to control others. If you score low in Machiavellianism, you are probably less controlling and more susceptible to the interpersonal persuasion attempts of others.

Where Does Power Come From?

In each of your key relationships, who holds the power?

Power is relational. The person who has power derives it from the social relationship itself. Another individual assents, overtly or covertly, to its use. The greater our power, the greater our abilities to make things happen and to prevent those things we do not want to happen from happening. When we have power, we simply are better able to control what happens to us when we interact with others. The amount of power you judge yourself or another to have is based on the resources you or the other person control, and determines the extent to which either one of you feels dependent in the relationship.

Power Categories

Researchers have identified six categories of power that we use to control and influence others: reward, coercive, expert, legitimate, referent, and persuasive (see Table 10.1).[2]

Reward Power

Reward power is held by one party to a relationship who controls something that is valued by the other party. The person who possesses reward power knows what the other person wants, is able to retain it or provide it, lets the other party know that this ability exists, and reveals what needs to be done for the reward to be released. Rewards can be tangible (job, money, "perk") or intangible (friendship, security, love). The extent to which one individual values the rewards determines the amount of power the offeror is able to exercise. An individual having the ability either to deliver positive consequences or to remove negative ones will be more likely to get others to comply with his or her requests. The individual whom we perceive to control physical or emotional resources has the power.

Every relationship we maintain usually implies some degree of reward power. The more fulfilling we find the relationship, the more we perceive it to have reward power.

Coercive Power

Unlike reward power, **coercive power** is typically associated with force. A person who has coercive power can deliver negative consequences or remove

TABLE 10.1
Types of Power

	Definition	Example
Reward power	One party in the relationship controls something valued by the other party.	Instructors hold reward power in the form of a grade over their students.
Coercive power	One party in the relationship can deliver negative consequences in response to the actions of another.	Individuals who threaten to boycott a business unless certain actions are taken hold coercive power over the owners.
Expert power	One party in the relationship possesses special knowledge or skill that another individual believes he or she needs.	Physicians hold expert power in the eyes of patients in the form of specific diagnoses or treatments.
Legitimate power	Because of his or her position, one party in the relationship is able to control the other party.	Employers hold legitimate power over their employees.
Referent power	Because of the respect and admiration accorded him or her, one party in the relationship is able to convince others.	An older sibling may have referent power over a younger brother or sister.
Persuasive power	One party in the relationship is able to persuade another to believe or act as he or she wants.	Through the use of logic, well-conceived and developed arguments, and emotional appeals, lawyers hold persuasive power over jurors.

 Theory

Powerful People

In a relationship, the more powerful person is the one who is in control of the situation.

1. Think of five different relationships you currently share. For each, identify the relationship's nature; is it primarily based on friendship, family ties, work, or health needs?

2. Compare and contrast the amount of power you perceive each person in the relationship wields. In each instance, whom do you consider to be the more powerful person and why?

3. Indicate your perceptions of the amount of power each of you has on the continuum below by marking the points for each of the five relationships. In which of your relationships is power balanced? In which is it imbalanced? How do you account for the difference?

You have more power	Power is balanced	The other person has more power

|——————————————•——————————————|

Are you willing to respect the power someone holds when it is based on knowledge and experience in a field?

positive ones in response to the actions of another. People who use coercive power need to be prepared both to continually escalate the threats they make and to have others resent or dislike them for threatening them in the first place. To exercise coercive power, you need to identify the specific consequences an individual fears most, have the ability to mete out those consequences at will, let the other person know that you possess that ability, and convince him or her that unless he or she behaves as you want, you will certainly act accordingly.

As a result of exercising physical or psychological coercive power, individuals can compel us to maintain a relationship that we might otherwise choose to end. Because we fear the punishment another person can inflict—whether that fear is of being ignored, demeaned, or something else—the threats of another can be a powerful interpersonal motivator.

Expert Power

An individual who has **expert power** is presumed to possess a special knowledge or skill others believe they need. People we perceive to have expert power have the ability to influence us because of their training, background, or accomplishments. Expert power is further enhanced when we believe the expert source to be unbiased, with nothing to gain personally from influencing our behavior. For example, a physician may persuade us to follow specific instructions concerning our health once we are convinced that her credentials allow her to dispense such medical advice, and allow us to believe in the correctness of her prescription and to trust that she will not profit unduly if we follow her advice. If, on the other hand, we find that a presumed expert will profit personally as a result of gaining our behavioral compliance, the perceived expertise of that individual will decline in our eyes. If, for instance, a salesperson recommends you purchase a product for which he earns a higher fee, you might doubt his actual expertise.

Legitimate Power

Legitimate power exists when one person's position enables him or her to control another. Most of us believe that some people have a right to exert power over us merely because of the roles they perform, who they are, or a position they hold. For example, students perceive their teachers to have legitimate power, law-abiding citizens perceive the police to have legitimate power, and employees perceive their employers to have legitimate power. Often used to reduce conflict, legitimate power convinces those with less power to adhere to the requests of the more powerful.

in **Context**

Power Plays on the Job

Each of the six categories of power comes into play as individuals relate to each other at work.

1. Describe how each power category can be used by employers and employees as they interact to solve work-related problems.

2. Which category do you find most effective in motivating others to think or behave as you would like? Explain.

3. Which type of power do you find most persuasive in influencing your thoughts and actions? Explain.

Referent Power

When a person has **referent power,** we do as he or she requests because we identify with him or her, respect or like him or her, and want him or her to like us as well. The relationship is a simple one. As our desire to be like someone increases, so does that individual's referent power in our eyes. The more attractive we find someone, the more we respect and admire him, and the greater is our tendency to mirror that individual's behavior rather than contradict his actions and to do as he wants rather than to fail to conform with his wishes. Thus, a person who serves as our referent can get us to do many things we might not otherwise ordinarily do.

Persuasive Power

Sometimes a person has power because others believe that he or she has the ability to persuade by conveying information in well thought-out arguments. The individual's power is based on the logic or reasonableness of his or her arguments or the demonstrated superiority of his or her knowledge. Called **persuasive power,** this kind of power enables one person to persuade another through the presentation of well-reasoned arguments. Persons who possess persuasive power need not be experts. They only need to know how to use speech powerfully and to be able to reason intelligently.

Although any of these types of power can be used in a relationship, some are more effective and less damaging than others to the sense of self of the less powerful member of a dyad. By analyzing the type of power that characterizes each of our meaningful relationships, we gain insight into how balanced or unbalanced, personally costly or beneficial, effective or ineffective the use of power is in our lives.

Preparing to Exercise Power: Exploring How Attitudes, Beliefs, and Values Influence Persuasibility

How frequently do you succeed in exercising power and persuading those with whom you share a relationship to see things your way? How frequently do you give in to others whom you perceive to have more power and agree to do things their way? Once we understand how and why we are able to influence others and how and why others are able to influence us, our effectiveness as interpersonal communicators will markedly improve.

How have others helped mold the attitudes you currently hold?

What are we doing when we attempt to influence another person? Usually we are trying to modify that individual's thinking, feelings, or behavior so they become more compatible with our own.

Today, more than ever before, we are concerned with being able to exert personal influence. We are so preoccupied with this that a central aim of many of our interpersonal contacts is to create similarity of thought, feeling, and behavior between ourselves and those with whom we interact. To this end, let us explore the role attitudes, beliefs, and values play in this process, and how attitudes, beliefs, and values are internalized, maintained, or changed through person-to-person interaction.

The Role of Attitudes

Although we are unable to see, hear, or touch our attitudes or those of another person, we can see, hear, or touch the behavior that is attributable to the influence of attitudes. We communicate our attitudes with both verbal and nonverbal cues. Our facial expressions, postures, and gestures are attitude revealers. Each time we socialize, attend class, or go to a meeting, we display our attitudes. They affect who we are and how we relate to others.

Defining and Measuring Attitudes

How do your attitudes influence communication preferences?

Most psychologists define an **attitude** as a mental set or readiness that causes us to respond in a particular way to a given stimulus. Each of our attitudes represents a predisposition to react positively or negatively toward certain people, ideas, things, or situations. In other words, our attitudes represent our evaluations. They help us sort our perceptions into categories ranging from extremely favorable to extremely unfavorable.

In large measure, our behavior and communication preferences are determined by the attitudes we hold. Our attitudes lead us and others to behave in certain ways and increase the likelihood that specific kinds of reactions will occur.

Where Do Our Attitudes Come From?

We act according to pictures we carry in our heads—pictures that do not necessarily correspond with reality. To understand why we hold the attitudes we do, we can try to "dig out" the roots of our pictures. In the process we will identify the forces that help us to create and sustain our attitudes.

The roots of our attitudes extend in many directions. Among the forces feeding them and causing them to grow are our family, religion, education, economic and social class, and culture.

Family. Few of us escape the strong influences exerted by our families. Our parents communicate their attitudes to us, and eventually we acquire and hold at least a number of them. Researchers confirm: "It is the family that bends the tender twig in the direction it is likely to grow."[3]

Religion. Religion affects both believers and nonbelievers. In fact, religion's impact is becoming even more widespread as churches strive to influence our attitudes on such social issues as violence in the media, abortion, the roles of men and women, and the welfare system.

Schools. We attend school for more years now than ever before. Many of us start before we are five years old and attend until we are well into our twenties or older. In addition, adults are returning to school in increasing numbers, either to complete or advance their education. What we are taught, who teaches us, the books we are assigned to read, and the videos we are shown all help shape our attitudes.

Economic and Social Class. Our economic and social backgrounds also shape our attitudes. Our economic status helps determine the social arena we frequent. What we think of the world and its problems is similarly influenced by the company we keep and the money we have.

Culture. We learn our culture. It is transmitted to us, and the messages it considers important are constantly reinforced for us. Culture is "our theory of 'the game' being played in our society."[4] Once we share a culture, we also share similar meanings. Our culture, passed on to us by our family, friends, and the groups we belong to, helps coordinate our behavior and the norms and rules we live by.

professional contacts

Are You Like "Some People"?

To what extent, if any, do you see yourself reflected in this passage from "Some People," an essay by Maurice Nicoll?

Some people stay very much in the same places all their lives, in their vast, inner, unmanifested, psychological country. It is as if one lived internally in a small village and always took the same walk. Every day the same thoughts and feelings repeat themselves, every day the same attitudes are at work, the same mechanical prejudices, the same buffers, the same automatic sentences. As we take time to become aware of the attitudes, beliefs, and values we prize, those we would be willing to stand up for in and out of the classroom, we are also taking time to change for the better and become more effective interpersonal communicators.

The Role of Beliefs

Although the term "attitude" is sometimes used interchangeably with the term "belief," the two are distinguishable. While we have internalized many attitudes, we have formed an even greater number of beliefs.

Identifying and Measuring Beliefs

Beliefs and attitudes are related to one another as buildings are related to the bricks used to construct them. In other words, **beliefs** are the building blocks of attitudes; they provide the basis or foundation for the attitudes we hold.

Whereas attitudes are measured on a favorable–unfavorable or good–bad continuum, beliefs are measured on a true–false or probable–improbable continuum.

Practice

Attitude Assessment

Use the two scales below to indicate your evaluations of the following people and issues. For example, if you hold an extremely favorable attitude toward the concept or person being evaluated, then you would indicate that by circling the words "extremely favorable" on the first scale as well as by choosing a 90 or a 100 on the positive scale and a 0 or a 10 on the negative scale.

Physicians

Scale 1	Extremely favorable	Fairly favorable	Neutral	Fairly unfavorable	Extremely unfavorable
Scale 2					
Positive	0 10 20 30 40 50 60 70 80 90 100				
Negative	0 10 20 30 40 50 60 70 80 90 100				

Marriage

Scale 1	Extremely favorable	Fairly favorable	Neutral	Fairly unfavorable	Extremely unfavorable
Scale 2					
Positive	0 10 20 30 40 50 60 70 80 90 100				
Negative	0 10 20 30 40 50 60 70 80 90 100				

Your best friend

Scale 1	Extremely favorable	Fairly favorable	Neutral	Fairly unfavorable	Extremely unfavorable
Scale 2					
Positive	0 10 20 30 40 50 60 70 80 90 100				
Negative	0 10 20 30 40 50 60 70 80 90 100				

Your boss

Scale 1	Extremely favorable	Fairly favorable	Neutral	Fairly unfavorable	Extremely unfavorable
Scale 2					
Positive	0 10 20 30 40 50 60 70 80 90 100				
Negative	0 10 20 30 40 50 60 70 80 90 100				

Your parents

Scale 1	Extremely favorable	Fairly favorable	Neutral	Fairly unfavorable	Extremely unfavorable
Scale 2					
Positive	0 10 20 30 40 50 60 70 80 90 100				
Negative	0 10 20 30 40 50 60 70 80 90 100				

Premarital sex

Scale 1	Extremely favorable	Fairly favorable	Neutral	Fairly unfavorable	Extremely unfavorable
Scale 2					
Positive	0 10 20 30 40 50 60 70 80 90 100				
Negative	0 10 20 30 40 50 60 70 80 90 100				

Long-distance relationships

Scale 1	Extremely favorable	Fairly favorable	Neutral	Fairly unfavorable	Extremely unfavorable
Scale 2					
Positive	0 10 20 30 40 50 60 70 80 90 100				
Negative	0 10 20 30 40 50 60 70 80 90 100				

Divorce

Scale 1	Extremely favorable	Fairly favorable	Neutral	Fairly unfavorable	Extremely unfavorable
Scale 2					
Positive	0 10 20 30 40 50 60 70 80 90 100				
Negative	0 10 20 30 40 50 60 70 80 90 100				

Telecommuting

Scale 1	Extremely favorable	Fairly favorable	Neutral	Fairly unfavorable	Extremely unfavorable
Scale 2					
Positive	0 10 20 30 40 50 60 70 80 90 100				
Negative	0 10 20 30 40 50 60 70 80 90 100				

1. Which scale enabled you to better clarify the nature of your attitudes? Why?

2. To what extent did your attitudes show absolute conviction (0 on one measure, 100 on the other)?

3. To what extent were your attitudes mixed or ambivalent?

Thus, if we say that we think something is true, we are really saying that we believe it. Beliefs help us describe the way we view our environment and reality.

Why do we believe or fail to believe what others tell us? Why do we believe or fail to believe our physician? our friends? our coworkers? the media?

We believe information for a variety of reasons. Sometimes we believe it because we read it somewhere or saw it on the news, and we have "blind faith" in what we read or see, never recognizing that the author or reporter may be wrong or biased. Other times, we believe information because an authority "says it is so," because our best friend says it so, because "everyone else believes it," or simply because "that's the way it really is." It is important that we recognize that our beliefs are not necessarily logical. Rather, in large part, we hold them as a result of what we want or need to believe, what we are able to believe, or what others teach us to believe. For reasons such as these, we don't always require proof to believe the things we do. Instead, we allow our beliefs to influence our interpretations; we use them to manipulate or distort what we see and hear. We act in ways that are consistent with what we think is true. As a result, at least to some degree, what we believe restricts what we perceive.

Psychologist Milton Rokeach notes that our belief system is made up of everything with which we agree.[5] It includes all the information and biases we have accumulated since we were born. Formed along with our belief system is our disbelief system. It is composed of all the things with which we disagree. Together, the two systems influence our processing of information.

in Practice

Belief Survey

1. Develop a list of five things you believe and five things you disbelieve about someone important to you.

2. Identify your reasons for each belief.

3. Describe how each belief influences your behavior toward that person, affecting what you do or say.

4. Indicate how your behavior might change if you did not believe what you say you believe and believed what you say you do not believe.

The Role of Values

Like attitudes and beliefs, the values we and others internalize influence our communication with each other. Let us examine values to determine how they affect our relationships (see Figure 10.1).

When was the last time you acted on a value?

Defining and Characterizing Values

We can define values as our ideas about what is important in our lives. Our values represent our feelings about the worth of something.

The value graph in the "In Practice" box is based on the work of Edward Spranger, a German scholar. In his book *Types of Men*, Spranger argues that we each have one predominant value system drawn from the following six major value types:

Theoretical: Values the pursuit and discovery of truth, the intellectual life
Economic: Values that which is useful, practical
Aesthetic: Values form, harmony, and beauty
Social: Values love, sympathy, warmth, and sensitivity in relationships with others
Political: Values competition, influence, and personal power
Religious: Values unity, wholeness, and a sense of purpose above human beings

Our **values** provide us with a relatively persistent framework for deciding what we think is right or wrong, which goals to aspire to, whom to listen to, and how to live. They provide us

FIGURE 10.1
Interpersonal Influencers

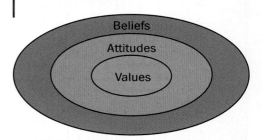

We exert interpersonal influence by tapping into the attitudes, beliefs, and values of others.

in Practice

Graphing Your Values

The box below describes six different types of people.

1. Read each description and then rank them from 1 to 6, with 6 representing the description that most closely resembles you and 1 representing the description that least resembles you.

A. You value the pursuit and discovery of truth—the intellectual life.
B. You value that which is useful and practical.
C. You value form, harmony, and beauty.
D. You value love, sympathy, warmth, and sensitivity in relationships with people.
E. You value competition, influence, and personal power.
F. You value unity, wholeness, a sense of purpose above human beings.

2. Next, plot the numbers you just entered in the preceding box in the appropriate place on the graph below. For example, if you gave sentence A a 4, put an X in the box at 4A. Once you connect the dots you will have your personal value profile—a visual representation of six dimensions of your personal system of values. Note the graph's high and low points. These reveal which of the preceding values are most and least central in your life. Provide examples that help demonstrate either the graph's accuracy or inaccuracy by revealing the extent to which your responses have been influenced by those values most important to you.

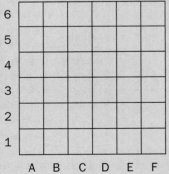

3. Use the following charts to compare and contrast the ranking of males and females in your class. Enter the number of males and females who made each choice in the appropriate column.

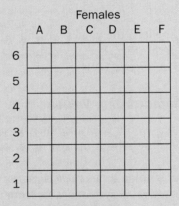

4. To what extent, if any, was there a difference in ranking by sex? To what do you attribute this difference or lack of difference?

5. In what ways can you apply the information you have learned about yourself and others? Identifying whether an individual's value system is theoretically, economically, aesthetically, socially, politically, or spiritually based can facilitate interpersonal persuasion by influencing susceptibility to personal-influence attempts.

Our value system helps us decide what is important in life.

with criteria for evaluating people, ideas, and actions. Our values indicate what we find desirable and to what extent, and, consequently, what we are willing to strive for.

Gaining Compliance in Interpersonal Relationships: The Promotion of Attitudinal and Behavioral Change

Because we are always forming new relationships and encountering new experiences, we often find it necessary or at times expedient to change or adjust our attitudes. Sometimes, for example, we interact with individuals whose actions conflict with our beliefs. When this occurs we may try to take steps to reduce or eliminate the conflict. We work hard to gain compliance so that we are able to maintain internal consistency or balance among our actions, feelings, and beliefs.

What relationship do you find most reinforcing? least reinforcing?

Strategies for Gaining Compliance

We use a variety of persuasive strategies to gain compliance from those with whom we share relationships. For example, we may attempt to influence another person toward a particular action, attitude, or belief by making a *direct request*

literary contacts

The Diary of a Young Girl

The following is a page from *Anne Frank: The Diary of a Young Girl*. How would you compare it to a page from your own diary? To what extent do our innermost thoughts and feelings help reveal our values?

Saturday, 15 July, 1944

"For in its innermost depths youth is lonelier than old age." I read this saying in some book and I've always remembered it, and found it to be true. Is it true then that grownups have a more difficult time here than we do? No. I know it isn't. Older people have formed their opinions about everything, and don't waver before they act. It's twice as hard for us young ones to hold our ground, and maintain our opinions, in a time when all ideals are being shattered and destroyed, when people are showing their worst side, and do not know whether to believe in truth and right and God.

Anyone who claims that the older ones have a more difficult time here certainly doesn't realize to what extent our problems weigh down on us, problems for which we are probably much too young, but which thrust themselves upon us continually, until, after a long time, we think we've found a solution, but the solution doesn't seem able to resist the facts which reduce it to nothing again. That's the difficulty in these times: ideals, dreams, and cherished hopes rise within us, only to meet the horrible truth and be shattered.

It's really a wonder that I haven't dropped all my ideals, because they seem so absurd and impossible to carry out. Yet I keep them, because in spite of everything I still believe that people are really good at heart. I simply can't build up my hopes on a foundation consisting of confusion, misery, and death. I see the world gradually being turned into a wilderness. I hear the ever approaching thunder, which will destroy us too. I can feel the sufferings of millions and yet, if I look up into the heavens, I think that it will all come right, that this cruelty too will end, and that peace and tranquility will return again.

In the meantime, I must uphold my ideals, for perhaps the time will come when I shall be able to carry them out.

Yours, Anne

SOURCE: From *Anne Frank: The Diary of a Young Girl* by Anne Frank, translated by B. M. Mooyaart-Doubleday, copyright 1952 by Otto H. Frank. Used by permission of Doubleday, a division of Random House, Inc.

such as "Will you drive me to the library so that I can get a research article I need on genetics?" This is the most straightforward way to gain compliance. Studies demonstrate that simply asking someone for something that they can easily comply with succeeds 90 percent of the time. For example, when a person asked people waiting in line if she could cut ahead of them because she was in a rush, most acquiesced. More than 60 percent also let the person in when the reason offered was weak: "I have to make some copies."[6] We might strengthen our request by adding *supporting evidence:* "I really would like to be able to put the latest research into my report, and to do that I need to get an article in the latest issue of the *Journal of Genetics* at the library." Or we might offer a *trade-off* such as "If you drive me to the library, I'll cook a great dinner." The norm of reciprocity—the fact that we often feel obligated to return another's favor—even if the person is someone we are not crazy about, often precipitates compliance.[7] On the other hand, instead of trying to strike a deal, we might attempt to *coerce* the other person into complying with our request by threatening him or her with a punishment for inaction: "I can't believe you're hesitating. I'm only asking you to drive me to the library, not around the world. If you don't take me, I won't go with you to that dinner that's so important to you."

TABLE 10.2
Compliance-Gaining Strategies

Which of the interpersonal persuasion strategies do you consider ethical? Which are you comfortable using? Which have you found work the best?

Strategy	Example
Make a direct request	Will you drive me to the airport and pick me up when I return?
Strengthen a request with supporting evidence	Will you drive me to the airport so that we can complete our discussion of what needs to be done while I'm away? And will you pick me up so that you can fill me in on how things went while I was gone?
Strike a deal/offer a trade	If you drive me to the airport and pick me up when I return, I'll treat you to a great dinner at that restaurant you wanted to go to.
Exert coercion	I can't believe that you haven't offered to drive me to the airport and pick me up. If you don't help out, I'll complete the report while I'm away and I won't put your name on it.
Identify compliance benefits	If you drive me to the airport and pick me up, I'll be more likely to have time to get your ideas on the project you'd like to be involved in, which means I'll be able to recommend you to the president.
Use emotion-laden statements	I really want to be able to recommend to the president that you be a part of the special team that's being formed, but I won't be able to unless I'm able to learn more about how you think. I just wish you'd take me to the airport and pick me up so I'm able to do a good job with that recommendation.
Instill empathy with an appeal directed at your welfare.	Come on. Take me to the airport and pick me up. I know that you care about how I do on this trip. If I'm rested, my chances of succeeding are greater. I know that's important to you.

Similarly, we might attempt to describe *another benefit*—that is, we might choose to offer one or more reasons that enable the other person to perceive what he or she stands to gain from helping us: "If I get that article, I'm much more likely to get a good grade, which will lead to my qualifying for a research assistantship, which means I won't have to get a second job, and I'll have more time to spend with you."

At times, however, we might find it more desirable to adopt an indirect approach, during which we use *emotion-laden statements* designed to help us maintain face: "You know I really wanted to get a good grade on my research assignment, but I won't be able to do it without that article. I just wish I could get to the library." Or we might aim to *instill empathy* for our need by appealing to the other person's love and concern for our welfare: "Come on," we might say, "We always help each other out because my doing well is important to you and your doing well is equally important to me."[8] Being successful at persuading others increases our sense of personal power and helps to facilitate our psychological balance (see Table 10.2).

Balancing Our Attitudes

Balance is a state of psychological health or comfort in which our actions, feelings, and beliefs are related to each other as we would like them to be. When we

Which of your current relationships causes you to feel balanced? unbalanced?

the party holding the rally. The second, the need for reassurance, ensures that we will seek out information and social support to confirm that we made the right decision. This explains why, after being persuaded to make a significant purchase, such as a car, you might pore over copies of *Consumer Reports,* seek feedback from a friend, or notice that others have bought cars like yours as well. The third, minimal justification for action, suggests that small rather than large incentives are more effective at creating dissonance and inducing attitude change. Of the three mental processes, the third runs counter to what we might expect. What it reveals, however, is that because the incentive to alter behavior is so small, we really do have to change our attitude to bring it in line with our behavior. Doing so also allows us to appear reasonable to ourselves. Our attitudes, it seems, follow our behavior when we have invested substantial effort. Thus, if you know someone who exhibits a behavior or holds an opinion that you find objectionable, the way to reduce the dissonance you feel is not to promise your friend significant rewards for changing or dire consequences if she or he fails to change. Instead, you are more likely to be successful if you offer your friend just enough encouragement (minimal justification) to alter the current behavior or way of thinking.

Routes to Interpersonal Influence

Which influence route do you think you travel—a peripheral or short-hand route or a central, more thoughtful route? Before you answer, realize that we are exposed to so many persuasive messages during our interpersonal encounters with others that we are compelled to take the lazy approach unless the subject is one in which we are personally involved.

Those of us who are more easily influenced than others are likely to respond to what psychologist Robert Cialdini calls trigger cues—a "click, whirr" programmed response to the persuasive appeals of others.[11] These cues are: *reciprocation*—"You owe me one"; *consistency*—"This has always worked before"; *social proof*—"The whole administration is in favor of this approach"; *liking*—"Love me, support my ideas"; *authority*—"Because I want you to"; and *scarcity*—"Hurry, before it's no longer possible for you to do so." The trigger cues lead us to take a cognitive short-cut, or a peripheral route that requires little or no scrutiny, effort, or thought.

According to psychologists Richard Petty and John Cacioppo, "A more thought-ful alternative cognitive process, the central route, involves message elaboration, the careful thinking about issue-relevant arguments contained in a persuasive communi-cation."[12] Once we opt to travel this route, a number of other factors, among them our motivation and ability to concentrate and resist distractions, determine whether we will be successful.

 Diversity and Culture Contacts

Diversity, Values, and Relational Power

According to theorist Gerte Hofstede, culture influences and modifies four value dimensions: individualism-collectivism, uncertainty avoidance, masculinity and femininity, and power distance.

One of the key variables that determine human action is whether one's primary orientation is individual or collective in nature. In individualistically oriented countries such as the United States, Great Britain, and Australia, the individual is of central importance; independence is stressed, with personal goals taking priority over allegiance to a group; personal achievement is rewarded; and uniqueness is an asset. In collectively oriented countries such as Taiwan, Columbia, and Pakistan, the individual is dependent on the in-group, the views and needs of the in-group are valued over the views and needs of the individual, a "we" consciousness prevails, and the individual sacrifices personal rights and places trust in group decisions.[13] A number of cocultures in the U.S., including Mexican Americans and African Americans, are collectively oriented.[14]

The second key variable for Hofstede is uncertainty avoidance, or the extent to which persons within a culture perceive uncertainty or ambiguous situations as threatening. This orientation, predominant in countries such as Japan, Portugal, and Greece, leads people to develop written rules and regulations and hold rituals and ceremonies that add structure to life. In contrast, countries such as the United States, Denmark, and Ireland, with their low tolerance for structure, have a low uncertainty-avoidance need. These countries instead value initiative and risk more highly.

By masculinity-femininity, Hofstede refers to the extent to which a country values masculine (male-oriented) or feminine (female-oriented) traits. Among the countries that value such masculine traits as ambition, achievement, and the acquisition of money are Ireland, Japan, and Mexico. In countries such as these, men are taught to be assertive, ambitious, and domineering. In contrast, femininity-valuing cultures such as Sweden and the Netherlands stress caring, nurturing, and sexual equality.[15]

Different cultures endow the parties to a relationship with different levels of social power or status. In some cultures, for example, wealth gives individuals more power, whereas in others age, education, occupation, or even family background is the source of power. Whereas some cultures minimize social or class inequalities, others emphasize them, sometimes even asserting that each individual has a protected place in the culture's social order, that hierarchical relationships are appropriate, and that when one has social status, he or she has the right to use his or her power as he or she sees fit. Such variations are a measure of **power distance,** the extent to which the members of a culture believe that institutional and organizational power should not be shared equally and that all decisions by power holders must be accepted.[16] A power distance index (PDI) indicates where a culture rests on the power distance scale. At one end of the scale are cultures such as Israel and Denmark, which believe in minimizing social or class imbalances, challenging authority figures, and using power only for legitimate purposes. On the other end of the scale are Arab countries, which prefer the maintenance of large power distances (see Table 10.3).

Individuals who grow up in cultures in which a large culture distance is preferred learn not to question authority, expect to be told what to do, and tend to conform readily

Practice

Where Does the Power Lie?

Divide into groups and assign each member to interview one person from a different culture. Ask each person interviewed to consider a relationship he or she shares with a parent, coworker, and boyfriend/girlfriend.

1. Who in each relationship tends to have the power?

2. What kind of power does he or she use most?

3. What, if anything, does the less powerful member in the relationship do to balance the power?

TABLE 10.3
Power-Distance and Behavior

Behaviors Characteristic of Low-Power-Distance Cultures	Behaviors Characteristic of High-Power-Distance Cultures
Minimizing class and social differences	Treating power as a fact of life
Challenging authority figures	Accepting inequalities in society
Using power for legitimate purposes only	Bypassing subordinates in decision making

to established norms. They learn to do as they are told without questioning the reasons for the requests. Because such individuals see power as a basic fact of life, the use of coercive or referent power is quite common.

In contrast, individuals who grow up in cultures in which a small culture distance is preferred value their independence and are less apt to conform to expectations that others have for them. Because they think that power should be used only when appropriate, such individuals prefer expert or legitimate power. These people need to understand why they should follow the directions of others before doing so.

In some cultures individuals are encouraged to take the reins of power when they feel it is rightfully theirs rather than allowing others to have power over them. In other cultures such verbal assertions of power on the part of individuals are repressed. Members of cultures that have a nonverbal rather than a verbal tradition do not tell others that they seek power; rather, these individuals believe that they can intuit where the power lies. Thus, for such people, power does not need to be claimed. If they have power, others will know. Unlike North American cultures, where power can be enhanced through communication, in Eastern cultures, members believe such communication is unnecessary and out of place.[17] Whatever an individual student's cultural background, however, when females are questioned about power relationships, they describe men as being more concerned both with power and content than with relational issues.[18]

 Gender Contacts

Gender and the Balance of Power

The societal view of women as less powerful influences the nature of relationships between men and women. Some women and men persist in holding the belief that men should be more powerful.[19]

For example, many women and men expect men to earn more than women and to achieve more status than women.[20] When these expectations go unmet, the relationships are apt to suffer. Current economic realities place increased pressure on men today as it becomes more and more difficult for them to be the sole or even the prime wage earners in their families.

Although women are now contributing to family income, they still have primary responsibility for seeing that domestic responsibilities are met. Research tells us that

.*in* *Theory*

Power Issues by Gender

Researchers report that in families where both wife and husband work full-time, the wives average over twenty-six hours a week in household labor, while the men complete an average of ten. When housework and employment hours are combined, women average sixty-nine hours a week, while men average fifty-two hours.* With these statistics in mind, consider how power is distributed in your family.

1. How many hours per week does each family member work?

2. How many hours per week does each family member spend performing household chores?

3. Which members of the household are given the power to decide who engages in what activities, how money is spent, how leisure time is spent, and so forth?

4. To what extent, if any, do you perceive in your family a relationship between the exercise of power and gender?

*D. Spain, *Gendered Spaces,* Chapel Hill: University of North Carolina Press, 1992.

only in approximately 20 percent of dual-career families do husbands equally share homemaking, child-care, and parent-care responsibilities with their partners. Such an inequitable gender-based workload is apt to lead to relationship resentment, dissatisfaction, or dissolution. In contrast, relationship satisfaction and stability are more closely allied with equitable out-of-home and in-home workload divisions.[21]

Women are expected to be work specialists, home specialists, health specialists, and life-cycle specialists. Women are supposed to monitor relationships and make sure things get done when they are scheduled to, yet accede to or comply with the preferences or beliefs of their partners whenever their opinions differ. Thus, while women may be gaining increased access to resources, they still are hesitant to use them independently.[22]

In general men engage in more efforts to exert control and dominate in relationships than do women.[23] However, according to researchers Patricia Darlington and Becky Mulvaney, women are showing that they conceive of power differently than men. Powerful women, these researchers contend, are not just men walking around in dresses. Instead of practicing male patterns of behavior in their efforts to gain and maintain power, many women seek alternative means of exerting power. Thus, in contrast to most men, when questioned about their perceptions of power in relation to their positions in American society, many women do not epitomize attributes such as control and domination that are so prominent in the traditional power displays of men but practice power based on a model of personal authority, empowerment, or reciprocal empowerment instead.[24]

Media and Technology Contacts

Power Shifts

How important are the media and technology in shaping our perceptions of power in relationships?

Media Power

Because women are consistently underrepresented in the media, we may be left with the impression that men hold the power, are typically in charge, occupy more high-status positions, and hold the cultural standard. Men, not women, are consistently held up to us by the media as the authorities. Even in broadcasting, there are more male than female news anchors, reinforcing our impression that men are in the position of authority. This fact is reinforced in commercials, where male voice-overs predominate, emphasizing the belief that women depend on men for direction.[25] In contrast, when they are portrayed in positions of power, women are often depicted as lonely or embittered.

Minorities fare even worse. Minority men are often cast in stereotypical roles and presented as lazy and unable to handle authority, and minority women are frequently shown misusing power in an effort to dominate others or as sex objects.[26] In addition, the media far too frequently present us with distorted depictions of the elderly, causing us to see them as sickly and powerless members of society.

The media encourage us to perceive women, minorities, and the elderly as less powerful, less active, and more dependent than men, nonminorities, and the young. They also cause men to believe that they are entitled to exert power over others and to force others to conform to their will.

Technological Power

According to researchers, some 35 million American and Canadian citizens are connected to the Internet. Estimates of Internet use around the world surpass 50 million. More than 65 percent of those with direct Internet access are male; more than 50 percent are between the ages of 18 and 34; and a majority are upscale, educated professionals with household incomes of more than $80,000. In addition, Internet users spend more time on-line each week than TV viewers spend with their TVs—an average of five hours.[27]

In the cyberspace age, those who don't have rapid access to information will lose power and fall behind. As Kathryn W. Wingard explains: "Power: That's what you get on the Internet. The people who have access to information are going to be successful. The people who don't are going to be out of the power structure."[28]

The Internet is color-blind and gender-blind. As a result, women who use the Internet to communicate are apt to find themselves with more listeners and receiving more respect than those who insist on communicating in more traditional ways.

Today some people prefer to interact with others via computer. Some teenage boys are more comfortable making contact with girls through the Internet than in person. Teachers also find the computer interpersonally empowering, saying it helps shy students come out of their shells and

··· Theory

The Lure of On-Line Power

In what ways is life on-line addictive? Some researchers say that by shutting out the world to dwell in cyberspace, cybersurfers get hooked on electronic chatting. According to Dr. Howard Shaffer, associate director of the division of addictions at Harvard University Medical School, "In some cases, users start showing tolerance and increase their on-line time. They become isolated and ignore other aspects of life."* He believes that life on-line can be habit forming.

1. Does life on-line seem to increase your sense of personal power at the same time that it actually decreases power by insulating you from intimate settings?

2. Once on-line, are you able to leave easily? Why or why not?

*Mollie O'Neill, "The Lure and Addiction of Life On Line," *New York Times*, March 8, 1995, p. C1.

allows students of different races, looks, and talents to get to know one another. Yet others question whether on-line interactions increase our personal power or decrease our ability to influence others because we are not actually face to face.[29]

The Internet also tends to enhance the personal power senior citizens feel by increasing the amount of contact they are able to have with others. Though limited because most senior citizens do not know how to use computers, the social implications that on-line services have for the nation's mushrooming elderly population are becoming increasingly apparent. In addition to giving senior citizens a sense of interpersonal power and the ability to share their ideas and concerns, cyberspace connections are used by senior citizens to help them attain control and handle or overcome health problems that would otherwise have left them isolated and lonely. Although computers surely cannot replace human warmth or touch, the on-line elderly become cyberpals and form lasting friendships. There's even love in cyberspace.[30]

By taking people away from television, will computers also decrease the amount of power the traditional media are able to exert? We think so. Welcome to the future!

Gaining Communication Competence

In order to become more interpersonally competent, you need to observe the following guidelines.

Controlling Relationships

Use Power Wisely

We have the option of using different kinds of power in relationships. The kinds we or others choose say a lot about the nature of the relationships we share. What kinds of power willingly and unwillingly bind us to others? What kinds of power enable us to make the most of relational opportunities? What kinds limit or debilitate us? Having a range of effective power and influence strategies can make it easier for us to satisfy our relational needs.

Understand How Beliefs, Values, and Attitudes Affect Interpersonal Interactions

Interaction with others is facilitated if we understand not only our own attitudes, beliefs, and values but also the attitudes, beliefs, and values of the people with whom we share relationships. It is important that we recognize how we and others respond when our significant beliefs are challenged. While some beliefs will be more meaningful to others than they are to us, the more central a belief is, the harder each of us works to defend it, the less willing we are to change it, and the more resistant we are to compliance-gaining efforts.

Capitalize on the Need for Balance

It is important to be able to recognize the extent to which our drive for consistency influences the nature and tone of our interpersonal interactions. When we want to convince an individual to think and feel as we do, we can create or point out an imbalance in their lives and then demonstrate how thinking or feeling as we do will help restore a sense of internal consistency.

daily
contacts

Wrap-Up

Meet again in pairs or with your discussion group. Turn back to the case study at the beginning of the chapter and reconsider the questions that followed it. How have your answers changed or become more focused? Based on what you have learned about interpersonal power, what advice would you give Tonja now?

Critical Thinking Contacts

Examine the following cartoon. Based on your understanding of interpersonal power, what advice can you offer these characters about the nature of their relationship and how to improve it?

Just Like Me

"It would work with us, Francine. We share the same narrow personal interests and concerns."

Summary

Power permeates all of our relationships. The amount of power a person has depends on the resources he or she is able to control. Six kinds of power are used to control and influence others: reward, coercive, expert, legitimate, referent, and persuasive.

Attitudes, beliefs, and values also affect the nature and tone of our interpersonal relationships. Communicated through behavior, they influence whose company we seek, with whom we are most comfortable interacting, and what we need to do to maintain a state of internal consistency or balance.

Gender, cultural expectations, the media, and technological innovations influence our perceptions of power and our readiness and ability to use it.

Terms to Talk About

power *(p. 290)*

reward power *(p. 292)*

coercive power *(p. 292)*

expert power *(p. 294)*

legitimate power *(p. 295)*

referent power *(p. 295)*

persuasive power *(p. 295)*

attitude *(p. 296)*

beliefs *(p. 297)*

values *(p. 299)*

balance theory *(p. 304)*

cognitive dissonance *(p. 304)*

power distance *(p. 307)*

Suggestions for Further Reading

Robert B. Cialdini, *Influence: Science and Practice*, 4th ed., Boston: Allyn and Bacon, 2001. An engaging account of how to exercise influence and defend yourself against those who wield it.

Joseph P. Folger, Marshall Scott Poole, and Randall K. Stutman, *Working through Conflict*, 2nd ed., New York: HarperCollins, 1993. A very interesting discussion of power and the balance of power.

J. R. P. French and B. H. Raven, "The Bases of Social Power." In *Studies in Social Power*, D. Cartwright, ed. Ann Arbor, MI: Institute for Social Research, 1959. An excellent overview of power sources.

Joyce L. Hocker and William W. Wilmot, "Power in Interpersonal Conflict," in *Interpersonal Conflict*, 3rd ed., Dubuque, IA: William C. Brown, 1991. A readable description of power and its uses.

Michael Korda, *Power! How to Get It: How to Use It*. New York: Ballantine, 1975. Though almost 30 years old, this book provides a wealth of information on power and its effects.

11

Conflict

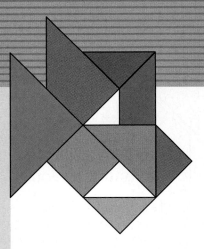

*Not everything that is faced can be
changed but nothing can be
changed until it is faced.*

—James Baldwin

After completing this chapter, you should be able to:

❚ Define conflict and identify its sources.

❚ Explain the difference between competitive and cooperative conflict
orientation.

❚ Identify the benefits of handling conflict effectively.

❚ Identify the consequences of handling conflict ineffectively.

❚ Explain the differences among assertion, nonassertion,
and aggression.

❚ Discuss the ways men and women differ in how they handle conflict.

❚ Provide examples of the way culture influences the handling of
conflict.

❚ Discuss how media portrayals affect perceptions of conflict.

❚ Identify behaviors that can be used to effectively resolve conflicts.

daily contacts

Jim and Jack Joust

Jim and Jack share an apartment. After reading their story, decide whether their pairing was a match or a mismatch.

Jim likes to rise early and enrolls for 8 A.M. classes. Jack likes to sleep in; he carries a heavy late afternoon and evening course load. Jim likes a quiet place to study. Jack loves to read with his expensive stereo system playing full blast. Jim is a neat freak. Jack leaves his things wherever he happens to drop them.

As roommates, the relationship shared by Jim and Jack could be described as tenuous at best, until . . .

It was about 2 A.M. Jim had been asleep for about three hours. Jack came in and immediately turned on the stereo — blasting it and virtually knocking Jim out of his bed. Jim yelled at Jack to turn it off. Jack yelled back at Jim to get a life. Jim was so angry that he hurled a book across the room; it hit the ceiling and set off the fire alarm. As the engines arrived, Jack and Jim began to wonder if they might consider alternatives to screaming and throwing things at each other.

Divide into pairs or small groups and consider these questions:

1. Will Jack and Jim survive a year together?
2. What can they do to develop a more positive and cooperative relationship?
3. What specific steps should they take to resolve their conflict?

Conflict is an inevitable part of life and sooner or later touches us all. Every one of our relationships of any significance has conflict—whether we want it to or not. In fact, a conflict-free relationship is a paradox; when a relationship is conflict-free it probably is not genuine.[1]

The Meaning of Conflict

Identify a recent conflict in which you were involved. What precipitated it? How did you handle it?

In this chapter we will explore what conflict is, how it arises, how it affects us, and what we can do to manage it more effectively. In the process, you will develop skills to deal more productively with conflict in your interpersonal relationships.

Conflict Defined

Interpersonal conflict is a struggle between interdependent parties that occurs whenever one individual's thoughts or actions are perceived to limit or interfere with those of another individual.[2] For example, when you and a friend want to play the same position on a team, or go to a function with the same date, or do a paper on the same book, your attempt to maximize your satisfaction or meet your needs may interfere with your friend's ability to do the same. Because both parties to the conflict are aware of a disagreement and recognize the incompatibility of their goals, each does his or her best to prevail. It doesn't matter if their goals aren't in fact incompatible; what matters is that one or both of them perceive the goals to be incompatible or mutually exclusive and believe that there isn't enough of something to satisfy them both.[3]

Conflict develops for a variety of reasons and assumes a variety of forms. Whatever its nature, however, one thing is certain: interpersonal conflict is based on interaction. Conflict is created by and maintained through our behavior, and it will test every relationship as well as help us assess each one's health. Upon discovering you are in conflict with another person, for example, do you tend to become aggressive and shout or strike out at each other, compete with each other, suppress your feelings, negotiate the situation, or deal with it directly? Do you escalate the conflict, seek to avoid it, demonstrate your inflexibility, or use constructive patterns that will allow you to manage it effectively?

Feelings about Conflict

Conflict exists in every relationship of any significance. If there were no conflicts, there could be no such thing as a meaningful relationship. Although we do not often look at conflict in a positive light, when we come to realize that we can look at it as a means to grow and develop in our interpersonal relationships, we are on the way to finding satisfying solutions to our problems, rather than letting the problems escalate and destroy our relationships.

Where have your feelings about conflict come from? Dictionaries tell us that conflict is disagreement . . . war, battle, collision. Such definitions suggest that conflict is a negative force that, of necessity, leads to undesirable consequences. Some of us also may have been led to believe that conflict is "evil," one of the prime causes of divorce, disorder, or violence, and that to disagree, argue, or fight with another person will either dissolve whatever relationship exists or prevent one from forming. Others may have grown up thinking that nice people don't fight, don't "make waves." We've developed fears that if we don't smile and act cheerful, others won't like us. The more awful we think conflict is, the worse it gets. It is not necessarily the conflict that creates the problem, but rather, the way conflict is approached and dealt with.[4] The reality is that conflict, in and of itself, is neither a positive nor a negative force. How we perceive it and how we handle it—whether it becomes functional or dysfunctional—determines, in part, the health of our interpersonal relationships and our satisfaction with them.[5]

How comfortable are you facing conflict? Do you agree with the following statement by Benjamin Disraeli? "My idea of an agreeable person is a person who agrees with me."

Functional Conflict

There are actually real benefits to conflict. When we handle conflicts well they become **functional conflicts,** helping us to develop a clearer understanding of each other's needs, attitudes, or beliefs and, in the process, to strengthen and cement our relationships.

According to conflict experts, when handled well, conflict serves a number of functions:

Describe and give examples of functional and dysfunctional conflicts in which you have been involved.

1. Each conflict helps us learn better ways of handling future conflicts and thereby reduces or eliminates the probability of more serious conflicts.

2. Conflict fosters innovation by helping us acquire new ways of looking at things, new ways of thinking, and new behaviors.

3. Conflict develops in us a new sense of cohesiveness and togetherness by increasing our understanding of each other, as well as our perceptions of closeness and trust.

4. Conflict provides us with invaluable opportunities to assess the viability of our relationships.

5. Conflict, once resolved, can help us strengthen our relationships.[6]

People who approach conflict with a functional orientation demonstrate their willingness to listen to opposing viewpoints, are willing to change troublesome behaviors, and accept differences in others. Conflicts that are functional are constructive; they do not damage relationships.

Dysfunctional Conflict

When we handle conflicts poorly we cause them to escalate, allowing them to become dysfunctional. **Dysfunctional conflicts** create serious relationship problems and often result in personal pain, emotional strains or schisms, and lasting resentment. People engaged in a conflict that has become dysfunctional characteristically rely on threats, deception, force, and violence to achieve their goals, which typically include defeating or hurting the other person.

Participants in dysfunctional conflicts demonstrate rigid inflexibility. In addition, they attempt to meet their own needs and serve their own interests by undercutting those of the other person and making him or her look bad. As a result, dysfunctional conflicts frequently grow worse, tend to be destructive, and badly damage or destroy relationships.[7]

in Practice

Considering Conflict

Think about several situations in which you were in conflict with another person, and the feelings you had at the time.

1. Use the following scale to measure your feelings about conflict. For example, for the first item, "good" versus "bad," if you feel that the conflict was completely good, circle "1." If you feel that the conflict was completely bad, circle "5." If you feel neutral about the conflict, circle "3."

Conflict

good	1	2	3	4	5	bad
rewarding	1	2	3	4	5	threatening
normal	1	2	3	4	5	abnormal
constructive	1	2	3	4	5	destructive
necessary	1	2	3	4	5	unnecessary
challenging	1	2	3	4	5	overwhelming
desirable	1	2	3	4	5	undesirable
inevitable	1	2	3	4	5	avoidable
healthy	1	2	3	4	5	unhealthy
clean	1	2	3	4	5	dirty

2. Compute your score by adding up your total.

Total Score

10–14	You think conflict is definitely a positive experience.
15–20	You think conflict can be helpful.
21–30	You don't like to think about conflict; you have very ambivalent feelings toward it.
31–40	You think conflict is something to avoid.
41–50	You think conflict is definitely a negative experience.

3. Determine the average male and female scores in the class. How do they compare? If they are different, what do you believe caused the difference? How does your score compare to the average score for your sex?

Psychologist George Bach believes that **crazymaking** behavior is often at the root of a dysfunctional conflict. Conflict-producing techniques that can drive a partner crazy are included under Bach's crazymaking label. For example, visualize the effects of the following conversation between a husband and wife after the husband has been waiting at a taxi-stand for his wife, who arrives late:

HE: Why were you late?

SHE: I tried my best.

HE: Yeah? You and who else? Your mother is never on time either.

SHE: That's got nothing to do with it.

HE: The hell it doesn't. You're just as sloppy as she is.

SHE: You don't say! Who picks your dirty underwear off the floor every morning?

HE: I happen to go to work. What do you do all day?

SHE: I'm trying to get along on the money you don't make, that's what I do all day.

HE: Why should I knock myself out for an ungrateful ?!*#!? like you?

This exchange illustrates what Bach refers to as *gunnysacking*, signifying that the user saves all his or her complaints in a gunnysack and then makes a mess of things when she or he empties the sack and complaints cascade out of it. When we visit our "psychiatric museums" and drag into a conflict irrelevant past issues such as the mother-in-law mentioned in the conflict above, we end up venting pent-up aggressions by exchanging insults. Thus, after being served remarks about her mother by her husband, the wife then complains about her husband's lack of substantial income.

Crazymakers typically involve the use of passive–aggressive behavior that both catches a person off guard, confusing them, and arouses their anger. Instead of constructively addressing a relational complaint, crazymakers use insidious approaches instead. Among examples of other kinds of crazymaking behavior are *guiltmaking, beltlining, avoiding,* and *withholding.* Guiltmaking occurs when one party makes the other party responsible for causing pain: "It's okay; don't worry about me," whines the guiltmaker. Beltlining involves the voicing of comments that "hit below the belt," such as bringing up a person's unattractive physical attributes or perceived lack of intelligence. Avoiding occurs when a party to a conflict refuses to face an issue, leaving the other party to the conflict frustrated because no one will discuss the issue. Finally, withholding involves the keeping back of affection, humor, a material possession, or some other desirable thing or behavior because of the conflict. Any of one of these inappropriate responses to conflict can build up relationship resentments.[8] (See the section on Conflict-Generating Behaviors on pages 322–323 for additional insight into behaviors that fuel conflict.)

In lieu of exhibiting crazymaking behavior, researchers suggest applying the following five steps:

1. Be specific when you introduce a complaint.
2. Ask for change that will make the situation better.
3. Be tolerant of your partner.
4. Attack the issue, not the other person.
5. Think about what you have to say before you say it.[9]

in Theory

Who's the Crazymaker?

Analyze the Cathy cartoon below. What crazymaking ploys do Cathy and Irving use? What steps might each of them take to get their interactions with one another back on track?

The win-lose nature of sports is the source of many conflicts.

Thus conflicts can have both constructive and destructive outcomes. The outcome of a conflict depends on the interactive communication strategies the parties to it employ to resolve it. The first step toward handling conflict more effectively is to be open to its positive values.

Sources of Conflict

Conflicts can be started by anyone and may occur in any setting. Forces within us that oppose each other can build to create a conflict, or we may find ourselves experiencing tension as outside forces combine to create a conflict. An **intrapersonal conflict** can originate within a single person. For example, a person who is going to school full-time while raising children may feel conflicted about whether to spend time studying or watching a child's Little League game. **Interpersonal** conflict originates between two or more interdependent people. For example, conflict occurs between people in all types of interpersonal relationships: parents and children, brothers and sisters, coworkers, bosses and subordinates, friends and lovers.

Interactions among Individuals

Interpersonal conflicts always involve communication situations in which the people involved are *interdependent*—that is, the actions or beliefs of one individual are likely to have some impact on the other.[10] Conflict is apt to occur whenever we:

1. Perceive an *individual difference* such as a difference in beliefs, opinions, perceptions, values, needs, assumptions, interests, or goals. For example, you may believe that taking personal risks and moving to accept a new job is necessary for you to grow and develop in your career, whereas your partner believes that stability and roots are more important. The difference in the way you think is apt to produce conflict.

2. Observe a *scarcity of certain resources* or rewards such as time, money, power, popularity, space, or position. For example, you may feel that a shared bank account is keeping you from realizing your personal goals. If you had your own bank account, you tell yourself, you would be better able to fulfill your personal needs. Thus, the shared bank account becomes a source of relational conflict.

3. Are party to *a rivalry*—a situation in which there is competition with someone else. For example, if you and a friend are competing for one job, conflict may arise between you.

4. *Disagree* over how to define a relationship. For instance, you and a partner may define your roles in a relationship differently. While you want to stay just friends, he or she may want more. Your disagreement over the nature of your relationship can trigger conflict between you.

5. *Misinterpret* another's intent. For instance, when you misunderstand the intention of another, you assume certain things that can lead to conflict. If, in actuality, a friend doesn't call because he or she wants to surprise you, but you think—erroneously—that he or she simply doesn't want to talk to or see you, conflict may result from your beliefs.

A conflict can result from real differences or from a misunderstanding, anger, or expecting too much or too little from another person.

Conflict-Generating Behaviors

Can you think of situations in your own life that illustrate the causes of conflict identified here?

When another person acts to block our goals, a conflict can be generated. The following are among the behaviors apt to precipitate relational conflict.

Preemptive Striking

As one partner walks through the door, without warning, the other partner attacks him or her verbally or physically. Because the just-entering partner is

Practice

What Sets You Off?

The actions another person takes can cause conflict between the two of you.

1. Compile a list of conflict-generating behaviors, both your own and your partner's.

2. Rank your list from most to least disturbing.

3. In groups take turns role-playing the various conflict-generating behaviors you have identified. Focus on the nonverbal and verbal cues being sent and received by both parties. Then discuss the following:

   a. What was the disagreement about?
   b. Why did the disagreement occur?
   c. In what ways did both parties communicate during the conflict?
   d. Create a simile to represent your behavior and a simile to represent your partner's behavior. For example, you may have come across "like a locomotive" while your partner came across "like a wilting flower."

unprepared to handle the conflict, the conflict is likely either to escalate or to be postponed by the entering person's immediate departure.

Forcing

When one partner forces his or her position on the other, conflict is apt to develop. We don't like to feel compelled to do something. Nor do we enjoy feeling that we cannot extricate ourselves from a situation. When this occurs, a relationship can suffer serious damage.

Blame

When one partner blames the other for some wrong suffered, conflict between the two is often inevitable. Blame does nothing to resolve a relationship problem, but it does expose the raw feelings that one party is experiencing. Blame relies on the delivery of messages that attack rather than messages that attempt to resolve disagreements.

Classifying Sources of Conflict

We can classify interpersonal conflicts in several different ways: by the nature of their *goal, level of intensity,* or *general character.* Let us explore each in turn.

The Nature of the Goal

We can categorize a conflict based on whether the goal sought by the parties is perceived to be a **shareable goal** or a **nonshareable goal.** A goal is shareable if both parties to the conflict possess some of it; it is nonshareable if it must be fully claimed and possessed by only a single individual. Two people competing for the same job are competing for a nonshareable goal; two people competing for the highest score on a test are competing for a shareable goal.

Jeremy Shockey Is Living Large

How does the following story about Giants football player and tight-end Jeremy Shockey, as reported in *New York Magazine* by Chris Smith, illuminate the differences between destructive and constructive conflict? In what ways, if any, does conflict as it occurs on a playing field differ from conflict as it occurs off the field? To what extent, if any, can a word or words (verbal rather than physical aggressiveness) function as a producer of conflict? To what extent, if any, can a displayed *attitude* function as a conflict escalator? What role do the media play in stoking or allaying conflicts like the one described below? In your opinion, should conflict be defined differently for athletes when they are "off the playing field"? Keep these questions in mind as you read this passage:

Jeremy Shockey looks small. This is weird, because Shockey stands six feet five inches tall, weighs 260 pounds, and has biceps as thick as suspension-bridge cables. . . . For the past six months, Shockey has been gulping down the attention that comes from being twenty-two, single, and one of the N.F.L.'s brightest new stars. . . . From his first exhibition game in August 2002 when he flattened three Houston Texan would-be tacklers on one 48-yard catch-and-run, Shockey was electrifying. By mid-season his No. 80 jersey was a national best seller. The papers chronicled every snip of his gelled blond hair.

"The only guy who was hating me was Parcels," Shockey says. As head coach of the Giants, Bill Parcels won two Super Bowls; last season, he was a commentator for ESPN. "I never watch TV," Shockey says. "But my buddies were like, 'Why does Bill Parcels hate you so much?' He's talking about, 'I never seen a player get so much hype off doing nothing.'"

Shockey's backbone straightens. His blue eyes narrow to slits.

"Parcels is not my kinda guy. He says he quits, then he wants to come back and coach. Do something! Stay in commentary or stay in football or get the hell out of everybody's life."

This year, after "final" stints leading the New England Patriots and then the Jets, Parcels has unretired again. He brings the Dallas Cowboys to Giants Stadium. . . . Shockey looks ready to take them on right here, right now: "All my buddies are like, 'Why's he dogging you? After you

catch a pass on him this year, you oughta throw it right at his fat head!'"

Shockey's chest swells. "Let's see how much Parcels wins this year," he spits. "I'll make him pay when we play them. The homo . . . ."

"You can't have it both ways," (Giants Coach) Jim Fassel says. "You can't have a bunch of choir boys and expect them to go out and fight their @!#?! off on the field. As a coach, what you're trying to figure out is, are they a bad person, or are they a good person that just kind of drifts a little bit? Shockey is a good guy. But you're gonna have to live with the edge in Shockey if you want him to be the player he is. You don't like that edge, then don't have him on your team. Me, I want him on my team in the worst way."*

Following the publication of this article, Coach Fassel reprimanded Shockey for the disparaging remarks he made about Coach Parcels. If you were advising Shockey, what recommendations would you make to him and the Giants regarding his role in the conflict? What comments would you make about the impact of verbal aggressiveness? What skills or strategies could Shockey benefit from learning to be better able to cope with conflict-arousing situations? For example, how might he communicate his ideas without displaying a bullying attitude or becoming verbally aggressive?

Finally, how do you imagine Shockey would score on the following verbal aggressiveness inventory? How do you score?

Inventory of Verbal Aggressiveness

When answering the questions below, use the following scale: 1 (almost never true), 2 (rarely true), 3 (occasionally true), 4 (often true), 5 (almost always true).

____ 1. I attempt not to attack someone's intelligence when I attack their ideas.

____ 2. In order to counter a person's stubbornness, I use insults.

____ 3. I try to preserve someone's self-concept as I try to influence him or her.

*Excerpts from Chris Smith, "Jeremy Shockey Is Living Large," *New York Magazine*, August 18, 2003. Reprinted by permission of New York Magazine; Inventory of Verbal Aggressiveness adapted from Dominic A. Infante and Charles J. Wigley III, "Verbal Aggressiveness: An Interpersonal Model and Measure," *Communication Monographs*, Volume 53, March 1986, p. 64. Reprinted by permission of Taylor & Francis Ltd., http://www.tandf.co.uk/journals/titles/03637751.html, and Professor Dominic A. Infante.

_____ 4. When someone has no reason that I can see for refusing to complete a task that I think is important, I tell the person how unreasonable he or she is.

_____ 5. When others do things I perceive to be stupid, I'm gentle in telling them what I think.

_____ 6. I attack the characters of others when I think they deserve it.

_____ 7. When I don't like how someone is behaving, I insult him or her to wake him or her up.

_____ 8. Even when I think another person's ideas are stupid, I'll try to make them feel good about him- or herself.

_____ 9. When people are fixed in their ways of thinking or acting, I lose my temper and say things to them I shouldn't say.

_____ 10. I take criticism well and do not retaliate by criticizing others.

_____ 11. I enjoy telling others off after they insult me.

_____ 12. When I do not like someone, I try not to show it.

_____ 13. To stimulate their intelligence I enjoy belittling people who do what I consider to be stupid things.

_____ 14. I try not to harm another person's self-concept even when I attack his or her ideas.

_____ 15. I go out of my way not to offend persons I try to influence.

_____ 16. When others are cruel or mean, I attack their character in an effort to correct their behavior.

_____ 17. I won't engage in an argument that involves personal attacks.

_____ 18. Yelling and screaming work to involve others I am trying to influence when all else fails.

_____ 19. When I am unsuccessful refuting the positions of another person, I'll make him or her feel defensive to try and weaken his or her position.

_____ 20. When an argument becomes a personal attack, I try to change the subject.

Follow the following steps to compute your verbal aggressiveness score:

1. Add the scores on items 2, 4, 6, 7, 9, 11, 13, 16, 18, 19.
2. Add the scores on items 1, 3, 5, 8, 10, 12, 14, 15, 17, 20.
3. Subtract the step 2 score from 60.
4. Add the score from step 1 to the score you computed from step 3.

If you scored between 59 and 100, you are highly verbally aggressive.

If you scored between 39 and 58, you are somewhat verbally aggressive.

If you scored between 20 and 38, you are rarely verbally aggressive.

Does your score surprise you? Do you think it would surprise others with whom you interact frequently? Ask them. Do their responses confirm or contradict your beliefs? If you scored high in verbal aggressiveness, what might you do in order to share your ideas with others without becoming verbally combative?

The Intensity Level of the Conflict

We can also categorize conflict by *intensity level.* The level of intensity that we bring to a conflict depends on how strongly we feel about winning. Interactants engaged in a **low-intensity conflict** do not usually seek to destroy one another; instead, they devise a strategy to help control their communications and permit them to discover a solution that is beneficial to each of them. Where to eat dinner may constitute a low-intensity conflict. In a **medium-intensity conflict,** although each interactant wants to win, winning itself is seen as sufficient. Interactants still do not want to destroy each other in the process. Competing with a friend to be captain of a sports team you are both on may create a medium-intensity conflict. On the other hand, in a **high-intensity conflict,** one party to the conflict aims to destroy or at least seriously debilitate the other. Winning is no longer enough; victory must be total. Individuals engaged in a highly contested divorce may find themselves in a high-intensity conflict.

The Character of the Conflict

In addition to the intensity level, it is important to consider the character of the conflict—the basic disagreement at the root of the problem. When we categorize a conflict by its character, we identify it as a *pseudoconflict,* a *content conflict,* a *value conflict,* or an *ego conflict.*

A **pseudoconflict,** while not really a conflict, gives the appearance of one. It occurs when one individual mistakenly believes that two or more goals cannot be achieved simultaneously by each interactant. Typically, pseudoconflicts revolve around erroneous either–or judgments (either you win or I win) or around simple misunderstandings (failing to perceive that you and the other person actually agree). A pseudoconflict is resolved when the parties to it realize they are not actually involved in a conflict. For example, suppose Aalyiah and Buffy are going to spend an evening watching DVDs. Aalyiah wants to watch one DVD, and Buffy wants to watch another. If one of them is willing to delay watching the one she wants until a little later, they can watch both. In this way both parties' goals can be met.

Pseudoconflicts can also exist due to a misunderstanding that results from a lack of clarity. For example, a person who is chronically late can be handled with little difficulty, as follows:

MAYA (on a cell phone): I'm running late. I won't be there for a while.

ELIJAH (on a cell phone): What do you mean by "a while." What time do you think you'll get here? I have a number of things to do today and not enough time to do them.

MAYA: It should be about twenty minutes.

ELIJAH: Oh, that's pretty soon, but it does give me time to run an errand before you arrive. See you in twenty minutes.

A **content conflict** occurs when individuals disagree over matters of fact: the definition of a term, the solution to a problem, the accuracy of information. Once interactants accept that facts can be verified, inferences tested, definitions checked, and solutions evaluated against established criteria, they are then able to settle their conflict rationally. If you and a partner disagree about how much money is in your joint savings account, a trip to the bank can resolve your disagreement.

A **value conflict** exists when individuals hold disparate views on an issue important to each of them—welfare, for example. An individual who values individual independence and self-assertion (standing up for one's rights while respecting the rights of others) is apt to possess very different opinions about welfare than someone who believes that we are all ultimately accountable for the well-being of others. If interactants can agree that it is all right to disagree, they will be able to discuss the issue, share insights, understand each other's position, and learn from one another, even though they might continue to disagree.

Of all the conflict categories, **ego conflicts** have the greatest potential to destroy a relationship. Individuals involved in an ego conflict seek to win at all costs because they think that losing will damage their self-worth or prestige or others' perception of their competence. Because the individual believes that his or her credibility is on the line, it is no longer the issue itself that is important. Rational decision making suffers as interactants strive to win in an effort to protect themselves.

Conflict-generating behavior affects each of us differently and elicits different kinds of responses as we seek to cope with or resolve it.

Conflict Resolution Strategies

A number of different paradigms have been defined to help us understand and represent the strategies we use as we try to resolve conflicts. Among the most popular is Blake and Mouton's **conflict resolution grid.**

Conflict Styles

Theorists Robert Blake and Jane Srygley Mouton originated the concept of preferred conflict resolution style.[11] By identifying five distinct types of conflict behavior and representing them on a grid, they were able to represent graphically the different ways people resolve conflict. The grid depicts the extent to which individuals employ *assertive strategies,* in which individuals attempt to satisfy their own concerns, or *cooperative strategies,* in which individuals attempt to satisfy the concerns of another as a means of resolving a conflict. (We'll talk more about learning to be assertive later in the chapter.)

What conflict-resolving strategies do you regularly use?

The grid has two scales (see Figure 11.1 below). The vertical scale, assertiveness, measures the extent to which a person acts to attain personal goals, and the horizontal scale, cooperativeness, represents the extent to which that individual exhibits behavior intended to satisfy a concern for others. The interface between the two

FIGURE 11.1
Blake and Mouton's Conflict Resolution Grid

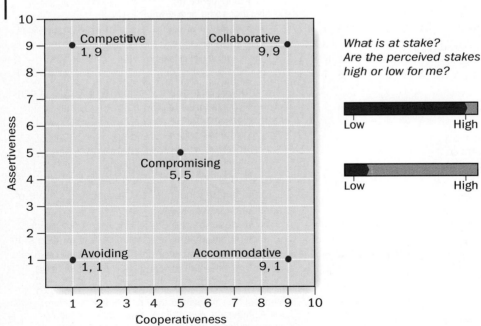

What is at stake?
Are the perceived stakes high or low for me?

SOURCE: Adapted from Robert R. Blake and Jane Srygley Mouton, "The Fifth Achievement," *Journal of Applied Behavioral Science,* Vol. 6, No. 4, 1970, p. 418. Copyright © 1970 by NTL Institute for Applied Behavioral Science. Reprinted by permission of Sage Publications, Inc.

Theory

Where Do You Fit into the Grid?

Think about how you characteristically respond to conflicts that you and a relational partner face. Then use the accompanying scales to respond to each question, where 1 indicates that you strongly *disagree* with the written statement and 7 indicates that you strongly *agree* with it.*

| | Disagree | Agree |

1. I discuss the problem to try to reach a mutual understanding.　1 2 3 4 5 6 7

2. I stick to my argument until I prove my point.　1 2 3 4 5 6 7

3. I give in to my partner to keep my relationship satisfying.　1 2 3 4 5 6 7

4. I sometimes sacrifice my own goals so my partner can meet her or his goals.　1 2 3 4 5 6 7

5. I try to find a new solution that will satisfy all our needs.　1 2 3 4 5 6 7

6. I usually try to win arguments.　1 2 3 4 5 6 7

7. I do not like to talk about issues of disagreement.　1 2 3 4 5 6 7

8. I am willing to give up some of my goals in exchange for achieving other goals.　1 2 3 4 5 6 7

9. I try to get all my concerns and my partner's concerns out in the open.　1 2 3 4 5 6 7

10. I usually try to forget about issues of disagreement so I don't have to confront my partner.　1 2 3 4 5 6 7

11. I try to think of a compromise that satisfies both our needs.　1 2 3 4 5 6 7

12. I argue until my ideas are accepted.　1 2 3 4 5 6 7

13. It is important to get both our points of view out in the open.　1 2 3 4 5 6 7

14. I try to convince my partner that my position is right.　1 2 3 4 5 6 7

15. I try to meet my partner half way.　1 2 3 4 5 6 7

16. If the issue is very important to my partner, I usually give in.　1 2 3 4 5 6 7

17. I attempt to work with my partner to find a creative solution we both like.　1 2 3 4 5 6 7

18. I usually let my partner take responsibility for bringing up conflict issues.　1 2 3 4 5 6 7

19. I would rather not get into a discussion of unpleasant issues.　1 2 3 4 5 6 7

20. I avoid bringing up certain issues if my arguments might hurt my partner's feelings.　1 2 3 4 5 6 7

21. I might agree with some of my partner's points to make my partner happy.　1 2 3 4 5 6 7

22. I avoid talking with my partner about disagreements.　1 2 3 4 5 6 7

23. I try to find a "middle ground" position that is acceptable to both of us.　1 2 3 4 5 6 7

24. I try to influence my partner so he or she will see things my way.　1 2 3 4 5 6 7

25. I believe that you have to "give a little to get a little" during a disagreement.　1 2 3 4 5 6 7

In order to determine your preferred style of conflict, add your scores for the following items:

3, 4, 16, 20, 21	(accommodating)	_____
7, 10, 18, 19, 22	(avoiding)	_____
1, 5, 9, 13, 17	(collaborating)	_____
2, 6, 12, 14, 24	(competing)	_____
8, 11, 15, 23, 25	(compromising)	_____

Higher scores indicate that you possess more of a particular conflict style.

As we describe the Blake and Mouton conflict grid and its five styles, keep your preferred style(s) in mind in an effort to determine if those you habitually use are effective in resolving relational conflicts.

*This inventory, based on the work of Blake and Mouton, appears in "Put Yourself to the Test," in L. K. Guerrero, Peter A. Andersen, and Walid A. Afifi, *Close Encounters: Communicating in Relationships,* New York: McGraw Hill, 2001, p. 384–385. Copyright © 2001 by The McGraw-Hill Companies, Inc. Reprinted by permission of The McGraw-Hill Companies, Inc.

scales represents how strongly an individual feels about each component—that is, how his or her concern is actually apportioned or how he or she behaves. On the basis of this measure, Blake and Mouton identified five key **conflict styles.**

Avoidance

A person with an *avoiding style* (1,1) is unassertive and uncooperative. The individual's behavioral approach to a conflict is to withdraw or "lose and walk away." He or she may actually physically flee or leave the scene of the conflict. The avoider aims to maintain the appearance of indifference. Avoiders view conflict as a useless and potentially punishing endeavor. Rather than face it and have to handle the frustrations that may accompany it, they physically and mentally separate themselves from the situation. By withdrawing and refusing to deal with the conflict, they relieve themselves of the psychological relational burdens imposed by it. Avoiders also give up their personal goals and sometimes their relationships.

Because they are nonconfrontational, adherents of the avoiding style diminish both the importance of the conflict and the interests of both parties. Instead, they deal with the conflict by acting as if they don't care, by changing the topic, and by joking. Such avoidance responses can precipitate a demand–withdraw interaction pattern, a particularly ineffective means of conflict management in which avoiders become intransigent in their efforts to withdraw from interacting with conflict engagers, who become increasingly persistent in their attempts to confront and resolve the problems they perceive.[12]

Competitive

A person with a *competing style* (1,9) is high in assertiveness and low in cooperation. Competers strive to force their position on the other person; they aim to attain their personal goals while ignoring the concerns of others. Competers, who possess a "win–lose" mind-set, exhibit an overwhelming need to win or defeat those with whom they are in conflict. They fight to defend their position, often confronting others, attacking their self-concepts, and compelling them to concur by physical force or psychological domination. Competers do this despite the cost incurred, the harm caused, or the fact that others may find them destructive in their handling of the conflict.

According to Papa and Canary, users of the competing style seek to maximize the importance of their own needs by minimizing the needs of other persons.[13] In their fight to achieve dominance, competing-style individuals make threats and accusations, engage in name calling, act in a confrontational manner, deny responsibility for any and all wrongdoing, and generally do everything they can to prove how right they are. Primarily because of their lack of motivation to treat their partners appropriately, adherents of the competing style exhibit low levels of effective communication.[14]

Compromising

Someone who has a *compromising style* (5,5) is in the middle range in both assertiveness and cooperativeness. Compromisers aim to find the middle ground by working to permit each party to a conflict to gain something. While that may happen, each also gives up something to reach the agreement. Also known as

Have you ever left the scene of a conflict? In your opinion, how does "walking away" affect the situation?

"sharing" or "horse-trading," this style leaves individuals only partially satisfied. In fact, it is sometimes referred to as the "lose–lose" approach. Part of a goal or a relationship is sacrificed to reach agreement for the common good.

Compromisers tend to appeal to fairness and negotiate tradeoffs in the effort to find a reasonably quick solution to the conflict they face. As such, compromising is only moderately effective, requires sacrifice on the part of both parties to the conflict, and precludes the search for more creative solutions.

Accommodative

A person with an *accommodative style* (9,1) is unassertive and cooperative. Accommodators typically "give in and lose." Because they typically overvalue the maintenance of relationships and undervalue the attainment of their own goals, accommodators' main concern is to do what they must to smooth things over and ensure that others accept them, like them, and will maintain a relationship with them. Because they believe conflict should be avoided in favor of harmony, accommodators are appeasers; in an effort to preserve the relationship, they smooth over disagreements and conceal ill feelings. Their actions can precipitate an uneasy, tense relational state characterized by a weak, self-sacrificing approach and even nervous laughter.

Persons who use a cooperative strategy to work out a conflict view the situation as a problem to be solved.

Indirect and passive in their approach to conflict, the accommodators tend to trivialize conflict by glossing over differences in an effort to downplay disagreements. The style is perceived as generally ineffective if only because its users usually feel powerless and fail to meet their personal goals, which typically adds to the strains their relationships are under.

Collaborative

A person with a *collaborative style* (9,9) is high in both assertiveness and cooperation. Collaborators, who exhibit a "win–win" orientation, are problem solvers who actively seek to satisfy their own goals as well as those of others. People who exhibit this style seek to integrate the needs of both parties to the conflict so that each attains full satisfaction with the solution. Collaborators see conflicts as a means of improving relationships. As problem solvers they recognize that conflicts are normal and can be helpful and that every person involved in a conflict holds an opinion that deserves to be aired and considered. Collaborators are able to openly discuss differences without resorting to personal attacks. They are not satisfied until they discover a solution that achieves both their own goals and those of the other person. Collaborators tend to be highly competent communicators who work to ensure that lines of communication are open, thereby preserving and promoting opportunities for sharing and continued interaction.

Each of the five styles has its place and can be useful given different relationships, circumstances, and contexts. People also use one strategy or another at different times and with different partners. In the cartoon above, Garfield seems to be most interested in satisfying his goals at the expense of others. Where would he fit on the conflict resolution grid?

How important achieving your personal goals is to you and how significant you perceive a relationship to be affects how you behave during conflicts. For example, avoidance may be the best approach to use when a conflict is minor, or the risk you face by confronting it is too great. Likewise, accommodation may be an appropriate choice when the outcome of the conflict is more important to the other person than it is to you. Forcing may be an appropriate strategy when you do not expect to need the continued goodwill and cooperation of the other person. By becoming more mindful of such possibilities, we can vary our responses according to what will work best in a given situation. In other words, by understanding Blake and Mouton's conflict resolution behaviors, we become better equipped to select the approach or behavioral strategies that are most appropriate for us to use to resolve a specific conflict.

Conflict Management Behaviors

As we seek to resolve conflict, we need to avoid exhibiting the kinds of behaviors that destroy relationships. By learning how to eliminate destructive communication behaviors from our behavioral repertoire and substitute constructive communication behaviors in their place, we will be better able to manage interpersonal conflict.

Destructive Communication Behaviors

When a conflict first develops, one of the variables affecting its outcome is whether the participants intend to cooperate or compete to resolve it. If both individuals bring a competitive orientation to the conflict, then each will tend to be ego-involved (see his or her self-concept at stake) and view winning the conflict as a test of personal worth and competence. When parties to a conflict are deceitful rather than open, when they fail to respect each other or view each other as equals, when they don't try to understand the nature of the conflict from the other person's point of view, when they neglect to ask questions, or when they ignore or fail to clarify the assumptions under which they are operating, they are also likely to employ strategies that suppress rather than encourage the free exchange of ideas. They will thereby impede, rather than facilitate, the identification of a mutually satisfactory solution.

Parties to a conflict who lack openness are usually not concerned with the feelings of the other person, believing that it is unnecessary that each party to the conflict benefit from a positive outcome. They tend instead to place blame for the conflict on the other person in an effort to absolve themselves of any responsibility for the creation of the conflict in the first place. In addition, they are apt to resort to using power techniques that further inhibit freedom of expression at the same time that they inflict psychological pain on or damage the self-image of the other person.

For better or for worse, competing with, even striving to defeat another person with whom we perceive ourselves to be in conflict, is common in U.S. society. Even the terminology supports this orientation: people speak of "out-smarting" another person, of getting "one up," of doing whatever is necessary to win at the sport of social "gamesmanship."

Constructive Communication Behaviors

When parties to a conflict define it as a mutually noncompetitive endeavor—a "win–win" opportunity—through which both individuals can gain, they express their ideas openly and honestly, view each other as equals, and respect and work to understand the position taken by the other person. In order for both parties to win, both must use effective listening techniques (see Chapter 4) and perception validation techniques (see Chapter 3) to ensure understanding of the other person's perspective on the problem. They must encourage a free exchange of ideas, an open discussion of alternatives, and the integration of their needs in an effort to identify a mutually satisfactory solution.

As a result of using constructive conflict resolution behaviors, each party to a conflict avoids behaving in a way that could escalate the problem by making the other party defensive or combative. Instead, individuals seek to view the conflict through the eyes of the other party. Employing **role reversal** is one way to learn conflict resolution strategies. Through this technique, in which each person imagines him- or herself as the other, the parties to the conflict are better able to understand each other, discover creative ways to integrate their interests and concerns, and work toward a common goal. Once statements like "you're wrong," "you're stupid," "I hate you," or "that's ridiculous" are replaced with statements like "what you believe is not what I believe," individuals are on their way to developing a cooperative conflict resolution orientation through effective communication.

To be sure, we all compete with others at one time or another. In school we compete for grades. At work we compete for jobs. In social settings we compete for attention, friendship, or even love. The question is, how do we behave and what kind of expressive style do we exhibit when faced with such conflicts?

.in *Practice*

Grid Analyses

Consider three conflict situations that you have experienced.

1. Answer the following questions for each situation:
   a. With whom were you in conflict?
   b. What was the conflict about?
   c. How much did you perceive to be at stake?
      Very little 1 2 3 4 5 6 7 8 9 A great deal
   d. How concerned were you with maintaining a good relationship with the other party to the conflict?

Not concerned 1 2 3 4 5 6 7 8 9 Very concerned

   e. To what extent were you and the other person involved in this conflict satisfied with the results?
   f. To what extent did the conflict style you employed differ between situations? Why?

2. Graph your conflict resolution style for each of the three conflict situations using three different colored pencils on the grid below, corresponding to your assertiveness and cooperativeness level for each situation.

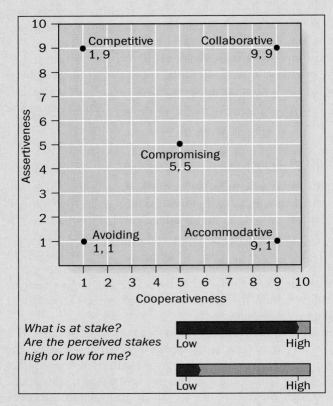

DESC Scripts

A strategy that can help us manage and resolve our conflicts is illustrated by the **DESC script,** a way of expressing our feelings and understanding the feelings of another person.[15] DESC is an acronym for *describe, express, specify,* and *consequences.* Every DESC script contains characters (in this case, the parties to the conflict), a plot (why at least one of the participants finds the current situation dissatisfying), a setting (the time and place of the interaction), and a message (the words and nonverbal cues of the interactants).

Describe

You initiate a DESC script by *describing* as specifically and objectively as possible why the situation troubles you. While describing the situation, you also give yourself the opportunity to examine and define your personal needs and goals. Once you identify what it is that you perceive as negative about the situation, you are in a better position to resolve it. During your description of the situation, it is important that the words you use be simple, concrete, specific, and unbiased. For example, instead of yelling, "You're always embarrassing me, you piece of dirt!" try saying, "I don't like to be embarrassed in front of my friends." Instead of assuming you understand someone's motives and saying, "You're infatuated with Danielle; when she's around, you wish I'd disappear," observe, "The last two times we've been with Danielle, you've ignored me."

Express

The second step in the DESC approach is to *express* how you feel about the nature of the situation. Here it's important to use personal statements that make it clear you are expressing what *you* feel and what *you* think. The key to making a personal statement is to use the pronouns "I," "me," or "my"; for example, use phrases such as "I feel," "I believe," "My feelings are," "It appears to me." You can name a feeling: "I feel disappointed"; "I feel angry." You can use comparisons: "I feel like a piece of trash." Or you can indicate the type of action your feelings prompt you to display: "I feel like running away." By disclosing your feelings, you can make the other person aware of your position without alienating him or her.

Specify

Once you have described the problem and expressed your feelings about it, your next step is to discuss changing. You *specify* how you would like to see the situation resolved. In effect, you request that the other person stop behaving one way and start behaving another, for instance: "When you know you will be late, please call to warn me."

Consequences

All behavioral changes have *consequences* (punishments or rewards). In the last phase of DESC, you spell out the consequences of the status quo or the change, or both. When possible, emphasize positive rather than negative outcomes. For example, it is probably more effective to say, "If you stop belittling me in front of Nick and Alisha, I'll feel better and we'll have more fun," than it would be to say, "If you continue to make fun of me, I'll have to start making fun of you."

The following example illustrates how one person, Emma, used a DESC script in an attempt to resolve the relationship difficulties she was having with her friend Destiny and reconcile with her:

DESCRIBE: Destiny, we hardly see or speak to each other any more. It's been weeks since we've IM'd, phoned each other, or gone out for a drink.

EXPRESS: I feel bad about how our schedules are making it difficult for us to get together, especially since I value your friendship, and I believe our friendship can be a strong one.

SPECIFY: Could we get together for a latte and see how we can make more time for each other?

CONSEQUENCES: If we can find a way to schedule friendship breaks like others schedule coffee breaks, I think we'd feel better and not find ourselves so stressed.

Similarly, an employee, Cole, had the following conversation with his supervisor, Alexa, in an effort to refuse what he perceived to be an unreasonable demand.

DESCRIBE: We have been swamped with work every day, yet almost every day right before I'm ready to leave you have asked me to complete a number of extra special assignments as well. I'm becoming exhausted.

EXPRESS: I feel overworked, overstressed, and overwhelmed.

SPECIFY: I typically complete the morning's assignments about a half hour before I take a lunch break. If you let me know then what additional work you need me to do, and which assignment has the highest priority, I'll take care of it then.

CONSEQUENCES: I can handle my regular responsibilities and the extra work without becoming stressed or overwhelmed if you'll give me enough notice. I think that would make us both feel relieved.[16]

Your Expressive Style: Nonassertive, Aggressive, or Assertive

There are three ways to handle conflict-producing situations: nonassertively, aggressively, or assertively (see Figure 11.2). Let's explore the characteristics of each approach. How would you respond if faced with the following situations?

> *Your friend is taking a public speaking class. She asks to borrow the speech you gave when you were enrolled in a similar course.*
>
> *You are in line waiting to buy concert tickets and another person pushes in front of you.*
>
> *You are not given the promotion you believe is due you.*
>
> *You are chosen to represent your school at a national conference that you have neither the time nor the desire to attend.*

Before we look at nonassertiveness, aggression, and assertiveness in detail, complete the "In Practice: A Self-Assessment" activity on pages 338–339 to evaluate your own conflict behavior.

Nonassertiveness

When we are fearful or hesitate to express our feelings and thoughts, we exhibit a **nonassertive expression style** in which we don't try to satisfy our own concerns. When we adopt such an avoidance-based strategy, we allow others to intimidate us and usually ensure that our own feelings will remain bottled up inside us and that our needs will go unmet. Because we are afraid to cause a problem, we often fail to

FIGURE 11.2
Expressive Style Scale

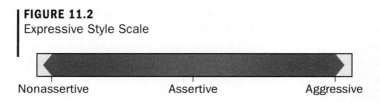

Nonassertive   Assertive   Aggressive

inform another person of our displeasure, and we don't take whatever steps are needed to improve an unsatisfying relationship. For one reason or another, we offer excuse after excuse; we never quite find the right time or the right words to express how we really feel, and we avoid confronting the individual or situation that is causing us discomfort. Thus a nonassertive style can contribute to our paying too much for a meal, performing a favor for someone when we don't have time to do it, or staying in a relationship that demeans us. Why would we not assert ourselves?

Why We Don't Assert Ourselves

A number of factors account for our nonassertiveness. Sometimes it is our *inertia*— we are merely lazy; it is, after all, easier for us to do nothing. Assertion takes energy. Other times, it is not because of laziness that we behave nonassertively; it is merely because *we don't care enough* to assert ourselves. The issue at stake is either not important enough or not salient enough to move us to take constructive action. Yet other times, it is our *fear* that compels us to adopt a nonassertive style. We may, for example, fear rejection, making another person angry, or their becoming unhappy with us. *Shyness* is also a factor that can precipitate a nonassertive response. People who are shy devote an excessive amount of time worrying about what others think of them, less time letting others know what they think, and more time as a victim.

Who makes you reluctant to assert yourself?

Nonassertive Language

Suppose, for example, a shy individual (*A*) wanted to get another person (*B*) to help him or her plan a party for a friend. Their conversation might proceed as follows:

A: Uh, pardon me. This really isn't important, uh, you know I was wondering if you would be willing to take a few minutes and help me plan Angela's party.

B: (*Head buried in a book*) Can't do it now. I'm busy.

A: Oh, sure. Sorry.

Various nonverbal and verbal behaviors are associated with shy or nonassertive behavior. Nonassertive nonverbal behaviors include downcast eyes or evasive eye contact, excessive head nodding, body gestures such as hand wringing, slouched posture, and a low, whining, hesitant, or giggly voice. Nonassertive verbal behaviors include fillers like "uh, um" and "you know"; negators such as "This really isn't important but," and "You'll probably think I'm stupid"; qualifiers such as "just," "I guess"; an overuse of apologetic words; and a disconnected speech pattern. In general, nonassertive behaviors reduce the impact of what the nonassertive person is saying, which is one reason why individuals who fear rejection use them. Remember, the nonassertive individual aims to appease others.

Aggressiveness

In contrast to nonassertive individuals, people who exhibit an **aggressive expression style** openly express their needs, wants, and ideas even if doing so hurts others. In an effort to stand up for themselves, aggressive individuals often ignore or violate the rights of those with whom they conflict. As a result, aggressive communicators get more of their needs met than nonassertive communicators, but at another's expense. The aggressor's aim is to dominate and win in a relationship; merely breaking even is not enough.

Sometimes it's worse to win a fight than to lose.

— Billie Holiday

in Practice

A Self-Assessment

Respond to the following statements to assess the extent to which you characteristically respond assertively to interpersonal conflict. Use the scale to evaluate the degree to which each statement typifies your behavior.

1. For each statement, assign a score of 5 to 1, according to the following criteria:

   5 If you almost always display the behavior

   4 If the behavior occurs about 75 percent of the time

   3 If you have a 50–50 chance of displaying the behavior

   2 If you sometimes, but not frequently, behave in this manner

   1 If you almost never display the behavior

2. Add the values in each of the sections below to determine your total score.

   You and a friend disagree over who works harder to make your friendship work. You:

   _____ try not to make your friend feel guilty.

   _____ calmly let your friend know what upsets you about his or her behavior.

   _____ avoid blaming your friend for any relationship problems.

   _____ look directly at your friend when talking to him or her.

   _____ make no assumptions about how your friend feels.

   _____ question your friend in an effort to avoid misunderstanding him or her.

   _____ avoid using sarcasm as a communication strategy.

   _____ refrain from becoming anxious about discussing the problem.

   _____ use appropriately forceful voice tone, body language, facial expressions, and gestures to support your feelings.

   _____ avoid cursing and using obscenities to make your point.

   _____ present your thoughts in an organized manner.

   _____ consider the impact of your actions.

   _____ Total

You and your boss disagree over the kind of job you are doing. You:

_____ try not to make your boss feel guilty.

_____ calmly let your boss know how you feel.

_____ avoid blaming your boss for the disagreement.

_____ look directly at your boss when speaking to him or her.

_____ make no assumptions about your boss's feelings.

_____ question your boss to avoid further misunderstanding.

_____ avoid using sarcasm during the interaction.

_____ refrain from becoming anxious about letting your boss know what you think.

_____ use appropriately forceful voice tone, body language, facial expressions, and gestures to support your feelings.

_____ avoid cursing or using obscenities to make a point.

_____ present your thoughts in an organized manner.

_____ consider the impact of your actions.

_____ Total

You and a professor disagree about a grade. You:

_____ try not to make the professor feel guilty.

_____ calmly let the professor know why you are upset.

_____ avoid blaming the professor for the grade.

_____ look directly at the professor when speaking to him or her.

_____ make no assumptions about the professor's reasons.

_____ question the professor to avoid a misunderstanding.

_____ avoid using sarcasm during your interaction.

_____ refrain from becoming anxious about speaking up and letting the professor know what you think.

_____ use appropriately forceful voice tone, body language, facial expressions, and gestures to support your feelings.

_____ avoid cursing or using obscenities to make a point.

_____ present your thoughts in an organized fashion.

_____ consider the impact of your actions.

_____ Total

3. If you consistently score near 60 for each situation, you are probably comfortable handling interpersonal conflict. If you consistently score near 12, you probably are not. Re-examine each set of responses. With which person were you most effective? most ineffective? Why? Circle the questions to which you responded with a 1, 2, or 3. These are the behaviors you may want to work on.

Aggressive Language

The message sent by the aggressive person is selfish: "This is the way I feel about . . . . You're dumb for feeling differently." "This is what I want; what you want doesn't count and is of no consequence to me." Now suppose an individual who exhibits an aggressive style (*A*) was attempting to convince a friend (*B*) to help him or her plan a party for another friend. Their conversation might proceed as follows:

A: I'm fed up with you. I'm sick of listening to you tell me you don't have time to plan this party. You'd better make time to plan this party with me now!

B: (*Head buried in a book*) Can't do it now. I'm busy.

A: You're wrong. You can do it now. You're just selfish. You don't have time for anyone but yourself.

B: Not so.

A: That's a lie. Who always does everything? I do. All you ever do is read or watch videos. You're just a lazy waste. I'm sick and tired of talking to you.

B: Oh, just cool down.

Compared to the nonassertive person, who starts hesitantly, the aggressive person begins by attacking and uses nonverbal and verbal behaviors to support the effort. Nonverbal cues include "stare down" messages; a raised, harsh, strident voice; a cold, sarcastic, or demeaning tone; excessive finger pointing, fist pounding, and a willingness to invade the personal space of another individual. Characteristically, the verbal messages of an aggressive person also spell p-u-t-d-o-w-n. Aggressors frequently interrupt or answer before others finish speaking, using threats such as "You'd better," "If you don't stop . . . ," or "I'm warning you." They are also prone to making evaluative judgments and uttering accusative statements such as "That's bad," "You're wrong," "Your approach is clearly inferior," and degrading comments such as "You can't be serious," "You're joking," and "Shut up." In some exchanges involving an aggressor, the conversation escalates out of control because the target of the aggressor's communication feels a need to retaliate. When this happens we reach a stalemate, and no one wins.

Why We Act Aggressively

Individuals act aggressively for a number of reasons. First, we may lash out simply because we feel ourselves become *vulnerable*; we make an effort to protect ourselves from the perceived threat of powerlessness. Second, *unresolved, emotionally volatile experiences* can trigger an aggressive reaction, causing an overreaction in the face of a conflict. Third, we may firmly believe that *the only way* for us to get our ideas and feelings across is through aggression. For some reason, we may be convinced that another will neither listen to nor react to what we say if we are mild-mannered in our approach. Fourth, we may not have learned *how to channel or handle our aggressive impulses.* Finally, our aggressive style may be related to repeated past incidences of nonassertive behavior. The hurt, the disappointment, the bewilderment, and the *sense of personal violation* that accompany a nonassertive response style may have reached a boiling point. No longer able to contain these feelings, we abruptly vent them. As a result, aggression may damage or destroy a relationship.

Assertiveness

While the intent of an individual who exhibits a nonassertive style is to avoid any kind of conflict, even if it means sacrificing needs and wants, and the intent of an individual who exhibits an aggressive style is to dominate in a relationship, even if this domination means that someone else will be hurt, the intent of the individual who exhibits an **assertive expression style** is to communicate honestly, clearly, and directly, and to stand up for what he or she believes without harming others or him- or herself.

When we assert ourselves, we meet more of our interpersonal needs, make more of our own decisions, and think and say what we believe without apologizing, dominating, infringing on the rights of others, or violating their dignity. In the process, we protect ourselves from becoming a "victim." Such behavior promotes a healthy interpersonal climate for the handling of conflict.

Acting assertively tends to be rewarding. We feel good when we begin to accomplish our goals in a relationship and when we act in our own best interest without harming or depreciating another. We are pleased when we elicit a positive response from someone and we can openly express our feelings and thoughts.

Learning Assertive Behavior

In order to stop yourself from sending nonassertive or aggressive messages when such behavior would be inappropriate, you need to learn assertiveness skills. By attending to feelings and using specific verbal and nonverbal skills, you can resolve interper-

Peanuts reprinted by permission of United Feature Syndicate, Inc.

sonal conflict. Nonassertive individuals create a power imbalance by giving everyone more rights than they give themselves, and aggressive individuals create an imbalance by giving themselves more rights than they give others. Assertive individuals try to balance social power and thereby equalize the nature of the relationships they share.

Assertive Language

As with nonassertion and aggression, there are particular nonverbal and verbal cues that characterize assertion. Good eye contact is an essential component of an assertive style. When we avoid eye contact we send the message that we are nervous, anxious, uncomfortable, or perhaps even incompetent. When we stare at another person, our gaze suggests that we hold him or her in contempt. However, when we look at another with interest and focus on him or her during a conversation, we communicate that we are concerned. Likewise, a strong, well-modulated, steady voice signals that we are in control of ourselves and sincere. We saw in Chapter 8 that using "I" language helps people accept responsibility for their feelings. In similar fashion, the verbal characteristics of assertive people include an ability and willingness to send "I" messages and "we" messages. Assertive individuals let us know what they think and feel ("I want," "I don't like,") and are willing to cooperate with another for the betterment of a relationship ("Let's," "We can"). When we communicate assertively we also use empathic statements of interest such as "What do you think?" or "How do you see this?" Absent from the conversations of assertive individuals are such wishy-washy statements as "I guess," fillers such as "um," and self-demeanors such as "I know this sounds dumb, but . . . ." In addition, when we display an assertive style, we rarely utter blame statements or send a "you" message. Instead, we express ourselves in ways that are personally fulfilling and interpersonally effective.

This assertive approach is exhibited in the following exchange, during which an assertive person (*A*) attempts to convince another person (*B*) to help him plan a party for a friend.

A: It's March and that means it's time to begin planning Tim's party.

B: (*Head buried in a book*) Oh, not yet! It's only March 1st.

A: I think the party will have a better chance of succeeding if we give ourselves plenty of time to get organized.

B: It's going to be impossible for me to give it much thought.

A: I've already jotted down some preliminary ideas. I hope you'll look at them when you finish the chapter you're reading.

B: Do I have to do it today?

A: Is there another day that would be better for you?

B: Oh, I don't know.

A: Well, let's talk about it when you complete the chapter. Are we agreed?

B: All right.

A: Good! It shouldn't take more than 30 minutes, and I'll really feel better when we've at least gone over these ideas.

The ability to communicate assertively can put you at an advantage during interpersonal conflict. Your view of your role in the relationships you share affects your choice of conflict-resolution strategy. Each of the following examples offers responses representing a nonassertive, an assertive, or an aggressive approach. Which response would you offer for each dilemma? Answer honestly.

You and Sheila work for the same company. Sheila asks you to pick her up and drop her off at the train station every day. You feel this will cause you unnecessary delays. You respond:

1. *"Um, well, I guess it's possible. . . . Oh, all right." (nonassertive)*
2. *"You're kidding! You really have nerve! Why should I do that for you?" (aggressive)*
3. *"I know it takes you a while to walk to the station, but I really don't want to be delayed by taking you there." (assertive)*
4. *"I would really be happy to do this for you if I didn't have to stop at my mom's on the way home." (nonassertive)*
5. *"You need a ride, huh? What's the problem? Your legs won't support the weight you've put on?" (aggressive)*
6. *"I understand you get tired of having to walk to the station every day, but still, I'd rather not commit myself to picking you up and driving you there every day. I'd be glad to help you out once or twice a week." (assertive)*

Your physician makes a sexist remark while examining you. You:

1. *Say, "Who the hell do you think you are?" (aggressive)*
2. *Say nothing. (nonassertive)*
3. *Laugh and say, "Oh, now really, doctor!" (nonassertive)*
4. *Storm out of the office, slamming the door behind you. (aggressive)*
5. *Say, "I think that remark is sexist. I can't believe you meant it." (assertive)*

You are attending a business meeting on possible company changes. One of your supervisors speaks up, urging the committee not to change the existing system, and gives inaccurate data in an attempt to convince committee members of her position. You disagree. You:

1. *Shout, "You're a liar! You've distorted everything on purpose!" (aggressive)*
2. *Keep silent. (nonassertive)*
3. *Quietly inform the person sitting next to you that your supervisor is presenting an inaccurate picture. (nonassertive)*
4. *Quietly say, "Well, uh, I know I'm just an employee, and I really don't know anything about the proposal, but . . . ." (nonassertive)*
5. *State, "I've listened to what you've said, and I disagree. Now I would like you to listen to my position." (assertive)*
6. *Say, "Wait a minute! You can't take advantage of your employees any longer. We've had it with your fuddy-duddy approach to business." (aggressive)*
7. *Say, "I see why you're worried about changing the total system, but I believe we can preserve its integrity and still develop innovative approaches." (assertive)*

For each situation, was your response assertive, nonassertive, or aggressive?

in Context

Ready—Aim—Fire

Form groups of three to four people. Take turns role-playing aggressive, nonassertive, and assertive expression styles in the following situation:

Your coworker has taken the data you spent weeks preparing and analyzing to write a report without crediting you.

1. Pay attention to the types of language both partners use in each expression style. Did "I" language or "you" language predominate? What nonverbal behavior did you notice?

2. Discuss the rewards and costs of aggressive, assertive, and nonassertive behavior. In which situations was an effective solution to the conflict formed?

As these examples illustrate, we can be assertive, nonassertive, or aggressive in many different ways. When we interact with another, we can communicate nonassertiveness by demeaning ourselves, by keeping silent, or by hesitating when we state a position. We can communicate aggressiveness by being openly hostile, sarcastic, or rude. And we can communicate assertiveness by standing up for our rights, openly expressing our beliefs, and stating our position in an open and direct fashion. Although there is no one way we must act in every interpersonal encounter, the choice of how we act should be our own.

Diversity and Culture Contacts

Culture and Conflict Resolution

Because it is the lens through which we view the world, our cultural background appears to influence our response to conflict. For example, individuals from individualist cultures such as the United States prefer to deal directly with conflict, and people from collectivist cultures such as Japan are more comfortable dealing indirectly with conflict. People from individualist cultures use controlling and overt confronting strategies, whereas people from collectivist cultures prefer to use smoothing or avoidance strategies in an effort to help those with whom they are in conflict save face.[17]

In the United States, for example, emphasis is placed on an individual's rights, mainly on whether a person's needs and rights are given their proper due. In contrast, most Latin American and Asian countries emphasize the concerns of the group instead of the rights and needs of individuals.[18] In one study, cited by gender

---

professional contacts

Now You Have a Conflict, Now You Don't

What does the following excerpt from Edward de Bono's book *I Am Right—You Are Wrong* suggests about how the Japanese handle conflict?

Every day the leading executives in the Japanese motor industry meet for lunch in their special club. They discuss problems common to the whole motor industry. But as soon as lunch is over and they step over the threshold of the club, out into the street, they are bitter enemies seeking to kill each other's business by marketing, technical changes, pricing policy, etc. For the Japanese, who do not have the tradition of Western logic, there is no contradiction at all between "friend" and "enemy." They find it easy to conceive of someone as a friend-enemy or enemy-friend.*

Would American business associates be likely to function in the same way? Why or why not?

*Edward de Bono, *I Am Right—You Are Wrong*, New York: Viking, 1991, p. 196.

in Context

Comparing Approaches to Conflict

1. Write down what you perceive to be your personal strengths and weaknesses when confronted with work-related, friend-related, and significant other–related discords.

2. Write down what you perceive to be the strengths and weaknesses of your coworker, friend, and/or significant other. (If possible, ask your partner from each context to do the same.)

3. Select images to compare the approaches that you and your coworker, friend, and/or significant other characteristically employ. (If possible, ask them to do the same.)

4. What do your selected images suggest about how comfortable you and your partner(s) are handling conflict in each context?

5. What, if anything, do you believe that each of you could do to enhance your conflict-handling effectiveness?

researcher Deborah Tannen, university students from different cultures were asked whether or not they would permit aggressive behavior in their children to help protect what they perceived to be rightfully theirs. The highest percentage of affirmative responses came from U.S. parents (61 percent).[19]

Cultures are also distinguished by whether they use high- or low-context communication. Cultures employing **high-context communication** systems are tradition bound, emphasizing politeness and indirectness in relationships with others. In contrast, members of cultures with **low-context communication** systems exhibit a more direct communication style. Thus, people from low-context cultures like the United States tend to interact in an open and direct way, whereas members of high-context cultures like Japan and Korea prefer to avoid confrontation and to preserve a sense of harmony in an effort to enable others to maintain their self-esteem.

Because conflict is inevitable in a relationship, people from different cultures need to recognize and acknowledge the differences. By becoming less ethnocentric and more culturally aware and

Japanese executives will ignore a conflict at dinner but will compete aggressively outside the restaurant.

competent, we can learn to handle conflicts with people from different cultures as effectively as we handle conflicts with people from our own culture. The next time you are involved in a conflict with a person from a different culture, ask yourself the following questions:

1. Which of my behaviors is my partner having difficulty understanding or accepting?
2. Which of his or her behaviors am I having difficulty with?
3. To what extent is this person more cooperative or competitive than I am?
4. To what degree is this person more open, direct, and assertive or more reticent, indirect, and nonassertive than I am?

By making an effort to understand how the experiences of people from different cultures lead them to develop perspectives on conflict that differ from your own, you can develop the flexibility necessary to resolve conflicts.[20]

When it comes to age as a cultural variable, developing the ability to empathize can bridge the generation gap that fuels many intergenerational conflicts. Older people complain that members of younger generations stereotype them as "old geezers," making them feel worthless and discarded. Members of the "sandwich generation" complain about the burden they have to shoulder in caring for and "parenting" their aged parents, who have "aches and pains" and from their adult children's perspective rarely seem to be content. If members of the older and younger generations could empathize with each other, that is, identify with and understand each other's feelings and motives, and could share thoughts, a fuller, more meaningful understanding might develop between them.[21]

Gender Contacts

Gender and Conflict Resolution

Can men and women work together effectively to resolve conflicts? When it comes to alleviating conflict, are the priorities of men and women the same or different?

Studies of how boys and girls handle conflicts during their early years indicate differences in their approaches to frustrating situations. Conflicts between boys tend to be short-lived but characterized by physical and verbal aggressiveness, while girls who face similar situations tend to engage in sustained negotiations with each other instead.[22] Boys tend to have fights; girls tend to try to avoid fighting.[23] In addition, boys tend to exhibit single-voice discourse, pursuing their own self-interests without orienting themselves to their partners' perspectives, sometimes relying on physical force or their powers of intimidation to accomplish their goals. Girls, in contrast, are more likely to exhibit double-voice discourse, using language to try to get what they want while also attempting to meet the needs of others.[24]

Researcher Julia Wood reports that men and women tend to respond to conflict in dissimilar ways. She notes that while women may specialize in communication that builds support, men tend to focus on task-related issues.[25] However, both kinds of behaviors can actually complement each other and can work together to resolve conflicts.

Yet neither men nor women may be fully aware of the contributions they are making and the strategies they are employing. As they are growing up boys are taught to use communication to solve problems and assert a given point of view. They see talk as a means to establish their superiority and win the respect of others. For women, conversation provides the means to work out conflicts and relationship problems. Whereas men use talk to negotiate for power and influence, women use it to build connections and include others. Men put priority on outcomes, and women put priority on the relationship itself. As a result, while men may be better at staying focused on the goal to be gained from resolving a conflict, women are probably better prepared to interpret the feelings, moods, and needs of those with whom they are in conflict. They are better at asking questions and avoiding the putdowns that make conflict resolution a challenge.[26]

Men and women also differ in how committed they are to resolving conflict. Some researchers report that men are much quicker than women to withdraw from conflict. Women may want to talk it out, but men may simply want to be done with it—often by leaving.[27] Research revels that, at times, both men and women are apt to overreact or withdraw from conflict because of a physiological response that causes them to lose control and experience rage. According to J. M. Gottman, *flooding* occurs when the man or woman becomes surprised, overwhelmed, or disorganized by the partner's expression of negative emotion.[28] Upon experiencing flooding, a person's heart rate increases, blood pressure rises, and it becomes difficult to process new incoming information. Fight or flight is the usual response. While stress or physical exertion can trigger emotional flooding, humor and affection can help allay its impact. Women also tend to do more compromising and accommodating than men, who are likely to use somewhat more forceful and direct means to get their way. It is most important that men and women recognize that they each bring different orientations to a conflict that will influence the responses each sex exhibits.

in *Theory*

The Lessons Learned from the Media and Technology

Choose a film, video, or computer game that focuses on the handling of an interpersonal conflict, for example, *Cold Mountain, The War of the Roses, Used People, The Prince of Tides, Kramer vs. Kramer, Boyz 'n the Hood, Mrs. Doubtfire, Street Fighter, Final Fight,* or *Mortal Kombat.*

1. Describe a major conflict presented in the film, video, or computer game.

2. Discuss how the characters involved attempt to handle the conflict, noting both negative and positive behaviors.

3. Describe the outcomes of the conflict and the extent to which its resolution strengthened or weakened the relationship.

4. In your opinion, to what extent, if any, should media and computer programmers discourage the use of violence as a means of resolving interpersonal conflict?

Media and Technology Contacts

Conflict Resolution Models or Madness

How do we arrive at solutions regarding interpersonal conflict? Is it solely by trying one approach after another and then weighing the consequences of each option? Or do we also acquire our behavioral dispositions by relying on the power of example and then acting it out? That is, do we also learn vicariously? According to Albert Bandura's **social learning theory**, we do learn at least some of what we know by observing others and then modeling the behaviors we have observed. Through observation and modeling we learn a wide range of behaviors and solutions to problems that we might otherwise not have had the money, inclination, or time to learn. Thus, the media and computer games can help us learn to exhibit certain behaviors or inhibit our use of other behaviors.

Bandura and other media effects theorists note specifically that "children and adults acquire attitudes, emotional responses, and new styles of conduct through filmed and televised modeling."[29] Bandura's message is that the prevalence and perceived usefulness of televised violence demonstrate to those who watch that violence is a solution to human problems and a strategy for life. In other words, by watching television programs and participating in computer games in which violent behavior gets results, we learn to be violent. Consequently, as a result of their vicarious observations, viewers and game players may also at times accept that aggression is a valid means of resolving conflict. From Bandura's perspective, the media and new technologies help make the once unthinkable more thinkable.

On the other hand, use of some of our newer technologies can help diffuse conflict. Persons who are very angry with one another may find that e-mail and instant messaging help them to communicate because both vehicles allow them to avoid an inevitable shouting match were they in the same room. Interacting in cyberspace frees individuals to communicate with one another by lowering the tension level so as to reduce the number of potentially hurtful and thoughtless retorts and by slowing things down a bit so that persons are able to think things through before responding.

Recognizing Reality

The media influence the way their consumers view conflict in another way. The media improve on "real life" by tying up into neat packages situations that in reality would often leave us feeling confused. To suit entertainment needs—for example, most television programs fit time slots of 30, 60, or 120 minutes—the media do not reflect life as we know it. Few, if any, conflicts go unresolved within those time periods. Rarely are we left hanging or in despair. Instead, we are presented with fabricated versions of conflict

Theory

Covering Conflict

Working with a current newspaper, look for articles focusing on various kinds of conflict. For example, news stories may describe gang fights, instances of domestic violence, management–union disputes, political rivalries, examples of terrorism, or war-front battles. Keep a tally of which conflict-focused articles have a positive resolution and which have a negative resolution.

Does your informal analysis of conflict-related content reveal that most conflicts reported in the newspaper are resolved positively or negatively? How might your finding affect the attitudes that the newspaper's readers have towards the effects and value of conflict?

resolution. To be sure, many of us realize that reality-based dramas and real life are not the same thing. However, others may not be able to adequately separate fantasy from reality.

Gaining Communication Competence

By applying the principles of effective communication, we can resolve interpersonal conflicts more productively. When we use effective communication techniques, we reduce the likelihood that our behavior will escalate a conflict. Learning to handle conflict successfully is an obtainable goal that can lead to increased self-confidence, improved relationships, and a greater ability to handle stressful situations. The following guidelines summarize the ways we can productively use our interpersonal communication skills to resolve conflict.

Recognize That the Conflict Can Be Resolved Rationally

Sometimes when we step back from a situation we find the perspective we need to realize that we can resolve a conflict. A conflict might be settled rationally if we don't withdraw when we should confront, smooth when we should merely compromise, or force when it would be more appropriate for us to smooth. At times, deciding who needs a goal most, and letting that person have it, is the rational choice. Similarly, withdrawing or postponing a discussion of the conflict until you are in control of your emotions can be the most rational decision, just as smoothing or apologizing when you feel that to engage in conflict would be wrong may well be the most rational way to end the conflict. Of course, meeting in the middle and facing the conflict head on are also valid approaches. Recognizing when to use which behavior, and sensing when a behavioral choice will be productive or not are first steps in learning to handle conflict more effectively. Being able to switch approaches according to what will work best is essential to conflict resolution.

Agree on a Definition of the Conflict

Once we acknowledge that a conflict can be handled rationally, we are ready to identify the reason for the conflict by asking questions such as: What is the nature of our conflict? Which of us feels more strongly about the issue? What can we do about it? Communication during this stage will be more effective if, when sharing their feelings and reactions, individuals send "I" messages ("I don't like having to do all the work") rather than "you" messages, and avoid sending "blame" messages ("You will destroy us"). This stage has no place for labeling, accusing, or insulting. Instead, it is important that both sides be specific regarding the reasons for the conflict and in explaining that both would like to discover a beneficial solution—a solution in which neither will lose and both will win. In other words, if we find a way to define the conflict as a mutual problem to be solved rather than as a win–lose battle, it will be easier to resolve. Defining a conflict is like baking a cake: once we make a mistake, the recipe won't work.

Exchange Perceptions: Describe, Express, Specify, and Note Behavioral Outcomes

To resolve a conflict effectively, each party to it needs to be able to explain his or her feelings, assumptions, and frame of reference to the other. After stating a tentative position, each person needs to listen to the tentative position and feelings expressed by the other. Only by understanding what the other person's interests and feelings are and by seeing things from his or her perspective will we be able to identify the differences between our underlying goals and demonstrate the flexibility necessary to meet each other's needs.

Communicate Tentative Solutions That Illustrate Cooperative Intentions

To the extent each party to the conflict proposes solutions that underscore the intention to cooperate, defensiveness and egocentrism levels are reduced. Such solutions require that each party understand the other person's perspective and be able to keep it as well as his or her own in mind as the sides resolve the differences between them. To settle a conflict, each party must understand—but not necessarily agree with—the motivation behind the other person's actions. Only by taking the perspective of another can we invent an array of possible solutions (propose options for mutual gain) based on a clear understanding of each side and the emotional force underlying each position.

To avoid gunnysacking, deal with the conflict now. Bear in mind the biblical warning: "Let not the sun go down upon your anger" (Ephesians 4:28).

Assess Alternative Solutions and Choose the One That Seems Best

Once possible solutions have been invented, it's necessary to determine the solution each party to the conflict considers best. Explore which solutions let one side "win" at the other's expense, which make everyone "lose," and which let everyone "win." Identify solutions that are totally unacceptable, and those that are mutually acceptable. The conflict is resolved when the participants select a solution that satisfies both of them and to which they agree to abide. This usually is the solution that has the most advantages and the fewest disadvantages for each side—the one that appears to be most fair when measured against agreed-on criteria.

Implement and Evaluate the Selected Solution

During this stage we test the chosen solution. We identify who is doing what, when, where, and under what conditions. We want to determine whether the adopted solution has alleviated the causes of the conflict, and whether the outcome has been as rewarding as anticipated. If it has not, then it is time to restart the conflict resolution process. Agreements that don't improve the ability of the individuals to relate to each other typically fail because they are usually inconsistent with, rather than supportive of, each person's needs and goals.

Wrap-Up

Meet again in pairs or small groups. Turn back to the case study at the beginning of the chapter and reconsider the questions that followed it. How have your answers changed or become more focused? Based on what you have learned about interpersonal conflict, what advice would you give Jack and Jim now?

Critical Thinking Contacts

Examine the following cartoon. Use your knowledge of conflict and its management to explain the nature of the relationship shared by the two characters. In what ways, if any, would you have handled this situation differently?

Flowers

"Don't you dare apologize to me!"

Summary

Conflict is inevitable in any relationship. Anyone can start a conflict, and it can occur in any setting. It can involve a single person (intrapersonal conflict) or two or more persons (interpersonal conflict). It is important that we understand what conflict is, how it arises, how it affects us, and what we can do to handle it more effectively.

Conflict occurs whenever the thoughts or actions of one person are perceived by another to limit or interfere with his or her own thoughts or actions. Once aware of the disagreement between them and the incompatibility of their goals, each party to the conflict tries to prevail.

Conflict itself is neither a positive nor a negative force; it is, however, functional or dysfunctional. Conflicts that are functional are constructive; they help us better understand others, as well as strengthen the relationship we share. Conflicts that are dysfunctional, in contrast, damage or destroy relationships.

Conflicts develop over perceived individual differences, a scarcity of resources, rivalries, relationship disagreements, or misinterpretations. Every conflict can be described according to the nature of its goal (shareable or nonshareable), its level of intensity (low, medium, or high), and its general character (pseudoconflict, content conflict, value conflict, or ego conflict).

Among the most popular means to depict preferred conflict resolution styles is Blake and Mouton's conflict grid. The five styles depicted in the grid are avoidance, accommodative, competitive, compromising, and collaborative.

Individuals can handle conflict-producing situations in three ways: nonassertively, aggressively, or assertively. The intent of an individual who exhibits a nonassertive style is to avoid any kind of conflict, even if this means giving up his or her own needs and wants; the intent of an individual who exhibits an aggressive style is to dominate in a relationship, even if this means someone else is hurt; and the intent of the person who displays an assertive style is to communicate honestly, clearly, and directly with another, and to stand up for what he or she believes without harming the other person or him- or herself.

Both gender and culture influence the way we respond to conflict. Also, we learn at least some of what we know about how to handle conflict through observing media characters, though much of it is exaggerated.

As a result of studying conflict and applying principles of effective communication when we find ourselves involved in a conflict, we will be better able to develop solutions that are more consistent with each person's needs and goals.

Terms to Talk About

interpersonal conflict *(p. 316)*

functional conflicts *(p. 317)*

dysfunctional conflicts *(p. 318)*

intrapersonal conflict *(p. 321)*

shareable goal *(p. 323)*

nonshareable goal *(p. 323)*

low-intensity conflict *(p. 325)*

medium-intensity conflict *(p. 325)*

high-intensity conflict *(p. 325)*

pseudoconflict *(p. 326)*

Relationship Dynamics

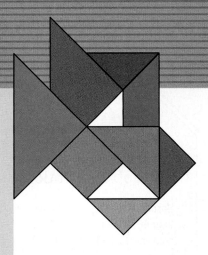

*To suggest that one simply starts
a friendship, courtship, romantic
partnership or marriage and "off it
goes" is simple-minded. It is like
believing that one can drive down
the street merely by turning the
ignition key, sitting back and letting
the car take care of itself.*

— Steve Duck

After completing this chapter, you should be able to:

▌ Identify the different types of relationships.

▌ Define and distinguish among the needs for inclusion, control, and affection.

▌ Describe, compare, and contrast the relationship model of Knapp and Vangelisti with the friendship model of Rawlins.

▌ Identify the characteristics of a love-based relationship.

▌ Define and identify the variables that influence interpersonal attraction.

▌ Identify ways that gender expectations influence communication.

▌ Discuss how culture influences relationship development.

▌ Discuss how technology influences the way we communicate.

▌ Identify specific techniques to facilitate the mastery of relationship dynamics.

daily
contacts

The Job Promotion

Susan and Bob are a two-career family. Both work more than 40 hours per week. Though Bob tries to share household chores, he typically lets Susan shoulder most of the burden.

It was Susan who figured out how the kids would get to and from soccer or softball practice, where they would go after school, or how they would spend their time on weekends. This seemed fair to Bob, since he made more money or, as he put it, "brought home the lion's share of the bacon."

And now this! Susan wondered how Bob would handle the latest development.

Susan had nearly stumbled out of her boss's office. Not only had she been promoted, she had also been given a substantial salary increase. Yet the excitement and pride

she felt was tinged with some regret and uncertainty. She sat down at her desk, took a deep breath, and dialed Bob at work. What should she say to him? She wanted to let him in on the good news that they would now have significantly more money to spend on those little extras that could make life easier. They could take a great family vacation, perhaps even hire a housekeeper. But now that she would make more money than he did, she just wasn't sure how he would react.

Divide into pairs or small groups and answer the following questions:

1. Should Susan reveal the truth to Bob?
2. If you were Bob, how would you respond? Be specific.
3. In what ways, or to what extent, do you think Susan's new position and salary will change Bob and Susan's relationship?

"The Bachelor," "The Bachelorette," "Joe Millionaire," "Blind Date," "High School Reunion," and "Married by America" offer testimony to our fascination with relationships. Among the most highly rated shows during the 2002–2003 TV season, they allowed us to watch as the people featured in them developed relationships with one another, figured out relationship ground rules, and then either terminated or opted to take their relationships to another level.

Our lives derive meaning from the relationships we share. In fact, how happy we are depends more on how satisfied we are with our relationships than anything else. Whether we are friends or family, linked romantically or through our careers, our relationships help shape our lives. In order for us to better understand the impact that our relationships have, let us first explore the different kinds of relationships.

Types of Relationships

The term **relationship** refers to a wide array of social connections that to varying degrees meet our interpersonal needs. Thus, when we speak of interpersonal relationships we are concerned with the relationships we share with our

How do the relationships we share with friends and family members differ from those we share with our coworkers and employers?

parents, spouse, siblings, friends, employer or employees, physician, and instructors, among others. The kind of interpersonal communication we use with another person reflects the nature, importance, and effectiveness of that particular relationship.

In what ways do your rules and goals change among relationships?

Our expectations for all of our relationships depend on the nature of each, as well as on the specific needs we would like each to fulfill. For example, we probably have different relational expectations for a doctor, coworker, friend, lover, or family member. We use different rules to guide our behavior with each individual, and we measure each relationship's effectiveness according to somewhat different criteria that we establish based on our goals for that particular relationship.

Our goals reflect the kind of interaction we expect to share. When interacting with a physician, for instance, our goals are probably different from those we have when interacting with a friend. Our expectations for a work relationship are probably different from those for a romantic relationship. Despite this, however, we might discern certain commonalities in the way we approach each other and communicate during each interaction. For example, do we need to feel we are in control? Do we need to feel that the other person is in some way committed to us? Do we need to feel that by communicating we will be brought closer together? With which individuals do we seek a close, long-term relationship? Whom do we look to for companionship? for intimacy? for intellectual stimulation? Who do we hope will help us fulfill an obligation or complete a task?

Why We Enter into Relationships: Relational Roles and Functions

Every relationship we share helps us meet a personal goal. Perhaps we are lonely and seek an outlet from our isolation. Maybe we feel a need to release pent-up tensions, discuss our interests, or share our concerns and feelings with others. Perhaps we want to complete a project or change the beliefs or attitudes of another. Or maybe we simply aspire to learn more about ourselves and those with whom we share a world. Whatever the personal impetus that propels us to reach out to another human being, the desire to interact with and develop meaningful relationships with others lives in all of us. In fact, it helps define our humanness. The fact is, we need interpersonal contact to survive. Table 12.1 illustrates the key functions our relationships serve.

Relationships Preserve Happiness and Health

There is a correlation between our happiness and the effectiveness of our relationships. According to researchers, problems such as depression, failed marriages, family violence, and job dissatisfaction often are the result of a lack of relational attention and poorly handled relationship problems.[1] The fact is that our family, friends, and associates can function as social support and help us get through the stresses and challenges of life events.

Not only do relationships help preserve our mental health, they also affect our physical well-being. Research reveals that people caught in problematic relationships tend to experience more medical problems than do those who share effective relationships. The incidence of heart attacks and injury in traffic accidents is higher among those in failing relationships than it is among those in thriving ones.[2] According to one researcher, mortality is higher in people who don't have good social support systems, who don't feel they are part of a group or a family or that they "fit in" somewhere.[3] Patients with terminal illnesses tend to die sooner if they have the support of only a small group of friends rather than

---

TABLE 12.1
Relationships Function to Help Us Meet Our Personal Goals

Relationships:

Preserve our happiness and health.

Prevent our isolation.

Meet our needs for inclusion, control, and affection.

Offer a point of reference to check whether our behavior and emotional responses are culturally acceptable.

Function as a communication pipeline.

Maintain our sense of worth.

a large array of family members and friends on whom they can rely for support. Widowed men who do not remarry have higher mortality rates than married men. The resilience of women also suffers after the death of a spouse. The immune systems of widows tend to be weaker than their married counterparts. People who are lonely die sooner and younger. Thus, loneliness is a hazard to our health, and involvement with others is a help. This is a greater problem for men than for women because men have fewer close friendships than women.

Relationships Prevent Isolation

We all need person-to-person contact. When we are cut off from others, we suffer. Even our dreams reflect our desire to end our loneliness and feelings of isolation. For example, hermits are prone to hallucinations that other people are present and speaking to them, the bereaved are apt to imagine their dead partner is there with them, and those who are incarcerated tend to dream about meeting other people and their loved ones on the outside.[4] When our social surroundings fail to reflect our wishes, we try to manufacture situations that do reflect them, even if only subconsciously.

Relationships Meet Needs for Inclusion, Control, and Affection

According to theorist William Schutz, we meet three of our basic interpersonal needs, for *inclusion, control,* and *affection,* through our relationships. To various degrees, we each have a need to include others and be included, to control others and be controlled, and to love others and be loved.[5] Inclusion is about our perception of whether we are "in" or "out," control is concerned with whether we are "on the top" or "on the bottom," and affection measures how "close" we are to or how "far" we remain from another.[6]

Inclusion relates to the extent to which we feel the need to establish and maintain a feeling of mutual interest with others—the degrees to which we take an interest in others, and vice versa. Wanting to be included is a feeling most of us experience. We want others to acknowledge us and hope they want to learn more about us. Most of us know what it feels like to be excluded—to be the last person asked to join a team or work on a project, to be the last person asked out, or to have to eat alone in the cafeteria because no one asked us to join them. When our need for inclusion goes unmet we feel isolated and lonely; our health may even deteriorate. In contrast, when our need for inclusion is satisfied, we develop a sense of enhanced self-worth; we feel fulfilled.

Control relates to our need to establish and maintain relationships that allow us to experience satisfactory levels of influence and power. To varying degrees, we need to feel that we are capable of being in charge or capable of having someone in charge of us. We differ in our levels of how necessary it is for us to be a controlling or a supportive player. When our control needs remain unfulfilled, we may conclude that others fail to value or respect our abilities and that, consequently, we are unable to make sound decisions, direct our future, or influence the future of another.

Describe how specific relationships help you meet your needs for inclusion, control, and affection.

Affection relates to the need we have to give and receive love and to experience emotionally close (intimate) relationships. Should our need for affection go

Literary **contacts**

By Yourself

In the following excerpt from *Newsweek* magazine, the "silencing" or isolation experienced by a West Point cadet is described.

As his name was called, James J. Pelosi . . . drew in his breath and went to the podium—steeling himself for one last moment of humiliation. The slender, bespectacled young man accepted his diploma, then turned to face the rows of starched white hats and—so he expected—a chorus of boos.

Instead, there was only silence. But when he returned to his classmates, the newly fledged lieutenant was treated to something new—a round of handshakes. "It was just as if I were a person again," he said. Thus ended one of the strangest and most brutal episodes in the long history of the corps.

Nineteen months ago, the Long Island cadet was hauled up before the West Point Honor Committee and charged with cheating on an engineering exam. In spite of conflicting testimony given at his trial and his own determined plea of innocence, the third-year cadet, one of the most respected in his company and himself a candidate for the Honor Committee, was convicted. Pelosi's case was thrown out by the Academy superintendent after his military lawyer proved there had been undue influence over the proceeding by the Honor Committee adviser, but that wasn't the end of it. The Academy honor code reserves a special fate for those thought by the majority to be guilty even when there is insufficient evidence to convict. It is called Silencing.

Pelosi's fellow cadets voted to support the Honor Committee sentence. And so for most of his third and all of his fourth year at West Point, Pelosi was ostracized. He was transferred by the Academy to what one friend called a "straight-strict" company—"one of the toughest in the corps." He ate alone each day at a table for ten; he lived by himself in a room meant for two or three; he endured insult and occasional brickbats tossed in his direction; he saw his mail mutilated and his locker vandalized. And hardly anyone, even a close friend who wept when he heard the Silencing decision, would talk to him in public. Under those conditions, most cadets resign. But even though he lost 26 pounds, Pelosi hung tough. "When you're right," he said later, "you have to prove yourself. . . . I told myself I didn't care."

And in the end, James Pelosi survived—one of only a handful of Academy cadets in history to graduate after Silencing. He may even be the last, since six other cadets are now in the process of suing the Academy over its honor system. Now that he is out, and even though he faces the possibility of Silencing by some West Point graduates for the rest of his life if he stays in the Army, Lieutenant Pelosi is almost dispassionate in his criticism of the Academy and his fellow cadets. About as far as he will go is to say that "Silencing should be abolished. It . . . says cadets are above the law. This attitude of superiority bothers me." As for his own state of mind during the order he told Newsweek's Deborah Beers last week: "I've taken a psychology course and I know what isolation does to animals. No one at the Academy asks how it affects a person. Doesn't that seem strange?"

1. Would you have survived the treatment accorded James Pelosi? Why or why not?
2. How does Pelosi's experience compare with that of Shannon Faulkner, the first woman to enter the all-male Citadel? Unlike Pelosi, Faulkner found the isolation untenable and resigned her assignment after only a few days.

unfulfilled, we are apt to feel unlovable. We are left longing for meaningful relationships and fear that we will remain emotionally detached from others. On the other hand, when our affection need level is met, we are comfortable sharing relationships that are intimate and friendly. We understand that not every relationship develops into one based on love.

Person-to-person contact is a lifelong need that helps to prevent feelings of isolation.

Typically, it is our need for inclusion that impels us to seek to develop relationships. Once we have done so, our needs for control and affection are usually met through the relationships. It is the extent to which these needs are felt and realized that varies from person to person. In fact, we can classify people according to the specific "need levels" they exhibit.

Different people express their needs for inclusion, control, or affection in varying ways and at varying levels. If individuals rarely attempt to satisfy a specific need, we say that their need level is deficient. On the other hand, if they are obsessed or consumed with trying to satisfy a specific need, we say that their need level is excessive. People who are deficient in their needs for inclusion, control, or affection are called, respectively, "undersocial," an "abdicrat," or "underpersonal"; people in whom these needs are excessive are called, respectively, "oversocial," an "autocrat," or "overpersonal." **Undersocial** people try to avoid interacting with others; they covet privacy. **Oversocial** people, in contrast, seek to be with others continually. It is interesting to note that undersocial and oversocial individuals experience similar fears—both fear being ignored or left out; they simply compensate for their fear in different ways. Likewise, **abdicrats** typically assume submissive or subordinate roles in relationships, while **autocrats** go to the other extreme and attempt to dominate those they are around. Again, however, both abdicrats and autocrats fear having others view them as incapable or irresponsible; they simply work to handle the fear in different ways. Finally, individuals who are **underpersonal** try to keep all their relationships superficial, while individuals who are **overpersonal** exhibit the opposite behavior—trying to become very close to others. Both are motivated by an overpowering need for affection and a fear of being rejected; however, as with the other types, they express this feeling differently.

Who has the greater need for inclusion, control, and affection—men or women?

Unlike people in the above groups, many of us are quite satisfied with the relationships we share; we find our need levels fulfilled and we express them comfortably and naturally. People in this group are called *social* (we are comfortable with people or alone), *democratic* (we are willing to give or take orders depending on the situation), and *personal* (we are at ease sharing both close and distant relationships).

Relationships Serve as Behavioral Anchors

In addition to meeting our needs for inclusion, control, and affection, our relationships serve as points of reference for appropriate behavioral and emotional responses. They help us express grief, happiness, and a host of other reactions in culturally acceptable ways. By comparing the way we react with the ways our friends and family react, and noting the common threads in our reactions, we become more comfortable with ourselves and gain a greater sense of emotional stability. Thus, our contacts help us see how we stand in relationship to others and let us know whether or not we are in or out of sync with various norms.

Practice

How Important Is Being In/Out, Up/Down, or Close/Far to You?

Interview both men and women from at least three different cultures and ask the following questions:

1. How important is it to you to feel included as part of a group?
   _____ Extremely important
   _____ Very important
   _____ Neither important nor unimportant
   _____ Very unimportant
   _____ Extremely unimportant

2. To what extent is your need to be included currently fulfilled?
   _____ Totally fulfilled
   _____ Very fulfilled
   _____ Somewhat fulfilled
   _____ Very unfulfilled
   _____ Extremely unfulfilled

3. How important is it to you to be able to exert power and control in a relationship?
   _____ Extremely important
   _____ Moderately important
   _____ Neither important nor unimportant
   _____ Moderately unimportant
   _____ Extremely unimportant

4. To what extent is your need to exert influence and power currently fulfilled?
   _____ Totally fulfilled
   _____ Very fulfilled
   _____ Somewhat fulfilled
   _____ Very unfulfilled
   _____ Extremely unfulfilled

5. How important is it to be involved in a close or an intimate relationship—one based on love?
   _____ Extremely important
   _____ Very important
   _____ Neither important nor unimportant
   _____ Very unimportant
   _____ Extremely unimportant

6. To what extent is your need for love fulfilled?
   _____ Totally fulfilled
   _____ Very fulfilled
   _____ Somewhat fulfilled
   _____ Very unfulfilled
   _____ Extremely unfulfilled

To what degree do men and women from different cultures feel each need is important or unimportant, fulfilled or unfulfilled? Compare and contrast your responses with those of others.

Relationships Provide Communication Conduits

Our relationships function as a communication pipeline; they become the place where communication about anything can occur. They give us the opportunity to talk about the important and the trivial, the meaningful and the seemingly insignificant. They provide us with an audience for our self-disclosures. They provide us with the "someones" to talk to as we attempt to make sense of ourselves and our experiences.

Relationships Help Us Maintain Our Sense of Worth

By supporting us, attending to us, and providing us with a sense of community, those with whom we share relationships help us preserve our self-esteem and sense of worth.

Relationship Characteristics

Every relationship we share is differentiated from all other relationships by various characteristics. Among these are the relationship's *duration, frequency of interpersonal contacts,* how much people *reveal to each other,* the kind of *support they offer each other,* the *variability of interactions,* and the *goals* the individuals have for the relationship itself.

Relationship Duration

How long was your longest relationship to date? Your shortest relationship to date? Why did one relationship thrive while the other withered? Meaningful relationships require significant attention if they are to endure. In general, the stronger a relationship, the more time it has to develop and the longer it lasts.

Contact Frequency

Duration and contact frequently go hand-in-hand. We tend to engage in frequent interactions with those to whom we are personally tied. The more often we have contact with someone, the greater are our opportunities to understand them and to develop an ability to predict their behavior. Compare, for example, your ability to predict the behavior of a close friend with your ability to predict the behavior of an acquaintance. Probably because you have had a greater number of interactions with your close friend, you have come to know that person better and thus are more accurate in your predictions of his or her behavior.

Sharing

The longer a relationship lasts, and the more frequent our contacts, the more information we are apt to share with each other about ourselves. Usually this sharing of our innermost thoughts and feelings does not occur early in a relationship, but gradually, over a significant period of time.

≋ *Theory*

What Do You Expect?

We have different expectations for different relationships.

1. Spend some time thinking about what you expect of your relationships with a specific friend, parent or other relative, coworker, health care provider, and instructor.

2. Identify one or two specific goals or expectations for each person.

3. Ask each person (if possible) what he or she expects from you.

4. Finally, compare your expectations of each other.

Support

When we think about the needs of another person and act to help meet those needs, we provide support. For instance, we alleviate the stress felt by another person or help him or her cope with problems or handle anxieties. We provide support by alleviating someone's sense of isolation or loneliness and by being there physically or emotionally whenever we are needed.

Interaction Variability

When there is significant variability in the kinds of contacts we have with a single individual, our relationship tends to have greater breadth. For example, we, the authors, work together writing books, socialize together, and live together. Thus our interactions are characterized by greater variability than they would be if we were merely coauthors.

Relationship Goals

We have different goals or expectations for different relationships. We expect those with whom we share relationships to be interested in us and in our welfare. We expect them to support us, rather than to frustrate us, to help alleviate our fears rather than add to them. We expect significant others to be attentive to us, to be honest with us, and to help us develop and understand ourselves. We also expect certain people to feel affection for us, to want to be with us, to enjoy our company, and, as we get closer, to want to share themselves with us.

Relationship Evolutions

Why are relationships both important and intriguing?

The more we can learn about the origins and causes of relational success and failure, the better we can deal with a range of important personal and social issues.

— Steve Duck

Throughout our lives we will come into contact with a wide assortment of people. Some we will simply meet and never see again. Our relationships with such people will never progress beyond superficiality; for all practical purposes, they will remain strangers to us. Others we will want to get to know better. Some of these individuals will become acquaintances; we will connect with them briefly whenever an opportunity arises, but our interactions with them will be limited in quality and quantity. In time, we will drift away from them. Others, however, will develop into longlasting meaningful friendships and/or romantic relationships.

What are the forces that draw us toward some people and keep us together? What keeps us from developing relationships with others or ultimately pushes us apart? What factors precipitate relationship escalation

Researchers have identified patterns to describe the ways relationships develop. During the initiating stage of a relationship, communication is usually brief or ritualistic.

and deescalation? What behaviors cause a relationship to blossom? What behaviors contribute to its deterioration?

The Ten-Stage Model

Our relationships are in a constant state of flux: ever-changing, they grow either stronger or weaker over time. As they strengthen or weaken, rise or fall, they pass through some or all of the ten **relationship stages** that Mark Knapp and Anita Van-gelisti identified and that we can use to characterize the nature of a relationship at any particular moment in its evolution (see Figure 12.1.)[7] As you read about these stages, consider how, without labeling it either good or bad, you would describe a romantic relationship or friendship you currently are in. We will introduce another relationship model, W. K. Rawlins's model of friendship, a little later in this chapter.

FIGURE 12.1
Relationship Stages

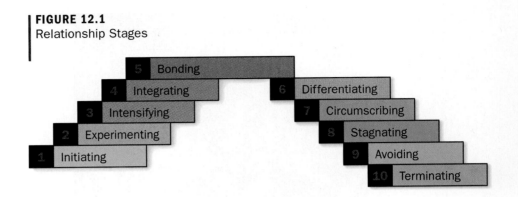

Stage 1: Initiating

During the **initiating stage** of a relationship, we ask ourselves whether someone is appealing enough for us to initiate interaction with him or her. If the answer is affirmative, we display an interest in making contact with this person and attempt to show why this individual would, in turn, enjoy interacting with us. In other words, we do what we can to make him or her perceive us as affable and friendly.

Communication during this phase is typically brief and frequently formulized or ritualistic. We greet each other with a handshake, we engage in **phatic communication** (superficial, casual interaction designed simply to open the channel between us, using such greetings as "How ya doing?" or "What's up?"), and we search for an appropriate conversation opener, often opting to talk about an

Peanuts reprinted by permission of United Feature Syndicate, Inc.

insignificant topic such as the weather as a means of continuing contact. Our goal is to make it possible to establish a relationship with the other person. At the same time we begin to make judgments about each other.

Stage 2: Experimenting

Once contact is initiated, we start the **experimenting stage,** in which our objective is to find out whether the relationship is worth pursuing. We attempt to reduce our uncertainty about the other person. Researchers even call the theory that describes the need individuals have for sharing information *uncertainty reduction.*[8]

At this stage, we keep our interaction casual as we probe the unknown in an effort to find out more about the other person. During our search for common ground, we use cultural, sociological, and psychological information as we attempt to make decisions about continuing the interaction. We are also likely to engage in small talk about a wide variety of subjects such as the news, books we're reading, courses we're taking, where we live, and hobbies we have. In effect, we "audition for friendship."[9] During this process we may also discover possible areas for more meaningful conversation.

Identify relationships you have shared that illustrate different developmental stages.

Stage 3: Intensifying

As we become closer and closer friends, our relationship enters the **intensifying stage,** and the amount of information we are willing to disclose to one another increases. We talk about more serious ideas, share secrets, become better at predicting each other's behavior, use nicknames or expressions of affection when addressing each other, and adopt similar postures or clothing styles. As we increase the closeness or intimacy of our relationship, we disclose much more personal information, which also increases our personal vulnerability. It is during this stage that we begin to transform ourselves from individual "I"s into a "we."

Stage 4: Integrating

During the **integrating stage,** we become a couple and are perceived by others as a "pair," a "package," or a "social unit," as the fusion of one "I" and another "I" is more fully realized. Our **interpersonal synchrony** also increases as we exhibit similar preferences for dress and begin to act, speak, and think more alike and also become more willing to share relaxation time, a car, or even a bank account. As a result of the relationship's strengthening, we begin to develop an even greater understanding and knowledge of each other, expect more from each other, and interact with each other in a wider array of settings.[10]

Stage 5: Bonding

In stage 5, **bonding,** we announce our commitment to each other in a public ritual that also lets the world in on the exclusive nature of our relationship. The relationship that exists between us is now formally recognized by such means as a wedding license or a prenuptial agreement. Our relationship begins to take on a new character because it is now guided by specific rules and regulations established by custom or law. Sometimes this change precipitates in us initial discomfort or rebellion as we attempt to adjust to it. In an effort to be acknowledged

literary contacts

The Message

What does the poem "After the Beep" by Alan Devenish suggest about modern technology's ability to foster or impede the development of relationships?

Hello, this is the Preston residence
and this is she speaking.
Sorry I'm not broadcasting live but do
    leave a message
and I or my machine will get back to you
or your machine.

Please wait
until the cannonade from Tchaikovsky's
    1812 Overture
completes its third volley and the strains
of the Marseillaise stir faintly in the
    background
before starting your message.

Kindly repress the urge to be cute or
    cryptic.
On the other hand don't make it ten years
    long either.
I would also ask that you refrain
from rhetorical questions and long
    subordinate clauses.

Just be yourself, keeping in mind
this is the late twentieth century
and literary flourishes tend to disgust.

Now, if you're the guy I met out jogging,
    I'm sorry but
forget it. It was all a mistake and
    anyway
I'm into squash now.

If however this is about an appointment
or interview which could advance my
    career
please speak distinctly and don't make any
    decisions
until I can process your message.

Lastly, if you've gotten my number
from any other source except me
    personally
you'd better have a good story.

So, until I get back to you, have a nice day
or should I decide to ignore your call,
a nice rest of your life.

SOURCE: Alan Devenish, "After the Beep," *College English*, November 1987. Reprinted by permission of the author.

as having formally bonded, homosexuals are petitioning that same-sex marriages be accorded the same formal recognition and sanctioning accorded heterosexuals.

Stage 6: Differentiating

Differentiating involves the attempt we make to reestablish or regain our unique identities. Instead of continuing to exist as a "we," we ask, "How am I different from you?" In this way, we make an effort to reassert an "I" orientation; individual differences, no longer similarities, become the focus of our attention.

As we differentiate ourselves from each other, we are apt to experience an increase in relational fights or conflicts.[11] Our joint possessions become reindividualized; "*our* friends" may revert to "*my* friends," "*our* bedroom" becomes "*my* bedroom," and "*our* children" become "*your* children" or "*my* children," depending on whether they have been good or bad.

Although recognizing the differences between individuals who have bonded is not unusual as partners strive to regain some privacy, this stage can also signal that a relationship is experiencing stress that needs to be addressed, that a means to preserving commitment to the relationship while allowing for independence needs to be identified or, if it persists, that the process of uncoupling is underway.

Stage 7: Circumscribing

During the **circumscribing stage**, the relationship between two people has begun to deteriorate, and a process of depenetration starts; as a result, we constrict both the amount (we talk less about fewer topics) and the quality of our communication (we reveal less and less of our feelings). We make a conscious effort to limit the subjects of discussion to those we consider "safe." Questionable or sensitive areas are considered taboo and are avoided. Phrases such as "Let's not talk about that," "That's not your concern," or "Let's just focus on . . . " are typical during this stage.

In what ways are learning to drive a car and handling a relationship similar?

As a result, we revert to interacting with each other in a more superficial way; our conversations begin to lack depth as we avoid exchanging meaningful information or personal opinions, being careful to avoid making intimate disclosures. In effect, we begin to withdraw both physically and mentally from the relationship.[12] We talk with each other only when we have to, no longer because we want to. Our relationship suffers from fatigue; we lack interest in it and feel exhausted by it.

Stage 8: Stagnating

Relationships in the **stagnating stage** no longer grow; instead, they remain virtually motionlesss—they stagnate. Stagnating relationships are inactive relationships with communication between the parties at a virtual standstill. Although two partners may still share a common space, they no longer share each other. They feel that because there is no real reason to talk with each other, they might as well say nothing. Interactions become superficial as we close ourselves off to each other. In sum, we have lost our enthusiasm for maintaining the relationship, and it becomes a shell of its former self. Exchanges feel strange and awkward. Our conversations become stilted; we may even stiffen when in each other's presence. We now perceive the individual who was once our partner as a stranger.

Stage 9: Avoiding

During the **avoiding stage** of what is now a deteriorating relationship, we do our best to close relationship channels; because of our desire to stay away from each other, we take whatever steps necessary to ensure that we won't have to relate in any way with each other. In effect, we do what we must to avoid coming together or making contact because we know that should we get together, it would be unpleasant, unfriendly, and antagonistic.

The running theme of a relationship in this stage is "I don't want to see you anymore; I don't want to speak to you anymore; I don't want to continue the relationship." The relationship's end is in sight.

Stage 10: Terminating

Stage 10, **terminating**, finds the ties that once held the relationship together in shreds. The relationship is over. Depending on how both parties to the relationship

in Context

At Which Stages Are Your Relationships?

Focus on three key relationships that you have shared with other persons, at least one of which involved someone with whom you work. For each relationship:

1. Identify whether the relationship passed through each of the ten stages or whether it skipped stages or stabilized at a particular stage.

2. To what extent were you and each partner able to agree on the optimum stage for relationship stabilization?

3. For the work-based relationship, in what ways, if any, did the fact that you and the other person worked together complicate or simplify the nature of your relational interactions?

feel about ending it, this stage can be short-lived or prolonged, cordial or bitter. It can occur soon after the relationship started or after many, many years. It is important to realize that both parties to a relationship may not necessarily want to move through all ten relationship stages at the same time, and hence a partner who wants out of a relationship often finds that the other person doesn't—at least not yet.

People say good-bye in different ways: with a note, over the phone, in person, or with a legal notice. While some couples who end a relationship part friends, others expect—and want—never to speak to or see each other again. While some are grateful for the good times together, others resent the fact that they will now be replaced by another. All of our relationships terminate eventually (death terminates a relationship); however, that doesn't mean that saying good-bye comes easily or is always pleasant for us.

Of course, not every relationship we share goes through each stage; many of our relationships never move beyond the experimenting stage, while others stabilize or are maintained at the intensifying stage, the bonding stage, or some other stage. Stabilization occurs at the level we both agree is satisfying and meets our needs. It is also possible for us not to proceed through the stages sequentially, but to skip one or more stages and jump ahead toward greater intimacy or backward toward less intimacy. It is when partners are at odds regarding the optimum point for relationship stabilization that relationship difficulties may develop.

We need also to recognize that our relationships can progress and retreat through the ten stages. We may advance in a relationship only to discover that we were more comfortable interacting at a more superficial level. Our relationships also grow and ebb at different rates. While some take a long time to deepen, others, especially those in which we perceive that we have little time to get to know one another, develop at a faster pace. The rate at which we grow toward or away from another person is dependent on our individual needs and desires.

The Relationship Spectrum: Communicating with Acquaintances, Friends, Lovers, and Others

It is impossible to have a close relationship with everyone we meet. Each relationship we have can be characterized according to the amount and kind of closeness that we and that relationship partner share. By exploring different kinds of relationships, we can also enrich our understanding of the nature of intimacy and the balance we strike between intimacy and distance with different people in our lives.

The Nature of Intimacy

Intimacy is a measure of closeness.[13] The closeness may involve *physical contact* (we touch, hug, or hold each other), *intellectual sharing* (we share ideas), *emotional disclosing* (we share feelings), and *participation in shared activities* (we do things together not because we have to, but because we want to). While some intimate relationships exhibit all four qualities, others exhibit only one or two. The amount of intimacy we share with acquaintances differs from the amount of intimacy we share with our friends, which, in turn, differs from the amount of intimacy we share when involved in a romantic relationship. Our communication expectations for each type of relationship also differ. For example, we expect close friends and romantic partners to display more caring, make more of an emotional investment, engage in more self-disclosure, and work harder to understand us than we would expect mere acquaintances, colleagues at work, or our casual friends to exhibit. We simply count on the former group of people more, are more influenced by them, and believe that the roles they play in our lives cannot easily be replaced by others. (We will discuss intimacy in greater detail in Chapter 13.)

Is more disclosure necessarily better? Why or why not?

The Nature of Acquaintanceships

Acquaintances are people we know, usually by name, with whom we converse when given the opportunity, but with whom our interaction is typically limited in scope and quality. Unless we harbor a desire to become more than acquaintances, rarely do we go out of our way to see an acquaintance, preferring to leave our meetings to chance.

 *Practice*

Measuring Intimacy

Think of five friends.

1. Locate each friend on the following relationship continuum according to the level of intimacy you share.

Names ____ ____ ____ ____ ____

       10 9 8 7 6 5 4 3 2 1

Strongly agree   Strongly disagree

   a. This person and I reveal our deepest feelings and thoughts to each other ___ ___ ___ ___ ___

   b. This person and I understand each other ___ ___ ___ ___ ___

   c. This person and I rely on each other for help and support ___ ___ ___ ___ ___

   d. This person and I trust each other ___ ___ ___ ___ ___

   e. This person and I accept each other as we are ___ ___ ___ ___ ___

   f. This person and I expect our relationship to last a long time ___ ___ ___ ___ ___

   g. This person and I share a lot in common ___ ___ ___ ___ ___

   h. This person and I enjoy doing things together ___ ___ ___ ___ ___

   i. This person and I meet each other's needs ___ ___ ___ ___ ___

   j. This person and I enjoy each other's company ___ ___ ___ ___ ___

2. Compute a total score for each individual. Based on your responses, with whom do you share the most intimacy? the least intimacy? In most cases, the higher the score, the greater your interdependence with this person and the more important and significant is the role this individual plays in your life.

The Nature of Friendship

Over time, some acquaintanceships develop into **friendships.** Unlike acquaintances, however, friends voluntarily seek each other out, enjoy each other's company, and display a strong mutual regard for each other. Friends accept each other, confide in each other, trust each other to keep the confidences each has disclosed, understand and provide emotional support for each other, share significant interests with each other, and expect their relationship to endure.[14]

We are closer to some friends than to others. Our closest friends are those to whom we confide our innermost feelings and thoughts. They are the ones with whom we share a greater degree of intimacy, as evidenced by our willingness to become emotionally close to them and our desire to continue to learn more about them and to share personal aspects of ourselves with them.

Friendships develop over time. People who were once strangers can become intimate friends. As we progress from the initial stages of contact into a more planned but still casual friendship, we begin to increase our knowledge of and trust in each other, and both the depth and breadth of the relationship increase. As our friendship continues to intensify, we become more "other-oriented," which we demonstrate by going out of our way for each other, becoming more open and expressive with each other, and being more accepting of each other.

Earlier in this chapter we looked at Mark Knapp and Anita Vangelisti's ten-stage model of relationship formation (see Figure 12.1). That model, together with communication researcher W. K. Rawlins's six-stage model of friendship, explain how relationships develop.[15] Notice in Table 12.2 how the six friendship stages correspond to the steps in Knapp and Vangelisti's ten-stage model.

TABLE 12.2
Models of Relationship and Friendship

Rawlins's Six-Stage Model of Friendship	*Knapp and Vangelisti's Ten-Stage Model of Relationships*
Role-limited interaction	Initiating
Friendly relations	Experimenting
Moving toward friendship	
Nascent friendship	Intensifying
Stabilized friendship	Integrating
	Bonding
Waning friendship	Differentiating
	Circumscribing
	Stagnating
	Avoiding
	Terminating

Role-Limited Interaction

Friendships usually start with a **role-limited interaction**—with two individuals making initial contact in some context. For example, we might meet someone at a sporting event, at work, in a restaurant, on a train, or in class. Our initial meeting represents the first stage of interaction and, perhaps, friendship. During this stage, because we are unsure of how or if our relationship will develop, we are somewhat tentative in our relating to each other. We don't possess much personal knowledge about each other, and we are reluctant to reveal personal information. We tend to rely on polite exchanges, stereotypes of social roles, and standard scripts when carrying on initial conversations.

Friendly Relations

During the next interaction stage, **friendly relations,** we continue to consider each other in an effort to determine whether we share enough in common to continue building a relationship. We increase the amount of small talk we engage in as we test the waters to see whether our interest in interacting is reciprocated. We become somewhat less guarded, a bit more openly expressive, and more interested in having the other person respond to our overtures.

Moving Toward Friendship

As our desire to be **moving toward friendship** increases, we cautiously step beyond conventional social rules and role playing, make small disclosures in an effort to demonstrate that we'd like to expand our friendship, and invite the other

person to voluntarily spend time with us in a context outside the naturally occurring one we've shared to this point. We might, for example, ask a classmate if he'd like to study with us for a test, or ask someone we work with if she'd like to stop at a coffee bar on the way home; we might even ask someone to join us at a party or to take in a movie. Once we have the opportunity to interact more personally with each other, we also have a better opportunity to reveal naturally and in a more relaxed setting our attitudes, beliefs, and values to each other.

Nascent Friendship

As our moves toward friendship are reciprocated, we begin to consider ourselves friends. At this point, **nascent friendship,** significant changes in the way we communicate with each other, occur. We drop the social stereotypes and standards that once regulated our interactions and we begin to work out our own rules. We may, for instance, choose to get together to play tennis every Thursday afternoon, go to a movie Friday night, or have dinner together some Sundays. We select the activities we will participate in together, and our interactions become more regularized or patterned.

Stabilized Friendship

Once we begin to assume that our friendship with each other will continue and that we can count on the other person to be there without our specifically planning to meet, we have reached the **stabilized friendship** stage in our relationship. We are willing to trust each other and to respond to each other in ways that confirm our trustworthiness. We interact with each other more frequently and across a greater number of settings; we display our emotional support for each other, share more intimate information with each other, and reveal fears or vulnerabilities that we would keep secret from most other persons. We expect our friendship to continue for a long time.

 ın Theory

Why Did Friendship End?

Think of three people whom you used to consider friends but no longer do.

1. Identify the reasons you believe each friendship ended. Be as honest as you can in identifying the causes for each friendship's waning.

2. Compare and contrast the reasons you've given for friendships ending. Do the reasons tend to fall into specific categories? If so, identify them.

3. Compare your reasons with others in your class. Do men and women offer different reasons for ending friendships? If so, what accounts for this difference?

Waning Friendship

Friendships do not maintain themselves; individuals need to work at them. Once individuals begin to take a friendship for granted, or make less of a personal effort or investment to keep it going, it may begin to move to the **waning friendship** stage.

Why do individuals drift apart? Interests, careers, or personal or family obligations may change. Each change can alter our friendship needs as individuals begin to participate in new activities and evidence new interests. In other cases, violations of trust may have occurred, or unspoken rules may have been broken, causing individuals to become less willing to disclose, or more protective of personal information. A third reason friendships wane is because individuals simply tire of or become bored with each other; when this happens, the friendship is apt to dissolve. Having run its course, it simply comes to an end.

The Nature of Romantic Relationships

The love we feel for the person we choose to have a **romantic relationship** with is different from the love we feel for our friends or family. Even though statistics reveal that approximately 50 percent of all marriages in the United States end in divorce, when we enter into marriage we expect it to be permanent, and that expectation of permanence, at least in part, is what distinguishes a romantic relationship from other kinds of relationships.

What other characteristics differentiate romantic relationships from other kinds of relationships? According to Robert Sternberg, the ingredients necessary to build a love-based relationship are **commitment** (your intention to remain in the relationship even if trouble occurs), **passion** (intensely positive feelings of attraction that motivate you to want to be with the other person), and **intimacy** (sustained feelings of closeness and connection).[16]

Sternberg's triangular theory of love posits that intimacy, passion, and commitment combine to create different types of love (see Figure 12.2).[17] Every love relationship, says Sternberg, contains these three elements in various amounts. For some of us intimacy dominates, with commitment and passion playing a supporting role. For others, there is little commitment to the relationship but an abundance of passion and intimacy.

Sternberg contends that *intimacy,* often the most central component within a love relationship, is the component that provides the foundation for love's development. It remains relatively stable over the course of a relationship—or at least until the relationship partners no longer find the relationship satisfying and no longer feel emotionally close. Think of the warm and affectionate feelings you get when hugging someone you love. You feel close and connected. This is manifest intimacy. But we can also experience feelings of intimacy or connection that are not directly apparent to others; this is latent intimacy.

Passion, according to Sternberg, is love's "hot" component. Included in passion are sexual attraction and arousal, as well as motivation. Passion is the ingredient whose role is most important at the beginning of a love relationship since it functions as an initial attractor. This doesn't mean that long-term relationships lack passion but that in developed relationships passion tends to occur in "sparks and spurts" rather than at a sustained high level.

The third component in Sternberg's love triangle is the "cooler" ingredient of commitment. A decision to love someone requires a commitment to maintain and sustain that love. Because commitment is based on decision making, it tends to be the most stable ingredient in the triangle and is the strongest predictor of relational satisfaction. Although any one element can exist without the others, all three are necessary for a romantic relationship and consummate love to exist.

Like friendships, romantic relationships tend to develop in stages that are based on each party's perception of the amount of self-disclosing that is occurring and the kind of intimacy shared. As we saw in our discussion of Knapp and Vangelisti's ten-stage model, we perceive our romantic relationships as either escalating/intensifying, stabilizing, or deteriorating/atrophying over time as we grow closer and more intimate with each other, become exceedingly comfortable with our **relational culture** (the rules or routines we have worked out for our relationship), or grow more distant or apart from each other.

FIGURE 12.2
The Triangle of Love

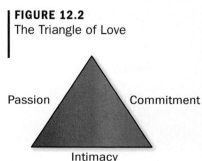

Relationship Attractors: Who Is Attracted to Whom?

Until we actually meet a person we cannot have a relationship with him or her. How do we decide whom we would like to meet? Why are we drawn to some people but not others? How do we identify those forces that make us want to get to know some "strangers" a lot better than others?

When it comes to choosing whom we will develop relationships with, interpersonal attraction plays a role. In fact, interpersonal attraction is the main reason we initiate contacts that, in time, may develop into more meaningful relationships. Why are we attracted to some people but not to others? Researchers identify a number of variables that may influence how attracted or drawn we feel to another person. Included among these are *physical attractiveness, social attractiveness, task attractiveness, proximity, reinforcement, similarity,* and *complementarity* (see Table 12.3).

Before exploring these attraction variables, we need to add a note of caution: attraction is not necessarily mutual (we may find ourselves drawn to someone who does not reciprocate our feelings). Attraction is not necessarily long-lived (we may discover that we were wrong about the qualities that we thought a person possessed, or we may discover that the qualities that drew us toward a person were unable to sustain our relationship with that person). As interpersonal theorist Steve Duck notes, "When the attraction stage goes badly, then the rest of the potential relationship never materializes."[18]

We need to also recognize that the amount of attraction we feel for another person depends on the kind of relationship we share. We feel differently about our casual and best friends, as we do about someone we hardly know and someone with whom we would like to be or have been intimate. Intimacy and attraction tend to positively correlate. We are likely to be highly attracted to a person with whom we have become extremely close. As the nature of our relationships changes, so do our feelings of attraction.

TABLE 12.3
Relationship Attractors

Physical attractiveness	Physical appeal can lead to the initiation of a relationship.
Social attractiveness	Personality and demeanor can be engaging.
Task attractiveness	When we enjoy working together, we seek more interpersonal contact.
Proximity	We are apt to enjoy interacting with people who work or live near us.
Reinforcement	We tend to persist in interacting with people whose company we find personally rewarding.
Similarity	We are apt to like people whose way of thinking resembles our own.
Complementarity	We find ourselves attracted to people who are different from us but whose personalities complement ours in some way.

Physical Attractiveness

Perceived **physical attractiveness** appears to be one means we use to determine who we want to interact with. How someone looks, whether it's eyes, clothing, body shape, or some other aspect of appearance, determines whether or not we will find ourselves drawn to him or her. For the most part, we tend to prefer to initiate relationships with people we find physically appealing. Of course, there is no one universal standard of what this "attractive person" looks like; cultural norms help set it. In many cultures, men judge physical attractiveness to be more important in a partner than do women. In Japan, for example, diminutive females are judged to be the most attractive, whereas American males tend to prefer tall, slender women.[19]

In Theory

What Do I See in You?

1. Identify three people with whom you currently share a close interpersonal relationship.

2. For each, identify those factors that you think initially attracted you to the person—that is, what led you to want to become better acquainted with or develop a more substantial relationship with each one? Be specific.

Social Attractiveness

We also consider a person's **social attractiveness.** People we judge to be socially attractive have the ability to engage us in contact with them. From our vantage point, they possess the kind of personality or interpersonal demeanor we admire. We simply feel comfortable interacting with them. Again, what is deemed to be socially attractive varies among cultures. Asian men, for example, are said to be more likely to find themselves attracted to women who appear introverted, gentle, or acquiescent.[20] What is interesting is that perceptions of physical attractiveness correlate with favorable personality attributions such as kindness, warmth, and intelligence.[21]

What makes us want to develop personal relationships with some people but not others?

Task Attractiveness

Task attractiveness is another factor in determining when we seek the company of another. If we enjoy working with a person, we are apt to want to have more contact with him or her. We value the individual's presence not just because he or she is adept at doing a job or enhances our productivity, but also because we find him or her engaging, and thus we want to sustain the interaction. As a result, what starts off solely as a business relationship may in time develop into a social friendship.

Proximity

Proximity also influences relationships. If you think about those people with whom you enjoy interacting, you may find that, for the most part, they are individuals who work or live close to you. Physical nearness influences feelings of attraction. Simply living or working in the same area increases the opportunities you will have to interact, talk, share experiences, and form an attachment. Common sense tells us that we are more apt to interact with people we see frequently.

The more we interact with someone, the more familiar we become with him or her, and the greater our chances of discovering other areas of common interest that could further increase that person's attractiveness in our eyes. Thus, the closer two people are geographically, the more likely it is they will be attracted to each other and develop an intimate relationship. This is not to say that familiarity cannot also breed contempt. In fact, sometimes it does. According to researchers Ellen Berscheid and Elaine Walster, the more closely people live, the greater the likelihood that they can come to dislike each other. Berscheid and Walster note, "While propinquity may be a necessary condition for attraction, it probably is also a necessary condition for hatred."[22] To what extent, if any, have your experiences revealed the truth of this claim?

Reinforcement

Another factor mentioned in most theories of interpersonal attraction is **reinforcement.** We enjoy sustaining contacts that are rewarding, and we refrain from maintaining contacts we judge to be punishing. Consequently, all things being equal, we enjoy being in relationships that yield personal rewards. We like people who praise us more than people who criticize us, we are attracted to individuals who like us more than those who dislike us, and we seek to be in the company of people who cooperate with us more than we want to be among those who compete with or oppose us. But as is so often the case, too much of a good thing can backfire. Too much reinforcement can make us question the sincerity or the motivation of the reinforcer. If people become overzealous in their praise of us, or disingenuously fawn over us, we begin to wonder what they really want. As social psychologist Eliot Aronson cautions, "We like people whose behavior provides us with a maximum reward at minimum cost."[23] In other words, we are attracted to those with whom we can share a relationship that has few negative aspects (costs), yet yields numerous incentives. When the opposite is true—the costs of a relationship outweigh its positive aspects (rewards)—we tend to find the relationship unattractive.

To what extent do you seek out people who can give you rewards?

Similarity

Similarity is another attraction variable. In general, we tend to feel more attracted to persons whose appearance, behavior, values, attitudes, experiences, beliefs, ideas, and interests are similar to our own and who like and dislike the same things we do. Typically, we like people whose way of thinking resembles our own more than we like those who disagree with us, especially when the issue under consideration is important to us. In fact, the more salient the issue, the more important our being similar becomes. Similarity presents us with "social validation": it provides us with the input we need to confirm the "correctness" of a stance we have taken. We also expect people whose attitudes are similar to our own to like us more than would those whose attitudes are substantially different from ours. By associating with and establishing relationships with people we perceive to be most like us, we play it safe. In fact, according to the *matching hypothesis,* although you may be attracted to the most physically attractive people, you will most likely date and enter into a long-term relationship with someone who is similar to yourself in physical attractiveness.[24] The same holds true for those who hold ideas similar to our own; our attraction for each other tends to grow over time. We become "peas in a pod."

Complementarity

Not all research suggests that we seek to develop relationships only with people who are like us. **Complementarity,** the last of the variables affecting attraction we will consider, suggests just the opposite. At times, instead of falling for someone who is our carbon copy, we find ourselves attracted to a person who is different from us. It may be because he or she exhibits one or more characteristics we admire but do not ourselves possess. Thus, an introverted male might be attracted to an extroverted female, or a submissive female might be interested in a dominant male. You may enjoy conversing with someone whose position on an issue is diametrically opposed to your own. Interacting with our "opposites" can help us learn different ways of thinking. Opposites can be attracted to each other, just not as commonly or as easily as people who are more alike.

 Theory

Attractors

To whom are you attracted? Use the following rating scale to identify why you find yourself attracted to a friend, coworker, and past or present romantic partner by placing each name in each blank and answering the questions with each person in mind. Attempt to determine what dimensions your attraction for each of your chosen subjects is based on. For example, is it based on physical, social, task, and/or other dimensions?*

For each question, use this scale to make your ratings:

Agree   Disagree
1 2 3 4 5

1. I think _____ is particularly pretty or handsome.

2. I find _____'s looks appealing in whatever she/he wears.

3. I find spending time with _____ fun.

4. _____ fits in well with my other friends.

5. I have confidence in _____'s ability to get a job done.

6. I believe _____ is an asset in most work situations.

7. I find living near _____ makes it easy for me to get together with _____.

8. Living near _____ has made me like him/her more.

9. _____ makes me feel good about myself.

10. I really think that _____ likes me.

11. I have a lot in common with _____.

12. _____ and I have similar attitudes on important issues.

13. _____ and I are like night and day.

14. _____ helps me learn new ways of thinking.

Did you find that your attraction for each person was based exclusively on one category, or was your attraction to each person based on an amalgam of factors? How does the nature of your attraction for each of these persons influence the kind of relationship you share? Explain.

*See C. H. Tardy, ed., *A Handbook for the Study of Human Communication: Methods for Observing, Measuring, and Assessing Communication Processes,* Norwood, NJ: Ablex, 1988.

Diversity and Culture Contacts

Connections

Culture influences how we form relationships. Although we all have a need to make contact and form connections with other people, it is culture that leads us to do it in different ways. Culture even guides us in deciding whether we will speak to strangers. Similarly, it teaches us how to spend our time and what to value. For instance, whereas some cultures value work as an end (Japan, for example), other cultures perceive work as a means to an end (Mexico, for example).[25]

Culture can also guide us in understanding relationship customs and practices around the world. For example, the way we define the word *stranger* reveals some of the challenges we face as we interact with persons from diverse cultures. In cultures that promote individualist values, the idea of *stranger* is easier to penetrate than it is in cultures that promote collectivist values that work to create strong in-group bonds to separate insiders from outsiders. As an example, in Greek the word for "non-Greek" translates as "stranger," and in Korea, strangers are seen as "nonpersons."[26]

In most cultures, only loose connections exist between acquaintances. Because acquaintances don't usually confide in each other, they are limited to engaging in ritualistic small talk. However, even topics deemed appropriate for small talk may be culturally regulated. For example, although it may be perfectly acceptable in the United States to inquire about one's spouse, in some Arab countries it is viewed as a breach of etiquette to ask a male acquaintance about his wife.

Intercultural conceptions of friendship may also vary. In some countries, such as Thailand, a friend is one whom another accepts completely or not at all; for example, if you disapproved of any aspect of the behavior or another person, that person could not be your friend.[27] In contrast, in the United States, we may simply choose not to discuss those aspects of our friends to which we take exception or with which we disagree, such as political or religious beliefs.

Cultural expectations for friendships differ in other ways as well. Whereas cultures with individualist orientations refer to friends as "friends," cultures with collectivist orientations refer to friends with labels we typically reserve for members of our family: brother, sister, or cousin. The latter labels suggest that the bonds of friendship will not be transient, but longlasting.

Cultural customs about romance and marriage also vary from country to country. For example, in some countries such as India and Afghanistan, parents arrange the marriages of their children; as a result, dating prior to marriage in these countries is rare. The same is true in many Middle Eastern countries,

in Context

The Ties That Bind

Although an emphasis on social relationships is conductive to cooperation and group harmony, it can also stifle individual initiative and independence. Interview two employees from American-owned corporations and two employees from Japanese-owned corporations to determine the feelings of each about their relationships to their employers, their satisfaction with their jobs, and their thoughts about their own importance to their organizations.

In some cultures family members arrange marriages and play integral parts in a couple's courtship. How does this pattern of family love relationships compare and contrast with your own?

although in some countries, such as Iran, it is against the law even to date others. In Central and South America, most males and females do not date until they are well into their teens, while in Japan and Korea, significant dating first begins during college. In many European countries, dating is not an individual but a group event.[28]

Because culture affects the way we communicate, it also affects how we respond to those whose cultures are different from our own. If we are to interact more effectively with people from diverse cultures, then we need to be able to answer a series of questions about potential cultural barriers that, if unanswered, could pose problems.

Does Your Culture Place More Stress on Individuals or on Social Relationships?

Whereas some cultures emphasize social relationships, others stress individualism. To determine what your culture has taught you, ask yourself if, when you interact with others, you give preference to your own private interests or the interests of the collectivity. In other words, do you tend to feel emotionally independent or dependent in the company of others? According to researchers, individualism lies at the very heart of American culture, while for members of other cultural groups, such as those from East Asian countries, it is the social relationship that is paramount.[29]

Theory

Gender Expectations

Think about what you were taught about men's and women's roles growing up and how you currently see them.

1. Which of your gender role expectations, if any, have undergone changes in recent years? What led to the changes? If none have changed, how do you account for the constancy of your gender perceptions?

2. How do your past and current expectations influence your view of the behaviors exhibited by males and females and your own gender orientation?

Does Your Culture Promote the Development of Short- or Long-Term Relationships?

While Americans may find it easy to drop in and out of relationships or organizations, Far Eastern cultures believe that relationships ought to be longlasting and that individuals should show loyalty to others simply because we are all obligated to each other. Because East Asian cultures share such a perspective, business and personal relationships tend to be mixed together, last for longer periods of time, and are based on mutual expectations of reciprocity and congeniality. Thus, whereas Americans tend to want to get right down to business, individuals from East Asian countries feel more comfortable if their business interactions occur on a more personal level. The belief is that for an effective business relationship to develop, a warm personal relationship must first exist.

Does Your Culture Value Results or the Interactional Process Itself?

Americans also tend to be highly results-oriented, often wanting instant answers—even from a relationship. They tend to be more spontaneous in their interactions and more apt to reveal themselves to others. In contrast, in most Asian countries, people tend to be less revealing of themselves and more willing to devote significantly longer periods of time to getting to know each other.

Gender Contacts

Roles and Rules

Gender affects the way we are taught to communicate. It influences both our **roles,** the parts we play when interacting, and the **rules,** or behavioral norms, that guide those interactions and determine how we play our roles.

We learn the roles we perform; we are not born knowing how to enact them. Our learning, however, starts very early—virtually as soon as we are born. For example, studies reveal that U.S. hospital nursery nurses handle boy and girl babies differently, raising the pitch of their voices as much as a third higher when talking to girls, and using larger gestures when interacting with boys.[30]

In part because of the ways many in U.S. society interact, we are apt to develop different expectations for males and females. As a result, we may expect the members of each sex to behave differently, dress differently, play differently, and perform different jobs. On the other hand, people who have grown up in families that treat males and females as equals will develop or acquire very different views of their prospective roles.

In general, U.S. culture teaches that males perform **instrumental roles** and females perform **expressive roles.** The male is supposed to focus on getting things done, whereas the female is expected to focus on helping, supporting, nurturing, and being responsive to the needs of others. Consequently, male communication is primarily *task-oriented* and female communication is primarily *relationship-oriented.*

Recently, however, many have attempted to make it possible and acceptable for males and females to be more **androgynous**—that is, to share in performing both instrumental and expressive roles. As our *perceptions of* men and women change, so do our *expectations for* them. When we view men and women as androgynous, we make it feasible for them to be behaviorally flexible and display an array of what were previously more limited sex-typed characteristics. Thus, men can be both nurturing and competitive, and females can be both assertive and submissive. Our gender expectations thus influence the nature of our person-to-person contacts.

When it comes to friendship, women choose women friends they can confide in.[31] Female friendships tend to be expressive, centering on sharing disclosures and developing loyalty and trust. Women focus on relational matters and are sensitive to what happens to their friends. Males, in contrast, have chumships.[32] Instead of basing their friendships around talk, men tend to befriend other males with whom they share hobbies, play sports, and so forth. Whereas the friendships of women emphasize face-to-face interaction, those of men emphasize side-to-side interaction. On the other hand, male–female friendships tend to be more active and less intense than female friendships and more emotionally fulfilling and expressive than male friendships.

When women and men begin to date, women typically want to talk more than the men would like. While men tend to approach conversation functionally, with the goal of sharing information or solving problems, women are more likely to view conversation as an ingredient essential to the development of their relationship. Thus, it is often the woman who keeps the conversation going. Deborah Tannen explains, women use *rapport* talk while men use *report* talk. Women talk to establish and negotiate relationships; men talk to preserve independence and negotiate status.[33]

When selecting partners for a romantic relationship, men tend to look for stereotypically feminine women—women who are attractive, slim, and sexy, and women are likely to look for men with stereotypically masculine qualities—men who are ambitious, energetic, and strong.[34] Many American women also report that they expect their spouse to be their superior in intelligence, ability, education, and job success.[35]

Media and Technology Contacts

Exploring Social Worlds

Media and Gender

The media tend to reflect our cultural expectations for gender. As such, they further influence how we perceive men and women and shape our views regarding what constitutes effective communication. For the most part, the media communicate that women are dependent and men are independent, that incompetent women need to rely on men to succeed, that men are the bread-winners and women the caregivers, and that men are the aggressors and women the victims.[36] These depictions weave their way into our consciousness and may, over time, further cause us to limit our perception of ourselves and perpetuate unrealistic images of what we should be like and how we should interact with others.

More specifically, stereotypical depictions of women and men abound in advertisements. Advertisers still tend to portray men as central to women's lives, and women as overly concerned with relationships, obsessed with appearance and youth, and emotionally dependent.[37] They tend to depict women as sex objects—desirable not because of their personal qualities but because of their bodies. Men are also held up as the authorities, while women are depicted as the consumers who need to be told by male authorities the products they should be using.

Television and film also perpetuate stereotypes of men and women. The ratios of men and women in film and television offerings remain unbalanced, with males predominating, leaving viewers to conclude that men are more important. Males are portrayed as aggressive, dominant, and engaged in exciting activities, while females are portrayed as caregivers and nurturers who are dependent on men. Women are depicted as preoccupied with and talking about romance, while men are shown engaged in more instrumental activities.[38]

Media producers stereotype us as well. For example, films targeted at female audiences emphasize feelings, bonding, romance, and conversation, whereas male-targeted films emphasize carnage, zingy one-liners, and sex.

Technology: Meeting by Modem

Have you ever used the computer as a substitute for face-to-face communication? Did it suffice? Why or why not?

Technology also affects the way men and women communicate. According to Neil Postman, we now live in a **technopoly,** a society in which all forms of cultural life are subordinate to technology, and men, for the most part, have led the way.[39]

The Internet has brought another social world into our lives. The on-line world is the context in which some of our friendships and romantic relationships now develop. While singles bars, parties, cruises, and ads still are used to meet people, the twenty-first century finds us also relying on a proliferation of commercial Websites, such as Match.com, eHarmony.com, or friendster.com, to facilitate relationship building. Friendster is an on-line community of over 200,000 members that creates a personal network based on all the people who know people you know. In December 2003, over a quarter of a million Americans visited Friendster or other on-line dating sites. In June 2003, that number had jumped to over 40 million Americans.[40] While women are more likely than men to form personal relationships on-line, both men and women use cyber-space to form friendships and romantic relationships, some of which transfer into real space.[41]

Why did on-line socialization take off? Why does it serve growing numbers of us as a surrogate form of interpersonal communication? Unlike society, the Internet is blind to gender, race, and appearance. At least until people send a digitized

professional

contacts

The Distorting Mirror

According to gender researcher Julia Wood, the media present us with a distorted view of cultural life in the United States. Wood notes the following demographic trends in characters portrayed in the U.S. media today:

White males make up two-thirds of the population. The women are less in number, perhaps because fewer than 10% live beyond 35. Those who do, like their younger and male counterparts, are nearly all white and heterosexual. In addition to being young, the majority of women are beautiful, very thin, passive, and primarily concerned with relationships and getting rings out of collars and commodes. There are a few bad, bitchy women, and they are not so pretty, nor so subordinate, and not so caring as the good women. Most of the bad ones work outside of the home, which is probably why they are hardened and undesirable. The more powerful, ambitious men occupy themselves with important business deals, exciting adventures, and rescuing dependent females, whom they often then assault sexually.*

How have the media helped shape your views of the roles and communication characteristics of males and females? Give specific examples. To what extent, if any, have the media provided you with depictions of men and women that were not societally endorsed?

*Julia T. Wood, *Gendered Lives*, Belmont, CA: Wadsworth, 1994; p. 232.

photo or meet face-to-face, looks are placed on the back burner. Now instead of having to probe during initial face-to-face encounters to find those with similar interests, we are able to log on quickly at any time of day to a bulletin board and "talk" directly with people around the world who share our interests.[42] For this as well as other reasons, some people find it easier to interact with others on-line than in real life, asserting that it is easier to tell people more via computer than in person or by phone.[43]

Some people find it easier to communicate when not in the physical presence of others. For example, one teenager noted: "It's easier to talk to girls on the Internet than in school. Sometimes I can't talk well in person. It doesn't come out like I want it."[44]

The Internet is also helping the housebound and the lonely get "out" and communicate with others. Though currently only approximately 5 percent of those who subscribe to on-line services are over age 65, senior citizens' use of on-line services has a number of important social implications. In addition to chatting, senior citizens are using the anonymity of cyberspace to learn about and overcome health problems that left them isolated and lonely. Gerontologists report that loneliness is a prime factor in elderly suicides. According to one gerontologist, "Our clients are so lonely that anything would make a difference."[45] Instead of having to ride a bus long distances to be in the company of other people, or going months at a time without talking to a single person, senior citizens can now make contact with others.

Although the computer is not a substitute for face-to-face contact, the support groups and friendships that start on-line can transfer to the real world. The fact is

The Internet is extending the social reach of the elderly and homebound. Do you think the Internet is capable of functioning as a viable source of interpersonal contact?

that many people today depend on computer modems to make contacts, strike up friendships, or just stay in touch.

.≈ *Theory*

Is It Better On-Line?

A number of people think the Internet makes it possible for people who are withdrawn to come out of their shells and mingle.

1. Is on-line communicating providing an outlet for loners?

2. Does the Internet help build social skills or does it just provide us with an escape from difficult personal interactions?

3. Is it easier for us to write to each other than to speak to each other? Would you, for example, rather ask someone out on-line or off-line?

"Away messaging," a function of instant messaging, adds another dynamic as the social tool people use to keep in touch when they aren't available to chat. Similar to a personal bulletin board, the away message also functions like a computer answering machine by letting others know that the person they seek is unable to reply immediately. Away messages also function as emotional outlets containing everything from quotations to song lyrics, jokes, insults, confessions, or complaints. For some persons they will be filled with meaning and let them know what a friend is up to or thinking, while others may not understand their significance. Researchers believe that the real message in away messaging is between the lines. The person does not want to be left out of the loop. They also allow people to exert control over the impressions others have of them. For example, you can post a "social butterfly"-type message even if you are home watching a video. Or you can make one boy- or girlfriend think you're out with someone else when you are not. The best part of the away message experience is to return to a screen full of messages sent in response to the away message. The worst part is to return to an empty screen. Thus, away messaging can serve as a litmus test of social capital.[46]

While many believe that the Internet can be used to strengthen friendships as well as enhance interaction with relatives, doubts persist. Some worry about *lurkers*—individuals who are reluctant to establish on-line relationships but browse or read through others' comments without actually posting, sharing, or revealing their presence. Others question whether heavy Internet use substantially reduces face-to-face contact with others, ultimately contributing to a sense of alienation and actually precipitating rather than preventing feelings of loneliness.[47] What do you think?

Gaining Communication Competence

Relationships are complex phenomena. The more we can find out about how we form them and why they do or do not work, the better able we will be to deal with them. What can we do to improve the relationships we share? How can we learn to develop better-balanced relationships? What sort of relationship future do the media and technology forecast and what can or should we do about it?

Mastering Relationship Basics

Understand That Relationships Don't Just Happen

Working to improve relationships is a lifelong endeavor. We can work to develop meaningful relationships or we can let them falter or wither away. By focusing on the nature of our relationships and why we have them in the first place, we can learn what it is we really miss when our relationships go awry.

Recognize Why We Need Other People

What happens to people who are cut off from others? Feelings of isolation increase our risk of death. The fact is that lonely people die younger.[48] By being in relationships with others, we combat loneliness and experience a sense of belonging. Relationships provide us with a sense of inclusion. When they are lacking, we are often left with a sense of doom.

 Theory

Something's Missing

What is it you miss when a relationship goes wrong? What exactly is it that you feel you are losing?

1. Identify two relationships you have shared that no longer exist.

2. Cite the problems you encountered, and what you felt when each relationship was disrupted or dissolved.

Understand the Nature of Friendship

People in healthy relationships note that they enjoy the following six characteristics:

1. They look forward to being together because they enjoy each other's company.

2. They accept each other as they are, feel free to be themselves, and make few — if any — demands that the other person change.

3. They trust each other and are willing to put themselves in the hands of the other person because each assumes that the other will act in his or her best interest.

4. They share a high level of commitment and are willing to help and support each other.

5. They respect each other.

6. They are willing to share personal information and engage in high levels of self-disclosure; as a result, they are better able to predict each other's behavior or response.

Meet the Challenge Posed by the Media and New Technologies

Our relational repertoire changes as new ways of interacting are made possible by the media and technological innovations. The ways we develop and grow relationships in the future may change from the way we grew and nurtured them in the past. We may become attracted to people in different ways and for different reasons. Pacing or repairing a relationship begun on the Internet may require different skills than pacing or repairing one established face-to-face. What is important, however, is that we remain open to making the most of every opportunity for a meaningful relationship.

 *daily* **contacts**   **Wrap-Up**

Meet again in pairs or small groups. Turn back to the case study at the beginning of the chapter and reconsider the questions that followed it. How have your answers changed or become more focused? Based on what you know about relationships, what advice would you give Susan now?

Critical Thinking Contacts

Examine the following cartoon. What advice can you give Ziggy about the basics of establishing interpersonal relationships and the functions such relationships serve? Be specific.

Nothing Personal

Summary

The expectations we have for each relationship we share depends on its specific nature and the functions we hope the relationship will fulfill. We meet three basic needs through our relationships: inclusion, control, and affection. When those needs go unmet, we are apt to feel isolated, powerless, and unloved. We all differ in our need levels as well as in the ways we express our needs.

Through their tenure, our relationships evolve, growing weaker or stronger over time. Researchers such as Knapp and Vangelisti, and Rawlins, perceive relationships as developing in stages. Sternberg's triangular theory of love explores love as a combination of intimacy, passion, and commitment.

The primary reason we initiate a relationship is attraction. Among the variables influencing the amount of attraction we feel for another are physical attractiveness, social attractiveness, task attractiveness, proximity, reinforcement, similarity, and complementarity.

Gender and cultural expectations influence the roles we perform and the rules we use to guide our interactions. In addition, the media and technology shape our image of an effective relationship and can help broaden our concept of acceptable means of interacting.

Once we are able to acknowledge that relationships don't just happen, to recognize how much we need people, and to display our ability to meet the challenges posed by the media and newer technology, we will be on our way to demonstrating our mastery of relationship dynamics.

Terms to Talk About

relationship *(p. 356)*
inclusion *(p. 359)*
control *(p. 359)*
affection *(p. 359)*
undersocial *(p. 361)*
oversocial *(p. 361)*
abdicrats *(p. 361)*
autocrats *(p. 361)*
underpersonal *(p. 361)*
overpersonal *(p. 361)*
relationship stages *(p. 365)*
initiating stage *(p. 366)*
phatic communication *(p. 367)*
experimenting stage *(p. 367)*
intensifying stage *(p. 367)*
integrating stage *(p. 367)*
interpersonal synchrony *(p. 367)*
bonding *(p. 367)*
differentiating *(p. 368)*
circumscribing stage *(p. 369)*
stagnating stage *(p. 369)*
avoiding stage *(p. 369)*
terminating *(p. 369)*
acquaintances *(p. 371)*
friendships *(p. 372)*

role-limited interaction *(p. 373)*
friendly relations *(p. 373)*
moving toward friendship *(p. 373)*
nascent friendship *(p. 374)*
stabilized friendship *(p. 374)*
waning friendship *(p. 374)*
romantic relationship *(p. 375)*
commitment *(p. 375)*
passion *(p. 375)*
intimacy *(p. 375)*
relational culture *(p. 375)*
physical attractiveness *(p. 377)*
social attractiveness *(p. 377)*
task attractiveness *(p. 377)*
proximity *(p. 377)*
reinforcement *(p. 378)*
similarity *(p. 378)*
complementarity *(p. 379)*
roles *(p. 382)*
rules *(p. 382)*
instrumental roles *(p. 383)*
expressive roles *(p. 383)*
androgynous *(p. 383)*
technopoly *(p. 384)*

Suggestions for Further Reading

Steve Duck, *Understanding Relationships*, New York: Guilford Press, 1991. An excellent summary of friendships, families, acquaintances, and romantic encounters.

John Harvey and Ann L. Weber, *Odyssey of the Heart*, Mahwah, NJ: Lawrence Erlbaum, 2002. Explores how the path of a relationship is a wandering course.

David W. Johnson, *Reaching Out: Interpersonal Effectiveness and Self-Actualization,* 5th ed., Boston: Allyn and Bacon, 1995. A highly involved look at the specific skills that facilitate effective interpersonal interaction.

Michael Monsour, *Women and Men as Friends,* Mahwah; NJ: Lawrence Erlbaum, 2002. Explores how friendship between men and women can be encouraged throughout the life span.

John Stewart, ed., *Bridges Not Walls, A Book about Interpersonal Communication,* New York: McGraw-Hill, 1995. A popular reader that contains a wide range of articles on communication.

Julia T. Wood, *Relational Communication, Continuity and Change in Personal Relationships,* Belmont, CA: Wadsworth, 1995. Explores the skills and understanding needed to develop and maintain intimate relationships.

13

Intimacy
and Distance

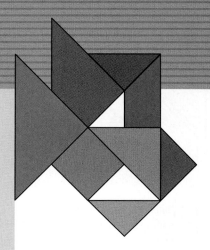

I believe we're all secretly happy we can't figure our relationships out. It keeps our minds working.

—Jerry Seinfeld

After completing this chapter, you should be able to:

▐ Define self-disclosure and intimacy.

▐ Explain social penetration theory.

▐ Draw and explain the Johari window.

▐ Define and explain relationship dialectics.

▐ Explain when and how to repair a relationship versus when to terminate a relationship.

▐ Define toxic communication and identify the four stages of an abusive relationship.

▐ Describe how technological innovations are making it easier to maintain long-distance relationships.

▐ Compare and contrast the ways in which gender influences male and female preferences for developing and maintaining intimacy.

▐ Identify how culture influences notions of intimacy.

▐ Discuss strategies to handle closeness and distance more effectively in relationships.

daily contacts

The Plane Trip

Samantha sat down in her first-class seat. Though her company had paid for her to travel coach, she had used some of her frequent flyer miles to treat herself to a first-class return flight. After all, she told herself, she had sold more than anyone in her division, and she really deserved a treat.

The first-class seats were *so-o-o* comfortable. As she read the paper and sipped her ice coffee, Samantha gazed out the window and watched the last-minute preparations of the ground crew. Then Tom arrived and sat in the seat next to hers. From his opening greeting, Samantha knew that the flight might not be the dream flight she envisioned, but would be awkward and uncomfortable instead.

"What are your plans for tonight?" Tom asked Samantha nonchalantly. At first, Samantha thought Tom must be joking, and she smiled faintly. But he wasn't joking. He continued, "I have tickets to the hockey game. Wanna go?"

Samantha answered that she had other plans, but added, "Thank you, anyway." Tom, however, pressed on: "I've just broken up with my girlfriend. Are you seeing anyone? Even if you are, what about tomorrow night, sweetheart?"

It wasn't just his sexist language that bothered her. It was the tone and content of the conversation. Tom acted as if they were together, as if he could confide in her, and she would confide in him, when they didn't even know each other. Not only had he skipped any rapport-building stages, he was attempting to move too quickly for friendship between them to ever have a chance of developing.

Samantha was unsure how to handle the situation. Should she ask to change her seat? Should she simply tell Tom that he was bothering her and that his manner was offensive? She turned away from him and looked out the window.

Suddenly, the decision was no longer hers. Tom stood up and asked to change his seat. As the plane slowly pulled away from the gate, Samantha heard him asking someone else, "Would you like to go to a hockey game?"

Divide into pairs or discussion groups and answer the following questions:

1. If you'd been in Samantha's position, how would you have responded to Tom?
2. What relationship-building mistakes do you think Tom made?

Some of us are satisfied with our relationships and some of us are not. Some of us have good relationships that complete or fulfill us, while others of us have poor relationships beset with problems and dangers that challenge us. What happens when we want to deepen a friendship, develop a romantic relationship, extricate ourselves from a relationship we no longer find satisfying, or terminate a relationship we believe to be dysfunctional?

In Chapter 12, we looked at the different kinds of interpersonal relationships we share with others. In this chapter, we delve into those qualities that distinguish our close, interpersonal relationships from our more superficial or distant ones, and our more satisfying relationships from those that are dysfunctional. When they are very good, close relationships can help make us healthier and extend our lives, but when they are very bad and handled poorly, they threaten both our health and our happiness.

In this chapter, we will explore how we know when a relationship is worth maintaining or deepening, how we can tell when a relationship is in need of repair or termination, and what we need to do in order to accomplish our relational objectives. We will also look at how the death of a person with whom we have shared an intimate relationship affects us and what we steps we need to take to be able to rescue ourselves from the grief we experience so that we can cope and continue.

Let us begin by looking at those qualities that differentiate our intimate and satisfying relationships from our more superficial or distant ones.

Self-Disclosure and Intimacy

When and with whom are you most comfortable talking about yourself? Under what conditions and to whom do you deliberately reveal information about yourself of which another person would not normally be aware? **Self-disclosure** refers to the act of willingly making known to others information about yourself. By definition, messages of self-disclosure generally include those personal facts about ourselves that people would be unlikely to discover on their own. At least among Westerners, self-disclosure is a measure of closeness.[1] For this reason—and also because we don't usually intentionally reveal significant personal details about ourselves to many people—self-disclosure aids in the achievement of feelings of closeness, or **intimacy.** Thus, as we disclose more about ourselves, our communication becomes more interpersonally intimate; similarly, as we refrain from self-disclosing or attempt to backtrack in revealing personal information, our communication with others becomes less intimate and more impersonal.

Sometimes we use self-disclosure as a tool to get to know other people.[2] Persons skilled in the art of establishing relationships will offer self-disclosures of their own that make it easier for a partner to reciprocate. They know that there are different depths of information and that the depth of disclosures should correlate positively with the appropriate relationship stage.

Self-disclosure can be risky: by revealing our likes, dislikes, feelings, fears, strengths, and weaknesses we increase our vulnerability. For that reason, we typically first reveal small amounts of low-risk information, saving more risky disclosures until we confirm that the other person is willing to match both the level and the nature of our disclosing behavior—that is, act in accordance with the **norm of reciprocity.**[3] According to the norm of reciprocity, we expect to experience self-disclosure equity in our relationships—that our self-disclosures will be returned in kind by the other person. When the other person reveals the same kind of information, we are more apt to feel safe, display a greater willingness to move our self-disclosing to a deeper level and, over time, become even more willing to relate increasingly intimate information. In contrast, lack of reciprocation indicates that the other person is not yet ready to disclose anything to us, that things need to proceed more slowly, or that the relationship may be one-sided and not likely ever to fully develop. The revealing of our most intimate information is typically reserved for only our very closest ongoing relationships.

If we are careless and inadequately or inappropriately engage in self-disclosure, others may view us negatively. The satisfactory development of our relationships hinges on our appropriate use of self-disclosures that typically occur incrementally during the course of a positive relationship. In fact, a way we judge the strength of our relationships is by assessing the breadth and depth of the information we share with others.

Social Penetration Theory: Depth, Breadth, Intimacy, and Distance

We can describe every relationship we share in terms of its *breadth* and *depth*. **Relationship breadth** is a measure of how many topics you discuss with another individual. **Relationship depth** is a measure of how central the topics discussed are to your self-concept and how much you reveal about yourself and your feelings in the process.

The Social Penetration Model

The model depicted in Figure 13.1 is used by social psychologists to describe how breadth and depth of communication relate to each other. In the model, the outer circle represents the complete individual, composed of many different aspects (e.g., religion, work, school, social life). The aspects are, of course, different for each individual. Each wedge-shaped section of the circle represents one aspect of that person's life. The concentric rings indicate the information the person reveals about him- or herself during conversation, with the outer circles representing casual conversations and the inner circles representing very intimate conversations. By noting which segments of the circle are active in any relationship, we can use this model to illustrate the level of intimacy in a relationship.

To understand how the model works, it is important to understand **social penetration theory**.[4] According to this theory, the relationships we share typically begin with relatively narrow breadth (we discuss few topics with each other) and shallow depth (our conversations about these topics remain relatively superficial). This type of relationship is shown in Figure 13.2 as a casual relationship. Over time, however, increases in the amount of intimacy we share (how close we become) and the amount of intensity we feel (how strong are our feelings for each other) are reflected in the overall breadth and depth of our relationship. As a result, highly intimate relationships reveal themselves to have significant amounts of both breadth and depth as interactants extend the range of topics they discuss and reveal more about themselves and their feelings. Such changes are shown in Figure 13.2. The breadth and depth of a more intimate relationship are also shown in Figure 13.2.

FIGURE 13.1
Altman and Taylor's Social Penetration Model: Breadth and Depth in Relationships

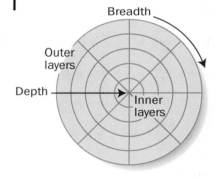

FIGURE 13.2
Social Penetration in a Casual and an Intimate Relationship

Casual relationship

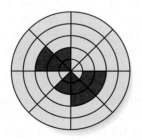

Intimate relationship

Looking at Relationships with the Social Penetration Model

The social penetration model is useful for a number of reasons. First, it helps us visualize our relationships by providing us with a depiction of the range of topics we talk about as well as the extent to which we reveal ourselves through our conversations. Second, it enables us to understand why some of our relationships seem stronger than others. As a relationship increases in strength, we become more willing to discuss particular subjects with a person and more comfortable revealing more about ourselves. Rather than limiting someone's access to us (and our relationship circle), we give that person greater access by allowing him or her to move away from our circle's periphery and venture inward, toward its center. This increases the relational bonds between us. Thus, when your communication with another person is lacking in breadth or depth, although your relationship may be satisfying, it will remain quite casual; to change that, you would need to take steps to enhance the scope and nature of your interactions.

in Practice

Social Penetration—Casual and Intimate Relationships

Think about the conversations that you engage in four different relationships:

    a. a new friendship
    b. a longlasting, meaningful friendship
    c. a current relationship with a parent
    d. a romantic relationship

1. For each relationship, label the pie-shaped wedges of each diagram with the various aspects of your life. Then color in the segments that correspond to the level of self-disclosure you share with that person.

2. The resulting diagrams will illustrate graphically the amount of social penetration you have with each person. How do the similarities and differences in the diagrams explain the different types of relationships you share?

A. a new friendship

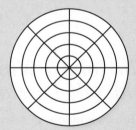

B. a long-lasting, meaningful friendship

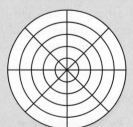

C. a current relationship with a parent

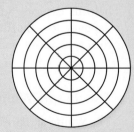

D. a romantic relationship

At times our desire to get to know someone better causes us to discuss topics at a depth that we would normally reserve for those with whom we share a more intimate relationship. When such disclosures or revelations occur prematurely—before individuals are fully ready for a more intense relationship—they may contribute to feelings of discomfort in either one or both parties. On the other hand, when individuals are ready to deepen the relationship, increases in breadth and depth occur naturally and cause little, if any, relational discomfort.

Research reveals that we are likely to judge individuals who reveal too much to us too soon as indiscreet, untrustworthy, or just plain odd. In addition, we perceive individuals who try to get us to do more disclosing than we are ready for as pushy and overbearing.[5]

The response to one's self-disclosure of positive and negative information is also time-related. Research reveals that we tend to dislike those individuals who disclose positive information about themselves to us in the very early stages of our relationship. In contrast, the disclosure of negative information early in a relationship can be positive because, for some reason, we tend to be attracted to those who are willing to be honest and take responsibility for their actions.[6]

Of course, it is neither possible nor desirable for us to have a close relationship with every individual with whom we interact; every relationship has an optimal level. Relationships that are currently more distant in scope and tone, if given the right opportunities, may in time become deeper and more significant. We need time to absorb information about each other. The satisfactory development of a relationship—whether it is a friendship or one more intimate and romantic in nature—depends on our being able to properly pace or time our self-disclosures.

The Johari Window and Self-Disclosure

The **Johari window** is a second model we can use to help understand the roles that self-awareness and self-disclosure play in relationship building. The window (whose name was created by combining the first names of its two creators: Joseph Luft and Harrington Ingham[7]) contains four panes that help us explore how self-awareness and self-disclosure are relationship dependent—that how we view ourselves and how much we are willing to reveal about ourselves varies among relationships.

FIGURE 13.3

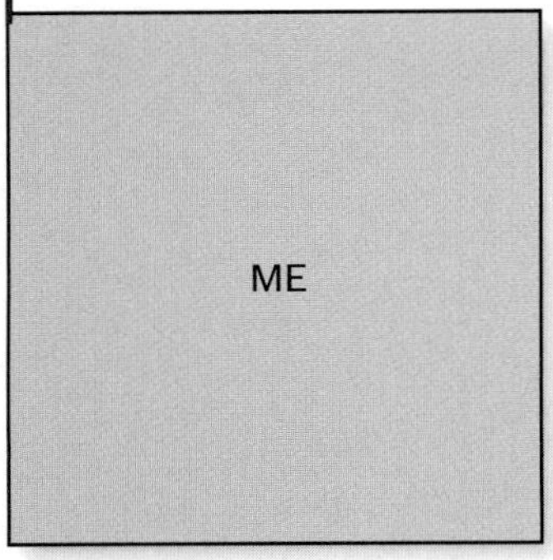

ME

The Johari Window Model

The window represents your self (see Figure 13.3). It is divided into two axes, creating four panes. The first axis includes what you do and do not know about yourself, and the second axis includes information that a specific other person does or does not know about you. Let's look at the four panes. The window represents the self.

By dividing this window in half with an axis, we can depict what we do and do not know about ourselves (see Figure 13.4). Then by dividing the window still again with a horizontal axis, we can represent what other people do and do not know about us (see Figure 13.5). Finally, by putting these two axes together in the same model, we create four panes that are descriptive of the relationship we share with another person (see Figure 13.6).

Pane 1, the *open* area, contains information about you that is known to both you and the other person. For example, you may have divulged your religious background, tastes in food, or career aspirations. As you and the other person become closer, the size of the open area grows larger.

Pane 2, the *blind* area, contains information about you that the other person is aware of but that you are not. For example, you may consider yourself to be very confident, while another perceives you to be extremely insecure. We learn of information in the blind area primarily through feedback. At times, we may feel we know so little about ourselves that we find it necessary to seek outside help to reduce the size of our blind area.

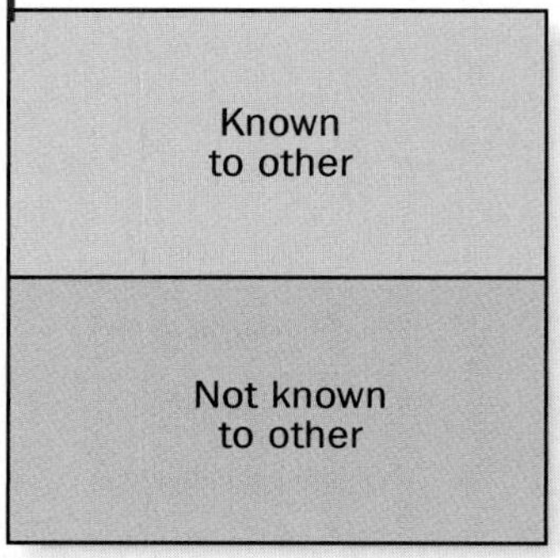

Pane 3, the *hidden* area, contains information that you know about yourself but are unwilling to reveal to another. For example, you may hesitate to reveal to another your fear of being left alone, out of concern that he or she would reject you and your fear would be realized. Items in the hidden area usually only become known as a result of self-disclosure, during which we reveal information about ourselves to another person that he or she would not otherwise have known. During this process, information is moved from pane 3 to pane 1, the open area. Thus, as you share more about yourself to another person, the size of pane 3 shrinks as the size of pane 1 grows.

FIGURE 13.4

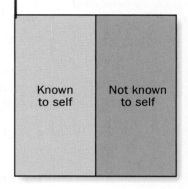

Known to self	Not known to self

FIGURE 13.5

Known to other
Not known to other

FIGURE 13.6
The Johari Window

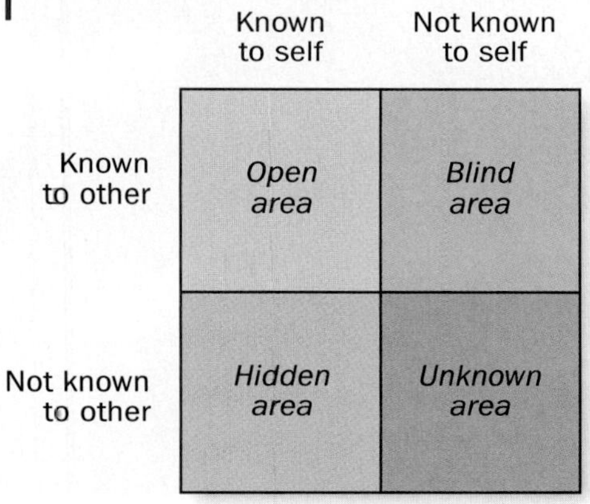

	Known to self	Not known to self
Known to other	*Open area*	*Blind area*
Not known to other	*Hidden area*	*Unknown area*

SOURCE: Joseph Luft, *Group Processes: An Introduction to Group Dynamics*, Third Edition. Palo Alto, CA: Mayfield, 1984, p. 60. Copyright © 1984, 1970, and 1963 by Joseph Luft.

What new things have you recently discovered about yourself?

Pane 4, the *unknown* area, contains information unknown to both you and the other person. Pane 4 exists because we constantly learn new things about ourselves. Over time, education or life experience succeeds in bringing some of the mysteries contained in this pane out into the open. For example, we may discover that we have an unknown fear, prejudice, or talent. The more introspective we are, the smaller the size of our unknown area tends to be.

Because developing self-awareness depends on our being able to gain information about ourselves, we need to be open to learning more about our blind and unknown areas. By understanding how others see us, we can develop greater insight into ourselves.

Looking at Relationships with the Johari Window

Just as we can represent each of our relationships with a social penetration model, so can we represent each with the Johari window. The relative size of each pane reveals how we feel about another person and how comfortable we are revealing personal information to him or her. Usually, as we begin a new relationship, we begin by disclosing relatively superficial information about ourselves to another person. If that person responds positively and reciprocates with disclosures of his or her own, we are apt to continue disclosing information about ourselves to him or her, and the relationship we share will increase in trust, the depth of knowledge we have about each other, and feelings of closeness. However, when two people in a relationship share little, if any, open area, interpersonal communication at any depth is, for all

While self-disclosure and relationship success are positively correlated, we do need to evaluate the level of self-disclosure appropriate to each of our relationships.

FIGURE 13.7
Relationship Windows

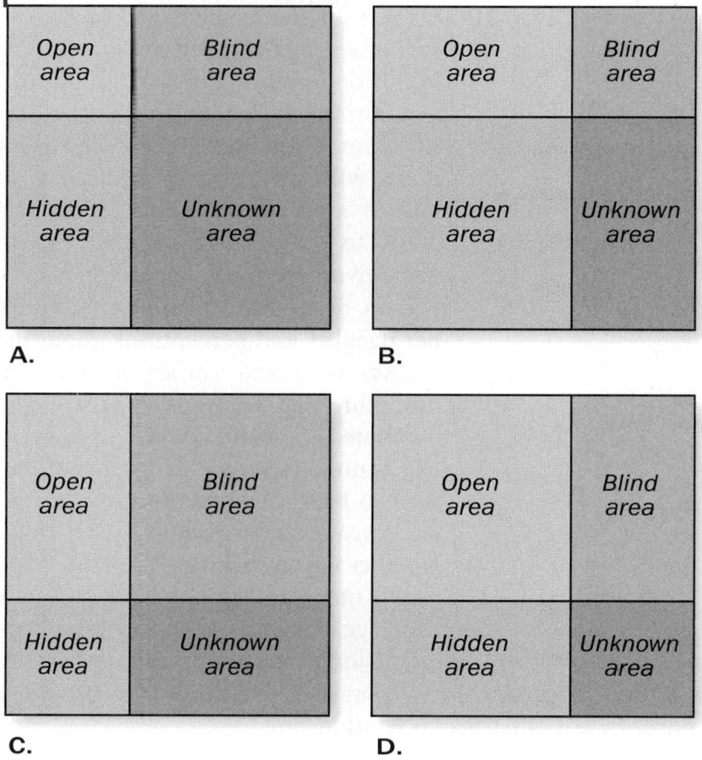

Which window most represents you and another person with whom you interact?

practical purposes, impossible. Because the less open person in a relationship typically is the one who blocks relationship-building attempts, he or she usually also functions to limit the amount of interpersonal communication possible.

Window A in Figure 13.7 shows a relationship that is fairly impersonal. The relatively large size of the unknown area and the relatively small size of the open area tell us that the individuals involved in this relationship are not particularly introspective, are apt to withdraw from contact with each other, refrain from self-disclosing, and probably project an image that announces their desire to be noncommunicative and not reveal a great deal of information to each other.

Window B shows a relationship in which the hidden area is dominant. This tells us that an individual involved in such a relationship fears exposure of some weakness and lacks trust in the other person, believing that he or she might exploit any information that is revealed. The individual is likely to feel that it is necessary to create and maintain a facade in an effort to pretend to be what he or she is not.

Window C shows a relationship in which the blind area is dominant. When we become involved in such a relationship, we are unaware of how we are affecting or being perceived by the other person because we are overly concerned with our own self-presentation in our interactions.

Window D depicts a relationship in which the open area is particularly large. A relationship such as this usually involves significant self-disclosing and is

What kind of window would you draw for someone who was afraid to take risks? for someone who was very trusting?

.≋ *Practice*

Window Gazing

Think again of the four relationships you analyzed in the previous "In Practice" box: a new friendship; a longlasting, meaningful friendship; a current relationship with a parent; and a romantic relationship.

1. For each relationship, draw a Johari window.

2. What does the relative size of each pane in each of your windows tell you about yourself in relation to the other four people?

3. For each relationship, consider the extent to which you think the other person's window would mirror the window you drew. Then ask each person to draw one. Compare and contrast the windows drawn with your own drawings. How do similarities and differences help explain the relationship you share with each person?

characterized by candor, openness, and sensitivity to the needs and insights of the other person.

Thus, when we choose not to disclose information about ourselves to others, our windows will have smaller open areas and larger hidden, blind, or unknown areas. In contrast, when we feel comfortable with another person and want to maintain or increase our closeness, our windows will have larger open areas and smaller hidden areas. In addition, as our relationships allow us to grow closer, the size of our blind unknown areas are apt to shrink as the other person reveals an increasing number of his or her insights and perceptions about us to us.

As we noted earlier in this chapter, self-disclosure and relationship success are positively correlated. The higher the quality of our self-disclosures, the more satisfying our relationships tend to be. Feeling comfortable being honest and self-revealing is a keynote of relationship health, whether we are talking about the health of a marriage or grandchild–grandparent interaction.[8]

Who limits a relationship— the person who is more or the person who is less open?

That does not mean that we should engage in self-disclosure without considering the risks of doing so—remember our discussion of the importance of trust in Chapter 9. There are a series of questions for us to answer to help us evaluate the level of self-disclosure appropriate to a particular relationship:

1. Do we want to take the relationship to a deeper level?

2. Do we feel comfortable and safe doing so?

3. Is the disclosing we intend to do appropriate and relevant?

4. Will our partner reciprocate?

5. Will the disclosure have a positive impact on our relationship?

If these five questions cannot be answered with a "yes," then this may not be the right time to engage in self-disclosure.

Always keep in mind that there is some risk in revealing personal information—both for you and for the person to whom you disclose yourself. This person may reject you or form a negative impression of you because of your revelation. In addition, as a result of your self-disclosure, you may reveal a previously unknown weakness. Revealing the weakness may also leave you with less control over the course of the relationship. While what you disclose may help you feel more honest and forthcoming, the truth you tell may hurt your partner. Or you may end up telling your partner more than she or he wishes to know.

On the other hand, self-disclosing to the right people often brings benefits that help to strengthen relationships. Of course, developing mutually satisfying relationships depends on more than reciprocal self-disclosures. Relationships worth having evolve and, as they do so, they need to be maintained.

Relationship Maintenance

Though we may find the relationships we share satisfying and mutually rewarding, we still have to make a commitment to work to maintain each one—that is, we need to work constantly at **relationship maintenance.** Should we grow lazy or careless and expect a relationship to take care of itself, the relationship could begin to suffer from a lack of nourishment and, unless tended to, ultimately waste away.[9]

What is it that we must do to keep our relationships healthy? First, we cannot let any important relationship go untended. We need to be mindful of each one, make time for it, and demonstrate our commitment to it. According to Kathryn Dindia and Leslie Baxter, there are at least five strategies we should use to maintain a healthy relationship:

1. We need to take time to talk to one another and share our feelings and concerns in an open and honest manner.

2. We need to talk about the way we talk to each other—that is, engage in **metacommunication.**

3. We need to rely on prosocial approaches, including showing our partner that we affirm, support, and value him or her; being cheerful in each other's presence; and refraining from criticizing each other.

4. We need to celebrate the relationship itself by engaging in activities that mark the relationship's very existence and confirm its importance.

5. We need to have fun simply spending time together.[10]

Does a relationship need to be fair to be satisfying? How many of your relationships would you characterize as fair and unfair?

In addition, if we want to invest in and work at maintaining a relationship, both partners need to feel that they are being treated fairly by the other. According to **equity theory,** we and our partner need to feel equally committed to preserving the relationship, that we can trust one another, that neither party is taking advantage of the other, and that the resources we have are being shared equitably.

As a relationship grows in strength, the partners become more secure and feel less pressure to reciprocate every relationship contribution equally or quickly. Instead of focusing on the short-term relationship balance sheet, they are able to focus on the relationship's long-term future and thus feel confident enough to postpone the personal rewards they expect to receive from the relationship to a later time. This does not mean, however, that the fairness quotient of the relationship can stay unbalanced too long without causing partners to explore the nature of their interactions and to suggest

in Theory

What Is Relationship Maintenance?

Because relationship maintenance means different things to different people, it is important to consider the meaning it has for you.

1. Describe the behaviors you use to maintain three important relationships in your life. For example, do you phone the individual often? Do you do frequent favors for him or her?

2. Compare and contrast the behaviors on each list. Based on your lists, which relationship requires more work to maintain at this point? Was there ever a time when that relationship required less work on your part? Explain.

3. In your opinion, which of the three relationships is the most healthy? the least healthy? Why?

in Theory

How Fair Is Fair?

To evaluate a relationship, we often try to assess whether it is based on fairness or is one-sided.

1. Consider a relationship you're currently in and one that has been terminated. Compare and contrast them based on the extent to which you and your current and former partners:
   a. experienced feelings of being let down.
   b. felt rewarded.
   c. shared resources.
   d. felt pressured to reciprocate the good deeds of the other.
   e. believed the relationship survived only because of your efforts or the efforts of your partner.
   f. handled and resolved relational problems and conflicts fairly.

2. Is fairness an important factor in maintaining a satisfying relationship?

changing the state of equity. By periodically assessing the equity and quality of the relationships we share, we demonstrate our interest in the general state or climate of the relationship, not merely in what either partner is presently gaining or losing by maintaining it.[11]

For those relationships that have the healthiest climates and make us feel the happiest, most rewarded, and most secure, researchers report that we tend to perceive ourselves and our partners as making equal investments in the relationship's well-being and future. In contrast, when we believe we are investing more in a relationship than a partner is, we tend to become resentful and might even conclude that we are being "used." At the same time, when we realize that our partner is making more of a psychological or physical investment than we are, we are apt to experience guilt. Either perceived imbalance reduces our satisfaction with the relationship, can erode its effectiveness, and limits its future or curtails it.[12] Once we conclude a relationship has no future, we no longer see a need to weather bad times together, and suddenly problems and conflicts we once would have handled easily or responsibly attempted to work out now appear insurmountable and not worth our time or effort. When this point is reached, we are also likely to trust each other less and tell each other less, and as a result continue to drift apart.

Relationship Dysfunctions: Toxic Communication

A woman is battered by an intimate partner approximately every fifteen seconds. Every day, four women die from violence committed by persons close to them. As many as 50 percent of women are physically or emotionally abused by a partner.[13] When a sexual relationship goes awry, why does it sometimes culminate in physical or domestic violence?

Despite the fact that we tend to think of all romantic relationships as love-based, some, unfortunately, are **dysfunctional**. They are unhealthy, destructive, and characterized by episodes of **toxic communication**, including consistent *verbal abuse* (one individual repeatedly relates verbally to another in ways that debilitate by attacking the person's physical appearance, intellectual capabilities, or emotional stability; lowering the person's self-esteem; and weakening, damaging, and ultimately destroying the person's sense of self) and *physical violence* (one person physically attacks and injures another's body). Both forms of abuse are relationally toxic and leave psychological scars that are difficult for victims to recover from. For the most part, the violence is committed by men against women and, though extreme in form, underscores the unequal balance of power in male-female relationships. It is

Have you ever been verbally abusive or verbally abused? How did you or the other person respond?

precipitated by the fact that men are socialized to assert themselves, compete, and focus on outcomes, whereas women are conditioned to defer, compromise, and focus on nurturing. Though spousal abuse is all too common, the highest incidence of such violence actually occurs among unmarried cohabiting couples.[14]

Why do some men enter into abusive relationships, and why do some women remain in them? Perhaps it is because society teaches us "love can jump hurdles." Research suggests that as the media fill our minds with romantic fantasies of Prince Charming and the Beast, some of us are apt to become dependent and tolerate abuse, contributing to increased physical and emotional risk.[15] Romanticized notions encourage the abused to downplay

In Theory

It Hurts

Every 12 seconds in the United States a woman is beaten by a man. Researchers assert that this abuse is promoted by cultural norms that espouse that males should be aggressive, in control, and dominant, and women should be submissive, loyal, and deferential.

1. Have you or anyone you know ever been involved in an abusive relationship?

2. To what extent, if at all, do you believe the abuse was gender generated?

relational violence by blaming it on anger that got out of control or too much alcohol rather than on the abuser. As a result both the victim and the aggressor ignore or reframe the incident. Research also reveals that abusive persons have strong masculine gender orientations, relish controlling others, and aggressively seek to dominate others. Women who remain in such unhealthy relationships have likely been socialized into combining the emotionally supportive feminine role with one of learned helplessness and fear. Additionally, they more than likely have also been socialized to be deferential and to value interpersonal harmony. Research by Lloyd reveals that when in a courtship relationship, the predominant theme a man enacts is control, while the predominant theme the woman enacts is dependence.[16] Men who commit violence also take pains to isolate their partners from financial resources, leaving them without access to cash, checking accounts, or credit cards.[17] See Figure 13.8.

FIGURE 13.8
The Cycle of Abuse

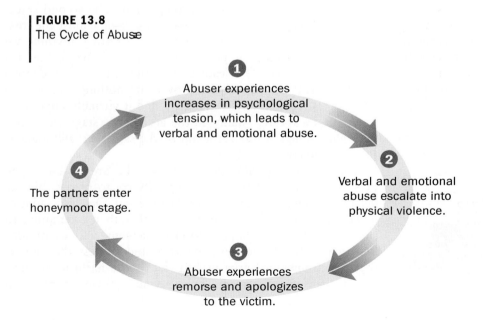

1 Abuser experiences increases in psychological tension, which leads to verbal and emotional abuse.

2 Verbal and emotional abuse escalate into physical violence.

3 Abuser experiences remorse and apologizes to the victim.

4 The partners enter honeymoon stage.

Like friendships and romantic relationships, dysfunctional relationships pass through a predictable cycle of stages: during the first stage, relational tensions build in the abuser, who blames a partner for problems or for not being supportive and looks for an excuse to vent anger. In the second stage, the tensions erupt into violence and one or more battering incidents occur. In the third stage, the abuser experiences remorse and resolves to make it up to the victim, typically promising that it will never happen again. In the fourth stage, there is a lull in violent activity, and the victim again feels loved until relational tensions build and the cycle of abuse repeats itself.[18]

For abuse to persist, the woman usually must be isolated from her family and friends who would otherwise offer her solace, support, and a means of escape.[19]

Why do people stay in relationships that are happy? They stay because they want to. Why do people stay in relationships that are abusive? Most stay because they *think* they have to.[20]

Relationships and Death: The Grief Process

While all relationships ultimately end, not all relationships terminate due to a decision made by one or both relationship partners. Some terminate due to the death of a loved one. Many report death as the most painful of all relationship endings. When a loved one dies, the surviving partner is left with the feelings of loneliness and despair that can damage psychological and physical health. According to James Lynch, bereaved persons are at greater risk for health and related psychological and immune system problems.[21]

What steps can we take to rescue ourselves from grief? An understanding of the **grief process** may help us answer this question. The grief process is composed of a series of stages (see Figure 13.9).

The first stage in the grief process, denial, finds us trying to deny what has happened. Reality prompts us to acknowledge the magnitude of our loss and the feelings of loneliness and social isolation that accompany it. The second stage, anger, leaves us feeling both helpless and powerless as we rage against the loss. During the third stage, grief, we turn our anger inward, regretting anything we might ever have done or said to hurt the person who has died. We feel as if a chapter in our lives is left unwritten. This leads us into the fourth stage, depression, during which we feel as if our former life is over and nothing will ever be right for us in the future. In fact, we find it virtually impossible to envision a future. Finally, in the acceptance stage we realize that while things will never again be the same, we will make it through and continue life.[22]

FIGURE 13.9
Working through Grief

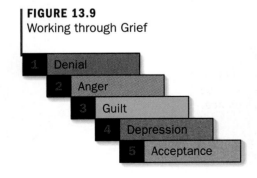

1 Denial
2 Anger
3 Guilt
4 Depression
5 Acceptance

During the mourning period, those who are closest to the person who has suffered a loss typically try to protect him or her by shielding him or her from feeling sad. Denying sadness, however, rarely makes it go away. Rather than attempting to suppress or ignore feelings of sadness, persons who are mourning need to be allowed to experience and express the sadness they feel. Submerged grief usually does more harm to an individual than its expression. By allowing grieving persons to process their feelings, we help free them to continue with their lives.[23] Here, a social support network can play a critical role.[24]

An erroneous stereotype of a partner's death is that women grieve while men replace. Actually, significant numbers of men and women over time form new, intimate relationships after recovering from the death of their loved one.

Relational Dialectics

As some relational forces pull us toward intimacy, opposing forces may pull us in the opposite direction. The road to a happy relationship does not always proceed smoothly. Partners don't necessarily want the same thing at the same time from the relationship. **Relational dialectics** captures the ups and downs, pushes and pulls, that dynamic, healthy relationships experience.

While some models portray our relationships developing in stages—recall both Knapp and Vangelisti's ten-stage model of relationships and Bill Rawlins's six-stage model of friendship discussed in Chapter 12—others perceive that there is more to developing a relationship than whether a relationship we share is new, has existed for some years, or has lasted for decades. Some theorists suggest that rather than proceed through a series of stages, relationships never really stabilize but evolve and change over time as the parties to a relationship repeatedly reevaluate and redefine their goals and needs as they seek to manage its course. Since the context of a relationship is ever changing, relational partners will need to resolve a series of dialectical tensions—the opposing tensions or conflicts created when the goals and expectations of one relationship partner clash with the goals and expectations of the other relationship partner.

Among the dialectical forces that make relationship maintenance a challenge are the push and pull partners feel toward integration versus separation, stability versus change, and expression versus privacy.[25] According to the theory's formulator, Leslie Baxter, the dialectics have both internal (the tensions experienced between relational partners, including how they communicate with each other) and external manifestations (the tensions between partners and other dyads or society). Let us look at each in turn. Dialectical tensions can occur in any interpersonal relationship in any context.

Integration–Separation

The dialectic of integration–separation focuses on the tension between a person's desire to be socially integrated but also self-sufficient. From an internal perspective, a person's desire for connection clashes with the need for autonomy. For example, we may want to be close to our partner (be connected) but independent of him or her (be autonomous). If you've ever felt smothered by a relationship partner and desired your freedom as a result, you were likely experiencing a need for more autonomy. On the other hand, if you ever felt like your relationship partner was ignoring you or not giving you enough attention, you were probably expressing your desire for greater connection.

Externally, we express this pull–push dialectic by wanting to introduce a partner to others and wanting to keep a partner away from others, or the inclusion–seclusion tension. Wanting to have our relationship included in a larger social network clashes with our desire to keep it private and personal.

Stability–Change

The internal manifestation of the stability–change dialectic suggests that we experience tension between desiring sameness or comfort in our relationships and desiring novelty or newness. For relationships to last, some stability and predictability need to be present. We need to be able to count on each other to perform certain relational roles; our lives need to have some nonvarying routines or we would experience chaos on a daily basis. Contrastingly, when our lives are filled with too much routine, we feel we know everything about the persons with whom we share a relationship; predictability rules, life becomes stale, and we find ourselves longing for excitement and something different. On the other hand, relationships characterized by too much novelty or surprise may leave us feeling overwhelmed by a lack of control.

Externally, we express this second pull–push dialectic by experiencing tension between a desire to have conventional relationships that conform to social expectations and norms and a desire to demonstrate a unique relationship.[26] For example, in the United States, we act in conventional ways by working to fulfill the American dream. We have a well-paying job with a dependable organization, own a home, and support a family. We challenge this norm when we opt not to settle down, drift from place to place, or choose not to have children.

Expression–Privacy

Do we disclose or keep things to ourselves? The internal manifestation of the expression–privacy dialectic finds us desiring openness in our relationships but also feeling a need to keep information private. The tension between relational openness and "closedness" determines how much partners reveal to one another.[27] The push–pull here is between wanting to get closer to others by revealing thoughts and feelings, and wanting to protect ourselves from criticism by withholding personal information that could increase our vulnerability.

The external manifestation of this dialectic focuses on the revelation-concealment tension. If your boss asks you what you think of the performance of a coworker, do you tell him or her the truth or keep your thoughts to yourself? What do you tell your best friend about a dysfunctional romantic relationship? Do you tell him or her about the abusive relationship or keep that information to yourself? While we may want to reveal the relationship, we may think it best to conceal it from public scrutiny, fearing what could happen if others intervene. Unfortunately, such fears could cause the abusive relationship to continue.[28]

Working Through Dialectical Tensions

Which of the preceding relational dialectics cause the most problems for you? If you're like most young married couples, the dialectic that produces the most tension in your close relationships is autonomy–connection, followed in descending order by predictability–novelty, inclusion–seclusion, openness–closedness, conventionality–uniqueness, and revelation–concealment.[29] Other researchers support the preeminence of autonomy–connection but believe that tensions surrounding the openness–closedness dialectic also significantly influence relational progress or deterioration.[30]

The question is not which of the dialectics causes you problems but rather how you manage the problems created by the contradicting pushes and pulls you experience. Researchers identify a number of ways of handling these dialectical tensions practically.[31] Among them are denial, disorientation, spiraling alteration, segmentation, balance, integration, recalibration, and reaffirmation.

When you practice *denial,* you respond to one pole of a dialectical challenge while ignoring the other. For example, were you caught between the conflicting desires for autonomy and connection, you might opt only for connection, choosing to spend all your time with your partner. You satisfy one need while denying the other.

When you practice *disorientation,* you feel overwhelmed and opt to give in to feelings of utter helplessness. This response is nonfunctional because all dialogue between relational partners stops.

The response of *spiraling alteration* finds you caught in a repetitive cycle of alternating tensions, causing you to move repeatedly from one side of the dialectic to the other. You might choose to draw close emotionally, then argue that you need more space, only to draw close once more.

When you engage in *segmentation* you and your partner choose to isolate different relationship aspects and deal with them in separate situations of relational life. For example, you may choose to share activities but have independent interests in other life-spheres. You might choose to emphasize different sides of the dialectic depending on the topic being discussed or the context in which you find yourselves. For example, you might be open to discussing everything except politics or religion.

Balance is another compromise approach in which both partners see dialectical tension poles as legitimate and attempt to balance their opposing needs by submerging their full strength. By engaging both sides of the dialectic—choosing to be moderately open or moderately connected, you strive to reach a midpoint that tips in neither direction.

Integration finds you responding to opposing forces without denying or diluting them. You might, for example, relish certainty but embrace its opposite by doing something new that you've never done before on weekends.

When you *recalibrate* a relational tension, you reframe it. Though this tactic does not ensure a solution to the tensions, it does allow partners to redefine the nature of the challenge facing them so that it is not perceived as a permanent oppositional pull or contradiction.

Finally, *reaffirmation* involves the realization by both partners that dialectical tensions

Theory

Try to See It My Way

The prevalence of popular expressions or adages reflecting contradictory impulses is testimony to the presence of relational dialectics in daily life. Identify sayings such as "I need my space," or "Out of sight, out of mind" that reflect or allude to the pull–push nature of relational dialectics.

will persist in relationships if only because our relationships are rich and complex. Working through tensions becomes a promise of what the relationship can accomplish rather than a threat to its survival.

Relationship Repair: Renegotiation or Dissolution

Have you ever tried to repair a relationship that seemed beyond repair? What happened?

When a relationship fails to satisfy us or is no longer as satisfying as it once was, we need to decide whether we want to work to salvage or repair it, and if so, how to go about it. Of course, before we can take steps toward **relationship repair** or dissolution, we should identify what caused our relationship's communication climate to become negative in the first place.

Identifying the Problem

Our first task is to identify, as clearly as possible, why the relationship isn't working. What is our problem? What exactly is it that we or our partner find dissatisfying?

As you learned in Chapter 2, primary among the factors that contribute to the establishment of relationship problems and the creation of a negative relationship climate is the sending of *disconfirming* rather than *confirming* messages. Whereas **confirming messages** show that we value the relationship and

Some relationships are dysfunctional and characterized by episodes of toxic communication including verbal or physical abuse.

the other person, **disconfirming messages** show our disregard for them. When we send disconfirming messages, we exhibit a lack of recognition of the other person or his or her needs, we fail to acknowledge his or her ideas or feelings, we refrain from exhibiting support for him or her, and we limit the amount of information we share. In effect, disconfirming messages announce to another that we are now of a mind to diminish or dismiss him or her in our eyes. By our behavior, we let the other person know that we are ignoring him or her; that the person is unworthy of our serious attention; that because we now believe the person to be insignificant, we are able to display a basic lack of concern for his or her needs. We may verbally abuse the individual, continually complain about his or her shortcomings, ignore the person by pretending he or she isn't present, and make a concerted effort to prove our own importance by demonstrating that whatever we do matters, while the other person's words and actions don't count. Over time, the absence of confirmation curtails effective communication and reshapes the relationship into one that is very uncomfortable.

Identifying Strategies to Repair the Problem

Next we need to agree on what we can do to restore the relationship to a state that our partner will find rewarding and reinforcing, one that affirms his or her presence. This is the point at which we ask what kinds of changes, if any, we each would be willing to make in our own behaviors that could improve our satisfaction with the relationship, including its emotional tone or communication climate. For example, we take a giant step toward confirming the importance of our relationship with another individual if we:

1. Demonstrate our willingness to acknowledge the significance of that person;

2. Work to sustain both a verbal and a nonverbal dialogue with the person that demonstrates our respect for him or her;

3. Reflect back to that person that we care about, understand, and respect his or her feelings; and

4. Encourage him or her to share thoughts and feelings with us.

Deciding to Dissolve or Save the Relationship

Relationship repair depends on partners' being able to talk to each other about what they want from the relationship and what they feel about each other. When a relationship is under stress, the parties tend to exchange and

.in *Theory*

What's Wrong?

Identifying the problem is a first step toward relationship repair.

1. To what extent, if any, do you or a partner exhibit any of the following behaviors in relationships that you believe have a problem or are in need of repair?
   a. Engage in verbal abuse in an effort to psychologically harm the other person
   b. Continually complain about what the other person does or does not do
   c. Interrupt or ignore the other person in an effort to short-circuit his or her communication with you
   d. Intentionally seek to confuse the other person as a means of maintaining a one-up position

2. What can each of you do to help ensure that you both feel better about your relationship?

perceive a lot more negativity than they used to; their comments to each other become tinged with sarcasm, they argue more, and problems tend to escalate rather than be resolved to both sides' mutual satisfaction.[32] When partners fail to receive the rewards they expect, see no purpose in maintaining the relationship, or are unable to handle the strain imposed on them that trying to maintain the relationship presents, the relationship is liable to break up.

Unless it is mutually agreed to, breaking up with another person is rarely easy. However, two key strategies can avoid an ugly scene when severing a relationship. First, do not overpersonalize the relationship's end by feeling a need to blame yourself or the other party for the breakup. Asking questions such as, "What's wrong with him or her?" or "How could I have been so stupid?" usually solves nothing. Most likely nothing is wrong with either person, and probably neither you nor he or she was "stupid," either. Thus there is no need to derogate or bad-mouth yourself or the other person. The fact is that sometimes circumstances rather than people cause relationships to end.[33] Second, keep a sense of perspective and recognize that relationships that do not survive probably were not meant to be pursued. When you are no longer able to meet each other's needs, or when you feel that the relationship is stifling your personal growth, it is better to end the relationship.

On the other hand, when one or both partners are motivated to repair a relationship, by questioning themselves and each other about the relationship and by making a commitment to change the dynamics of the way they relate to each other, they can renegotiate their relationship, transform it, and facilitate its continued growth.

Diversity and Culture Contacts

Getting Closer through Interpersonal Connections

Notions of intimacy vary from one culture to another. The Japanese, for example, use friendship as a pathway to greater intimacy, while Americans rely more on romantic relationships to attain intimacy. Thus, the Japanese perceive best-friend relationships to be more intimate than boy- or girlfriend relationships. On the other hand, both the Japanese and Americans perceive strangers to be the least intimate kind of relationship, see acquaintance relationships as less intimate than relationships with friends, and view best-friend relationships as more intimate than relationships with those who are just friends. This similarity in perception suggests that the stages of relationships discussed previously may cut across cultures.[34] Within the United States, African Americans and Caucasians hold the most permissive sexual attitudes, while individuals from Asian, Latino, and Middle Eastern cultures typically display more conservative attitudes.[35] Similarly, both Caucasians and African Americans believe that talking about sexual intimacy is a sign of a strong relationship, while Asian and Hispanic Americans are much less likely to discuss their more intimate relationships.[36]

Notions of disclosure also vary among cultures. Natives of the United States are most disclosing, even demonstrating some willingness to disclose information about themselves to strangers.[37] This may explain why Americans seem particularly easy to meet, are proficient at cocktail party conversation, and are perceived as exhibitionists by persons from more nondisclosing cultures. Conversely, Japanese tend to do little disclosing about themselves to others except to those few people with whom they are very close. In general, Asians do not reach out to strangers. They do, however, demonstrate great care for each other during interactions, since they view harmony as essential to relationship nurturance. To this end, they work hard to prevent those whom they perceive to be outsiders from obtaining information they believe to be unfavorable. Latinos also focus on the importance of relational support.

Cultures with a strong group orientation do not value privacy as much as do cultures with an individualistic orientation. Thus, members of Arabic, Greek, and Spanish cultures have a lesser need for privacy in a relationship than do members of Western or North American cultures.[38] Similarly, members of Western cultures tend to rely on verbal disclosures to build trust, whereas members of Asian cultures depend on actions rather than words to cement trust. Westerners tend to perceive commitment as a bond connecting two people. Asians, Hispanics, and African Americans perceive commitment as a bond linking groups.[39]

Different cultures also express grief differently. Duck reports that in some cultures it is acceptable to fall to the ground, cover oneself with dust, and wail loudly; others emphasize public composure and view the showing of such emotion as unacceptable. Even how we cope with grief is culturally bound.[40]

 ## *Gender Contacts*

Intimacy and Distance

Understanding alternative ways of developing and maintaining intimacy is important if we are to sustain relationships in our lives. While both women and men value friendships and romantic relationships, they are apt to express closeness in different ways.

Whereas most men define intimacy in terms of what two people *do* together (*instrumental activities*), most women define it in terms of what they *talk about* together (*personal talk*). According to researchers, men engage in shared activities as a means to achieve closeness, while women participate in shared emotional talk.[41] Men assume the value of a relationship; they don't feel a deep need to talk about it. Women, in contrast, feel that discussing the dynamics of a relationship is important. This can create relationship problems because as men attempt to develop intimacy with women, they will plan activities, whereas women might prefer to be in a situation in which they would have an increased opportunity for talking and self-disclosing, not just doing.[42]

If given the choice, would you rather actively do something with a date or spend time talking? Why?

Additionally, men and women assign different weights to autonomy and connection. Because men are more likely to be socialized towards independence, they tend to prefer autonomy to interrelatedness; women, in contrast, tend to need autonomy less but covet connection more. This preference disparity can lead the woman to think that her partner does not value their relationship and lead the man to think that the woman wants to consume his time with intrusive talk.

Feelings

In the poem "To Women, as Far as I'm Concerned,"
D. H. Lawrence expresses his opinion of feelings.

> *The feelings I don't have, I don't have.*
> *The feelings I don't have, I won't say I have.*
> *The feelings you say you have, you don't have.*
> *The feelings you would like us both to have, we neither of*
>   *us have.*
> *The feelings people ought to have, they never have.*
> *If people say they've got feelings, you may be pretty sure*
>   *they haven't got them.*
> *So if you want either of us to feel anything at all*
> *You'd better abandon all idea of feelings altogether.*

1. Which of his observations—if any—do you agree with?
2. In what ways do you think his perceptions express
   a male point of view? Explain.

SOURCE: "To Women, as Far as I'm Concerned" by
D. H. Lawrence, from *The Complete Poems of D. H. Lawrence*
by D. H. Lawrence, edited by V. de Sola Pinto & F. W. Roberts,
copyright © 1964, 1971 by Angelo Ravagli and C. M. Weekley,
Executors of the Estate of Frieda Lawrence Ravagli. Used by
permission of Viking Penguin, a division of Penguin Group
(USA) Inc.

What creates comfort for most women is the opposite of what creates comfort for most men. Women also tend to disclose more intimate information to their partners than do men. Perhaps this is because women have been encouraged to be more personal and open about their thoughts, feelings, and fears than men. Thus, men tend to ask women more questions about themselves than women ask of men. At the same time, women hope that their male partners will voluntarily reciprocate with self-disclosures of their own.[43] When it comes to disclosing intimate information, however, women lead in revealing more information to their partners.

Women, in general, tend to watch the progress of their relationships more carefully than men do. As a result, women also tend to detect relationship troubles sooner and, except in relationships based on equality, are apt to surpass men in both expressing feelings of vulnerability and providing emotional support. Whereas women are more comfortable revealing their feelings and providing overt expressions of caring, men tend to be at ease using covert caring signals such as teasing, joking, and providing companionship.

Contrary to the image presented in romance novels and films, research reveals that men are more likely to initiate a declaration of love in a relationship than women.[44] They are also more likely to fall in love first.[45] More often than not, women wait until they hear the male say the "I love you" phrase to reciprocate with a declaration of love of their own. Men are socialized to take the lead in love, while women are socialized to be reactive.

Media and Technology Contacts

The Psychological Shortening of Long-Distance Relationships

The Internet lets us communicate with and maintain ties with people who live at a distance, some of whom we may never meet face-to-face, potentially making it the ultimate, noncontact, person-to-person network.[46] This is particularly important since **long-distance relationships** are an increasingly common fact of contemporary life. Today's economic environment has turned us into a more transient society; in increasing numbers, we find ourselves compelled to move wherever job opportunities lead us, travel extensively for our jobs, and venture to distant training or retooling centers that require us to spend a significant length of time away from home. As a result, we and our friends, family, or partner with whom we are romantically involved may either reflect the transience of our society by ending relationships whenever we move to a new site or may commit ourselves to "staying together" psychologically though we are geographically apart.

Today, more than ever before in our history, we are technologically equipped to survive the challenges that relating across the miles presents us. In the past, when individuals had to carry on long-distance relationships, they were aware how the geographical distance created a special fragility in their relationships, which they tended to characterize as tenuous and uncertain. Research reveals that long-distance partners lack something we all tend to take for granted: *routine interactions about nothing*—that is, talk about routine, seemingly unimportant daily events or activities.[47] Being able to maintain more frequent low-cost contact with each other, contact that actually facilitates a form of small talk, might tend to increase a relationship's health, durability, and survivability.[48] The fact that we can now communicate with each other via the Internet and e-mail has made long-distance relationship partners more accessible to each other. Letters and more costly telephone calls are increasingly being supplanted by the immediacy computer-mediated communication allows us. This sense of immediacy may enable us to nurture and sustain our long-distance relationships by allowing us to continue to feel a sense of relational commitment and continuity. Thus, because such relationships no longer engender the decreased contact they once did, rather than concluding that the distance between us requires us to end long-distance relationships, we may now feel better able to cope with them. Although the computer is not a genuine substitute for face-to-face involvement, it can provide us with that instant connection that allows us to continue to weave our daily lives together. Even though we may be far apart, we can now feel close and continue to add depth to our relationship.

On-line communication, especially instant messaging, facilitates relationship development and maintenance in other ways, too. People tend to become more talkative when instant messaging. There are no awkward silences or embarrassing moments. Many report that the biggest allure of instant messaging is that users feel less vulnerable talking about their feelings than they do when face-to-face.[49] Do you think these perceptions will change now that instant messaging can also incorporate audio and video?

Inwardly focused on-line journals, also known as weblogs or blogs, now serve as vehicles persons use to purge their emotions; because writers often solicit reader feedback and can read each other's entries, these journals also bring people closer together. By writing about painful traumas, "bloggers" pour their most painful feelings out on a computer screen, which also helps improve their health as well as enhance their insight into themselves.[50]

in Context

At a Distance

In today's culture, work demands are compelling more and more people to experience long-distance relationships.

1. Have you experienced or do you expect to experience a long-distance relationship because of the demands of your job or the job of a significant other?

2. If you have experienced one, describe what such a relationship feels like, how you adjust to it, and what you consider to be the greatest hurdles to overcome.

Gaining Communication Competence

Deciding How to Handle Closeness and Distance in Relationships

By now it should be apparent that negotiating the amount of closeness or distance in a relationship is not a simple matter. By considering the following questions you will be better able to select the level of closeness that's appropriate for you.

How Important Is the Other Person to You?

We tend to want to get closer to and share more about ourselves with those whose friendship or romantic involvement is important to us. One measure of how important an individual is in your life is the extent to which you are willing to invest time, effort, and energy to build and maintain your relationship with him or her.

Do You Create a Climate That Fosters Information Seeking and Giving?

No matter how interested you are in another person or he or she is in you, you stand little chance of developing a meaningful relationship unless you begin to communicate with each other. If either of you hesitates or for some reason is unable to initiate contact, you are less likely to construct the foundation necessary for an effective relationship. Thus, it is necessary to use appropriate conversation openers that make the following situation unlikely:

> *I decided to marry her. Courtship would be a mere formality. But what to say to begin the courtship? "Would you like some of my gum?" sounded too low-class. "Hello," was too trite a greeting for my future bride. "I love you! I am hot with passion!" was too forward. "I want to make you the mother of my children," seemed a bit premature.*
>
> *Nothing. That's right. I said nothing. And after a while, the bus reached her stop, she got off, and I never saw her again.*
> *End of story.*[51]

How Much and What Kind of Intimacy Do You Want?

Many of us hope to realize emotional closeness with our friends and lovers. We expect to reveal our inner selves and hope that they will reciprocate. The ways in which we express intimacy, however, depend on our background. Some of us will build intimacy through expressive disclosure talk, while others will build it instrumentally by participating in activities together and by being there and doing things for one another.

How Accepting Are You of the Other Person?

To what degree are you able to accept the other person for who he or she is and what he or she represents, or do you feel that in order for you to accept him or her, the other person must change? With our friends and lovers, we should feel that we can be ourselves, that we do not need to dissemble or put on a false front, and that we can reveal our feelings without having them or ourselves rejected.

In What Ways Are You Willing to Support the Other Person?

Support is a basic expectation of most relationships based on friendship or love.[52] We show support in different ways: by listening, talking through problems, empathizing, or being there in times of need or even when we disagree.

Do You Recognize That Relationship Will Change?

Changes in relationships are natural and a continuous part of the life cycle. Our relationships are constantly evolving and dynamic. The relational changes we experience may upset us, thrill us, or challenge us. We may welcome them or curse them, feel delighted or disoriented by them. But they will continue to happen. The people whose lives we touch, and vice versa, will influence us and change us in ways we cannot predict. The relationship choices we make, and whether we manage or mismanage them (expecting instant gratification or having the patience necessary for a meaningful relationship to grow) will affect and transform us as well as those with whom we have contact in the future.

Would Your Relationship Survive the Distance Test?

While we are likely to remain close to those people we see regularly, what do you imagine would happen to your friendships and romantic relationships if you had to move to a different part of the country or the world? Which of your relationships do you think would survive the test of distance? What specific steps would you take to secure closeness and to ensure the relationship's maintenance? How would you keep your lives interwoven?

Do You Know When to End a Relationship?

Not every relationship should be sustained or maintained. When a relationship is destructive, deteriorates into verbal or physical violence, or drains our energy and our self-confidence, we need to end it before it does irreparable harm. However, there are some relationships that we do not want to end, such as family relationships. In these cases, we may need to seek professional help.

daily contacts

Wrap-Up

Meet again in pairs or small groups. Turn back to the case study at the beginning of the chapter and reconsider the questions that follow it. How have your answers changed or become more focused? Based on your knowledge of intimacy and distance in relationships, what advice would you give Samantha now?

Critical Thinking Contacts

Examine the following cartoon. Based on your understanding of relationship flux, what advice can you offer the two characters regarding the life of a relationship?

"You can't leave. Your role in this relationship is pivotal."

Summary

Self-disclosure is the term used to refer to willingly telling people things about ourselves that they would not otherwise know. How much you reveal about yourself to another is a measure of closeness, or intimacy, in a relationship.

Each of our relationships involves a different amount of intimacy and distance. In fact, every relationship we share can be described in terms of its breadth (the number of topics we talk about) and its depth (how central the discussed topics are to our self-concept and how much we reveal about ourselves during our conversations). According to social penetration theory, most of our relationships begin with relatively narrow breadth and shallow depth. As the relationships grow and increase in strength, however, both breadth and depth increase also.

The Johari window is a model to explore the nature of our relationships with other people. Our relationships with others are characterized by the amount and kind of intimacy or closeness we share. Although closeness is limited in acquaintanceships, it intensifies in friendships and becomes most pronounced in love-based relationships.

Unfortunately, not all of our relationships are characterized by the presence of healthy patterns of communication. The use of toxic communication is common in dysfunctional relationships, which are also noted for the use of verbal or physical abuse.

While some relationships we want to end, others end not because we want them to but because of the death of a loved one. When this happens we need to take steps to work through and recover from grief.

While some relational forces pull us toward intimacy, others pull us in the opposite direction. Relational dialectics explores the dynamic nature of relational ties and tugs such as integration–separation, stability–change, and expression–privacy, tensions that we need to resolve. Sometimes, if we cannot renegotiate a relationship satisfactorily, we need to dissolve it.

Long-distance relationships are on the rise. Though advances in technology continue to make it easier for us to sustain such relationships, they still require extensive commitments from both partners to survive.

Both gender and culture influence the expression of intimacy and distance in relationships. Sensitizing ourselves to these differences can facilitate interactions between both men and women and people from diverse backgrounds.

Learning how to handle closeness and distance in our relationships is not a simple task, but by asking and answering a series of questions, we can begin to identify what we need to do to secure closeness.

Terms to Talk About

self-disclosure *(p. 395)*

intimacy *(p. 395)*

norm of reciprocity *(p. 395)*

relationship breadth *(p. 396)*

relationship depth *(p. 396)*

social penetration theory *(p. 396)*

Johari window *(p. 398)*

relationship maintenance *(p. 402)*

metacommunication *(p. 403)*

equity theory *(p. 403)*

dysfunctional *(p. 404)*

toxic communication *(p. 404)*

grief process *(p. 406)*

relational dialectics *(p. 407)*

relationship repair *(p. 410)*

confirming messages *(p. 410)*

disconfirming messages *(p. 411)*

long-distance relationships *(p. 414)*

Suggestions for Further Reading

Steve Duck, *Human Relationships,* 2nd ed., Newbury Park, CA: Sage, 1992. An excellent overview of personal relationships.

B. Aubrey Fisher and Katherine L. Adams, *Interpersonal Communication: Pragmatics of Human Relationships,* New York: McGraw-Hill, Inc., 1994. Focuses on patterns of interaction that define our relationships and bind individuals together.

L. Edna Rogers and Valentin Escudero, eds., *Relational Communication,* Mahwah, NJ: Lawrence Erlbaum, 2004. Offers a step-by-step guide to studying relationships from a cross-cultural perspective.

Brian Spitzberg and William Cupech, eds., *The Dark Side of Close Relationships,* Hillsdale, NJ: Lawrence Erlbaum, 1998. An investigation of physical and psychological abuse and other messages that hurt. A followup to *The Dark Side of Interpersonal Communications.*

Julia T. Wood, *Relational Communication: Continuity and Change in Personal Relationships,* Belmont, CA: Wadsworth, 1995. Focuses on the exploration of intimate personal relationships, including how current social trends influence their development, maintenance, and chances for survival.

Relationships in Our Lives: Exploring Family-, Work-, and Health-Related Concerns

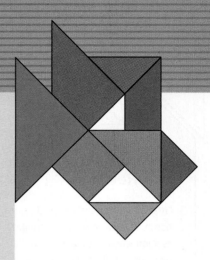

They always say that time changes things, but you actually have to change them yourself.

— Andy Warhol

After completing this chapter, you should be able to:

❚ Compare and contrast definitions of family and family types.

❚ Compare and contrast problematic/unhealthy and productive/nurturing patterns of family communication, organizational communication, and health communication.

❚ Explain the types of relationships shared by family members, subordinates and superiors at work, and health practitioners and patients.

❚ Discuss how stereotypical views of gender influence communication in the family, at work, and in health care settings.

❚ Give examples of the ways in which the media and technology influence family, job, and health communication.

❚ Identify steps you can take to improve communication in your family, on the job, and in health care settings.

daily
contacts

The Reunion

"It seemed like such a good idea!" Jade moaned to her husband, Dominic. "I thought hosting a family reunion would be such fun and succeed in getting all of us together. Now I just want to call the whole thing off!"

Jade and her husband both worked full-time jobs. Taking their two kids, ages 6 and 10, to school and an array of weekend activities, juggling sitters, and—since they lived the closest—serving as caregivers for an ailing grandparent (taking him to and from doctor visits), plus a host of other responsibilities, made it difficult for them to stay in touch with all the members of their respective families. They saw their siblings, parents, aunts and uncles, and assorted others far less frequently than they had expected they would when they married fifteen years ago. A family reunion seemed like the perfect solution. So Jade had sat at her computer and dashed off invitations.

As soon as invitations were mailed and delivered, their phone began to ring. From questions about the date and the food she would serve to requests for transportation, from inquiries regarding who else was invited to complaints about who should not

have been invited, it seemed that everyone had a different agenda.

No one had told Dominic's parents in advance about the reunion, so they had already planned a vacation cruise. Uncle Fred called to ask if cousin Jennifer was invited, because if she was, he would not attend—they were no longer on speaking terms. Cousins Olivia and Jason were going to be on a business trip. Nieces Jana and Keri and nephews Elijah and Connor were committed to playing in assorted Little League and soccer games. Jade's mother would not come if it meant having to stay overnight at Jade's home. Aunt Tessie would love to come, but she was under a doctor's care and needed someone to fly down and escort her to the reunion.

Jade and Dominic were ready to cancel the reunion when their children started whining that they wanted to have a party.

Divide into pairs or small groups and consider these questions:

1. What advice would you give Jade and Dominic?
2. Have you or someone you know been in a similar situation? How was it resolved?
3. What kinds of attitudes or behavioral orientations would turn this experience into a positive one?

Family, work, and health care settings are three communication contexts in which many of our most important interactions occur. How we interact with others and the kinds of relationships we share in each of these settings influence our personal, economic, mental, and physical wellbeing. What happens in our family, on the job, and with health providers affects our sense of self, influences the kind of interpersonal communicator we are likely to become, and determines how comfortable we are as communicators and whether we feel prepared to meet the daily challenges that life presents us as interpersonal communicators.

Let us begin by exploring how the family influences interpersonal interaction. After all, much of what we know about communication we initially learned from our family. Whatever kind of training took place is reflected in the ways we relate to others both at work and play. From our family we learn family functions, effective and ineffective communication patterns, and roles and responsibilities. It is in the family that we first learn how to create, maintain, and end relationships; how to express ourselves; how to argue; how to display affection; how to choose acceptable topics for mixed company; how work affects home life; how to cope with illness; and more. What it means to be a member of a family and how our family affects our interpersonal health and relationships expectations are important questions to consider.

.. *Theory*

Considering Characteristics

Every member of our family affects us differently.

1. Identify the members of your immediate family.

2. Use a series of words and images to describe each family member. For example, you might use *wired*, *tight*, and *frenetic* to describe a sibling and choose a jack-in-the-box to represent your image of him or her.

3. Provide an example that illustrates how, to some extent, each member of your family affects the ways you currently relate to other people.

The Nature of Familial Communication

How do you define "family"? Researchers in family communication define a family in several ways. The following are samples:

Networks of people who share their lives over long periods of time; who are bound by ties of marriage, blood, or commitment, legal or otherwise; who consider themselves as family; and who share a significant history and anticipated future of functioning in a family relationship.[1]

An organized, relational transaction group, usually occupying a common living space over an extended time period, and possessing a confluence of interpersonal images that evolve through the exchange of meaning over time.[2]

A group of intimates, who generate a sense of home and group identity, complete with strong ties of loyalty and emotion, and an experience of a history and a future.[3]

A group of two or more individuals who are perceived as interdependent based on blood connections, legal bonds, and/or explicit verbal commitments.[4]

What is your definition of family? Compare and contrast it with those given here.

Some define family narrowly, while others define it more broadly. We think family should be defined in terms of what it means to individuals. Thus, when you list the members of your family, in many ways you are revealing what family means to

Peanuts reprinted by permission of United Feature Syndicate, Inc.

As the developmental stage of a family changes, persons who were once advice givers may find they have become advice takers.

How would you describe your own family?

you.[5] Definitions of family need to be flexible and reflective of the diverse forms of contemporary families that currently exist in society.

For many of us the concept of family brings to mind a picture of a traditional **nuclear family,** one that includes a mother (a wife), a father (a husband), and one or more children. At times we might also include brothers and sisters, grandparents, aunts and uncles, in-laws, and nieces and nephews. However, there are other types of families today. Among these are **blended families,** which include two adults—gay, lesbian, or heterosexual—and children (biological or adopted) from one or both of the adults' previous marriages, as well as perhaps more from the current marriage; **single-parent families,** in which the mother or father who was formerly married, divorced, or never married is solely responsible for a biological or adopted child; childless couples, persons of the same or different sex who have made some type of publicly recognized commitment to each other, either through marriage or through a commitment ceremony; **live-in couples,** in which different or same-sex individuals live together with or without their own or adopted children and cohabit as if they were married; **integrated families,** in which the parents (different or same sex) or the children (biological or adopted) are of different races or religions; **boomerang families,** families containing adult children who the family thought had left permanently but unexpectedly return home; and extended families, groups of relatives—such as aunts, uncles, cousins, or grandparents—who share blood, legal, or surrogate ties and are considered part of the family unit.

These categories are neither exhaustive nor unchangeable. New family forms such as **commuter families,** those families composed of one or more members who commute from a primary residence to a work location in a distant city and remain there for a period of time, continue to emerge. Actually, as long as we are legally or emotionally connected to one or more people, we may consider ourselves part of a family.

The Family as Communication System

It is virtually impossible to assign a beginning or an end to communicative exchanges between family members; although every family member interprets experience on the basis of his or her point of view or personal perspective, in actuality these points are considered in process and are continually changing or evolving.[6] Family members are actively engaged in the continuous give-and-take of person-to-person interaction. As a result, the family provides us with a unique context for the study of communication.

There is a dynamic interplay between the two or more individuals that compose a family when they communicate with each other. Thus, according to **systems theory,** family members' behavior can be understood only in relation to each other and to the functioning of the family as a whole.[7] In other words, *every member of a family is interdependent with other members of the family.* The behavior of one family member affects the behavior of every other family member, both in and out of the family setting. Consequently, *the verbal and nonverbal actions of one family member cannot be fully understood in isolation from those of other family members.* (See also the discussion of Watzlawick's axioms of communication in Chapter 1.)

To fully grasp the concept of interdependence, picture family members connected to each other by pieces of rope. As one member moves, his or her movement tugs on or affects other members. Sometimes family members tie each other up in knots; other times they try to pull away from each other; while still other times they give each other enough rope to experience the freedom necessary for personal growth.

No family member's actions occur in a vacuum. When one member of a family acts out, all have to adjust to the behavior; any change in one part of the family system compels the entire system to adapt. Each family member can keep the system operating as it is or cause it to revise its ways of dealing with situations including the new and different. Any change in the family precipitates change in all its members, and change in any one member precipitates change in the family.

Describe an incident that illustrates how the behavior of one family member influenced the behaviors of other family members.

professional
contacts

Peoplemaking

Virginia Satir is a family therapist and the author of *Peoplemaking* and *The New Peoplemaking*. In the following excerpt from the latter book, she shares her thoughts about the nature of "family." After you read her comments and consider the questions she poses, ask yourself to what extent, if any, you would like to change the nature of your family.

> When I was five, I decided that when I grew up I'd be a "children's detective on parents." I didn't quite know what I would look for, but I realized a lot went on in families that didn't meet the eye. There were a lot of puzzles I did not know how to understand.
>
> Now, many years later, after working with some thousands of families, I find there are still a lot of puzzles

I have learned from my work, and learning opens up new possibilities and new directions for discovery. It is now clear to me that the family is a microcosm of the world. To understand the world, we can study the family: issues such as power, intimacy, autonomy, trust, and communication skills are vital parts underlying how we live in the world. To change the world is to change the family. . . .

> Does it feel good to you to live with your family right now? . . .
>
> Do you feel you are living with friends, people you like and trust, and who like and trust you? . . .
>
> Is it fun and exciting to be a member of your family?

SOURCE: Reprinted by permission of the author and publisher: *New Peoplemaking*, Virginia Satir. Science & Behavior Books, Inc. 800.547.9982.

Recall from Chapter 1 that the principle of *nonsummativity* tells us that *the whole is greater than the sum of its parts.* Summing up the characteristics of individual family members does not allow us to understand the family. We need, instead, to attend to how family members function as a whole, the ways in which they are connected to one another, and the patterns of interaction they exhibit. By becoming more aware of the family system, and discovering their part in it, including who they are and the connections between themselves and other elements in the system, family members open the way to talking about their respective perceptions and any desire they have to reshape either the roles family members assume or their family's interaction patterns. Families are complex and constantly in flux. Thus, *family systems need to be adaptive.* Because they are made up of people, and people change as they grow and age, families are continually involved in dealing with change, processing new information, negotiating meaning, meeting the needs of individual members, and adapting to transitions while attempting to maintain a sense of stability and a balanced state that facilitates the maintenance of the family system itself. This is not easy. Change frequently leads to unresolved feelings, stress, and conflict. Families' attempts to meet such challenges and to realize their goals reveals much about how they communicate. The systems process of *equifinality,* which asserts that initial inputs of a system don't determine outputs, reminds us that different families may reach similar goals using different pathways.[8]

Families are engaged in the complex process of *mutual influence.* As family members decode, create, and share meaning, they interact with each other and

To what extent, if any, has a deceased family member influenced your family?

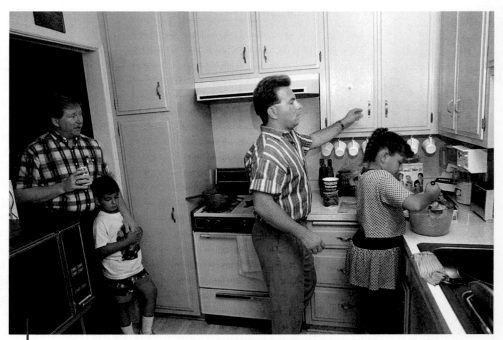

Researchers are broadening the definition of family in order to reflect the wide range of relationships people include as family today.

work out the nature of their relationships. (Every member of a family, whether dead or alive, has the ability to influence the family.) Memories of deceased family members may play as great a role as present family members do in the here and now of family life because all members of a family are interconnected.

After exploring the process of family communication and practicing effective communication skills, you should become better able to increase the satisfaction you derive from communicating with the members of your own family. It is through interpersonal communication that we exhibit our understanding of or frustration with family members; help resolve or elevate family conflicts; establish more intimate or autonomous relationships; handle differences in power; and cope with change, stress, and decision making.[9]

Communication Functions and Dysfunctions: A Look at Family Communication Rules

Whatever the nature of the basic family unit, each family has characteristics that define its nature. Let's consider them.

Family Members Perform Roles

The members of a family are expected to play certain roles in relation to each other and to the family as a whole. A role is a term that describes a set of prescribed behaviors. Among the roles family members perform are wage earner, homemaker, financial manager, child-care provider, social planner, and so on. In some families these roles are shared; in others, each is the primary responsibility of a single family member. Whereas some families exhibit significant role versatility and turn-taking in role performance, other families adhere more strictly to more traditional or stereotypical role definitions. The family system itself sustains

in Practice

Role-Call

Which of the following roles do you perform in your family?

1. Indicate your answers with an X.

   ___ wage earner
   ___ housekeeper
   ___ cook
   ___ wife/husband
   ___ mother/father
   ___ son/daughter
   ___ sister/brother
   ___ conflict mediator
   ___ limit tester
   ___ child-care provider
   ___ elder-care provider
   ___ achiever
   ___ clown/tension reliever

2. List any others not identified above:

   _____

3. Do you share any roles? Do family members take turns performing some roles?

the roles that family members play. In modern families, family members are expected to play an increasing number of roles, a demand that may result in increased stress.

In healthy families the role relationships of family members are not static, but constantly change as family members grow and develop and enter different life stages. As the developmental stage of a family changes, different family members may perform different roles. For example, some family members may assume more responsibility while others assume less. Family members who used to be advice givers may become the advice takers, and vice versa. The late essayist and humorist Erma Bombeck referred to this switch in roles and power in an essay titled "When Did I Become the Mother, and the Mother Become the Child?"

> *When will the baby catch up with the mother?*
> *When indeed.*
> *Does it begin one night when you are asleep and your mother is having a restless night and you go into her room and tuck the blanket around her bare arms?*
> *Does it appear one afternoon when, in a moment of irritation, you snap, "How can I give you a home permanent if you won't sit still? If you don't care how you look, I do!" (My God, is that an echo?)*
> *Or did it come the rainy afternoon when you were driving home from the store and you slammed on your brakes and your arms sprang protectively between her and the windshield and your eyes met with a knowing, sad look?*
> *The transition comes slowly, as it began between her and her mother. The changing of power. The transferring of responsibility. The passing down of duty. Suddenly you are spewing out the familiar phrases learned at the knee of your mother.*[10]

Consider these questions: What roles do you play in your family? Are you satisfied with them? Would you like to negotiate a different role for yourself? Why or why not?

Family Members Have Responsibilities

Family members have expectations for each other; the realization of such expectations increases family member satisfaction. For example, family members are expected to pull together to preserve the family unit and ensure its viability by helping each other survive everyday life and meeting each other's financial and emotional needs. All family members expect to receive emotional support from one another. We expect our family members to support us no matter what. To this end, we reserve time for each other and recognize the obligation we have to help other family members by offering them social support and doing whatever we can to help them deal with the realities of everyday life. What relational contributions do you make to the members of your family? What relational benefits do you derive from being a member of your family?

One of the challenges facing today's families is providing emotional support for parents who become dependent on their children. As Americans live longer, the parent–child relationship will endure for a very long time. Thus elder care, as a form of nurturance, is assuming as important a role in society as child care.[11] The sandwich generation is responsible for both simultaneously.

Family Members Share a Past, Present, and Future

Families evolve through time. Members share a history and the prospect of a future. Their past interactions, rituals, and celebrations pave the way for present exchanges and indicate the potential for mutually influential relationships to continue into the future. What changes have you perceived in your family? In your opinion, what can cause family relationships to thrive or break off?

Family Members Share Living Space

People who perceive themselves to be a family usually occupy the same living space. Thus, they have a need to adapt to each other's personalities, expectations, and interaction styles. How have you adapted to accommodate the members of your family? How have they adapted to accommodate you?

Families Have Rules

Implied or spoken understandings or *rules* guide communication within families. Through repeated exposure, we learn to recognize and internalize these rules just as we learn to recognize and internalize the rules of our culture.[12] Some rules are passed down through the generations; others are new and are negotiated directly by present-day family members.

The rules of a family help regulate family interaction and, among other things, let members know how family members divide tasks, who is in charge of what, who talks and listens to whom, when, where, why, and under what conditions. For example, which, if any, of the following rules were understood by the members of your family?

> Children should be seen but not heard.
> Children should speak only when spoken to.
> Don't talk about family matters outside the family.
> No arguing at the dinner table.
> Never go into Mom and Dad's room.
> Don't lie.
> Don't answer back when being disciplined.
> Never raise your voice when talking.
> Don't show when you've been hurt.
> Don't express fear.
> Don't ask for attention or affection.
> Don't ask for the car when Dad's in a bad mood.
> Don't interrupt a parent when he or she is speaking.

Identify five rules that guide communication within your family. How happy are you with them? Which, if any, would you like to change?

Through sustained interaction, we develop expectations regarding how family members behave in relation to each other and to us. Understanding these rules and their effects leads us to understand whether we and other members of our family communicate as effectively as we could with each other, and what rules, if any, we would like to renegotiate to improve family communication. To survive in most families you need either to follow or to successfully renegotiate the rules that prescribe and limit family members' behavior.

literary
contacts

"Growing Up"; "To a Daughter Leaving Home"

In the first selection, "Growing Up," author Russell Baker describes his relationship with his aging mother. As you read the piece, notice how the son's perceptions of his aging mother influence the way he interacts with her and chooses to remember her. Then consider this question: What means has the son devised to cope with impending and significant family changes?

In the second selection, "To a Daughter Leaving Home," author Linda Pastan reverses roles and offers us a mother's perception of a growing child. In your opinion, what do the two selections have in common? What do they tell us about each subject's view of family?

Growing Up
Russell Baker

At the age of eighty my mother had her last bad fall, and after that her mind wandered free through time. Some days she went to weddings and funerals that had taken place half a century earlier. On others she presided over family dinners cooked on Sunday afternoons for children who were now gray with age. Through all this she lay in bed but moved across time, traveling among the dead decades with a speed and ease beyond the gift of physical science.

"Where's Russell?" she asked one day when I came to visit at the nursing home.

"I'm Russell," I said.

She gazed at this improbably overgrown figure out of an inconceivable future and promptly dismissed it.

"Russell's only this big," she said, holding her hand, palm down, two feet from the floor. That day she was a young country wife with chickens in the backyard and a view of hazy blue Virginia mountains behind the apple orchard, and I was a stranger old enough to be her father.

Early one morning she phoned me in New York. "Are you coming to my funeral today?" she asked.

It was an awkward question with which to be awakened. "What are you talking about, for God's sake?" was the best reply I could manage.

"I'm being buried today," she declared briskly, as though announcing an important social event.

"I'll phone you back," I said and hung up, and when I did phone back she was all right, although she wasn't all right, of course, and we all knew she wasn't.

She had always been a small woman—short, light-boned, delicately structured—but now, under the white hospital sheet, she was becoming tiny. I thought of a doll with huge, fierce eyes. There had always been a fierceness in her. It showed in that angry, challenging thrust of the chin when she issued an opinion, and a great one she had always been for issuing opinions.

"I tell people exactly what's on my mind," she had been fond of boasting. "I tell them what I think, whether they like it or not." Often they had not liked it. She could be sarcastic to people in whom she detected evidence of the ignoramus or the fool.

"It's not always good policy to tell people exactly what's on your mind," I used to caution her.

"If they don't like it, that's too bad," was her customary reply, "because that's the way I am."

And so she was. A formidable woman. Determined to speak her mind, determined to have her way, determined to best those who opposed her. In that time when I had known her best, my mother had hurled herself at life with chin thrust forward, eyes blazing, and an energy that made her seem always on the run.

To a Daughter Leaving Home
Linda Pastan

When I taught you
at eight to ride
a bicycle, loping along
beside you
as you wobbled away
on two round wheels,
my own mouth rounding
in surprise when you pulled
ahead down the curved
path of the park,

*I kept waiting
for the thud
of your crash as I
sprinted to catch up,
while you grew
smaller, more breakable
with distance,
pumping, pumping
for your life, screaming
with laughter,*

*the hair flapping
behind you like a
handkerchief waving
goodbye.*

SOURCES: From *Growing Up* by Russell Baker, pp. 1–2. Reprinted by permission of Don Congdon Associates, Inc. Copyright © 1982 by Russell Baker; "To a Daughter Leaving Home," from *The Imperfect Paradise* by Linda Pastan. Copyright © 1988 by Linda Pastan. Used by permission of W. W. Norton & Company, Inc.

Communication Patterns

Families evolve habitual patterns of communication. Some patterns facilitate effective interaction between family members and others impede such interaction from developing.

Problematic Family Communication Patterns

The rules of some families are too restrictive or limiting to be healthy. The term used to describe a family with a problematic communication pattern is **dysfunctional**. When a family's rules prohibit a member from adequately expressing certain feelings or needs, they also prevent

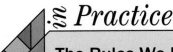 *in* Practice

The Rules We Live By

Individually interview every member of your immediate family, if possible, asking the following questions:

1. What are the rules that guide our life as a family?
2. Where did the rules come from?
3. What are your feelings about these rules?
4. What new rules would improve the balance or operation of our family?

Once the interviews are complete, identify those rules that were agreed on by all, and those rules that at least one family member thought unfair or in need of revision.

him or her from sharing important aspects of him- or herself. Inhibiting individuals can be emotionally devastating and may harm them in ways that will not become apparent for years.[13] For example, if every time we bring a problem to a parent he or she explodes with rage, we soon learn not to bring him or her our problems. We also learn an improper use of anger.

In addition, some families suffer from frequent episodes of *communication confusion* or chaos. Instead of supporting each other, family members continually crash into each other. Instead of exhibiting family cohesion and pulling together emotionally, they appear to be coming unglued or emotionally torn. The communication characteristics of dysfunctional families enable at least one family member to systematically inflict pain on or denigrate one or more other members.

.² *Theory*

Dysfunctional Communication

The following excerpt is from an article that appeared some years ago in the *New York Times*. Although it is an extreme example of dysfunctional family communication, it shows how an inability to communicate effectively can precipitate troubled relationships.

Linda failed to return home from a dance Friday night. On Saturday she admitted she had spent the night with an Air Force lieutenant. The Pratts decided on a punishment that would "wake Linda up." They ordered her to shoot the dog she had owned about two years. On Sunday, the Pratts

and Linda took the dog into the desert near their home. They had the girl dig a shallow grave. Then Mrs. Pratt grasped the dog between her hands and Mr. Pratt gave his daughter a .22 caliber pistol and told her to shoot the dog. Instead, the girl put the pistol to her right temple and shot herself. The police said there were no charges that could be filed against the parents except possibly cruelty to animals.

1. What communication problems does this story illustrate?

2. How might such a family tragedy have been avoided?

Using the print and broadcast news media as sources, provide an example of dysfunctional family communication.

Among the harmful messages communicated are physical, sexual, or emotional abuse; messages of worthlessness, intimidation, and manipulation; or the belief that one person has a right to use any and all compliance-gaining or power strategies to fully control the behavior of another. The targets of problematic or dysfunctional communication often blame themselves for precipitating such behavior in the first place. As a result of their labeling themselves inadequate and believing they are powerless to control their lives, they frequently do not possess the inner strength or self-confidence to counter the abuse they receive.

The behaviors of family members contain clues regarding family system issues and underlying family problems. To operate successfully as part of a family we need to take steps to ensure that the costs of family life for its members do not exceed its rewards. Parents and children who are insensitive to each other's needs often take increasingly dangerous steps to maintain their delicate sense of balance and assert control. This can lead to destructive, self-defeating behavior on both sides, behavior that demonstrates little, if any, concern how it will affect family members. When we lack interpersonal sensitivity and fail to consider the feelings and needs of those with whom we live, our relationships suffer and deteriorate.

Productive Family Communication Patterns

The promotion of more **productive** or **healthy family communication patterns** occurs in families in which members have the freedom to express their feelings. The members of such families are:

1. able to offer emotional and physical support to each other,

2. comfortable revealing their feelings and thoughts to each other,

3. confident about the family's ability to meet each member's needs, and

4. flexible and open enough to adapt and respond to situations that produce conflict or unexpected change.

Communication is the greatest single factor that determines the health of family members and how they will interact.[14] Families whose members communicate effectively are healthy and are also more adaptable to changes in the family's power structure, role relationships, and rules.[15] They also are more willing to negotiate seemingly incompatible goals.

Observe and Map Your Family Network

Family therapist Virginia Satir suggests that we can learn a lot about how our family communicates by drawing a map of our **family network**.[16]

1. One family member should tack a large sheet of paper to the wall where all can see it clearly.

2. Family members begin the family map by drawing a circle for each person who is a part of it, using a felt-tipped pen. If the family currently includes a grandparent or other person as part of the household, a circle is added for that person on the row with the other adults. If someone was a part of the family but is now gone, that person is represented with a filled-in circle.

3. To show how the members of the family are connected, lines are drawn between the different pairs or roles. For example, a family may have marital pairs, parent–child pairs, or sibling pairs (see Figure 14.1).

4. Identify what each role means to each family member.

5. Family members compare and contrast how close family member role definitions or views of prospective roles are. After sharing their ideas with each other, family members may develop new understanding about the members of their family and the relationships they share.

6. Family members add network lines to the map by linking every family member with every other family member. As the lines are drawn, each individual needs to think about the particular relationship he or she has with each other member of the family; in other words, each person needs to describe how he or she feels about each connection.

The lines reveal that in families of more than two people, we do not live in pairs; we live in triangles. As Satir explains:

> *A triangle is always a pair plus one and, since only two people can relate at one time, someone in the triangle is always the odd one out. . . . The odd person in a triangle always has a choice between breaking up the relationship between the other two, withdrawing from it, or supporting it by being an interested observer. The odd person's choice is crucial to the functioning of the whole family network."*[17]

Consider how a triangle looks from the point of view of each family member. To be sure, family living is a complicated affair, and every family develops its own patterns.

In more nurturing families, these relationships and the perceptions of family members are available and open to discussion by everyone. In less nurturing families, family members are unaware of these networks and their effects, and are

FIGURE 14.1
The Family Network: How Families Are Connected

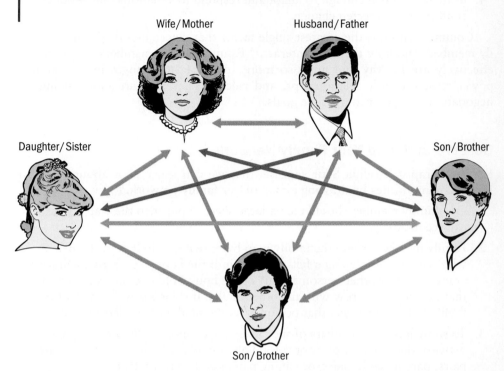

SOURCE: Reprinted by permission of the author and publisher: *New Peoplemaking,* Virginia Satir. Science & Behavior Books, Inc. 800.547.9982.

either unwilling or unable to discuss them. By discussing connections, however, the family unit can develop the insights needed to function more effectively.

Diversity and the Family

Although the concept of family is universal, the nature of families is not. Because culture shapes families, family means different things to different people.

> *Families do not develop their rules, beliefs, and rituals in a vacuum. What you think, how you act, even your language, are all transmitted through the family from the wider cultural context. This context includes the culture in which you live, and those from which your ancestors have come.*[18]

Varying Family Composition

One group or culture's definition of the family should be no more correct or acceptable than another's—except, of course, to the specific group or culture itself. In many cultures the extended family is the norm. For example, in Mexico it is common for grandparents to live with the family, not in a retirement development. In the United States, the nuclear family was viewed as the ideal for quite a long time. Recently, however, population statistics have revealed significant changes. The chances are now better than 50-50 that rather than living as part of a nuclear family, U.S. citizens may find themselves living alone, being divorced, or being a stepparent.

Varying Communication Styles

It is important to acknowledge that families from diverse cultures produce children with communication styles and beliefs that may be different from yours. Family life differs among cultural groups. Thus, members of different cultures often differ regarding the extent to which they believe in extended families, practice traditional sex roles, tolerate uncertainty and change, share or disclose their feelings and affections, retain individual identities, enjoy personal space and privacy, seek to avoid or confront conflict, and assert individual rights.[19]

Describe the extent to which your cultural background has influenced your communication style and beliefs about family life.

For example, Mexicans provide family members with a very supportive environment; Mexican children need not be terribly self-reliant to survive. Whereas children in the United States are taught that they will achieve because of individual ability or initiative, Mexicans believe they will achieve because of the family.[20]

Varying Family Roles

Some families are more position-oriented than they are person-oriented, and vice versa. In **position-oriented families,** family roles are more rigidly related to sex and age than they are in person-oriented families. **Person-oriented families** nurture flexible family roles—preferring to match a role with an individual's comfort level and needs rather than with his or her family position. In some cultures, the sex of the parent determines who will be in charge and possess the authority and power to influence the other members of the family.

In significant ways, the family influences perception and communication. Chinese children are taught to respect and feel a lifelong obligation to their parents. The Chinese proverb "To forget one's ancestors is to be a brook without a source, a tree without a root," reflects this belief. In other cultures, such as India, it is common for males to be perceived as the superior sex, for men and women to eat separately, or for the women to eat after the men have finished. In Indian culture, boys are given significantly more freedom of expression than are girls.[21] In cultures such as in Japan, China, and Korea, the father is the ultimate authority, and other family members are subservient to him, while the nurturing and caregiving are provided by the mother.

The experiences that one person had in his or her family may be very different from those of another. As a result, when two people from different families decide to create a new family of their own, they may possess different value systems, role definitions, and rule definitions. Unless we talk about our differences and reveal our expectations to each other, we will fail to clarify and check assumptions, clash regarding the roles we ought to take and the responsibilities we ought to fulfill, be unable to negotiate the differences between us, and, more than likely, fail to meet many of the challenges of family communication.

Gender and the Family

The family is an important source of our attitudes regarding gender and what it means to be male or female. Different families deal with such issues as gender identity and male and female authority and power in different ways. Through both overt and unconscious communication, families contribute to the **role assignments** we make for males and females. Consider your own family for a moment. To what extent do the notions it espouses regarding household roles, occupational choices, areas of responsibility, sources of emotional support, and the ways males and females should interact with sons and daughters and with each other reveal its feelings concerning gender issues?

in Context

Gender Role Assignments

Consider who held or holds the primary responsibility for wage earning, household, and other family tasks in your family.

1. In the column preceding the function below, indicate whether the primary responsibility for each of the identified activities belonged to a male, a female, or was shared in your family.

2. Now consider your current feelings about whether you believe primary responsibility for each of the identified activities should belong to a male or a female or should be shared by both. Indicate your responses in the second column.

Your family   Your current feeling

_____ a. cooking   _____

_____ b. cleaning   _____

_____ c. paying bills   _____

_____ d. making investments   _____

_____ e. decorating   _____

_____ f. arranging/providing   _____
      child care

_____ g. buying/maintaining   _____
      a car

_____ h. maintaining and   _____
      repairing the home

_____ i. planning the   _____
      social calendar

_____ j. making travel plans   _____

How many members of the family are wage earners? To what extent, if any, does a family member's wage earning level affect which other responsibilities he or she is expected to perform? Discuss your answers.

Families serve five functions that require the performance of specific family roles:

1. the provision of basic resources such as food, clothing, and money;

2. the provision of nurturance and support;

3. the meeting of sexual needs;

4. personal and social development; and

5. the maintenance and management of the family unit itself, including decision making.

Identify who in your family performs each role identified here. How happy are you with your role assignments?

While men traditionally were given primary responsibility for providing the financial needs of the family, today many women contribute to the fulfillment of this role. Similarly, while women have traditionally been more likely than men to provide comfort, care, and warmth for family members, today many men share this responsibility. Despite this trend, research reveals that women still devote significantly more time to housework and child care than do men.[22] In any case, the role expectations your parents and other family members held for you, the kinds of activities they encouraged you to engage in, and the kind of emotional behaviors they expected you either to exhibit or refrain from displaying influenced your personal perception of what is and is not appropriate.

In what ways has your family influenced your perceptions of male and female roles and male and female strengths?

In addition to the role assignments, communication from parents also reflects *gender expectations* by reinforcing cooperation, helpfulness, and nurturance in girls, and competition, independence, industriousness, and assertiveness in boys.[23] Thus, parents often treat boys more roughly and urge them to be aggressive while they treat girls more gently and urge them to be more emotional but more physically reserved. Families that observe traditional sex-role behaviors are more apt to develop children who stereotype the sexes than are families who urge less traditional sex-role behaviors, and who thereby encourage their children to exhibit a broader view of sex roles and a broader communication repertoire.[24] Indeed, families that require women to relegate themselves to expressive social-emotional roles and men to instrumental task roles may end up reducing the economic and decision-making power of women in the family and may make it more difficult for men to establish truly intimate relationships by compelling them to be too emotionally distant.

Parents communicate their gender expectations to their children in the way they relate to them, the clothes and toys they buy, the chores they assign them, and the way they speak to them. For example, girls are often assigned to help take care of and be responsible for *others,* whereas boys often find themselves assigned to take care of *things.*[25] Boys are often spoken to in a

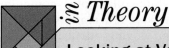

Theory

Looking at Values

Think about the ways U.S. society treats men and women differently.

1. Do you think U.S. society works harder to convince males of the importance of being masculine than it does to convince females of the importance of being feminine, or vice versa?

2. Does U.S. culture value masculinity more than femininity, or vice versa? Why do you think this is so?

more active manner, with the content focused around their activities, while girls are spoken to for longer periods of time and in softer tones, with the focus of the conversation on their thoughts and feelings.[26] In addition, boys are more rigidly socialized regarding the importance of being masculine than girls are regarding the importance of being feminine.

Of course, today multiple role demands are causing increasing numbers of men and women to share roles more than they characteristically did in years past. This is very likely a positive change. Sharing tasks correlates positively with increased disclosure and relationship maintenance.[27]

Media and Technology Contacts

It's Magic

What lessons do we derive from the media, particularly television situation comedies, concerning family communication? According to some researchers, the family is the primary consumer of television, and the images presented to us by television frequently offer distorted views of communication in the contemporary family; they may even contribute to our evaluating our own families as less positive, and ourselves as failed siblings, parents, children, or spouses because of the comparisons we make between us and the more idealistic **mediated images of family**.[28] For example, think of the members of your own family. How do you see each person? To what extent do those images compare favorably with the images of families projected by your favorite shows?

Though television presents us with a variety of family types today, this was not always the case. In years past, the predominant television family consisted of a legally married couple and their children. We had, for example, "The Adventures of Ozzie and Harriet," the Cleavers of "Leave It To Beaver," "The Donna Reed Show," and "The Dick Van Dyke Show." These TV families lived in spotless homes; the mothers packed lunches, the fathers worked in white-collar jobs; communication was, for the most part, conflict-free; there were few really serious problems; and the general image was of a stable, warm, loving family.[29] During the 1950s this model of working father, housewife mother, and two or more school-age children represented 60 percent of all families; according to more current statistics, it now represents a mere 7 percent.[30]

As the years passed, although we were still shown images of conventional families in such programs as "The Cosby Show" and "Family Ties," alternatives came from an increasing number of nonnuclear families. For example, we were offered shows featuring single parents, such as "One Day at a Time"; divorced parents, such as "Kate and Allie"; male caregivers, such as "My Two Dads"; integrated families, such as "Diff'rent Strokes"; and blended families, such as "Eight is Enough." Whatever the situation or conflict depicted in the program, however, invariably the problem was quickly resolved within its half-hour time slot—typically without disrupting family harmony. Rarely were we shown families with serious money problems, parents juggling two or more jobs to survive, or the child-care problems of dual-income families.

Although the trend of airing images of idyllic families with charming children and parents who had to face only minor problems or resolve only minor disputes persisted in the 1980s and 1990s, that time also provided us with shows that contrasted dramatically with such wholesome images. We saw working class families in which family life was radically deglamorized; in shows such as "Roseanne," "Married with Children," and "The Simpsons," family members are overworked, disagree, complain, speak disrespectfully to each other, lack social graces, have to cope with economic hard times, and are threatened by impending unemployment.[31] Finally, the twenty-first century saw shows like "Will and Grace" that featured a gay individual contemplating having children with a heterosexual woman; programs like "The Real World" that created artificial, temporary families composed of young people who were relationship-challenged, job-challenged and health-challenged; shows like "Six Feet Under" in which families worked out real life work, health, and relationship problems; and shows like "Sex and the City" in which women took health risks as they searched for the right man with whom to create a family. To what degree, if any, do media images of families influence the image of the kind of family you would like to be able to create, were you able to do so?

Practice

Spotlighting a TV Family

1. Watch a television sitcom that depicts a family. As you watch it, identify:
   - The members of the family, their roles and relationships to each other;
   - The factors that seem to hold the family together;
   - The subjects family members communicate about;
   - The nature of a conflict they experience; and
   - How the conflict is resolved.

2. Compare the television family to your own family. To what extent, if any, could the communication between members of the television family be improved? Based on your observation of the television family, fantasize a sitcom episode involving your own family.

3. What conclusions can you draw about the nature of communication in your own family?

The Importance of Interpersonal Communication at Work

Like the role it performs in families, interpersonal communication sustains our job relationships. Whether we occupy an entry-level position or function as CEO, our work-related activity depends on some form of interpersonal communication. How well we communicate with others at work can make the difference between career success and career failure. Because the need to communicate is central to all that we do, it should not come as a surprise that we communicate interpersonally with others every day on the job. In fact, it is difficult to imagine any work-related activity that does not depend on some form of interpersonal communication. Thus, in this chapter we will explore the role that interpersonal communication plays in the work world. We will look at the effects of different work environments and networks; the ways in which diversity, gender, the media, and technology influence interaction; leadership and management styles; the increasing use of work teams; and steps you can take to improve your on-the-job relationships.

Economic needs compel most of us to go to work every day. In fact, chances are that we will spend most of our adult lives working within or for some organization. What does it mean to be a member of an organization? How does the nature of the organization affect the way we relate to others? What are the most important skills we need to be successful on the job? Whether we are concerned about management–employee relations, conflict resolution, negotiating, problem solving, decision making, work-team participation, or leadership, good interpersonal communication skills are necessary. It takes the ability to communicate effectively with others to make our work experiences personally and professionally satisfying.[32] Though continued technological advancements have made obtaining and moving information faster than ever before, we have realized less progress toward greater understandability. Distortions in communication, misunderstandings, and shortcomings in corporate cultures precipitate numerous examples of missed opportunities for meaningful interaction. Yet today's typical executives and employees must spend much of the work day involved in face-to-face interactions. In fact, we could say that *relationships are the organization.*

To communicate effectively, we need to take the time to develop the skills that ensure that individuals in the organizations are able to work in **supportive**

Give an example of a missed opportunity for meaningful interaction that you personally observed or experienced.

The ability to communicate effectively with others enriches our work experiences.

environments, meaning those that build trust and maintain each person's sense of personal worth and importance. To this end, we need to develop patterns of communication that allow us to increase worker morale, improve job satisfaction, and enhance job performance. Determining why some organizations function well and "feel alive" while others "feel dead" may be as simple as identifying the kinds of interpersonal relationships and dynamic connectedness that the people who work in them have.[33]

Relationships Are the Organization

People who work in organizations share interdependent relationships with each other and with their setting. In effect, unless people interact, there is no organization.[34] Organizations whose members possess relationship savvy and are knowledgeable about how to build person-to-person relationships become better able to nurture both individual and organizational growth. Organizations that value employees who know how to listen and facilitate work groups recognize that these are among the talents needed to precipitate strong relationships. Rugged individualism no longer dominates the thinking of successful organizations; instead, team players are now what's important, indicating that more relationships are in store for us at work. Consequently, it is essential that we take the time to examine how a workplace organizes and energizes employee relationships.

> Very few ideas and very few projects of any significance are implemented by one person alone.
>
> —*Rosabeth Moss Kanter*

On-the-job satisfaction depends on the nature of the work relationships we share. What kind of relationships do you think the persons in this work group share?

The Quality of Relationships Influences Outcomes

Each individual who works in an organization is an important player. By participating in ongoing conversations with other employees, each one helps the organization grow.[35] It is up to us to ensure that we as individuals do not go off in different directions, but rather realize our potential to work together to develop meaningful partnerships with many others in our organization. Such behavior allows for the development of a more diverse pool of ideas from which the organization can draw. The more participants engage in the life of an organization, the smarter, or more effective, the organization becomes.[36] When we feel part of a **participative organization,** we perceive ourselves to have greater ownership of our work and, consequently, a greater emotional investment in it. We are also more apt to support the organization that we have helped create.

The Dyad and the Organization

As you saw in Chapter 1, the dyad, or two-person relationship, is the most basic level of interpersonal interaction. Numerous examples of dyadic communication occur daily in the organizational setting as, for example, we interact with our coworkers, superiors, and subordinates when we send and receive information. The relationship level is where most of the work of the organization gets done, and also is where most of the difficulties are encountered. Let's begin by exploring the nature of on-the-job relationships.

A Question of Dependence and Independence

In any organization we find work relationships in which some people are subordinates and other people are their superiors. A superior gives orders to another person and that person reports to him or her. A **subordinate** is someone who receives orders and reports to another person. Although superiors and subordinates depend on each other, people in the superior positions are usually able to exert varying degrees of control or power over those in the subordinate positions.

Superiors and subordinates spend much of their time interacting. When their interactions are perceived as supportive, open, and honest, subordinates tend to be more satisfied with their jobs. Another contributor to subordinate job satisfaction is the degree of *argumentativeness* present in the communication styles of superiors and subordinates. Argumentativeness is not a negative; rather, it is the tendency to recognize controversial issues in communication situations, to present and defend positions on the issues, and to question the positions others have taken.[37] When subordinates perceive their superiors to be high in argumentativeness and low in verbal aggressiveness (that is, they exhibit behavior that neither blames the subordinate nor denies him or her the right to disagree), they tend to exhibit higher levels of job satisfaction. Similarly, when superiors see the same traits in their subordinates, they tend to value them more. Thus, the nurturance of *independent-mindedness* (people are free to express their opinions and interests without denying those of others) appears to play an important role in the relational satisfaction of both superiors and subordinates.[38]

This is not to suggest that we don't want to work with people who see things the way we do. It is comfortable to work with those who share similar goals and values. As you learned in Chapter 12, the more alike two people are, the more likely they are to interact with each other. Yet to sustain relational satisfaction (having relationships meet our needs), we also need to be comfortable expressing differences. Thus, we also find it desirable to work with and for people who have a high tolerance for disagreement.[39]

A Question of Trust

When subordinates, superiors, and coworkers perceive an organization's climate as trusting and supportive, their relational satisfaction is generally good. In addition, the corporate culture of openness makes possible genuine expressions of ideas and feelings. In contrast, if an employee fears punishment for revealing his or her true feelings, he or she will tend to suppress them. Trust in one's superior and one's coworkers is the most important determinant of open communication. We are more likely to trust those people who are consistent in their behavior and who increase our own feelings of security.

Trust is built through risk and confirmation and destroyed through risk and disconfirmation (see Chapter 9). When we disclose our thoughts and feelings to a coworker, superior, or subordinate and that person responds with acceptance, support, and cooperation, then reciprocates by disclosing his or her own feelings, we are more apt to trust that person. To accept, support, and display cooperative intentions toward another, we do not necessarily have to agree with everything the other person says. What we must do, however, is display our trustworthiness by refraining from exploiting others' vulnerabilities. That means we do not reject them, ridicule them, or refuse to share our ideas with them.

A Question of Perception

Subordinates and superiors who understand each other's job responsibilities and requirements, as well as the problems inherent in each other's jobs, tend to exhibit higher morale and openness than those whose perceptions differ.[40] When communicating, employees who are overly ambitious, exhibiting a burning desire to achieve and be promoted, are more likely to distort information as it is passed up to the superior to ensure that it pleases him or her. Thus, a subordinate's answer to a question may be based on what he or she thinks the boss wants to hear, not on what he or she actually thinks. Superiors, on the other hand, may at times discount positive information about a subordinate and pay more attention to information that may be critical of him or her.[41] Remember from Chapter 3 that individuals see and hear what they expect to see and hear. Our perception influences our interpretations of events and person-to-person interactions. Differences in perception cause us to respond in different ways.

> Not everything that is faced can be changed, but nothing can be changed until it is faced.
>
> —*James Baldwin*

Networks and Interaction: Influencing Relationship Satisfaction

Networks reveal communication path options. They determine the amount and type of communication individuals will send and receive. In addition, they establish the extent to which ideas and feelings are able to flow freely through an organization.

Networks can be formal and describe the structured, established, official lines of contact—that is, they reveal who should be talking to whom and about what. On the other hand, networks can be informal and describe the unofficial channels of communication, who is in fact talking to whom and about what.[42] Just as in a family, an organization's network indicates the extent to which every member functions not as an isolated element, but as an active part of a relationship; they also show us that every meeting can produce a different outcome. Because effective interactions are necessary for an organization to realize its desired outcomes, we need to explore how networks can influence and create the organization's capacity to grow, change, renew itself, and evolve.

The first studies of **organizational networks** or communication paths were done by the sociological researchers Bavelas and Leavitt.[43] Bavelas explored the effects of four communication patterns: the *circle*, the *line* (or chain), the *wheel* (or star), and the *Y* (see Figure 14.2). He measured the time it took group members to solve a simple problem using each pattern, as well as the satisfaction of group members with the operation of their groups. Bavelas discovered that the Y pattern was the most efficient; members restricted to using that network were able to solve the problem presented to them in the shortest time. However, he also learned that groups restricted to using the circle network had the highest group morale. Significantly, Bavelas found that individuals who occupied the central positions in each network were more satisfied with the group's operation than were members who occupied the network's peripheral positions because the centrality of their positions allows them to perceive themselves as exerting more influence on the group.

Leavitt explored the same four patterns of communication. In his study, members of each type of network had to discover a common symbol found on cards Leavitt gave them. He determined that the network with the greatest degree of **shared centrality**—the circle—produced the highest morale among network

FIGURE 14.2

Four Types of Organizational Networks or Communication Paths

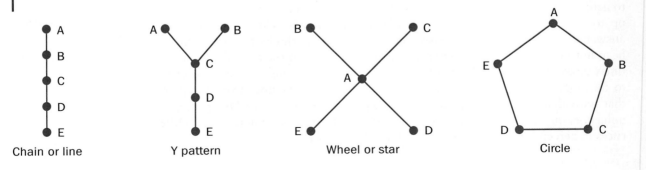

Chain or line   Y pattern   Wheel or star   Circle

participants; the network with the lowest degree of shared centrality—the wheel—required the shortest time to come up with a correct answer. In most of the networks Leavitt studied, the person who occupied the most central position was identified as the group's leader. While the circle groups had shared leadership, each of the other groups had one clearly emergent leader.

Network studies reveal that the type of communication pattern or pathway individuals use to create and exchange messages determines which communication channels are open and thus who interacts regularly with whom. In Figure 14.3 the all-channel network reveals itself to be the one in which all available information is communicated to all members, allowing each member to feel fully included in the group's functioning.

Networks also affect morale within the organization. When employees are not allowed to interact, individual satisfaction suffers. Further, it is through person-to-person interactions that new information is generated and exchanged. Organizations that foster the freedom for workers to circulate and make new connections enable this to happen naturally, whereas organizations that tightly control such activity limit not only normal human interaction but also the organization's potential to receive and generate new information. Because new information is an organization's primary source of "nourishment" and a sign of organizational health,[44] using networks that foster an array of interpersonal connections (as does the all-channel network in Figure 14.3) increases the overall intelligence of an organization, its ability to harvest new ideas, and its capacity to develop new projects.

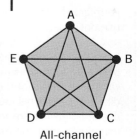

FIGURE 14.3
The All-Channel Organizational Network

All-channel

Working in Teams: Strategies for Success

Despite the fact that interaction at the dyadic level may serve as the most basic unit for exploring interaction in the organization, communication within and between groups is also central to the organization.[45]

Create Healthy Working Climates

In the now classic book *Communication within the Organization,* Charles Redding notes that an effective working climate is characterized by (1) supportiveness, (2) participative decision making, (3) trust among group members, (4) openness and candor, and (5) high performance goals.[46] The healthier the work group's climate, the more effectively the group is able to work. Likewise, Douglas McGregor, an expert in organizational communication, attributes the effectiveness of work groups to the following characteristics:

1. The working atmosphere tends to be informal, comfortable, and relaxed.

2. There is ample discussion pertinent to the task at hand, in which virtually all participate.

3. Members understand, accept, and commit themselves to the group's task or objective.

4. Members listen to each other. Every idea put forth is given a fair hearing.

Many of us are more capable than some of us . . . but none of us is as capable as all of us!

—*Ziggy*

.⋮ *Practice*

How Central Are You?

Form groups of five members each. Each group will use only one of the networks shown in Figures 14.2 and 14.3. Assign a letter to each group member based on the diagrams in the figures. Group members may communicate via written messages only with the member or members to whom they are directly linked. This means that only in the all-channel network are the lines of communication completely free and open.

Each group member will receive five playing cards from a standard deck. The group's task is to create the single best poker hand possible by selecting one card from every group member's cards. Ask your instructor for help if you don't know how to play poker or, better yet, follow the chain of communication in your group until you find someone who does. After the group has a

poker hand, record the time it took group members to reach a decision. Members should respond to the following questions:

1. To what extent did you enjoy being part of your network?

   Not at all   1   2   3   4   5   Very much

2. What was your network's average level of enjoyment? (To compute this, add the individual scores from item 1 together and divide by five, the number of people in your group.)

3. How did your network's enjoyment level compare with the enjoyment levels of groups using other networks?

4. To what extent do you think your group's network facilitated or impeded your collective ability to complete the task as quickly as possible? as effectively as possible?

5. Disagreements are not suppressed. Rather, the reasons for disagreement are carefully examined, as the group seeks to resolve them rationally rather than dominate dissenters.

6. Most important decisions are reached by a kind of consensus in which it is clear that everyone generally agrees and is willing to support the group's decision.

7. Criticism is frequent, frank, and relatively comfortable. There is little evidence of personal attack, either overt or hidden.

8. Members are free to express their feelings about the problem and the group's behavior.

9. When action needs to be taken, clear assignments are made and accepted.

10. The group's chairperson does not dominate the group; nor does the group defer unduly to the chairperson. In fact, the group's leadership shifts from time to time, depending on the circumstances. The issue is not who controls the group but how the job is done.

11. The group is cognizant of its own operation.[47]

Encourage Effective Decision Making

How well the group works together also depends at least in part on the nature of its decision-making process. Groups that work effectively tend to rely on a number of methods designed to increase problem-solving effectiveness: among these are reflective thinking, brainstorming, and the conscious avoidance of groupthink.

Reflective Thinking Framework

The **reflective thinking** framework, first proposed by John Dewey in 1910, is probably still the most commonly adopted sequence used by problem-solving teams. It consists of six basic steps:

1. What is the problem?
2. What are the facts of the situation? Analyze the problem.
3. What criteria must an acceptable solution meet?
4. What are the possible solutions?
5. Which is the best solution?
6. How can the solution be implemented?

If the reflective thinking framework is to work effectively, team members need to suspend judgment and open themselves to all available ideas, facts, and opinions. To ensure that this occurs, as they make their way through the framework, team members ask themselves questions such as the following:

1. Are we using all of the group's resources?
2. Are we using our time to advantage?
3. Are we open to fact finding and inquiry?
4. Are we listening to each other and demonstrating respect for each other?
5. Are we resisting pressuring those who disagree to conform?
6. Is the atmosphere in which we work supportive, trusting, and cooperative?

Brainstorming

Brainstorming was devised in 1957 by communication practitioner Alex Osborn and is still used by many work teams today.[48] Brainstorming promotes the free flow of ideas during the problem-solving process. To ensure that brainstorming sessions are successful, the following guidelines must be followed:

1. Judgment is temporarily suspended. When initially put forth, ideas are neither evaluated nor criticized. Adverse criticism is forbidden.
2. Freewheeling thinking is encouraged. It is easier to tame a wild idea than to give life to an inert idea.
3. Quantity of ideas is stressed. The greater the number of ideas, the better the group's chance of finding a good one.
4. Ideas put forth are built on by other members of the group. Ideas are modified, combined, and mixed together to generate different combinations or patterns.
5. All ideas are recorded. No idea censorship occurs.
6. Only after brainstorming is completed do members evaluate ideas for their usefulness and applicability.

You know . . . everybody is ignorant, only on different subjects.

—Will Rogers

In what ways does this quotation justify the use of teams to solve problems?

Many groups kill good ideas during the decision-making process. By following these guidelines, brainstorming groups do not shoot down ideas before they have had a chance to fully consider them. Defeatist phrases such as "That won't work" or "You've got to be kidding" are not included in the group's communication repertoire.

Avoidance of Groupthink

According to Irving Janis, "Groups can bring out the worst as well as the best in human decision making." What can you do to ensure that they bring out only the best?

The third strategy, the avoidance of **groupthink,** means making a conscious effort to refrain from instances in which some of the group members exert pressure on individual members to conform to the majority opinion and reach consensus.[49] Instead, the group works to ensure that a realistic appraisal of alternative courses of action is thoroughly explored and that minority or unpopular views are expressed fully and listened to—not suppressed by inappropriate pressures. To eliminate the threat, individuals who work in groups need to be alert to the following symptoms of groupthink:

1. There is the *illusion of invulnerability.* Members feel so secure about a group decision that they ignore warning signs that the decision may be wrong. Instead they let excessive optimism and risk-taking lead the way.

2. Members use *rationalizations* as a means to discount warnings.

3. There is an unquestioned belief in the *inherent morality* of the group and its actions.

4. Those who disagree with the group are *stereotyped* as evil, weak, or stupid. A "we" versus "they" attitude is fostered.

5. The group applies direct *pressure* to any members who question the stereotypes. The guiding ethic is that if you are a loyal member of the group, you will not question the direction in which the group is proceeding.

6. *Self-censorship* occurs as members strive not to be perceived as deviating from the group's consensus.

7. The *illusion of unanimity* causes group members to interpret silence as agreement.

8. Members serve as self-appointed *mind guards* in an effort to protect the group from adverse information.

Groups that engage in groupthink let a desire for consensus interfere with the need to think critically. The mental efficiency of the group deteriorates when groups exhibit defensive avoidance and when healthy disagreements and conflicts are suppressed. There is little doubt that work groups that consciously seek to avoid becoming trapped by the dynamics of groupthink produce better decisions.

≈ *Theory*

The Effects of Groupthink

Some attribute the bombing of Pearl Harbor in 1941, the Bay of Pigs invasion in 1961, the Vietnam War (1964–1967), and the fatal explosions of the space shuttles in 1986 and 2003 to groupthink.

1. In groups, research any one of these incidents—or another of your own choosing—to discover which, if any, groupthink processes were factors in each tragedy.

2. Do you think it would have been possible for the decision-making group to have taken another course of action?

Culture and the Workplace

As we have noted, our world is shrinking and requires that we employ new communication strategies. Although many people from other cultures now have some common language because of the growing acceptance of English as the international business language, there remain myriad differences in the way people from various countries relate to each other at work.

For example, the **participative leadership** style evidenced by many American managers may be less effective with people who are from countries where **authoritarian leadership** is the norm.[50] Authoritarian leaders use a dominating and directive communication style as they determine the policies and make the decisions that other team members then abide by. Participative leaders, in contrast, act as guides to team members who are free to identify their own goals, establish their own procedures, and reach their own conclusions. In organizations with participative leaders, virtually any leadership function may be fulfilled by any member of the organization.

Similarly, managers who reward the best workers with bonuses may find that such rewards do not work with Japanese workers, who are not accustomed to being singled out and who do not like such individual attention, which is contrary to the norms and values instilled in them by their culture.[51] Nor are they accustomed to the bluntness and independence of U.S. business people.

We can all benefit from an increased understanding of how cultural differences affect on-the-job relationships. As we explore these, however, keep in mind that characterizing a national work culture does not mean that every person in that country ascribes to that culture; individual variations and differences will always exist.

> The more voices we allow to speak about one thing, the more eyes, different eyes we can use to observe one thing, the more complete will our concept of this one thing . . . be.
>
> — *Nietzsche*

Are Workers Dominant or Submissive?

Some cultures instill in people a desire to dominate their environment, while other cultures instill in them a desire to live in harmony with it. People from the United States, for example, interact directly with each other and typically seek to dominate their environment, while people from Asian cultures work instead to preserve a sense of harmony and thus interact with each other in a much more indirect and often less offensive fashion. United States business people prefer that those with whom they communicate "get to the point" and "put all their cards on the table."[52] In contrast, Asian business people try not to reveal their emotions, may practice avoidance, use third-party intermediaries, and go out of their way to help others save face.

Are Workers Individualistic or Collectivistic?

Whereas some countries of the world, such as the United States, Great Britain, and Canada, encourage individualism, other countries, such as Japan, China, and Israel, emphasize group harmony and loyalty. As discussed in Chapter 7, in *high collectivist cultures*, people tend to show considerable allegiance to their organization, while in *high individualist cultures*, individuals tend to think more of themselves, their individual goals, their personal potential for success, professional

contacts

Culture Can Shock

In "The Japanese Manager's Traumatic Entry into the United States: Understanding the American–Japanese Cultural Divide," published in the November 1993 issue of the *Academy of Management Executive,* Richard G. Linowes describes the following scene:

> Around a conference table in a large U.S. office tower, three American executives sat with their new boss, Mr. Akiro Kusumoto, the newly appointed head of a Japanese firm's subsidiary, and two of his Japanese lieutenants. The meeting was called to discuss ideas for reducing operating costs. Mr. Kusumoto began by outlining his company's aspiration for its long-term U.S. presence. He then turned to the current budgetary matter. One Japanese manager politely offered one suggestion, and an American then proposed another. After gingerly discussing the alternatives for quite some time, the then exasperated American blurted out: "Look, *that* idea is just not going to have much impact. Look at the numbers! We should cut this program, and I think we should do it as soon as possible!" In the face of such bluntness, uncommon and unacceptable in Japan, Mr. Kusumoto fell silent. He leaned back, drew air between his teeth, and felt a deep longing to "return East." He realized his life in this country would be filled with many such jarring encounters, and lamented his posting to a land of such rudeness.

1. What similar experiences, if any, have you or individuals you know experienced?
2. What, if anything, could be done to limit such incidents?

and the needs of their immediate family. Whereas individuality, independence, and self-reliance are important, making the "I" most important in individualist cultures, it is the "we" that is stressed in collectivist cultures. In individualist cultures decisions are based on what is good for the individual, but in collectivist cultures decisions that juxtapose the benefits to the individual and the benefits to the group are based on what is best for the group. The emphasis is on belonging rather than on the self and individual initiative. Members of individualist cultures are apt to use confrontational strategies when dealing with interpersonal problems; in contrast, because they believe that "the nail that sticks up gets pounded," members of collectivist cultures characteristically do not.

Do Workers Have a Space Need?

Different cultures perceive space differently. In the United States, for example, employees prefer private space and have a greater need for personal space than do persons of other cultures. The harder it is to gain access to someone who works in an organization, the more important that individual is perceived to be. In Japan, however, bosses and their employees often share the same space. Middle Eastern cultures also have a public orientation, preferring to mix workers and managers together in one space.

FIGURE 14.4
Preferred Furniture Arrangements: U.S. and Asian Cultures

| Preferred by people in the United States | | Preferred by Asian cultures |

Face-to-face   Right angles   Side-by-side

People often use furniture to communicate their space needs. When people from the United States meet to talk they generally prefer a face-to-face arrangement or to have chairs placed at right angles. People from Asian cultures, however, generally prefer a side-by-side arrangement; their desire to avoid direct eye contact may account for this preference.[53] What advantages and disadvantages do you see for each type of arrangement for effective communication (see Figure 14.4)?

How Do Workers Perceive Time?

How we look at time is at least in part culturally determined. While persons in some societies are oriented toward the past, in others, such as the United States and Canada, persons tend to place more emphasis on the present or the future. Business strategists from these countries are not as concerned with where they have been as they are with where they are now and where they will be five to ten years from now. Asian countries are even more future-oriented in their outlook. The Chinese, for example, share a very long-term future-oriented perspective:

> A Chinese official matter-of-factly informed an ARCO manager that China would one day be the number one nation in this world. The American said he did not doubt that, considering the size of the country and its population, and the tremendous technological progress that will be made, but he asked, "When do you think that China will be number one?" The Chinese responded, "Oh, in four or five hundred years."[54]

Cultural preferences regarding time also affect whether a person thinks it rude to do two things at once, such as reading a newspaper during a meeting. Countries that follow monochronic time such as the United States, Germany, and Switzerland think it's best to do only one thing at a time, whereas those that follow polychronic time, including Latin American and Arabic countries, believe it is acceptable to work on several activities simultaneously.

The significance of being on time also differs among cultures. Being punctual for business meetings is very important in the United States, Germany, and Switzerland.

In Latin American and Arabic countries, however, business people typically display a much more casual approach to punctuality. Arabs, for instance, believe that God, not people, decides when things get accomplished.[55] This orientation often becomes a source of frustration for those who would like to take control by making sure things get done in a timely fashion.

How Do Interpersonal Needs and Skills Differ?

Asian cultures emphasize the importance of meeting collective needs, but in the United States the meeting of individual needs usually is a priority. Thus, in the United States Abraham Maslow's hierarchy, a schema that suggests that human needs fall into five hierarchical categories, each of which needs to be fulfilled before we are able to concern ourselves with the next, puts self-actualizing needs at the apex (see Figure 14.5). In Asian societies self-actualizing needs might well be deemphasized and belonging needs stressed instead. The needs for a sense of responsibility and personal achievement differ by culture. Although all cultures have a hierarchy of needs, the ordering of these needs is not necessarily the same in each.[56]

Agree or disagree with the following: Tomorrow's effective organizations will be those that have learned to be productive with a diverse work force.

Similarly, workers and managers across cultures differ in the practice of interpersonal skills. Managers in some countries such as Spain and Portugal tend to be more aware of workers' feelings and more concerned with the welfare of their subordinates, whereas managers from other countries such as Germany and France are less so. Whereas the Dutch appear quite willing to cooperate with others, the French are frequently the least willing. The Japanese tend to rely on objectivity in decision making, but other countries, including those in Latin America, appear to rely more on intuition. According to researchers, managers in the United States and Latin America have greater interpersonal competence than managers in other countries. This does not mean they are perfect. Consider the following:

A U.S. supervisor on an oil rig in Indonesia, in a moment of anger, shouted at his timekeeper to take the next boat to shore. Immediately, he was surrounded by

FIGURE 14.5
Maslow's Hierarchy of Needs versus an Asian Society's Hierarchy of Needs

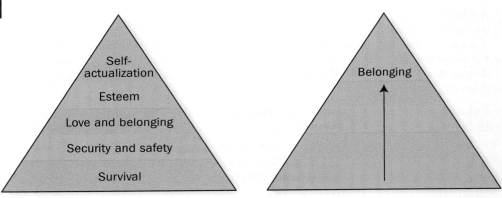

Maslow's hierarchy   Asian society emphasizes the collective

SOURCE: Based on Abraham Maslow, *Toward a Psychology of Being.* New York: Van Nostrand Reinhold, 1968.

a mob of outraged, ax-carrying, Indonesian coworkers of the timekeeper. The supervisor had to barricade himself in his quarters in order to escape the mob. He learned an important cultural lesson, however: Never berate an Indonesian in public.[57]

Gender and the Workplace

Cultural views of gender influence communication in the organization.[58] By fostering different prescriptive roles for men and women, the world of work reflects its expectations for them. The sexual division of labor has long been a fundamental feature of work, as has the devaluation of women's work and the gendering of the workplace. When sex is made a prominent issue even though it is irrelevant and actions are taken based on stereotypical assumptions, then the workplace becomes an arena for gender inequality.[59]

Stereotypes of Women

According to organizational communication researcher Rosabeth Moss Kanter, some organizations exhibit a tendency to classify women into one of four roles: sex object, mother, child, or iron maiden.[60] While the accuracy and applicability of these stereotypes continue to be debated, let us explore each in turn.

The stereotype of *women as sex objects* is revealed in interactions occurring between male and female coworkers, and between male supervisors and their female subordinates. Conversations between such dyads often focus on the women's appearance rather than her work performance. In addition, according to researchers, potentially 90 percent of the female work force has fallen prey to sexual harassment.[61] The Supreme Court has defined sexual harassment as "unwelcome sexual advances, requests for favors, and other verbal or physical conduct of a sexual nature" when submission to or rejection of the conduct enters into employment decisions and/or the conduct interferes with work performance or creates a hostile work environment. The Tailhook incident involving Navy officers and the accusations against then U.S. Senator Robert Packwood that resulted in his resigning from the U.S. Senate are just two incidents that illustrate how prevalent the treatment of women as sex objects is in our society and history.

The stereotype of *women as mothers* also influences their treatment in organizations. When male coworkers or supervisors are in need of support or sympathy, they characteristically seek to interact with a woman rather than with another man. Even in the corporation women are expected to support and take care of others. Also, in U.S. culture, working women who have children are believed to be less committed to their work than are working men with children. Consequently, women are passed over more frequently than are men for training and advancement opportunities.[62]

The stereotype of *women as children* reinforces men's need to protect women. By asserting that women are not mature enough to make difficult decisions, men restrict women and frequently prevent them from holding leadership positions. The stereotype of *women as iron maidens* reflects the belief that women who succeed in achieving positions of power got there because they are unwomanly and are independent, ambitious, tough, and forceful—characteristics typically associated with men.[63]

What steps have you personally taken to avoid stereotyping men and women in the work place?

literary
contacts

Paths to Power

The following passage appears in *Paths to Power* by Natasha Josefowitz. To what extent have you ascribed to or witnessed others ascribing to the sex-role stereotypes described here? Be specific. What other descriptions of gender-based behaviors have you heard?

Impressions from an Office

The family picture is on HIS desk:
    Ah, a solid, responsible family man.
HIS desk is cluttered:
    He's obviously a hard worker and a busy man.
HE's not at his desk:
    He must be at a meeting.
HE is talking with his coworkers:
    He must be discussing the latest deal.
HE's not in the office:
    He's meeting customers.
He's having lunch with the boss:
    He's on the way up.
The boss criticized HIM:
    He'll improve his performance.
HE got an unfair deal:
    Did he get angry?
HE's getting married.
    He'll get more settled.
HE's having a baby:
    He'll need a raise.

HE's going on a business trip:
    It's good for his career.
HE's leaving for a better job:
    He knows how to recognize a good
    opportunity.

The family picture is on HER desk:
    Umm, her family will come before her career.
HER desk is cluttered:
    She's obviously a disorganized scatterbrain.
SHE's not at her desk:
    She must be in the ladies' room.
SHE is talking with her coworkers:
    She must be gossiping.
SHE's not in the office.
    She must be out shopping.
SHE's having lunch with the boss:
    They must be having an affair.
The boss criticized HER:
    She'll be very upset.
SHE got an unfair deal:
    Did she cry?
SHE's getting married:
    She'll get pregnant and leave.
SHE's having a baby:
    She'll cost the company money in
    maternity benefits.
SHE's going on a business trip:
    What does her husband say?
SHE's leaving for a better job:
    Women are undependable.

SOURCE: Reprinted with permission of the author from *Paths to Power: A Woman's Guide from First Job to Top Executive* by Natasha Josefowitz. Reading, MA: Addison-Wesley, 1980, p. 60. Copyright © 1980 by Natasha Josefowitz. Permission conveyed through Copyright Clearance Center, Inc.

Each of these stereotypes prevents women from advancing in their careers. Either because of their perceived incompetence or lack of femininity, women are frequently held back from realizing their full potential.

According to researchers Nader and Nader, women are condemned because of their communication patterns, which is like "blaming the victim for being abused."[64]

Women are constrained from reaching the top of the corporate ladder because of sex-role stereotypes held by those in power that women don't possess the personality characteristics needed for top leadership positions. The feeling is that because many women are naturally affiliative and nurturing, they are less able to make tough decisions, are not assertive enough, and are too concerned about disappointing others to be effective.[65]

in Theory

Stereotypes and Individuals

Stereotyping the people we work with can limit our perception of their actual abilities and behaviors.

1. Which, if any, of the stereotypes discussed in this section, do you think is valid? Why?

2. Based on your experience and the experiences of people you know, provide examples of male and female behavior that contradict each stereotype.

Stereotypes of Men

Men are also stereotyped in organizations. However, researcher Julia Wood finds that while still limiting, the stereotypes linked to men tend to be more positive: men are seen as sturdy oaks, fighters, and breadwinners.[66]

The stereotype of *men as sturdy oaks* indicates that men who are tough, self-sufficient, and in control of their feelings are "real men" and are thus of more value to the organization than are men who lean on others, complain, or more readily give in to their fears. As a result, men often feel compelled to hide mistakes and suffer stress-related ailments in silence.

The stereotype of *men as fighters* reflects the training they have had to be aggressive and committed in their efforts to defeat any competition. Thus, to illustrate their toughness, men wage war, figuratively and literally. For men, the battleground is work, and it, not family, often come first.

The stereotype of *men as breadwinners* indicates the expectation society has for men to be the primary wage earners. A man's ability to earn a good income is a measure of his success. This perception puts enormous pressure on men to perform.[67] In fact, according to psychiatrist Willard Gaylin, "men commit suicide at a rate of seven to eight times as frequently as women in our culture, and they do it invariably because of perceived social humiliation that is almost exclusively tied to business failures."[68]

These stereotypes, while having little if any validity, do limit women's chances for growth in the work world and men's chances for a satisfactory and fulfilling family life.

Leadership and Management Style

A survey conducted for the International Women's Forum reveals that individuals perceive significant differences in the management styles of men and women. Male managers describe their style in terms of a series of exchanges involving rewards or punishments for the actions of subordinates. In contrast, female managers are more concerned with exhibiting *interactive leadership*—in encouraging and sharing both power and decision making with subordinates and coworkers.[69] In addition, although both men and women enjoy being leaders, women are considered to be most effective when they display sensitivity during interactions, but less effective when they display the traits traditionally associated with more assertive or

If you were you given the choice, would you choose to work for a male or a female? Why?

in Context

Gender and Style

Interview two female managers and two male managers regarding their perceptions of how the communication styles of male and female managers are similar to and different from each other. Ask the following questions:

1. In what ways, if any, is the increased presence of women in the work force affecting the nature of your on-the-job person-to-person interactions?

2. What examples can you give of how the communication style of a male or a female prevented or facilitated his or her and your attainment of a goal?

3. What steps, if any, would your organization have to take to ensure that the careers of men and women employees were developed with equal attention? Is this a valid objective? Why or why not?

dominating male managers.[70] Consequently, women leaders use more collaborative, participative communication to accomplish goals, and men rely on more directive communication strategies. It is interesting to note that characteristics associated with males such as assertiveness, competitiveness, and instrumentality are valued in leaders, but so are supportiveness, receptiveness, participation, and collaboration—the communication skills more typically attributed to women.

Facing Each Other

Can men and women work well together in organizations? The answer, according to Julia Wood, is yes, despite all stereotypes. *Mixed-sex work teams* tend to be more productive, produce better quality decisions, and result in greater member satisfaction than do *single-sex work groups*. It appears that when men and women work together they complement and enhance each others' performance.[71] Whereas women may excel in exhibiting communication that supports and builds cohesion, men may initiate more communication that focuses directly on the task at hand. Both kinds of communication are important.

Media and Technology Contacts

Reflecting and Refracting Images

How have the pervasiveness of the media and technology influenced our perceptions of what it is like to work and communicate in organizational settings? In what ways do they help bind us together or tear us apart? How have they contributed to global thinking and personalization (demassification)? To what extent are they helping those who work in organizations to live up to or surpass their potential?

Prime-Time Portrayals

An analysis of prime-time television programming presents us with an interesting picture of males and females. According to media researcher Marvin Moore, men's roles tend to be "exaggerated, with a large number of male single-parent portrayals and an emphasis on the family roles over work roles."[72] Moore finds that although television programs depict men in nontraditional roles, infusing us with the impression that men have the freedom to travel many different roads,

Practice

Prime Time Presents

Divide the class into groups of four and assign one network—NBC, CBS, ABC, or Fox—to each group member. Each student should watch two different hours of prime-time programming on the assigned network and collect the following data:

1. List the gender and profession of each character.

2. Is each character presented in a positive, a negative, or a neutral way?

Pool the information you have collected and then discuss the following questions:

3. What kinds of messages about the professional lives of men and women in our society are being communicated by each network's shows?

4. To what extent, if any, do you believe any or all of these shows are maintaining or contradicting sex-role stereotyped portrayals of males and females and/or traditional prescriptions for gender?

5. Provide specific examples to support your position.

women's changing roles have tended to receive much less attention. Moore determined that mothers and wives in family series were rarely identified as having occupations outside the home. When women were shown working, often they were shown operating businesses from their homes.[73]

Other media researchers echo this observation by noting that the professionalism exhibited by working women is rarely the focus of a story line. Instead, working women are typically shown having trouble juggling work and personal relationships.[74] When shown in their places of business, women are often presented discussing relationships with men, problems with children, clothing, or other nonwork issues. Researchers agree that in years past, there has been a dearth of story lines that emphasize the professional development and contributions of women.

More recently, however, there have been some signs of change. A number of story lines have focused on the working lives of women characters. Shows such as "Star Trek: Deep Space Nine" highlight women performing leadership roles in what were traditionally male-dominated professions.[75]

Other media critics point out that the prime-time jobs of both males and females may now be superfluous. For example, in a number of 1990s shows, jobs became character accessories. What mattered most to characters was not their work, but their personal lives and their friends. While some describe this as a backlash to the "me, me, me" philosophy of the 1980s, when the job was everything, others believe that the shows are designed instead to provide viewers with a greater sense of community. What it has created, however, are characters who earn a lot of money but play a lot harder than they work. Will television ever reveal "the truth" about work and jobs?[76]

Technological Realities

The media we use to interact with each other on the job are expanding. No longer are we limited to traditional means of interacting such as face-to-face communication, the telephone, or paper memos. Rather, we now send e-mail and faxes regularly, and even hold video conferences. While they are extensions of the older, more familiar ways of interacting, these newer technologies are, at least to some extent, redefining the way we live and work.

Many of us now spend a significant portion of our days in front of laptop computers, on cellular phones, and in general less tied to the once familiar notion of office. In fact, some believe that the office, in its traditional sense, is on the way to becoming a relic. We can now telecommute from home—linked to others by a network of computers—and yet still function as a member of a work team. A number of companies, recognizing the extent to which technology is reinventing the work place, are taking steps to combat the lack of face-to-face interaction among employees by setting up coffee-bar-like conference rooms in which employees can meet for casual interchanges and bounce ideas off each other.[77]

What steps do you need to take to prepare yourself to interact effectively in tomorrow's work environment?

Companies now habitually employ virtual teams comprising persons who live in different countries, locations, and time zones. Since these team members do not have to assemble physically to work together, virtual teams have proven themselves capable of accomplishing some assignments more quickly than real-time-and-place teams.[78]

In years to come we may reassess the kinds of communicative interactions we need to master to advance professionally. Newer interactive technology may well influence who has status and power in an organization. Because we will no longer be affected to the same degree by the cues provided us during in-person encounters, we may be more apt to trust those whom we may not have trusted before.[79] We may find ourselves reacting more to the content of a message than to the credibility of the messenger. Dress, eye contact, facial expression, vocal qualities, and postural demeanor may wane in importance. Consequently, those who excel at personal communication skills may need to learn new skills to perform as successfully in a computer-mediated work place.

Interpersonal Communication and Health

Just as interpersonal effectiveness can enhance our family and work-related relationships, so can it enhance the ease with which we interact with health providers as well as improve their abilities to interact with us. In fact, whether we are successful at maintaining our own health or helping others maintain theirs may well depend on the following three factors:

1. How effective we are at interacting interpersonally in different health care settings,

2. How capable we are at developing and maintaining effective health care relationships, and

3. How adept we are at using interpersonal communication to resolve health-related conflicts and solve health communication problems.

While we recognize the importance of formal health care providers, we have to recognize that the bulk of the communicative interactions we will have about health will probably not occur in formal health care settings. Many of our health-related interactions will occur in more informal settings such as in our home, on the phone, over the Internet, or in our office conversing with a coworker to whom we offer our social support. According to researchers, offering social support reveals to others that we value and care for them.[80] We probably offer others more social support than we realize. When we comfort a friend who is stressed and finding it difficult to cope, we offer social support. When we listen to a grieving parent, we offer social support. When we help someone log onto WebMD to conduct a search, we offer social support. These acts of social support may do more to affect the health of other people than we may realize. Research reveals that social support can enhance healing, reduce stress, and build feelings of self-worth. In addition, the person offering the support often benefits as much as the person receiving it.[81] Thus, the support of family members and friends can do much to enhance health; however, we still need to consider the contributions and impact that health care providers have on our ability to cope with and recover from an illness.

The Link Between Health Care Consumers and Providers

Health communication is the study of human interaction in the health care process.[82] There are four key functions of communication in relation to health care provider–patient communication.[83] To a large extent, the fulfillment of each function involves interpersonal communication:

Which of these functions is most important? Why?

> *Function 1—Diagnosis* requires data gathering, data interpretation, and problem-solving skills.
>
> *Function 2—Obtaining compliance or gaining cooperation* requires skills in developing quality interactions that facilitate effective provider–patient relationships; involves eliciting consumer consent, including the following of measures prescribed for patients' care.
>
> *Function 3—Counsel* relates to the provider's role as therapist and his or her effectiveness as a deliverer of therapeutic communication.
>
> *Function 4—Education* involves the provider in disseminating information to individuals in an effort to reduce health risks and increase the overall effectiveness of health care.

Identify behaviors that have led you to be satisfied or dissatisfied with a particular health care provider.

How can we as patients or future providers improve our abilities to interact with each other and thus precipitate the maximum realization of these functions? What steps can we take to ensure that sufficient information is shared to facilitate the correct diagnosis, the needed cooperation, and the proper treatment of medical problems?

The key to answering these questions lies not in what we do alone, but in what we do together. Whether we function as patients or choose a career as a provider, we influence each other mutually in the encounters we share.[84]

in Context

What Is Your Role?

When it comes to interacting with a physician, how do you see your role? Answer the following questions:

1. Which of the following words would you use to describe yourself in relation to your physician? Why?

   a patient   *a consumer*   *a client*

   Why do some researchers advocate a change in vocabulary from *patient* to *consumer* or *client*? To what extent do you agree with them?

2. How would you differentiate among a patient, a consumer, and a client?

3. Provide examples of times during which communication between you and your physician was satisfactory and unsatisfactory. Identify the kinds of behavior contributing to each kind of interaction.

Gathering data for a diagnosis is just one aspect of the ongoing communication process between doctor and patient to ensure effective health care.

Certainly, developing a sensitivity to each other's needs, an awareness of mutual expectations, a knowledge of the ways in which manner of interaction influences communicator confidence and comfort, and a recognition of the myriad ways one's own communication behaviors affect those of others play an integral part.

Even today, while medical advances are significant, charges of insensitivity, an inability to empathize, a lack of trust, and poor listening skills continue to be leveled against health care providers by some consumers. (*Consumer* is preferred by some, a term that implies a more active role than that of patient, that individuals have the right to "shop around" for service they find satisfying.[85]) What is fast becoming apparent is that effective interpersonal communication, combined with trust in the medical abilities of the provider, is essential to the creation of satisfactory provider–client relationships.[86] When it comes to *health communication*—the informing, influencing, and interpretation of health-related messages—how the messages are encoded and who encodes them is as important as how they are perceived and interpreted and who perceives and interprets them.[87]

Demonstrating Sensitivity

When communication between health care provider and consumer is characterized by insensitivity, the outcome, typically, is dissatisfaction. In contrast, interpersonal sensitivity, awareness of the variables that are likely to facilitate full and honest disclosure during discussions, is of vital importance to the maintenance of effective client–practitioner relationships. Practitioners who carry extremely

Once I heard a hospital nurse describing doctors. She said there were beside-the-bed doctors, who were interested in the patient, and foot-of-the-bed doctors, who were interested in the patient's condition. They unconsciously expressed their emotional involvement—or lack of it—by where they stood.

—*Edward T. Hall*

heavy workloads tend to be the most vulnerable; they become exasperated and burn out, exhibit more of a callous outlook, and consequently are apt to exhibit less responsiveness to the needs of their patients.

Consumers who seek information and reassurance when paired with a provider who is stressed out often conclude that they are being ignored or short-changed and, in turn, display an insensitivity to the needs of their providers. Because we perceive our personal problems to be paramount, as consumers, we make demands on providers that are difficult for them to fulfill, and we become even more upset and apprehensive when significant attention is not paid immediately to our concerns.

Insufficient interpersonal sensitivity and caring thus lead to increased levels of provider and consumer dissatisfaction and the breakdown of health care relationships. In contrast, when interpersonal sensitivity and caring are high, client satisfaction and compliance with provider recommendations tend to increase.

Identify a health care professional whom you feel possesses superior interpersonal communication skills. Identify the characteristics that cause you to rate him or her highly.

Encoding the Message Clearly

Communication apprehension, fear, or anxiety over communicating on the part of either the health provider or the client can impede effective interaction. To develop the ability to be open with and trusting of each other, practitioners and consumers need to become more skilled at exchanging messages.[88]

Finding the right words to use when communicating about health—particularly sexual health—is difficult for health practitioners and consumers alike. The latter sometimes assume that health care providers will tell them what they need to know without being asked; health care providers sometimes assume that the sexual lives of their patients are just too personal to ask about. Yet research shows that effective communication is necessary for meaningful behavioral change to occur. Not talking about safe sex increases the chances that individuals will engage in risky behavior rather than exhibit healthful sexual attitudes and practices.[89]

In addition, health care practitioners are frequently unaware of how the messages they send to consumers frighten or confuse them, and consumers often find it difficult to fully describe or clearly explain their health-related symptoms or problems to practitioners, who then may not be able to interpret them correctly. Thus, both sides often feel apprehensive, frustrated, or dissatisfied with the messages they do exchange and the relationship they ultimately create. Effective message sending is necessary for consumers to explain their symptoms and physical problems to the provider; the provider must be able to communicate instructions that allow **client compliance**, so the consumer is able to relieve or manage the specific situation.

Contributing to this clarity problem is an overreliance by health care providers on jargon, which makes it even more likely that consumers will misinterpret practitioner instructions or misunderstand a diagnosis or treatment regimen, and thus be unable to comply with what the provider orders because they do not understand the messages. Thus, willingness to comply is influenced by specific message-sending strategies. Among these are the *emphasizing of expertise* ("If you comply with my recommendations to take time off and take the prescribed medication, your anxiety level should decrease") and, if the client resists, *threats* ("If you fail to follow my recommendations, you're a prime candidate for a stroke").

Along with verbal messages, providers also employ a wide range of nonverbal communication behaviors—some that enhance and some that unintentionally undermine client compliance. By moving physically closer to a client, smiling, or exhibiting pleasant facial expressions, head nods, or vocal reinforcers such as "uh-huh," providers communicate high sensory involvement and caring and enhance client compliance. In contrast, by maintaining excessive distance between themselves and clients, frowning, or speaking in a cold voice, providers cause clients to become less willing to follow instructions.

Overcoming Perceptual Barriers

In what ways have you stereotyped a health care provider?

In addition to misunderstanding each other, health care providers and consumers both frequently misperceive or stereotype each other. This further complicates the relationship.

As consumers, for instance, we may approach health care professionals with unreasonable performance expectations—counting on them to pull a miracle cure out of a hat much like a magician pulls out a rabbit. In our eyes, the provider is a hero who can conquer any problem. Such perceptions make it highly unlikely that he or she will be able to measure up to or surpass our expectations.

But at the same time, providers stereotype clients. Providers, for example, may underestimate the intelligence of their clients, or, based on assumptions related to age, sex, or level of attractiveness, fail to work with them to foster an honest exchange of information and feelings.

| *A Closer Look at the Characteristics of Therapeutic Relationships*

When our interpersonal relationships are therapeutic, they enable us to increase our levels of interpersonal health. By fostering the development of personal insights, **therapeutic relationships** also make it possible for us to participate in future encounters in more satisfying ways.[90]

To the extent that we are willing and able to provide one another with honest feedback, we are each better able to redirect our behavior in ways that enable us to achieve personal insight and realize our personal goals while underscoring the spirit of cooperation that exists between us. Once this occurs, the relationship we share can be described as *therapeutic*.

Problems are likely to arise when health care practitioners ignore how patients react *emotionally*, attending only to the physical symptoms. Medical personnel who fail to recognize that emotional state can play a significant role in both illness vulnerability and recovery can be linked to the lack of emotional intelligence (see also Chapter 8).[91] Among the variables essential to the development of a therapeutic relationship are empathy, trust, honesty, confirmation, caring, and humor.

Empathy refers to the ability to understand another individual's condition and feelings and to communicate that understanding to the person. During health care provider–consumer interaction, empathy can be demonstrated by accurately acknowledging and stating the perceived feelings of the consumer. This can be done both verbally and nonverbally. Nodding one's head, maintaining eye contact, and mirroring nonverbal cues lets the consumer know that the provider is following and understanding what's being communicated.

Trust is the belief that an individual will respect another's needs and concerns and interact with him or her in a responsible and predictable manner (see also Chapter 9). When we trust another person we exhibit *trusting behavior*—that is, we are willing to take a chance by disclosing information about ourselves to that individual in a way that could increase our vulnerability. We assess whether our trust was warranted or misplaced by the person's response. Unless consumers trust their health care providers, they will not be likely to communicate with them about uncomfortable subjects or to reveal vital personal information.

. **Practice**

Looking at Relationships

A number of movies have focused on the relationship between consumers and providers, including *The Doctor* or *Whose Life Is It Anyway?* Tapes of these or similar films can easily be obtained from a local video store or public library.

1. Watch a video of a movie that focuses on the provider–consumer relationship.

2. Discuss in class what the video reveals about provider–consumer relations and the modern health care system.*

*Based on an exercise in the syllabus of Ellen W. Bonaguro; see the 1995 SCA summer conference proceedings, p. 53.

Honesty refers to how willing we are to communicate truthfully and sincerely. In health care relationships, honest self-disclosure facilitates effective treatment.

Confirmation occurs when we feel as though what we have to say or what we are is accepted and respected by another. In health care relationships, when individuals carefully listen to and respond to what's said to them, they acknowledge each other's importance and confirm each other.

Caring refers to the level of emotional involvement we convey to one another. When we pay attention to the other person and exhibit emotionally supportive nonverbal cues, we communicate our willingness to help him or her work through his or her problems.

Humor refers to the ability to make another person smile or laugh, in this case despite the seriousness of his or her medical condition. By diffusing fear and infusing a dose of laughter, we enable the individual to better cope with his or her situation.

It is not surprising that, as consumers, we prefer providers who appear caring, friendly, and expressive. By exhibiting such behaviors physicians enhance their credibility in our eyes and do much to create a more favorable provider–client relationship.

The Practitioner–Client Dyad: Experiencing the Relationship

How the practitioner and the client relate to each other depends in part on how each views his or her own and each other's roles, and how much responsibility they believe each should assume.

The Continuum of Decision Making

How decisions are made and who makes them can affect patient satisfaction, compliance with a prescribed treatment, and recuperation. The **continuum of**

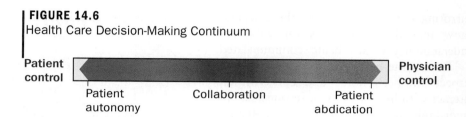

FIGURE 14.6
Health Care Decision-Making Continuum

Use this scale to indicate where you fall in relation to your provider.

Patient control — Patient autonomy — Collaboration — Patient abdication — Physician control

decision making seen in Figure 14.6 identifies three key provider–patient relationships.[92]

At the *physician control* end of the continuum is *patient abdication,* in which the physician is responsible for all decision making. This was the most common model of physician–patient interaction in the past. The mind-set is that because the physician has superior knowledge and abilities, the patient must trust him or her. Because the patient lacks the medical knowledge and is unwilling or lacks the competence to take responsibility for making a decision, the physician is probably the best person to make the decision. In such a relationship, the physician does most of the talking, asks the majority of questions, frequently interrupts the patient, changes topics abruptly, or even ignores the

professional
contacts

It Could Have Been You

Gary L. Kreps and Barbara C. Thornton offer the following story in their book: *Health Communication: Theory and Practice.*

The young woman needed four wisdom teeth extracted. The procedure was a routine one that could be performed in the dentist's office. Nitrous oxide was administered as an anesthetic. The woman's mother accompanied her but was directed to sit in the waiting room, with the promise that she would be called if needed. During the course of the treatment, the woman had a drug reaction. She began to experience terror and wanted her mother. The client tried to ask for her mother, only to find that she was unable to talk. Feeling helpless only increased her terror.

At no time during the one-hour dental procedure did the dentist or the dental assistant inquire into the client's comfort. After the procedure, the client had several psychological reactions, including nightmares which persisted for several months. Today, almost six years later, she continues to feel aversion toward dentists. The dentist and his assistant, questioned by the parent as to why they had not inquired into the client's comfort, explained that they typically become so involved in the procedure that they often do not inquire; also, they felt at a loss as to how they should approach the client during a procedure.

If you were the parent, how would you have responded to the practitioners?

patient completely. In other words, the physician dominates and controls the interaction.

At the opposite end of the continuum is *patient autonomy*. In such a relationship, the patient exercises his or her right to self-determination and assumes complete responsibility for decision making. Though the physician does possess the knowledge and willingly shares it with the patient, the patient makes all major decisions. Physician–patient interaction in this type of relationship is the opposite of that in a patient-abdication relationship.

At the scale's midpoint is *collaboration*. When the health care provider and patient share this kind of relationship, both work actively, share information, negotiate perspectives, and reach a mutually satisfactory decision. In a relationship based on collaboration, the consumer, not just the physician, is actively involved in decision making. The thinking is that the patient has the right to participate fully in decisions affecting his or her health. Typically more time-consuming, this approach allows more balanced opportunities for interaction, cooperation, negotiation, and consensus building. Clients are not passive participants in the medical relationship; they take an active role, sometimes even challenging the authority and control of their physicians.

Regardless of how active or inactive a role the patient assumes in decision making for his or her health care, patient participation through open communication with the health care provider is very important.

The Interview

Another important aspect of the provider–consumer relationship is the interview in which the nature of the medical problem is revealed to the practitioner. The interview is an important context for the exchange of information and thus the primary tool the practitioner and client tend to rely on, at least initially. The interview typically occurs because the client seeks treatment and the practitioner needs information. The interview sets the stage for the development of the health care relationship and establishes the guidelines for communication between practitioner and consumer.

Interviews range from directive to consumer-centered. **Directive interviews** are more tightly controlled and orchestrated so that the practitioner is able to prescribe an appropriate course of action for the client. In contrast, **client-centered interviews** are less directive and call on practitioners to assume the role of helper as they attempt to help clients achieve insight and find solutions to the problems facing them. The type of interview selected depends not on a formula but on the needs and strengths of both the professional and the client. Whatever interview type is used, however, for the interview to be successful, practitioners and patients need to be familiar with both approaches and be ready to use and respond to a mixture of question types. *Closed-ended questions* are restrictive, limit answer options, and allow practitioners to elicit specific information. Examples include "Are you currently taking any prescription drugs?" or "When was your last physical?" *Open-ended questions* allow the client to answer without much direction and therefore to offer additional information. Examples include "How do you feel?" or "What does the pain feel like?" *Primary questions* introduce topics

How many questions did you ask during your last visit to a doctor?

or new areas such as "What were you doing when you started feeling sick?" *Secondary questions* are designed to elicit more information such as "What else happened?" *Mirror or summary questions* that summarize a question series are designed to ensure that responses are processed accurately: "Let's see if I have this right. Your stomachaches occur after you eat foods high in acid." *Reflective probing questions* are used to correct inaccuracies, such as "Didn't you say your grandfather was color-blind?" In addition, during the interview patients need to carefully articulate their conditions. Practitioners must listen equally carefully to these explanations, do their best to let the clients choose the rate and amount of self-disclosure, and resist interrupting.

Interviews work best when the consumer also asks questions. Because a patient's unanswered questions can add to his or her stress and compound his or her feelings of vulnerability and uncertainty, it is important that the patient be prepared to ask questions. It is also helpful if the physician can encourage the patient to ask questions.

It is at the interpersonal level that meaningful relationships will or will not be established between individuals who seek and those who provide health care services.

Communicate about AIDS with Each Other

 .ﷺ Theory

Talking about AIDS

It is estimated that one in 500 college students in the United States is infected with HIV, the virus that causes AIDS. Because most individuals at this stage are asymptomatic and often unaware of their HIV-positive status, they may be likely to infect others. Thus many college students are at risk, though they may neither recognize it nor feel personally vulnerable.

1. Working in pairs, develop a series of communication strategies you could employ to encourage reflection on perceptions and relationships affecting health.

2. Specifically, identify what you can do to dispel misconceptions about lack of risk, overcome stereotypes and gender role expectations, resist undue influence, enhance dialogue between you and others, build a supportive climate for discussion, and protect your own health.

AIDS is an important health care issue about which many people feel uneasy communicating. The inability of U.S. society to communicate effectively on this issue is leading to a very dangerous situation. Parents today wonder if talking to their children about sex will put ideas in their heads. Teenagers are reluctant to question their parents about sex because their parents never bring it up. Sexual partners focus on relationship maintenance rather than the risk of acquiring a sexually transmitted disease.[93] There is little doubt that some of us are engaging in high-risk activities and, for one reason or another, far too many of us feel relatively little personal risk.

One of the main obstacles to developing a dialogue that can lead to more healthy intimate interactions is our hesitancy to negotiate preventive behaviors with our partners. As with other interpersonal communication contexts, our willingness to self-disclose, our reaction to media depictions, our perceptions of gender roles and differences, and our feelings about openness and deception play a part in our ability to take an active role in protecting our own health.[94]

literary **contacts**

"Death of Innocence"

In this article, published by the Knight–Ridder News Service on March 8, 1992, reporter Frank Bruni reveals why high school student Jennifer Swartout felt that she had to help get the AIDS message to her classmates.

Listening to the wild stories her classmates brought back from the beaches of spring break last year, Jennifer Swartout feared some of them were true.

She wasn't jealous.

She was panicky.

The boys who counted their sexual conquests, the girls who gulped birth control pills, didn't they know?

Swartout did.

She had watched AIDS lay waste to her favorite uncle, her godfather, left emaciated and addlebrained by the disease at age 35.

He died last September.

In November, Swartout made an appointment with her high school principal, Rodney Hosman, at Livonia Churchill High. . . .

She told Hosman that this year, the week before spring break, there should be a senior class assembly about AIDS.

It should be blunt and forceful, because she didn't want any of her friends ever to get the gruesome disease. They should learn a little fear, a lot of caution.

Swartout offered to coordinate the project. That night, she phoned the president of the school's Parent, Teacher, and Student Association, a woman she had never met.

In subsequent days, she talked to health teachers. She told them that whatever AIDS education she had gotten in the 10th grade wasn't gripping enough—she couldn't even remember it. How could the assembly go further?

She got answers and help. Next month, just before school lets out for a week's recess, most of the 388 seniors will gather in the auditorium, listen to guest speakers infected with the virus that causes AIDS, and be told how to save themselves.

They also will hear Swartout's story. The 17-year-old girl will stand up before her classmates and talk about losing her uncle to AIDS, an experience she felt compelled to keep secret while it was happening because some people view the disease as a shameful curse.

. . . Hosman believes the assembly is important. He said that while most teenagers have a good scientific grasp of what AIDS is, they don't feel its threat or impact in any direct way.

For Swartout, it was particularly important for teenagers to know. They seemed oblivious to AIDS.

"They hear about it so much it becomes part of the background noise," she said. "It blends in with all the other crises in the world.

"But if you've watched a person die this way, it just becomes so urgent that people understand how serious it is."

If you were a parent, how would you explain the seriousness of AIDS to your child?

SOURCE: From Frank Bruni, "Communicating About AIDS," March 8, 1992. Copyright, 1992, Knight-Ridder/Tribune Media Services. Reprinted with permission.

Diversity and Culture Contacts

The Role of Culture

The odds are increasing that the cultural backgrounds of patients and professional caregivers will be different. While this does not necessarily cause problems, problems can surface if both fail to recognize how culture and prevailing stereotypes influence communication about health.

Speakers try to help members of the public become more comfortable discussing AIDS. In your opinion, are they succeeding?

When it comes to health and perceptions of illness, the importance of an individual's beliefs, values, and attitudes within his or her own cultural framework needs to be considered. Our beliefs influence which symptoms we are prone to consult a physician about, what we expect the physician to do, and how we are apt to react when faced with a medical problem. By asking questions such as "What most concerns you?" "How is this illness affecting your life?" and "What do you think is happening to you?" practitioners become better able to understand diverse world views.[95] We cannot focus on individuals in isolation from their cultural contexts.

Due to both the ethnocentrism of health care providers and the bureaucratic nature of the Western health system, health providers often sound as if they are proselytizing to patients—spouting technical phrases their patients do not understand when discussing the patient's treatment. Such an approach, because of its tendency to disparage the beliefs of others, may cause patients to resist rather than cooperate with and follow the instructions of their physicians. When it comes to health and illness, the diverse beliefs of those involved influence reactions and outcomes. Misunderstandings complicate things when persons from different cultures have conflicting ideas regarding the nature of disease and the meaning of illness. For example, physicians who fail to comprehend that persons from Asian cultures may perceive mental illness as dishonoring their family and their community may be confused when an Asian patient strongly denies being depressed even though all his symptoms suggest that as a diagnosis.[96]

Practitioners also need to realize that patients from different cultures vary in how they cope with and attempt to reduce the uncertainty that an illness presents. Here Gudykunst's uncertainty reduction theory plays a role. In high-context cultures such as Japan, uncertainty reduction predicts whether persons will follow *group* norms, while in low-context cultures (as in America), the focus is on the predicting of individual, rather than group, behavior. It is important that health care practitioners also have contact with relatives and mutual friends of a patient from a high-context culture to reduce their uncertainty.[97]

Cultural awareness can facilitate health improvements. For example, knowing that in a Hispanic family the grandmother or mother decides health-related matters could facilitate patient treatment or organ donation, just as knowing that in Hispanic culture, blood relationships supersede legal ones.[98]

Because we know that personal biases influence interaction, clearly consumers would benefit if health care professionals would work to eliminate negative personal prejudices that could affect the quality of care they deliver. For example, stereotyping the elderly, men versus women, or members of certain ethnic or racial groups can pose serious health care problems. Losing patience with a Hindu who won't eat meat or with an African who wears an amulet will not help solve that person's medical situation.

Consumers will benefit if practitioners sensitize themselves to client preferences. When working with clients who are members of other cultures, practitioners would be wise to spend time posing such questions as: What are the individual's space needs? Does he or she respond to touch? What kind of eye contact will help establish trust? Are there any special rules of protocol that should be adhered to? Are there any role models that will increase the chances of treatment compliance? Knowing the answers to such questions would allow the practitioner to better understand how the patient feels about and is dealing with the problem.

Theory

Perception, Culture, and Health

Read the following scenario.

I was standing outside the school with my friend when I saw Alex. Alex was wearing a black shirt and jeans and had short hair. As Alex walked away my friend turned to me and said, "Alex has AIDS."

1. What sex do you think Alex is?

2. How old do you think Alex is?

3. To what cultural group do you think Alex belongs?

4. Of what socio-economic group do you think Alex is a member?

5. What questions would you like to ask Alex?

6. In your opinion, to what extent, if any, do any of these answers influence your perception of Alex and his or her health?

Gender Contacts

Health Care

Although American prime-time health-related television shows do contain more interesting professional women than they used to years ago, such portrayals are still underrepresented. In addition, the female professionals who are shown tend to be young, are less frequently seen than the men, and are rarely in charge. No healthy woman can avoid turning 40, but that is the age at which women begin to disappear from media offerings.[99] Such media messages reinforce inappropriate gendered identities.

The depiction of men as sexual aggressors and women as sex objects also contributes to the pathologizing of women's bodies and the legitimizing of unhealthy and destructive behaviors, both self- and other-inflicted, ranging from anorexia to battering. It is not safe for us to regard healthy, functional bodies as deficient or abnormal. Yet mediated images have persuaded millions of us that what every medical source considers "normal body weight" and "normal aging" are to the rest of society abnormal and cause for diets or cosmetic surgery.[100]

Additionally, MTV's, rock music's, and even prime-time television's emphasis on eroticism and sex helps create a societal atmosphere conductive to risky sex, which ultimately leads to our endangering ourselves, and to frustration and disappointment.[101]

In addition to influencing how our own self-images affect our health, gender influences health care in other ways. Consider the following interchange between a male obstetrician and his pregnant patient:

> *Several years ago, Dr. Faith Frieden watched in dismay as a fellow obstetrician checked a patient who had begun bleeding during her pregnancy.*
> *"Well," the doctor announced matter-of-factly, "you've miscarried."*
> *His words of comfort? "These things happen. Some women miscarry before they even know they're pregnant."*
> *True, Frieden thought, but if patients wanted merely a clinical explanation, they could consult a medical encyclopedia. What about a little kindness?[102]*

Would you prefer to have a male or a female health care provider? Why? To what extent do the responses of males and females differ?

in Theory

Is It an Issue of Gender?

Think about the ways gender affects health care issues.

1. In what ways, if any, does being a male or a female increase your health risks?

2. Which gender perceives itself as more at risk and why?

3. Which gender is more at ease discussing health care problems?

4. To what extent do gender roles influence expectations regarding sexual behavior? Explain.

Do male and female health care providers relate differently to patients? On average, women spend more time with patients, interrupt less frequently, are more empathic, elicit more medical information, and are more responsive to issues related to reproduction and sexuality. That's not to say that men do not also do these things; the research simply shows that women do them more. Female providers also work harder to create a positive interpersonal climate with their patients. According to Dr. Fred Palace, former president of the Medical Society of New Jersey: "Women are by social training more equipped to emphasize listening."[103] In contrast, male providers tend to interrupt their patients when they speak. Female providers also ask more questions about medical and psychosocial issues and encourage patients to talk more than do their male colleagues. While visits with male providers last an average of 22 minutes, visits with female providers last an average of 28 minutes; 20 percent of visits to male internists last 10 minutes or less, only 5 percent of visits to female internists are that brief.[104] Such gender differences are making themselves felt. More medical schools today grade male and female students not only on their ability to elicit patient information, but also on their ability to maintain comfortable eye contact, hold an interested posture and facial expression, and respond empathically to each patient's concerns. Greater emphasis is now being placed on the need for provider and patient to communicate with each other.

How patients react to their caregiver may depend on cultural expectations. For example, because verbal aggressiveness is considered to be more acceptable in men, patients are likely to view female physicians who violate this expectation negatively and are therefore less likely to take the advice they offer. The same is probably true for male physicians who violate patient expectations.[105]

Media and Technology Contacts

The Media's Messages and the Influence of New Technology

In addition to influencing the way we perceive and interact with health care providers, the media and technological innovations influence other factors that have an impact on our health: what we eat and drink and how we live.

Media Messages

Prime-time television continues to present us with high levels of sexual and occupational stereotyping; even now, on most prime-time programs, nurses are females and physicians are males.[106] The portrayal of medical practitioners also contributes to our developing a distorted picture of illness and available medical treatments. Rarely does television deal with the long-term consequences of illnesses; instead, week after week, it bombards us with examples of acute illnesses, crisis situations, and injuries.

In addition, unlike their real-life counterparts, television doctors hardly ever make diagnostic errors; in fact, far too frequently, they display an almost clairvoyant ability to diagnose and cure the strangest patient ailments.[107] Television practitioners also tend to rely on biomedical treatments including drugs to cure patients in lieu of interpersonal or home-based means of dealing with illness in which the patient takes an active part in the treatment. Consequently, children who are heavy viewers of television exhibit great concern about getting sick and have distorted perceptions of the help they can get from medicine.[108] They simply do not see media images of patients taking an active role in health care—because they are so rare.

Television also shows eating and drinking practices that in many cases are not conducive to the maintenance of good health. Prime-time programs contain numerous references to food, show characters eating snacks rather than meals, and show them drinking a lot of alcohol and coffee.[109] Despite the fact that characters on television eat fattening foods and unbalanced diets, they rarely are portrayed as overweight or out of shape. Instead, for the most part, they stay thin

in Theory

Media and Your Health

Think about the various health-related themes and health practitioners you see portrayed on television and in films.

1. In your opinion, are most of the messages the entertainment media present promoting healthy or unhealthy behaviors? Provide specific examples in support of your stance. When the messages the entertainment media present are unhealthy, do they also show us the consequences that the unhealthy behavior produces? Again, support your position with examples.

2. Describe the extent to which specific entertainment offerings influence your perception of medical practitioners and health-related behavior. Specifically, in what ways, if any, have portrayals you have observed vicariously via the entertainment media influenced your opinion of medical personnel and treatments you or others have actually experienced? In what ways, if any, have entertainment portrayals encouraged behaviors in yourself or others that could be deemed risky or unhealthy? Do you believe that the entertainment media should take a more active role in promoting safer and more healthful behavior among audience members? At the very least, do you think they should show the realistic consequences of unhealthful actions? If yes, why? If no, why not?

Which TV doctor would you most like to have as your own? Why?

and physically fit. As we should know, real life is not so kind. In fact, there is some evidence that frequent viewers are more apt to gain weight, to have dental problems, and to be less active than occasional viewers.

Television is not the only medium that influences our attitudes and our behavior toward health. Radio talk shows on health care also play an active role. Consider the following:

> *Hello, Barbara from New Jersey. You're on the air.*
> *"Hi, doctor. I had my third knee operation. I've been diagnosed with reflex sympathetic dystrophy. I've developed severe inflammation. My doctor wants to inject the knee, or go back in. Is there anything I can take naturally to reduce the inflammation?"*
> *Barbara from New Jersey is talking to Dr. Ronald Hoffman—but she's also talking to 300,000 listeners of WOR-AM (710). The show is "Health Talk." And Barbara is calling to get medical advice from a doctor she has never met, will never pay, and likely will never talk to again.*[110]

Doctors today fill the airwaves. Some are hired by radio stations to do talk shows; others use radio to promote alternative medicine or their own health products. Such shows are popular because they allow people who don't have the opportunity for sustained contact with health care providers or who don't get information from them to think they can receive the information they need to control their own treatements—without prescriptions or surgery—and be entertained in the process.

Commercially available medical videotapes and CD-ROMs also influence our health care. Some providers even offer these services as part of their patient education. "To see THE DOCTOR, press 'play.'"[111] In an effort to facilitate patient education without increasing the amount of time a physician spends with a client, videos and CD-ROM offerings brief patients on the risks and benefits of various treatment options. In addition, they enable patients to learn about health away from the tensions of the examining room. The hope is that the use of such media will not replace the one-to-one nature of the provider–patient relationship, but rather will be another resource to be combined with face-to-face counseling.

New Technology

The Internet has also entered the health care arena. There are over 25,000 Internet sites related to health.[112] For example, *Healthnet* allows patients to chat with nurses on-line. In addition, the existence of electronic communities facilitates patient research and patient-to-patient interaction. Individuals can now more easily explore medical literature and compare notes with other patients suffering from the same afflictions. By communicating directly with others, a number of patients have been able to determine that they received a placebo rather than real medication when participating as part of a drug study. Such discoveries have caused some patients to drop out of studies and prompted others to seek alternative treatments.[113] Thus, the Internet is enabling those patients who want to do so to take more control over their own medical futures.

Support groups on the Internet are also playing a new role in health communication. People can join support groups that deal with a wide range of issues, from cancer and alcoholism to attention deficit disorder or depression.[114]

Evidence regarding the impact of virtual communities is mixed. Certainly, our busy schedules and the desire for anonymity make the ease of on-line research a benefit for some. On the other hand, on-line interaction with a health practitioner is not an effective substitute for personal interaction.[115] In addition, the quality of advice offered on computer bulletin boards, while often compassionate and practical, is not a replacement for the kind of social support that can be offered face-to-face.

Gaining Communication Competence

Across Contexts

In our highly mobile, stress-filled technological society, life rarely remains static, whether it is family life, work life, or health. Change is the one constant. Old family relationships are dissolved; new ones are created. Some family members experience health problems or die. Others willingly leave the family due to divorce or relocation. New members are born or voluntarily enter the family. These deaths, departures, and arrivals may give rise to deep-seated grief, lasting resentments, happiness, jealousy, or fear. Similar comings, goings, and health-related challenges occur in organizational life. As we move through the life cycle, individuals and circumstances inevitably change. We are challenged to work though or renegotiate the nature of our relationships in order to adapt successfully. This can be accomplished through constructive observation, verbalization and discussion, problem solving, and joint decision making—keystones of effective interpersonal communication.

Learn to Deal with Conflicts across Contexts

We have a disagreement with a friend down the street, and we choose to simply walk away. We disagree with the mechanic about the cost of repairing our car, but we decide to pay and tell ourselves as we do so that we'll never bring our car there to be fixed again. It's not so easy to walk away from or escape family conflicts, work conflicts, or disagreements with health practitioners. Thus, to avoid creating "pressure-cooker" environments that boil over, resulting in unresolved situations, we need to learn to use effective problem-solving and conflict resolution techniques (also see Chapter 11). To help realize this, it is important to establish rules that clarify rather than distort communication. The following rules are suggested to help in the sharing of perceptions:

1. Respond to what is going on rather than what you *think* is going on; clarify all ambiguous messages by describing any discrepancies between the words spoken and the nonverbal message and asking for clarification.

2. Ask for help and emotional support when you need it.

3. Express your dreams and vision for the future.

4. Refrain from blaming and judging others.

5. Express your feelings directly without concealing them or becoming physically or verbally aggressive.

6. Observe your own behavior by noticing what you say, how you sound, and what you feel during an interaction.

Recognize That We Can't Always Be Happy or Healthy, or Stay the Same

Whether it is in a family, job, or health-related setting, persons who can communicate honestly with each other are able to admit when they have problems and seek help when they are unable to resolve their problems alone. In order to deal with issues as they emerge, they:

1. Share responsibilities.

2. Maintain a high level of self-disclosure and trust.

3. Deal directly with unmet or unrealized expectations.

4. Deal directly with changing rules and role conflicts.

5. Ask questions.

6. Listen more, paying attention to verbal and nonverbal cues.

7. Remain open to change—and willing to relate to the person or condition that is, rather than the person or condition that was.

Take Time to Share and Learn about Each Other

Persons who share effective interpersonal family, work, and health care relationships talk about important issues; they do not merely engage in surface chatter. Instead, they focus on and explore issues that will help them adapt to change and face new situations and circumstances. They also exhibit an other-orientation, focusing not just on themselves but on the perceptions of others as well. They offer support when it is needed, take a sincere interest in the welfare of others, use productive methods for coping with stress and illness, and prepare themselves to use the Web to help maintain social and work networks and to acquire knowledge relevant to their and others' wellbeing. In addition, they are sensitive to how cultural customs affect them and others and are aware that they influence how they perceive and interact across contexts.

daily contacts

Wrap-Up

Meet again in pairs or small groups. Turn back to the case study at the beginning of the chapter and reconsider the questions following it. How have your answers changed or become more focused? Based on what you know about issues in family, organizational, and health communication, what advice would you offer?

Critical Thinking Contacts

Examine the cartoon below. Use your knowledge of family, organizational, and health communication to analyze the dynamics at work in the scene.

Over Breakfast

"Your mother and I think it's time you got a place of your own. We'd like a little time alone before we die."

Summary

Interpersonal communication plays a key role in family-, work-, and health-related settings. The family is the core of early communicative and socialization experiences, and family members engage in continuous interaction. As Virginia Satir notes, "The family is the factory where the person is made."

According to systems theory, at any point in time, the behavior of any one family member can be understood only in relation to every other family member's behavior. Families are defined in different ways because so many kinds of families are common today. In any family, however, members perform roles and have responsibilities. Besides sharing living space, they also share a past, present, and future. They also create rules that guide family communication and help regulate interaction between family members.

As in a family, those who work in an organization share interdependent relationships. The dyad, or two-person relationship, is the most basic level of interaction in a family, in an organization, and in a health-related setting. The dyad is at the heart of not only peer but also superior/subordinate or leader/follower relationships. The kinds of communication that occur between and within groups also play a central role in fostering or impeding an organization's success. In addition, the use of different networks or communication paths affects the organization's ability to fulfill its functions, complete its tasks, and facilitate worker morale and job satisfaction.

Like persons in families and organizations, persons communicating in health-related settings also rely on interpersonal communication as they present, process, and react to health-related messages. No matter what the setting, several aspects are crucial: sensitivity to each other's needs, an awareness of mutual expectations, an understanding of how our manner of encoding messages and interacting with others influences relationships, and a recognition of how to overcome perceptual barriers. In addition, cultural differences, beliefs about gender, media portrayals, and technological advances affect and influence the nature of communication between family members, workers on the job, and health professionals.

Whatever the context, the promotion of constructive observation, verbalization and discussion, problem solving, and joint decision making all enhance communication.

Terms to Talk About

subordinate *(p. 442)*

organizational networks *(p. 444)*

shared centrality *(p. 444)*

reflective thinking *(p. 447)*

brainstorming *(p. 447)*

groupthink *(p. 448)*

participative leadership *(p. 449)*

authoritarian leadership *(p. 449)*

health communication *(p. 459)*

client compliance *(p. 461)*

therapeutic relationships *(p. 462)*

empathy *(p. 462)*

continuum of decision making *(pp. 463–464)*

directive interviews *(p. 465)*

client-centered interviews *(p. 465)*

Suggestions for Further Reading

Alan Booth and Ann C. Crouter, ed., *Just Living Together: Implications of Cohabitation on Families, Children, and Social Policy,* Mahwah, NJ, Lawrence Erlbaum, 2002. One of the first books to focus on different aspects of cohabitation.

Athena du Pre, *Communicating About Health: Current Issues and Perspectives,* Mountainview, CA: Mayfield Publishing, 2000. Explores how gender, race, age, language, and culture influence interaction in health-related situations.

Mary Anne Fitzpatrick and Anita L. Vangelisti, eds., *Exploring Family Interactions,* Thousand Oaks, CA: Sage, 1995. A detailed overview of communication processes and family functioning.

Gary L. Kreps and E. N. Kunimoto, *Effective Communication in Multi-Cultural Health Care Settings.* Thousand Oaks, CA: Sage, 1994. Explores culture as a health care variable.

Peter G. Northouse, *Leadership: Theory and Practice,* 3rd ed., Thousand Oaks, CA: Sage, 2003. An excellent overview of leadership theories and their implications for real-world organizations.

Gary N. Powell and Laura M. Graves, *Women and Men in Management,* 3rd ed., Thousand Oaks, CA: Sage, 2002. Provides a comprehensive review of the literature on gender and organizations.

Janet Yerby, Nancy Buerkel-Rothfuss, and Arthur P. Bochner, *Understanding Family Communication,* 2nd ed., Scottsdale, AZ, Gorsuch Scarisbrick, 1995. An introduction to foundational concepts in family communication and an overview of family systems theory.

Glossary

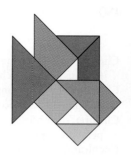

Abdicrat: one who has little need to control others

Accenting: nonverbal cues that underscore or emphasize parts of a verbal message

Acquaintances: people one knows and may converse with, but with whom interaction is typically limited in scope and quality

Active listening: the paraphrasing of a speaker's thoughts and feelings

Adaptors: unintentional movements of the body that reveal information about psychological state or inner needs, such as nervousness

Affect displays: unintentional movements of the body that reflect the intensity of an emotional state of being

Affection need: the need to give and receive love and to experience emotionally close relationships

Affectors: factors that color responses to stimuli including, but not limited to, culture, roles, biases, emotional state, past experiences, physical limitations, and capabilities

Ageism: discriminating against persons because of their age

Aggressive expression style: the open expression of one's needs, wants, and ideas even at the expense of another person

Allness: a perceptual fallacy that allows one to believe he or she knows everything about something

Allocentric orientation: a perspective displayed by people who are primarily collectivist in their thinking and behaving

Androgynous: having both masculine and feminine traits

Appreciative listening: listening that gives pleasure

Argot: the language used by members of a coculture

Articulation: how individual words are pronounced

Assertive expression style: honest, clear, and direct communication

Attending: the willingness to organize and focus on particular stimuli

Attitude: a mental set or readiness that causes one to respond in a particular way to a given stimulus

Attribution theory: the theory that posits we assign meaning to behavior by ascribing motives and causes

Authoritarian leadership: a group with a leader who uses dominating and directive communication

Autocrat: one with a great need to control and dominate others

Avoiding stage: the stage during which relationship channels are closed as individuals attempt to refrain from contact with each other

Axioms of communication: a paradigm used for understanding communication

Backchannel signals: verbalizations we use to tell another person that we are listening

Balance theory: a mode of attitude change that demonstrates our desire to live in a state of equilibrium

Behavioral pattern: a series of behavioral events that occur within a given context

Beliefs: the building blocks of attitudes; one's assessment of what is true or false, probable or improbable

Blended family: a family with two adults and children from one or both of the adults' previous marriages, as well as possibly from the current marriage

Blinders: the unconscious adding of restrictions that do not actually exist

Bonding stage: a stage of relational development during which individuals symbolically demonstrate for others that their relationship exists

Boomerang families: families containing adult children who the family thought had left permanently but unexpectedly return

Brainstorming: a technique designed to encourage idea generation

Bypassing: a problem that occurs when individuals think they understand each other but actually miss each other's meaning

Caring: the level of emotional involvement we convey to one another

Channel: a medium or passageway through which a message travels

Chronemics: the study of how humans use time to communicate

Circumscribing stage: a stage of relational development during which partners start to lessen their degree of contact with each other and commitment for each other

Client-centered interview: an interview during which the interviewer/practitioner helps the interviewee/client achieve his or her own insights and find solutions to problems he or she faces

Client compliance: the following of measures prescribed for one's care by a health care provider

Closed-ended question: a question that forces the respondent to choose a specific response

Closure: the process by which one fills in a missing perceptual piece

Coculture: a group of people who live within a society but outside its dominant culture

Coercive power: the ability to deliver negative consequences in response to the action of another; power derived from force or the threat of force

Collectivist culture: a culture in which group goals are given a higher priority than individual goals

Commitment: the intention to remain in a relationship even if trouble occurs

Commuter family: a family comprising one or more members who commute from a primary residence to a work location in a distant city and remain there for a period of time

Comparison level for alternatives: a comparison of profits and costs derived from one relationship with those that might be derived from another relationship

Competitive relationship: a relationship characterized by the presence of defensive and threatening behavior; a relationship in which one party aims to win, beat, or outsmart the other party

Complementarity: attraction for one who is different

Comprehensive listening: listening to gain knowledge

Computer-mediated communication: communication that uses the computer as a means of linking individuals

Confirmation: communication that tells another person that his or her self-image is affirmed

Confirming messages: messages that convey our value for another person

Conflict resolution grid: a model that measures one's preferred conflict resolution style

Conflict style: one's characteristic approach to a conflict with respect to measures of assertiveness and cooperativeness

Connotative meaning: subjective meaning; personal meaning

Contact cultures: cultures that encourage nonverbal displays of warmth, closeness, and availability

Content conflict: a conflict that revolves around a matter of fact

Context: the setting in which communication takes place

Continuum of (health care) decision making: a measure of the three provider–patient relationships: physician control, patient control, and collaboration

Control need: the need to establish and maintain relationships that allow one to experience satisfactory levels of influence and power

Conversation: a relatively informal social interaction in which the roles of speaker and listener are exchanged in a nonautomatic fashion under the collaborative management of all parties

Conversation deprivation: a lack of aural communication

Conversational blunder: a faux pas; the uttering of something someone is apt to find objectionable

Conversational maintenance: the smooth and natural flow of conversation

Conversational rules: behaviors that are established, preferred, or prohibited during social exchanges

Conversational structure: a format for conversation comprised of the greeting, topic priming, the heart of the conversation, preliminary processing, and the closure

Conversational turn taking: the exchanging of the speaker and listener roles during a conversation

Cooperative relationship: a relationship based on supportiveness, sharing, interdependent efforts, and trust

Coping: the managing of emotions

Cost–benefit theory: the theory that states that we work to sustain relationships that give us the greatest total benefit; the belief that a relationship will be sustained only as long as perceived benefits outweigh emotional expenditures

Counterfeit relationship: a relationship based on a lie

Crazymaking: behavior believed to be at the root of dysfunctional conflict

Cultural awareness: understanding the role cultural prescriptions play in shaping communication

Cultural lens: the ability of culture to influence perception

Cyberspace: the space that exists in an on-line or computer environment

Debilitative emotions: emotions that impede a person's ability to function effectively

Deception detection: identifying a person's behavior that contradicts his or her words

Defensive climate: the climate that results when a party to a relationship perceives or anticipates a threat

Denotative meaning: dictionary meaning; emotion-free meaning

DESC script: an acronym for describe, express, specify, and consequences; a way of expressing our own feelings and understanding the feelings of another

Describing feelings: revealing how another's behavior affects you without judging that behavior

Dialogue: an interactive process involving speaking and listening

Dialogic listening: the give and take between interactants as they co-create a relationship

Differentiating stage: a stage of relational development in which the parties reestablish their personal identities

Directive interview: an interview that is tightly controlled and orchestrated by the interviewer or practitioner

Disconfirmation: communication that denies another person's significance

Disconfirming messages: messages that convey our disregard for another person

Displacement: a defense mechanism by which one releases anger or frustration by communicating feelings to people or objects perceived to be more accessible and less dangerous than the person who precipitated the feelings

Displaying feelings: the overt enactment of feelings

Dissonance: an aversive drive that propels us toward consistency

Dominant culture: the culture that has the most power

Double message: the message that is communicated when words say one thing and nonverbal cues another

Dyad: two individuals interacting; a two-person relationship

Dynamic process: a process that is ongoing, continuous, and in a state of constant flux

Dysfunctional conflict: conflict that creates one or more serious relationship problems

Effect: the result of a communication episode

Ego conflict: a conflict that revolves around one's self-worth

Emblems: deliberate movements of the body that are consciously sent and easily translated into speech

Emotion state: an emotion of limited endurance

Emotion trait: a persisting emotion

Emotional contagion: the ability to respond in kind or to exhibit a parallel response

Emotional ineptitude: the inability to handle and control one's emotional response

Emotional intelligence: the ability to motivate oneself or to persist in the face of frustration; to control impulse and delay gratification; to regulate one's mood and keep distress from swamping the abilities to think, empathize, and hope

Emotions: the feelings one experiences in reaction to one's surroundings

Empathic concern: the ability to convey an altruistic concern for another person

Empathic responsiveness: the experiencing of an emotional response that corresponds with the emotions a speaker is experiencing

Empathy: the ability to understand another's thoughts and feelings and to communicate that understanding to the person; the ability to comprehend another's point of view

Equivocal language: words that have more than one interpretation

Ethnocentrism: the tendency to perceive what is right or wrong, good or bad, according to the categories and values of one's own culture

Euphemism: the substitution of less direct or inoffensive language for language that is blunt

Evaluative feedback: feedback that reveals one's feelings or reactions to what one heard; it provides a positive or a negative assessment

Experimenting stage: an early relational development stage during which individuals search for common ground

Expert power: power derived from knowledge; one person possesses special knowledge or skill that another thinks he or she needs

Expressive roles: roles focused on helping, supporting, nurturing, and being responsive to the needs of others; relationship-oriented roles

Extensional orientation: the type of orientation displayed when one is not blinded by labels

Face saving: the practice of giving indirect answers to avoid hurting another person

Facilitative emotions: emotions that promote effective functioning

Fact–inference confusion: the tendency to treat observations and assumptions similarly

Family network: a map of family relationships and connections

Feedback: information received in exchange for a message sent

Feedforward: a variant of feedback sent prior to a message's delivery as a means of revealing something about to follow

Field of experience: the sum of all the experiences that a person carries with him or her when communicating

Figure–ground principle: a strategy that facilitates the organization of stimuli by enabling one to focus on different stimuli alternately

Fixed feature space: the permanent characteristics of an environment

Friendly relations: a stage of friendship during which an effort to preserve and strengthen the friendship is made if individuals have enough in common to build a relationship

Friendship: the voluntary seeking out and the displaying of a strong, mutual regard between two people

Frozen evaluation: the perceptual fallacy that discourages flexibility and encourages rigidity; an evaluation of a person that ignores changes

Functional conflict: a conflict that develops a clearer understanding of needs, attitudes, or beliefs

Fundamental attribution error: overemphasizing internal or personal factors

Gender differences: social definitions and views of masculinity and femininity

Gender-lect: Deborah Tannen's term for language differences attributed to gender

Gender prescription: the ability of one's culture to influence one's view of male and female roles and behaviors

Grief process: a five-stage process during which the feelings an individual experiences range from denial to anger to guilt to depression to acceptance

Groupthink: a dysfunction in which some group members attempt to protect the group's harmony by exerting irrational pressures on one or more members so that the voicing of genuine opinions is suppressed

Halo effect: the perceiving of positive qualities in a person we like

Haptics: the study of how touch communicates

Hearing: an involuntary physiological process by which sound waves are transformed into electrical impulses and processed by the brain

High-intensity conflict: extreme conflict in which one party aims to destroy or debilitate the other.

Horn effect: the perceiving of negative qualities in a person we dislike

"I" messages: a nonevaluative form of feedback that reveals a speaker's feelings about the situation faced by an other

Idiocentric orientation: an orientation displayed by people who are primarily individualistic in their ways of thinking and behaving

Illustrators: bodily cues designed to enhance receiver comprehension of speech by supporting or reinforcing it

Impression management: exercising control over selected behaviors in an effort to make the desired impression

Inclusion need: the social need to feel a sense of belonging or mutual interest in relationship to others

Individualist culture: a culture in which individual identity is paramount

Informal space: the invisible space each person carries around

Initiating stage: the first stage in relational development during which two individuals express interest in each other

Instrumental roles: roles focused on getting things done; task-oriented roles

Integrated family: a family in which the parents and/or the children are of differing races and/or religions

Integrating stage: a stage of relational development in which the identities of the parties begin to merge

Intensifying stage: a stage of relational development during which the amount of contact and self-disclosure the parties have increases

Intensional orientation: the type of orientation displayed when one responds to a label rather than to what the label actually represents

Interactive leadership: leadership that encourages the sharing of both power and decision making with subordinates and coworkers

Interpersonal communication: a relationship; the act of interacting with another; the process of behaving with another or of creating a social relationship

Interpersonal competence: the ability to use appropriate communication to build and maintain an effective interpersonal relationship

Interpersonal conflict: a struggle between interdependent parties that occurs whenever one individual's thoughts or actions are perceived to limit or interfere with those of another; conflict that originates between two or more interdependent people

Interpersonal deception theory: a theory that explains deception as a process based on falsification, concealment, or equivocation

Interpersonal relationship: an association between two people through which the parties may or may not meet each other's social needs

Interpersonal synchrony: the exhibition of similarities; the interpersonal fusion of two individuals

Intimacy: a measure of closeness; sustained feelings of closeness and connection

Intimate distance: between skin contact and 18 inches from another person; the distance usually used by people who trust each other or who share an emotional bond or closeness

Intimate relationship: a relationship that involves a high degree of personal closeness or sharing

Intrapersonal conflict: conflict that originates within a single person

Johari window: a model containing four panes (the open area, the blind area, the hidden area, and the unknown area) that is used to explain the roles that self-awareness and self-disclosure play in relationship building

Kinesics: the study of human body motion

Language: a code or system of arbitrary symbols shared by a group and used by its members to communicate with each other

Legitimate power: the type of power in which one party in a relationship controls the other

Lie: the deliberate distorting or concealing of information; intentionally deceiving another person into accepting what one knows to be untrue

Listening: a voluntary psychological process composed of the following stages: sensing, attending, understanding/interpreting, evaluating, responding, and remembering

Live-in couple: a family in which individuals live together with or without children and cohabit as if they were married but are not

Long-distance relationship: a relationship between individuals who are geographically separated

Low-intensity conflict: a conflict in which interactants devise strategies to create a solution beneficial to both

Make-believe media: the ability of the media to make us believe things that are not necessarily true

Media models: the images we see depicted in the media

Mediated images of family: the family as portrayed in the media

Mediated reality: the reality depicted for us in the media we see, hear, and read

Medium-intensity conflict: a conflict in which each interactant wants to win

Message: the content of communication

Metacommunication: communication about communication

Metaconversation: conversation about conversation

Microfacial/micromomentary expression: an expression lasting no more than one-eighth to one-fifth of a second that usually occurs when an individual consciously or unconsciously attempts to disguise or conceal an emotion and that reveals an actual emotional state

Monologue: A process lacking in interactivity during which one person speaks while another person listens

Moving toward friendship: the point at which we make small disclosures in an effort to expand friendship

Nascent friendship: the stage during which rules for regulating interaction are worked out

Negative Pygmalion: an individual who negatively influences one's perceptions of one's own abilities

Noise: anything that interferes with or impedes the ability to send or receive a message

Nonassertive expression style: displaying hesitation in expressing one's feelings and thoughts

Noncontact cultures: cultures that discourage the use of nonverbal displays of warmth, closeness, and availability

Nonevaluative feedback: feedback that is nonjudgmental

Nonfluencies: hesitation phenomena; a nonlinguistic verbalization

Nonlistening: a kind of deficient listening behavior in which the receiver tunes out

Nonshareable goal: a goal that can be fully claimed and possessed by a single individual only

Nonverbal communication: that form of communication that does not include words; messages expressed by nonlinguistic means; people's actions or attributes, including their use of objects, sounds, time, and space, that have socially shared significance and stimulate meaning in others

Norm of reciprocity: the expectation of self-disclosure equity in relationships

Open-ended question: a question that allows the respondent free rein in answering

Organizational networks: patterns of communication in organizations

Overattribution: the attributing of everything an individual does to a single or a few specific characteristics

Oversocial: one with an overriding need for inclusion

Paralanguage: messages sent by the voice

Participative leadership: a group with a leader who acts as a guide to others who remain free to identify their own goals, establish their own procedures, and reach their own conclusions

Participative organization: an organization in which individuals perceive themselves to have significant ownership of and emotional investment in their work

Passion: intensely positive feelings of attraction that motivate one person to want to be with another

Perception: the process we use to make sense of experience

Perceptual constancy: the tendency to maintain the way one sees the world

Perceptual set: a readiness to perceive; a tendency to perceive stimuli in ways to which we have been conditioned

Perceptual shortcuts: the kind of perception exhibited by lazy perceivers who rely on stereotypes to help them make sense of experience

Personal distance: between 18 inches and 4 feet from a person; the distance at which we are most apt to converse informally

Person-oriented family: a family in which flexible roles are nurtured

Perspective taking: the ability to adopt the viewpoint of another person

Persuasive power: the ability of one party in a relationship to persuade the other party to act in a desired way

Phatic communication: superficial interaction designed to open the channel between individuals

Physical attractiveness: physical appeal that may lead to the initiation of a relationship

Pitch: the highness or lowness of a voice

Polarization: the describing of experience in either–or terms

Position-oriented family: a family in which roles are rigidly related to sex and age

Positive Pygmalion: an individual who positively influences one's perceptions of one's own abilities

Power: the potential to influence others

Power distance: the extent to which individuals are willing to accept power differentials

Prejudiced talk: the making of racist, sexist, or ageist comments

Presentational facial expressions: facial expressions that are consciously controlled

Probing: a nonevaluative technique in which one solicits additional information from another

Productive/healthy family communication patterns: family communication styles that facilitate the expression of members' feelings and wants

Pronunciation: the conventional treatment of the sounds of a word

Proxemics: the study of how space and distance are used to communicate

Proximity: physical nearness

Pseudoconflict: a nonexistent conflict

Public distance: a distance of 12 feet and beyond; the distance we use to remove ourselves physically from interaction, to communicate with strangers, or to address large groups

Purr words: words that register social approval

Rate: the speed of speech

Rationalization: providing oneself with a logical or reasonable explanation for an unrealistic thought or feeling

Reasoned sense making: the ability to predict the behavior of a particular person and account for that behavior with reasons

Red-flag word: a word that triggers emotional deafness in the receiver, dropping listening efficiency to zero

Referent power: one person's ability to encourage another to do or think as he or she desires because of the second person's identification with or respect for the first

Reflected appraisal theory: a theory that states that the self we present is in large part based on the way others categorize us, the roles they expect us to play, and the behaviors or traits they expect us to exhibit

Reflective thinking: a problem-solving system designed to encourage critical inquiry

Regulators: cues intentionally used by communicators to influence turn taking and to control the flow of conversation

Reinforcement: behavior that is personally rewarding

Rejection: the negation of or disagreement with a self-appraisal

Relational culture: how individuals work out the rules or routines of a relationship

Relational dialectics: the push or pull partners feel toward integration versus separation, stability versus change, and expression versus privacy

Relationship: a wide array of social connections that, to varying degrees, meet our interpersonal needs

Relationship breadth: a measure of how many topics individuals discuss

Relationship depth: a measure of how central discussed topics are to the self-concepts of the individuals involved and how much people are willing to reveal about themselves and their feelings

Relationship maintenance: the work needed to keep a relationship healthy

Relationship repair: work that is needed when a relationship fails to satisfy

Relationship stages: points used to characterize the nature of a relationship at any particular moment in its evolution

Representational facial expressions: exhibited facial expressions that communicate genuine inner feelings

Repression: the forgetting or denial of a disturbing stimuli

Retrospective sense making: the ability to make sense of our own behavior once it occurs

Reward power: the kind of power in which one party in a relationship controls something valued by the other party

Role assignments: the parts individuals play

Role limited interaction: an early stage of friendship characterized by a reliance on polite exchanges and standard scripts

Role reversal: imagining or acting by one party in a relationship or an exchange that he or she is the other party

Roles: the parts we play when interacting

Romantic relationship: a love-based relationship built on commitment, passion, and intimacy

Rules: behavioral norms; implied or spoken understandings

Sapir–Whorf hypothesis: a theory that proposes that language influences perception by revealing and reflecting one's world view; language is determined by the perceived reality of a culture

Schemata: the mental templates or knowledge structures we carry with us

Scripts: the general ideas we have about persons and situations and how things should play out

Selective attention: the focusing on certain cues while ignoring others

Selective exposure: exposing oneself to people and messages confirming existing beliefs, values, or attitudes

Selective perception: the tendency to see, hear, and believe what we want to

Selective retention: the recalling of things that reinforce thinking and the forgetting of things we find objectionable

Self-concept: the relatively stable set of perceptions each of us attributes to ourselves

Self-disclosure: information about the self that is willingly made known to others

Self-esteem: one's appraisal of his or her own self-worth

Self-fulfilling prophecy: a prediction or expectation that comes true simply because one acts as if it were true

Self-serving bias: the overemphasizing of external factors

Semi-fixed feature space: the use of moveable objects to identify boundaries and promote or inhibit interaction

Shareable goal: a goal that both parties to a conflict can possess

Shared centrality: a communication network in which the ability to influence others is shared

Silence: the absence of vocal communication

Similarity: attraction or social validation that comes from a like way of thinking

Single-parent family: a family in which one parent is solely responsible for a biological or adopted child or children

Small talk: spontaneous conversation that lays the foundation for an interpersonal relationship

Snarl words: words that register social disapproval

Social attractiveness: having an engaging personality and demeanor

Social distance: an interpersonal distance that extends from 4 feet to 12 feet; usually used to conduct business or discuss nonpersonal issues

Social learning theory: a theory that asserts that we learn at least some of what we know by observing others and then modeling the behaviors that we have observed

Social penetration theory: the theory that states that the relationships we share typically begin with relatively narrow breadth and shallow depth and develop both over time

Speech–thought differential: the difference between the rate of speech and the rate at which speech can be comprehended

Spotlighting: the highlighting of a person's sex for emphasis

Stabilized friendship: the stage during which individuals behave as if they expect their friendship to continue for a long time

Stagnating stage: a stage of relational development characterized by one person's decreasing interest in the other

Standpoint theory: the theory that one's place in the power hierarchy influences the accuracy of his or her perception of social life

Stereotypes: rigid perceptions that are applied to all members of a group or to an individual over a period of time, regardless of individual variations

Subordinate: the person who reports to a superior

Substituting: nonverbal cues that take the place of verbal cues

Supportive climate: a climate in which the level of threat individuals experience is reduced

Supportive environment: an environment that builds trust and maintains each person's sense of personal worth

Supportive feedback: nonevaluative feedback that indicates that we view another's problem as important

Symbol: something that stands for something else

Sympathetic responsiveness: feeling for, rather than with, a speaker

Systems theory: an approach to communication that stresses the interaction of all elements

Task attractiveness: pleasure in working with another that leads one to seek increased interpersonal contact with the other

Technopoly: a culture whose thought-world is monopolized by technology

Telepresence: the ability of virtual reality to allow one to have the sense of physically being in a different place or time

Terminating stage: the stage of relational development during which the parties decide the relationship is over

Territoriality: the space one claims or identifies as one's own

Therapeutic relationship: a relationship that increases one's level of interpersonal health

Toxic communication: communication that is verbally or physically abusive

Triangle of meaning: a model that demonstrates the relationship that exists among words, things, and thoughts

Trust: the belief that one can rely on another; made up of two components: trusting behavior and trustworthy behavior

Trusting behavior: acting in accordance with the belief that another will not take advantage of one's vulnerabilities

Trustworthy behavior: behaving so as not to take advantage of another's vulnerabilities

Tunnel vision: seeing what one expects to see

Turn-denying signals: paralinguistic and kinesic cues that signal a reluctance to switch speaking and/or listening roles

Turn-maintaining signals: paralinguistic and kinesic cues that suggest that we are not yet ready to give up the speaking role

Turn-requesting signals: paralinguistic and kinesic cues that let the speaker know the listener would like to switch roles

Turn-yielding signals: paralinguistic and kinesic cues that indicate readiness to exchange the role of speaker for the role of listener

Uncertainty reduction theory: a theory espousing that by monitoring our social environment we learn more about each other

Undelayed reaction: the tendency to jump to conclusions

Underpersonal: one with little need for affection

Undersocial: one with little need for inclusion

Understanding: a form of nonevaluative feedback during which we attempt to comprehend what another person has told us by paraphrasing what we have heard

Value conflict: a conflict that revolves around the importance of an issue

Values: one's ideas about what is important in life

Virtual community: a community that exists in cyberspace

Visual dominance ratio: a figure derived by comparing the percentage of looking while speaking with the percentage of looking while listening

Volume: the power of a voice, its loudness or volume

Waning friendship: the drifting apart of friends

Word mask: ambiguous language meant to confuse

Word wall: language use that impedes understanding

Answers to Questions

Answers to "Facts and Inferences" exercise, page 84.

1. T
2. ?
3. ?
4. F
5. ?

Answers to "Dots" exercise, page 86.

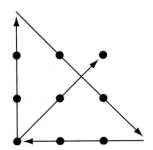

End Notes

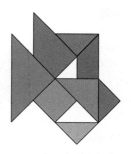

Chapter 1

1. See, for example, *New York Times,* July 3, 1991, p. A17.
2. See, for example, Julia T. Wood, *Communication Theories in Action: An Introduction,* 3rd ed., Belmont, CA: Wadsworth, 2004, p. 16; W. W. Wilmot, *Relational Communication,* New York: McGraw Hill, 1999.
3. William W. Wilmot, *Dyadic Communication,* 3rd ed. New York: Random House, 1987.
4. See, for example, S. G. Lakey and D. J. Canary, "Actor goal Achievement and Sensitivity to the Partner as Critical Factors in Understanding Interpersonal Competence and Conflict Strategies," Paper presented at the International Communication Association conference, Washington, D.C., May 2001.
5. For a review of the research on interpersonal communication competence, see J. M. Wiemann and M. O. Wiemann, *Interpersonal Competence,* Newbury Park, CA: Sage, 1991.
6. For background on this topic, see Gerald R. Miller, "The Current State of Theory and Research in Interpersonal Communication," *Human Communication Research,* 4 (1978): 164–178.
7. I. Lau, C. Chiu, and Y. Hong, "I Know What You Know: Assumptions about Others' Knowledge and Their Effects on Message Construction," *Social Cognition,* 19, 2001, pp. 587–600.
8. Steve Duck, "Relationships as Unfinished Business: Out of the Frying Pan and into the 1990s," *Journal of Social and Personal Relationships,* 7 (1990): 5.
9. See Thomas Hora in Paul H. Watzlawick et al., *Pragmatics of Human Communication: A Study of Interaction Patterns, Pathologies and Paradoxes,* New York: Norton, 1967.
10. See N. Bolger and S. Kelleher, "Daily Life in Relationships," in Steve Duck (ed.), *Understanding Relationship Processes, 3: Social Context and Relationships,* Newbury Park, CA: Sage, 1993, pp. 100–108. See also S. Cohen, "Psychosocial Models of the Role of Social Support in the Etiology of Physical Disease," *Health Psychology,* 7 (1988) pp. 269–297.
11. Willam Schutz, *The Interpersonal Underworld,* Palo Alto, CA: Science and Behavior Books, 1966.
12. See, for example, Kay Deaux, Frances C. Dave, and Lawrence S. Wrightsman, *Social Psychology,* 5th ed., Belmont, CA: Wadsworth, 1993; and Fathali M. Moghaddam, Donald M. Taylor, and Stephen C. Wright, *Social Psychology in Cross-Cultural Perspective,* New York: W. H. Freeman, 1993.
13. C. R. Berger, *Planning Strategic Interaction: Attaining Goals through Communicative Action,* Mahwah: Lawrence Erlbaum. 1997
14. B. Aubrey Fisher, "The Pragmatic Perspective of Human Communication," in Frank Dance, ed.,

Human Communication Theory, New York: Harper & Row, 1982.
15. B. Aubrey Fisher and Katherine L. Adams, *Interpersonal Communication: Pragmatics of Human Relationships,* 2nd ed., New York: McGraw-Hill, 1994, p. 15.
16. Paul H. Watzlawick, Janet H. Beavin, and Don D. Jackson, *Pragmatics of Human Communication: A Study of Interaction Patterns, Pathologies and Paradoxes,* New York: Norton, 1967.
17. See, for example, Daniel G. Bates and Fred Plog, *Cultural Anthropology,* 3rd ed., New York: McGraw-Hill, 1990.
18. Edward T. Hall, *The Silent Language,* New York: Fawcett, 1959.
19. See William B. Gudykunst, *Bridging Differences,* 2nd ed., Thousand Oaks, CA: Sage, 1994.
20. Julia T. Wood, *Gendered Lives,* Belmont, CA: Wadswoth, 1994, p. 15.
21. Elizabeth Fox-Genovese, *Feminism without Illusions,* Chapel Hill, NC: University of North Carolina Press, 1991, p. 20.
22. See, for example, J. A. Doyle, *The Male Experience,* 2nd ed., Dubuque, IA: William C. Brown, 1989.
23. Marshall McLuhan, *Understanding Media: The Extension of Man.* New York: McGraw-Hill, 1964.
24. Marc Peyser, Andrew Murr, and Rob French, "Don't 'Chat' to Strangers," *Newsweek,* June 19, 1995, p. 42.
25. Steven G. Jones, *Cybersociety,* Thousand Oaks, CA: Sage, 1995, p. 17.
26. See K. O'Toole, "Study Takes Early Look at Social Consequences of Net Use," *Stanford Online Report,* February 16, 2000. **http://www.stanford.edu/dept/news/report/news/february16/internetsurvey-216 html** "Stanford Institute for the Quantitative Study of Society," *New York Times,* February 16, 2000, p. A-18.
27. "Pew Internet and American Life Project," Pew Charitable Trusts, May 2000. **http://www.pewinternet.org/.**
28. See, for example, Josh Meyrowitz, "Media Theory," in Eric P. Bucy, *Living in the Information Age,* Australia: Wadsworth, 2002, p. 32.
29. Jan Samoriski, *Issues in Cyberspace,* Boston: Allyn & Bacon, 2002, p. 37.
30. "Who Wins in the New Economy?" *The Wall Street Journal,* June 27, 2000, p. B4.
31. D. Kirkpatrick, "Here Comes the Payoff from PCs," *Fortune,* March 23, 1992, pp. 93–102.
32. Sherry Turkle, *Life on the Screen: Identity in the Age of the Internet,* New York: Simon & Schuster, 1995.
33. Michael James, Edward Wotring, and Edward J. Forrest, "An Exploratory Study of the Perceived Benefits of Electronic Bulletin Board Use and Their Impact on Other

Communication Activities," *Journal of Broadcasting and Electronic Media,* 39, 1 (1995): 30–49.

34. Neil Postman, *Technopoly: The Surrender of Culture to Technology,* New York: Vintage. 1992.

Chapter 2

1. See Don Hamacheck, *Encounters with the Self,* 3rd ed., Fort Worth, TX: Holt, Rinehart & Winston, 1992, pp. 5–8.
2. S. I. Hayakawa & Alan R. Hayakawa, *Language in Thought and Action,* 5th ed., New York: Harcourt Brace Jovanovich, 1990.
3. See Thomas C. Palmer, Jr., "Self-Esteem: Self-Defeating?" *Boston Globe,* March 31, 1996, p. 79.
4. Ibid.
5. Hamachek, *Encounters with the Self,* pp. 3–5.
6. Ibid.
7. See Lauren Slater, "The Trouble With Self-Esteem," *The New York Times Magazine,* February 3, 2002, pp. 44–47.
8. R. Baumesister, L. Smart, and J. Boden, "Relation of the Threatened Egotism to Violence and Aggression: The Dark Side of High Self-Esteem," *Psychological Review,* 103, 1996, pp. 5–33.
9. R. Brooks and S. Goldstein, *Raising Resilient Children,* New York: Contemporary Books, 2001.
10. William James, *The Principles of Psychology,* New York: Dover Publications, 1890.
11. C. H. Cooley, *Human Nature and the Social Order,* New York: Scribner's, 1912.
12. Leon Festinger, "A Theory of Social Comparison Processes," *Human Relations* 2 (1954): 117–140.
13. L. B. Whitbeck and D. R. Hoyt, "Social Prestige and Assortive Mating: A Comparison of Students from 1950 and 1988," *Journal of Social and Personal Relationships,* 11 (1994): 137–145.
14. See, for example, W. Weiten, *Psychology Themes and Variations,* 4th ed., Pacific Grove, CA: Brooks/Cole, 1998.
15. D. M. Tice, and J. Faber, "Cognitive and Motivational Processes in Self-Presentation," in J. P. Forgas, K. D. Williams, and L. Wheeler, eds., *The Social Mind: Cognitive and Motivational Aspects of Interpersonal Behavior,* Cambridge: Cambridge University Press, 2001, pp. 139–156.
16. Paul Watzlawick, Janet H. Beavin, and Don D. Jackson, *Pragmatics of Human Interaction: A Study of Interactional Patterns, Pathologies and Paradoxes,* New York: Norton, 1967.
17. See Kim Giffin and Bobby R. Patton, "The Search for Self Identity," in *Fundamentals of Interpersonal Communication,* New York: Harper & Row, 1971; and G. H. Mead, *Mind, Self and Society,* Chicago: University of Chicago Press, 1934, pp. 144–164.
18. Len Sandler, "Self-Fulfilling Prophecy: Better Management by Magic," *Training Magazine* (February 1986).
19. Robert Rosenthal and Lenore Jacobson *Pygmalion in the Classroom,* New York: Holt, Rinehart and Winston, 1968.
20. George Bernard Shaw, *Pygmalion,* New York: Dover Publications, 1994.

21. See Michael L. Hecht, Ronald L. Jackson II, and Sidney A. Ribeau, *African American Communication: Exploring Identity and Culture,* Mahwah, NJ: Lawrence Erlbaum Associates, 2003.
22. Richard Brislin, *Understanding Culture's Influence on Behavior,* Orlando, FL: Harcourt Brace Jovanovich, 1993, p. 47.
23. "Hey, I'm Terrific," *Newsweek,* February 17, 1992, p. 48.
24. Larry Samovar and Richard E. Porter, *Communication between Cultures,* Belmont, CA: Wadsworth, 1991, p. 91.
25. William B. Gudykunst and S. Ting-Toomy, *Culture and Interpersonal Communication.* Newbury Park, CA: Sage, 1988.
26. S. Kitayama and H. R. Markus, "Culture and Self: Implications for Internationalizing Psychology," in N. R. Goldberger and J. B. Veroff, eds., *The Culture and Psychology Reader,* New York: New York University Press, 1995, p. 44.
27. Harry C. Triandis, K. Leung, M. Villareal, and F. Clack, "Allocentric vs Idiocentric Tendencies," *Journal of Research in Personality,* 19, 395–415.
28. J. A. Vandello and D. Cohen, "Patterns of Individualism and Collectivism Across the United States," *Journal of Personality and Social Psychology,* 77, 1999, pp. 279–292.
29. See, for example, W. B. Gudykunst, Y. Matsumoto, S. Ting-Toomy, T. Nishida, K. Kim, and S. Heyman, "The Influence of Cultural Individualism-Collectivism, Self-Construals, and Individual Values on Communication Styles Across Cultures," *Human Communication Research,* 22, 1996, pp. 510–543.
30. For a second discussion of cultural variations see J. N. Martin and T. K. Nakayama, *Intercultural Communication in Contexts,* 2nd ed., Mountainview, CA: Mayfield, 2000.
31. Robert Atkinson, "The Universal Teenager," *Psychology Today* (October, 1988).
32. Darlene Powell Hopson and Derek Hopson, *Different and Wonderful: Raising Black Children in a Race-Conscious Society,* Saddle River, NJ: Prentice Hall, 1991.
33. Yvone Shinhoster Lamb, "Self Esteem is Skin Deep," *Washington Post,* 1992.
34. J. McWhorter, *Losing the Race: Self-Sabotage in Black America,* New York: Free Press, 2000.
35. N. R. Branscombe and N. Ellemers, "Coping with Group-Based Discrimination: Individualistic Versus Group-Level Strategies," in J. K. Swim and C. Stangor, eds., *Prejudice: The Target's Perspective,* San Diego: Academic Press, 1998, pp. 243–266.
36. Angie Williams and Jon F. Nussbaum, *Intergenerational Communication Across the Life Span,* Mahwah, NJ: Lawrence Erlbaum, 2001; and Joel Wells, *Who Do You Think You Are,* Chicago: The Thomas More Press, 1989, p. 90.
37. See, for example, J. Coupland, J. F. Nussbaum, and N. Coupland, "The Reproducing of Aging and Ageism on Intergenerational Talk," in N. Coupland, H. Giles, and J. Wiemann, eds., *Miscommunication and Problematic Talk,* Newbury Park CA: Sage, 1991, p. 85; K. A. Gainor and L. Forrest, "African American Women's Self Concept: Implications for Career Decisions and

Career Counseling," *Career Development Quarterly,* 39:3, March, 1991, pp. 262–272; and F. E. Obiakor, "Self-Concept of African-American Students: An Operational Model on Special Education," *Exceptional Children,* 59:2, October, 1992, pp. 160–167.

38. Dawn O. Braithewate, "Viewing Persons with Disabilities as a Culture," in Larry A. Samovar and Richard E. Porter, eds., *Intercultural Communication: A Reader;* Belmont, CA: Wadsworth, 1994, p. 151.

39. Kevin Kilbane, "This Girl Got Her Wish," *The Record* (Hackensack, NJ), December 22, 1993, p. A18.

40. David Firestone, "While Barbie Talks Tough, G. I. Joe Goes Shopping," *New York Times,* December 31, 1993, p. A12.

41. L. M. Brown and Carol Gilligan, *Meeting at the Crossroads: Women's Psychology and Girls' Development,* Cambridge, MA: Harvard University Press, 1992; and P. Orenstein, *School Girls,* New York: Doubleday, 1994.

42. Julia T. Wood, *Gendered Lives: Communication, Gender, and Culture,* Belmont, CA: Wadsworth, 1994, p. 21.

43. See Sally Quinn, "Look Out. It's Superwoman," *Newsweek,* February 15, 1993, pp. 24–25.

44. Douglas Kellner, "Cultural Studies, Muliculturalism, and Media Culture," in G. Dines, J. M. Humez, eds., *Gender, Race and Class in Media,* 2nd ed., Thousand Oaks, CA: Sage, 2003, pp. 9–20.

45. Michael Parenti, "The Make Believe Media," *The Humanist* (November–December, 1990).

46. "This Is a Job for Wonder Woman," *The Record,* (Hackensack, NJ), December 31, 1993, p. D3.

47. "Hey, I'm Terrific," p. 46.

48. Stuart Ewen, *All Consuming Images,* New York: Basic Books, 1988, p. 89.

49. Mark Caro, "Virtual Reality Is The Real Thing—Or Is it?" *The Record,* May 25, 2003, O1, O4.

50. A. Lenhart, L. Rainie, and O. Lewis, "Teenage Life Online," Washington, D.C.: Pew Internet and American Life Project, 2001.

51. Turkle, p. 12.

52. Turkle, pp. 14, 178.

53. D. Myers, "Anonymity Is Part of the Magic: Individual Manipulation of Computer-Mediated Communication Contexts," *Qualitative Sociology,* 19, 3 (1987): 251–266.

54. Lynda Edwards, "What Might Have Been," *New York Times,* January 2, 1994, Section 9, p. 1.

55. Claudette Mackay-Lassonde, "Butterflies, Not Pigeonholes," *Vital Speeches of the Day,* January 1, 1994, p. 183.

Chapter 3

1. Mark Caro, "Virtual Reality is the Real Thing—Or is It?" *The Record,* May 25, 2003, O1, O4.

2. Ibid.

3. Stephen R. Covey, *The Seven Habits of Highly Effective People,* New York: Simon & Schuster, 1990, p. 28.

4. See P. H. Collins, "Learning from the Outsider Within," *Social Programs,* 33, 1986, pp. 514–532.

5. S. Harding, *Whose Science? Whose Knowledge? Thinking from Women's Lives,* Ithaca, NY: Cornell University Press, 1991.

6. V. Manusov, "It Depends on Your Perspective: Effects of Stance and Beliefs About Intent on Person Perception," *Western Journal of Communication,* 57, 1993, pp. 27–41.

7. Ibid.

8. Sharon Begley, "The Memory of Sept. 11 Is Seared in Your Mind; But Is It Really True?" *The Wall Street Journal,* September 13, 2002, B1.

9. S. Kassin, *Psychology,* Upper Saddle River, NJ: Prentice-Hall, 1998.

10. Larry A. Samovar and Richard E. Porter, *Communication between Cultures,* Belmont, CA: Wadsworth, 1991, p. 104

11. Ibid., p. 106.

12. Donald R. Atkinson, George Morten, and Derald Wing Sue, "Minority Group Counseling: An Overview," in *Intercultural Communication: A Reader,* 4th ed, Larry A. Samovar and Richard E. Porter, eds., Belmont, CA: Wadsworth, 1982, p. 172.

13. "A Newspaper Apologizes for Photos," *The New York Times,* August 31, 2002, A9.

14. See, for example, R. Buttny, "Reported Speech in Talking Race on Campus," *Human Communication Research,* 23, 1997, pp. 477–506.

15. Richard Benedetto, "Differences in Perceptions Fuel Mistrust," *USA Today,* March 5, 2002, 11A.

16. Irene V. Blair, Charles M. Judd, Melody S. Sadler, and Christopher Jenkins, "The Role of Afrocentric Features in Person Perception: Judging by Features and Categories," *Journal of Personality and Social Psychology,* 83: 1, July, 2002.

17. See, for example, M. E. Hill, "Color Differences in the Socioeconomic Status of African American Men: Results of a Longitudinal Study," *Social Forces,* 78, 1437–1460.

18. Blair, Judd, Sadler, and Jenkins.

19. See Alison L. Chasteen, "The Role of Age and Age-Related Attitudes in Perceptions of Elderly Individuals," *Basic and Applied Social Psychology,* 22:3, September 2000.

20. S. T. Fiske and S. L. Neuberg, "A Continuum of Impression Formation, from Category-Based to Individuating Processes: Influences of Information and Motivation on Attention and Interpretation" in M. P. Zanna, ed., *Advances in Experimental Social Psychology,* New York: Academic, volume 23, 1990, pp. 1–74.

21. See, for example, K. Speas and B. Obenshain, *Images of Aging in America,* Washington, D.C.: American Association of Retired Persons, 1995.

22. M. Snyder and P. K. Miene, "Stereotyping of the Elderly: A Functional Approach," *British Journal of Social Psychology,* 33, 1994, pp. 63–82.

23. Ibid.

24. William V. Haney, *Communication and Organization Behavior,* Homewood, IL: Richard D. Irwin, 1973, p. 318.

25. Alfred Korzbski, *Science and Sanity,* 4th ed. San Francisco, CA: Institute of General Semantics, 1980.

26. Irving J. Lee, *How to Talk with People,* San Francisco, CA: International Society for General Semantics, 1982.

27. Haney, *Communication and Organization Behavior,* p. 336.

28. Mary Morain, ed., *Classroom Exercises in General Semantics,* San Francisco, CA: International Society for General Semantics, 1980, pp. 17–18.

29. Marshall Singer, "Culture: A Perceptual Approach," in Larry A. Samovar and Richard E. Porter, *Intercultural Communication: A Reader,* 4th ed., Belmont, CA: Wadsworth, 1985, pp. 62–69.

30. Samovar and Porter, *Communication between Cultures,* p. 105.

31. J. W. Bagby, "A Cross-Cultural Study of Perceptual Predominance in Binocular Rivalry," *Journal of Abnormal and Social Psychology* 54 (1957): 331–334.

32. Covey, p. 277.

33. S. A. Basow, *Gender: Stereotypes and Roles,* 3rd ed., Pacific Grove, CA: Brooks/Cole, 1992, p. 159.

34. "Study Reports Sex Bias in News Organizations," *New York Times,* April 11, 1989, p. C22.

35. Wood, *Gendered Lives,* p. 238.

36. David Evans, "The Wrong Examples," *Newsweek,* March 1, 1993, p. 10.

37. C. Hoffner et al., "The Third-Person Effect in Perceptions of the Influence of Television Violence," *Journal of Communication,* 51, June 2001, pp. 283–299.

38. See G. Gerbner, L. P. Gross, M. Morgan, and N. Signorielli, "The 'Mainstreaming' of America: Violence Profile No. 11," *Journal of Communication,* 30, 1980, pp. 10–29; and G. Gerbner, "The Politics of Media Violence: Some Reflections," in C. Hamelink & O. Linne, eds., *Mass Communication Research: On Problems and Policies,* Norwood, NJ: Ablex, 1994.

39. See, for example, R. Spears, T. Postmes, M. Lea, and S. E. Watt, "A SIDE View of Social Influence," in J. P. Forgas & K. D. Williams, eds., *Social Influence: Direct and Indirect Processes,* Philadelphia: Psychology Press, 2001, pp. 331–350.

40. Julia T. Wood, *Gendered Lives,* Belmont, CA: Wadsworth, 1994, pp. 21, 131.

41. Ibid.

42. See Judy Cornelia Pearson, *Gender and Communication,* Dubuque, IA: William C. Brown, 1985.

43. L. M. Harasim, ed., *Global Networks,* Cambridge, MA: MIT Press, 1993.

44. J. Jensen, *Redeeming Modernity,* Newbury Park, CA: Sage, 1990, p. 71.

45. Sharon Begley, "The Kid Flunked, but He Sure Pays Attention," *The Wall Street Journal,* May 29, 2003, B1, B8.

46. Sandra Blakeslee, "Video-Game Killing Builds Visual Skills, Researchers Report," *The New York Times,* May 29, 2003, A1, A25.

Chapter 4

1. A. Wolvin and C. G. Coakley, *Listening,* 5th ed., Dubuque, IA: Brown & Benchmark, 1996.

2. See, for example, Larry Barker, R. Edwards, C. Gaines, K. Gladney, and F. Holley, "An Investigation of Proportional Time Spent in Various Communication Activities by College Students," *Journal of Applied Communication Research,* 8 (1981): 101–109; and Andrew Wolvin and Carolyn Coakley, "A Survey of the States of Listening

Training in Some Fortune 500 Corporations," *Communication Education,* 40 (1991): 152–164.

3. For a thorough discussion of listening, see the classic work by Ralph Nichols and Leonard Stevens, *Are You Listening?* New York: McGraw-Hill, 1957.

4. A. Robertson, *The Language of Effective Listening,* Carmel, IN: Scott Foresman Professional Books, 1991, pp. 44–45.

5. Lyman K. Steil, J. Summerfield, and G. deMare, *Listening: It Can Change Your Life.* New York: Wiley, 1983.

6. See, for example, M. Snyder, "A Gender-Informed Model of Couple and Family Therapy: Relationship Enhancement Therapy," *Contemporary Family Therapy: An International Journal,* 14 February 1992, pp. 15–31; and B. I. Omdahl, *Cognitive Appraisal, Emotion, and Empathy,* Mahah, NJ: Lawrence Erlbaum, 1995.

7. L. A. Sapadin, "Friendship and Gender: Perspectives of Professional Men and Women," *Journal of Social and Personal Relationships,* 5, 1988, pp. 387–403.

8. J. B. Weaver III and M. B. Kirtley, "Listening Styles and Empathy," *Southern Communication Journal,* 60, 1995, pp. 131–140.

9. See D. Johnson, "Helpful Listening and Responding," in K. M. Galvin and P. Cooper, eds., *Making Connections: Readings in Relational Communication,* Los Angeles: Roxbury, 1996, pp. 91–97.

10. R. Preiss and L. Wheeless, "Affective Responses in Listening," *The Journal of the International Listening Association,* 3 (1989): 72–102.

11. See, for example, J. B. Bavelas and T. Johnson, "Listeners as Co-Narrators," *Journal of Personality and Social Psychology,* 79, 2000, pp. 941–952.

12. John Stewart and M. Thomas, "Dialogic Listening: Sculpting Mutual Meanings," in J. Stewart, ed., *Bridges Not Walls: A Book about Interpersonal Communication,* 6th ed., New York: McGraw-Hill, 1995, pp. 184–201.

13. Larry A. Samovar and Richard E. Porter, *Communication between Cultures,* 5th ed., Belmont, CA: Wadsworth, 2003, pp. 211–212.

14. William B. Gudykunst, *Bridging Differences,* 14th ed., Thousand Oaks, CA: Sage, 2004, pp. 196–197.

15. Deborah Tannen, *You Just Don't Understand: Women and Men in Conversation.* New York: Morrow, 1990.

16. S. Petronio, J. Martin, and R. Littlefield, "Prerequisite Conditions for Self-Disclosing: A Gender Issue," *Communication Monographs,* 51 (1984): 268–272.

17. M. Booth-Butterfield, "She Hears . . . He Hears: What They Hear and Why," *Personnel Journal,* 44, 36–42.

18. J. B. Stiff, J. P. Dillard, L. Somera, H. Kim, and C. Sleight, "Empathy, Communication, and Prosocial Behavior," *Communication Monographs,* 55 (1988): 198–213.

19. Diana K. Ivy and Phil Backlund, *Exploring Gender Speak,* New York: McGraw-Hill, 1994, p. 225.

20. N. Newcombe and D. B. Arnkoff, "Effects of Speech Style and Sex of Speaker on Person Perception," *Journal of Personality and Social Psychology,* 37:8, 1999, pp. 1293–1303.

21. A. Mulac, C. R. Incontro, and M. R. James, "Comparison of the Gender-Linked Language Effect and Sex Role

Stereotypes," *Journal of Personality and Social Psychology,* 49:4, 1985, pp. 1098–1109.

22. See, for example, Robert Kubey and Mihaly Czikszent-mihaliyi, *Television and the Quality of Life: How Viewing Shapes Everyday Experience,* Hillsdale, NJ: Erlbaum, 1990.

Chapter 5

1. Michael L. Hecht, Ronald L. Jackson II, and Sidney A. Ribeau, *African American Communication: Exploring Identity and Culture,* 2nd ed., Mahwah, NJ: Lawrence Erlbaum Associates, 2003.
2. C. K. Ogden and I. A. Richards, *The Meaning of Meaning,* New York: Harcourt Brace Jovanovich, 1930.
3. William Safire, "Traffic Talk," *New York Times,* February 28, 1982.
4. I. Strecker, "Cultural Variations in the Concept of 'Face,'" *Multilingua,* 12, 1993, pp. 119–141.
5. William Lutz, *Doublespeak Defined,* New York: Harper Resource, 1999; and National Council of Teachers of English, "The 1999 Doublespeak Awards," *ETC,* 56:4, Winter 1999–2000, p. 484.
6. See, for example, M. Schwartz and the Task Force on Bias-Free Language of the Association of American University Presses, *Guidelines for Bias-Free Writing,* Bloomington: Indiana University Press, 1995; J. Lever, "The 1995 Advocate Survey of Sexuality and Relationships: The Women, Lesbian Sex Survey," *The Advocate,* 687–688, 22–30, 1995; Michael L. Hecht, Ronald Jackson II, and Sidney A. Ribeau, *African American Communication: Exploring Identity and Culture,* 2nd ed., Mahwah, NJ: Lawrence Erlbaum Associates, 2003.
7. See William V. Haney, *Communication and Organizational Behavior,* 3rd ed., Homewood, IL: Richard D. Irwin, 1973, pp. 247–248.
8. Benjamm Lee Whorf, "Science and Linguistics," in John B. Carroll (ed.), *Language, Thought and Reality: Selected Writings of Benjamin Lee Whorf,* Cambridge, MA: MIT Press, 1996.
9. William B. Gudykunst, "Uncertainty and Anxiety," in Y. Y. Kim and W. B. Gudykunst, eds. *Theories in Intercultural Communication,* Newbury Park, CA: Sage, p. 129.
10. Dean C. Barnlund, *Public and Private Self in Japan and the United States: Communicative Styles in Two Cultures.* Yarmouth, ME: Intercultural Press, 1989, p. 57.
11. David G. Mandelbaum, ed., *Selected Writings of Edward Sapir,* Berkeley: University of California Press, 1949, p. 162.
12. E. M. Rogers and T. M. Steinfatt, *Intercultural Communication,* Prospect Heights, IL: Waveland Press, 1998, p. 135.
13. B. L. Whorf, *Language, Thought, and Reality: Selected Writings of Benjamin Lee Whorf,* J. B. Carroll, ed., Cambridge, MA: MIT Press, 1940/1956, p. 239.
14. D. G. Mandelbaum, ed., *Selected Writings of Edward Sapir,* Berkeley and Los Angeles: University of California Press, 1949, p. 162.
15. W. Johnson, *People in Quandaries,* New York: Harper and Row,

16. F. Cowie, *What's Within? Nativism Reconsidered,* New York: Oxford University Press, 1999.
17. Larry A. Samovar and Richard E. Porter, *Communication between Cultures,* Belmont, CA: Wadsworth, 1991, p. 152.
18. Richard Brislin and Tomoko Yoshida, *Intercultural Communication Training: An Introduction.* Thousand Oaks, CA: Sage, 1994.
19. S. I. Hayakawa and Alan R. Hayakawa, *Language in Thought and Action,* 5th ed., San Diego, CA: Harcourt Brace Jovanovich, 1990, p. 116.
20. N. M. Henley, "Molehill or Mountain? What We Know and Don't Know About Sex Bias in Language," in M. Crawford & M. Gentry, eds., *Gender and Thought: Psychological Perspectives,* New York: Springer-Verlag, pp. 59–78.
21. See, for example, J. Gastil, "Generic Pronouns and Sexist Language: The Oxymoronic Character of Masculine Generics," *Sex Roles,* 23, 1990, pp. 629–643, and J. Y. Switzer, "The Impact of Generic Word Choices: An Empirical Investigation of Age- and Sex-Related Differences," *Sex Roles,* 22, 1990, pp. 69–82.
22. A. Sheldon, "Kings are Royaler Than Queens: Language and Socialization," *Young Children,* January 1990, pp. 4–9.
23. See "No Sexism Please, We're Webster's," *Newsweek,* June 24, 1991, p. 59.
24. Julia T. Wood, *Gendered Lives,* Belmont, CA: Wadsworth, 1994, p. 127.
25. Deborah Tannen, "Gender Differences in Conversational Coherence: Physical Alignment and Topical Cohesion," in B. Dorval, ed., *Conversational Organization and Its Development,* vol. 38, Norwood, NJ: Ablex, 1990, pp. 167–206.
26. Wood, *Gendered Lives,* pp. 139–144.
27. J. Coates, *Women, Men and Language,* New York: Longman, 1986.
28. Deborah Tannen, *You Just Don't Understand: Women and Men in Conversation,* New York: Morrow, 1990, p. 42.
29. L. Tamir, *Men in Their Forties: The Transition to Middle Age,* New York: Springer, 1982.
30. J. Harwood, H. Giles, S. Fox, E. B. Ryan, and A. Williams, "Patronizing Young and Elderly Adults: Response Strategies in a Community Setting," *Journal of Applied Communication Research,* 21, 1993, pp. 211–226.
31. Naomi Wolf, *The Beauty Myth.* New York: Morrow, 1991.
32. "Study Reports Sex Bias in News Organizations," *New York Times,* April 11, 1989, p. C22.
33. A. R. Stone, "Will the Real Body Please Stand Up?" in M. Benedikt, ed., *Cyberspace: First Steps,* Cambridge, MA: MIT Press, 1991, pp. 81–118.
34. H. Reingold, "A Slice of Life in My Virtual Community," in L. M. Harasim, ed., *Global Networks,* Cambridge, MA: MIT Press, 1993, p. 61.
35. Margaret L. McLaughlin, Keery K. Osborne, and Christine B. Smith, "Standards of Conduct on Usenet," in Steven G. Jones, *Cybersociety,* Thousand Oaks, CA: Sage, 1995, p. 103.

Chapter 6

1. See Dale Leathers, *Successful Nonverbal Communication,* 2nd ed., New York: Macmillan, pp. 5–7.
2. Ibid., p. 19.
3. See Paul Ekman, *Telling Lies: Clues to Deceit in the Marketplace, Politics, and Marriage.* New York: Norton, 1992.
4. Ibid., p. 43.
5. See, for example, M. Zuckerman and R. E. Driver, "Telling Lies: Verbal and Nonverbal Correlates of Deception," in A. W. Siegman and S. Feldstein, eds., *Multichannel Integrations of Nonverbal Behavior,* Hillsdale, NJ: Lawrence Erlbaum, 1985, pp. 129–147.
6. See Paul Ekman, "Mistakes When Deceiving," in Thomas A. Sebeok and Robert Rosenthal, eds., *The Clever Hans Phenomenon: Communication with Horses, Whales, Apes, and People,* New York: New York Academy of Sciences, 1981, pp. 269–278.
7. David B. Buller and Judee K. Burgoon, "Interpersonal Deception Theory," *Communication Theory,* volume 6, 1996, pp. 203–242.
8. See, for example, Paul Ekman, *Emotions Revealed: Recognizing Faces and Feelings to Improve Communication and Emotional Life,* Henry Holt: New York, 2003; and Malcolm Gladwell, "The Naked Face," *The New Yorker,* August 5, 2002, pp. 38–49.
9. Leathers, *Successful Nonverbal Communication,* p. 32.
10. Daniel Goleman, "Sensing Silent Cues Emerges as Key Skill," *New York Times,* October 10, 1989.
11. See H. D. Ellis and A. W. Young, "Are Faces Special?" in A. W. Young and H. D. Ellis, eds., *Handbook of Research in Face Processing,* Amsterdam: North Holland, 1989, pp. 1–26.
12. M. D. Alicke, R. H. Smith, and M. L. Klotz, "Judgments of Physical Attractiveness: The Role of Faces and Bodies," in *Personality and Social Psychology Bulletin,* 12 (1986): 381–389.
13. D. S. Berry, "What Can a Moving Face Tell Us?" *Journal of Personality and Social Psychology,* 58 (1990): 1004–1014.
14. See J. L. Keilerman, J. Lewis, and J. D. Laird, "Looking and Loving: The Effects of Mutual Gaze in Feelings of Romantic Love," *Journal of Research in Personality,* 23 (1989): 145–161.
15. E. H. Hess and J. M. Polt, "Pupil Size as Related to Interest Value of Visual Stimuli," *Science* (1960): 349–50.
16. See C. L. Kleinke, "Gaze and Eye Contact: A Research Review," *Psychological Bulletin,* 100 (1986): 78–100.
17. M. Argyle and J. Dean, "Eye Contact, Distance, and Affiliation," *Sociometry,* 28 (1965): 289–394.
18. See A. Abele, "Functions of Gaze in Social Interaction: Communication and Monitoring," *Journal of Nonverbal Behavior,* 10 (1986): 83–101.
19. See, R. Bandler and J. Grinder, *Frogs into Princes: Neuro Linguistic Programming,* Real People Press, 1979; R. Dilts, *Roots of NLP,* Capitola, CA: Meta Publications, 1983; and W. Buckner, E. Reese, and R. Reese, "Eye Movement as an Indicator of Sensory Components in Thought," *Journal of Counseling Psychology,* 34:3, 1987.
20. See M. LaFrance and C. Mayo, *Moving Bodies: Nonverbal Communication in Human Interaction,* 2nd ed., New York: Holt, 1978.
21. P. Ekman and W. Friesen, *Unmasking the Face: A Guide to Recognizing Emotions from Facial Expressions,* Englewood Cliffs, NJ: Prentice-Hall, 1984.
22. "Girl's Surgery Is Performed for a Smile, Doctors Hope," *New York Times,* December 15, 1995, p. 8.
23. P. Ekman and W. V. Friesen, "The Repertoire of Nonverbal Behavior: Categories, Origins, Usage and Coding," *Semiotica,* 69 (1969): 49–97.
24. M. Argyle, *Bodily Communication,* 2nd ed., London: Methuen, 1988.
25. See P. D. Krivonos and M. L. Knapp, "Initiating Communication: What Do You Say When You Say Hello," *Central States Journal,* 26 (1975): 115–125; and M. L. Knapp, R. P. Hart, and G. W. Friedrich, "Nonverbal Correlates of Human Leave Taking," *Communication Monographs,* 40 (1973): 182–198.
26. M. Knapp, "Nonverbal Communication: Basic Perspectives," in John Stewart, ed., *Bridges Not Walls: A Book about Interpersonal Communication,* 5th ed., New York: McGraw-Hill, 1990.
27. See G. Collier, *Emotional Experience,* Hillsdale, NJ: Erlbaum, 1985; and Leathers, *Successful Nonverbal Communication,* p. 71.
28. See M. Hodgins and K. Miyake, "The Vocal Attractiveness Stereotype: Replication and Elaboration," *Journal of Nonverbal Behavior,* 14 (1990): 97–112.
29. R. N. Bond, S. Feldsteen, and S. Simpson, "Relative and Absolute Judgments of Speech Rate from Masked and Content-Standard Stimuli: The Influence of Vocal Frequency and Intensity," *Human Communication Research,* 14 (1988): 548–568.
30. Leathers, *Successful Nonverbal Communication,* p. 169.
31. Ibid., p. 93.
32. Edward T. Hall, *The Hidden Dimension,* New York: Doubleday, 1969.
33. A. G. Halberstadt, "Race, Socioeconomic Status, and Nonverbal Behavior," in A. W. Siegman and S. Feldstein eds., *Multichannel Integrations of Nonverbal Behavior,* NJ: Lawrence Erlbaum, 1985, pp. 195–225.
34. See J. K. Burgoon, "Privacy and Communication," in M. Burgoon, ed., *Communication Yearbook 6,* Beverly Hills, CA: Sage, 1982, pp. 206–249; J. K. Burgoon and L. Aho, "Three Field Experiments on the Effects of Violations of Conversational Distance," *Communication Monographs,* 49 (1982): 71–88; and J. K. Burgoon and J. B. Walther, "Nonverbal Expectations and the Evaluative Consequence of Violations," *Human Communication Research,* 17, 2 (1990): 232–265.
35. See Edward T. Hall, *The Hidden Dimension,* New York: Doubleday, 1969; and A. Rapoport, *The Meaning of the Built Environment,* Beverly Hills, CA: Sage, 1982.
36. G. Collier, *Emotional Experience,* Hillsdale, NJ: Erlbaum, 1985.
37. See U. J. Derliga, R. J. Lewis, S. Harrison, B. A. Winstead, and R. Costanza, "Gender Differences in the Initiation and Attribution of Tactile Intimacy," *Journal of Nonverbal Behavior,* 13 (1989) 83–96.

38. See D. F. Fromme, W. E. Jaynes, D. K. Taylor, E. G. Hanold, J. Daniell, J. R. Roundtree, and M. Fromme, "Nonverbal Behaviors and Attitudes toward Touch," *Journal of Nonverbal Behavior*, 13 (1989): 3–14.

39. S. E. Jones and A. E. Yarbrough, "A Naturalistic Study of the Messages of Touch," *Communication Monographs*, 52 (1985): 19–56; and M. Argyle, *Bodily Communication*, London: Methuen, 1986.

40. Nancy Henley, *Body Politics: Power, Sex and Nonverbal Communication*, New York: Simon & Schuster, 1986.

41. S. Kaiser, *The Social Psychology of Clothing: Symbolic Appearances in Context*, 2nd ed., New York: Macmillan, 1990.

42. J. Malloy, *New Dress For Success*, New York: Warner, 1988.

43. See, for example, M. S. Singer and A. E. Singer, "The Effect of Police Uniforms on Interpersonal Perception," *Journal of Psychology*, 119 (1985): 157–161.

44. Max Luscher, *The Luscher Color Test*, New York: Simon & Schuster, 1980; and Max Luscher, *The Four Color Person*, New York: Simon & Schuster, 1980.

45. Deborah L. Jacobs, "The Titans of Tint Make Their Picks," *New York Times*, May 29, 1994, p. 7.

46. Robert Levine, "Waiting Is a Power Game," *Psychology Today* (April 1987): 30.

47. Peter Andersen, "Exploring Intercultural Differnces in Nonverbal Communication," in L. Samovar and R. Porter (eds.), *Interpersonal Communication; A Reader*, 5th ed., Belmont, CA: Wadsworth Publishing, 1998, pp. 272–282.

48. L. A. Samovar, R. E. Porter, and L. A. Stefani, *Communication Between Cultures*, 2nd ed., Belmont, CA: Wadsworth, 1998, p. 159.

49. Michael L. Hecht, Ronald L. Jackson II, and Sidney A. Ribeau, *African American Communication*, 2nd ed., Mahwah, NJ: Lawrence Erlbaum Associates, 2003.

50. M. P. Orbe and T. M. Harris, *Interracial Communication Theory Into Practice*, Thompson Learning, 2001.

51. Judith A. Hall, *Nonverbal Sex Differences: Communication Accuracy and Expressive Style*, Baltimore: Maryland: Johns Hopkins University Press, 1984, p. 3.

52. B. Veland, "Tell Me More: On the Fine Art of Listening," *Utne Reader* (1992): 104–109; A. Mulac, "Men's and Women's Talk in Some Gender and Mixed Gender Dyads: Power or Polemic?" *Journal of Language and Social Psychology*, 8 (1989): 249–270.

53. J. F. Dovidio, S. L. Ellyson, C. F. Keating, K. Heltman, and C. E. Brown, "The Relationship of Social Power to Visual Displays of Dominance between Men and Women," *Journal of Personality and Social Psychology*, 54 (1988): 233–242.

54. K. Floyd, "Affectionate Same-Sex Touch: The Influence of Homophobia on Observers' Perceptions," *The Journal of Social Psychology*, 140, 2000, 774–788.

55. See, for example, Nancy Briton and Judith Hall, "Gender Based Expectancies and Observer Judgments of Smiling," *Journal of Nonverbal Behavior*, 19:1, Spring, 1995, p. 49; and Diane Hales, *Just Like a Women*, New York: Bantam Books, 1999, p. 270.

56. Julia T. Wood, *Gendered Lives*, Belmont, CA: Wadsworth, 1994, p. 154.

57. Antonia Abbey, Catherine Cozzarelli, and Kimberly McLaughlin, "The Effects of Clothing and Dyad Sex Composition on Perceptions of Sexual Intent: Do Women and Men Evaluate These Clues Differently?" *Journal of Applied Social Psychology*, 17 (1987), pp. 108–126.

58. See, for example, Bill Puka, "The Liberation of Caring: A Different Voice for Gilligan's Different Voice," *Hypatia*, 5, 1990, pp. 59–82, and J. A. Hall, "Gender, Gender-Roles, and Nonverbal Communication Skills," in R. Rosental, ed., *Skill in Nonverbal Communication: Individual Differences*, Cambridge, MA: Oelgeschlager, Gunn and Hair, 1979.

59. Carol Gilligan, *In a Different Voice: Psychological Theory and Women's Development*, Cambridge, MA: Harvard University Press, 1982; and Carol Gilligan, W. Lyons and T. Hanmer, *Making Connections*, Cambridge, MA: Harvard University Press, 1990.

60. See, for example, J. Leland and E. Leonard, "Back to Twiggy," *Newsweek*, February 1, 1993, pp. 64–65.

61. Wood, *Gendered Lives*, p. 239.

62. Suzanne Stefanic, "Sex and the New Media," *NewMedia*, (April 1993): 38–45.

63. Aaron Wolfgang, *Everybody's Guide to People Watching*, Yarmouth, ME: Intercultural Press, 1995, p. 19.

64. H. S. Hodgkins and C. Belch, "Interparental Violence and Nonverbal Abilities," *Journal of Nonverbal Behavior*, 24, 2000, pp. 3–24.

65. See, for example, N. Miczo, C. Segrin, and L. E. Allspach, "Relationship Between Nonverbal Sensitivity, Encoding, and Relational Satisfaction," *Communication Reports*, 14, 2001, pp. 39–48.

Chapter 7

1. Steve Duck, *Understanding Relationships*, New York: Guilford Press, 1991, p. 16.

2. Gerald Coffee, "Beyond Survival," Chicago, IL: Nightingale-Conant Audio, 1990.

3. Margaret McLaughlin, *Conversation: How Talk Is Organized*, Newbury Park, CA: Sage, 1984.

4. Susan Shimanoff, *Communication Rules*, Newbury Park, CA: Sage, 1980, p. 57.

5. S. Duck, *Human Relationships*, 3rd ed., Thousand Oaks, CA: Sage, 1998, p. 7.

6. See, for example, S. Jacobs and S. Jackson, "Speech Act Structure in Conversation: Rational Aspects of Pragmatic Coherence," in R. T. Craig and K. Tracy, eds., *Conversational Coherence: Form, Structure and Strategy*, Newbury Park, CA: Sage, 1983, pp. 47–66.

7. For a discussion or criteria used to assess conversational effectiveness, see D. Canary, M. J. Cody, and V. L. Manusov, *Interpersonal Communication: A Goals-Based Approach*, Boston, MA: Bedford/St. Martin's, 2003, pp. 520–523.

8. T. E. Murray, "The Language of Singles Bars," *American Speech*, 60 (1985): 17–30.

9. Chris Kleinke, *Meeting and Understanding People*, New York: W. H. Freeman, 1986.

10. Alan Garner, *Conversationally Speaking: Testing New Ways to Increase Your Personal and Social Effectiveness*, New York: McGraw Hill, 1981.

11. Gregory Stock, *The Book of Questions,* New York: Workman, 1987.

12. Mark L. Knapp et al., "The Rhetoric of Goodbye: Verbal and Nonverbal Correlates of Human Leave Taking," *Speech Monographs,* 40 (August 1973): 182–198.

13. H. P. Grice, "Logic and Conversation," in *Syntax and Semantics,* vol. 3, *Speech Acts,* P. Cole and J. L. Morgan, eds., New York: Seminar Press, 1975, pp. 41–58; and K. Lindblom, "Cooperating with Grice: A Cross-Disciplinary Metaperspective on Uses of Grice's Cooperative Principle," *Journal of Pragmatics,* 33, 2001, pp. 1601–1623.

14. M. L. McLaughlin, *Conversation: How Talk Is Organized,* Newbury Park, CA: Sage, 1984, pp. 88–89.

15. See, for example, K. Midooka, "Characteristics of Japanese Style Communication," *Media, Culture and Society,* 12, 1990, pp. 477–489; and Y. Gu, "Polite Phenomena in Modern Chinese," *Journal of Pragmatics,* 14, 1990, pp. 237–257.

16. P. Brown and S. Levinson, *Politeness: Some Universals in Language Usage,* Cambridge, England: Cambridge University Press, 1987.

17 William B. Gudykunst, *Bridging Differences,* 2nd ed., Thousand Oaks, CA: Sage, 1994, p. 83.

18. Ibid., p. 139.

19. T. S. Lebra, "The Cultural Significance of Silence in Japanese Communication," *Multilingua,* 6 (1987): 343–357.

20. M. L. Morris, *Saying and Meaning in Puerto Rico,* Elmsford, NY: Pergamon, 1981, pp. 135–136.

21. H. Yamada, "Topic Management and Turn Distributions in Business Meetings: American versus Japanese Strategies," *Text,* 10 271–295.

22. See, for example, L. K. Acitelli, "Gender Differences in Relationship Awareness and Marital Satisfaction among Young Married Couples," *Personality and Social Psychology Bulletin,* 18 (1992): 102–110; and Julia T. Wood and C. C. Inman, "In a Different Mode: Masculine Styles of Communicating Closeness," *Journal of Applied Communication Research,* 21 (1993): 279–295.

23. Deborah Tannen, *You Just Don't Understand: Women and Men in Conversation,* New York: Morrow, 1990.

24. Alice Greenwood, "Discourse Variation and Social Comfort: A Study of Topic Initiation and Interruption Patterns in the Dinner Conversation and Pre-Adolescent Children," doctoral dissertation, City University of New York, 1989.

25. Tannen, *Gender and Discourse,* pp. 61–67.

26. Bruce Kluger, "Why Do Mean-Spirited TV Shows Lure Americans?" *USA Today,* January 30, 2003, 13A.

27. Corey Kilgannon, "Even Host Is Offended by Talk on Imus Show," *The New York Times,* June 18, 2001, C7.

28. Phyllis M. Japp, "Gender and Work in the 1980s: Television's Working Women as Displaced Persons," *Women's Studies in Communication,* 14 (1991): 49–74.

29. The documentary *American Tongues,* distributed by the Center for New American Media, explores the attitudes people have about regional, social, and ethnic differences in American speech.

30. Steve Lohr, "Reluctant Conscripts in the March of Technology," *New York Times,* September 17, 1995, p. 16.

31. Geoff Dougherty, "Summit Guests Told Internet Can Advance Women's Rights," *The Record* (Hackensack, NJ), October 2, 1995, p. A3.

32. Ibid.

33. Scott McCartney, "For Teens, Chatting on Internet Offers Comfort of Anonymity," *Wall Street Journal,* December 8, 1994, p. B1.

34. Joan E. Rigdon, "Now Women in Cyberspace Can Be Themselves," *Wall Street Journal,* March 18, 1994, p. B1.

35. Crispin Sartwell, "We Are Losing Our Voices As We Merge With Machines," *Philadelphia Inquirer,* April 26, 2000.

36. Ruth Padawer, "Teens Get Closer From Afar with Instant Messages," *The Record,* June 17, 2003, A1, A8.

37. Janet Kornblum, "Tapping Into Text Messaging," *USA Today,* June 3, 2003, 1D, 2D.

Chapter 8

1. Daniel Goleman, *Emotional Intelligence,* New York: Bantam Books, 1995, p. x.

2. Ibid., p. 34.

3. R. Lazarus, *Emotion and Adaptation,* New York: Oxford University Press, 1991.

4. Carroll E. Izard, *Human Emotions,* New York: Plenum, 1977, p. 10.

5. See Howard Gardner, *Multiple Intelligences: The Theory in Practice,* New York: Basic Books, 1993, p. 9.

6. I. Ruisel, "Social Intelligence: Conception and Methodological Problems," *Studia Psychologica,* 34, 1992, pp. 281–196.

7. See, for example, H. Gardner, *Multiple Intelligences,* New York: Basic Books, 1993.

8. J. D. Mayer and P. Salovey, "The Intelligence of Emotional Intelligence," *Intelligence,* 17, 1993, pp. 433–442.

9. Adapted from Goleman, *Emotional Intelligence,* p. 43.

10. Paul Ekman, *Darwin and Facial Expression,* New York: Academic Press, 1973.

11. Goleman, *Emotional Intelligence,* p. 6.

12. E. Nagourney, "Blow a Gasket For Your Heart," *The New York Times,* February 11, 2003, F6.

13. American Psychological Association, **http://helping.apa.org/daily/anger.html.**

14. Stephanie Armour, "After 9/11, Some Workers Turn Their Lives Upside Down," *USA Today,* May 8, 2002, A1, A2.

15. Daniel Goleman, "A Feel-Good Theory: A Smile Affects Mood," *New York Times,* July 18, 1989, p. C1.

16. R. Plutchik, "Emotions: A General Psychoevolutionary Theory," in K. R. Scherer and P. Ekman, eds., *Approaches to Emotion,* Hillsdale, NJ: Lawrence Erlbaum Associates, 1984, pp. 197–219.

17. See, for example, Daniel Goleman, "Happy or Sad, a Mood Can Prove Contagious," *New York Times,* October 15, 1991, p. C1; and Ellen O'Brien, "Moods Are as Contagious as the Office Cold," *The Record* (Hackensack, NJ) November 15, 1993, p. B3.

18. B. Aubrey Fisher and Katherine L. Adams, *Interpersonal Communication: Pragmatics of Human Relationships,* New York: McGraw-Hill, 1994, p. 290.

19. Ibid.

20. Izard, *Human Emotions,* p. 5.

21. Goleman, "Happy or Sad."

22. Lazarus, *Emotion and Adaptation.*

23. Albert Ellis and R. Harper, *A New Guide to Rational Living,* North Hollywood, CA: Wilshire Books, 1977.

24. Joseph P. Forgas, "Affect and Person Perception," in Joseph P. Forgas, ed., *Emotion and Social Judgments,* New York: Pergamon, 1991, p. 288.

25. Sandra Metts and John Waite Bowers, "Emotion in Interpersonal Communication," in Mark L. Knapp and Gerald R. Miller, eds., *Handbook of Interpersonal Communication,* 2nd ed., Thousand Oaks, CA: Sage, 1994.

26. J. W. Pennebaker, B. Rime, and V. E. Blankenship, "Stereotypes of Emotional Expressiveness of Northerners and Southerners: A Cross-Cultural Test of Montesquieu's Hypotheses," *Journal of Personality and Social Psychology,* 70, 1996, pp. 372–380.

27. Julia T. Wood and C. Inman, "In a Different Mode: Recognizing Male Modes of Closeness," *Journal of Applied Communication Research* (August 1993).

28. S. Swain, "Covert Intimacy: Closeness in Men's Friendships," in B. J. Risman and P. Schwartz, eds., *Gender and Intimate Relationships,* Belmont, CA: Wadsworth, 1989, pp. 71–86; and D. Scherrod, "The Influence of Gender on Same-Sex Friendships," in C. Hendrick, ed., *Close Relationships,* Newbury Park, CA: Sage, 1989, pp. 164–186.

29. See, for example, E. J. Coats and R. S. Feldman, "Gender Differences in Nonverbal Correlates of Social Status," *Personality and Social Psychology Bulletin,* 22, 1996, pp. 1014–1022.

30. D. J. Goldsmith and P. A. Fulfs, "You Just Don't Have the Evidence": An Analysis of Claims and Evidence in Deborah Tannen's *You Just Don't Understand,* in M. E. Roloff, ed., *Communication Yearbook,* 22, Thousand Oaks, CA: Sage, 1999, pp. 1–49.

31. See, for example, J. Swenson and F. L. Casmir, " The Impact of Culture-Sameness, Gender, Foreign Travel, and Academic Background on the Ability to Interpret Facial Expression of Emotion in Others," *Communication Quarterly,* 46, 1998, pp. 214–230.

32. J. Hall, *Nonverbal Sex Differences: Communication Accuracy and Expressive Style,* Baltimore: Johns Hopkins University Press, pp. 182, 184.

33. R. A. Buhrke and D. R. Fuqua, "Sex Differences in Same- and Cross-Sex Supportive Relationships," *Sex Roles,* 17 (1987): 339–352.

34. D. Witmer and S. Katzman, "On-Line Smiles: Does Gender Make a Difference in the Use of Graphic Accents?" *Journal of Computer-Mediated Communication* (On Line) 2:4, 1997.

35. Anthony Pratkanis and Elliot Aronson, *Age of Propaganda: The Everyday Use and Abuse of Persuasion,* New York: W. H. Freeman, 1991, p. 52.

36. Ibid., p. 54.

37. A. Ellis, "Why Rational-Emotive Therapy to Rational Emotive Behavior Therapy?" *Psychotherapy,* 36:2, 1999, pp. 154–159.

38. A. Ellis, *A New Guide to Rational Living,* North Hollywood, CA: Wilshire Books, 1977.

39. C. Peterson, M. E. P. Seligman, and G. E. Vaillant, "Pessimistic Explanatory Style Is a Risk Factor for Physical Illness: A 35-Year Longitudinal Study," *Journal of Personality and Social Psychology,* 55, 1988, pp. 23–27.

Chapter 9

1. See, for example, James Jaska and Michael S. Pritchard, *Communication Ethics: Methods of Analysis,* Belmont, CA: Wadsworth, 1988.

2. Abraham Maslow, *Motivation and Personality,* New York: Harper & Row. 1970.

3. F. Luskin, *Forgive For Good,* San Francisco: Harper Collins, 2002.

4. Fred Luskin, "Four Steps Toward Forgiveness," *Healing Currents Magazine,* September/October, 1996, **http://www.coopcomm.org/essay_luskin.htm.**

5. Linda Berlin, "Forgive: Stanford Program Teaches How to Let Go of Grudges," **http://www.sfgate.com/cgibin/article.cgi?file=chronicle/archive/1999/09/24/PN75893.DTL.**

6. F. Luskin and C. Thoresen, "The Effect of Forgiveness Training on Psychosocial Research," December 1998, **http://www.learningtoforgive.com/Research.htm.**

7. F. Luskin, "Four Steps Toward Forgiveness," *Healing Currents Magazine,* September/October 1996, **http://www.coopcomm.org/essayluskin.htm.**

8. Jennifer Kavanaugh, "Getting Down to the Heart of Forgiveness," *Palo Alto Weekly,* February 10, 1999.

9. See J. W. Thibaut and H. H. Kelly, *The Social Psychology of Groups,* New York: Wiley, 1959; and K. J. Gergen, M. S. Greenberg, and R. H. Willis, *Social Exchange: Advances in Theory and Research,* New York: Plenum, 1980; Dalmas Taylor and Irwin Altman, "Self-Disclosure as a Function of Reward-Cost Outcomes," *Sociometry,* 38 (1975): 18–31.

10. Ellen Bersheid, "Interpersonal Attraction," in G. Lindzey and E. Aronson, eds., *Handbook of Social Psychology,* New York: Random House, 1985, 413–484.

11. Stephen R. Covey, *The Seven Habits of Highly Effective People,* New York: Simon & Schuster, 1989, p. 188.

12. Jack R. Gibb, "Defensive Communication," *Journal of Communication,* 2 (1961): 141–148.

13. See Anatole Rapoport and Albert Chammah, *Prisoner's Dilemma,* Ann Arbor: University of Michigan, 1965; Harold H. Kelly and John W. Thibaut, *Interpersonal Relationships,* New York: Wiley, 1978; and John W. Thibaut and Harold H. Kelly, *The Social Psychology of Groups,* New York: Wiley, 1959.

14. See Sissela Bok, *Lying,* New York: Pantheon, 1978; Sissela Bok, *Secrets,* New York: Random House, 1989; and Steven A. McCormack and Timothy R. Levine, "When Lies Are Uncovered: Emotional and Relational

Outcomes of Discovered Deception," *Communication Monographs,* 57 (June 1990): 119.

15. Michael Lewis and Carolyn Saarni, ed., *Lying and Deception in Everyday Life,* New York: Guilford Press, 1993, p. 7.

16. Ibid., p. 8.

17. C. Camden, M. T. Motley, and A. Wilson, "White Lies in Interpersonal Communication: A Taxonomy and Preliminary Investigation of Social Motivations," *Western Journal of Speech Communication,* 48 (1984): 309–325.

18. See, for example, Jennifer Coates, "Gossip Revisited: Language in All-Female Groups," and Jane Pilkington, "Don't Try to Make Out that I'm Nice! The Different Strategies Women and Men Use When Gossiping," in Jennifer Coates, ed., *Language and Gender: A Reader,* Blackwell Publishers, 1998, pp. 226–253 and pp. 254–269; and Lubna Abdel Aziz, "Why We Gossip," Al-Ahram Weekly online, November 28–December 4, 2002, **http://weekly.ahram.org.eg/2002/614/pe2.htm.**

19. S. Eggins and D. Slade, *Analyzing Casual Conversation,* Washington, D.C., Cassell, 1997.

20. J. Levin and A. Arluke, *Gossip—The Inside Scoop,* New York: Plenum Publishing, 1987.

21. Robin Dunbar, *Grooming, Gossip, and the Evolution of Language,* Cambridge, MA: Harvard University Press, 1998.

22. William B. Gudykunst, *Bridging Differences,* 2nd ed., Thousand Oaks, CA: Sage, 1994, pp. 74–75.

23. See, for example, M. Hecht, S. Ribeau, and M. Sedane, "A Mexican-American Perspective on Interethnic Communication," *International Journal of Intercultural Relations,* 14 (1990): 31–55.

24. J. Holmes and J. Rempel, "Trust in Close Relationships," in C. Hendrick, ed., *Close Relationships,* Newbury Park, CA: Sage, 1989.

25. See, for example, E. Goodman and P. O'Brien, *I Know Just What You Mean: The Power of Friendship in Women's Lives,* New York, Simon and Schuster, 2000; and P. M. Nardi, ed., *Men's Friendships,* Newbury Park, CA: Sage, 1992.

26. Bella M. DePaulo, Jennifer A. Epstein, and Melissa M. Wyer, "Sex Differences in Lying: How Women and Men Deal with the Dilemma of Deceit," in Michael Lewis and Carolyn Saarni, eds., *Lying and Deception in Everyday Life,* New York: Guilford Press, 1993, pp. 126–147.

27. Ibid., p. 19.

28. D. Sherrod, "The Influence of Gender on Same-Sex Friendships," in C. Hendrick, ed., *Close Relationships,* Newbury Park, CA: Sage, 1989, pp. 164–186.

29. For example, see the Jean Kilbourne video *Killing Us Softly.*

30. Louis A. Day, *Ethics in Media Communications: Cases and Controversies,* Belmont, CA: Wadsworth, 1991, p. 279.

31. Susan Faludi, *Backlash: The Undeclared War against American Women,* New York: Crown, 1991.

32. Amitai Etzioni, "E-Communities Build New Ties, But Ties That Bind," *The New York Times,* February 10, 2000, G7.

33. See, for example, Bruce E. Johansen, "Race, Ethnicity, and the Media," in Alan Wells, ed., *Mass Media and Society,* Lexington, Mass: D.C. Heath, 1987, p. 441.

34. James E. Murphy and Sharon M. Murphy, "American Indians and the Media: Neglect and Stereotype," in Ray Heibert and Carol Reuss, eds., *Impact of Mass Media,* 2nd ed., New York: Longman, 1988, pp. 312–322.

35. Jim Puzzanghera, "Love Is in the Air—and On Line, Too," *The Record* (Hackensack, NJ), May 13, 1996, p. B1.

36. Dan Rosenbaum, "You Have the Right to Remain Silent . . . " NETGUIDE (July 1996), 49–50.

37. Jonathan Coleman, "Is Technology Making Us Intimate Strangers?" *Newsweek,* March 27, 2000, p. 12.

Chapter 10

1. http://www.socialphobia.org.

2. John R. French and Bertram Raven, "The Bases of Social Power," in *Studies in Social Power,* D. Cartwright, ed., Ann Arbor: University of Michigan Press, 1959, pp. 150–167, and "The Bases of Conjugal Power," in *Power in Families,* R. E. Cromwell and D. H. Olson, eds., New York: Halstead Press, 1975, pp. 217–237.

3. Scott Cutlip and Alan Center, *Effective Public Relations,* Englewood Cliffs, NJ: Prentice-Hall, 1985, p. 122.

4. William B. Gudykunst, *Bridging Differences,* 2nd ed., Thousand Oaks, CA: Sage Publications, 1994, p. 37.

5. See Milton Rokeach, *The Open and Closed Mind,* New York: Basic Books, 1960; and Milton Rokeach, *Beliefs, Attitudes and Values,* San Francisco, CA: Jossey-Bass, 1970.

6. E. J. Langer, "Rethinking the Role of Thought in Social Interaction," in J. H. Harvey, W. J. Ickes, and R. F. Kidd, eds., *New Directions in Attribution Research,* vol. 2, Hillsdale, NJ: Lawrence Erlbaum Associates, 1978, pp. 35–58.

7. Cialdini, 2001.

8. See, for example, G. Miller, F. Boster, and D. Siebold, "MBRS Rekindled: Some Thoughts on Compliance Gaining in Interpersonal Settings," in M. E. Roloff and G. R. Miller, eds., *Interpersonal Processes: New Directions in Communication Research,* Newbury Park, CA: Sage, pp. 89–116.

9. Fritz Heider, *The Psychology of Interpersonal Relations,* New York: Wiley, 1958.

10. Leon Festinger, "Social Communication and Cognition: A Very Preliminary and Highly Tentative Draft," in *Cognitive Dissonance: Progress on a Pivotal Theory in Social Psychology,* Eddie Haron-Jones and Judson Mills, eds., American Psychological Association, Washington D.C., 1999, p. 361.

11. R. B. Cialdini, *Influence: Science and Practice,* 4th ed., Needham Heights, MA: Allyn and Bacon, 2001.

12. Richard Petty and John T. Cacioppo, *Communication and Persuasion: Central and Peripheral Routes to Attitude Change,* New York: Springer-Verlag, 1986, p. 7.

13. G. Hofstede, *Culture's Consequences: International Differences in Work-Related Values,* Beverly Hills: Sage, 1980.

14. M. L. Hecht, M. J. Collier, and S. A. Ribeau, *African American Communication: Ethnic Identity and Interpretation,* Newbury Park, CA: Sage, 1993, p. 97.

15. Hofstede, *Culture's Consequences*, 1980.

16. See Geert Hofstede, *Cultures and Organizations: Software of the Mind*, London: McGraw-Hill, 1991.

17. Jan Servaes, "Cultural Identity in East and West," *The Howard Journal of Communication I* (Summer 1988): p. 64.

18. See M. J. Collier, "Conflict Competence within African, Mexican, and Anglo-American Friendships," in S. Ting-Toomy and F. Korzenny, eds., *Cross Cultural Interpersonal Communication*, Newbury Park, CA: Sage, 1991.

19. J. M. Steil and K. Weltman, "Marital Inequality: The Importance of Resources, Personal Attributes, and Social Norms on Career Valuing and the Allocation of Domestic Responsibilities," *Sex Roles*, 24 (1991): 161–179.

20. W. Farrell, "Men as Success Objects," *Utne Reader* (May/June 1991): 81–84.

21. J. J. Suitor, "Marital Quality and Satisfaction with the Division of Household Labor across the Family Life Cycle," *Journal of Marriage and the Family*, 53 (1991): 221–230.

22. Graham Allen, *Family Life*, New York: Blackwell, 1993.

23. P. S. E. Darlington and B. M. Mulvaney, *Women, Power, and Ethnicity: Working Toward Reciprocal Empowerment*, New York: The Haworth Press, 2003.

24. J. Sweet, L. Bumpass, and V. Call, *National Survey of Families and Households*, Madison, Wisconsin: Center for Emography and Ecology, University of Wisconsin, 1988.

25. S. A. Basow, *Gender: Stereotypes and Roles*, 3rd ed., Pacific Grove, CA: Brooks/Cole, 1992.

26. "Sights, Sounds, and Stereotypes," *Raleigh News and Observer*, October 11, 1992, pp. G1, G10.

27. Steve Lohr, "Who Uses Internet? 5.8 Million Are Said to Be Linked in U.S.," *New York Times*, September 27, 1995, p. D2; and Jared Sandberg, "Internet's Popularity in North America Appears to Be Soaring," *Wall Street Journal*, October 30, 1995, p. B3.

28. Geoff Dougherty, "Summit Guests Told Internet Can Advance Women's Rights," *The Record* (Hackensack, NJ), October 2, 1995, p. A3.

29. Scott McCartney and Joan E. Rigdon, "Society's Subcultures Meet by Modem," *Wall Street Journal*, December 5, 1994, p. B1.

30. Debra Lynn Vial, "Electronic Friendship, Information— Even Love," *The Record* (Hackensack, NJ), April 3, 1994, p. A1; and Mary Jo Layton, "Seniors on the Net," *The Record* (Hackensack, NJ), November 19, 1995, p. L1.

Chapter 11

1. See, for example, D. H. Cloven and M. E. Roloff, "Sense-Making Activities and Interpersonal Conflict: Communicative Cures for the Mulling Blues," *Western Journal of Speech Communication* 55 (1991): 134–158.

2. See J. L. Hocker and W. W. Wilmot, *Interpersonal Conflict*, 3rd ed., Dubuque, IA: William C. Brown, 1991, p. 12; Dudley Cahn, "Intimates in Conflict: A Research Review," in Dudley D. Cahn, ed., *Intimates in Conflict: A Communication Perspective*, Hillsdale, NJ: Erlbaum,

1990; and Joseph P. Folger, Marshall Scott Poole, and Randall K. Stutman, *Working through Conflict*, 2nd ed., New York: HarperCollins, 1993.

3. See G. L. Welton, "Parties in Conflict: Their Characteristics and Perceptions," in K. G. Duffy, J. W. Grosch, and P. V. Olczak, eds., *Community Mediation: A Handbook for Practitioners and Researchers*, New York: Guilford Press, 1991, pp. 105–118.

4. See, for example, Lavinia Hall, ed., *Negotiation: Strategies for Mutual Gain*, Newbury Park, CA: Sage, 1993.

5. See R. Fisher and S. Brown, *Getting Together: Building Relationships as We Negotiate*, Boston, MA: Houghton Mifflin, 1988.

6. Alan C. Filley, *Interpersonal Conflict Resolution*, Glenview, IL: Scott Foresman, 1975; and Mark L. Knapp and Anita Vangelisti, *Interpersonal Communication and Human Relationships*, 2nd ed., Boston, MA: Allyn & Bacon, 1994.

7. Folger, Poole, and Stutman, *Working through Conflict*, pp. 8–10.

8. G. R. Bach and P. Wyden, *The Intimate Enemy: How to Fight Fair in Love and Marriage*, New York: William Morrow, 1969, p. 3.

9. G. R. Bach and R. Deutsch, *Pairing*, New York: Peter Wyden, 1970; G. Bach, *Stop! You're Driving Me Crazy*, New York: Putnam Publishers, 1985.

10. John Stewart, ed., *Bridges, Not Walls: A Book about Interpersonal Communication*, New York: McGraw Hill, 1995, p. 401.

11. R. R. Blake and J. S. Mouton, *The Managerial Grid*, Houston, TX: Gulf Publishing, 1964.

12. J. M. Gottman and R. W. Levenson, "The Social Psychophysiology of Marriage," in P. Noeller and M. A. Fitzpatrick, eds., *Perspectives on Marital Interaction*, Philadelphia: Multilingual Matters, 1988, pp. 182–200.

13. M. J. Papa and D. J. Canary, "Communication in Organizations: A Competence-Based Approach," in A. M. Nicotera, ed., *Conflict and Organizations: Communicative Processes*, Albany, NY: State University of New York Press, 1995, pp. 153–179; and J. L. Hocker and W. W. Wilmot, *Interpersonal Conflict*, 5th ed., Dubuque, IA: Brown and Benchmark, 1998.

14. M. A. Gross and L. K. Guerrero, "Managing Conflict Appropriately and Effectively: An Application of the Competence Model to Rahim's Organizational Conflict Styles," *International Journal of Conflict Management*, 11, 2000, pp. 200–226.

15. Sharon Bower and Gordon Bower, *Asserting Yourself*, Reading, MA: Addison-Wesley, 1977.

16. Adapted from S. A. Bower and G. H. Bower, *Asserting Yourself: A Practical Guide for Positive Change*, Reading, MA: Perseus Books, 1991, pp. 111–113.

17. S. Ting-Toomey, "A Face Negotiation Theory," in Y. Kin and William Gudykunst, eds., *Theories in Intercultural Communication*, Newbury Park, CA: Sage, 1988.

18. See, for example, S. Ting-Toomey, "Managing Conflict in Intimate Intercultural Relationships," in D. D. Cahn, ed., *Conflict in Personal Relationships*, Hillsdale, NJ: Lawrence Erlbaum, 1994.

24. K. J. Prager, *The Psychology of Intimacy*, New York: Guilford Press, 1995.

25. L. A. Baxter, "The Social Side of Personal Relationships: A Dialectical Perspective," in S. Duck, ed., *Understanding Relationship Processes*, Newbury Park, CA: Sage, 1993, pp. 139–165.

26. L. A. Baxter, "The Social Side of Personal Relationships: A Dialectical Perspective."

27. S. Patronio, "The Boundaries of Privacy: Praxis of Everyday Life," in S. Petronio, ed., *Balancing Secrets of Private Disclosure*, Mahwah, NJ: Erlbaum, 2000, pp. 37–49.

28. R. Klein and R. M. Milardo, "Third-Party Influence on the Management of Personal Relationships," in S. Duck, ed., *Understanding Relationship Processes: Social Context and Relationships*, Newbury Park, CA: Sage, 1993, pp. 55–77.

29. D. R. Pawlowski, "Dialectical Tensions in Marital Couples' Accounts of Their Relationships," *Communication Quarterly*, 46, 1998, pp. 396–416.

30. L. A. Baxter and L. A. Erbert, "Perceptions of Dialectical Contradictions in Turning Points of Development in Heterosexual Romantic Relationships," *Journal of Social and Personal Relationships*, 16, 1999, pp. 547–569.

31. See, for example, L. A. Baxter, "Dialectical Contradictions in Relationship Development," *Journal of Social and Personal Relationships*, 7, 1990, pp. 69–88; and E. M. Griffin, *A First Look at Communication Theory*, 5th ed., New York: McGraw Hill, 2003, pp. 157–170.

32. K. A. McGonagle, R. C. Kessler, and I. H. Gotlib, "The Effects of Marital Disagreement Style, Frequency, and Outcome on Marital Disruption," *Journal of Social and Personal Relationships*, 10 (1993): 385–404.

33. Duck, *Understanding Relationships*, pp. 168–169.

34. W. B. Gudykunst, "The Influence of Cultural Variability on Perceptions of Communication Behavior Associated with Relationship Terms," *Human Communication Research*, 13, 1986, pp. 147–166.

35. S. Sprecher and K. McKinney, *Sexuality*, Newbury Park, CA: Sage, 1993.

36. R. Crooks and K. Baur, *Our Sexuality*, Pacific Grove, CA: Brooks/Cole, 1999.

37. W. B. Gudykunst, "The Influence of Cultural Variability on Perceptions of Communication Behavior Associated with Relationship Terms," *Human Communication Research*, 13, 1986, pp. 147–166.

38. Carol Dolphin Zinner, "Beyond Hall: Variables in the Use of Personal Space," *The Howard Journal of Communications*, I, Spring 1988, pp. 28–29.

39. S. Gaines, Jr., "Relationships Among Members of Cultural Minorities," in Julia T. Wood and Steve W. Duck, eds., *Understanding Relationship Processes*, Thousand Oaks, CA: Sage, 1995, pp. 51–88.

40. S. Duck, *Understanding Relationships*, New York: Guilford Press, 1991, p. 12.

41. S. Swain, "Covert Intimacy: Closeness in Men's Friendships," in B. J. Riesman and P. Schwartz, eds., *Gender and Intimate Relationships*, Belmont, CA: Wadsworth, 1989, pp. 71–86; and E. Paul and K. White, "The Development of Intimate Relationships in Late Adolescence," *Adolescence*, 25 (1990): 375–400.

42. Julia T. Wood and C. C. Inman, "In a Different Mode: Masculine Styles of Communicating Closeness," *Journal of Applied Communication Research*, 21 (1993): 279–295.

43. See, for example, J. C. Pearson, L. H. Turner, and W. Todd-Mancillas, *Gender and Communication*, 2nd ed., Dubuque, IA: William C. Brown, 1991, pp. 170–171.

44. W. F. Owen, "The Verbal Expression of Love by Women and Men as a Critical Communication Event in Personal Relationships," *Women's Studies in Communication*, 10, 1987, pp. 15–24.

45. S. S. Brehm, *Intimate Relationships*, 2nd ed., New York: McGraw-Hill, 1992.

46. M. M. Kazmer, C. Haythornthwaite, "Juggling Multiple Social Worlds: Distance Students Online and Offline," *American Behavioral Scientist*, 45:3, November, 2001, pp. 510–530.

47. Steve Duck, *Understanding Relationships*, p. 163.

48. M. Rohlfing, "Doesn't Anybody Stay in One Place Anymore? An Exploration of the Understudied Phenomenon of Long-Distance Relationships," in Julia T. Wood and Steve W. Duck, eds., *Understanding Relationship Processes, 6: Off the Beaten Track: Understudied Relationships*, Thousand Oaks, CA: Sage, 1995, pp. 173–196.

49. Ruth Padawer, "Teens Get Closer From Afar With Instant Messages," *The Record*, June 17, 2003, A1, A8.

50. Michael Liedtke, "'Blogging' May Launch Internet's Next Wave," *The Record*, March 10, 2003, L5, L8; and Marilyn Elias, "You've Got Trauma, But Writing Can Help," *USA Today*, July 1, 2002, G6.

51. Alan Garner, *Conversationally Speaking*, New York: McGraw-Hill, 1981, p. 69.

52. See B. R. Burleson and W. Samter, "A Social Skills Approach to Relationship Maintenance: How Individual Differences in Communication Skills Affect the Achievement of Relationship Functions," in D. J. Canary and L. Stafford, eds., *Communication and Relational Maintenance*, Orlando, FL: Academic Press, 1994.

Chapter 14

1. Kathleen M. Galvin and Bernard J. Brommel, *Family Communication and Change*, 4th ed., New York: HarperCollins, 1996, p. 4.

2. Judy Pearson, *Communication in the Family*, 2nd ed., New York: HarperCollins, 1993, p. 14.

3. Patricia Noller and Mary Anne Fitzpatrick, *Communication in Family Relationships*, Englewood Cliffs, NJ: Prentice-Hall, 1993.

4. Laurie P. Arliss, *Contemporary Family Communication: Messages and Meanings*, New York: St. Martin's, 1993, p. 7.

5. See also Jane Jorgenson, "Where is the 'Family' in Family Communication? Exploring Families' Self-Definitions," *Journal of Applied Communication Research* 17 (1989): 27–41.

6. Janet Yerby, Nancy Buerkel-Rothfuss, and Arthur P. Bochner, *Understanding Family Communication*, 2nd ed., Scottsdale, AZ: Gorsuch Scarisbrick, 1995, p. 38.

7. Arliss, *Contemporary Family Communication,* p. 57.
8. L. Von Bertalanffy, *General Systems Theory: Essays on Its Foundation and Development,* New York: Brazilier, 1968.
9. Judy C. Pearson, *Communication in the Family,* 2nd ed., New York: HarperCollins, 1993, p. 30.
10. Erma Bombeck, "When Did I Become the Mother and the Mother Become the Child?" in *If Life Is a Bowl of Cherries, What Am I Doing in the Pits?* New York: McGraw-Hill, 1978.
11. Arliss, *Contemporary Family Communication,* p. 14.
12. Galvin and Brommel, *Family Communication.*
13. Matthew McKay, Martha Davis, and Patrick Fanning, *The Communication Book,* Oakland, CA: New Harbinger Publications, 1983.
14. Virginia Satir, *The New Peoplemaking,* Moutainview, CA: Science and Behavior Books, 1988, p. 79.
15. D. Olson and H. McCubbin, *Families: What Makes Them Work,* Beverly Hills, CA: Sage, 1983.
16. Virginia Satir, *The New Peoplemaking,* pp. 182–193.
17. Ibid.
18. See Monica McGoldrick, "Ethnicity, Cultural Diversity, and Normality," in *Normal Family Processes,* Froma Walalish, ed., New York: Guilford Press, 1973, p. 331.
19. See Patricia Noller and Mary Anne Fitzpatrick, *Communication in Family Relationships,* Englewood Cliffs, NJ: Prentice-Hall, 1993.
20. John W. Santrock, *Life Span Development,* 4th ed., Dubuque, IA: William C. Brown, 1992, p. 261.
21. Serena Nanda, *Cultural Anthropology,* 5th ed., Belmont, CA: Wadsworth, 1994, p. 137.
22. Pearson, *Communication in the Family,* p. 80.
23. Julia T. Wood, *Gendered Lives,* Belmont, CA: Wadsworth, 1994, pp. 69–70.
24. R. L. Repetti, "Determinants of Children's Sex-Stereotyping: Parental Sex-Role Traits and Television Viewing," *Personality and Social Psychology Bulletin,* 10 (1984): 457–468.
25. Wood, *Gendered Lives,* p. 71.
26. N. L. Buerkel-Rothfuss, A. M. Covert, J. Keith, and C. Nelson, *Early Adolescent and Parental Communication Patterns,* paper presented at the annual meeting of the Speech Communication Association, Chicago, IL, November 1986.
27. S. Yogev and J. M. Brett, "Patterns of Work and Family Involvement among Single and Dual Earner Couples," *Journal of Applied Psychology,* 70 (1985): 754–768.
28. See, for example, Ray L. Birdwhistell, "The Idealized Model of the American Family," in *The Family: Functions, Conflicts and Symbols,* Peter Stein et al., eds., Reading, MA: Addison-Wesley, 1977, pp. 310–335; and Mary Strom Larson, "The Portrayal of Families on Prime Time Television," paper presented at the annual meeting of the Speech Communication Association, Boston, MA, November 5–7, 1987.
29. F. Earl Barcus, *Images of Life on Children's Television: Sex Roles, Minorities, and Families,* New York: Praeger, 1983.
30. Galvin and Brommel, *Family Communication.*
31. Arliss, *Contemporary Family Communication,* pp. 258–262.
32. Dan B. Curtis, Jerry L. Winsor, and Ronald D. Stephens, "National Preferences in Business and Communication Education," *Communication Education,* 38 (1989): 11.
33. Margaret J. Wheatley, *Leadership and the New Science,* San Francisco, CA: Barrett Koehler, 1994, p. 23.
34. See, for example, Karl Weick, *The Social Psychology of Organizations,* New York: Random House, 1979, p. 223.
35. Peter Senge, *The Fifth Discipline: The Art and Practice of the Learning Organization,* New York: Doubleday/Currency, 1990.
36. Marvin Weisbord, *Discovering Common Ground: How Future Search Conferences Bring People Together to Achieve Breakthrough Innovation, Empowerment, Shared Vision, and Collaborative Action,* San Francisco, CA: Berrett-Koehler, 1992.
37. D. A. Infante and A. S. Rancer, "A Conceptualization and Measure of Argumentativeness," *Journal of Personality Assessment,* 45 (1982): 72–80.
38. D. A. Infante and W. I. Gorden, "Superiors' Argumentativeness and Verbal Aggressiveness as Predictors of Subordinates' Satisfaction," *Human Communication Research,* 12 (1985): 117–125; and D. A. Infante and W I. Gorden, "Superior and Subordinate Communicator Profiles: Implications for Independent-Mindedness and Upward Effectiveness," *Central States Speech Journal,* 38 (1987): 73–80.
39. Virginia P. Richmond and James C. McCroskey, *Organizational Communication for Survival,* Englewood Cliffs, NJ: Prentice-Hall, 1992, p. 125.
40. Gerald M. Goldhaber, *Organizational Communication,* 5th ed., Dubuque, IA: William C. Brown, 1990, p. 214.
41. F. Dansereau and S. E. Markham, "Superior-Subordinate Communication: Multiple Levels of Analysis," *Handbook of Organizational Communication,* Newbury Park, CA: Sage, 1987, pp. 343–353.
42. Richmond and McCroskey, *Organizational Communication,* p. 26.
43. See A. Bavelas, "Communication Patterns in Task Oriented Groups," *Journal of the Acoustical Society of America,* 22 (1950): 725–730; and H. J. Leavitt, "Some Effects of Certain Communication Patterns on Group Performance," *Journal of Abnormal Social Psychology,* 46 (1951): 38–50.
44. Wheatley, *Leadership,* p. 107.
45. See S. W. Littlejohn, *Theories of Human Communication,* 4th ed., Belmont, CA: Wadsworth, 1992.
46. Charles Redding, *Communication within the Organization,* New York: Industrial Communication Council, 1972.
47. Douglas McGregor, *The Human Side of Enterprise,* New York: McGraw-Hill, 1960.
48. Alex F. Osborn, *Applied Imagination,* New York: Scribner's, 1957.
49. Irving Janis, *Groupthink,* Boston, MA: Houghton Mifflin, 1982.
50. See, for example, Lisa A. Mainiero, "Participation? Nyet: Rewards and Praise? Da!" *Academy of Management Executive* (August 1993): 87; and Diane H. B. Welsh,

Fred Luthans, and Steven M. Sommer, "Managing Russian Factory Workers: The Impact of U.S. Based Behavioral and Participative Techniques," *Academy of Management Journal* (February 1993): 57–79.

51. Nancy J. Adler, Robert Doktor, and S. Gordon Redding, "From the Atlantic to the Pacific Century: Cross-Cultural Management Reviewed," *Journal of Management,* 12, 2 (1986).

52. Lillian H. Chaney and Jeanette S. Martin, *Intercultural Business Communication,* Englewood Cliffs, NJ: Prentice-Hall, 1995, p. 41.

53. Ibid., p. 59.

54. L. Copland and L. Greggs, *Going International: How to Make Friends and Deal Effectively in the Going Market-place,* New York: Random House, 1985, p. 10.

55. C. Engholm, *When Business East Meets Business West,* New York: Wiley, 1991.

56. See Nancy J. Adler, *International Dimensions of Organizational Behavior,* 2nd ed., Boston, MA: PWS-Kent, 1993.

57. See B. M. Bass and P. C. Burger, *Assessment of Managers: An International Comparison,* New York: Free Press, 1979.

58. Gary N. Powell, *Women and Men in Management,* 2nd ed., Thousand Oaks, CA: Sage, 1993.

59. Barbara Reskin and Irene Padavic, *Women and Men at Work,* Thousand Oaks, CA: Pine Forge Press, 1994.

60. Rosabeth Moss Kanter, *Men and Women of the Corporation,* New York: Basic Books, 1977.

61. Julia T. Wood, "Telling Our Stories: Narratives as a Basis for Theorizing Sexual Harassment," *Journal of Applied Communication Research,* 4 (1992): 349–363; and Gary N. Power, *Gender and Diversity in the Workplace: Learning Activities and Exercises,* Thousand Oaks, CA: Sage, 1994, pp. 53–54.

62. See, for example, Deborah Tannen, "The Real Hillary Factor," *New York Times,* October 12, 1992, p. A19.

63. B. Garlick, S. Dixon, and P. Allen, eds., *Stereotypes of Women in Power: Historical Perspectives and Revisionist Views,* Westport, CT: Greenwood Press, 1992.

64. J. K. Nader and L. B. Nader, "Communication, Gender and Intraorganizational Negotiation Ability," in L. P. Stewart and S. Ting-Toomy, eds., *Communication, Gender, and Sex Roles in Diverse Interaction Contexts,* Norwood, NJ: Ablex, 1987, pp. 119–134.

65. L. P. Stewart and D. Clarke-Kudless, "Communication in Corporate Settings," in L. P. Arliss and D. J. Borisoff, eds., *Women and Men Communicating: Challenges and Changes,* Fort Worth, TX: Harcourt Brace Jovanovich, 1993, pp. 142–152.

66. Julia T. Wood, *Gendered Lives,* Belmont, CA: Wadsworth, 1994, pp. 266–270.

67. W. Farrell, "Men as Success Objects," *Utne Reader* (May/June 1991): 81–84.

68. Willard Gaylin, *The Male Ego,* New York: Viking, 1992.

69. Judith B. Rosener, "Ways Women Lead," *Harvard Business Review* (November/December 1990): 110–125.

70. P. W. Lunneborg, *Women Changing Work,* Westport, CT: Greenwood Press, 1990.

71. Wood, *Gendered Lives,* pp. 277–278.

72. Marvin L. Moore, "The Family as Portrayed on Primetime Television, 1947–1990: Structure and Characteristics," *Sex Roles,* 26 (1992): 41–61.

73. Ibid.

74. See, for example, P. M. Japp, "Gender and Work in the 1980s: Television's Working Women as Displaced Persons," *Women's Studies in Communication,* 14 (1991): 49–74, and L. R. Vande Berg and D. Streckfuss, "Primetime Television's Portrayal of Women and the World of Work: A Demographic Profile," *Journal of Broadcasting and Electronic Media,* 36 (1992): 195–208.

75. M. A. Luong, "Star Trek: The Next Generation: Boldly Forging Empowered Female Characters," paper presented at the annual meeting of the Speech Communication Association, Chicago, IL, October, 1992.

76. Dana Andrew Jennings, "In TV Land, Work Involves a Lot of Play," *New York Times,* October 1, 1995, p. F12.

77. Claudia H. Deutsch, "Companies Using Coffee Bars to Get Ideas Brewing," *New York Times,* November 5, 1995, p. 13.

78. See, for example, B. S. Bell and S. W. J. Kozlowski, "A Typology of Virtual Teams: Implications for Effective Leadership," *Group and Organizational Management,* 27:1, 2002, pp. 14–49.

79. Judith A. Perrolle, "Computer-Mediated Conversation," *National Forum* (Summer 1991), pp. 21–22.

80. M. K. Barnes and S. Duck, "Everyday Communicative Contexts for Social Support," in B. R. Burleson, T. L. Albrecht, and I. G. Sarason, eds., *Communication of Social Support: Messages, Interactions, Relationships, and Community,* Thousand Oaks, CA: Sage, 1994, pp. 175–194.

81. See S. Cohen and T. A. Wills, "Stress, Social Support, and Buffering Hypothesis," *Psychological Bulletin,* 98, 1985, pp. 310–357; T. Ferguson, "Health Care in Cyberspace: Patients Lead a Revolution," *The Futurist,* 31:6, November–December 1997, pp. 29–34.

82. Gary, L. Kreps and Barbara C. Thornton, *Health Communication: Theory and Practice,* 2nd ed., Prospect Heights, IL: Waveland Press, 1992, p. 2.

83. See D. E. Costello, "Health Communication Theory and Research: An Overview," in B. Ruben, ed., *Communication Yearbook I,* New Brunswick, NJ: Transaction Books, 1977, pp. 557–567.

84. P. Arntson, "Future Research in Health Communication," *Journal of Applied Communication Research,* 13 (1985): 118–130.

85. See Barbara C. Thornton and Gary L. Kreps, *Perspectives on Health Communication,* Prospect Heights, IL: Waveland Press, 1993, p. 1.

86. Kreps and Thornton, *Health Communication.*

87. L. Donohew and E. Berlin Ray, "Introduction: Systems Perspectives on Health Communication," in E. Berlin Ray and L. Donohew, eds., *Communication and Health,* Hillsdale, NJ: Erlbaum, 1990.

88. T. L. Thompson, "Patient Health Care: Issues in Interpersonal Communication," in E. Berlin Ray and L. Donohew, eds., *Communication and Health,* Hillsdale, NJ: Erlbaum, 1990, pp. 27–50.

89. Peggy Clarke, "Finding the Words to Communicate about Sexual Health," *Communication and Health,* from the 1995 Speech Communication Association summer conference proceedings and prepared remarks, Washington, DC, July 19–23, 1995, p. 2.

90. D. Barnlund, "Therapeutic Communication," in D. Barnlund, ed., *Interpersonal Communication,* Boston, MA: Houghton-Mifflin, 1968, pp. 613–645.

91. Daniel Goleman, *Emotional Intelligence,* New York: Bantam, 1995, p. 165.

92. See D. Ballard-Reisch, "A Model of Participative Decision Making for Physician-Patient Interaction," *Health Communication,* 2, 2 (1990): 91–104.

93. Clarke, "Finding the Words," p. 2.

94. S. P. Bowen and P. Michal-Johnson, "The Crisis of Communication in Relationships: Confronting the Threat of AIDS," *AIDS and Public Policy Journal,* 4, 1 (1990): 10–19.

95. Kreps and Thornton, *Health Communication,* pp. 167–168.

96. Athena du Pre, *Communicating About Health: Current Issues and Perspectives,* Mountainview, CA: Mayfield, 2000, p. 157.

97. G. L. Kreps and E. N. Kunimoto, *Effective Communication in Multicultural Health Care Settings,* Thousand Oaks, CA: Sage, 1994.

98. See, for example, T. Randall, "Key to Organ Donation May Be Cultural Awareness," *The Journal of the American Medical Association,* 285:2, 1991, pp. 176–178.

99. "Women on TV: The Picture Still Needs Some Tuning, Study Says," *Charlotte* (NC) *Observer,* October 20, 1990, pp. B1, B2.

100. Germaine Greer, *The Change: Women, Aging, and Menopause,* New York: Knopf, 1992.

101. J. Shapiro and L. Kroeger, "Is Life Just a Romantic Novel? The Relationship between Attitudes about Intimate Relationships and the Popular Media," *American Journal of Family Therapy,* 19 (1991): 226–236.

102. Ruth Padawer, "Warming Trend: Increase in Female Doctors Brings a More Personal Touch to Medical Care," *The Record* (Hackensack, NJ), October 9, 1995, pp. H1, 2.

103. Ibid.

104. Ibid.

105. C. J. Conlee, J. Olveera, and N. N. Vagim, "The Relationships Among Physician Nonverbal Immediacy and Measures of Patient Satisfaction with Physican Care," *Communication Reports,* 6, Winter 1993, pp. 25–33.

106. An early study formally documented the dichotomy of occupational portrayals. See P. A. Kalisch and B. J. Kalisch, "Sex-role Stereotyping of Nurses and Physicians on Prime-time Television: A Dichotomy of Occupation Portrayals," *Sex Roles,* 10, 7/8 (April 1984): 533–553.

107. Michael Parenti, *Make-Believe Media: The Politics of Entertainment,* New York: St. Martin's, 1992, p. 109.

108. Aletha C. Huston et al., *Big World, Small Screen: The Role of Television in American Society,* Lincoln, NE: University of Nebraska Press, 1992, pp. 66–67.

109. Ibid., pp. 67–68.

110. Carol Ann Campbell, "Alternative Radio: Physicians and Others Promote Non-Traditional Remedies," *The Record* (Hackensack, NJ), October 30, 1995, pp. H1, 2.

111. Martin Chase, "Videotapes Educate People about Disease Minus Bedside Manner," *Wall Street Journal,* October 30, 1995, p. B1.

112. T. Ferguson, 1997.

113. Bill Gates, *The Road Ahead,* New York: Viking, 1995, p. 212.

114. S. C. Alexander, J. L. Peterson, and A. B. Hollingshead, "Help at Your Keyboard: Support Groups on the Internet," paper presented at the National Meeting of the National Communication Association, November 4–7, 1999.

115. A. du Pre, 2000, p. 143.

Photo Credits

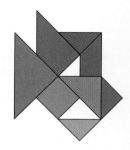

Part 1 opener: ©Royalty-Free/Corbis. **Chapter 1** opener: ©Spencer Grant/Photo Edit. Page 7: ©Jennie Woodcock/Reflections PhotoLibrary/Corbis; 11: ©David Young-Wolff/PhotoEdit; 13: ©Spencer Platt/Getty Images; 18: ©David Raymer/Corbis. **Chapter 2** opener: ©Stuart McClymont/Stone/Getty Images. Page 41: ©Michael Newman/PhotoEdit; 47: ©David Young-Wolff/PhotoEdit; 53: ©Mia Foster/PhotoEdit; 61: ©David Young-Wolff/PhotoEdit. **Chapter 3** opener: ©Richard Elliott/Stone/Getty Images. Page 74: ©Sygma Collection/Corbis; 80: ©Mark Ludak/The Image Works; 87: ©Monika Graff/The Image Works.

Part 2 opener: ©Spencer Grant/PhotoEdit. **Chapter 4** opener: ©Jeff Greenberg/PhotoEdit. Page 109: ©Jeff Greenberg/PhotoEdit; 119: ©Michael Newman/PhotoEdit; 127: ©Jose Luis Pelaez, Inc./Corbis. **Chapter 5** opener: ©Jim Cummins/Taxi/Getty Images. Page 144: ©Orjan F. Ellingvag/Corbis; 153: ©Felicia Martinez/PhotoEdit; 163: ©Kathy Ferguson/PhotoEdit. **Chapter 6** opener: ©Michael Keller/Corbis. Page 177: ©Chuck Savage/Corbis; 187: ©Will Hart/PhotoEdit; 198: ©Jeff Greenberg/PhotoEdit. **Chapter 7** opener: ©Robert Brenner/PhotoEdit. Page 213: ©Bill Aron/PhotoEdit; 217: ©Yellow Dog Productions/The Image Bank/Getty Images; 221: ©Michael Newman/PhotoEdit.

Part 3 opener: ©Andrew Lichtenstein/The Image Works. **Chapter 8** opener: ©Jeff Greenberg/The Image Works. Page 237: ©Helen Norman/Corbis; 238: ©Gerhard Steiner/Corbis. **Chapter 9** opener: ©Mike Powell/Allsport Concepts/Getty Images. Page 258: ©Michael Newman/PhotoEdit; 263: ©Rolf Bruderer Studio/Corbis; 264: ©Sonda Dawes/The Image Works; 270: Photofest. **Chapter 10** opener: ©Jeff Greenberg/PhotoEdit. Page 294: ©Bob Krist/Corbis; 301: ©Jonathan Andrew/Corbis. **Chapter 11** opener: ©Bruce Ayres/Stone/Getty Images. Page 321: ©Reuters NewMedia Inc./Corbis; 330: ©Laura Wiley/The Image Works; 331: ©Dennis Mac-Donald/PhotoEdit; 344: ©Michael S. Yamashita/Corbis.

Part 4 opener: ©George Shelley/Corbis. **Chapter 12** opener: ©Steve Mason/Photodisc Green/Getty. Page 357: ©Spencer Grant/PhotoEdit; 361: ©David Butow/Corbis Saba; 365: ©Ian Shaw/Stone/Getty Images; 381: ©Alison Wright/Corbis; 386: ©Tiffany M. Hermon/Journal-Courier/The Image Works. **Chapter 13** opener: ©Photodisc Green/Getty. Page 400: ©Don Smetzer/PhotoEdit; 410: ©David Young-Wolff/PhotoEdit. **Chapter 14** opener: ©Elyse Lewin/The Image Bank/Getty Images. Page 424: ©Roy Morsch/Corbis; 426: ©Mark Richards/PhotoEdit; 440: ©Ed Bock/Corbis; 441: ©Jim Craigmyle/Corbis; 460: ©A. Ramey/PhotoEdit; 468: ©Jeff Greenberg/The Image Works.

Index

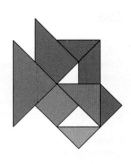